CITIES OF GOD

Cities of God

THE RELIGION OF THE ITALIAN COMMUNES
1125–1325

AUGUSTINE THOMPSON, O.P.

The Pennsylvania State University Press
University Park, Pennsylvania

Unless otherwise noted, all photographs are by David Sundt.

Library of Congress Cataloging-in-Publication Data

Thompson, Augustine.
Cities of God : the religion of the Italian communes, 1125–1325 /
Augustine Thompson, O.P.
p.   cm.
Includes bibliographical references and index.
ISBN 0-271-02477-1 (alk. paper)
1. Italy—Church history.
I. Title.

BX1210 .T48   2005
282'.45'09022—dc22
2004015965

The Pennsylvania State University Press
is a member of the Association of American University Presses.

It is the policy of The Pennsylvania State University Press
to use acid-free paper. Publications on uncoated stock
satisfy the minimum requirements of
American National Standard for Information Sciences—
Permanence of Paper for Printed Library Materials, ANSI Z39.48–1992.

Contents

Abbreviations

The references to published sources, especially city statutes or liturgical texts, would require confusing and cumbersome short citations if these followed standard forms. So I have used short descriptive tags rather than the actual titles found in the printed editions. For example, I use "Vicenza Stat." for the collection published as *Statuti del comune di Vicenza MCCLXIV* and "Bologna Stat. 1" for the collection *Statuti di Bologna dell'anno 1245 all'anno 1267*. When the source has book, chapter, and verse or other division numbering, this is given before the page reference [e.g., 1.1.1, pp. 1–11]. When the date of a statute or document can be determined, I include it in parentheses for the reader's convenience, as I also do for chronicle sources. At the first citation of a manuscript source, I similarly give the approximate dates of the codex and of the original copied, if relevant. This dating is occasionally silently corrected when library catalogue dates are clearly wrong.

ACGOP *Acta Capitulorum Generalium Ordinis Praedicatorum* I: *Ab Anno 1220 usque ad Annum 1303*, ed. Benedictus Maria Reichert, MOPH, 3 (Rome: Polyglotta, 1898)

AFH *Archivum Franciscanum Historicum*

AFP *Archivum Fratrum Praedicatorum*

AIMA *Antiquitates Italicae Medii Aevi*, ed. Lodovico Antonio Muratori, 6 vols. (Milan: Societas Palatina, 1738–42; rpt., Bologna: Forni, 1965)

AMDSPPR *Atti e memorie della Deputazione di storia patria per le province di Romagna*

Aquileia Constitutiones *Constitutiones Provinciales Aquilejenses Bertrandi Patriarchae Anno 1339*, Mansi 25:1109–32

AS *Acta Sanctorum quotquot Toto Orbe Coluntur vel a Catholicis Scriptoribus Celebrantur ex Latinis et Graecis Aliarumque Gentium Antiquis Monumentis Collecta, Digesta, Illustrata*, 2d ed., ed. Godefridus Henschenius et al., 60 vols. in 70 (Paris: Palme, etc., 1867–1940)

ASOB *Acta S. Officii Bononie ab Anno 1291 usque ad Annum 1310*, ed. Lorenzo Paolini and Raniero Orioli, 2 vols. (Rome: Istituto Storico Italiano per il Medio Evo, 1982)

BF *Bullarium Franciscanum Romanorum Pontificum*, ed. Giovanni Giacinto Sbaraglia, 7 vols. (Rome: Propaganda Fidei, 1758–68)

Biella Stat. *Statuta Comunis Bugelle et Documenta Adiecta*, ed. Pietro Sella (Biella: Testa, 1904)

Bol. Pop. Stat. *Statuti delle società del popolo di Bologna*, ed. Augusto Gaudenzi, Fonti per la storia d'Italia: Statuti secolo XIII, 4–5, 2 vols. (Rome: Istituto Storico Italiano, 1889/96)

Bologna Stat. 1 *Statuti di Bologna dell'anno 1245 all'anno 1267*, ed. Lodovico Frati, 3 vols. (Bologna: n.p., 1869–77)

Bologna Stat. II *Statuti di Bologna dell'anno 1288*, ed. Gina Fasoli and Pietro Sella, Studi e testi 73 and 85, 2 vols. (Vatican City: Biblioteca Apostolica Vaticana, 1937–39)

Bologna Synod (1310) "Costituzioni della chiesa bolognese emanate nel sinodo diocesano del 1310 al tempo del vescovo Umberto," ed. Leandro Novelli, *Studia Gratiana* 8 (1962): 448–552

BOP *Bullarium Ordinis Fratrum Praedicatorum*, ed. Thomas Ripoll and A. Brémond, 8 vols. (Rome: Mainardi, 1729–40)

Brescia Stat. *Statuti di Brescia*, ed. Federico Odorici (Turin: Paravia, 1877)

CCB *Corpus Chronicorum Bononiensium*, ed. Albano Sorbelli, *RIS²* 18:1, incl. *Cronaca*

A detta volgarmente Rampona [*CCB:* A], *Cronaca B detta volgarmente Varignana* [*CCB:* B], *Cronaca detta dei Bolognetti* [*CCB:* Bol.], Pietro and Floriano da Villola, *Cronaca* [*CCB:* Vill.]

Cremona Cath. Stat. "Gli statuti dei canonici della cattedrale di Cremona del 1247," ed. Francesco Novati, *Archivio storico lombardo* 30 (1903): 451–60

Cremona Stat. *Dei documenti storici e letterari di Cremona,* ed. Francesco Robolotti (Cremona: Feraboli, 1857), 99–111

Ferrara Clergy Const. *Constitutiones Factae a Parochis Civitatis Ferrariensis pro Suae Congregationis Regimine, Anno 1278, AIMA* 6:433–40

Ferrara Stat. (1287) *Statuta Ferrariae Anno MCCLXXXVII,* Deputazione provinciale ferrarese di storia patria: Monumenti 3 (Modena: Casa di Risparmio di Ferrara, 1955)

Florence Stat. *Statuti della Repubblica Fiorentina,* ed. Romolo Caggese, 2 vols. (Florence: Galileiana, 1910–20)

Grado Council *Concilium Gradense in quo Plura tum ad Disciplinam Ecclesiasticam cum ad Divinorum Officiorum Ritus Clerive Mores Pertinentia Sancita Sunt et Synodus Torcellana in qua Praedicti Gradensis Concilii Constitutiones Promulgatae Sunt,* Mansi 24:1163–72

Gratian, *Decretum* *Decretum Magistri Gratiani,* vol. 1 of *Corpus Iuris Canonici,* 2d ed., ed. E. Friedberg (Leipzig: Tauchnitz, 1879)

Matteo Griffoni Matteo Griffoni, *Memoriale Historicum de Rebus Bononiensium,* ed. Lodovico Frati and Albano Sorbelli, *RIS*² 18:2

Lucca Stat. *Statuto del commune di Lucca dell'anno MCCCVIII,* ed. Salvatore Bongi and Leone Del Prete, Memorie e documenti per servire alla storia di Lucca, 3:3 (Lucca: Giusti, 1867)

Lucca Synod (1253) *Dei sinodi della diocesi di Lucca: Dissertazioni,* ed. Paolino Dinelli, Memorie e documenti per servire all'istoria del ducato di Lucca, 7 (Lucca: Bertini, 1834), 54–58

Lucca Synod (1300) *Constitutiones Domini Lucani Episcopi,* in "La sinodo lucchese di Enrico del Carretto," ed. Raoul Manselli, *Miscellanea Gilles Gérard Meersseman,* ed. Michele Maccarrone et al., Italia sacra, 15 (Padua: Antenore, 1970), 1:210–46

Lucca Synod (1308) *Lucana Synodus sub Henrico Lucensi Episcopo circa Annum 1308 Habita,* Mansi 25:173–98

Mansi Giovanni Domenico Mansi, ed., *Sacrorum Conciliorum Nova et Amplissima Collectio,* 54 vols. (1901; rpt., Graz: Academische Druck, 1960)

Mantua Stat. *Statuta Dominorum Raynaldi Botironi Fratrum de Bonacolsis, Anno 1303,* ed. Carlo d'Arco, *Studi intorno al municipio di Mantova dall'origine di questa fino all'anno 1863; Ai quali fanno seguito documenti inediti o rari* (Mantua: Gaustalla, 1871–74), 2:45–309; 3:5–299

Manuale Ambrosianum *Manuale Ambrosianum ex Codice Saec. XI olim in Usum Canonicae Vallis Travalliae,* ed. Marco Magistretti, Monumenta Veteris Liturgiae Ambrosianae, 2–3, 2 vols., (Milan: Hoepli, 1904–5)

Meersseman, *Dossier* *Dossier de l'ordre de la pénitence au XIIIᵉ siècle,* ed. Gilles Gérard Meersseman, Spicilegium Friburgense, 7 (Fribourg: Editions Universitaires, 1961)

Meersseman, *Ordo* *Ordo Fraternitatis: Confraternite e pietà dei laici nel Medioevo,* ed. Gilles Gérard Meersseman, with the collaboration of Gian Piero Pacini, Italia Sacra, 24–26, 3 vols. (Rome: Herder, 1977)

Mem. Pot. Reg. *Memoriale Potestatum Regiensium,* ed. Lodovico Antonio Muratori, *RIS* 8:1071–180

MGH.SS *Monumenta Germaniae Historica inde ab Anno Christi Quingentesimo usque ad Annum Millesimum et Quingentesimum:*

Scriptores, ed. Georg Heinrich Pertz et al., 33 vols. in 36 (1826–1913; rpt., Stuttgart: Hiersemann, 1976)

Milan Council (1287) *Concilium Mediolanense in Causa Disciplinae Ecclesiasticae Habitum Anno Domini 1287*, Mansi 24:867–82

Modena Stat. (1306/7) *Respublica Mutinensis (1306–1307)*, ed. Emilio Paolo Vicini (Milan: Hoepli, 1932)

Modena Stat. (1327) *Statuta Civitatis Mutine Anno 1327: Testo*, ed. Cesare Campori, Monumenta di storia patria delle province modenesi: Serie degli statuti, 1 (Parma: Fiaccadori, 1864)

MOPH Monumenta Ordinis Fratrum Praedicatorum Historica

Novara Battuti Stat. (XIV) *Regula et Constituciones Regule Congregationis et Elemosine Fratrum Sancte Marie Nove cum Indulgentie eidem Regule Concesse in Novara*, ed. Pier Giorgio Longo, in "Penitenti, battuti, devoti in Novara tra XIII e XVI secolo (Documenti e appunti per uno studio)," *Bollettino storico per la provincia di Novara* 72 (1981): 278–85

Novara Synod I "Per la storia della chiesa novese: Gli statuti del vescovo Gerardo (1209–1211) con le aggiunte del vescovo Sigebaldo (1249–1268)," ed. Carlo Salsotto, *Bollettino storico per la provincia di Novara* 44 (1953): 28–35

Novara Synod II *Canones Episcopales Ecclesiae Novariensis*, ed. Giuseppe Briacca, *Gli statuti sinodali novaresi di Papiniano della Rovere (a. 1298)* (Milan: Vita e Pensiero, 1971), 168–279

Ordo Senensis *Ordo Officiorum Ecclesiae Senensis ab Oderico eiusdem Ecclesiae Canonico Anno MCCXIII Compositus*, ed. Giovanni Crisostomo Tombelli (Bologna: Longi, 1766)

Padua Stat. *Statuti del comune di Padova dal secolo XII all'anno 1285*, ed. Andrea Gloria (Padua: Sacchetto, 1873)

Padua Synod *Constitutiones Paduanae ab*

Ildebrandino Paduano Episcopo in Synodo Anni 1339 Conditae, Mansi 25:1131–44

Parma Stat. I *Statuta Communis Parmae Digesta Anno 1255*, Monumenta Historica ad Provincias Parmensem et Placentinam Pertinentia, 1 (Parma: Fiaccadori, 1856)

Parma Stat. II *Statuta Communis Parmae ab Anno 1266 ad Annum circiter 1304*, Monumenta Historica ad Provincias Parmensem et Placentinam Pertinentia, 1 (Parma: Fiaccadori, 1857)

Parma Stat. III *Statuta Communis Parmae ab Anno 1316 ad 1325*, Monumenta Historica ad Provincias Parmensem et Placentinam Pertinentia, 1 (Parma: Fiaccadori, 1859)

Piacenza Battuti Stat. (1317) *Liber Vite*, ed. C. Mesini, in "Statuti piacentini-parmensi dei disciplinati," *Archivio storico per le province parmensi* 12 (1960): 55–70

Piacenza Stat. Cler. *Statuta Clericorum Placentiae, Statuta Varia Civitatis Placentiae*, Monumenta Historica ad Provincias Parmensem et Placentinam Pertinentia, 1 (Parma: Fiaccadori, 1855), 529–55

Pisa Stat. *Statuti inediti della città di Pisa dal XII al XIV secolo*, ed. Francesco Bonaini, 2 vols. (Florence: Vieusseux, 1854–70)

PL *Patrologiae Latinae Cursus Completus*, ed. Jean-Paul Migne, 221 vols. (Paris: Garnier, 1878–90)

Pont. Rom. (XII) *Pontificale Romanum Saeculi XII, Le pontifical romain au Moyen Âge*, 1, ed. Michel Andrieu, Studi e testi, 86 (Vatican City: Biblioteca Apostolica Vaticana, 1938), 123–302

Pont. Rom. (XIII) *Pontificale secundum Consuetudinem et Usum Romanae Curiae, Le pontifical romain au Moyen Âge*, 2, ed. Michel Andrieu, Studi e testi, 87 (Vatican City: Biblioteca Apostolica Vaticana, 1939), 327–522

Pont. Rom. (Durandus) *Pontificale Guillielmi Durandi, Le pontifical romain au Moyen Âge*, 3, ed. Michel Andrieu, Studi e testi, 88 (Vatican City: Biblioteca Apostolica Vaticana, 1940), 327–662

Rat. Dec. Aem. *Rationes Decimarum Italiae nei secoli XIII–XIV: Aemilia, le decime dei secoli XIII e XIV,* ed. Angelo Merati et al., Studi e testi, 60 (Vatican City: Biblioteca Apostolica Vaticana, 1933)

Rat. Dec. Ven. *Rationes Decimarum Italiae nei secoli XIII–XIV: Venetiae-Histria, Dalmatia,* ed. Pietro Sella and Giuseppe Vale, Studi e testi, 96 (Vatican City: Biblioteca Apostolica Vaticana, 1941)

Ravenna Council (1286) *Concilium Ravennate I Causa Reformandae Disciplinae Celebratum Anno Domini 1286,* Mansi 24:615–26.

Ravenna Council (1311) *Concilium Ravennate II pro Disciplina et Moribus Ecclesiae Reformandis Celebratum Anno 1311,* Mansi 25:449–76

Ravenna Council (1314) *Concilium Ravennate III de Disciplina Ecclesiastica Celebratum Anno 1314,* Mansi 25:535–50

Ravenna Council (1317) *Concilium Ravennate IV Celebratum Bononiae Anno 1317,* Mansi 25:599–628

Ravenna Stat. *Statuto del secolo XIII del comune di Ravenna,* ed. Andrea Zoli and Silvio Bernicoli (Ravenna: Ravegnana, 1904)

Reggio Stat. *Consuetudini e statuti reggiani del secolo XIII,* ed. Aldo Cerlini (Milan: Hoepli, 1933)

RIS Rerum Italicarum Scriptores, ed. Lodovico Antonio Muratori, 25 vols. in 28 (1723–51; rpt., Bologna: Forni, 1965)

*RIS*² *Rerum Italicarum Scriptores: Raccolta degli storici italiani dal cinquecento al millecinquecento,* ed. Giosue Carducci et al., 103 vols. in 142 (Città di Castello: Lapi, 1908–16)

Salimbene, *Cronica* Salimbene of Parma, *Cronica,* ed. Giuseppe Scalia (Bari: Laterza, 1966); trans. Joseph L. Baird et al., *The Chronicle of Salimbene de Adam,* Medieval and Renaissance Texts and Studies, 40 (Binghamton, N.Y.:

Center for Medieval and Early Renaissance Studies, 1986)

San Gimignano Stat. "Statuti del comune di San Gimignano compilati nel 1255," ed. Luigi Pecori, *Storia della terra di San Gimignano* (Florence: Galileiana, 1853), 662–741

Siena Stat. I *Il constituto del comune di Siena dell'anno 1262,* ed. Lodovico Zdekauer (Milan: Hoepli, 1897)

Siena Stat. II *Costituto del comune di Siena volgarizzato nel MCCCIX–MCCCX,* ed. Alessandro Lisini, 2 vols. (Siena: Lazzari, 1903)

Treviso Stat. *Gli statuti del comune di Treviso,* ed. Giuseppe Liberali, Monumenti storici pubblicati dalla Deputazione di storia patria per le Venezie, n.s., 4, 2 vols. (Venice: Deputazione di Storia Patria, 1951)

Vercelli Stat. *Statuta Communis Vercellarum ab Anno MCCLXI,* ed. Giovambatista Adriani, Historiae Patriae Monumenta 16: Leges Municipales, 2:2 (Turin: Regius, 1876), cols. 1089–389

Verona Stat. I *Liber Juris Civilis Urbis Veronae,* ed. Bartolomeo Campagnola (Verona: Bernum, 1728)

Verona Stat. II *Gli statuti veronesi del 1276 colle correzioni e le aggiunte fino al 1323 (Cod. Campostrini, Bibl. Civica di Verona),* ed. Gino Sandri, Monumenti storici pubblicati dalla Deputazione di storia patria per le Venezie, n.s., 3. (Venice: Deputazione di Storia Patria, 1940)

Vicenza Stat. *Statuti del comune di Vicenza MCCLXIV,* ed. Fedele Lampertico, Monumenti storici pub. dalla Deputazione veneta di storia patria, ser. 2: Statuti 1 (Venice: Deputazione Veneta, 1886)

Volterra Stat. *Statuti di Volterra (1210–1224),* ed. Enrico Fiumi (Florence: Casa di Risparmio, 1951)

X Decretalium D. Gregorii Papae IX Compilatio [Liber Extra], *Decretalium Collectiones,* vol. 2 of *Corpus Iuris Canonici,* 2d ed., ed. E. Friedberg (Leipzig: Tauchnitz, 1881)

Note on Style

I have in my notes reproduced Latin and medieval Italian texts from the printed editions and manuscripts, with all their peculiarities of spelling and grammar. For manuscripts, I have modernized the punctuation and the capitalization, but have not attempted to introduce accents and apostrophes lacking in the original, since these are transcriptions, not editions. As a result, the texts look very peculiar and sometimes downright ungrammatical. This is probably all to the good, since it gives the reader a more immediate contact with the written words of the people under consideration. All translations into English are mine, unless otherwise noted.

I normally give proper names, whether from Latin or Italian sources, in their likely vernacular dress. The presence of the word *fu* between a given name and a following patronymic, as in "Giovanni di fu Pietro," means that the father was dead at the time of writing. Sometimes a name is preceded by "Don" or "Donna," representing *dominus* and *domina* in the original Latin. These courtesy titles were used by honorable laypersons and by the clergy, especially priests. If the cleric was a monk, I have rendered the title as "Dom," following the common English usage. "Fra," meaning *frater* (Latin), indicates a member of a mendicant order or a lay penitent (the earlier use). The female form of this title is "Sor" or "Sora." More aristocratic laymen are sometimes titled "Ser" (like the English "sir"), which is a bit more exalted than "Don."

I have made some exceptions. If the name indicated a place of origin, as in Giovanni di Vicenza or Guido da Vicenza, I have converted the proposition to "of," since that is its meaning. I give the names of Church Fathers, famous saints, and popes in English. But I have given the names of communal lay saints in Italian dress because that is how their neighbors knew them. I make an exception for the lay saint Francis of Assisi. It would have been very distracting to do otherwise.

The money in thirteenth-century records generally indicates money of account, rather than actual coins. In theory the "denominations" were as follows: £ = *libra* (*lira;* in English, "pound"); s. = *solidus* (*soldo;* in English, "shilling"); d. = *denarius* (*denaro;* in English, "penny"). £1 = 20s. = 240d. A typical money of account was the "imperial lira" (£ imp. = *libra imperialis*). Cities had their own hypothetical currencies: £ bon. = *libra bononinorum,* the lira of Bologna; £ fer. = the lira of Ferrara; £ flor. = the lira of Florence; £ flor. parv. = the smaller lira of Florence; £ mil. = the lira of Milan; £ mut. = the lira of Modena; £ parm. = the lira of Parma; £ pis. = the lira of Pisa; £ placen. = the lira of Piacenza; £ rav. = the lira of Ravenna; £ reg. = the lira of Reggio; £ ven. gros. = the larger lira of Venice; £ ven. parv. = the smaller lira of Venice. Three of these lire were usually equal to one imperial lira. North Italian records sometimes merely indicate lire, without any reference to specific type. In fact, the coins struck by most cities were nearly always the traditional silver pence (*denari*). The north Italian cities began to mint larger denari, called *grossi,* in the early 1200s. These contained about two grams of fine silver—four to twenty-six times the amount in the older *piccoli.* These *piccoli* and *grossi* are reflected in the larger and smaller denominations of the moneys of account listed above. This means that the money of account, the "lira" of each city, was of different value, and the differences varied as cities debased their coin. Changing "exchange rates" for the different Italian coinages after the mid-1200s are tabulated in Peter Spufford's *Handbook of Medieval Exchange* (London: Boydell & Brewer, 1986), which is an excellent resource for those needing further information. As to buying power, a modest house in the city of Bologna was worth about £200 bon. in the 1290s, after a century of moderate inflation. The typical stipend for Mass in thirteenth-century Bolognese statutes was 6d. bon., and it was supposed to provide the priest with one day's material needs.

Acknowledgments

In writing this book I have incurred countless debts. To single out institutions or individuals for special thanks might be invidious, but it is necessary. Above all, I thank the University of Oregon at Eugene, whose grant of a sabbatical year in 1997–98 allowed me to do most of the research. A summer research grant in 2003 from the University of Virginia's College of Arts and Sciences allowed a trip to Italy to prepare the illustrations. During my research, the Dominican communities of Bologna, Florence, Milan, Oakland, and San Francisco offered the most gracious of hospitality. My colleagues at the Religious Studies Department of the University of Virginia, Charlottesville, have supported the work in countless ways, not the least by never grumbling about my summers spent off grounds writing and doing research. The friars of my province have been the best of brothers and the most critical of readers. I thank Fr. Stanley Fabian Parmesano, Bro. Augustine Hilander, and especially Mr. Keith Monley, for their careful editing. Katherine Ludwig Jansen, Duane Osheim, Daniel Bornstein, Frances Andrews, and James Gordley read and commented extensively on all or most of the text, as did both Richard Sundt, who photographed most of the illustrations in the "terrarium" of a hot Italian summer, and Barbara Pike Gordley, who originally suggested the project. I would also like to thank Diana Webb of King's College, London, who graciously consented to my appropriation of this book's title from a very fine article of hers. Finally, this book owes its very existence to Mr. Peter Potter and the Pennsylvania State University Press, who graciously agreed to consider a very long manuscript on what is hardly a bestseller topic, a kind of risk taking that is sadly becoming less and less common among academic presses.

Introduction

This is a book about the religious life of ordinary laypeople in high medieval Italy. As such, it is an excursion into a mostly uncharted world, the lived experience of orthodox religion in the Italian cities. Some readers might find this characterization surprising, even shocking. Nothing could be better known than what it meant to be "Catholic" Christians in the Italy of Saint Francis and Dante. So historians of medieval religion have directed their gaze and research elsewhere. During my first venture into the world of thirteenth-century Italian religion, more than fifteen years ago, I was surprised to discover how little the day-to-day orthodox world had been studied. Older scholarship produced studies of papal politics and scholastic theology, but these treated only an ecclesiastical elite. In his classic study of medieval religious movements, Herbert Grundmann first suggested that high medieval heresy, the mendicants, and women's mysticism all formed part of a single whole and deserved more attention.[1] Subsequent scholarship focused, almost exclusively, on those three phenomena. A glance at the treatment of medieval religion in the Einaudi handbook of Italian history, itself the work of an eminent scholar, shows an odd religious landscape.[2] Traditional scholarly divisions rule: a section on the Gregorian Reform is followed by sections dedicated to heresy and repression (pp. 609–733), the mendicant orders (pp. 734–874), and the Church's institutional crises of the 1300s (pp. 874–974). Heretics, popes, theologians, Franciscans, and saints. Where is everyone else?

1. Herbert Grundmann, *Religiöse Bewegungen im Mittelalter*, 2d ed. (Hildesheim: Olms, 1961), translated by Steven Rowan as *Religious Movements in the Middle Ages* (Notre Dame: University of Notre Dame Press, 1995).

2. For bibliography, see Giovanni Miccoli, "La storia religiosa IV: Limiti e contraddizioni della restaurazione postgregoriana," *Storia d'Italia* 2:1 (Turin: Einaudi, 1974), 431–1079, and Alba Maria Orselli, "Vita religiosa nella città medievale italiana tra dimensione ecclesiastica e 'cristianesimo civico': Una esemplificazione," *Annali dell'Istituto storico italo-germanico in Trento* 7 (1981): 361–98, esp. 361–68.

Among Grundmann's areas of interest, heretics were the first to generate a scholarly industry, already vital in the 1960s. The bibliography on heresy in medieval Italy is vast and ever expanding.[3] There is also a growing recognition that heresy cannot be understood apart from the religion it rejected.[4] In spite of their prominence in modern scholarship, heretics represented only a tiny fraction of the medieval Italian population. Since 1980 Grundmann's interest in thirteenth-century mysticism has been transformed, in great part by the work of André Vauchez, into a rich and expanded field of study, that of saints and holiness.[5] But again, as in the case of heretics, saints represented only a tiny fraction, albeit an important one, of those living in the medieval Italian cities. New studies on "popular religion" and "lay piety" initially appeared to be very promising.[6] But the religious experience studied in these books tends to dissolve into a disembodied piety; day-to-day realities are lost in generalizations and abstraction. This book is a study of neither the "popular religion" nor the "lay piety" showcased in such books. It is, I hope, something greater, a recovery of the religious world of all in the Italian cities who considered themselves orthodox Christians. Medieval lay piety is incomprehensible without the sacraments and the clergy, but "popular religion" is seldom treated as part of the larger world of orthodox worship and belief. Perhaps its very "legality" and ordinariness make the garden variety of Christian life so elusive.[7] The scarcity of sources and the opacity of those

3. Carl T. Berkhout and Jeffrey B. Russell, *Medieval Heresies: A Bibliography, 1960–1979*, Subsidia Mediaevalia, 11 (Toronto: PIMS, 1981); Eugène Dupré Theseider, "Problemi di eresiologia medioevale," *Bollettino della Società di studi valdesi* 76 (1957): 3–17; Raoul Manselli, "Les hérétiques dans la société italienne du 13ᵉ siècle," *Hérésies et sociétés dans l'Europe pré-industrielle, 11ᵉ–18ᵉ siècles*, ed. Jacques Le Goff (Paris: Mouton, 1968), 199–202; Mariano D'Alatri, " 'Eresie' perseguite dall'inquisizione in Italia nel corso del duecento," *The Concept of Heresy in the Middle Ages (11th–13th C.)*, Mediaevalia Lovaniensia, ser. 1, stud. 4 (Louvain: Louvain University Press, 1976); id., *Eretici e inquisitori in Italia: Studi e documenti* (Rome: Istituto Storico dei Cappuccini, 1986); Grado G. Merlo, *Eretici ed eresie medievali* (Bologna: Il Mulino, 1989); on the Waldensians, id., *Valdesi e valdismi medievali* (Turin: Claudiana, 1984), and Gabriel Audisio, *The Waldensian Dissent: Persecution and Survival, c. 1170–c. 1570*, trans. Claire Davison (Cambridge: Cambridge University Press, 1999); on Catharism in Orvieto, Carol Lansing, *Power and Purity: Cathar Heresy in Medieval Italy* (New York: Oxford University Press, 1998).

4. So Gabriele Zanella, "Malessere ereticale in valle padana (1260–1308)," *Hereticalia: Temi e discussioni* (Spoleto: Centro Italiano di Studi sull'Alto Medioevo, 1995), 60. "Orthodoxy" could include anticlericalism and even private doubt: Walter L. Wakefield, "Some Unorthodox Popular Ideas of the Thirteenth Century," *Medievalia et Humanistica*, n.s., 4 (1973): 25–35.

5. See, above all, André Vauchez, *La sainteté en Occident aux derniers siècles du Moyen Âge d'après les procès de canonisation et les documents hagiographiques*, Bibliothèque des Écoles françaises d'Athènes et de Rome, 241 (Rome: École Française de Rome, 1981), translated by Jean Birrell as *Sainthood in the Later Middle Ages* (New York: Cambridge University Press, 1996). In Einaudi's *Storia d'Italia*, 2:1, the saints now appear, pp. 807–9.

6. André Vauchez, *Les laïcs au Moyen Âge: Pratiques et expériences religieuses* (Paris: Cerf, 1987), now happily available in English as *The Laity in the Middle Ages: Religious Beliefs and Devotional Practices*, ed. Daniel E. Bornstein, trans. M. J. Schneider (Notre Dame: University of Notre Dame Press, 1993); Raoul Manselli, *La religion populaire au Moyen Âge: Problèmes de méthode et d'histoire* (Quebec: Institut d'Études Médiévales Albert-le-Grand, 1975); Rosalind Brooke and Christopher Brooke, *Popular Religion in the Middle Ages* (London: Thames & Hudson, 1984); and Bernard Hamilton, *Religion in the Medieval West* (London: Arnold, 1986).

7. Judith Maltby, *Prayer Book and People in Elizabethan and Early Stuart England* (Cambridge: Cambridge University Press, 1998), 5.

that exist cannot excuse the failure to pursue such a study, although they are often so used.[8] Indeed, Vauchez has already pointed the way toward recovering the concrete, lived religion in Italy in spite of the lack of sources.[9]

The communes were simultaneously religious and political entities. This may sound like a commonplace, but given the trajectories of modern scholarship, this perspective represents something of a reorientation. Historians of communal Italy once focused on the cities as a precursor for the centralized states of early modern Europe, and this political perspective still obscures the religious nature of communal Italy for many modern observers.[10] Recently, historians of medieval Italy have gone beyond a story of political progress and emphasized instead the factiousness, primitiveness, oligarchy, particularism, and agrarian dependence of the cities, their "archaic" nature.[11] All to the good. Yet in histories of the communes, religion remains oddly alien to the civic life.[12] In Philip Jones's recent 673-page study of the Italian city-states, the author dedicates a mere seventeen pages to their religious life—and these are mostly dedicated to conflicts over ecclesiastical and secular jurisdiction.[13] The best short overview of the communes available in English asserts: "The Italian communes . . . were essentially secular contrivances whose particularism flourished in spite of a universal religion and the claims of a universal empire."[14] No, I do not think so. What this opposition of clerical and lay realms obscures is that the city was a single entity, however jurisdiction and government were divided. And its lay government, far from being "secularized" by its separation from the cathedral and bishop, came to express and understand itself through ever more explicitly religious rhetoric and rituals. The communes were able to distance themselves from the medieval empire because they, like the empire, claimed a sacred legitimacy. It has been argued that the proximity of the papacy and wars with the popes forced the communes to develop this religious identity—to justify political

8. E.g., Raffaello Morghen, "Vita religiosa e vita cittadina nella Firenze del duecento," *La coscienza cittadina nei comuni italiani nel duecento, 11–14 ottobre 1970*, Convegni del Centro di studi sulla spiritualità medievale, 11 (Todi: Accademia Tudertina, 1972), 197.

9. André Vauchez, "Reliquie, santi e santuari, spazi sacri e vagabondaggio religioso nel Medioevo," *Storia dell'Italia religiosa 1: L'antichità e il Medioevo*, ed. André Vauchez (Rome: Laterza, 1993), 455–83, esp. 460–63.

10. For bibliography on the communes, see Antonio Ivan Pini, *Città, comuni e corporazioni nel Medioevo italiano* (Bologna: CLUEB, 1989), 47–55, 59–65.

11. See Elena Fasano Guarini, "Center and Periphery," *The Origins of the State in Italy, 1300–1600*, ed. Julius Kirshner (Chicago: University of Chicago Press, 1995), 79, 83, on the changes this has meant for Einaudi's *Storia d'Italia* series.

12. See Diana Webb, *Patrons and Defenders: The Saints in the Italian City-States* (London: Tauris Academic Studies, 1996), which captures the right relation of Church and commune, and Enrico Cattaneo, *Città e religione nell'età dei comuni* (Milan: Vita e Pensiero, 1979), but see the review of this book in *Rivista di storia della Chiesa in Italia* 33 (1979): 609.

13. *The Italian City-State: From Commune to Signoria* (Oxford: Clarendon Press, 1997), 423–40.

14. J. K. Hyde, *Society and Politics in Medieval Italy: The Evolution of the Civic Life, 1000–1350*, New Studies in Medieval History (London: Macmillan, 1973), 8. Cf. Jones, *Italian City-State*, 423–25: "In the communes before all states in Europe government and politics were altogether secularized" (425).

policies independent of the papacy.[15] But this flies in the face of the political policies and communal identity of the first Lombard League. Rather, it was the cities' wars with the empire that encouraged their citizens to sacralize the commune. The cities exploited religious forms of organization, they sought legitimacy through the cult of patron saints, they conceptualized their time and space in sacred terms, and these religious realities in turn formed the people. The Italian city as a living religious entity deserves greater attention.

I should note from the onset that I have chosen to keep the Franciscans on the sidelines and so let the piety that produced Francis speak for itself. There is probably no period and place in Christian history where ordinary people had a greater impact on forms of devotion than in the communal republics of Italy. The world of the communes came between the rule of the count-bishops of the old empire and the later rule of the princes. The cities produced a religious culture truly their own. Communal Italy also produced the single largest concentration of lay saints in Christian history, the modern age included. This book is meant to be about the people who produced Saint Francis, not his imitators or those whom he influenced.

Scholars of ancient and early modern religion have already produced fine reconstructions of Christians and their lived piety—their rituals, their beliefs, and their devotions.[16] These accomplishments challenge the way we Italian medievalists do our work. Such a study is long overdue for communal Italy. If my book has succeeded in recapturing this lost world, even in part, then good. If it has failed, then I hope it will convince others to renew the attempt.

PART I: SACRED GEOGRAPHY
The first part of this book presents a religious geography of the communes, the self-governing republics of Italy, during their classical period, 1125–1325.[17] My geographical choice was not arbitrary, as will become clearer as the book goes on. Until books like this one appear for France, England, Germany, Spain, and the rest of Italy, sustained comparisons are impossible. But it is already clear that in many ways the religious life of the Italian communes was unique. Only in central and northern Italy did the public cult focus on a revival of the ancient practice of mass Easter baptisms conducted by the bishop. Elsewhere in Europe the dioceses were simply too large for such consolidation.[18] Scholars working on southern Italy assure me

15. See Diana M. Webb, "Cities of God: The Italian Communes at War," *The Church and War*, ed. W. J. Sheils, Studies in Church History, 20 (Oxford: Ecclesiastical History Society, 1983)," 111–14.

16. And not only for Christianity; on lived ancient Judaism, see E. P. Sanders, *Judaism: Practice and Belief, 63 B.C.E.–66 C.E.* (London: SCM, 1992). On Christianity I have especially in mind Eamon Duffy's *Stripping of the Altars: Traditional Religion in England, 1400–1580* (New Haven: Yale University Press, 1992), 9–376, and Robin Lane Fox's *Pagans and Christians* (New York: Knopf, 1987), both of which have had great influence on my project.

17. For the political history of the communes, see Jones, *Italian City-State;* Hyde, *Society and Politics;* and Daniel Philip Waley, *The Italian City Republics*, 3d ed. (New York: Longman, 1989).

18. See Robert Brentano, *Two Churches: England and Italy in the Thirteenth Century*, 2d ed. (Berkeley and Los Angeles: University of California Press, 1988).

that it did not occur there; indeed, south Italian cities were quite different in their ecclesiastical, commercial, and political forms.[19] So, too, only in the region studied in this book did medieval cities construct great new monumental baptisteries for their Easter rites. This special focus of city religious life on the cathedral complex also distinguishes the religion of the large communes from the Italian countryside—where such consolidation was impossible.

Within north-central Italy, I focus principally on those cities that achieved practical autonomy during the twelfth-century struggles against German imperial rule. This means that I have little to say about Venice, so unique in many ways, or the cities in the States of the Church, with their unique relations to their nearby papal sovereign. At the risk of anachronism—for even today Italy is a land of fierce regionalism—I call, as a shorthand, the citizens of these cities "Italians." Although they certainly thought of themselves first of all as Florentines or Bolognese, Milanese or Sienese, these communes had marked cultural and political similarity, and they themselves had already begun to use the adjective *italiani* to distinguish themselves from their would-be German overlords.[20]

Chronological divisions, like those I have chosen, are always arbitrary, but mine provide a reasonable framework for the age of the republican city-states of Italy.[21] In 1125, the emperor Henry V died; two hundred years later, only two of the northern communes, Padua and Parma, still enjoyed republican independence. In 1328, they too fell into the hands of seignorial families, the della Scala and the Rossi. Henry's death signaled the decline of imperial power in the north and the establishment of independent governments, a process complete by 1140. Already before the fall of Padua and Parma, the age of princes had arrived and the republican era was gone. In Tuscany, as at Venice and Genoa, republican forms continued on, but these cities became oligarchies, having little in common with the popular communes of the 1200s. Ruling groups always employ public ceremony for their own purposes. The ritual world of late medieval Florence, so provocatively described by Richard Trexler, with its aristocratic flavor evocative of the Medici princes, feels quite different from that of the high medieval communes.[22] I suspect that the rise of princes and oligarchies lies behind this change, although this is still a conjecture waiting for another book to confirm it.

The first five chapters of this book map the religious and civic "geography" of the city-states. The first sketches the republics' ecclesiastical institutions and their relation to civic identity. The bishop, the cathedral, and the diocese predated the commune, and they outlived it. Historians have given

---

19. See Jones, *Italian City-State*, 262, on the contrasts between north and south.
20. See ibid., 478.
21. As in Hyde, *Society and Politics*, 59, 146.
22. See *Public Life in Renaissance Florence* (Ithaca: Cornell University Press, 1991), esp. 549–53.

much attention to the economic and political development of Italian bishop-rics.[23] We have much on church territory and jurisdiction, much on diocesan administration, but little on the people's identification with the church of the city.[24] I hope to go beyond these investigations and present bishops, cathe-drals, clergy, and parish organization as the context for the religious world of the citizens. I am especially interested in the ways in which they provided the backdrop for the creation and development of the early communes, polit-ically, culturally, and spiritually.

The rise of the communes presupposed the formation of voluntary associ-ations, in particular the religious associations that grew up in the penance culture populated by the *conversi*—lay penitents, often married—who sponta-neously took up a life of moderate asceticism while remaining in the world. Chapter 2 treats this movement and its forms. The chapter is founded on the well-known work of Fr. Giles Gérard Meersseman,[25] adding new items from manuscript sources only occasionally. Conversi had already begun to coalesce into groups half a century before they received a "rule" in 1210. Their societies and confraternities provided a model for other voluntary as-sociations, especially those that would form the corporations known as the Popolo (people) in the golden age of communal democracy.

The third chapter focuses on the popular commune itself and its religious self-understanding. The precocious democracy of the Italian communes is too well known to require much comment. Recently, scholars have reevalu-ated the ideology of the medieval republics and discovered a political theory of great sophistication, in comparison to which Renaissance "civic human-ism" looks rather restricted and oligarchic. But even the most evocative ap-preciations of communal political theory obscure its Christian character.[26] Ecclesiastical and civic institutions formed a single communal organism, and this chapter is meant as a complement, not a contrast, to my first chapter. Communal lay governments themselves magnified their "sacred" aspects, associating their cities with patron saints and, especially in the age of the Popolo, adopting wholesale religious language, rituals, and forms.[27] Bishop and commune, clergy and laity, feuded occasionally, but they inhabited the same space and shared the same culture.

Chapter 4 evaluates how the cities used ritual to form and "imagine"

23. See Cinzio Violante, "Sistemi organizzativi della cura d'anime in Italia tra Medioevo e Rinasci-mento: Discorso introduttivo," *Pievi e parrocchie in Italia nel basso Medioevo (sec. XIII–XV)*, ed. A. Erba et al. (Rome: Herder, 1984), 1:36, on tithing studies.

24. Antonio Rigon, "Congregazioni del clero cittadino e storia della parrocchia nell'Italia settentrio-nale: Il problema delle fonti," *La parrocchia nel Medio Evo, economia, scambi, solidarietà*, ed. Agostino Paravicini Bagliani and Véronique Pache, Italia Sacra 53 (Rome: Herder, 1995), 4; on diocesan administration, see Brentano, *Two Churches*.

25. See his *Dossier* and *Ordo*.

26. E.g., John Hine Mundy, "In Praise of Italy: The Italian Republics," *Speculum* 64 (1989): 815–35.

27. See Paolo Golinelli, *Città e culto dei santi nel Medioevo italiano*, 2d ed. (Bologna: CLUEB, 1996), 67–68, on the political aspects of patronal cults.

themselves.[28] Much has been done on ritual in late medieval Italy, but not in high medieval Italy.[29] I hope this chapter will break some ground in that direction. Processions, candle offerings, and bell ringing dominated the ritual expressions of public life in the Italian republics. Such ceremonies claimed a public space for the city's "natural" unit, the family, shaped the social ordering of neighborhoods, and finally gave identity to the city itself. Rituals made tangible the patterns and orderings of urban life. In them, the city spoke to itself about its composition, its sources of authority and power, and its boundaries.

Italian urban piety produced a peculiar kind of holiness. The final chapter of Part 1 focuses on the most distinctive spiritual characteristic of the communes, their lay saints. Medieval "sanctity" has also been the object of much historical and anthropological study in recent years. So, too, the urban context of medieval Italian saints is now getting the attention it deserves.[30] Still, the towering figure of Saint Francis of Assisi—and his order—so dominate the landscape that we easily forget that he exemplified a common lay style of holiness.[31] The holy men and women of the cities deserve a portrait in their own right because they represent the holiness venerated by their contemporaries. The saints are not a stand-in for ordinary lay piety. First, they were saints and, by that standard, exceptional. There is no question that a certain, more or less sizable, proportion of the lay population was not pious at all and perhaps even religiously indifferent.[32] Second, with a couple of exceptions, the saints were very much influenced by traditional monastic asceticism and so distanced themselves from many aspects of ordinary life, such as children and marriage. The exceptions include Saint Facio of Cremona, Saint Pietro Pettinaio of Siena, and Saint Omobono of Cremona. Ascetic as they were, they did not become full-fledged penitents. The lay saints were above all good neighbors, exceptional principally in the intensity with which they lived the common religiosity. The women saints did not enter cloisters or join organized religious orders. The men practiced worldly professions or dedicated themselves to organized charity. Even hermits, like

28. Enrico Cattaneo, "Il battistero in Italia dopo il Mille," *Miscellanea Gilles Gérard Meersseman*, ed. Michele Maccarrone et al. (Padua: Antenore, 1970), 1:182.

29. See, e.g., Trexler, *Public Life*; E. Muir, *Civic Ritual in Renaissance Venice* (Princeton: Princeton University Press, 1981); and Ronald F. E. Weissman, *Ritual Brotherhood in Renaissance Florence* (New York: Academic Press, 1982).

30. See Paolo Golinelli, "Agiografia e storia in studi recenti: Appunti e note per una discussione," *Società e storia* 19 (1983): 109–200 (with bibliography, 277–303); Sophia Boesch Gajano, "Il culto dei santi: Filologia, antropologia e storia," *Studi storici* 23 (1982): 119–32; and Vauchez, *Laity in the Middle Ages*, 51–72.

31. On Francis and his movement, see *Gli studi francescani dal dopoguerra ad oggi*, ed. Francesco Santi (Spoleto: Centro Italiano di Studi sull'Alto Medioevo, 1993).

32. At least that was the opinion of the six mendicant preachers studied in Alexander Murray's "Piety and Impiety in Thirteenth-Century Italy," *Popular Belief and Practice: Papers Read at the Ninth Summer Meeting and the Tenth Winter Meeting of the Ecclesiastical History Society*, ed. G. J. Cuming and Derek Baker, Studies in Church History, 8 (Cambridge: Cambridge University Press, 1972), 83–106, but then few moralizers underestimate the prevalence of sin.

Saint Giovanni Buono of Mantua or Saint Galgano of Siena, never ceased to be part of the city landscape. Their neighbors responded to these remarkable individuals by "canonizing" them, that is, by praying to them after death and expecting miracles. Cities collaborated in the cults, erecting shrines and fostering devotion. Sometimes devotees called in the papacy to validate a saint, but this was neither necessary nor common. A network of local shrines imposed a kind of "charismatic" overlay on the religious geography of civic and ecclesiastical institutions. The saint, living at home or supernaturally present at his shrine, was a fixture of urban religious geography.

Part I of this book draws heavily on city and ecclesiastical statutes, tithe lists, court litigation, and hagiography. Studies on the significance of the names that Italians gave their children, like those on the relative popularity of civic patron saints, I have used whenever available, though mostly by default, since little other evidence exists for religious institutions and attitudes.[33] The transition from legal and administrative texts to lived realities, and from hagiographic commonplaces to actual people, is fraught with pitfalls. Nonetheless, if particular saints did not perform the marvels ascribed to them, their biographers still had to assimilate the saints to conventional ways of holiness. And that is exactly our subject. Furthermore, when emphasizing the miraculous, biographers could not hide the very conventionality that recommended saints to the neighbors who canonized them. In legal texts, too, a society often speaks to itself about shared ideals and fears.

PART II: RELIGIOUS OBSERVANCE

Shared religion is shared behavior as well as space. Part II focuses on the shared behavior of communal Catholics, but it is not a study of "popular religion."[34] It is a study of communal—that is, urban—religion as experienced by all its practitioners, from the common people to the elites. The first three chapters of this section are liturgical history, understanding "liturgy" in its original Greek meaning as "the work of the people." I focus more on the laity than the clergy, even though the rituals described are mostly the formal cult of the Church, the sacraments of the Mass, penance, and baptism. I have foregrounded, in all three chapters, the "nave" and backgrounded the "choir." In church, movement, gesture, and sensation spoke

33. See Violante, "Sistemi," 40–41.

34. For criticism of the idea of "popular religion," see Jean-Claude Schmitt, "'Religion populaire' et culture folklorique," *Annales: Économies—sociétés—civilisations* 31 (1976): 941–53; Natalie Davis, "Some Tasks and Themes in the Study of Popular Religion," *The Pursuit of Holiness in Late Medieval and Renaissance Religion,* ed. Charles Trinkaus and Heiko A. Oberman, Studies in Medieval and Renaissance Thought, 10 (Leiden: Brill, 1974), 307–36; ead., "From 'Popular Religion' to Religious Cultures," *Reformation Europe: A Guide to Research,* ed. Steven Ozment (St. Louis: Center for Reformation Research, 1982), 321–42; Leonard Boyle, "Popular Piety in the Middle Ages: What Is Popular?" *Florilegium* 4 (1982): 184–93; and John Van Engen, "The Christian Middle Ages as an Historiographical Problem," *American Historical Review* 91 (1988): 512–52. In my opinion, the most trenchant critique of the "popular-religion" model remains Peter Brown, *The Cult of the Saints: Its Rise and Function in Latin Antiquity* (Chicago: University of Chicago Press, 1981), 12–20.

more eloquently than words to the laity. Nevertheless, words did matter. The unlettered "got" and "took away" much more from the chanted Latin than we give them credit for. The liturgy of the cities, except for Milan, with its Ambrosian Rite, was that of the Roman Church in a north Italian form.[35] I have privileged liturgical sources localized in that region. One witness has proved indispensable, Bishop Sicardo of Cremona, whose *Mitrale* is a trove of riches for Italian worship in the late 1100s.[36] Next to him in importance are the canons of Siena, who produced a revision of their early-twelfth-century ordo about 1210.[37] Equal in importance is the work of Rolando, a deacon of Pisa, who compiled his study of local Pisan usages in the late 1100s (fig. 49).[38] For the lay perspective on the rituals described by these clerics, I have drawn on hagiography and narrative sources.

The first of the three liturgical chapters focuses on the Divine Office and the Mass. These, and especially the latter, formed the shared devotional patrimony of medieval Italians, as they did for Christians throughout Europe. The next two chapters follow the liturgical year, that catechetical tool of the medieval Church. First, I examine the period from Christmas to Lent, briefly glancing at the feasts of the saints. Lent, especially after 1215, was the time for confession, and in this context I examine that sacrament and the pious practices that surrounded it. It is not my intention to reproduce the massive scholarship treating penitential and confessional manuals in the period. Rather, I try to recover the people's experience of going to confession and doing penance. The concentration of private confessions in Lent following Lateran IV and their linkage with public reconciliations had a transforming impact on the sacramental rite. The last liturgical chapter moves through Holy Week to Pentecost. Its centerpiece is the civic rite of the Easter vigil, with its mass baptism of infants, a ritual innovation distinctive of the communes. Baptism made the children citizens of both the commune and of heaven. At Easter the commune renewed itself and reaffirmed its identity as a sacred society. These rites came to be so closely associated with republican identity that they were among the first things to go as princes established seignorial rule in the early 1300s.

The ninth chapter focuses on the prayer life of ordinary people outside of

35. On Roman and Ambrosian liturgical customs, see Pierre-Marie Gy, "La papauté et le droit liturgique aux xiième et xiiième siècles," *The Religious Roles of the Papacy: Ideals and Realities, 1150–1300*, ed. Christopher Ryan (Toronto: PIMS, 1989), 229–45.

36. *Mitrale; seu, De Officiis Ecclesiasticis Summa*, PL 213:13–432. On the exemplarity of Sicardo for our period, see Enrico Cattaneo, "Lo spazio ecclesiale: Pratica liturgica," *Pievi e parrocchie*, ed. Erba et al., 1:475, and Webb, *Patrons*, 19–20.

37. For Sienese use about 1213, see *Ordo Senensis*, which edits Siena, Biblioteca Comunale degli Intronati, MS G.v.8 (late xii cent.); on which, see Lorenzo Ilari, *La biblioteca pubblica di Siena disposta secondo le materie* (Siena: Ancora, 1849), 5:74. See Mino Marchetti, *Liturgia e storia della chiesa di Siena nel xii secolo: I calendari medioevali della chiesa senese* (Roccastrada: Istituto Storico Diocesano di Siena, 1991), 45–60, on dating this manuscript; but cf. Webb, *Patrons*, 20–21.

38. Unedited, text in Bologna, Biblioteca Universitaria, MS 1785.

the liturgical context. Taken with the earlier chapters on sacramental life, this completes my overview of orthodox religious practice and experience within the spiritual geography described in the first part of the book. Narrative sources paint a vivid picture of the "lay Psalter," the practice of reciting a set number of Our Fathers and Hail Marys that would become the Rosary of the late Middle Ages and modern Catholicism. Manuscript collections of devotions and prayers dating as early as the 1200s suggest more bookish forms of piety. A final chapter focuses on death and the rituals that gave it meaning, linking the living to the faithful departed. Here I consider both the rituals of dying—making an edifying "good death"—and the web of relations and neighbors who assisted those dying and carried their bodies to the church and grave. Where they exist, I have drawn on published studies of Italian wills and testaments, especially for what these can tell us about deathbed charitable practices.[39] Communal Italians reaffirmed the community even in death by the performance of suffrages, prayers for the dead. I close the book by acknowledging how this practice linked the people of the city here on earth to their neighbors beyond the grave, creating a community transcending time.

I began this book hoping to write a history of communal religion that, without completely forgetting heretics and mendicants, left them mostly in the background so that the vast majority who were neither might be seen. As I worked on this book, I found it impossible to leave heretics and mendicants totally unremarked. So I have added an epilogue treating both. The mendicant orders arose in the world of communal piety and ultimately came to dominate it. In the Epilogue, I sketch the impact of the mendicants' rise to hegemony. The friars slowly replaced the lay penitents as the religious presence in city government. Their great churches refashioned the religious geography of the cities, and their spiritual authority remolded lay piety. By the end of the communal period, lay sainthood pretty much demanded affiliation with the mendicants through one of their "third orders." Ironically, the friars arose from the lay religiosity of the communes, but in the end, as clerics, they came to dominate it. Their role in the transformation of communal piety, which was a long progressive development, deserves a study of its own. The friars, often as inquisitors, became arbiters of orthodoxy and opponents of dissent. Their definition of deviance, like the papacy's, differed from that of the lay orthodoxy. By the late 1200s, the older freelance lay

---

39. Suggestive on this is *Nolens Intestatus Decedere: Il testamento come fonte della storia religiosa e sociale: Atti dell'incontro di studio (Perugia, 3 maggio 1983)* (Perugia: Editrice Umbra Cooperativa, 1985), esp. Robert Brentano, "Considerazioni di un lettore di testamenti," 3–9, which focuses on wills as a source for religious sensibilities. I have, with regret, chosen not to analyze systematically the many large deposits of unpublished Italian wills, such as that described for Bologna by Martin Bertram in "Bologneser Testamente I: Die urkundliche Überlieferung," *Quellen und Forschungen aus italienischen Archiven und Bibliotheken* 70 (1990): 151–233, and "Bologneser Testamente II: Sondierungen in den *Libri Memoriali*," *Quellen und Forschungen aus italienischen Archiven und Bibliotheken* 71 (1991): 193–240. To have done so would have made this already long book even longer.

spirituality that produced the communal saints began to look suspect and some of its most revered practitioners dubious. The conservatism, independence, and simple-minded rituals of lay spirituality looked unformed and perhaps adulterated by theological deviance. The mendicants aggressively directed urban religiosity in new ways. Shrines of dubious saints were destroyed; laypeople who escaped clerical tutelage became suspect. It was the inquisitors' harassment of the traditionally orthodox, with their old-fashioned piety and devotions, more than the burning of heretics that fed popular resentment against the Holy Office. As the civic religion of the Italian republics was transformed, the homely holiness it nurtured passed into oblivion, but not without protest. My epilogue concludes by recounting a conflict over orthodoxy that pitched the lay population of Bologna against the Dominican inquisition there in 1299. In the wake of that conflict, the inquisitors interrogated more than 350 laypersons and investigated, among other things, the ways in which they conceived of "practical orthodoxy"—the beliefs and practices that led people's neighbors to consider them members in good standing of the Catholic community of the city.

These laypeople's responses to the inquisitor nicely confirmed the image of day-to-day religiosity I had formed during my research on this project. This book is itself a homage to the lost holiness of the Italian republics; I dedicate it to the unexceptional Italian men and women who were its practitioners.

PART ONE

La Citade Sancta

SACRED GEOGRAPHY

Chapter One
The Mother Church

In a sermon on the Annunciation, the Dominican preacher Bartolomeo of Braganze, later bishop of Vicenza, digressed and praised hometowns, no matter how small. He contrasted Christ's little Nazareth with the great cities he had visited. "There was Paris, then he came to Bologna, then he went to Rome, and then he was sent to Jerusalem. But on this feast, the Son of God, through Gabriel, teaches us that we should glory in our own town more than all others. For God in the Gospel tells us: Go and sit in the lowest place!"[1] Bartolomeo had it right. For a thirteenth-century Italian no place could compare with his birthplace, however humble. The native city was itself sacred. Not that grand buildings, mighty walls, bustling commerce, a powerful militia, and a splendid location did not count. All the better! The twelfth- and thirteenth-century *Laudes Civitatum*, poems hailing Italian cities, tell us what citizens gloried in most: large and numerous churches, famous bishops, tombs of powerful saints, and grand public spectacles.[2] These proved the glory of the city, the pride of citizens. In churches, bigger was better, as, in saints, international renown outclassed mere local devotion. The Franciscan friar Salimbene of Parma visited the Black Monks of Cluny in 1247. He commented with chagrin that the French Benedictines outshone their brothers in Italy—they had the grandest church and monastery in Europe.[3]

---

1. Bartolomeo of Vicenza, *Sermones de Beata Virgine (1266)*, ed. Laura Gaffuri (Padua: Antenore, 1993), Sermo 55.4, p. 363: "Loca vero nobilia prima pronte nominantur ut: erat Parisius, venit Bononiam, ivit Romam, missus est in Ierusalem. Et per hoc Dei Filius per Gabrielem nos edocuit ut illa loca eligamus que possint de nobis magis quam nos de ipsis, gloriari. Propter quod Deus in evangelio consulit: vade et recumbe in novissimo loco [Luke 14:10]"; on this passage, see ibid., p. xvi.

2. Giorgio Cracco, "La 'cura animarum' nella cultura laica del tardo Medioevo (lo specchio delle 'Laudes Civitatum')," *Pievi e parrocchie*, ed. Erba et al., esp. 1:561, and Pini, *Città, comuni e corporazioni*, 177.

3. Salimbene, *Cronica* (1247), Baird trans., 203.

The Cultic Center

The city: the church. The church: the bishopric. When the north and central Italian cities shook off imperial control and established their unique form of government, the commune, the word they used for city (*civitas—citade*) said that the municipality was the seat of a bishop.[4] To have a bishop was to be complete as a church, complete as a city. The authority of the commune and its bishop together extended into the *contado*, the countryside. The city fathers of Parma used the words *episcopatus* (bishopric) and *civitas* (city) as synonyms in their podesta's oath and in laws and statutes.[5] Strictly speaking, the *episcopatus*, the seat of the bishop, was his cathedral. Therein and -about unfolded the splendid public ceremonies and rites beloved of the poets. Great episcopal liturgies made it the *Ecclesia Matrix*, the Mother Church, of the diocese (fig. 1). At Bergamo in 1187, during an inquest to identify the city's true Ecclesia Matrix, Canon Oberto of Mapello from San Vincenzo explained that in his church "the bishop is chosen, there the holy chrism is made, there ordinations take place, there the scrutinies are performed, and there public penances are given." His friend the sacristan, Don Lanfranco of Monasterolo, added that San Vincenzo was also the place for baptisms and, more ominously, for excommunications.[6] Baptism made lay Christians, ordination made the clergy. Both orders of people, clergy and laity, were born at the Mother Church, the womb of their city. Over these rites presided the bishop, the pastor of the city church.

The cathedral provided the model for the rest of the diocese. One could tell a Sienese church, however far out in the countryside, because it modeled its ceremonies and worship on those at the cathedral of the Glorious Virgin. The clergy of Piacenza agreed; Piacentine rites identified a Piacentine church.[7] Conformity to the ritual customs of the cathedral was an ancient rule, enshrined in canon law.[8] Did the village of San Cesario belong to Bologna or to Modena? One need only check the liturgical books of the parish: the feast of Saint Petronio of Bologna outranked that of Saint Giminiano of Modena. The place was Bolognese.[9] Liturgy more than geography mapped the countryside.

4. On the bishop's presence in the cities, see Maureen C. Miller, *The Bishop's Palace: Architecture and Authority in Medieval Italy* (Ithaca: Cornell University Press, 2000), and Carlrichard Brühl, "Il 'Palazzo' nelle città italiane," *La coscienza cittadina nei comuni italiani nel duecento*, 265–66; on city and bishopric, see Pini, *Città, comuni e corporazioni*, 16–17, and C. D. Fonseca, "'Ecclesia Matrix' e 'conventus civium': L'ideologia della cattedrale nell'età comunale," *La pace di Costanza, 1183: Un difficile equilibrio di poteri fra società italiana ed impero* (Bologna: Cappelli, 1984), 135–49.

5. E.g., Parma Stat. 1 (1250), 1, pp. 3 and 59.

6. "Instrumentum Litis de Matricitate," ed. Giangiuseppina Valsecchi (September 1187), 2.13 (Oberto) and 2.18 (Lanfranco), Giangiuseppina Valsecchi, *"Interrogatus . . . Respondit": Storia di un processo del xii secolo* (Bergamo: Biblioteca Civica, 1989), 148 and 152.

7. Piacenza Stat. Cler. (1298), pp. 530, 538.

8. *Ordo Senensis*, 2.106, p. 514, quoting the *Decretum Gratiani*, D. 12 c. 13.

9. On the vagueness of diocesan boundaries, see A. Benati, "Confine ecclesiastico e problemi circoscrizionali e patrimoniali tra Ferrara e Bologna nell'alto Medioevo," *AMDSPPR*, 3d ser., 27 (1980): 29–80.

In 1123, at Piacenza, Bishop Arduino, seemingly for the first time, made his cathedral the sole *pieve* (baptismal church) for the whole city. He ordered the congregations of all eighteen urban chapels *and* of the seven suburban churches henceforth to attend the Easter vigil and its baptisms at the duomo.[10] This would effectively have ended, for the suburban pievi at least, the practice most typical of a pieve—the administration of baptism. Bishop Lanfranco Civolla of Bergamo also tried, later in the 1100s, to concentrate pastoral functions at his cathedral church. He attempted to subordinate the four suburban chapels dependent on the church of Sant'Alessandro to the cathedral of San Vincenzo.[11] The result was that within and without the walls all attended the duomo for major feasts. Into the 1200s, however, the collegiate church of Santa Maria Maggiore, the "Cappella della Città," still rivaled the cathedral of San Vincenzo as the religious center of the city and diocese. That was truly exceptional at such a late date.[12] In 1136, Bishop Landolfo of Ferrara celebrated the consecration of his new cathedral— whose magnificent facade still delights visitors (fig. 2)—by issuing this edict: "Let no one, whether in town or in the suburbs, dare to baptize, confirm, give public penance, or probate wills," save by the will of the cathedral canons. So did he centralize the rites of baptism, penance, and death at his new cathedral,[13] and so began the displacement of the old baptismal churches in Ferrara's suburbs. During the decades that followed, Ferrarese priests, like Don Giovanni of San Marco di Fossanova in 1143, might still occasionally bring their parishioners' infants to the old cathedral of San Giorgio for the scrutinies during Lent and for baptism at Easter. Bishop Landolfo allowed such exceptions merely as a gesture of respect to the ancient church, where, after all, he still lived. By 1200, however, the great rites of baptism had become the monopoly of one place, his new Santa Maria, the Mother Church of Ferrara.[14]

The cathedral canons of Ferrara zealously vindicated their new exclusive claim on baptism. In 1211, priests of Santa Maria in Vado, an old baptismal church, started doing baptism at Easter again. Previously they had conformed and come to the new cathedral for baptisms and for the major feasts

---

10. Giovanni Felice Rossi, "Battistero della chiesa piacentina dalle origini a metà del secolo XVI," *Atti del convegno di Parma (1976)*, Ravennatensia, 7 (Cesena: Santa Maria del Monte, 1979), 61–62.

11. Valsecchi, *Interrogatus*, 52–54.

12. See Giuseppina Zizzo, "S. Maria Maggiore di Bergamo 'Cappella della Città': La basilica bergamasca nei secoli XII e XIII," *Archivio storico bergamasco* 2 (1982): 216–19, and Miller, *Bishop's Palace*, 185–87. Another exception would be Forlì, with its two baptismal churches.

13. Document edited in Antonio Samaritani, "Circoscrizioni battesimali, distrettuazioni pastorali, congregazioni chiericali nel Medioevo ferrarese," *Analecta pomposiana* 4 (1978): 94–96. On the cathedral and city of Ferrara, see *La cattedrale di Ferrara: [Atti del Convegno nazionale di studi storici organizzato dalla Accademia delle scienze di Ferrara . . . , 11–13 maggio, 1979]* (Ferrara: Belriguardo, 1982).

14. Document to this effect by Landolfo, edited in Samaritani, "Circoscrizioni," 99. For the cathedral's monopoly over baptism and rites of Easter at Pisa, see Mauro Ronzani, "L'organizzazione della cura d'anime nella città di Pisa (secoli XII–XIII)," *Istituzioni ecclesiastiche della Toscana medioevale*, ed. C. Fonseca and C. Violante (Galatina: Commissione Italiana per la Storia delle Pievi, 1980), 49–52.

of the Church year. Ritually, their recommencement of baptisms put them in competition with the cathedral. It seems their excuse for recommencing baptisms was the fortieth anniversary of a Eucharistic miracle that was supposed to have happened in their church. But miracles did not count against the Ecclesia Matrix in this dispute. The court ordered the priests of Santa Maria in Vado to desist and return to the cathedral—under pain of excommunication.[15] At Bergamo, the ancient collegiate church of Sant'Alessandro shared baptismal rights with the cathedral of San Vincenzo. Then, in the 1180s, the cathedral clergy went to court against Sant'Alessandro to vindicate their exclusive right to the title of Ecclesia Matrix. Cardinal Adelardo of San Marcello, legate of Pope Urban III, heard the case. On 23 December 1189 he resolved the dispute in favor of the cathedral and merged the two groups of clergy into a single body.[16] The cathedral became the unique religious head of the city. As in ritual, so in civil law. In 1224, Volterra promulgated new statutes and decreed of their cathedral: "As that church is the head and authority for all the city of Volterra and its district, so it follows, to the honor of the Blessed Virgin and the city and district of the Commune of Volterra, that we should first discuss church matters found in its constitutions."[17] They did not linger long over the cathedral's statutes, but their legal point had been made. The cathedral came first in authority and honor. Almost everywhere by 1200 the concentration of major religious rites at the cathedral was complete. This consolidation of ritual and sacramental life at the cathedral gave the bishop the exclusive responsibility over the care of souls in his city. One might read this as episcopal imperialism, with the bishops seeking to regain in the spiritual sphere the civil authority they were losing to the commune.[18] But the identification of church and city made the commune's secular consolidation and the bishop's spiritual consolidation two sides of one coin.

The *citade* was a single sacred entity. The bishop was its pastor; his cathedral was its parish church: the "house" (*duomo*) of the city. No communal government ever doubted this. At Bologna in 1222, Saint Francis of Assisi gave his famous sermon to a packed crowd in the piazza of the commune.[19] The Bolognese duomo, San Pietro, was a few blocks away in its own piazza. This separation of space was precocious. Until the late 1200s, when most cities completed their communal palazzi, the piazza of the duomo and pi-

---

15. Samaritani, "Circoscrizioni," 116.

16. See Valsecchi, *Interrogatus*, esp. 49–53. On the city and cathedral of Bergamo, see Zizzo, "S. Maria Maggiore di Bergamo," 207–29.

17. Volterra Stat. (1224), 1–2, pp. 108–10: "Quoniam ecclesia est caput et principium totius Vulterrane civitatis eiusque districtus, sequitur ergo quod, ad honorem Dei et beate Marie Virginis et totius comunis Vulterrane civitatis eiusque districtus, de negotiis ecclesiarum in constitutionibus istis prius tractare debeamus."

18. So Miller, *Bishop's Palace*, 6, who rejects the idea that this activity shows the bishops as involved in a power struggle with the commune: ibid., 142.

19. Matteo Griffoni, 8; *CCB*: Vill., 86.

azza of the commune were the same. The piazza of the duomo was a privileged area, different from all others.[20] Buildings fronting it, sometimes even small churches, were removed at city expense to enhance its size and beauty. When the demolition involved an old church, however, the city erected a covered cross on the spot to remind passersby that they trod on consecrated ground.[21] At Parma and Pisa, the duomo and its piazza were a single legal entity, with carefully defined boundaries, protected by special laws against violence and insult.[22] At Modena, perpetual banishment punished those who profaned the duomo or its piazza.[23] The Sienese podesta's oath of office committed him, first of all, to protect physically and legally the religious spaces and institutions of the city, above all the duomo of the Glorious Virgin.[24] When an outrage occurred in the cultic center, reaction could be visceral and violent. At Bologna in 1262, robbers carrying off money and church plate murdered Don Enrico, the sacristan of San Pietro, and his nephew Bernardino. The seven perpetrators were apprehended while attempting an escape to the roof. Citizens threw one malefactor to his death from the top of the episcopal palace; four they quartered (*stasinati*) in the piazza. The remaining two escaped by night from prison. The man set to guard them, a servant of the bishop, was tortured for information. He died on the rack.[25] The site of the crime more than its victims triggered this savage retribution.

Like most cities, Padua made do with heavy fines to keep its cultic center pure, clear of noisome leavings.[26] In other cities, the bishop and commune collaborated and hired a custodian to police the area and clean up trash.[27] By 1277, Brescia had hired a *vir religiosus* to keep the church of San Pietro cleared of wood and swept clean.[28] This city bound the podesta under oath to prevent scrap parchment from being thrown out the windows of the city offices onto the duomo. He could fine litterbugs up to 40s.[29] The city fathers of tiny Biella near Vercelli protected the dignity of their religious center with a vigor equal to that of the great communes. In 1245, they imposed a fine of 22s. on anyone who dared to climb the facade of a city church—one can imagine small boys!—unless, of course, the climber was doing repairs.[30] Not atypically, Biella excluded gamblers and prostitutes from its cultic center.[31]

20. On the civic role of the piazza duomo, see Pini, *Città, comuni e corporazioni*, 29–32.
21. *CCB:* A (1285), 227: At Bologna, Santa Maria de Rustigani in Piazza Maggiore came down this way.
22. Parma Stat. 1 (by 1255), pp. 286–87, 295–96. Pisa Stat. 1 (1286), 1.23, pp. 81–82.
23. Modena Stat. (1327), 4.18, pp. 388–89, for *insulto* or *mislancia*—that is, for insult or assault.
24. Siena Stat. II (1310), 1.6–12, 1:48–64.
25. Matteo Griffoni (1262), 16.
26. Padua Stat. (pre-1236), 3.6, pp. 257–56, no. 781.
27. E.g., Parma Stat. 1 (1233), p. 320, and Brescia Stat. (1313), 1.109, col. 33.
28. Brescia Stat. (before 1277), col. (185).
29. Ibid. (1313), 1.35, col. 13.
30. Biella Stat., 1.3.13 (73).
31. Brescia Stat. (1313), 2.30, col. 72 (gambling); Lucca Stat. (1308), 3.152, p. 228–29 (prostitution).

The town strictly forbade unseemly activities there, especially rock fights between groups of youths, because of possible damage to precious city monuments.[32] Cities sought, in little ways, to protect the dignity of their Mother Church. At the end of the century, the archpriest of the duomo at Modena petitioned the city to purchase new clothing for Antonio, the poor fellow charged with sweeping, trimming the lights, and acting as night watchman in the duomo chapel of Saint Giminiano. The city was already providing for two other regular custodians to be properly attired, "to the honor of Saint Giminiano" and, of course, to the honor of Modena. They happily added Antonio to their subvention.[33]

The cathedral belonged as much to the city as to the bishop. Communes monopolized its construction, reconstruction, and embellishment. In 1267, the city fathers of Siena organized the Opera del Duomo, a board responsible for the material upkeep of their beloved Santa Maria. After first funding the city's vigil lamp before the altar of Mary, the fathers stipulated the officers, oaths of office, funding, and responsibilities of the board. By the 1290s, officials of the Opera were appointed directly by the Nine, the executive committee of the commune. Twice yearly they requisitioned all draft animals in the city for hauling marble to the construction at the duomo.[34] The city provided food for laborers and protection for their beasts of burden.[35] Other cities did likewise. In 1264, Vicenza hired a supervisor for its cathedral and established a yearly subsidy for its decoration and maintenance.[36] By 1286, Pisa had in place for the cathedral of Santa Maria Maggiore and its already famous tower a system even grander in scale than that at Siena. When the city named Giovanni Scorcialupo di Ser Ranieri director, they provided him with a secretary, a lawyer, three servants, two horses, and a house.[37] So important was his service that the city forbade him to engage in any other work or business during his tenure.[38] Cities competed for famous architects, painters, and sculptors. Modena had the good fortune to commission the famous Tommaso of Fredo to carve the cathedral pulpit.[39] Pisa boasted one of the greatest artists of the period, Giovanni di Nicola Pisano. The city ensured his services as *capomaestro* of Santa Maria by grant of a tax exemption and a promise to fire any staff member of the Opera with whom he could not get along.[40]

32. Vicenza Stat. (1264), 147; Pisa Stat. I (1286), 1.154, p. 263, and Pisa Stat. II (1313), 1.207, p. 221; Florence Stat. II (1325), 3.40, pp. 202–3.

33. Modena Stat. (1306/7), 2:203 and 1:102. On this period, see Carmen Vicini, *La caduta del primo dominio estense a Modena e la nuova costituzione democratica del comune (1306–1307)* (Modena: n.p., 1922).

34. Siena Stat. I (1262), 1.6–13, pp. 27–28; on draft animals, ibid., 1.17, p. 30.

35. Siena Stat. II (1290), 1.507–10, 1:319–20; ibid. (1297), 1.57–62, 1:85–87.

36. Vicenza Stat. (1264), 199. It amounted to £10.

37. Pisa Stat. I (1286), 1.154, pp. 268–69, 285.

38. Pisa Stat. II (1313), 1.207, pp. 220–21; ibid. (1333), pp. 1269–74, 1273.

39. *Annales Veteres Mutinenses ab Anno 1131 usque ad 1336*, ed. Lodovico Antonio Muratori (1322), *RIS* 11:80.

40. Pisa Stat. I (1275), p. 49; ibid. (1286), 1.154, pp. 273–74; Pisa Stat. II (1313), 1.265, pp. 261–62.

As a symbol of the city, the duomo came first in municipal charity. In 1262, Siena limited city poor alms to a mere 10d. a day, so they could divert funds to buy concrete for the cathedral.[41] They granted the Opera of Santa Maria fodder rights in the city woods and hired a night watchman for the construction site.[42] At Bologna a fire destroyed the old cathedral in 1131. When the bishop had still not begun reconstruction some thirty-four years later, the city fathers took control of the project. They completed the new building in just four years.[43] Chronicles and city legislation record Bologna's solicitude for its Mother Church. When the cathedral vaults collapsed on Christmas Day 1228, the city fathers engaged Maestro Ventura to restore them, a task he completed by 1232.[44] In 1250, they appropriated £15 bon.— allowing for cost overruns of up to £10—so that the new *capomaestro* Alberto might buy marble to enhance the duomo, as well as its tower and cloister.[45] The campanile got a lead roof in 1254.[46] Perhaps these projects proved too much for the organizational skills of the industrious Alberto. In 1259, the city ordered the return of all unspent funds within two months of the promulgation of the statute and commissioned an audit.[47] Their concern was to get value for money and get it promptly. Subsequent legislation showed no reluctance to lavish funds on the Mother Church. In 1260, the city charged Alberto to redo the piazza surrounding the baptistery of San Giovanni, which stood directly before the west portal of the cathedral, to allow for more light and thus show off the facade.[48] Once this construction was finished, they kept Alberto on the city payroll to provide maintenance and repairs.

Care of the ritual center, however, was a matter of concern to all, not just the city fathers, and private citizens garnered public gratitude and recognition by sharing in the work. Two women at Orvieto, Milita of Monte Amiata and her friend Giulitta, gained a reputation as great patrons of the duomo by funding a new roof. In gratitude, the clergy confraternity of the cathedral included their names in public prayers. Imagine the horror of Bishop Riccardo (1169–1200) when he discovered that both women were active Cathars and that their good citizenship had blinded people to their heterodox views.[49] If a good citizen of Orvieto, so also a good Catholic, the bishop had

41. Siena Stat. I (1262), 1.20, p. 31.

42. Siena Stat. II (1310), 1.13–14, 1:56–57.

43. Enrico Bottrigari Manzini, *Cenni storici sopra le antiche e sulla odierna cattedrale di Bologna* (Modena: Vincenzi, 1877), 26–43.

44. *CCB:* A, Vill. (1228), 94; Matteo Griffoni (1234), 10; *CCB:* A (1234), 103; on this collapse, see Manzini, *Cenni storici*, 32–34.

45. Bologna Stat. I (1250), 5.4, 1:442.

46. Matteo Griffoni (1254), 13.

47. Bologna Stat. I, 5.23, 1:457.

48. Ibid. (1260/67), 5.2, 1:440.

49. Giovanni of Orvieto, *Vita [S. Petri Parentii]*, 1.2, *AS* 18 (May v), 87. Grado G. Merlo, "Militia Christi come impegno antiereticale (1179–1233)," *Militia Christi e crociata nei secoli XI–XIII: Atti della undecima Settimana internazionale di studio, Mendola, 28 agosto–1 settembre 1989* (Milan: Vita e Pensiero, 1992), 364, considers the vita of Saint Pietro Parenzo a *manifesto antiereticale*. Pope Gregory IX in 1235 specifically

reasoned. Well, maybe not. In the end, their citizenship probably counted more to people than peculiar theological idiosyncrasies. The two women had proved their pride in the city and spent their money to the honor of Orvieto.

In the early 1200s Don Guidolino of Enzola, a wealthy citizen of Parma, retired to town so he could live near the cathedral and its splendid baptistery. Salimbene had seen him sitting in the piazza "thousands of times," in front of the cathedral of the Blessed Virgin:

> And every day he heard Mass in the cathedral and, when he could, the Divine Offices of both day and night. And when he was not attending the church Offices, he sat with his neighbors under the community portico near the bishop's palace, spoke of God, and listened to others speaking of him. He also used to stop the boys of the city from throwing stones at the baptistery and the cathedral, destroying the bas reliefs and frescoes. Whenever he saw any boy doing this, he would chase him down and whip him with his belt, acting as though he were the official custodian, though he did it purely out of zeal for God and divine love. . . . And once a week he prepared an open charity supper of bread, beans, and wine in the street near his house for all the poor of the city who wished to come.[50]

Don Guidolino's piety and civic pride were of a piece. Actions by the communes themselves exhibit a similar unity. When the commune of Parma financed renovations and construction on their duomo, they made sure to commemorate it with a memorial plaque.[51] Such benefactions beautified the church and reflected honor on the commune.

The House of the City

In the late 1100s and early 1200s, before the creation of the first communal public buildings, the cathedral served as site of the most important civic functions. This was natural, since the nave, uncluttered by the modern invention of pews, was certainly the largest interior space in the city. There, in the nave, the consuls and other government officials took their oaths of office; there the bishop and clergy blessed the banners of the army and its battle wagon, the *carroccio*. At Brescia, the carroccio itself was stored there; it stood against a pillar in the nave, secured by chains.[52] City assemblies delib-

forbade reception of alms from heretics: Bologna, Biblioteca dell'Archiginnasio, ms B.3695, doc. 1 (unedited original). On Milita and Giulitta, see Lansing, *Power and Purity*, 30–31.

50. Salimbene, *Cronica*, 887–88, Baird trans., 616–17. Translation slightly modified.
51. Miller, *Bishop's Palace*, 88.
52. Brescia Stat. (before 1277), col. (185).

erated there and officially proclaimed their treaties with other communes.[53] Consecration of an altar in the duomo could bring important personages from far away, enhancing the stature of the city. At Bologna in 1261, when Cardinal Ottaviano consecrated the new altar of San Pietro, the archbishops of Ravenna and Bari and no fewer than thirteen other bishops assisted him.[54] The installation of monumental doors for exclusive use in civic ceremonies made visible the link of commune and cathedral. Such a door exists to this day on the flank of the duomo at Modena (fig. 3), next to the smaller one for ordinary use. It opens off the south aisle into the Piazza Comunale. It was opened only once a year, when the city officers came in procession to offer candles to the city's patron, Saint Giminiano, at his tomb-altar in the crypt (fig. 4). Ferrara cathedral had a similar door, the Porta dei Mesi, of which only vestiges remain today (fig. 5). In 1222, the Bolognese constructed their ceremonial door on the south flank of San Pietro, the famous Porta de' Lioni.[55] Sadly, only the lions carved by Maestro Ventura remain, now displayed inside the west doors of the building (fig. 6).

The nave belonged to all the people of the city, not just its government. Various groups created their own semiprivate spaces there by constructing chapels off the side aisles and by endowing altars. Bologna's duomo had at least eight such chapels, each supplied with a chaplain.[56] Chapels multiplied in cathedrals and larger churches throughout the 1200s. City and commercial corporations built them; wealthy families endowed them as replacements for the older *cappelle gentilizie* in their own houses.[57] This switch marks, perhaps, the older aristocracy's integration into the new republican regime. Such chapels were tiny churches in themselves, separated from the aisle by an openwork iron or wooden grill, which left them visible to those outside. Inside, patrons found themselves in an intimate space, standing only a few feet from the altar. Each chaplain was obliged to perform the Office and Mass, and in this age when the quiet Low Mass did not yet exist, he sang them. Sometimes worshipers at one chapel service would have been aware of the music coming from other parts of the building. If the singers tried to match each other in volume, morning in the nave would have presented visitors with a holy dissonance.

After the morning services, the nave reverted to the laity. Here was a natural place to conduct business, at least when daytime services were not

---

53. L. Salvatorelli, *L'Italia comunale dal secolo XI alla metà del secolo XIV,* 318; on this, see Enrico Cattaneo, "Il battistero in Italia dopo il Mille," *Miscellanea Gilles Gérard Meersseman,* ed. Maccarrone et al., 1:186.

54. Matteo Griffoni (1261), 15.

55. Ibid. (1220), 8; *CCB:* A, Vill. (1220), 82. On this door, see Manzini, *Cenni storici,* 29–32.

56. Pietro Sella, "La diocesi di Bologna nel 1300," *AMDSPPR,* 4th ser., 18 (1927/28): 106–7: chapels dedicated to S. Andrea, S. Maria, S. Nicola, S. Petri, S. Biagio, S. Paolo, S. Vitale, and S. Martino were all rendering tithes in 1300. These would appear to be the chapels of the duomo. By 1315, they had been reduced to four: Mario Fanti, "Sulla costituzione ecclesiastica del bolognese IV: La decima del 1315," *AMDSPPR,* n.s., 17–19 (1965–68): 117.

57. Cattaneo, "Spazio ecclesiale," *Pievi e parrocchie,* ed. Erba et al., 1:472–73.

going on, never on Sunday, and, at least in Reggio Emilia, not on Saturday.[58] Faenza's expectation of such business in the nave was so compelling
that in 1195 the city had its linear measures cut in stone and mounted at the
church door (fig. 41).[59] In 1222, Volterra, although it did not seek to prevent
use of the cathedral as a market, did move to clear out wood stored in the
duomo at night.[60] By the mid-1200s, growing numbers voiced concern that
the clatter of buying and selling not detract from the sacrality of the building.
Reggio removed its official measures outside to the courtyard in 1259.[61]
Parma, too, in 1255, put a stop to storage in the duomo.[62] The clergy took
similar action in Ravenna, ordering that grain and animals no longer be
stored in the major church.[63] Any grain left there was confiscated. In 1262,
the city of Bologna charged Alberto to see to it that the duomo, the "head
of the same city," not be used as a market and that no wood or grain be
stored there.[64] Nonetheless, no thirteenth-century city but Bologna tried to
stop markets in the nave. That section was the laity's terrain and for their
use. When, in 1311, the provincial council of Ravenna finally tried to end
markets, community meetings, and secular trials in churches, the bishops
had to make an exception for times of necessity, such as war.[65]

East of the nave lay the choir, the clergy's part of the church. Galvano
Fiamma, a contemporary chronicler, gives extended descriptions of the interior of a large religious-order church from the communal period, Sant'Eustorgio at Milan.[66] As in many cathedrals, a chancel screen separated the
choir, which belonged to the clergy (here Dominican friars), from the nave,
which belonged to the people. In this large church, the screen was an imposing structure, taking the form of a high wall, pierced by a central door, which
was itself flanked by two large windows for viewing the elevation of the Host.
Paintings on it showed Saint Dominic dispatching his brothers to Milan. A
great pulpit for chanting the Gospel and preaching protruded from the
screen on the north side. The deacon entered it by a stair from the choir.
The screen had three nave altars attached to it for less solemn Masses with
the people. Above the door, in the center of the screen, stood the great
crucifix, showing the sacrifice of Christ (for an example, see fig. 7). The
solemn Mass on the high altar, visible just below the cross, through the

58. Reggio Stat., 21, p. 13.
59. Maestro Tolosano, *Chronicon Faventinum*, ed. Giuseppe Rossini, 121, *RIS²* 28:1:114.
60. Volterra Stat. (1210–22), 183, p. 95; ibid. (1224), 219, p. 218.
61. Reggio Stat., 4.26, pp. 253–54.
62. Parma Stat. 1 (by 1255), p. 320; the town of San Gimignano, ecclesiastically dependent on Florence, cleared its churches in the same year: San Gimignano Stat. (1255), p. 737.
63. Ravenna Stat., 169, p. 89; 338b, p. 158.
64. Bologna Stat. 1 (1262–57), 9.63, 2:612–13.
65. Ravenna Council (1311), 12, p. 457.
66. On this church, see Galvano Fiamma, *Cronica Maior Ordinis Praedicatorum*, ed. Gundisalvo Odetto,
in "La Cronaca maggiore dell'Ordine Domenicano di Galvano Fiamma: Frammenti inediti," *AFP* 10
(1940): 323, 326, 327, 330.

screen door, made that sacrifice present each day in the church's primary act of worship.[67] Sant'Eustorgio's choir contained twenty-eight stalls, fourteen on each side facing the center, for the clergy's chanting of the Office. During renovations in 1246, the prior, Peter of Verona, raised the high altar at the east end of the choir on several steps and embellished it with a fine altarpiece showing Saint George. He also repaved the choir and nave. After Peter's murder, the laity of the church commissioned a new altarpiece to show the martyr saint and decorated the walls of the nave with a fresco cycle showing his life. Even in a conventual church, the nave remained the special preserve of the laity.

Another common arrangement, again especially in larger churches and cathedrals, placed a raised choir over the crypt in the east end. This was an ancient and much copied model, originating with Pope Gregory the Great's renovations of old Saint Peter's in Rome. Entrance to the crypt was by a half-flight of stairs downward; people could ascend to the choir by half-flights in the aisles. Visitors can see such an arrangement today at the cathedral of Fiesole (fig. 8). Older monastic churches, such as that of San Miniato in Florence, preserve a similar arrangement. Even smaller churches, like the Chiesa del Crocifisso in the Santo Stefano complex at Bologna, might have this arrangement. The most striking example extant today is in the cathedral of Modena, where thirteenth-century choir furnishings remain intact (fig. 9).[68] There a knee-high wall topped with graceful paired columns and an architrave encloses the raised choir. Bishop Sicardo of Cremona, twelfth-century commentator on the liturgy, especially liked the idea of a divider of twinned columns, like that at Modena. To him these columns recalled the pairs in which the apostles set out to preach, just as the separation of clergy and laity recalled the many mansions in God the Father's house.[69] The Modena colonnade, which also extends across the front parapet of the choir, serves less to hide the choir than to delimit its space. Within the choir, on each side facing inward, are the choir stalls of the canons. The canons of higher dignity found their places on the north side, the direction toward which the deacon chanted the Gospel at Mass. Those with greater seniority found their assigned seats closer to the nave. The bishop, when he presided, however, had his throne in the center of the apse to the east.

At Modena, after ascending to the choir by the flanking stairs, the visitor enters an upper extension of the aisles, with access outward into private chapels and a view inward toward the high altar within the choir. Modena's

67. See Marcia Hall, "The *Tramezzo* in Santa Croce, Florence, Reconstructed," *Art Bulletin* 56 (1974): pl. 17.

68. On this structure, see Arturo Carlo Quintavalle, *Wiligelmo e Matilda: L'officina romanica* (Milan: Electa, 1991), 125–78.

69. Sicardo, *Mitrale*, 1.4, col. 21. On the symbolism of church buildings in Sicardo, see Joseph Sauer, *Symbolik des Kirchengebäudes und seiner Ausstattung in der Auffassung des Mittelalters* (Münster: Mehren u. Hobbeling, 1964).

is certainly a high altar, rising to chest height on a medieval man. Like ancient Christian altars, this altar is flat topped, unencumbered by a painted altarpiece or reredos. In the age of the commune, altar cloths, removable candlesticks, and reliquaries would have provided the vesture. During Mass with the bishop, the so-called pontifical Mass, its most exquisite decoration would have been Modena's great pontifical missal, which can still be seen in the Biblioteca Palatina at Parma.[70] This book's centuries of service in the duomo can be gathered from the faint grease stains on each folio's lower corner—the leavings of many years of episcopal fingers. The book is large, 225 by 300 millimeters, lavishly illustrated, and in a particularly fine, clear late-twelfth-century hand. Its legibility and the height of the altar must have been a godsend for elderly myopic bishops. The book is itself a monument to civic pride: the great miniature highlighting the Mass of the city patron, Saint Giminiano (fig. 10), is far larger and more splendid than the miniatures for Christmas and Easter. Behind the high altar stands the bishop's throne, rising above the choir and the nave. Although the bishop on his throne would not have been hidden from those in the nave, the canons in the choir, raised above the people's heads, would not have been visible during their chanting of the daily solemn Mass and Office. Unless they had climbed the stairs to the choir, worshipers would have experienced the pontifical liturgy principally through the melodies of the chant and the evocative odor of burning incense.

The cathedral as a whole recalled to Bishop Sicardo three realities. It was a model of the Tabernacle of Moses in which God came to dwell. It was a presentation of the whole order of the cosmos, the *machina mundi*. And its coordinated parts made it a representation of the "army of the people of God."[71] Taken as a whole, the cathedral made present the orders of the church, the society, and the commune. Medieval theologians saw in the Ecclesia Matrix the pattern of the heavenly Jerusalem come down to earth. This was the House of God, the Holy City, and the Gate of Heaven.

The Womb of the Commune

In 1187, when Don Lanfranco Mazzocchi, canon of the cathedral of San Vincenzo at Bergamo, was asked about the relation of his church to the baptistery church of Santa Maria, he explained that the two were a single entity, and since the baptisms for the city were performed in one, both together formed the Ecclesia Matrix, the Mother Church.[72] Baptism, above all else, identified the first church of the city. For thirteenth-century Italians, too, the religious heart of the commune was not the cathedral but the baptis-

---

70. Parma, Biblioteca Palatina, ms Par. 996 (late XII cent.).

71. Sicardo, *Mitrale*, 1.1, col. 15.

72. "Instrumentum Litis," 1.1, p. 132; on the civic significance of the font, see Pini, *Città, comuni e corporazioni*, 31.

tery.[73] In his *Commedia,* when Dante meets his ancestor Cacciaguida in heaven and speaks to him of their native city, the poet refers to his fellow Florentines as the "flock of San Giovanni," the offspring of the city baptistery:

> Tell me, my dear forbear, about your ancestors;
>> and what were the years like
>> that are accounted to your youth?
> Tell me about the flock of San Giovanni,
>> how large was it then, and who were those
>> in it worthy of highest rank.[74]

The attachment to the baptistery was almost physical, certainly experiential. As a small boy, the Franciscan Salimbene heard from his father, Guido di Adamo, how, when construction of the new Parma baptistery began in 1196, he and other men of the city put stones into the foundation as memorials of their families. The construction project was a long one; the Parma baptistery opened twenty years later for the Easter baptisms of 1216 (fig. 11).[75] Those who visit it today will agree it was worth the wait. Fra Salimbene's house was right next door.[76] In his chronicle, the friar proudly records his own baptism there at Easter in 1221.[77] Civic attachment to the baptistery survived to the end of the Middle Ages. In 1472, for example, the citizens of Perugia argued for restoration and repairs to their cathedral complex principally because of their shared baptism there.[78] The Mother Church's monopoly on baptisms itself perdured into the modern period. Bologna, for example, did not have baptismal churches in its suburbs until the late 1600s. Until the mid-1900s, all Florentines received baptism in the city baptistery of San Giovanni.

Baptism attached one to a place; the site of baptism determined tithing responsibilities.[79] The baptistery was not merely the site of baptisms. Other religious services, public and private, occurred there. Eventually it replaced the cathedral as the place to keep the carroccio and the city's military banners—and those captured from enemies in battle. The baptistery was the shrine of the republic. In 1262, after Vicenza had thrown off the yoke of the tyrant Ezzelino da Romano, one of the restored republican government's

---

73. Cf. Enrico Cattaneo, "La *Basilica Baptisterii* segno di unità ecclesiale e civile," *Atti del convegno di Parma (1976),* 29–31.

74. Dante, *Paradiso,* 16.22–27: "Ditemi dunque, cara mia primizia, | quai fuor li vostri antichi, e quai fuor li anni | che si segnaro in vostra püerizia: | ditemi dell'ovil di San Giovanni | quanto era allora, e chi eran le genti | tra esso degne di più alti scanni."

75. *Chronicon Parmense ab Anno 1038 usque ad Annum 1338,* ed. Giuliano Bonazzi (1216), *RIS²* 9:9:8–9.

76. Salimbene, *Cronica* (1285), 849–50, Baird trans., 590.

77. Ibid., 47, trans., 8.

78. U. Nicolini, "Pievi e parrocchie in Umbria nei secoli XIII–XV," *Pievi e parrocchie,* ed. Erba et al., 2:879–80.

79. Valsecchi, *Interrogatus,* 107 n. 315, commenting on Enrico Cattaneo, *Città e religione nell'età dei comuni* (Milan: Vita e Pensiero, 1979), 41.

first acts was to commission the construction of a new baptistery. They placed it in the piazza between the cathedral of Saint Mary and the episcopal palace. The space around the baptistery was sacred. no executions might be performed there.[80] Frescoes on the outside of the baptistery, as at Verona, commemorated important, and sometimes frightful, events in city history. Private citizens might decorate the interior walls with ex-voto paintings commemorating prayers fulfilled. Such ex-votos can still be seen in the baptistery at Parma (fig. 12). The Medici princes of Renaissance Florence recognized that their San Giovanni was a republican shrine: on seizing power they purged the baptistery of its communal paraphernalia, removing and destroying the votive images, banners, and candle offerings from the republican regime. Such artifacts were *cose pubbliche,* symbols of ancient victories and the city's expansion and defense of the contado—many loyal Florentines protested the sacrilege.[81]

Satan hated the font and was more likely to attack it than any other sacred object.[82] The waters of the font were powerful. Locked covers protected them, lest they be put to use in sorcery. Every Italian, high or low, was reborn a Christian in the same water, which, after being blessed at Easter, served for baptisms throughout the entire year. Only in emergencies could a minister use other—profane—water for baptism. Italians swore their most sacred oaths over the waters of the city font, as in times of invasion, when the commune was threatened. The chronicler Dino Compagni addressed his fellow Florentines before the font of their baptistery in 1301: "Dear and capable citizens, who have each of you taken holy baptism from this font, reason forces and constrains you to love each other like brothers; also, you possess the most noble city in the world. . . . Over this sacred font, whence you received holy baptism, swear to a good and perfect peace among yourselves, so that the lord who is attacking us finds all citizens united."[83] At Parma, when Berardo Oliverio di Adamo died at the Battle of San Cesario in 1229, fighting against the hated Bolognese, the commune could think of no greater honor than to place his body in state before the font in the baptistery.[84] When the exiled Dante imagined a return in triumph to Florence and acclaim as loyal citizen and honored poet, he envisioned the reception would take place in his beloved San Giovanni.[85] This Italian identification of the

80. So at Bologna: Bologna Stat. 1 (1250), 2.64, 1:321–22; and Vicenza: Vicenza Stat. (1264), 203–7. Bologna did allow flogging (*fustigatio*).

81. Filippo Rinuccini, *Ricordi storici dal 1282 al 1460,* ed. G. Aiazzi (Florence, 1840), 49; and, on the Medici's action, Trexler, *Public Life,* 453.

82. Didier Lett, *L'enfant des miracles: Enfance et société au Moyen Âge (XIIᵉ–XIIIᵉ siècle)* (Paris: Aubier, 1997), 72.

83. Dino Compagni, *Cronica delle cose occorrenti ne' tempi suoi,* 2.8 (Milan: 1965), trans. from Trexler, *Public Life,* 48.

84. Salimbene, *Cronica* (1229), 52, Baird trans., 11; he was Salimbene's father's first cousin.

85. Dante, *Paradiso,* 25.1–12. On San Giovanni, see also *Paradiso,* 15.135–36, 16.25–26, and 25.1–9.

baptistery with the city saved the massive freestanding communal structures from being pulled down after the Council of Trent, when baptismal churches proliferated and quiet private baptism became the Catholic norm.

Some Italian cities inherited ancient baptisteries and continued to use them.[86] Medieval Ravenna used the Neronian baptistery, which is found in the baptistery's usual ancient location, off the cathedral's north transept (fig. 13); the old Arian baptistery there had long since been converted into a church. Crema used its ancient baptistery into the fourteenth century; that at Pavia was in use until its demolition in 1488. Brescia used its ancient baptistery until the sixteenth century. Some cities, like Treviso, converted churches that happened to lie beyond the north transept into baptisteries (fig. 14). But most communal baptisteries were themselves products of a building boom during the twelfth and thirteenth centuries. The boom began with the construction of a new baptistery at Verona under Bishop Bernardo (1123–35). Pisa dedicated its famous baptistery in 1152. With the collapse of imperial control in the north, constructions started in earnest: Cremona in 1167, Parma in 1196, and, during the same period, the great constructions at Florence and Padua.[87] The thirteenth century saw cities improving and redecorating both ancient and twelfth-century baptisteries. Some cities felt the need of something more impressive than their early communal constructions and initiated projects to replace them. Bologna, in 1250, funded a project to take down the old structure in front of the duomo and build a more impressive one.[88] Nothing came of the project, but they did redo the old building under Bishop Ottaviano degli Ubaldini in 1272.[89] I have already mentioned work at Vicenza. Como rebuilt its Paleo-Christian baptistery in the 1270s. Siena, at the end of the century, replaced its old freestanding baptistery with a modern one under the apse of the duomo.

As princes replaced the republics in the fourteenth-century, the boom ended, although Modena drew up plans (never executed) to replace their old baptistery in 1326.[90] Bergamo completed a new building in 1340, perhaps the last monumental baptistery of the Italian Middle Ages. Under princely domination, the baptistery lost civic importance. Milan, under the Visconti, abandoned their ancient baptisteries of San Giovanni and Santo Stefano in 1387. By contrast, in the communal period, there is but one example of a decision to abandon a monumental baptistery, at Faenza in 1172. There they turned the building into a church and moved the font to a chapel in the

---

86. On baptistery construction, see Cattaneo, "Battistero," 173–90.
87. Annales Cremonenses (1167), ed. Georg Waitz, *MGH.SS* 31:186.
88. Bologna Stat. 1 (1250), 1:440.
89. Manzini, *Cenni storici*, 26.
90. Modena Stat. (1327), 6.1, p. 862; on this project, see Giuseppe Pistoni, "I battisteri della diocesi di Modena," *Atti del convegno di Parma (1976)*, 99. Nothing seems to have come of it: Modena Stat. (1327), 6.1, p. 682.

cathedral.[91] But then Faenza was a small commune, and its Mother Church never enjoyed a monopoly on baptisms.

The architectural developments in baptistery construction during the communal period are suggestive of the building's growing civic importance. The ancient arrangement, visible at Ravenna, had the baptistery flanking the cathedral, with easy access to the sacristy. This made sense in antiquity, when baptism was performed for unclothed adults. That rite was semiprivate. A handful of early communal baptisteries adhered to the old location. At Milan, as well as Verona, the oldest communal construction placed the baptistery off a north transept. At Lucca, the Paleo-Christian structure was off the north transept of a special baptismal church, distinct from the duomo. This position was preserved in the communal construction there. As time progressed, the favored site for baptisteries was directly before the west facade of the duomo. This is the arrangement of Volterra's lovely little baptistery (fig. 15); the most famous example is Florence's San Giovanni. Lost communal baptisteries were positioned before the west portal at Siena, Bologna, and Reggio.[92] We see the same position at Piacenza, where a column topped by a statue of the Blessed Virgin stands in an eight-sided flower bed beyond the western facade of the duomo to mark the site of the communal baptistery (destroyed in 1544) (fig. 16).[93] At Modena carvings over the doors on the inside of the west front show that they too opened toward a baptistery.[94] Dante's baptistery of San Giovanni seems small today compared to the late medieval duomo, Santa Maria del Fiore. But in the 1200s the old cathedral of Santa Reparata was a more humble structure, less than half the size of Santa Maria. In the days of the commune, the baptistery was by far the more impressive building, evidence of the structure's civic importance.

Desire to highlight new baptismal rituals on Easter Saturday probably urged the new positioning of the baptistery. By placing the new structures directly in front of the cathedral, in a large open space, the Easter processions circumambulating the baptistery from the cathedral became public spectacles. The carrying of newly baptized infants through the great west portal during the Easter vigil made their incorporation into the worshiping community far more impressive than the old route, which had slipped them in through the sacristy or north transept. But this new location did obscure the duomo's facade. Not surprisingly, a number of cities repositioned their baptisteries to the side of the piazza abutting the duomo. This kept the ritual

91. Ennio Golfieri, "Topografia medioevale delle aree intorno al duomo di Faenza," *Atti del convegno di Parma (1976)*, 29.

92. On Siena: Brian Kempers, "Icons, Altarpieces, and Civic Ritual in Siena Cathedral, 1100–1530," *City and Spectacle in Medieval Europe*, ed. Barbara A. Hanawalt and Kathryn L. Reyerson, Medieval Studies at Minnesota, 6 (Minneapolis: University of Minnesota Press, 1994), 95; on Bologna: Manzini, *Cenni storici*, 26; on Reggio Emilia: Vittorio Nironi, "La chiesa di san Giovanni Battista: Battistero di Reggio Emilia," *Atti del convegno di Parma (1976)*, 128–44.

93. Rossi, "Battistero, *Atti del convegno di Parma (1976)*, 65, pl. 4.

94. Pistoni, "Battisteri," 99; on the Modena baptistery generally, see ibid., 97–101.

benefits of the westward location and even improved on them. A position to the south of the duomo was preferred. Padua and Parma exemplify this arrangement, although Padua's structure is square and attached to the corner of the duomo (fig. 17). There the position showcases Easter rites and processions while permitting an unobstructed view of the Mother Church itself.

The communes inherited from antiquity the traditional form for a baptistery: an eight-sided building covered by a dome. The octagon aligned with the points of the compass; the dome brought the vault of heaven down to earth. Symbolically, the building stood at the center of terrestrial and celestial space. Very commonly, as at San Giovanni in Florence, there were three doors, facing east, north, and south. The west wall, the direction of darkness and the setting sun, was blind. That bay formed a niche for the baptistery altar. In Florence, the dome mosaics depict the biblical history from creation to the last judgment (fig. 18). This placed those baptized below in the center of time. At Padua, the Menabuoi frescoes in the baptistery accomplish a similar positioning of the participants in biblical time. At Pisa, the set of buildings in the cathedral complex, the Piazza dei Miracoli, positions worshipers at the center of time through a different strategy (fig. 19). The monumental cemetery represents the commune's past, the duomo its present, and the baptistery its future. At Pisa the cultic center has itself become a cosmic organism.

The single most important element in the baptistery was, and is, the font. Here, by immersion, one became a Christian, "baptized into Christ's death" by plunging into a watery tomb. Paleo-Christian fonts were excavated below the floor of the baptistery, creating a kind of wading pool.[95] The minister and those to be baptized entered the water down a series of steps. Such an ancient font may be seen in recent excavations next to San Clemente in Rome. The original fonts at Ravenna undoubtedly had this shape.[96] But no example of a wading-pool font has been dated to communal Italy. It would have been very awkward for the baptism of infants. In late antiquity, when adult baptisms became rare and then ceased, the old form disappeared. Something far less monumental replaced them. The early-eleventh-century font at Ferrara shows the new style: made of the monoblock base of a Byzantine column, it is not much larger than a modern font (fig. 20).[97] At Modena, the early-eleventh-century font is preserved in the Museo Civico, though now transformed into a well, probably for use in a garden (fig. 21).[98] It is 0.85 meter deep and 0.92 meter across; in shape, it may originally have been

95. Cattaneo, "Battistero," 181.
96. The font in the Neronian baptistery today is a reconstruction and does not reflect any historical font.
97. *Enciclopedia cattolica*, 5:1178, "Ferrara"; the Ferrara font is now a holy-water vessel in the narthex.
98. Museo Civico d'Arte Medievale e Moderna (inv. no. 119b); on this font, see Pistoni, "Battisteri," 100.

square. This font resided until about 1400 in a small chapel inside the west doors of the duomo, on the left. Piacenza has preserved its late antique font in the Cappella di Santa Caterina at the duomo. It is a bath-tub-shaped vessel of white Verona marble measuring 2.97 meters by 1.56 meters, with a depth of 0.74 meter.[99] Vicenza had a "Longobard" font similar in size to that at Ferrara. It was kept in a small baptismal chapel on the right as one entered the cathedral, and it continued in use there until the Napoleonic period.[100] None of these fonts was monumental; they were placed in small, cramped chapels. They were just large enough to baptize a single infant by the immersion method used in early medieval Italy.

During the baptistery building boom of the later twelfth and early thirteenth centuries, font style underwent a radical change. The best-known example of the new style is in the baptistery of Pisa (fig. 22). That font, which is larger than the ancient baptismal pools, is raised two steps above the floor. The eight-sided *vasca*, like the bays of the building, is oriented to the compass. At alternating angles of the octagon, four cylindrical stalls are attached to the inside of the font. These provided dry places, within but separated from the water-filled vessel, where clerics could stand while baptizing. The upper gallery of the Pisa baptistery offers a fine view of the font and actions in or around it (fig. 23). The large baptistery and vessel served, not for private individual baptisms, but for multiple, assembly-line baptisms during public rites. One can see a small version of the same type of font in the cathedral of Massa Marittima, where it is celebrated as the font in which Saint Bernardino of Siena was baptized. Unfortunately, a Renaissance font in the modern style, useful only for individual baptisms, has been imposed on top of the communal one, hiding most of the vessel and rendering the priests' stalls almost invisible. Dante's San Giovanni in Florence once housed a font of the same shape. To this day, the floor pavements there mark the site of a huge eight-sided *vasca*. In a famous passage of *Inferno*, Dante used the ministers' cylindrical stalls in this font as the model for the tubes into which the simoniacs were thrust head-downward.[101] The simoniacs suffered eternal death in an image of the very vessel from which they had sold the baptismal gift of eternal life. Like the new positioning of the baptistery in relation to the cathedral, these new fonts point to the baptisms of Easter Saturday as a great public rite of the city.

About 1140 the canonist Gratian, in Case 30 of his *Decretum*, envisioned baptism in the communal period. In Gratian's hypothetical case great crowds lined up before a font. The priest handed a newly baptized infant to the child's own father in the press of the crowd—thereby making the man his own son's godparent. Since this mistake gave the man spiritual affinity

99. Rossi, "Battistero," 65–70.
100. Vicenza Stat. (1264), 203–7 n. 1.
101. Dante, *Inferno*, 19.16–21.

with his wife, the event raised the question whether it would now be spiritual incest for the father to cohabit with his wife—Gratian concluded that it did not. To moderns, the accident and the legal issues it raised seem far-fetched, but both are perfectly at home in communal Italy, where mass baptisms and crowds were normal. Gratian's confused priest was probably baptizing in a font like that at Pisa, where the priest had to take the child from the parents, turn around, immerse him three times, turn back again, and then hand the child to the godparents. It must have been an awkward procedure, and many a priest certainly got confused. Gratian's weird mistake probably happened many times.

Baptismal logistics were more elegant further north. There two fonts survive from the early thirteenth century, both of similar form. In the nave of the baptismal church at Verona is a large eight-sided *vasca* carved from a single block (fig. 24). Instead of four individual stalls for the ministers, as in Tuscany, the pool has, in its center, a single quatrefoil well. Four priests could stand in it with their backs to the center, facing outward over the water-filled vessel. This avoided the awkward turning. Leaden plugs on the top of the eight panels forming the octagonal font fill what must have been the holes for attaching the cover that protected the sacred water from profanation. This cover also allowed the ministers to get over the water filled vessel into the central well before baptisms commenced. The side panels carry bas-reliefs depicting the life of Christ up to his baptism by John in the Jordan. This particular panel greets us as we enter through the church's ceremonial door. The image identifies those reborn in the font with Christ himself. The second example of a northern font is at Salimbene's baptistery in Parma, where it is part of the structure's intact medieval decorations (fig. 25). This font's imposing size is magnified by its elevation three steps above the floor. Its pink Veronese marble becomes a vibrant red when wet. The Parma baptistery contains a second thirteenth-century font of smaller size, intended for individual private baptisms (fig. 26). On the wall above the smaller font is a fresco that depicts the small font in use (fig. 27). To one side of the image a deacon baptizes a child by immersion while the godparents look on. On the other side, a bishop baptizes, again by immersion, a king, perhaps Constantine. The parallel is clear: the baby citizen is sacramentally equal to a king or emperor, born of the same water. This small font was used for children whose poor health counseled against waiting until the mass baptisms of Easter or Pentecost. Such a motive also explains the preservation of older small fonts even in cities that boasted monumental communal baptisteries with large impressive fonts.

NEIGHBORHOODS AND CHAPELS

If the cathedral complex was the heart of the Mother Church, the body extended throughout the area within the city walls and beyond, into the contado. Before the concentration of ritual activity at the Mother Church in the 1100s, there had already grown up, in city and countryside, a network of baptismal churches, or pievi.[102] Such pievi dot the Italian countryside, but in only one that I know of, San Giorgio in Brancoli, outside of Lucca, can one see an intact communal-period baptismal font (fig. 28). Around Ferrara, for example, some thirty-seven pievi existed before 1100.[103] The number of baptismal churches in the valley of the Po increased rapidly after 1100, and scholars have identified some four hundred.[104] The pievi of Italy north of Umbria had a nearly identical form and followed similar development.[105] In the tithe lists for Liguria, for example, the typical rural baptismal church was located in a population center. It was a collegiate church, that is, one staffed by an archpriest and several deacons. There might also have been one or more assistant priests.[106] Administratively, the archpriest had control over priests and clerics staffing the network of chapels (cappelle) surrounding the population center.[107] Baptisms and major feasts were conducted at the baptismal church, and the clergy and people of the chapels attended them.[108] Chaplains of the subordinate chapels were appointed from there, with the archpriest, or pievano, functioning something like the rural deans of contemporary England. Unlike the appointed subordinate chaplains, the pievano was elected by the people of the baptismal church, although the bishop did the ordination and actual appointment.[109] At Busto Arsizio in the diocese of Novara, which appears earlier merely as a "locus," a chapel was already in place in the 1100s. By 1212, the chapel was a pieve, with baptismal font and the right to elect the pievano. In 1343, the parish was divided and a second church built.[110] Pievi also served as secular administrative districts.[111] This administrative identification mirrored the popular view, according to which

102. On the pieve, see P. Zerbi, "Conclusione," *Pievi e parrocchie*, ed. Erba et al., 2:1200–202; for bibliography to 1988, see L. Mascanzoni, "Saggio di bibliografia storica," *Pievi e parrocchie in Italia 1: Italia settentrionale*, ed. A. Vasina (Bologna: n.p., 1988), esp. 285–97. On pievi in the Veronese contado, see Giuseppe Forchielli, *La pieve rurale: Ricerche sulla storia della costituzione della Chiesa in Italia e particolarmente nel Veronese* (Bologna: Zanichelli, 1938), 185–203.

103. Samaritani, "Circoscrizioni," 69–176, esp. 69–138.

104. Giancarlo Andenna, "Alcune osservazioni sulla pieve lombarda tra XIII e XV secolo," *Pievi e parrocchie*, ed. Erba et al., 2:682; Augusto Vasina, "Pievi e parrocchie in Emilia-Romagna dal XIII al XV secolo," ibid., 728.

105. Cinzio Violante, "Presentazione delle relazioni regionali dell'Italia centrale," *Pievi e parrocchie*, ed. Erba et al., 2:753.

106. Sabatino Ferrali, "Pievi e clero plebano in diocesi di Pistoia," *Bullettino storico pistoiese*, 3d ser., 8 (1973): 40, for Pistoia.

107. Geo Pistarino, "Diocesi, pievi, e parrocchie nella Liguria medievale (secoli XII–XV)," *Pievi e parrocchie*, ed. Erba et al., 2:637.

108. See Andenna, "Alcune osservazioni," 684, on Lombardy.

109. Brentano, *Two Churches*, 68–70, examines pievi in the Lucchese contado. Documents on rural pievi are edited in *La parrocchia studiata nei documenti lucchesi dei secoli VIII–XIII*, Analecta Gregoriana 47 (Rome: Gregoriana, 1948).

110. Andenna, "Alcune osservazioni," 690.

111. Pistarino, "Diocesi," 653, on Liguria; for another example, see Parma Stat. II (1266), 181, where the *loci* of the contado are also called interchangeably "plebatus" or "ecclesiae baptismales."

being of a place or people (*plebs*) meant worshiping together in a particular church.[112] Modern parishes, independent churches with baptismal rights, did not replace this system until well into the fourteenth century.[113] In Pistoia, division of the pievi happened only in the late 1400s.[114]

Within the city walls, a different system reigned. In the mid-1100s most pastoral care within the city was already divided among urban chapels (called *cappelle*) similar to the subordinate chapels of a rural pieve but dependent on the cathedral itself.[115] Although variations existed, city dwellers now used the term *parrocchia* (parish), as the canonist Gratian did in 1140, for the diocese, not their local chapel. In town, the single "parish" was that of the cathedral.[116] When tithe lists become available in the mid-1200s, the cathedral as single urban parish was the rule almost everywhere. The earliest datable tithe list containing sufficient information to reveal the network of city chapels is from Parma in 1230. That city had sixty-three urban chapels. All but twelve belonged either to the Ecclesia Matrix or to the bishop himself. Other chapels depended on the monasteries of San Paolo, Sant'Olderico, and San Giovanni.[117] In 1299, the date of next extant list showing chapel organization at Parma, the number of urban chapels had increased to sixty-eight. Of these, all but eight (still subject to the monastery of San Giovanni) were under the Ecclesia Matrix.[118] By then the contado had also been reorganized. The rural chapels had been consolidated into forty-five districts, each under an archpriest.

In spite of the consolidation of pastoral functions at the cathedral, the lower clergy of the city chapels and the outlying parishes remained essential to the day-to-day spiritual life of the people. These priests heard confessions and sang daily Mass; they visited the sick and buried the dead. The lower clergy's ministry was of concern to the commune itself. At Parma in the 1250s, after many of the clergy had fled their churches during a period of civil strife, one of the first acts of Gilberto de Gente, the new podesta of the reconciled city, was a negotiation with the bishop's vicar to get the clergy to

---

112. As at the pieve of Gavi in northern Liguria in 1227–28: Pistarino, "Diocesi," 660; there the phrase *habere parochiam et parochianos* ("to have a parish and parishioners") means *habere populum, et homines, et mulieres* ("to have people, both men and women"); *carere parochia et parochianis* ("to lack a parish and parishioners") means *carere populo* ("to lack people").

113. M. Tangheroni, "Vita religiosa e strutture ecclesiastiche nella Garfagnana del Trecento," *Pievi e parrocchie*, ed. Erba et al., 2:764, e.g., for the Garfagnana.

114. Ferrali, "Pievi," 42.

115. For this division and dating at Pisa, see Ronzani, "Organizzazione," 79–80. On the cappelle of Faenza, see G. Lucchesi, "I santi titolari delle parrocchie nella diocesi di Faenza," *Bollettino di diocesi di Faenza*, 27–28 (1940–41).

116. André Vauchez, "Conclusion," *La parrocchia nel Medio Evo*, ed. Paravicini Bagliani and Pache, 305–6, links "parishes" in the modern sense with the decree *Utriusque Sexus* (1215). The effect of this decree in Italy was designation of the *cappellano* of the neighborhood chapel as confessor for the community.

117. Rat. Dec. Aem. (Parma, 1230), 331–34.

118. Ibid. (Parma, 1299), 361–69.

return to their work. He was especially concerned to have the priests reconcile the excommunicated and penitents. He offered to help displaced parish priests recover their lost possessions.[119]

Parma contrasts with other dioceses, smaller and larger. In the little diocese of Forlì, out on the eastern Via Emilia, consolidation under the Ecclesia Matrix was not complete in the mid-1200s. There were still two urban pievi, both with baptismal fonts. One was the cathedral, with nine dependent chapels; the other was the church of San Mercuriale, with six chapels. Two collegiate churches also functioned as chapels, so the total number of neighborhood chapels was seventeen.[120] In Padua, a medium-sized church, we find another arrangement, although here more typical, since the only baptismal church was the cathedral. Padua had only twenty-five urban chapels, of which all but eleven were subject, not to the Ecclesia Matrix, but to one or another of the numerous urban monasteries.[121] The number of chapels seems low, but then Padua was well supplied with urban religious houses, which also provided daily services. In comparison, Ferrara, perhaps a slightly smaller city, had forty-seven chapels and some ten collegiate churches.[122] Tuscan tithe reports of the period are far less complete, but a glance at those of Pisa for 1276–77 shows the same kind of structure. In that city, there were fifty-seven chapels and collegiate churches, all apparently subordinate to the cathedral.

Records for Bologna give some idea of chapel organization in a larger city.[123] In the late thirteenth century, Bologna and its suburbs had ninety-four chapels. These had been grouped since 1223 into quarters, each named for its major gate: Porta San Pietro, Porta Stiera, Porta San Procolo, and Porta Ravennate.[124] Each quarter had twenty-two to twenty-seven chapels.[125] The Bologna tithe list compiled in 1300 by the papal collector, Bishop Lotterio della Tosa of Faenza, still exists.[126] It shows that the same division by quarters lasted into the early 1300s. The quarters were more than administrative districts. They also reflected the *consortia*, or confraternities, of the

---

119.　Parma Stat. 1 (1254), p. 74.

120.　Rat. Dec. Aem. (Forlì, 1290), 165–71.

121.　Rat. Dec. Ven. (Padua, 1297), 105–80.

122.　Rat. Dec. Aem. (Ferrara, 1300), 43–54.

123.　The tithe returns for Milan, *Rationes Decimarum Italiae nei secoli XIII–XIV: Lombardia et Pedemontium*, ed. Maurizio Rosada, Studi e testi, 324 (Vatican City: Biblioteca Apostolica Vaticana, 1990), 3–18, are not useful for such reconstructions. There are no Florentine returns until after our period.

124.　Girolamo de' Borselli, *Cronica Gestorum ac Factorum Memorabilium Civitatis Bononie*, ed. Albano Sorbelli (1223), *RIS²* 23:2:21. Such a quarter division was typical; see, e.g., Brescia Stat. (1313), 4.83, col. 278, which gives the quarters as S. Faustino, S. Giovanni, S. Stefano, and S. Alessandro.

125.　Bologna, Biblioteca dell'Archiginnasio, MS Gozz. 158, fol. 1ʳ: "Parrocchie di Bologna da una pergamena dell'Archivio della Vita." Its date "mccxxxiii"—1233—is wrong; the document represents parish structure of about 1300.

126.　In Archivio Vaticano, Collett. MS 199, fols. 159ᵛ–174ᵛ, which is edited in Sella, "Diocesi di Bologna," but see the dating in Fanti, "Sulla costituzione," 116–45, who edits the 1315 Bologna tithe. On Bologna, see also G. Lucchesi, "Pievi di S. Pietro e cappelle urbane nel Medioevo," *Parliamo della nostra città* (Castel Bolognese: Comune di Faenza, 1977), 113–25.

chapel clergy. The consortia each met in a major church or monastery of the quarter: San Prospero, San Donato, San Procolo, or Santo Stefano. The clergy within the walls had founded these consortia themselves, so they did not include priests from the suburbs. Each quarter took a distinct religious identity from its patrons. On the feast of a chapel patron, priests and laity of the quarter gathered for the services at that church. Outside the city walls, the suburbs of Bologna contained four "pievi" (*plebatus*) containing fifty-one chapels. These pievi were not independent baptismal churches; they all pertained to the "pieve of Bologna"; that is to say, their Mother Church was the duomo itself.[127] In the contado were another 535 chapels and altars, all but fifteen grouped into forty-two pievi, each under a rural baptismal church.[128] The chapels within the walls, the ones whose priests formed the consortia, numbered seventy-one. If the tithe assessed is any indication of chapel size, this varied considerably: some chapels paid as little as 10s. bon., while Sant'Ambrogio in the consortium of San Procolo, at £10, paid most. A typical tithe was between 20s. and 50s.[129]

City churches showed considerable variety in organization. Ferrara never completely abolished multiple baptismal fonts, in spite of Bishop Landolfo's decrees and his canons' legal efforts. In the Romagna the cities were small and did not flourish politically.[130] There the smaller communes of Imola, Forlì, Forlimpopoli, and Ravenna all had more than one urban pieve. Bologna may have been exceptional in the degree to which its cathedral dominated the liturgical life of the commune, but evidence at Padua and Parma suggests that Bologna was more typical of communal Italy than little Forlì. Besides, Ferrara, dominated throughout the 1200s by the Este family, never really developed a mature republican regime.[131]

Everywhere within the walls neighborhood chapels lay thick, very thick, on the ground. To pass from one to another was to walk only a couple of blocks. Until the earlier 1200s lay attachment to a neighborhood chapel was tenuous and boundaries fluid. At Florence in 1202, a dispute over chapel boundaries might be resolved by placing the men in one chapel and the women in the other.[132] But within a generation, the network of chapels reached its final form. By the 1250s, families had been attending the same chapel for at least two generations and in so doing become part of a small

---

127. Sella, "Diocesi di Bologna," 116–19; Fanti, "Sulla costituzione," 113–14, shows that these suburbs all belonged to the "Plebs Sancti Petri Episcopatus," that is, to the duomo. In 1315 the cathedral had over 150 subordinate chapels.

128. Sella, "Diocesi di Bologna," 119–54.

129. Ibid., 107–11; for Sant'Ambrogio, see ibid., 111.

130. Vasina, "Pievi e parrocchie," 738–39.

131. See Lodovico Antonio Muratori, *Delle antichità estensi ed italiane* (Modena: Ducale, 1717), 1:389–90, for the 1208 municipal law making Azzo IV d'Este "rector" and "dominus perpetuus" of the city; on the Este signoria, albeit later, see Trevor Dean, *Land and Power in Late Medieval Ferrara: The Rule of the Este, 1350–1450* (Cambridge: Cambridge University Press, 1988).

132. Trexler, *Public Life*, 13.

face-to-face community. Bologna's approximately 150 urban and suburban chapels of 1300–1315 divided an estimated population of about fifty thousand—a figure that includes the many transient university students.[133] This gives an average congregation of only 340 souls per chapel. Over half this population would have been children. A typical chapel served as few as thirty or forty households. Many chapels must have been smaller, considering the differences in tithes mentioned earlier. Some congregations must have had the feeling of small clubs.

Was Bologna typical? The population of late-thirteenth-century Vicenza may reliably be placed between fifteen and twenty thousand. Unfortunately, the state of the Vicenza tithe returns makes it impossible to calculate the number of chapels.[134] But Parma, which was not much larger than Vicenza, though population estimates are lacking, has detailed tithe reports. Generously assuming a population of twenty-five thousand for that city's seventy chapels yields an average of 360 individuals per chapel—a figure very close to that of Bologna.[135] In 1288, Bonvesin de la Riva, a member of the Milanese Humiliati, bragged that the very largest Milanese parishes had five hundred families,[136] so an average like that of Bologna or Parma seems reasonable there too. When population is considered, the network of urban chapels seems even denser than it first appeared. Nor was the small size of these congregations anomalous. Thirteenth-century canon law required a mere ten male inhabitants to found a new church.[137] To be of a place was to worship in its church, and so a neighborhood, however small, found its identity in its chapel.

The churches that served the cappelle were often miniature in size. Most of these medieval structures, if they survived the reforms of Trent, disappeared because of parish consolidation under the Napoleonic regimes of the early nineteenth century. An archaeological and architectural survey of suppressed parishes exists for Bologna, and it opens a vista into the physical realities of the cappelle.[138] The chapel of San Mamolo (founded between 1246 and 1255), for example, lies at the smaller end of the spectrum.[139] Located at what is now Via D'Azeglio 60, it was an aisleless structure only a

133. Antonio Ivan Pini, *Città medievali e demografia storica: Bologna, Romagna, Italia (secc. XIII–XV)* (Bologna: CLUEB, 1996), 135, and id., "Problemi di demografia bolognese del duecento," *AMDSPPR*, n.s., 17–19 (1965–68): 221, give that estimate for 1294.

134. Francesca Lomastro, *Spazio urbano e potere politico a Vicenza nel XIII secolo dal "Regestrum Possessionis Comunis" del 1262* (Vicenza: Accademia Olimpica, 1981), 61. The Vicenza returns of 1297, Rat. Dec. Ven., 215–25, do not include chapels subordinate to monasteries.

135. Rat. Dec. Aem. (Parma, 1299), 356–95.

136. Quoted by Hyde, *Society and Politics*, 155.

137. See Hostiensis (Enrico di Susa), *Summa Aurea* (Venice: Sessa, 1570), 3.54.6, fols. 314^v–315^r.

138. Luciano Meluzzi, "Le soppresse chiese parrocchiali di Bologna," *Strenna storica bolognese* 12 (1962): 113–40; 13 (1963): 167–97; 14 (1964): 165–88; 17 (1967): 291–317; 18 (1968): 227–39; 19 (1969): 141–72; 21 (1971): 141–74. Sadly Meluzzi did not include measurements.

139. Ibid., 17 (1967): 293–96.

few feet wider than its single western door. Five small bays deep, the east end terminated in a tiny rectangular sanctuary entered through an arch. It held perhaps fifty persons without excessive crowding. Even smaller was the church of San Marino della Croce dei Santi, built about 1142 and located at what is now Via Val d'Aposa 13.[140] Worshipers entered this church through a typical Bolognese portico a mere three arches broad. From the door to the main altar was no further than the width of the sidewalk under the portico. The space allowed a nave about twice as wide as it was deep. Again, columns and an arch opened into the minuscule sanctuary. A congregation greater than twenty would have found itself crowded. Both churches had room for no more than two secondary altars, one for each nave wall.

As in the cathedral and monastic churches, small chapels also had a screen dividing the choir and sanctuary from the nave. In a church belonging to a religious order, the divider or screen between the choir and nave was more or less solid, so that the friars or monks could chant the Office more privately.[141] Parish priests and their clerics chanted the Office too, but they placed no special emphasis on privacy. The screen in one of their buildings might consist of a row of columns with a beam on top or of open ironwork (*cancella;* fig. 29), both allowing a more or less unobstructed view of the altar. The screen was sometimes more solid, so worshipers viewed the altar through its door. Nevertheless, this barrier did not prevent the laity, or at least the men, from entering the sanctuary with relative frequency. Infants and mothers entered the sanctuary during the rite of thanksgiving for delivery (known in English as "churching"), and married couples received their nuptial blessing there. In Giotto's *Saint Francis at Greccio,* the viewer can see a group of pious laymen venerating the first Nativity crèche inside the screen near the main altar (fig. 30). The rear of the screen, with the steps up to the pulpit, and the reverse of the great painted crucifix mounted above the screen's door are clearly visible. The main altar in the image is typically medieval, square, flat-topped, and covered by a baldachino rising on four columns, each attached to a corner of the altar. Saint Francis lays the image of the Christ Child into the manger, and some of the friars sing Christmas chants. One can easily imagine similar scenes in the tiny, almost domestic chapels of medieval Bologna. Outside the screen lay the nave, the preserve of the people. They decorated the nave as they wished. Some congregations, if their means were sufficient, suspended crown-shaped chandeliers studded with gems between the columns to provide light and remind Christians of the crowns awaiting them in heaven.[142] Guilds or confraternities erected benches against the columns of the nave for the elderly or for use during their meet-

140. Ibid., 19 (1969): 164–67.
141. *ACGOP* (1249), 47.
142. Sicardo, *Mitrale,* 1.13, col. 51B.

ings.[143] Private individuals commissioned ex-voto frescoes of diverse sizes, shapes, and subjects to adorn the walls.

In the early 1200s, private corporations and craft guilds established their own churches, adding "intentional parishes" to the network of loosely geographical ones. In 1202, Bishop Gerardo Ariosti of Bologna entrusted a foundation stone to the consuls of the new merchants and money changers' society for their new church of San Bartolomeo.[144] Communes themselves added to the network. Siena provided funds to build a church at the baths of Petriolo, contingent upon approval from their bishop, Fra Tommaso Balzetti.[145] The place was becoming more populated and lacked pastoral care—or perhaps the city fathers had found the baths a congenial place to spend their Sundays and wanted a convenient place to go to Mass. The coming of the mendicants triggered further building projects and yet more new construction during the religious revivals they preached. In 1233, for example, Archdeacon Alberto of Reggio blessed the foundation stone of the new church of San Giacomo, for which the citizens themselves provided labor.[146] A sizable percentage of the new urban foundations in the late 1100s and early 1200s were collegiate churches, staffed by communities of priests and endowed. Bologna affords the example of the large church of Santa Maria Maggiore, which stands to this day.[147] Bishop Girardo Scannabecchi took a role in the foundation, and on 10 July 1187 he joined in the ceremonies of the church's consecration by Pope Gregory VIII.[148] The new collegiate churches certainly relieved the pressure to erect new urban chapels and, with such a large staff, lent their services a degree of solemnity lacking to neighborhood chapels. As new foundations continued in the thirteenth century, some consolidation of chapels occurred, such as that of the churches of San Silvestro and Santa Tecla at Bologna in 1222.[149]

The Padua tithe returns of 1297 list the clerics of each chapel, revealing how urban churches were staffed. In the duomo quarter, the larger-than-average chapel of Santa Lucia had two priests, Don Francesco (tithed at £5) and Don Corradino (£4). Assisting them had been two clerics, Antonio de' Guizi and Zeno (£3 4s.), but, unfortunately, Antonio had just died and no replacement had appeared.[150] By contrast, in the nearby tiny chapel of Sant'Agnese, assessed at £8 8s. 16d., the chaplain, Don Scalco, had to get

---

143. In 1253, the Società dei Quartieri installed two such benches in their church of Sant'Ambrogio: Bol. Pop. Stat., 1 (Quartieri, 1256, c. 18), 1:300.

144. Ibid., 2:485–86. This church later become the seat of the smiths; see ibid., 2 (Ferratori, 1248, c. 43), 190.

145. Siena Stat. 1 (1262), 3.270, p. 358.

146. Mem. Pot. Reg. (1233), col. 1107.

147. See Francesco Bocchi, "Il necrologio della canonica di Santa Maria di Reno e di San Salvatore di Bologna: Note su un testo quasi dimenticato," AMDSPPR, n.s., 24 (1973): 53–65, on this church.

148. CCB, 49–50.

149. CCB: A, Vill. (1222), 85.

150. Rat. Dec. Ven. (Padua, 1297), 109.

along without a cleric. Perhaps he was looking for help. On the other hand, the small San Clemente had a priest, Don Giovanni (£10), and a cleric, Bresciano (£8 1s. 4d.). This seems common: a single chaplain and one or two clerics. Occasionally, an ordained deacon or subdeacon replaced the cleric. In contrast, a rural pieve was home to a large community of priests. Outside the city walls, in the Paduan contado, at the pieve of Santa Maria of Merlaria, where Don Rolandino was prior, he supervised a staff of four priests, Don Giacomo, Don Floriano, Don Antonio, and Don Enrico.[151]

Within the city, collegiate church staffs rivaled in size those of the rural pievi. At Padua, again, the collegiate church of Sant'Andrea in the Ponte Altinate Quarter was home to the prior, Don Gerardo (who paid £16 in tithe), his assistant, Don Pietro Bagno (£8 24s.), and three nonpriest canons, Don Oliverio Rappresaglia, Don Manfredo Mascara, and Don Muzello de' Ingleschi.[152] Written constitutions governed the common life of a collegiate church. Bishop Girardo Scannabecchi's Santa Maria Maggiore at Bologna had new constitutions approved in 1310 by Bishop Uberto, and these afford a glimpse at the clerical life of a collegiate church.[153] Santa Maria had endowment for up to seven benefices. The prior, Don Giacobino (who received the revenues from two benefices), and his associates, Ubaldino, Tancredo, Bondo, and Andrea, divided these among themselves. The five priests also shared the rents that the church received on property.[154] Since these men were "secular" canons, not monks, each kept his finances for himself.[155] They received daily stipends at the celebration of the daily Office—prorated for Mass and the other hours. Absence from Mass or Office meant no stipend. These stipends totaled 6d. bon. on an ordinary day. There was a bonus on feasts—20s.—which certainly ensured better attendance in choir on those days. The canons had assigned rooms, and that of the prior (the best one) was guaranteed to his successor.[156] Each canon had an assigned duty. Along with prior, positions included treasurer, sacristan, and chaplain, of which the constitution accommodated two for the church.[157] With this large number of clerics, the neighborhood of Santa Maria Maggiore boasted a far more impressive ecclesiastical establishment and more ceremonious worship than little Sant'Agnese in Padua. Even more lavish than Santa

151. Ibid., 129.

152. Ibid., 109.

153. Bologna, Biblioteca Universitaria, MS 89.VI.5 (XVIII cent. copy of XIV cent. original), fols. 1ʳ–18ʳ: *Constitutiones Ecclesiae S. Mariae Majoris Anno 1310*.

154. Ibid., fols. 15ʳ–16ʳ.

155. For another example of statutes given to "regular" canons, see Milan, Biblioteca Trivulziana, MS 1335 (copied 1272), the *Costituzioni date ai canonici di S. Maria di Torello* promulgated by Guglielmo della Torre, bishop of Como in 1217. The constitutions treat the novitiate (1ᵛ–3ᵛ), choral office (3ᵛ–9ʳ), the practice of communal poverty (9ʳ–11ʳ, 11ᵛ–12ᵛ), and prohibitions of worldly involvements (15ʳ–16ᵛ). The canons also accepted *conversi*—lay brothers (17ʳ–18ᵛ). There is nothing on the laity or pastoral responsibilities.

156. Bologna, Biblioteca Universitaria, MS 89.VI.5, fols. 12ᵛ–14ᵛ.

157. Ibid., fols. 9ᵛ–10ᵛ.

Maria Maggiore was the staffing at the collegiate church of San Zeno at Pistoia, with six priests, three deacons, and two subdeacons.[158] The collegiate churches of the communes deserve a study in their own right.

The fabric of the Mother Church would be incomplete without the urban monasteries. These played an important role in city religious identity. In the early 1200s, the Paduans called the Benedictine prior Giordano of San Benedetto their spiritual father.[159] The religious houses were a public presence and not a mere cloistered preserve. When Cardinal Guglielmo Visconti consecrated a new abbot for San Prospero at Reggio on 13 June 1272, the abbey gave a dinner in the streets for all the clergy and leading laymen of the city.[160] Monasteries did not have formal congregations and normally did not undertake pastoral care, unless they had responsibility for dependent chapels. Although the monks were hidden behind a choir screen, anyone could attend monastic services, and the splendor of their monastic Offices attracted many. In thirteenth-century Bologna the Benedictine house of San Procolo developed special connections to the university law faculty, providing classrooms for rent and becoming, in fact, their cappella.[161] Large ancient monasteries were only the tip of the cloistered iceberg. The diocese of Bologna could count, inside and outside the city, some eighty-one monasteries, convents, hospitals, and religious houses.[162] Giovanni Villani, in his famous 1340 passage on the glories of Florence, bragged that his city could count 55 neighborhood chapels, 5 large monasteries of men, 24 convents of nuns, 10 houses of mendicants, and some 30 hospitals.[163]

Bologna to this day boasts a monastic complex that is simultaneously a religious and a civic shrine, the Olivetan monastery of Santo Stefano (fig. 31).[164] This foundation was the shrine of Bologna's patron saint, Petronio, and its "seven churches" were a sanctuary duplicating the holy places in Jerusalem.[165] A Bolognese did not need to go on pilgrimage to the Holy City in Palestine to visit the sites of Christ's Passion, death, burial, Resurrection, and Ascension. The monastery of Santo Stefano dates at least to the ninth century, when an imperial diploma of the emperor Charles the Fat mentions it briefly, but it did not become an important institution until the 1000s,

158. Ferrali, "Pievi," 45.

159. *Chronicon Marchiae Trevisinae et Lombardiae,* ed. L. A. Botteghi (1236), *RIS²* 8:3:12.

160. Alberto Milioli, *Liber de Temporibus et Aetatibus,* ed. Oswald Holder-Egger (1272), *MGH.SS* 31:542.

161. Massimo Giansante, "Insediamenti religiosi e società urbana a Bologna dal x ad xviii secolo," *L'Archiginnasio* 89 (1994): 214–16.

162. Sella, "Diocesi di Bologna," 111–16.

163. Giovanni Villani, *Cronica* (Rome: Multigrafica, 1980), 1:658; on this passage, see Anna Benvenuti Papi, "Pubblica assistenza e marginalità femminile," *In Castro Poenitentiae: Santità e società femminile nell'Italia medievale,* Italia Sacra, 45 (Rome: Herder, 1991), 635.

164. On this complex, see now Robert G. Ousterhout, "The Church of Santo Stefano: A 'Jerusalem' in Bologna," *Gesta* 20 (1981): 311–21, which summarizes the author's M.A. thesis, "The Church of Santo Stefano: A 'Jerusalem' in Bologna" (University of Cincinnati, 1977).

165. Albano Sorbelli, "La 'Sancta Jerusalem' stefaniana," *L'Archiginnasio* 35 (1940): 15–18.

when Pope Gregory VII praised it in one of his letters.[166] The sanctuary modeled on the Jerusalem holy places may date to the early Middle Ages, when the Constantinian basilicas there were destroyed by the Muslims, but no clear reference to the "Holy Jerusalem" sanctuary exists before 1017.[167] The layout of the complex matches the Jerusalem shrine as it was before the additions and modifications made by the crusaders, so the Bologna construction is certainly pre-twelfth-century. The complex became famous in the eleventh century as a repository of relics. To foster the relic cult, the monks of Santo Stefano concocted a vita for the saintly Bononio (d. 1026), a monk of the monastery who died as abbot of a monastery in Piemonte.[168] According to the legend, he made pilgrimages throughout the Mediterranean world collecting relics for Santo Stefano.[169] The monastery was soon on the shrine map of north Italy. When the Italian life of Saint Petronio appeared in the 1200s, the Holy Jerusalem was already very old and very celebrated.[170]

The sanctuary consisted of the round structure known today as the San Sepolcro, which mimicked the tomb of Christ. In its center stands a model of the Holy Sepulcher, since the fourteenth century the repository of Saint Petronio's relics (fig. 32).[171] The current aedicula, which dates after the communal period, is slightly off center, mimicking the position of its archetype in Jerusalem. The original tomb shrine was probably identical in size to the prototype.[172] To the east, as in the ancient shrine at Jerusalem, lies a courtyard with porticoes on three sides. In the 1200s a church dedicated to the Holy Cross (now replaced by a chapel dedicated to the Trinity) rose beyond the east end of this courtyard. Past the monastery walls to the north, probably near the modern post office, was a sanctuary identified with the Hakeldama, or "Field of Blood," considered the same as the Valley of Jehoshaphat in the Middle Ages. A "Pool of Siloam" could be found at this site. At what is now the church of San Giovanni in Monte, up the street from Santo Stefano, was a sanctuary named for the church of the Ascension.[173] Medieval Bolognese believed that the distance between Santo Stefano and San Giovanni was exactly the same as the distance between the two original shrines in Jerusalem. The Jerusalem shrine of the Ascension was an open-air circular

---

166. Ibid., 19.

167. Francisco Lanzoni, *San Petronio vescovo di Bologna nella storia e nella legenda* (Rome: Pustet, 1907), 103–4, 124.

168. Ousterhout, "Church of Santo Stefano," 312–13.

169. Bologna, Biblioteca Universitaria, MS 1473 (ca. 1180), fol. 161ʳ.

170. Bologna, Biblioteca Universitaria, MS 2060, c. 37, fol. 15ᵛ; Giuseppe Guidicini, *Vita di s. Petronio vescovo di Bologna, Notizie relative ai vescovi di Bologna da san Zama ad Oppizzoni* (Bologna: Compositori, 1883), 90; Maria Corti, ed., *Vita di san Petronio con un'appendice di testi inediti del secoli XIII e XIV* (Bologna: Commissione per i Testi di Lingua, 1962), 35–36; on this XIV cent. codex, see Lanzoni, *San Petronio*, 108–18.

171. On the Sepulcher church, see *Vita S. Petronii Episcopi et Confessoris*, 2.13, *AS* 50 (Oct. II), 455; Lanzoni, *San Petronio*, 231–32.

172. Ousterhout, "Church of Santo Stefano," 315.

173. The vernacular life of Saint Petronio says nothing about its appearance or symbolism; cf. Bologna, Biblioteca Universitaria, MS 2060, cc. 38–39, fols. 16ʳ–ᵛ; Guidicini, *Vita*, 90–91; Corti, *Vita*, 39–41.

structure of twelve columns. The medieval church of the Ascension in Bologna was, however, a cruciform structure quite different from the original in Jerusalem.[174] Petronio's Latin life tells us that during the thirteenth century the monks and city added further embellishments, making the sanctuary even more vividly a reproduction of Jerusalem. Among these was a "Column of the Flagellation" and a basin (extant today in the courtyard and actually Lombard) representing the "Washbowl of Pilate" (fig. 33).[175] With the complex complete in this form, the citizens of Bologna could experience the spiritual benefits of pilgrimage to the holiest sites of Christendom without ever leaving home. Santo Stefano assimilated the city of Bologna to the Holy City itself, and by that association suggested that the city was a representation on earth of the Heavenly City.[176] Until the coming of the mendicants, it was, after the duomo, the geographic locus of spiritual power in the city.

THE CITY CLERGY

People are as important to a city as buildings, indeed more important. The ecclesiastical geography of the communes included the clergy, a group of men who, as the canonist Gratian said, belonged to a "genus" of Christians distinct from the laity.[177] At their head stood the bishop. In 1260, when Bishop Giacomo Buoncambio of Bologna died suddenly at his country house in Massimatico, they brought him to the city for burial.[178] This somewhat trivial incident suggests that although the bishop was the chief priest of the diocese and the single most important figure of the Mother Church, he was not always a physical presence in the commune. To the average citizen, a bishop was most important ritually. As the universal baptizer of the city, he was everyone's spiritual father.[179] This did not mean, however, that people looked to him as a spiritual guide. Bishop Giacomo was somewhat exceptional. As a former Dominican with a reputation for piety, he would have given sage advice. He became bishop, in part at least, because his skills qualified him for the office. In contrast, well into the 1100s and beyond, aristocratic families monopolized election to the bishopric in most cities.[180] Politics played as large a role as piety in those elections.

In the precommunal order, the bishops were also agents of the imperial administration. This would change as the cities threw off imperial control. In Piacenza, the independent commune arrived with relatively little conflict.

---

174. Ousterhout, "Church of Santo Stefano," 315–16; see also Bologna, Biblioteca Universitaria, MS 1473, fols. 260ʳ⁻ᵛ—*Vita S. Petronii*, 2.14, *AS* 50 (Oct. II), 459—and Lanzoni, *San Petronio*, 232.

175. Bologna, Biblioteca Universitaria, MS 2060, c. 37, fol. 16ʳ; Guidicini, *Vita*, 90; Corti, *Vita*, 36–39; discussion: Lanzoni, *San Petronio*, 167–71.

176. On this dual significance of Jerusalem, see Sorbelli, "Sancta Jerusalem," 23–24.

177. Gratian, *Decretum*, C. 12 q. 1 c. 7.

178. Matteo Griffoni (1260), 15.

179. Cattaneo, "Battistero," 185–86.

180. See Mauro Ronzani, "Vescovi, capitoli e strategie famigliari nell'Italia comunale," *Storia d'Italia: Annali* (Turin: Einaudi, 1986), 9:103–48.

There, Bishop Arduino (1121–47) continued to use the imperial title of count until 1136 and even exercised some of his old prerogatives after the appearance of "consuls" heading a communal government. The transition was peaceful; bishop and commune maintained good relations and supported each other. Conflict arose later, under Arduino's successor, Giovanni (1147–55).[181] In contrast, at Vicenza, Bishop Ezzelino (1080–1104) sided with Henry IV against the commune; his equally imperialist successors, Giovanni Cacciafronte (1179–84) and Pistore (1184–1203) both paid with their lives for their opposition to the commune. By the thirteenth century such conflicts were mostly over. Later communal bishops were generally willing to bend the rules and cooperate with city governments, as, for example, at Parma, where in 1236 Bishop Grazio obligingly defrocked a cleric, murderer of one Gerardo dei Nauli, so the city could execute him. They boiled him in a pot on the Piazza Comunale.[182] Conversely, the cities returned such favors and enacted severe punishments for those who dared to molest or harm their prelates.[183]

Whether absentee, careerist, or imperialist, the bishop remained the spiritual head of the Mother Church and, as such, the representative and defender of the city. The model of a good bishop in the communal period included a role as protector of city independence. When Emperor Frederick Barbarossa attacked Gubbio, the city's saintly bishop Ubaldo went out, confronted the emperor, and gave him a stern lecture. Barbarossa asked his blessing and departed.[184] In a tiny diocese like Gubbio, the bishop lived as close to his flock as the rector of many a pieve. At least ritually, the bishop had to show his paternal care for his people and their needs. Saintly Bishop Lanfranco of Pavia set a model for later bishops by *personally* feeding twelve of the city poor at his table every day.[185] The good bishop was one who used his station for the welfare of his people and guided them wisely. After his death, Lanfranco appeared to his fellow citizens in dreams and visions to give them direction or rebuke, always clad in the full pontificals of his office.[186] Now that was a true spiritual father!

Charity like Lanfranco's befitted all prelates: the council of Ravenna later ordered that all bishops of the province feed the poor at their tables daily and that they and their chapters feed twelve paupers in memory of deceased

181. See Simona Rossi, "Piacenza dal governo vescovile a quello consolare: L'episcopato di Arduino (1121–1147)," *Aevum* 68 (1994): 323–38.

182. *Chronicon Parmense* (1236), 11. Cities also enforced episcopal rent collection; see, e.g., Siena Stat. 1 (1262), 4.23, p. 410.

183. E.g., Florence Stat. 11 (1325) 3.113, p. 268.

184. Giordano di Città di Castello, *Vita Beati Ubaldi Eugubini Episcopi*, ed. François Bolbeau, 15.1–4, in "La vita di sant'Ubaldo, vescovo di Gubbio, attribuita a Giordano di Città di Castello," *Bollettino della Deputazione di storia patria per l'Umbria* 74 (1977): 102.

185. Bernardo Balbi, *Vita [S. Lanfranci Episcopi Papiensis]*, 1.4, *AS* 25 (Jun. v), 534.

186. Ibid., 3–4, pp. 537–40.

bishops on the vigil of Saint Praxedes (21 July).[187] Such largess was fitting for those of means, but Italian bishops were in no way the grandees typical of northern European dioceses. None were distant potentates like the archbishop of York. When the bishop of Volterra defaulted in 1262 on the £215 he owed the Sienese, this may have been a sign of penury.[188] Many a communal bishop was a recognizable face about town, relatively accessible, like the secular officials of the commune. The relative modesty of Italian sees made the bishop more a man of his city than a lord over it. The rates of papal tithes are suggestive. At Forlì, for example, individual parish priests paid tithes as high as £10, while the tithe of the bishop of Forlì was only £50. He was not a great magnate. Even the bishop of a larger see, like Padua, was only assessed at £300. At Ferrara the bishop paid £100, not even twice the tithe of his wealthiest cathedral canon (£66). No Italian bishop was a prince in his own right, like the prince-bishops of Cologne and Trier in Germany.[189]

Nevertheless, outside a ritual context, Italians probably encountered their bishop mostly as a judge. Episcopal courts handled tithes, wills, marriages, and all manner of suits concerning the clergy. Before the 1230s, bishops' courts also handled cases of heresy; after that, at least in theory, they were to assist papally appointed inquisitors of heretical depravity, but they sometimes seem to have put little energy into this.[190] The bishop was an integral part of the city's legal institutions, and the communes recognized him as such.[191] Before the Fourth Lateran Council forbade the ordeal, bishops blessed the hot water and the hot iron for civil courts, a task common enough so that Bishop Ugo of Volterra had the ceremony copied into his personal ritual.[192] The late 1100s were a time of expansion for Italian episcopal courts, some hearing cases from far out in the contado.[193] Parishioners complained to the bishop's court about their priests.[194] At Pisa, the traffic at the episcopal court was brisk enough in 1286 that the city fathers formed a committee to

187. Ravenna Council (1311), 473, p. 30; 452, p. 3.

188. Siena Stat. 1 (1262), 3.376, pp. 390–91.

189. For Forlì: Rat. Dec. Aem., 165; for Padua: Rat. Dec. Ven., 105–9; for Ferrara: Rat. Dec. Aem., 43–44. See also Cinzio Violante, "Le istituzioni ecclesiastiche nell'Italia centro-settentrionale durante il Medioevo: Province, diocesi, sedi vescovili," *Forme di potere e struttura sociale in Italia nel Medioevo*, ed. G. Rossetti (Bologna: Il Mulino, 1977), esp. 83–111.

190. E.g., Innocent IV in 1253 wrote to the Lombard bishops, chastising them for not helping the inquisitors investigating the murder of Peter of Verona: Bologna, Biblioteca dell'Archiginnasio, MS B.3695, doc. 12 (28 January 1253).

191. E.g., Verona Stat. 1 (1228), p. 15; Verona Stat. II (1276), 2.38, p. 295; Bologna Stat. 1 (1250), 4.20, 1:403; Pisa Stat. II (1233), Usus 10, p. 848.

192. *Rituale di Hugo [di Volterra], secolo XII con aggiunte, De Sancti Hugonis Actis Liturgicis*, ed. Mario Bocci, Documenti della Chiesa volterrana, 1 (Florence: Olschki, 1984), 320–23.

193. Mary Kenefick, "Episcopal Justice and Lombard Law in the Contado: Evidence from Parma Around the Year 1200," *Atti dell'11° Congresso internazionale di studi sull'alto Medioevo, Milano, 26–30 ottobre 1987* (Spoleto: Centro Italiano di Studi sull'Alto Medioevo, 1989), 947–67, esp. 960–62.

194. Giovanni Cherubini, "Parroco, parrocchie e popolo nelle campagne dell'Italia centro-settentrionale alla fine del Medioevo," *Pievi e parrocchie*, ed. Erba et al., 1:382.

complain to Archbishop Ruggieri degli Ubaldini about court fees.[195] The bishop's court sometimes poached on the turf of the secular courts, bringing spates of jurisdictional conflict.[196] The bishop's court was a part of his household. When in town he almost lived above the shop—or close enough to it to give credence to an early-fourteenth-century Italian tale in which a parish priest, Pievano Porcellino, takes advantage of the proximity to extort a favorable decision from his disreputable bishop, Giovanni de' Mangiadori of Florence (1251–74). The wily Porcellino (accused of unchastity) sneaks from the courtroom directly into the bishop's bedchamber and finds him with a woman. The bishop lets him off.[197] One can understand why even saintly Bishop Giacomo Buoncambio preferred his residence at Massimatico over the busy episcopal palace in Bologna.

The bishop might come from elsewhere, but the core of his community, or *familia,* was the college of cathedral canons. These clerics were, sometimes by city law, hometown men.[198] They were the repository of the Mother Church's traditions. They were its tangible link to the city, its people, its past, and its identity. They acquired this status in the precommunal period, when bishops were often appointed by the distant German emperors.[199] The canons, in a sense, "owned" the cathedral, or at least their part of it, the choir.[200] They were a small elite group, with all the conscious identity of a private corporation. Parma in 1230 had 17 canons; Padua in 1297, 21; Ferrara in 1300, 18; Vicenza in 1297, 17.[201] Bologna in the thirteenth century counted between 12 and 15 canons. Bolognese cathedral canons' papal tithe assessments were in the range of those for wealthier city chaplains, between 30 and 50s. bon. The archdeacon was assessed at £5, the bishop at £150. So, although well-off, the canons, like their bishop, were not men of disproportionate wealth.[202]

Like those of the canons in collegiate churches, the duties of the cathedral canons were principally liturgical. They formed the bishop's splendid entourage when he celebrated the great feasts of the year. When Don Galdo, the dean of San Vincenzo in Bergamo, described the primary duties of the canons and bishop, he named their celebration of the great feasts of Christmas and its octave, Epiphany, Saint Vincent (the cathedral patron), Palm Sunday, Easter, Ascension, Saint John the Baptist, and the "other solemn

195. Pisa Stat. 1 (1286), Popolo 74, pp. 596–604.

196. Bologna Stat. 1 (1259–60), 11.94, 3:341–42, reasserts city tribunal jurisdiction over real estate.

197. *Novellino,* ed. Cesare Segre, 54, *La prosa del duecento,* La letteratura italiana: Storia e testi, 3 (Milan: Ricciardi, 1959), 840–41.

198. Bologna Stat. 1 (1250), 7.135, 2:140.

199. Miller, *Bishop's Palace,* 85.

200. Ibid., 219, suggests that construction of private episcopal chapels in the late 1100s resulted from the canons' dominance in the duomo.

201. Rat. Dec. Aem. (Parma, 1230), 328; Rat. Dec. Ven. (Padua, 1297), 105–9; Rat. Dec. Aem. (Ferrara, 1300), 43–44; Rat. Dec. Ven. (Vicenza, 1297), 215–25.

202. Sella, "Diocesi di Bologna," 107–8; cf. Fanti, "Sulla costituzione," 116.

feasts."[203] Cathedral constitutions required them to be on hand for such events and to be suitably attired—no bare feet and no wooden clogs allowed.[204] At these times, the bishop himself preached to his clergy and people. Bishop Nicola Maltraversi of Reggio was doing just that when the great earthquake hit at noon on Christmas in 1222.[205] No one forgot that sermon.

The neighborhood chaplain, or *cappellano*, was the people's minister.[206] In congregations as small as those typical of communal cities, chaplain and parishioners enjoyed a close, almost suffocating, relationship. The congregations of rural pievi elected the incumbent by canonical right. This was a jealously guarded privilege, at times defended by force.[207] More likely than not, the people of the urban cappella also presented candidates for the chaplaincy, at least informally. While city chapels subordinate to the Mother Church had no legal right of election, the new cappelle of the neighborhood societies (*società*) in the popular communes of the 1200s did, as did the associations of the arts for their churches.[208] In Pisa, where monasteries played a special role in the expansion of pastoral care during the 1100s, abbots appointed the rectors. But they usually did so in collaboration with important families of the chapel.[209] Synods legislated to ensure the propriety of parish elections and the rapid ordination of the candidates presented.[210] The city of Siena itself threatened to strip any citizen of his right to vote for cappellano if he broke into the church when the priest was away.[211]

The cappellani of the communes are elusive, but when we catch a glimpse, the image is not unflattering.[212] Consider poor Don Giacomo Benintendi, cappellano of San Tommaso del Mercato in Bologna, who in the 1290s brought an elderly ex-Cathar parishioner the sacraments, visited her

203. "Instrumentum Litis," 3.28, p. 170.
204. Cremona Cath. Stat. (1247), p. 453.
205. *Mem. Pot. Reg.* (1223), col. 1104; Alberto Milioli, *Liber* (1222), 504.
206. In Florence, however, "cappellano" also named the lay heads of the associations of the Popolo. I thank Prof. Katherine Jansen for calling this to my attention.
207. Cherubini, "Parroco," 382. This privilege lasted until the end of the Middle Ages: Denys Hay, *The Church in Italy in the Fifteenth Century: The Birkbeck Lectures, 1971* (Cambridge: Cambridge University Press, 1977), 24.
208. Cattaneo, *"Basilica Baptisterii," Atti del convegno di Parma (1976)*, 30.
209. Ronzani, "Organizzazione," 44–45; local families presented the candidates for rectors of chapels at Rieti: Robert Brentano, "Vescovi e collocazione socio-culturale del clero parrocchiale," *Pievi e parrocchie*, ed. Erba et al., 241; at San Gimignano, the patrons of the chapels presented the candidates: San Gimignano Stat. (1255), 4.30, pp. 725–26.
210. Grado Council (1296), 25, p. 1170, excommunicates any who rigged elections of priests. On rapid ordinations, see Lucca Synod (1308), 16, p. 178; Ravenna Council (1317), 3, p. 602; and Lucca Synod (1300), 15, p. 217.
211. Siena Stat. II (1310), 6.68, 2:259–60.
212. Charles M. De La Roncière, "Dans la champagne florentine au xive siècle: Les communautés chrétiennes et leurs curés," *Histoire vécue du peuple chrétien* (Toulouse: Pivat, 1979), 1:312–13; but cf. Grado G. Merlo, *Eretici e inquisitori nella società piemontese del trecento* (Turin: Claudiana, 1977), 130–31; Zelina Zafarana, "Cura pastorale, predicazione, aspetti devozionali nella parrocchia del basso Medioevo," *Pievi e parrocchie*, ed. Erba et al., 1:531–32. Andenna, "Alcune osservazioni," 703, suggests that the negative image of medieval parish priests in modern scholarship comes from historians' privileging of literary and moralizing sources. He places the rate of concubinage among rural clergy at 20 percent (ibid., 701–2).

as she lay dying, buried her at his own expense, and so incurred the wrath of the local inquisitor of heretical depravity, Fra Guido of Vicenza.[213] One extant episcopal visitation book, admittedly late, shows the cappellani as a group of men who generally responded well when questioned on sacraments, respect for the reserved sacrament, and Latinity.[214] Admittedly, the priest was a local man in a small community. Being well known and local did not guarantee piety, morality, or learning—perhaps just the opposite. Nonetheless, the ecclesiastical legislation of the communal period shows a greater concern for enhancing clerical dignity than for correcting vice. While clerical concubinage does appear as a topic of legislation, the synods of the communal period more often legislated to foster clerical identity and to separate priests from activities unsuitable to their state—such as playing dice and running taverns.[215] Synods concerned themselves with clerical dress, profane pastimes, and practice of secular professions, particularly that of lawyer.[216] Synods tried to increase clerical professionalism, exactly what one would expect when the priests were mostly local men. Above all, they expected the local clergy to take care of the elderly and indigent, to perform the sacraments, and to show a good example to their flock.[217] Don Giacomo comes immediately to mind.

When the lower clergy legislated for themselves, as they did in clerical confraternities like the consortia of Bologna, their own concerns took first place. Rome already had an association of the lower clergy in the tenth century.[218] Such clerical associations sprang up all over north and central Italy at the time of the foundation of the communes: Faenza (1120), Ferrara (1139), Bologna (1180s), Modena (1189), Rovigo (by 1200), Pisa (early 1200s), Parma (1224), and Florence (1311, which may be an error for 1131). Similar associations existed in Udine, Venice, Vicenza, Mantua, Lodi, Pavia, Parma,

213. On this incident, see pages 444–46 below.

214. Camerino, Archivio Storico Diocesano, MS Benedetto Chiavelli, *Liber Visitationis (1380–1386);* on this visitation book, see A. Fiecconi and E. Taurino, "Pievi e parrocchie nelle Marche del XIII e XIV secolo," *Pievi e parrocchie,* ed. Erba et al., 2:862–64. Antonio Rigon, "Organizzazione ecclesiastica e cura d'anime nelle Venezie: Ricerche in corso e problemi da risolvere," ibid., 720, agrees with this positive assessment.

215. For legislation on concubinage, see Lombardy (ecclesiastical province), *Constitutiones Domini Coelestini Legati in Lombardia* (1287), 8, Mansi 24:884, and Lucca Synod (1300), 24, p. 221 (which seems more about scandal caused by priests' housekeepers). The lack of legislation leads Cinzio Violante, "Sistemi organizzativi della cura d'anime in Italia tra Medioevo e Rinascimento: Discorso introduttivo," *Pievi e parrocchie,* ed. Erba et al., 1:29, to think that laypeople did not care about concubinage. It might just as well indicate that concubinage was not very common. However, absence of anticoncubinage laws does not prove one thing or the other. M. A. Kelleher, "Like Man and Wife: Clerics' Concubines in the Diocese of Barcelona," *Journal of Medieval History* 28 (2002): 350, suggests concubinage was "common."

216. On attire: Milan (ecclesiastical province), *Synodus Provincialis Pergami habita in Castono sive Cassono Mediolani Archiepiscopo anno MCCCXI,* ed. Carlo Castiglioni, RIS² 9:3:5–6; Ravenna Council (1314), 10, pp. 543–44; Ravenna Council (1317), pp. 603–4. On drinking, dicing, or profane speech: Grado Council (1296), 19, p. 1168; Lucca Synod (1308), 29, 38, 39, 68, 69, pp. 183–84, 193–94. On lawyering: Lucca Synod (1300), 36, p. 224; Verona Stat. II (1276), 1.120, pp. 105–6; Bologna Stat. II (1288), 6.39–40, 2:32–33.

217. Novara Synod II (1298), 1.1, p. 172.

218. See Tommaso di Carpegna Falconieri, *Il clero di Roma nel Medioevo: Istituzioni e politica cittadina (secoli VIII–XIII)* (Rome: Viella, 2002).

Reggio, Fiesole, Pistoia, Pisa, Lucca, and Volterra, although we lack foundation dates. Priestly confraternities were a product of communal society.
Their statutes paid special attention to admission and to internal self-gover-
nance, since the confraternities were democratic in organization.[219] In the
south, such associations were lacking until the later fourteenth century, and
in some places until even later.[220]

The confraternities were not guilds or unions, although their grassroots
nature made them a powerful instrument for defending the rights of the
lower clergy. In Siena, for example, the priest's confraternity protested the
bishop's demand that priests pay fees to participate in processions.[221] Like
the contemporary lay associations I discuss in the next chapter, the priestly
societies' focus was spiritual and devotional. In Florence, the clerical confraternity required all chaplains to recite the Votive Mass for Forgiveness of Sin
on Wednesday and that of the Holy Cross on Friday. On both days the
priests urged the laity to attend the Mass and contribute *i loro oboli* for poor
relief.[222] At Ferrara, where the city was divided into two sections, the clergy
of each section attended the patronal feasts of each chapel there. The priests
came together for Vespers of the vigil and for the Office and Mass of the
day. They urged their own parishioners to attend as well.[223]

The Conventus of the clergy of Ferrara is among the best documented of
such groups.[224] It included the archpriest of the duomo, the chaplains of the
urban cappelle, and the priors of collegiate churches. Its statutes mostly concern prayers, suffrages, funerals, and mutual charity.[225] The clergy of the
Conventus held monthly meetings, with sermon or exhortation. Sometimes
the group focused on the clergy's internal concord or on mediating disputes
between priests and parishioners.[226] Meetings rotated through the chapels of
the quarter, and each was a parishwide event at the church of the month.
All member priests attended Mass at the chapel of the convocation.[227] It fell

219. Rigon, "Congregazioni," 7–10; and on the associations in Padua specifically, see id., *Clero e città: "Fratalea Cappellanorum," parroci, cura d'anime in Padova dal XII al XV secolo*, Fonti e ricerche, 22 (Padua: Istituto per la Storia Ecclesiastica Padovana, 1988); and for Piacenza, see G. Bertuzzi, "Consorzio o congregazione dei parroci della città di Piacenza," *Indicatore ecclesiastico piacentino* 72 (1941): xxvii–xlii.

220. See Antonio Samaritani, "Il 'Conventus' e le congregazioni chiericali di Ferrara tra analoghe istituzioni ecclesiastiche nei secoli x–xv," *Atti del convegno di Parma (1976)*, 163–64.

221. Archivio di Stato, Diplomatico Opera della Metropolitana, 13 May 1197; cited by Mauro Ronzani, "Aspetti e problemi delle pievi e delle parrocchie cittadine nell'Italia centro-settentrionale," *Pievi e parrocchie*, ed. Erba et al., 1:344. By the late Middle Ages, confraternities became a vehicle for voicing lower-clergy grievances: Richard C. Trexler, "Diocesan Synods in Late Medieval Italy," *Vescovi e diocesi in Italia dal XIV alla metà del XVI secolo*, ed. Giuseppina De Sandre Gasparini et al. (Rome: Herder, 1990), 322–23.

222. Meersseman, *Ordo*, 1:186.

223. Ferrara Clergy Const. (1278), col. 436; similar legislation is found at Treviso in 1310: Rigon, "Congregazioni," 15, citing Treviso, Archivio della Curia Vescovile, Missaletum, pt. 2, fol. 1ᵛ.

224. Ferrara Clergy Const. (1278), col. 433.

225. E.g., ibid., cols. 433–40.

226. Samaritani, "Conventus," 173–74.

227. See, e.g., Antonio Rigon, "La congregazione del clero intrinseco di Verona e i suoi statuti (1323)," *Gli Scaligeri (1277–1387)*, ed. G. M. Varanini (Verona: Mondadori, 1988), 429–30.

to the resident cappellano to give the sermon and to exhort the congregation to pray for success of the meeting. At the close of the service all present sang psalms together.[228] These spontaneous associations and their activities evidence a real grassroots longing for priestly spiritual growth and professionalism. In the association at Verona, clergy who did not live up to the requirements of their state—by wearing secular garb, for example—were expelled from membership and denied charitable assistance.[229] Communes themselves fostered and encouraged their clergy's projects for professionalization in their own ways. At Verona in 1272, the city fathers promised to enforce contracts of the Congregationes Intrinsece et Extrinsece, the clerical association there.[230]

These societies were original creations of the lower clergy themselves. They are a better indicator of priestly discipline, piety, and esprit de corps than salty tales like that mentioned earlier about the mythical Pievano Porcellino. They also hint at the overlap between the spiritual aspirations of the clergy and those of the laity. Although they restricted full membership to priests, and sometimes only to rectors of churches, at Ferrara, Padua, Treviso, Verona, Piacenza, Bologna, and Faenza laypeople enrolled, not as members of the society admittedly, but as spiritual participants in the prayers and good works of their clergy.[231] Such groups and activities bound the clergy— and their congregations—together by a web of prayer. Lay demand for enrollment was constant, heavy, and seemingly spontaneous. The Treviso priestly society's prayer list for 1300 shows that 1,951 out of 2,076 participants were lay affiliates. Clerical members, the rectors of urban cappelle, numbered 125. The average, then, was sixteen lay members from each urban chapel.[232] The high level of enrollment, for both priests and laity, suggests that in the small neighborhood chapels religious and devotional life was neither bureaucratic nor formal. Rather, clergy and people sensed a joint ownership of buildings, rituals, and piety. This paralleled the sense of ownership felt by the commune for the Ecclesia Matrix herself. At every level, the city church was a "condominium of all the citizens."[233]

228. Ferrara Clergy Const. (1278), col. 435.

229. Verona, Archivio di Stato, Clero intrinseco, Reg. 1, cap. XIII; quoted and discussed in Rigon, "Congregazioni," 14–15.

230. Verona Stat. II (1276), 1.269, pp. 209–10.

231. Rigon, "Congregazioni," 11. And at Veroli in Lazio: Meersseman, *Ordo*, 1:179–80.

232. Rigon, "Congregazioni," 17–18.

233. The term is that of Vauchez, "Conclusion," *La parrocchia nel Medio Evo*, ed. Paravicini Bagliani and Pache, 308–9.

fig. 1 The Ecclesia Matrix: the duomo at Modena, nave, twelfth century.

fig. 2 The duomo at Ferrara, western facade after thirteenth-century communal additions.

fig. 4 The tomb-altar of Saint Giminiano (formerly in the crypt of the duomo at Modena), twelfth century. Modena, Museo Lapidario del Duomo.

fig. 3 The duomo at Modena, door for the city fathers, Porta Regia, ca. 1178.

fig. 5   The duomo at Ferrara, door for the city fathers, Porta dei Mesi, late 1100s (demolished 1737, vestiges visible above shops).

fig. 7 Giunto Pisano, *Crocifisso*, a great screen crucifix, 1250. San Domenico, Bologna.

fig. 6 Lion from the ceremonial Porta de' Lioni of the duomo at Bologna, 1220.

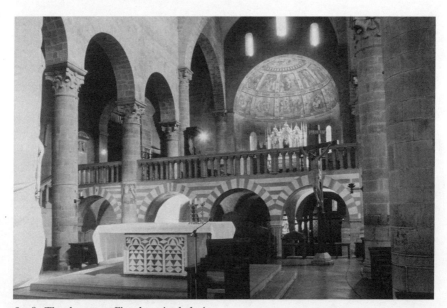

fig. 8 The duomo at Fiesole, raised choir.

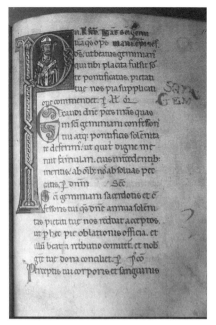

fig. 9 The duomo at Modena, choir, ca. 1100, and high altar, twelfth century.

fig. 10 The cathedral missal of Modena, Saint Giminiano miniature, late 1100s. Parma, Biblioteca Palatina, MS Par. 996, fol. 112ʳ.

fig. 11 The duomo at Parma, late twelfth century, and the baptistery, 1196–1216.

fig. 12 The baptistery at Parma, ex-voto paintings, fourteenth century.

fig. 13 Neronian baptistery, Ravenna, fifth century.

fig. 14   The baptistery at Treviso, thirteenth century.

fig. 15   The baptistery at Volterra, built after 1250.

fig. 16 Octagonal flower bed marking the site of the communal baptistery (demolished 1544) in the Piazza del Duomo, Piacenza.

fig. 17 The duomo at Padua and the baptistery, twelfth century, enlarged 1260–81.

fig. 18 The baptistery at Florence, dome mosaics, installed after 1225.

fig. 19 The cathedral complex at Pisa, eleventh–twelfth centuries, baptistery begun 1152.

fig. 21 Precommunal baptismal font, before the twelfth century. Modena, Museo Civico d'Arte Medievale e Moderna (inv. no. 119b).

fig. 20 The duomo at Ferrara, precommunal baptismal font, before the twelfth century.

fig. 22 The baptistery at Pisa, eight-sided font, 1246.

fig. 23 The baptistery at Pisa, eight-sided font, viewed from the gallery.

fig. 24 The baptistery at Verona, eight-sided font, early thirteenth century.
(photo: Gabriella Bovi)

fig. 25 The baptistery at Parma, eight-sided font, early thirteenth century.

fig. 26 The baptistery at Parma, font for individual baptisms, thirteenth century.

fig. 27   The baptistery at Parma, frescoes, thirteenth–fourteenth centuries.

fig. 28   San Giorgio, Brancoli, font, twelfth century.

fig. 29 San Miniato al Monte, Florence, ironwork screen, 1338.

fig. 30 Giotto, *Saint Francis at Greccio. Assisi,* upper basilica. (photo: Art Resource, New York)

fig. 31　Santo Stefano complex, Bologna, eleventh–thirteenth centuries.

fig. 32　Santo Stefano complex, Bologna, Holy Sepulcher, fourteenth century.

fig. 33 Santo Stefano complex, Bologna, Pilate's Washbowl, eighth century, in the Cortile di Pilato.

Chapter Two
From Conversion to Community

The laity of the communes created a spiritual geography of their own along-side the structures of the parish and diocese. What has been called medieval "penance culture" inspired this creation, although its roots are much older.[1] During the Gregorian Reform, some laypeople in northern Italy were al-ready seeking a more intense Christian life. By 1200, these individuals were calling themselves *conversi* (converts) or *penitenti* (penitents). The word *converso* originally denoted a layman who had attached himself to a monastic order and made a "conversion of life" or an "oblation" of himself. That is to say, he had become a member of the monastic "family" and served the monks as lay brother.[2] Strictly speaking, a "penitent" was a person on whom the Church had imposed public penance for serious sin. More loosely, this was a layperson who had more or less spontaneously taken up a life of asceticism. Throughout the 1100s, single and married people took up a variety of ascetic practices, sometimes on their own but often under spiritual direction, at a church or monastery. Documents of the early communal period record ex-amples of conversi who privately vowed "conversion of life" before their local priest but continued to live in their homes. By the early 1200s, the

1. On the origins of "penance culture," see Gilles Gérard Meersseman, "I penitenti nei secolo XI e XII," Meersseman, *Ordo*, 1:265–304, esp. 304. Bibliography: Gennaro Monti, *Le confraternite medievali dell'alta e media Italia*, 2 vols. (Venice: Nuova Italia, 1927) (on which, see James M. Powell, *Albertanus of Brescia: The Pursuit of Happiness in the Early Thirteenth Century* [Philadelphia: University of Pennsylvania Press, 1992], 104 n. 5); Meersseman, *Ordo*, and id., *Dossier* (on which, see André Vauchez, "Ordo Fraternitatis: Confraterni-ties and Lay Piety in the Middle Ages," *Laity in the Middle Ages*, 107–17); Ida Magli, *Gli uomini della penitenza: Lineamenti antropologici del Medioevo italiano* (Milan: Cappelli, 1967); Maria Giuseppina Muzzarelli, *Penitenze nel Medioevo: Uomini e modelli a confronto,* Il mondo medievale, 22 (Bologna: Pàtron, 1994); Giovanna Casa-grande, *Religiosità penitenziale e città al tempo dei comuni* (Rome: Istituto Storico dei Cappuccini, 1995); and, for Bergamo, Lester K. Little, *Liberty, Charity, Fraternity: Lay Religious Confraternities at Bergamo in the Age of the Communes* (Bergamo: Lubrina, 1988).

2. On monastic conversi in Tuscany, see Duane Osheim, "Conversion, *Conversi*, and the Christian Life in Late Medieval Tuscany," *Speculum* 58 (1983): 368–90.

distinction between conversi and penitents had become blurred, and the words were used interchangeably, as I will use them. Originally, married people could undertake penance only by separating, since the state of penitence demanded celibacy. In the communal period, married conversi rose to over 50 percent of self-oblations. At Lucca, for example, 53 percent of the conversi were married couples, 20 percent single women (more than half widows), and the remainder single men.[3] This was an important transformation and gave a great boost to the movement.[4] Not all of the married conversi availed themselves of the "rights" of marriage. Private vows of chastity were typical for couples past childbearing age and were not uncommon among unmarried conversi.

In the communal period, individuals practicing penance appear in Lombardy along the Via Emilia from Sant'Arcangelo below Cesena to Milan, in the Veneto north to Vicenza, and around Florence in Tuscany. Isolated examples exist also in Umbria, the Marches, and Rome, but the true homeland of penance culture was in central and north Italy.[5] After 1160 or so, conversi and penitents had begun "clubbing together" in associations for mutual spiritual and material support, and by 1210, they had already composed, with clerical help, written "rules," or forms of life.[6] Popes like Innocent III encouraged this lay asceticism, and the number of those entering the state multiplied rapidly. A defining moment came with Gregory IX's bull of 21 May 1227, in which he recognized a special canonical status for associations of conversi, calling them "Brothers and Sisters of Penance" for the first time.[7] By this bull the pope approved forms and practices at least a generation old and in so doing gave an ecclesiastical status to groups of penitents not dependent on a monastery or church. These communities of the Brothers and Sisters of Penance became a permanent fixture of communal life, remaining lay-run and independent of direct clerical control until the last decades of the thirteenth century.

CONVERSION TO PENANCE

Asceticism was the foundation of conversi life. The biographer of the lay saint Ranieri of Pisa tells us that a demon once appeared to the holy man and explained that even devils could have been saved, had they possessed bodies for doing penance. But since they had only a spiritual nature and no bodies to mortify, they were stuck forever in hell.[8] For a layperson to undergo "conversion," to become a converso, entailed the practice of asceticism, doing penance. In the later 1100s and early 1200s, conversion to

---

3. See ibid., 380.
4. As observed by Meersseman, "I penitenti," Meersseman, *Ordo*, 301–2.
5. See Meersseman, *Dossier*, 323.
6. For this dating, see Vauchez, *Laity in the Middle Ages,* 117.
7. Meersseman, "Penitenti," *I laici nella Societas Christiana,* 335 n. 121; bull in Meersseman, *Dossier,* 41.
8. Benincasa of Pisa, *Vita [S. Raynerii Pisani],* 6.70, *AS* 24 (Jun. IV), 361.

asceticism was an individual act, and organization was very informal. In 1204, chroniclers tell that a "Fra Alberto of Mantua" preached for six weeks in Bologna, and "many persons converted." Although many may have converted from heretical tendencies, this certainly meant that some were inspired to enter the "state of penance," that is, became conversi.[9] Francis of Assisi's almost contemporary conversion, when viewed against the background of the earlier conversi, looks remarkably traditional.[10] The saint, on renouncing his inheritance, took up a life of "penance" under the protection and jurisdiction of Bishop Guido of Assisi. This position granted Francis a *privilegium fori* at law, as an "ecclesiastical person."[11] When Francis's disciple Clare left her wealthy family to imitate the "Little Poor Man," she herself described her decision as entering a state of penance, that is, "doing penance" (*poentientiam facerem*).[12]

Some conversi adapted monastic forms of mortification, including practices extreme even for the most austere of monks. Benvenuta Bojani wore a hairshirt from the age of twelve, along with a chain discipline, which "miraculously" broke off as she grew. She avoided wine and never slept in a bed. She flagellated herself, at least until her confessor forbade it.[13] The young Pietro of Foligno also flagellated himself, apparently without objection from his confessor. His biographer tells that Pietro gave himself the discipline "in secret"—perhaps his clerical director did not know about it.[14] During his canonization process, witnesses to the life of the Mantuan converso Giovanni Buono all commented on his one threadbare robe, which he wore both summer and winter. They mentioned his naked feet, his wooden clogs, and the board on which he slept. Giovanni made no fetish of his poverty, but in simplicity he could rival any early Franciscan. His personal penances were savage. On one occasion, when tormented by the memory of a former lover, he drove splinters under his nails and beat the fingertips with a rock. He fainted for three days from the pain. After he revived, the temptations—thank goodness—left him permanently.[15] But no witness dwelt extensively on such extravagances. For them his regularity in prayer and fasting made him a saint. Moderate asceticism was the normal road to conversi holiness.

Simplicity was essential to the life of penance. This did not imply the absolute poverty typical of Francis, Clare, and others in the Franciscan movement. Although conversi practiced asceticism and took vows before a local priest, they remained laypeople and continued to live at home, earn a

9. *CCB* (1204), 67.

10. Meersseman, *Dossier*, 7; Giovanna Casagrande, "Un ordine per i laici: Penitenza e penitenti nel duecento," *Francesco d'Assisi e il primo secolo di storia francescana* (Turin: Einaudi, 1997), 246.

11. As noted by Meersseman, *Dossier*, 1–2, and id., *Ordo*, 1:355–56.

12. Meersseman, *Dossier*, 5; id., *Ordo*, 1:358.

13. Corrado of Cividale, *Vita Devotissimae Benevenutae de Foro-Julii*, 1.4–6, *AS* 61 (Oct. XIII), 153.

14. Giovanni Gorini, *[Legenda de Vita et Obitu Beati Petri de Fulgineo]*, 2.11, *AS* 31 (Jul. IV), 667.

15. Antonino of Florence, "De Joanne Bono Cive Mantuano" (*Chronicae*, 24.13.2), *AS* 57 (Oct. IX), 747.

living, and even conduct business affairs. Conversi needed sufficient resources to live on their own; they owned personal property.[16] When Umiliana dei Cerchi became a conversa, she distributed food and clothing,
including her bed linen, to the poor and arranged to have Mass said daily
for her sins, but she retained enough to live on.[17] When the ten-year-old
Bona of Pisa asked to become a *devota*, as female Pisan penitents called themselves, the pious women rejected her because she was young and did not
have the money to buy proper penitents' garb, much less support herself.[18]
At home, conversi could enjoy the benefits of other family members. Family
domestics waited on Umiliana dei Cerchi during her final illness, and she
continued to treat them as her own servants. One serving girl found Umiliana's constant demands for water so trying that she eventually hit the holy
woman on the head with a pitcher.[19]

Long before the 1220s, penitents had begun to pool their resources and
live in small communities. At Florence, female penitenti rented houses in the
area of Santa Maria Novella and received financial patronage from the Galli,
a Guelf family of the district.[20] They turned to the Dominicans for spiritual
guidance and became known as the "sisters and mothers of the friars of the
convent."[21] In organizational, financial, and material matters they remained
independent of the friars. Penitents might be objects of charity, as in Vicenza
during the 1260s, where the city provided alms to the poor Brothers of Penance living at the hospital of Santa Croce di Porta Nuova so they could
purchase bed linen.[22] A community of penitents might slowly transform itself
into something very much like a traditional religious order on a local scale.
Contemporary observers remarked on this, expressing hesitations about the
lack of ecclesiastical oversight.[23] Normally, however, penitents worked in the
marketplace to support themselves.

The penitents' individualistic charity could develop into institutionalized
social-service projects—the penitents Ranieri of Pisa and Raimondo of Piacenza eventually founded and ran hospitals. Documents between 1230 and
1244 recording the land purchases and donations relating to the hospital that
Florentine penitents established near Santa Maria Novella allow historians
to trace their transformation into a hospital confraternity.[24] This is an early
date for institutionalization on such a scale. By the 1260s, however, penitenti-

16. Casagrande, "Ordine," 252.
17. Vito of Cortona, *Vita [B. Humilianae de Cerchis]*, 1.2, *AS* 17 (May IV), 386.
18. *Vita [Sanctae Bonae Virginis Pisanae]*, 1.10, *AS* 20 (May VII), 145.
19. Vito of Cortona, *Vita [B. Humilianae]*, 3.49, p. 397.
20. Anna Benvenuti Papi, "I penitenti," *In Castro Poenitentiae*, 20–22.
21. Benvenuti Papi, "Donne religiose nella Firenze del due-trecento," *In Castro Poenitentiae*, 621: "so-
relle e madri dei frati del convento."
22. Vicenza Stat. (1264), 199.
23. E.g., Jacques of Vitry, *The "Historia Occidentalis" of Jacques de Vitry: A Critical Edition*, ed. John
Frederick Hinnebusch, Spicilegium Friburgense, 17 (Fribourg: University Press, 1972), 29, pp. 146–49.
24. "Cartulaire," 1–10, Meersseman, *Dossier*, 180–81.

run charities had become widespread. In some cities, like Bologna, the penitenti life always remained more individualistic, unstructured, and untied to
institutions like hospitals. Indeed, the Bolognese penitents do not seem even
to have established stable forms of organization for themselves until after
1250.[25] Even in the later 1200s, the penitents preserved the markings of their
spontaneous and lay origins.

Their ad hoc religious status never sat well with clerical authorities. The
Lucca diocesan synod of 1300 set out to regulate the city's conversi. Within
fifteen days of the promulgation of the statute, all claiming to be conversi
were to present themselves to the bishop and show written proof of their
vows, an *instrumentum conversarie* issued by the rector of their chapel. The
rectors had been receiving vows from conversi who continued to live at
home, conduct secular business, and work to support themselves.[26] The conversi might live on their own, even practice trade, but they were not to
handle money. One wonders how the synod expected them to meet their
needs—perhaps by barter.

Religious associations of devout laity with forms similar to those of the
communal period already existed in the late Carolingian period.[27] Perhaps
the earliest example of laypeople founding a society for devotional purposes
in an Italian context comes from the mid-900s at Modena. This society
produced a matricula, that is, a membership list, naming those who donated
1d. yearly for the group's votive lights in the local church.[28] Unlike the groups
of the communal period, the members of this association did not take up any
religious observances beyond paying for candles and oil. By the sixties of the
same century, a mixed clerical and lay confraternity dedicated to Saint
James, the Congregatio Sanctae Veronensis Ecclesiae, had come into existence at Verona, and by the 1170s this group had urban and rural branches.
The Congregatio was really a priestly confraternity, however. The laity
shared only in spiritual benefits, not in the governance or style of life.[29] At
San Cassiano d'Imola, about 1160, laypeople had founded a rural confraternity that met annually on the feast of Saint James. The ministers collected
donations and then went in procession to make candle offerings, attend solemn Mass in honor of their patron, and distribute alms to the poor. The
group also provided support for poorer members, should they become sick
or die.[30] In contrast to the other two examples, this association was virtually
identical, in activities and organization, to the first documented communities

25. So Mario Fanti, "Gli inizi del movimento dei disciplinati a Bologna e la confraternita di Santa
Maria della Vita," *Bollettino della Deputazione di storia patria per l'Umbria* 66 (1969): 183–85.
26. Lucca Synod (1300), 23, p. 220; 66, pp. 239–40; repeated, p. 246. Cf. Bologna Synod (1310),
508–9. On this legislation, see Osheim, "Conversion," 386–88.
27. Meersseman, *Ordo*, 1:34 (Carolingian parallels), pp. 35–67 (early rural confraternities), 68–112
(monastic examples), 113–36 (early urban examples).
28. Modena, Archivio Capitolare, MS O.II.7; discussed in Meersseman, *Ordo*, 1:97–98.
29. Meersseman, *Ordo*, 1:186.
30. Ibid., 1:65–66.

of lay penitents. The group's organization was also strikingly similar to that of the neighborhood corporations (*società*) that dominated the thirteenth-century communes. But this group had no penitential aspects or civil functions. One can only assume that the communal corporations derived their structures from pious societies like this one rather than vice versa.[31] I discuss the communal neighborhood societies in the next chapter.

Like the San Cassiano d'Imola group, early societies of conversi were rural foundations. A well-documented group of conversi gathered around the church of San Desiderio in the Vicentine contado. They were active from 1187 to 1236 and present a good example of the structure and goals of such a lay association.[32] These penitents formed a voluntary community and supported themselves by agriculture. Lowland flooding, which destroyed their livelihood, probably explains their disappearance in the late 1230s.[33] Members of this group married, had children, cultivated their fields in common, and practiced an asceticism based on that of canonical public penance (save for celibacy). The association was spontaneous and voluntary.[34] Their religious identity was paramount. They vowed conversion of life, wore a kind of habit (*saio*), recited the traditional hours, if literate, or the Pater Noster (as medievals knew the Our Father, or Lord's Prayer), if not. They met for periodic Masses, sermons, and chapters of faults. The group held common property, but they were not monks, nor were they attached to a monastery. A document of 21 November 1222 records the self-oblation of Adriano of Grancona and his wife, Richelda, to the San Desiderio community. The couple give their property, including Richelda's dowry, to the group, and the document carefully itemizes it. Fortunately, the document also includes the couple's ceremony of oblation. After offering their property, the conversi of the church wrapped the couple with cloths from San Desiderio's altar, thereby symbolizing that the group's patron had taken the new members under his protection.[35] This gesture is strikingly like that by Bishop Guido of Assisi, who wrapped his mantle around Saint Francis as a sign of ecclesiastical protection when that layman converted to penance and disburdened himself of property and clothing.

Although eleventh-century conversi were "freelancers," they sought sponsorship from local ecclesiastical authorities. The turn of the thirteenth century was a fertile time for such affiliation. Excepting their common

31. Cf. De Sandre Gasparini, *Statuti*, xlix–l, and Ronald Weissman, "From Brotherhood to Congregation: Confraternal Ritual Between Renaissance and Catholic Reformation," *Riti e rituali nelle società medievali*, ed. Jacques Chiffoleau, Lauro Martines, and Agostino Paravicini Bagliani (Spoleto: Centro Italiano di Studi sull'Alto Medioevo, 1994), 79.

32. Documents in Vicenza, Archivio di Stato, San Bartolomeo, Busta 1, on which, see Gilles Gérard Meersseman, "Penitenti rurali comunitari in Italia alla fine del XII secolo," Meersseman, *Ordo*, 1:305–54.

33. Meersseman, "Penitenti," 321.

34. Ibid., 335. On use of canonical penance forms, see Meersseman, *Ordo*, 1:326–27.

35. "Pergamene dei Penitenti di S. Desiderio" 25, Meersseman, *Ordo*, 1:349–51, esp. 350; on this ceremony, see ibid., 1:312.

ownership of property, the San Desiderio group's way of life closely resembled that found in the form of life approved by Innocent III for the Humiliati lay tertiaries (1201), a text drawn on for the earliest extant rule of the Brothers and Sisters of Penance (1221).[36] In 1188, the San Desiderio penitents received a church of their own from the cathedral chapter of Vicenza. This served as their cultic and administrative center. Possession of a church implied the exercise of jurisdiction, something laypeople could not possess. So the chapter took responsibility for the group, but the canons left day-to-day religious affairs to the members. The conversi had the right to find a priest-chaplain for themselves and present him to the chapter. The group symbolized its subjection to the chapter by an annual tax (*nomine census pro signo obedientie*) of 20s. This offering the society placed on the altar of the Virgin in the cathedral. Eventually the group received episcopal approbation.[37] The San Desiderio conversi were by no means unique. They were but one of the many associations of conversi that appeared in the late 1100s and early 1200s with ecclesiastical approval. The Catholic hierarchy even extended protection to penitent groups of reconciled heretics, such as the Poor Catholics (1208) and Poor Lombards (1210). Authorities asked only that the ex-heretics live their corporate life of penance as orthodox Christians within the bosom of the Church.[38]

By the early 1200s, the transition from penitents with private vows to rudimentary private association and finally to canonically erected religious institution was well advanced. Typically, the first move from private vows to a canonically recognized association happened when a group's membership reached thirteen—twelve members and a leader—the evangelical number of Christ and his apostles. This was the number specified in canon law and was the size reached by Saint Francis and his early followers when he first sought Church approbation.[39] In the early 1200s, voluntary lay associations were common enough so that notaries drew up formulas to create them for both religious and secular purposes.[40] Although the Lateran Council of 1215 forbade the composition of new "rules" for religious life, clerical and lay groups created new "constitutions" and "statutes" with abandon, encountering no real resistance from the ecclesiastical hierarchy.[41] Associations of conversi took their inspiration from earlier rural associations like that of San Desiderio, their legal language from notarial books, and their discipline from

36. Ibid., 1:313–14. Cf. "Propositum des Humiliés" (1201), Meersseman, *Dossier*, 276–82. On the borrowings from Humiliati, see Casagrande, *Religiosità*, 97–98. On Humiliati tertiaries, see Frances Andrews, *The Early Humiliati* (Cambridge: Cambridge University Press, 1999), esp. 100–106.

37. "Pergamene dei Penitenti di S. Desiderio" 3, Meersseman, *Ordo*, 1:309–11, 330–31; for episcopal approbation, see ibid. 1:347–48.

38. For these groups, see "Propositum des Pauvres Catholiques," Meersseman, *Dossier*, 282–84.

39. See Meersseman, *Ordo*, 1:153.

40. E.g., Boncompagno of Signa, *Cedrus, Briefsteller und Formelbücher des elften bis vierzehnten Jahrhunderts,* ed. Ludwig Rockinger (Munich, 1863), 122; on which, see Trexler, *Public Life*, 395.

41. Powell, *Albertanus*, 43.

canonical penance and traditional religious orders.[42] The multiplication of such groups did not go unnoticed by canon lawyers. In the mid–thirteenth century, the canonist Enrico of Susa, better known as Hostiensis, complained that it was "absurd" (*absurdum*) to allow the multiplication of freelance conversi and independent lay religious associations—the bishop should, he said, regulate the conversi and impose on them a standardized habit and rule.[43]

The lay penitents had already anticipated Hostiensis's complaint. The so-called "Propositum of the Lombard Penitents" of 1215 is the earliest recoverable collection of statutes for a group of Italian urban penitents and reflects the fertile legislative climate among religious groups of the early thirteenth century. Although the original text is lost, its form and contents are not hard to reconstruct from later legislation. The penitents enlisted an anonymous north Italian canonist to draft the document, probably in the wake of preaching by Saint Francis in north Italy during 1215. The canonist borrowed heavily from Innocent III's provisions for Humiliati lay tertiaries in 1201. The use of the money of Ravenna in the document suggests a Romagnol origin, perhaps Faenza.[44] The "Propositum" stipulated a monthly convocation for preaching and Mass in the association's patronal church. It organized aid for poor and sick members and required that all make a will "lest they die intestate." The members were to work for peace among themselves.[45] This legislation, reflecting that from pious associations of the previous century, was already notarial boilerplate. Identical provisions for Masses and votive lamps are found in statutes of "secular" associations, such as the association of the Bolognese teachers and students that contracted with Camoldolese monks to provide religious services for them at about the same time.[46]

The "Propositum" reflected the group's penitential life. As befitting converts from secular concerns, the "Propositum" forbade members to attend shows, dances, indecent parties, and other "worldly" activities.[47] The most rudimentary of habits, closed cloaks of undyed cloth, symbolized the members' commitment to a life of austerity.[48] The brothers bound themselves to the recitation of the Divine Office if they were literate and had the books to do so. Otherwise, if illiterate or when traveling, each said seven Pater Nosters and seven Gloria Patris for each hour. For Prime and Compline they added a Credo and the psalm "Miserere," if they had them memorized. All recited

---

42. Meersseman, *Dossier*, 86; for a typical statute formulary, see Boncompagno of Signa, *Cedrus*, 121–26; on which, see Meersseman, *Ordo*, 1:18–20.

43. Hostiensis (Enrico of Susa), *Summa Aurea* (Venice: Junta, 1581), 3.3, fol. 193[vb], reprinted in Meersseman, *Dossier*, 309.

44. Meersseman, *Dossier*, 83.

45. "Propositum," 19–22, ibid., 89.

46. Boncompagno of Signa, *Cedrus*, 125, used these statutes as a formula; on which, see Meersseman, *Ordo*, 1:189.

47. "Propositum," 5, Meersseman, *Dossier*, 88; cf. "Memoriale," 5, ibid., 95–96.

48. "Propositum," 1–4, Meersseman, *Dossier*, 88.

the Pater as grace before and after meals.[49] During Lent, and from the feast of Saint Martin (11 November) to Christmas, all attended Matins daily at their local church.[50] The statutes made provision for governance as well. Leadership was vested in two brothers, who served as "ministers." These ministers, the treasurer, and the messenger of the society solicited from the brothers annual nominations for the officers of the coming year. As their last act of governance, they appointed new leaders from the list of nominees. The officials examined candidates for membership, granted dispensations from various provisions of the rule when necessary, and served as the group's link to the local bishop. A new member needed permission from his wife to join. Each vowed himself to permanent membership unless he left to become a regular religious. The ministers had power to expel incorrigible members, whether for violations of the rule or heresy.[51] The "Propositum" made elaborate provision concerning suffrages for the dead. When a member died, the brothers engaged a priest to sing a Requiem Mass within the week of death; the literate members recited fifty psalms and the illiterate fifty Paters. Each year, priest affiliates said three Masses, the literate said the whole Psalter, and all others said a hundred Paters for the group's departed.[52]

Short and unelaborated, the "Propositum" imitates the structures and devotions of known eleventh-century rural confraternities. Later urban societies, whether religious confraternities or communal corporations, perpetuated the same forms. In practice, however, the move from ad hoc association to developed organization came slowly. The penitent movement arrived in Vicenza about 1222, where by midcentury wills and other records identify individual lay penitents. The oldest extant will, that of Fra Zilio di fu Alberto Ofredini of Marostica, is dated 17 December 1253. The Vicenza penitents remained very loosely organized. Only in the 1280s did they become institutionalized. By then, the brothers had a single "minister," Fra Giacomo of Vicenza, who attended the "general chapter" of Italian penitents at Bologna on 12 November 1289.[53] Even at this late date, the penitents were free of clerical control. Fra Giacomo was a lay penitent himself, not a friar or cleric.

ECCLESIASTICAL AND SECULAR RECOGNITION

The lay penitents' way of life, begun in the 1100s and systematized by the 1210s, received canonical form on 20 May 1221, with Pope Gregory IX's approbation of the *Memoriale* of the "Brothers and Sisters of Penance Living

49. "Propositum," 7–12, Meersseman, *Dossier,* 88; "Memoriale," 7, 12–14, ibid., 98, 99–100; cf. Gratian, *Decretum,* C. 33 q. 3 c. 20; and see Andrews, *Early Humiliati,* 104–5, on Humiliati practice.

50. "Propositum," 14, Meersseman, *Dossier,* 89; "Memoriale," 14, ibid., 100.

51. "Propositum," 27–38, Meersseman, *Dossier,* 90; "Memoriale," 28, 32–38, ibid., 106, 110–12.

52. "Propositum," 23–24, Meersseman, *Dossier,* 89; secular clergy complained about the alienation of burial fees: Meersseman, *Ordo,* 2:579.

53. On the Vicenza penitents, see Giovanni Mantese, "Fratres et sorores de poenitentia di s. Francesco in Vicenza dal XIII al XV secolo," *Miscellanea Gilles Gérard Meersseman,* ed. Maccarrone et al., 2:696, 700–701.

in their Own Houses." *Memoriale* here means "record of an intended way of life." The pope's recognition gave the penitents formal ecclesiastical status as a group, something they corporately lacked in the earlier period. Popes and bishops soon granted them a vast range of ecclesiastical privileges. In 1225, Honorius III, by letter to all the bishops of Italy, granted the penitents exemption from both episcopal and papal interdict. This gave them access to Mass and Divine Office when these were forbidden to a city or area. Provided that they did not admit excommunicates, they could conduct services behind closed doors, with low voices and no bells. This privilege included the right to funerals and Christian burial at such times.[54] Bishop Giacomo Calvacante of Città di Castello, in a common practice, granted indulgences to new penitents.[55]

Individual penitents remained "ecclesiastical persons," even when not affiliated with a local group. The "Memoriale" was not a piece of original legislation.[56] The group that had the "Memoriale" drafted probably arose during the preaching of Saint Francis in the Marches, Romagna, and Lombardy during 1209–10 and was probably already following the "Propositum" of 1215. The final document differs from the "Propositum" in its inclusion of legal glosses and elaborations, citation of the papal letter of approval, and a "Dominican" provision that the rule bind only under pain of penance, not sin.[57] Much of the document is borrowed from legal formularies and canon-law sources. Hardly a single line of the "Memoriale" lacks a model in an earlier rule or penitential canon.[58] As the document's full title indicates, the individuals living under it dwelt at home in their houses. They were "seculars" living on their own, not "regulars" enclosed in a monastery and holding their goods in common.[59] The lack of originality and the simplicity of this document and of similar confraternità and communal statutes led the notary Boncompagno of Signa to doubt whether such legislation deserved the name of statutes (*statuta*) at all.[60] Papal approval made this "Memoriale" the sole normative rule for all conversi and penitents until the 1290s. Local groups of

---

54. "Bullarium," 2 (Honorius III, 1 December 1225), Meersseman, *Dossier*, 42; for which, see also *BF* 1:19, and August Potthast, *Regesta Romanorum Pontificum* (Berlin: Decker, 1874–77), 7. Renewals of the privilege: "Bullarium," 7 (Gregory IX, 23 August 1229), Meersseman, *Dossier*, 47; "Bullarium," 10 (Gregory IX, 5 April 1231), ibid., 48; "Bullarium," 40 (Alexander IV, 15 July 1260), ibid., 67. The privilege applied to special groups: Lombard penitents: "Bullarium," 21 (Innocent IV, 15 March 1246), ibid., 57; women penitents: "Bullarium," 27 (Innocent IV, 15 September 1251), ibid., 60; Florentine penitents: "Bullarium," 30 (Innocent IV, 13 October 1251), ibid., 61; "Bullarium," 42 (Urban IV, 5 July 1264), ibid., 68; "Bullarium," 45 (Honorius III, 28 January 1286), ibid., 70–71.

55. "Cartulaire," 20–21, Meersseman, *Dossier*, 204–6.

56. Meersseman, *Dossier*, 6–7; Meersseman, *Ordo*, 1:359–60; Robert W. Stewart, *"De Illis qui Faciunt Penitentiam": The Rule of the Secular Franciscan Order: Origins, Development, Interpretation* (Rome: Istituto Storico dei Cappuccini, 1991), 183–84; Casagrande, *Religiosità*, 79–93.

57. Meersseman, *Dossier*, 11, 84, 112. See also later legislation, "Memoriale," 39; see Meersseman's comments in *Dossier*, 112 n. 39.

58. Meersseman, *Ordo*, 1:32; Meersseman, *Dossier*, 93–112.

59. "Memoriale," Meersseman, *Dossier*, 92–93.

60. De Sandre Gasparini, *Statuti*, xxi.

penitents adapted the rule to their needs through special legislation and affiliated with other local groups to form larger provinces. Later papal letters speak of a "Lombard Province" of the penitents and its specific legislation. Between 1266 and 1268, Saint Bonaventure spoke of the penitents as having "provincial superiors." Legislative acts of penitenti councils for Lombardy exist after 1280—in particular, those by Piacentine penitents in 1288 and those by the Bolognese penitents in November 1289.[61]

Before 1221, and even more before 1215, custom, not written law, governed conversi life. Over time, such custom was written down and added to the "Memoriale" as local legislation, but appearance in written form came late. Confraternity legislation postdating the "Memoriale" can suggest the customary practice that governed earlier piety and life. Even after the papacy and the hierarchy began to take an active role in supervising penitent groups, the laity maintained their autonomy and independence. From the beginning, groups of penitents had clerical advisors and visitators, but the laity chose and invited these priests themselves. Bishops did not appoint them. Nor did they appoint clerical supervisors for the penitents; these functioned as overseers for a whole diocese, not as directors of individual fraternities. The one exception is telling in its outcome. In 1248, Pope Innocent IV subjected all Lombard and Florentine penitents to supervision by Franciscan provincial superiors. The result was protest, and by 1260 Pope Alexander IV had restored the laity's right to choose their own visitators and chaplains.[62] Individual penitents related to provincial supervisors through the local lay leadership. The "Memoriale" specified that such "ministers" report the public faults of members to the regional visitator and, if the delinquent was male, to the rector of the city.[63]

Communal and ecclesiastical authorities recognized the "religious" status of individual, unaffiliated conversi. A Bolognese statute of 1288 provided for conversi who claimed canonical status without entering a religious house. The city required that they have their vows notarized within fifteen days of profession and place the document on record at the city offices. This process stopped imposters from defrauding the city through dissimulation.[64] The commune of Biella began auditing the books of male and female conversi groups in 1245 to prevent similar fraud.[65] The Bolognese wanted to ensure that no one claimed the rights of a penitent without the responsibilities, but for penitent status they did not require membership in an ecclesiastically

61. Meersseman, *Dossier*, 160; for extant acta, see ibid., 63–78.

62. Ibid., 8; Meersseman, *Ordo*, 1:363–64; for the legislation of Innocent IV and Alexander IV, see Meersseman, *Dossier*, 57, 123–25.

63. "Memoriale," 35, Meersseman, *Dossier*, 111; spouses were not required to report each other's faults: "Memoriale," 36, ibid., 111.

64. Bologna Stat. II (1288), 5.97, 1:452–53.

65. Biella Stat. 1.3.8 (60).

approved association, merely a certified profession of vows.[66] Some married conversi continued to live together, on their own, as a couple. In the mid-1200s, Bishop Guercio of Lucca ordered married couples who wished to enter the penitential state and pledge chastity to execute a legal instrument to that effect. Their parish priest would make this public by announcing, four times a year, the names of those so vowed.[67]

The older practice of married penitents, still active in secular life and work, declined slowly. Although the "Memoriale" of 1221 did not yet require abstinence from marriage, it had always been implicit in the assimilation of conversi to those under canonical penance. Gregory IX, Innocent IV, and Martin IV all assumed chastity as the normal state for penitents, although this may have extended only to abstinence on fast days.[68] Common opinion considered it pretty much normative for conversi to forsake marriage and take vows of celibacy. In 1228, Dominican leadership warned friars about accepting vows of celibacy from undirected young penitents.[69] The midcentury canonist Hostiensis concluded that, legally speaking, anyone—even a *rusticus*—who pledged chastity, even within marriage, and vowed obedience to the rector of a church or became a member of a hospital confraternity under direction of a bishop was entitled to the canonical status of a "religious," just like members of formal religious orders.[70] Celibate penitents commonly withdrew from worldly affairs and attached themselves to local churches.[71] If anything, the identification of celibacy with penance increased during the thirteenth century, perhaps because of the growing number of female penitents, since sexual abstinence was always more typical of women's piety than of men's.[72]

To churchmen, vows of celibacy made the penitent; to the city, it was forfeiture of private property and dependence on an ecclesiastical living. In 1233, Parma issued the earliest extant communal legislation on the privileges and obligations of penitents, at the request of the Franciscan Fra Gerardo of Modena. The city pledged generally to observe penitent privileges, without specifying any in particular. Legislation of 1248 shows that one privilege intended was exemption from military service. This was not granted, however, to penitents who remained householders, lived with their wives, and reared children.[73] Bologna considered someone a true "penitent," or "con-

66. "Cartulaire," Meersseman, *Dossier,* 180–220.

67. Lucca Synod (1253), 13, pp. 56–57, invoking *X* 2.24.23–25. For similar fourteenth-century legislation at Lucca, see Osheim, "Conversion," 374–76.

68. Meersseman, "Penitenti," 336–37.

69. Meersseman, *Dossier,* 22.

70. Hostiensis (Enrico of Susa), *Summa Aurea* (Venice: Junta, 1581), 3.3, fol. 193vb, reprinted in ibid., 309.

71. Meersseman, "Penitenti," 336; Meersseman, *Ordo,* 1:43–57.

72. Dyan Elliott, *Spiritual Marriage: Sexual Abstinence in Medieval Wedlock* (Princeton: Princeton University Press, 1993), 196–205.

73. Parma Stat. I, 200.

versus," only if the individual was the servant of a city church (part of its *familia*), wore a religious habit, and lived off the "proceeds of the altar" rather than from his own property.[74] The city fathers of Parma seemed to favor, by their restriction of privileges, withdrawal from secular affairs as typical, if not obligatory, for conversi.

No penitent privilege posed more problems for the communes than that exemption from military service. It was an integral part of public penance and, in ecclesiastical law, went back to Gratian's compilations (ca. 1140) and beyond.[75] The "Memoriale" made mandatory a penitent's abstinence from military activity.[76] From the late 1100s until the early 1200s communes did not protest this privilege. In the 1220s this changed, undoubtedly because the multiplication of penitents threatened the cities' ability to raise the urban militia. On 16 December 1221 Pope Honorius III wrote Archbishop Picino of Ravenna, asking him to intervene with the podesta of Faenza, who had violated the penitents' exception from military service. The penitents involved, the pope allowed, did live in the world (*in saeculo*), but they wore distinctive garb and dedicated themselves full-time to pious practices.[77] What came of the pope's intervention is unknown, but Pope Gregory IX also protested in 1227 and 1231 against the impress of penitents into military service.[78]

The archdeacon of Bologna wrote to Pope Innocent IV on the matter, at the request of the "council and commune of Bologna," in 1251. The pope explained that only individual penitents, not their children or grandchildren, were entitled to the military exemption.[79] Perhaps some convert couples had claimed their whole families as "penitents." Siena granted tax and military exemptions to the local penitent and holy man, Pietro Pettinaio, even when he remained in the world, practiced his trade, and supported his family. Bologna probably did not object to the exemption for conversi living at home, but they balked at extending it to their children and relatives. By 1260, Bologna exempted penitents who were properly vowed and enrolled in the matricula of the Brothers of Penance, even if they lived at home.[80] For reasons of self-interest, then, the cities supported papal and hierarchical moves to reduce the hordes of self-made penitents to groups of vowed celibates under ecclesiastical supervision.

The communes granted other privileges to penitents with less misgiving.

---

74. Bologna Stat. 1 (1250), 6.17 1:470; see also Modena Stat. (1327), 2.48, p. 265.

75. Gratian, *Decretum*, C. 33 q. 3 c. 5 (12 Toledo, c. 2); Meersseman, *Dossier*, 8 and 101 n. 16.; id., *Ordo*, 1: 363.

76. "Memoriale," 16, Meersseman, *Dossier*, 101.

77. "Bullarium," 1 (Honorius III, 16 December 1221), Meersseman, *Dossier*, 41; for which, see also Potthast, *Regesta*, 6736.

78. "Bullarium," 5 (Gregory IX, 26 May 1227), Meersseman, *Dossier*, 46–47; for which, see also *BF* 1:30; *BOP* 1:536; Potthast, *Regesta*, 7919. "Bullarium," 9 (5 April 1231), Meersseman, *Dossier*, 48.

79. "Bullarium," 32 (Innocent IV, 5 December 1251), Meersseman, *Dossier*, 62; for which, see also Potthast, *Regesta*, 14429.

80. Bologna Stat. 1 (1259–67), 6.14, 1:478 (military service); (1250), 6.18, 1:479–80 (taxes).

Siena and Bologna accepted testimony by penitents in legal cases without demanding the calumny oath—a privilege previously granted only to monks and bishops.[81] Like those under public canonical penance, lay penitents were forbidden to take oaths, unless there was "necessity" or a papal dispensation.[82] Popes construed necessity very broadly, allowing peace oaths, professions of faith, testimony in court, and making a will. For those performing public charity, cities granted tax exemptions without hesitation. They willingly granted such penitents alms from public funds.[83] Siena, typically, exempted penitents, there called *mantellati*, from service in public office.[84] The communes protected conversi, unarmed as they were, from those who would harass them or interfere with their self-government or autonomy.[85] As spontaneous and distinctively lay as the penitents' conversion of life was, both Church and commune recognized and respected it.

THE PENITENTIAL LIFE

The habit made the penitent; nothing obliged conversi to live together or even join a society or confraternity. There was little standardization in appearance. Umiliana dei Cerchi simply wore a black robe with a white veil, and so she appeared to one of her followers after her death.[86] When Margherita of Cortona decided to embrace the life of penance, she made herself a shift of white and gray check (*quadretto taccholino*) and placed over it a black mantle. She appears wearing this odd homemade habit on an early-fourteenth-century altarpiece in Cortona (fig. 34). She was very much the do-it-yourself conversa—in spite of later Franciscan attempts to claim her as one of their Gray Penitents.[87] The Sienese combmaker Pietro Pettinaio took up the habit of a penitent after the death of his wife, or perhaps a little before. That act made him a penitent. By the late 1200s, mendicant directors were pressuring penitents to adopt the "colors" of their particular orders. As for Pietro, the Franciscans claimed that his habit had been their color—gray—not the black of Dominican-sponsored penitents. The adoption of Pietro into the Franciscan family was postmortem wishful thinking. In life, his friend Salvi di Orlando rebuked him for his discolored mantle. Pietro replied that

81. Ibid. (1250), 4.23, 1:404; Siena Stat. 1 (1262), 1.88, p. 46.

82. "Memoriale," 17–18, Meersseman, *Dossier*, 101–2.

83. Parma Stat. 1 (1261), p. 431; "Capitoli inediti di una redazione statutaria pavese del secolo XIII: Documenti," ed. Renato Sòriga, 1.383, *Bollettino della Società pavese di storia patria* 22 (1922): 11; Pisa Stat. II (1313), 1.271, p. 264; Florence Stat. 1 (1322), 5.72, p. 270.

84. Siena Stat. 1 (1262), 1.93, p. 47.

85. As Florence did in 1325: Florence Stat. II, 2.80, pp. 147–48.

86. Vito of Cortona, *Vita [B. Humilianae]*, App. 63, pp. 401–2.

87. On her independence of the Franciscans, see Enrico Menestò and Roberto Rusconi, *Umbria: Una strada delle sante medievali* (Rome: Rai, 1991), 61, 62. On Margherita, see Daniel Bornstein, "The Uses of the Body: The Church and the Cult of Santa Margherita da Cortona," *Church History* 62 (1993): 163–77. On the saint's cult and image in art, see Joanna Cannon and André Vauchez, *Margherita of Cortona and the Lorenzetti: Sienese Art and the Cult of a Holy Woman in Medieval Tuscany* (University Park: Pennsylvania State University Press, 1997).

one should care about God, not worldly things.[88] His habit was gray-brown probably from dirt. Nothing in Pietro's life suggests that he understood his penance as somehow Franciscan. The "Memoriale" merely specified that the cloth for male penitents' clothing cost no more than 6s. rav. per yard. It vetoed fancy dress with slashes and required that the brothers' gowns be closed. For women, a bit of vanity was permitted: their cloth might cost 12s. rav. a yard, and they could carry a leather purse on a plain strap. Fripperies like embroidered belts, waistbands, and tooled straps were out, as were elaborate dress pleats. No penitents might wear furs. Rather, they were to be content with lamb's wool.[89] Penitents were to dress plainly, in a way that reflected their state. Nothing here suggests a standardized "habit." By the 1260s, legislation, admittedly rudimentary, standardized the color of the undyed cloth used in penitents' clothing. It excluded black; perhaps Franciscans, the Gray Friars, were behind this new regulation.[90]

Clothing new penitents with the habit was managed on an ad hoc basis by local lay leadership. The ministers simply examined each candidate and decided among themselves about admission. The "Memoriale" did little to standardize this procedure. It told the ministers to explain carefully the obligations of the society and make sure that a candidate was at peace with his neighbors and had no outstanding debts.[91] Elaborate statutory guidelines regarding admission and expulsion criteria do not appear until the early 1300s, although earlier examples may be lost.[92] The most important change in the rule of 1221, a change made by the later 1200s, was the provision for a one-year testing period, or novitiate, before the candidate committed himself to the life.[93] This reflects papal legislation, certainly not an imitation of the religious orders. Popes struggled to get orders like the Dominicans to postpone life profession of vows until after the year of testing in the novitiate.[94] If a penitent misbehaved, the ministers had discretion to punish him, but little or no statutory guidance. Specific statutory penalties for infractions, like those of the Lombard Penitents in 1280, came later. When they arrived, these took the form of fasts and fines.[95]

Legal privileges followed on wearing the habit. City fathers knew this. The Florentines promulgated statutes forbidding any but true *pinçocheri* (the local name for penitents) from wearing the *conversi* habit.[96] Church councils

---

88. Pietro of Monterone, *Vita del beato Pietro Pettinajo da Siena*, trans. Serafino Ferri, ed. Maestro de Angelis (Siena: Rossi, 1802), 2, pp. 12–13.

89. "Memoriale," 1–4, Meersseman, *Dossier*, 93–95.

90. "Expositiones Regule," 1, Meersseman, *Dossier*, 114; "Memoriale," 29.2, ibid., 107–8, prescribes the drab undyed material associated with public penance; on which, see ibid., 107–8 n. 292.

91. "Memoriale," 29.1–3, Meersseman, *Dossier*, 106–8.

92. E.g., for Padua; see De Sandre Gasparini, *Statuti*, xxxvi–xl, esp. xxxvi.

93. "Memoriale," 30.1, Meersseman, *Dossier*, 109.

94. See Simon Tugwell, *Way of the Preacher* (Springfield, Ill.: Templegate, 1979), 39–40.

95. "Chapitre de Pénitents Lombards" (1280), 1–12, Meersseman, *Dossier*, 163–65.

96. Florence Stat. II (1325), 5.9, p. 371.

also ordered penitents (and clerics) to wear distinctive garb.[97] On 24 July 1286 Bishop Giacomo Cavalcante of Città di Castello excommunicated anyone who wore the penitent's habit without making vows.[98] Bishop Giacomo's emphasis on vows indicates a somewhat clericalized view of penitent life. The laity had broader views on what it took to enter the state of penance. The penitents' earliest entrance ceremony was nothing more than the execution of a legal instrument accepting the rule of the society and the imposition of a penitent "habit." The "Propositum" of 1215, reflecting earlier practice, gave no regulations on the habit's appearance.[99] Use of a legal instrument, rather than a spoken vow, followed the norms of canonical penance rather than monastic practice.[100] Other rites of the penitents were equally nonmonastic. The blessing of the "habit" in one early penitents' ritual from Brescia has nothing in common with the analogous ceremony in the rite of monastic profession. It took the vestition prayers from the ancient rite for imposing public or voluntary penance. As in the old ritual, the penitents called their attire not a *habitus*, like that of religious, but by the primitive word *cilicium*, "hair shirt"—even though it was nothing of the kind.[101] Only after the 1260s do we find penitent profession rituals including spoken vows, now patterned on the rites of the religious orders. At Arezzo, the penitents vowed to accept the rule, replied to questions about their acceptance of the society's purpose by saying Amen, and then kissed the statute book of the society.[102] Also like ancient public penitents, a converso, once professed, could leave the life of lay penance only to enter a canonical religious order.[103]

Penitents were called to a higher standard of lay life, not a cloistered monasticism. The penitent habit represented no separation from the daily work of earning a living, but rather the self-discipline by which individuals sought to overcome sins and vices. The rules of the penitents and their offshoots proscribed blasphemy, dicing, tavern haunting, and womanizing. The 1261 statutes of the Frati Gaudenti, or Jovial Friars, a lay brotherhood founded by the Franciscan Ruffino Gorgone of Piacenza, captured the spirit of this legislation: "The [brothers] are not to loiter about at intersections and under porticoes, chatting in a worldly way, since this causes the integrity and reputation of their religious life to be very much denigrated."[104] Penitents

---

97. E.g., Pistoia, *Constitutiones Synodi Diocesanae Pistoriensis sub Episcopo Ermanno Editae Anno 1308*, 1, Mansi 25:170–71.

98. "Cartulaire," 19, Meersseman, *Dossier*, 203–4.

99. "Memoriale," 5–6, Meersseman, *Dossier*, 129–30.

100. See "Memoriale," 30.2, Meersseman, *Dossier*, 109. Cf. Gratian, *Decretum*, C. 20 q. 1 c. 16; C. 27 q. 1 c. 36; and *Rule of St. Benedict*, ed. Timothy Fry (Collegeville, Minn.: Liturgical Press, 1982), 46, p. 68. On the Humiliati tertiaries' ceremony, which combined a written instrument and spoken vows, see Andrews, *Early Humiliati*, 183–84.

101. Meersseman, *Ordo*, 1:449 (the Brescia penitents); see Meersseman on this rite, ibid., 1:420.

102. "Nuovo statuto della congregazione della Vergine di Arezzo" (1262), 7, ibid., 2:1021.

103. "Memoriale," 31, Meersseman, *Dossier*, 109; cf. Gratian, *Decretum, De poen*. D. 5 c. 3.

104. "Regula Militiae B. Mariae V. Gloriosae," 62, Meersseman, *Dossier*, 304: "In triviis aut porticis more seculari in coloquiis non morentur, quoniam ex hoc religiose vite honestas et fama posset non modicum denigrari."

followed, in their own lay style, the "counsels" of Christ, something pre-viously understood as the preserve of vowed religious alone. They foreswore taking oaths, bearing arms, going to court, and so on. Statutes disciplined public sins of members, such as breach of peace and concord, usury, gam-bling, tavern haunting, association with "dishonest" or "bad" places or per-sons, and blasphemy. But legislation on sexual sins and adultery is rare.[105]

Penance culture gave particular importance to sacramental confession and Communion, and all penitents sought to go beyond the norm of once-yearly confession established by the Lateran Council of 1215. The penitent associations linked the frequency of confession to the group's general Com-munions. All extant penitent statutes required members to confess more than the Lateran canonical minimum. Generally, conversi practiced the pre-1215 rule of confession and Communion thrice a year, at Christmas, Easter, and Pentecost.[106] Statutes allowed members to confess fewer times, but only for good reason and "if they had permission of their confessor."[107] At the end of our period there seems to have been an increase in the frequency of confes-sion among penitents and a loosening of its connection to general Commu-nions, portending, perhaps, the more individualistic Eucharistic piety of the later Middle Ages.[108]

Medieval spirituality closely connected the state of penance with fasting, and so did the penitents. But they did not carry this to excess. Conversi observed the traditional fasts of the Church, including those of Wednesdays and Saturdays and that during Saint Martin's Lent (11 November to Christ-mas), which had somewhat fallen out of use. To these traditional fasts, peni-tent legislation added fasting on the vigils of feasts and saints' days particular to them or their city. In Piacenza, penitents fasted on the vigil of Saint Fran-cis because he was patron of their city.[109] Penitents practiced a moderate asceticism, avoiding extravagance at table. In particular, they were to avoid *convivia*. As commentators on the "Memoriale" explained, this word meant meals where entertainers and singers (*ioculatores vel cantatores*) were present. The commentary forbade penitents to put on *convivia*, even as fund-raising events for poor relief (*ad utilitatem pauperum*).[110] Apparently someone had dis-

105. Giuseppina De Sandre Gasparini, "Laici devoti fra confessione e penitenze," *Dalla penitenza all'ascolto delle confessioni: Il ruolo dei frati mendicanti: Atti del XXIII Convegno internazionale, Assisi, 12–14 ottobre 1995* (Spoleto: Centro Italiano di Studi sull'Alto Medioevo, 1996), 243–44. "Memoriale," 26, Meersseman, *Dossier*, 106, places special emphasis on peacemaking. For typical "blue laws," see Lucca, Biblioteca Statale, MS 1310 (1299), fol. 8ʳ; Milan, Biblioteca Nazionale Braidense, MS AC.VIII.2, fol. 9ʳ; Piacenza, Biblioteca Comunale, MS Pallestrelli 323 (1317), fol. 7ʳ.

106. "Memoriale," 15, Meersseman, *Dossier*, 101; see Gratian, *Decretum, De cons.* D. 2, cc. 16, 19, for pre-Lateran IV norms. *Pace* De Sandre Gasparini, "Laici devoti," 215–16.

107. Lucca, Biblioteca Statale, MS 1310, fols. 5ᵛ–6ʳ: "per alcuna legiptima cagione della qual'avesse licentia dal suo confessore." "Gli statuti di un'antica congregazione francescana di Brescia," ed. P. Guer-rini, *AFH* 1 (1908): 549, requires confession twice a year.

108. E.g., the 1332 Pavia flagellant statutes in Milan, Biblioteca Nazionale Braidense, MS AC.VIII.2, fols. 9ʳ⁻ᵛ. On the Eucharistic piety of the penitents, see Weissman, "From Brotherhood," 90.

109. Piacenza, Biblioteca Comunale, MS Pallestrelli 323, fols. 6ᵛ–7ʳ.

110. "Expositiones Regule," 3, Meersseman, *Dossier*, 114.

covered a loophole in the rule against parties. But money saved by fasting helped the poor or could be laid up for famine relief.[111]

Individual penitents enjoyed freedom to elaborate on the generally observed fasts. Sora Pacifica de' Guelfuzzi of Assisi described Saint Clare's fasts, which seem typical of lay penitents. Clare fasted three days a week, on Monday, Wednesday, and Friday.[112] This was hardly extravagant; the later two days were already traditional days of penance. Margherita of Città di Castello, from the age of seven and while living privately at home, observed the traditional monastic fast from the feast of the Holy Cross (14 September) to Easter and added Saturday to the penitential days observed by Clare.[113] Typically, the penitent merely observed traditional and neglected fasts of the Church with greater devotion. Umiliana dei Cerchi, her biographer tells us, observed the "customary church fasts" and fasted on the same four weekdays as Margherita. Umiliana added the ancient "Apostles' Fast" after Pentecost, "Saint Martin's Lent" before Advent, and a short fast before the Assumption in August. She also fasted on the vigils of her favorite saints.[114] Even the "private" fasting of the penitents was itself traditional and liturgical in origin. Among the recorded practices, only the Monday fast lacks ecclesiastical inspiration. To fast or "do penance" was to do what any Christian might do. If a lay penitent wanted to fast, she did so according to "the mind of the Church." The penitents' discipline was rigorous, but hardly self-imposed starvation.[115] To fast did not mean absolute abstinence from food and water. Medieval Italians avoided flesh and dairy products, eating a single meal, usually in the early afternoon. That meal might include fish. Corporate fasting also followed the traditional fasts of the Church, often adding a social dimension lacking in private observances. A confraternity at Pavia, for example, observed only the Church fasts, adding that members unable to fast because of illness should provide enough food to feed a poor person for each day they were dispensed from fasting.[116]

Communities of conversi and penitents cared for the material as well as spiritual needs of their members. The "Memoriale" stipulated that when any member heard that another had fallen sick, he should tell the ministers so they could provide for a weekly sick-call visit and, if the sick member were poor, supply his needs from the common fund. Should the sick member die,

111. Meersseman, *Dossier*, 88; on which, see Powell, *Albertanus*, 95. Cf. Gratian, *Decretum*, D. 42 c. 1.

112. *El processo della canoniçatione de sancta Chiara*, ed. Zeffirino Lazzeri, 1.8, in "Il processo di canonizzazione di S. Chiara d'Assisi," *AFH* 13 (1920): 444.

113. *Legenda B. Margaritae de Castello*, ed. M.-H. Laurent, 11, in "La plus ancienne légende de la b. Marguerite di Città di Castello," *AFP* 10 (1940): 121.

114. Vito of Cortona, *Vita [B. Humilianae]*, 3.27, p. 392.

115. Cf. later extreme fasting practices in Caroline Bynum, *Holy Feast and Holy Fast: The Religious Significance of Food to Medieval Women* (Berkeley and Los Angeles: University of California Press, 1987), and Rudolf Bell, *Holy Anorexia* (Chicago: University of Chicago Press, 1985).

116. Milan, Biblioteca Nazionale Braidense, MS AC.VIII.2, fols. 8v–9r.

all were to attend the funeral.[117] Charity extended beyond sick members, at least in ritual ways. Not uncommonly, penitents fed a symbolic twelve poor men before their Palm Sunday banquet. The members ate later and separately from the poor, however, indicating the special community they shared among themselves.[118] This gesture did not imply that the penitents were an economically privileged group practicing noblesse oblige. If they observed the spirit of their rule, penitents followed a life, if not of poverty, at least of simplicity. Their behavior was to be humble enough so that they could be suitable recipients of alms themselves. Abuse through luxurious living seems to have happened only in individual cases, the result of the brothers' independence and the freelance quality of their life. Bologna exiled under a ban of £10 bon. any bogus penitent who falsely solicited alms in the morning and spent the rest of his day blaspheming in the tavern.[119] More typically, groups of simple-living penitents organized assistance for the indigent and served the sick. This identification of penitents with charitable service became marked in the period 1220 to 1250. Cities consequently increased their financial support for penitent groups in the same period. But hospital work and social service meant increased institutionalization.[120] The conversi's success in such corporate endeavors was always in tension with their origin as an individualistic lay movement.

Every group of penitents had a monthly solemn Mass and sermon at a particular church, whose titular they adopted as their saintly patron. Into the early 1200s, the church was usually the chapel of the neighborhood where they lived. The monthly Mass was the pivot and focus of the confraternity's devotional life, and attendance was mandatory.[121] The most common day for this Mass was the first Sunday of the month, a practice possibly derived from ancient Roman (and Jewish) observance of the new moon.[122] Individual groups added particular devotions to the Mass. The flagellants of Pisa met in the Dominican church of Santa Catarina on the fourth Sunday of the month. After hearing the monthly Mass and a sermon, the brothers went in procession, two by two, to the patronal altars and offered candles.[123] In addition, they celebrated the solemnities of Our Lady and the feasts of

---

117. "Memoriale," 22–23, Meersseman, *Dossier*, 103–4 (cf. Humiliati tertiaries' provisions ibid., 104 n. 23); "Statuti della Confraternita dei Servi di Dio e della s. Madre del Duomo" (Statuti D, 1298), 13, De Sandre Gasparini, *Statuti*, 15.

118. E.g., "Statuti della Confraternita dei Servi di Dio e della s. Madre del Duomo" (Statuti D, 1298), 24, De Sandre Gasparini, *Statuti*, 22.

119. Bologna Stat. 1 (1259–67), 8.97⁵, 2:285–86.

120. See Benvenuti Papi, "I penitenti," 25–39, esp. 30. See also ead., "Pubblica assistenza e marginalità femminile," *In Castro Poenitentiae*, 656–58, on Giovanni Villani, *Cronica*, 1:658, which speaks of hospital work as typical of women penitents.

121. On confraternities and parishes, see De Sandre Gasparini, *Statuti*, l; on monthly Mass, see Meersseman, *Ordo*, 2:583–84; and for legislation, see Piacenza, Biblioteca Comunale, MS Pallestrelli 323, fols. 7ʳ⁻ᵛ; Milan, Biblioteca Nazionale Braidense, MS AC.VIII.2, fol. 9ᵛ.

122. So Meersseman, *Ordo*, 1:24.

123. "Regula della 'vita' dei disciplinati e laudesi di Pisa" (1312), 4, ibid., 2:1051.

their patrons, Saint Dominic, Saint Peter of Verona, and Saint Catherine of Alexandria. At Bologna in the 1240s the confraternity dedicated to Saint Dominic met in the Dominican church where he was buried. Their monthly Mass and assembly were on the last day of the month. They celebrated their patron's feast with a solemn Mass and candle offering at his altar. Like other confraternities, they maintained a perpetual lamp before their patron saint's image.[124]

Religious confraternities, like the secular associations of their age, sealed their comradeship by table fellowship. Dinner followed the monthly Mass at the common time of the medieval Italian main meal, noon. The ministers of the society organized the Mass, meeting, and dinner. The treasurer paid the expenses from a collection taken up at the Mass; the "Memoriale" set each brother's contribution at 1d. The treasurer set aside any remainder to assist poor members and provide them with suitable funerals. Any further surplus became poor alms.[125] At Sant'Ilario near Florence, the peasants of one confraternity met at the local church and then dined under the direction of their rectors, who had responsibility for provisions and calculation of expenses. Local statutes usually included elaborate legislation governing distribution of food and drink and the sharing of expenses.[126]

Until the late 1200s, penitent groups met and prayed wherever was convenient, and that place determined their patron saint. One Padua confraternity celebrated its patronal feast of Saint Lucy with Mass, poor alms of 12d., and a candle offering. Their poor alms were a public affair and its date well known. The brothers sent a trumpeter around the city to announce the event, bringing in, one assumes, a significant crop of beggars. But when the parish was rededicated to Saint Rocco, they changed the patronal feast accordingly and moved the poor dole to the new day.[127] The Marian penitents who met in the church of Santa Margherita of Montici in Florence came for annual Mass on feasts of both the Virgin and Saint Margaret. When they moved to the cathedral in 1310, the brothers dropped Margaret as their patron, even though that meant forfeiting the indulgence of forty days that Bishop Francesco Monaldeschi had granted them in 1296 for devotions on her feast.[128] A local group took its identity from its place of assembly and that church's titular. Common penitential life and mutual fraternity gave the members their common identity, not some shared special devotion.

The "Memoriale" stipulated that a "pious man" (*vir religiosus*) preach in

124. "Statutum Fraternitatis S. Dominici" (1244), Meersseman, *Ordo*, 2:628–29; Lucca, Biblioteca Statale, MS 1310, fols. 6ʳ⁻ᵛ.

125. On the collection, see "Memoriale," 19–20, Meersseman, *Dossier*, 102, and Lucca, Biblioteca Statale, MS 1310, fols. 3ᵛ⁻4ʳ.

126. "Forma Statuti," 5, Meersseman, *Ordo*, 1:19.

127. "Statuti della Confraternita di s. Lucia" (Statuti L, 1334), 17 and 27, De Sandre Gasparini, *Statuti*, 71 and 73–74.

128. Raffaello Morghen, "Vita religiosa e vita cittadina nella Firenze del duecento," *La coscienza cittadina nei comuni italiani nel duecento*, 214–15.

conjunction with the monthly Mass and dinner. The priest engaged for Mass could have preached, but until late in the 1200s the preacher was commonly a gifted member of the society. He spoke at the meeting that followed Mass. We know that one lay penitent held the official position of *vir religiosus* for his Florentine confraternity in the 1220s.[129] He preached after Mass but before the dinner. Lay preaching focused on practical issues, the group's way of life, and exhortation to works of charity and devotion. Albertano of Brescia, the famous lay theologian, served in the same function, even if he never held the formal title. Albertano delivered his "First Brescian Sermon" to the lawyer's confraternity that met in the Franciscan church of San Giorgio at Brescia. He preached on the association's rule, the business of the meeting, and corporate devotional activities like purchasing oil for the votive lamps. He alluded to the common meal that would follow.[130] Such preaching required little theological sophistication, although Albertano, for one, had no lack of that. Lay preaching declined as the penitents came under supervision of the mendicant orders in the late 1200s. Members of the Franciscan and Dominican "third orders" had to listen to sermons by their clerically appointed spiritual directors instead of hiring a preacher of their own choice or giving sermons to each other. Lay preaching pretty much died out after 1300, but the flagellant confraternities, independent as always, refused to capitulate to any clerical monopoly. They shopped around, inviting preachers from the Augustinians, Dominicans, Franciscans, Carmelites, and secular clergy.[131]

PENITENTS AT PRAYER

Penitents adapted their individual daily prayers to the liturgical Office of the Church. After rising early, Umiliana dei Cerchi went to hear Matins. Afterward, she returned to her cell (a room in the family palazzo) and prayed by herself until dawn. On fast days, she extended her prayers until None, but otherwise she took a light meal at sunup and went to serve the indigent, whether at the local hospital or in their homes. In the evening, she returned home for prayer and sleep. A good penitent, she was never idle.[132] Many groups encouraged daily Mass.[133] But the more common devotion, practiced as well by Umiliana, was the Divine Office at a local church. The "Memoriale" specified recitation of this Office as the personal daily prayer of those who were literate, that is, able to read, if not understand, Latin. Those who

---

129. "Memoriale," 21, Meersseman, *Dossier,* 103. The Florentine Archivio di Stato document is published in Meersseman, *Dossier,* 181–83; on lay preaching, see ibid., 15.

130. Summarized in Powell, *Albertanus,* 92. Meersseman, *Ordo,* 3:1279–89, outlines five other sermons. For Albertano resources, see Angus Graham, *Albertano of Brescia: Resource Site,* 15 January 2000 <http://freespace.virgin.net/angus.graham/Albertano.htm> (accessed 25 October 2003).

131. Piacenza flagellant statutes of 1317, in Piacenza, Biblioteca Comunale, MS Pallestrelli 323, fols. 20ʳ⁻ᵛ.

132. Vito of Cortona, *Vita [B. Humilianae],* 2.10, p. 388.

133. E.g., Milan, Biblioteca Nazionale Braidense, MS AC.VIII.2, fols. 8ʳ⁻ᵛ (1332 Pavia flagellants).

could not sound out the Latin texts said Paters instead.[134] Italians much preferred the recitation of Paters to reading a "little Office" from a book. So-called books of hours from communal Italy are very rare indeed. The well-to-do Frati Gaudenti assumed that recitation of Paters would be the norm. They did change the balance somewhat, saying twelve Paters for Matins and twelve for Vespers. At Pisa, the Laudesi confraternity, a group dedicated to singing the lauds of the Virgin, recited the Pater and the Ave Maria (the Hail Mary, taken from Lk 1:28, 42) three times for each minor hour, and five for Lauds and Vespers.[135] Set numbers of Paters are the near-universal private prayer specified by confraternity statutes of the later 1200s and early 1300s. Associations changed the number and occasion of such recitation according to their needs and devotions.

The penitents' autonomy allowed them to develop devotions suited to their own particular tastes. Groups dedicated to the Blessed Virgin Mary already existed in the 1100s, usually connected to churches with that title. Mid-thirteenth-century Florentine confraternities that had spontaneously adopted the Blessed Virgin as patron gathered each evening at Santa Maria Novella to sing hymns in her honor. The early-fourteenth-century Marian confraternity at Pisa assembled *a cantare le laude* in the Dominican church of Santa Catarina.[136] Penitent groups with Marian devotion emphasized acts of piety, especially processions and candle offerings, rather than social service or charity. At Arezzo, the members of the Congregation of the Virgin each contributed 2d. to the society after attending Terce or None on the four great feasts of Mary, the Annunciation, Assumption, Nativity, and Purification. These collections underwrote the community's candle offerings and Mass on those days.[137] In Florence, during Mary's feasts, Marian groups erected votive altars before images of the Virgin in the city streets.[138]

At Milan, according to a record of 1273, each member of the *piccola schola* of the Virgin contributed 1d. monthly to pay for votive lights before images of Mary in the city's churches and streets. The group recited suffrages for dead members. That group counted a priest, Don Giovanni of Dugiano, and two brothers (probably Humiliati) among its twenty-eight members, but all the rest were laymen and women. Members' relatives, in particular the men's wives, enrolled as auxiliaries to share in the society's spiritual benefits without contributing money to the illumination project.[139] Devotional prac-

134. "Memoriale" (1223), 12.3–4, Meersseman, *Dossier*, 391.

135. "Regula Militiae B. Mariae V. Gloriosae" (1261), 34–36, Meersseman, *Dossier*, 296–97; Lucca, Biblioteca Statale, MS 1310, fol. 6ʳ (1299 Lucca flagellant statutes); "Regula della 'vita' dei disciplinati e laudesi di Pisa" (1312), Meersseman, *Ordo*, 2:1056–57. For similar practices at Brescia (1265–95) and Reggio Emilia (1295–1321), see Meersseman, *Ordo*, 2:945–46.

136. On these devotions, see Meersseman, *Ordo*, 2:960.

137. "Nuovo statuto della congregazione della Vergine di Arezzo" (1262), 18, ibid., 2:1025.

138. Meersseman, *Ordo*, 2:951.

139. The wives' names are found in a fragment of the group's matricula in Paris, Bibliothèque National, MS lat. 6512, fol. 103ʳ, ed. in Meersseman, *Ordo*, 1:21–22.

tices varied greatly, reflecting the confraternities' diverse membership. A Marian confraternity at Siena organized processions on twelve different feasts of the Virgin but also cultivated devotion to Christ Crucified. According to their legislation of 1267, the members recited, probably in the vernacular, John 8:21–29—Christ's prediction of his Passion—at the end of their monthly Mass of the Virgin.[140]

Perhaps as early as the 1230s, penitents produced the first vernacular hymns dedicated to the Virgin, the *laude*.[141] After midcentury, various Marian groups appeared spontaneously, sometimes the result of lay piety, but more commonly under clerical leadership.[142] Indulgences granted by Pope Alexander IV show such associations active at Orvieto, Recanati, Reggio, Bagnoregio, Osimo, and Toscanella.[143] A second wave of hymn composition followed in the 1260s.[144] Some confraternities made hymn singing their principal devotional focus. A passage in the life of Saint Ambrogio Sansedoni (+1268) mentions such a group, perhaps our earliest example.[145] During the 1260s, hymn-singing confraternities multiplied, first at Assisi, Gubbio, Borgo San Sepolcro, Orvieto, and Fabriano; later at Arezzo, Cortona, Urbino, Siena, Florence, and Rome.[146] In a letter of 2 September 1273, Bishop Bernardo de' Gallerani of Siena used, for the first time, the name by which they came to be known, Laudesi.[147] The Laudesi were mostly a Tuscan and central Italian phenomenon. Their heartland was Umbria, Spoleto, and Perugia.[148] That region is the provenance of the oldest extant hymn collections, the *Laudario di Cortona* (1260s), the compositions of Iacopone of Todi (admittedly a Franciscan and not a penitent), and the *Laudario urbinate*. The Laudesi's anonymous and vernacular hymns show a striking homogeneity in their piety and modes of expression.[149] They are a remarkable window into the lay Marian piety of the central Italian communes.

140. Meersseman comments on this recitation in *Ordo*, 2:958; for their statutes, see ibid., 1029–34, esp. 1032–33, on the processions.

141. The earliest example may be "Pianto della Virgine della Passione di Montecassino," ed. Mauro Inguanez, *Un dramma della Passione del secolo XII*, Miscellanea cassinese, 18 (Badia di Montecassino, 1939). For other examples, see Salimbene, *Cronica* (1233), Baird trans., 49; "Vita Fratris Aegidii," *Chronica XXIV Generalium Ordinis Fratrum Minorum*, Analecta Franciscana, 3 (Quaracchi: Collegium S. Bonaventurae, 1897), 101; and Francesco A. Ugolini, *Testi volgari abruzzesi del duecento* (Turin: Rosenberg & Sellier, 1959), 1–50 (1290s).

142. On rising clerical control after 1250, see Nicolas Terpstra, "Confraternities and Mendicant Orders: The Dynamics of Lay and Clerical Brotherhood in Renaissance Bologna," *Catholic Historical Review* 82 (1996): 5.

143. Meersseman, *Ordo*, 2:974.

144. See Emilio Pasquini and Antonio Enzo Quaglio, *Lo stilnovo e la poesia religiosa*, Letteratura italiana Laterza, 2 (Bari: Laterza, 1980), 151–53.

145. *AS* 16 (May III), 212, sect. 14; on which, see Meersseman, *Ordo*, 2:956.

146. Pasquini and Quaglio, *Stilnovo*, 154–58.

147. Meersseman, *Ordo*, 2:954–55.

148. Pasquini and Quaglio, *Stilnovo*, 158. For a non-Tuscan example, see "La Compagnia di s. Maria delle Laudi e di San Francesco di Bologna," ed. Candido Mesini, *AFH* 52 (1959): 361–72.

149. Recent editions: *Laudario di Cortona* (1260s), *Poeti del duecento* (Milan: Ricciardi, 1995); the *laude* of Iacopone of Todi, *Laudi, trattato, e detti*, ed. Franca Ageno (Florence: Felice le Monnier, 1954); and *Laudario urbinate*, "Il Laudario dei disciplinati di S. Croce di Urbino," ed. G. Grimaldi, *Studi romanzi* 12 (1915):

In the north, corporate hymn singing also appears in the 1260 statutes of
the Bolognese flagellants. These statutes describe the prayer book used in
their corporate devotions. It included lauds to Christ and the Virgin, as well
as prayers for the pope, the Christian faithful, the Roman Church, the city
of Bologna, those doing penance, pilgrims, benefactors, and even the group's
enemies (*illis qui fecerunt nobis iniuriam*).[150] Later devotional collections linked
to confraternities usually included indulgenced Latin prayers adopted from
the public liturgy of the Church and lists of indulgences granted for activities
like confession and general Communion, visits to the confraternity's patronal
altar, and even mere active membership.[151]

While manuscripts containing penitents' rituals, as opposed to hymns, are
lacking until the early 1300s, their creation is certainly older. In their developed form, their ritual books included hymns or laments in honor of Christ's
Passion, rituals for the washing of feet, *laude* in honor of the patron saint,
and prayers for the dead.[152] Bolognese confraternity prayers are less an ad
hoc collection than a lay version of the Church's liturgical prayers. Florentine and Mantuan flagellants included in their devotions vernacular bidding
prayers modeled on the Church's liturgy of Good Friday. During their rituals
the brothers knelt and recited a Pater and an Ave for each intention. These
intentions, like those in Bologna, followed the Good Friday order, invoking
God's grace on the hierarchy, civil authorities, the local group, and those in
need. At both Florence and Mantua, the Latin formula of the Paters and
Aves, along with collects lifted from the Church's liturgy, added hieratic
solemnity to a service in which the prayer intentions were pronounced in the
vernacular so they might be understood by all.[153]

Statutes of one Florentine Marian confraternity describe the liturgical devotions typical of monthly meetings in the confraternities of the late communal period.[154] This group ritualized their corporate penance by adaption of
a monastic practice known as the "chapter of faults." The group's leader, or

1–96. For a handlist of manuscripts and editions, see Ignazio Baldelli, "La lauda e i disciplinati," *Rassegna
della letteratura italiana* 64 (1960): 396–418, esp. 399–409.

150. "Statuto dei Disciplinati di Bologna" (1260), 28, Meersseman, *Ordo*, 1:490.

151. E.g., Piacenza, Biblioteca Comunale, ms Pallestrelli 323, fols. 4ᵛ–5ʳ (1317 Piacenza flagellant statutes); Milan, Biblioteca Nazionale Braidense, ms AC.viii.2, fols. 42ᵛ–45ᵛ (1332 Pavia flagellant statutes);
Florence, Biblioteca Nazionale Centrale, ms II.iv.686, fols. 34ʳ–36ʳ (statutes of Florentine flagellants from
the 1320s).

152. Summarized by Baldelli, "La lauda e i disciplinati," 405, whose sources are late, e.g., Assisi,
Archivio di San Rufino, ms 78 (dated to 1327). For an example of foot washing, see Milan, Biblioteca
Nazionale Braidense, ms AC.viii.2, fol. 27ʳ.

153. Florence, Biblioteca Nazionale Centrale, ms II.iv.686, fols. 3ʳ–9ʳ; for bidding prayers, see Giacomo Benfatti, *Li statuti et ordinatione per la compagnia de' fratelli disciplinanti in del loco de Sancta Maria de la
Misericordia*, ed. Augustine Thompson, in "New Light on Bl. Giacomo Benfatti, Bishop of Mantua, and
the Mantua Disciplinati," *AFP* 69 (1999): 167–69. On bidding prayers of other flagellants, see Giuseppe
Landotti, "La 'Preghiera dei fedeli' in lingua italiana da secolo xiii al secolo xx," *Ephemerides Liturgicae* 91
(1977): 101–9.

154. Florence, Biblioteca Medicea Laurenziana, ms Acq. e Doni 336 (xiv cent.), fols. 12ᵛ–14ʳ (on the
examination of faults), 14ʳ–18ʳ (on the prayers).

governatore, began the session by recalling Jesus' command that all should be reconciled to their neighbors before offering sacrifice. Members then sought out those they had offended since the last meeting and asked forgiveness. This completed, the leader summoned to the altar anyone who had transgressed the rule, so that he might impose penance on him (fig. 35). Transgressions punished included missing a meeting, neglect of monthly sacramental confession, and failure to recite morning and evening prayers. Especially punished were visits to taverns and worldly amusements such as jousting, dancing, and horse racing. Each delinquent received "some particular task" (*alcuno incaricho*) as a penance. Finally, the group knelt and collectively recited the Confiteor, the admission of sins from the Mass.

So prepared, the community began their devotions. They first recited the Ave Maria in Latin, doing so responsorially in the form of verses and responses and using the short form, ending at "the fruit of thy womb," as usual in that period. The principal liturgical exercise for those who could read came next, the little Office of the Virgin—unusual as a lay devotion at this date. All then recited the Salve Regina, which even the unlettered would have committed to memory. At the end of the little Office, the prayers returned to the vernacular and to the forms typical of other groups. The leader proposed prayer intentions in Italian, for each of which the group recited a Pater and an Ave. This bidding prayer, although similar to the liturgical form of Good Friday, followed an order wholly independent of the clerical version. The brothers prayed for the grace of penance and the needs of the members, the Church hierarchy, the sick, the founder of the society, their civil officials, their relatives, the whole Christian faithful, the crops, the faithful in purgatory, the leaders of Christendom, and last of all for peace. This bidding prayer ended with a Pater and an Ave, in responsorial form, and the usual Latin collects. *Qualche lauda spirituale*, "some vernacular hymn," ended the meeting. In their devotions, the group's "Marian" element, the little Office, was secondary to the lay liturgy shared by all confraternities of the period.

The bare outlines of confraternity prayer services can never express the texture of penitent prayers and devotions, something, alas, mostly lost to us. The rituals lack the penitents' tender devotion to the Virgin, their heartfelt need for penance amid the sins of life, and their call to praise God in action. One *laude* preserved in a book used by the Florentine flagellants of the early fourteenth century expresses their piety beautifully:

> This life is like a breeze,
> which passes in a moment;
> Whoever would be happy,
> let him invoke the Virgin Mary;

who is our advocate,
by us always to be praised. Amen.[155]

SERVICE TO CITY AND CHURCH

Communes called on penitents to fill positions in city administration, although the brothers and sisters theoretically enjoyed exemption from public
service.[156] Very early, the penitents themselves accommodated communal
needs. Parma statutes of the 1240s, among the earliest extant for any commune, show countless *fratres* (brothers) in city functions. From 1 September
to 29 September (the feast of Saint Michael the Archangel), two penitents
and a judge were annually sequestered to revise city statutes. The city provided them with a cook and messengers.[157] Another penitent, who was also
a notary, registered and took pledges for back taxes, while yet another kept
the city seals, receiving £5 imp. for the task.[158] Penitents assumed responsibility for keeping the city books and records in 1242.[159] The *dugarolus* in charge
of waterworks and drains was, from the early 1240s, always a penitent.[160] A
commission of four brothers, chosen by the podesta and his council, oversaw
weights and measures in consultation with the "minister" of the Parma penitents. Their broad commission gave them oversight of sales in grain, flour,
and wine. One brother ran the city office where people could bring bread to
have it tested for weight, quality, and color. At this brother's direction, the
commission could fine delinquent bakers up to £12 parm.[161] Brothers also
served in charitable tasks such as dispensing municipal alms.[162] Finally,
Parma relied on penitents for supervision of municipal elections until the
1260s.[163] By 1288, Parma penitents held the monopoly for bread and wine
sales during famine, to ensure that no one would lack food on account of
poverty.[164]

Though not as early or complete as those of Parma, the statues of other
communes show conversi in similar roles. At Bologna, the brothers served

155. Florence, Biblioteca Nazionale Centrale, MS II.IV.686, fol. 21ᵛ: "Questa vita e come vento, | che
in un ponto passa via. | Chi ci vole stare contento, | preghi la vergine Maria; | la quale e nostra avocata,
| da noi sempre sia laudata. Amen."

156. For papal assertion of exemption, see the 21 May 1227 decree of Gregory IX, in "Bullarium," 4,
Meersseman, *Dossier*, 43–45; and for later reaffirmations: Gregory IX, 27 March 1232 ("Bullarium," 12,
ibid., 49); Innocent IV, 30 July 1244 ("Bullarium," 19, ibid., 55); Gregory IX, 4 June 1230 ("Bullarium,"
8, ibid., 50; *BF* 1:65; Potthast, *Regesta*, 8565; Lucien Auvray, *Les registres de Grégoire IX* [Paris: Thorin,
1896–1955], 1:463); Gregory IX to the bishop of Siena, 20 April 1239 ("Bullarium," 17, Meersseman,
Dossier, 53–54); Innocent IV to Florence, 17 October 1251 ("Bullarium," 31, ibid., 62); Innocent IV to
Mantua, 31 May 1252 (ibid., 64).

157. Parma Stat. 1 (1241), p. 29.

158. Ibid. (1242), 114; (before 1241), 27.

159. Ibid. (1242), 125.

160. Ibid. (1243), 146–47.

161. Ibid. (1242), 157; (before 1243, perhaps before 1233), 26. The commission received £10 parm. a
year for their services.

162. Ibid. (1221), 31, and (1241), 18, where a frater supervised the list of those banned from the city.

163. Ibid., 14; cf. 414, for the year 1259, when mendicants replaced them.

164. *Chronicon Parmense* (1288), 55.

as lay chaplains to the municipal jail. They made and distributed bread to prisoners, a task for which the jail warden had to provide funds, lest he incur a penalty of 20s.[165] At Parma, the *fratres* maintained the books listing those banned, that is, exiled or condemned to death. Popes entrusted the penitents with peacemaking. When Innocent IV sent penitents to make peace at Florence, he excused the imposition, saying that such work was for them not a "burden" but rather that the penitents gave *subsidium* to the city.[166] Penitents served the cities in less sensitive matters, especially in public works. Reggio in 1267 gave oversight of walls, gates, canals, and bridges to a pair of lay penitents, providing them with a stipend of £8 reg. At Bologna, a committee of three or four brothers supervised road maintenance outside the walls and collected taxes on grain shipments, a service for which they each received 2s. bon. annually.[167]

Freelance *conversi* in government and administration easily assimilated to secular functionaries. This risked bringing the entire movement into disrepute. In 1262, at Parma, the minister of the brothers tried to reassert his proper control over *conversi* doing city work. The city agreed to appoint as municipal servants only brothers with the minister's explicit permission. He, in return, promised to make sure that they properly executed the work assigned—an exception being made for the aged Fra Uberto Blaxa, longtime servant of the commune. Too old and sick to work, he could remain on the city payroll in recognition of past service.[168] But with office came temptations. Secularization and loss of religious identity plagued penitents in government service during the later communal period. At Bologna and Florence, the city stripped penitents and Frati Gaudenti of their exemption from taxes on inheritances and real estate in 1288.[169] That the poor penitents were possessed of wealth sufficient to attract the attention of tax collectors is troublesome. In 1299, the podesta of Città di Castello expelled all penitents who claimed exemption from labor on the city walls.[170] At Bologna in 1289, the city excluded *conversi* from administrative, judicial, and financial responsibilities in neighborhood corporations.[171] At Verona and Brescia in the same period, the Humiliati lost their roles in city administration.[172] By the early 1300s, the *fratres* left the civil service, never to return.[173] The Church had for a long time been taking up the slack.

165. Bologna Stat. I (1252), 10.74, 3:169–71.

166. "Bullarium," 20 (Innocent IV, 21 January 1246), Meersseman, *Dossier*, 56.

167. Reggio Stat. (1267), 1.47, pp. 118–19; Bologna Stat. II (1288), 3.49, 1:142.

168. Parma Stat. I (1262), p. 445; reaffirmed later, ibid. (1264), p. 445. But penitents did take on new responsibilities, such as bridge construction and repair of the piazza of the commune: ibid. (1262), 447; (1264), 458.

169. Bologna Stat. II (1288), 9.10, 2:117; Florence Stat. II (1325), 5.42, p. 392.

170. Meersseman, *Dossier*, 27.

171. "Ordinatione Fratrum de Penitentia" (Bologna, 1289), 11, ibid., 175.

172. E.g., Verona Stat. II (1276), 1.69, p. 62; Brescia Stat. (before 1277), col. (170).

173. As noted by De Sandre Gasparini in *Statuti di confraternite*, lii–liii.

Dominicans had, from their arrival in Italy, directed penitents to take part in the detection of heresy.[174] The preacher Giacopino of Reggio founded the most famous antiheresy society, the Società della Beata Virgine, at Bologna in 1233. The city itself favored that society into the 1250s and enlisted the members in the struggle against heresy and sodomy. The *società* played such an important role in public morals and orthodoxy that the podesta and city officials consulted with the Dominicans in the appointment of its officers.[175] Also about 1233, at Parma, Fra Bartolomeo of Branganze founded the Militia of Jesus Christ, again dedicated to heresy hunting. It was an aristocratic organization open only to knights.[176] The militia and groups like it departed far from the freelance style of ascetic life typical of lay penitents. The militia assisted the communal committees who reported on heretics to the inquisitors. Secular princes also founded antiheresy organizations, such as Charles of Anjou's Società della Croce, described by the chronicler Salimbene of Parma.[177] At Milan, a committee of twelve members appointed by the podesta did this work. In 1252, a papal decree made such committees mandatory in the Lombard cities.[178] The antiheresy societies, while in form confraternities, did not reflect ordinary lay piety; they were police agencies. They tended to be highly aristocratic, closed corporations. Saint Peter of Verona's Societas Fidelium, formed to assist communes and inquisitors in detecting heresy, was exclusive, even covert.[179] Antiheresy societies might have broader goals. The Frati Gaudenti were antiheretical but also assisted the neighborhood corporation in peacemaking and peacekeeping. In form, one might consider them an offshoot of the penitents. But Salimbene, who considered the Jovial Friars a mere clone of Bartolomeo's militia, spoke for contemporaries (and modern historians) when he characterized the Gaudenti as indolent, self-serving, and lax.[180]

As penitents entered antiheresy work, they became attached to the mendi-

174. On Dominican Marian confraternities, see Gilles Gérard Meersseman, "Le congregazioni della Vergine," Meersseman, *Ordo*, 2:921–1117, esp. 927–32, on origins. On antiheresy confraternities, see Lorenzo Paolini, "Le origini della 'Societas Crucis,'" *Rivista di storia e letteratura religiosa* 15 (1979): 173–229.

175. Bologna Stat. 1 (1259), 1.145–47, 1:408–9; on this group, see Meersseman, *Ordo*, 2:828, 2:770, and Meersseman's publications of source documents for the *società* in *AFP* 18 (1948): 136–40; 21 (1951): 67–68, 120–21; 22 (1952): 90–92; 20 (1950): 11, 18, 70.

176. Salimbene, *Cronica* (1285), 891, Baird trans., 619. On these groups, see Gilles Gérard Meersseman, "Le varie Militie di Gesù Cristo," Meersseman, *Ordo*, 3:1233–70, rpt. of his "Études sur les anciennes confréries dominicaines iv: Les Milices de Jésus Christ," *AFP* 23 (1953): 275–308; and Merlo, "Militia Christi," 373–86.

177. Salimbene, *Cronica* (1250), 543, Baird trans., 376–77.

178. Innocent IV, *Ad Extirpanda* (15 May 1252), Meersseman, *Ordo*, 2:764.

179. On Peter of Verona's groups, see Meersseman, "Le confraternite di san Pietro Martire," Meersseman, *Ordo*, 2:754–920.

180. Salimbene, *Cronica* (1260/61), 678–80, Baird trans., 476–78; Matteo Griffoni, 15; for their rule, see "Regula Militiae B. Mariae V. Gloriosae" (1261), Meersseman, *Dossier*, 295–309; documents on the group at Bologna are collected in *Cronaca di Ronzano e memorie di Loderingo d'Anadalò, frate gaudente*, ed. Giovanni Gozzadini (Bologna: Società Tipografica Bolognese, 1851), 129–208. For the tomb of a wealthy Jovial Friar, see *Iscrizioni medievali bolognesi*, ed. Giancarlo Roversi (Bologna: Istituto Storico di Bologna, 1982), 216–17, no. 10 (San Giovanni in Monte).

cant orders.[181] Dominican-directed individual penitents promoted orthodoxy, which replaced the older focus on temporal works of mercy.[182] At
Vicenza in the 1280s, the most visible penitent was Sor Mabilia di fu fra
Guidone Zenoese, herself the daughter of a penitent, as her name implies.
She handled the confiscated goods of heretics convicted by the local Franciscan inquisition and, after the pope removed the Minorites for financial corruption, worked for the new Dominican-run tribunal. Sor Mabilia seems to
have done well for herself—detractors accused her of retaining confiscated
property. In 1305 she and her friend Sor Meltruda Bellasoro drafted wills
leaving money to a number of charities.[183] She requested burial in the Franciscan church of San Lorenzo, near the altar she herself had constructed in
honor of Saint Peter. The local Poor Clare abbess was her executor. We are
a long way from the poor rural penitents of San Desiderio.

LAY AUTONOMY AND THE MENDICANTS

By mid–thirteenth century, sexual segregation had become the norm among
the penitents. At Padua, confraternity statutes from the communal period
and later never mention women.[184] This is exceptional, since women penitents appear everywhere else and, by the late 1200s, probably outnumbered
the men.[185] Perhaps the male confraternities' growing involvement in government dictated this; perhaps it reflected increasing restrictions on women;
or, more likely, it arose from the women's aversion to elaborate organization
and their desire for autonomy. Because the female penitent style was more
independent and freelance than that of the men, their absence from statutes
means little. Women's desire for companionship and support encouraged
formation of more informal communities or, better, networks. "Microcon-
vents" and anchor-holds for individual *recluse* multiplied in many communes,
although their transience meant that they left few documents or records.[186]
Sibyllina Biscossi became a conversa on her own. She felt drawn to the
Dominican church at Pavia, met some friars there, and became a penitent
under their direction.[187] She never joined a group. Umiliana dei Cerchi lived
a life of penance at home. Eventually another conversa, Sobilia of Sasso,

181. Mariano D'Alatri, "I minori e la 'cura animarum' di fraternità e congregazioni," *I frati minori e il terzo ordine: Problemi e discussioni storiografiche, 17–20 ottobre 1982*, Convegni del Centro di studi sulla spiritualità medievali, 23 (Todi: Accademia Tudertina, 1985), 150–53; De Sandre Gasparini, "Laici devoti," 223.

182. See Meersseman, *Dossier*, 24; id., *Ordo*, 1:379.

183. Mantese, "Fratres et sorores," 697–98.

184. De Sandre Gasparini, *Statuti*, xl–xlii.

185. E.g., at Bergamo: Maria Teresa Brolis, "A Thousand and More Women: The Register of Women for the Confraternity of Misericordia Maggiore in Bergamo, 1265–1339," *Catholic Historical Review* 88 (2002): 231–46. On the feminization of the confraternities, see Casagrande, *Religiosità*, 211–314.

186. On such written records, see Benvenuti Papi, "Donne religiose," 614–15; for women penitents (and their male counterparts), see Casagrande, *Religiosità*, 28–33; and on penitents' networks and active life, see Maiju Lehmijoki-Gardner, *Worldly Saints: Social Interaction of Dominican Penitent Women in Italy, 1200–1500* (Helsinki: Suomen Historiallinen Seura, 1999).

187. Tomasso of Bossolasco, *Vita [B. Sibyllinae Papaiensis]*, 1.5, *AS* 9 (Mar. III), 68.

joined her as a companion. A priest, Fra Michele, guided her in spiritual matters.[188] This was sufficient "community" for Umiliana.

Ad hoc groups of pious women were more numerous—and probably more autonomous—than written sources suggest, and they have parallels elsewhere in Europe, such as the twelfth-century Beguines of the low countries.[189] Jacques of Vitry already mentions female penitent communities in Italy about 1217, almost certainly the later Poor Clares, still living like autonomous associations of individual penitents.[190] From the 1240s, small communities of pious laywomen left written records. They termed themselves in the vernacular *bizoche*—a term first found in Constantino of Orvieto's 1246 life of Saint Dominic.[191] In 1243, Dominican capitular legislation regulated the hearing of confessions from women called "Beguines." Within three years, Dominican chapter acts treated that word as synonymous with *bizoche*.[192] Called *bizoche*, Beguines, *mantellate*, and *pinzochere*, female penitents multiplied in the 1270s and after.[193] Their support networks can be traced through thirteenth-century wills.[194] Umiliana dei Cerchi was typical in her preference for an informal network of friends and supporters in her neighborhood.

Entrance into a cloister seemed the best option for a small percentage of female penitents. The widow Umiltà of Faenza, at first a freelance urban hermitess, finally found a more congenial home among the nuns at Vallombrosa. Some women penitents asked ecclesiastics for a rule and received public recognition. This effectively turned them into cloistered nuns. In 1284, Bishop Guidaloste of Pistoia gave a rule to a group of pious women in Prato. For all intents and purposes, the bishop made them conventual nuns, modifying the monastic rule only for their lesser literacy and lay status. They prayed small parts of the Divine Office in common but, like laywomen, mostly recited Paters and Aves. The sisters elected an *abbatissa* as moderator. Bishop Guidaloste put the convent under the patronage of Saint Francis of Assisi and subordinated the women to Franciscan control. The friars imposed on them a gray habit, white veil, and Franciscan cord.[195] Such a transformation was exceptional; most *bizoche* preserved their independence and autonomy—at least until the 1300s.

In 1260, at Perugia, the rise of the flagellants gave male penitents a new

188. Vito of Cortona, *Vita [B. Humilianae]*.

189. See Ernest W. McDonnell, *The Beguines and Beghards in Medieval Culture, with Special Emphasis on the Belgian Scene* (New York: Octagon Books, 1969).

190. See the text of Jacques of Vitry in Meersseman, *Dossier*, 21 n. 3; on which, see Maria Pia Alberzoni, "Nequaquam a Christi Sequela in Perpetuum Absolvi Desiderio: Clare Between Charism and Institution," *Grayfriars Review* 12 (1998): 81–122, and Werner Maleczek, "Questions About the Authenticity of the Privilege of Poverty of Innocent III and the Testament of Clare of Assisi," *Grayfriars Review* 12 (1998): 1–80.

191. "Vitae Sancti Dominici," MOPH, 16:350, § 120.

192. *Capitula Provinciae Romanae* (1243), MOPH 20:1; ibid. (1246), MOPH 20:5.

193. Meersseman, *Dossier*, 20–21; id., *Ordo*, 1:374–77.

194. E.g., Benvenuti Papi, "Donne religiose," 603, 619–20.

195. "Règle pour les Vestitae de Prato" (1284), Meersseman, *Dossier*, 138–42.

vehicle for doing penance in a traditional conversi fashion. Popular desire for peace in the wake of the bloody victory of Siena over Florence at Montaperti (4 September 1260) may have triggered this movement.[196] These penitents are famous, almost exclusively, for their practice of self-flagellation, a ritual they practiced in private and, most famously, in public processions.[197] An illumination in an early-fourteenth-century manuscript of their statutes from Pavia shows them kneeling before the Crucifix, robed in belted white tunics (the *sacco* of the document) with hoods that cover the head and face, save for two eye slits. They apply the "discipline," scourging their shoulders with cords though an opening in their tunics.[198] The weirdness of the image obscures the movement's profound continuity with earlier conversi and penitents. Reading their legislation, one might easily miss their distinctive penitential practice, so much do their statutes resemble earlier legislation. The preface to the statutes of the Pavia flagellants mentions their dedication to the Madonna and the court of heaven, as well as their fidelity to the overlord city of Milan, but never mentions flagellation. The 1299 introduction to the statutes of the Lucca flagellants speaks exclusively of their purpose, to honor the Passion of Christ.[199] Only much later in the document does the practice of self-flagellation appear. Arresting as flagellation might be to modern observers, the *disciplinati* speak of themselves as a traditional confraternity of penitents, albeit one practicing a distinctive form of penance.

Flagellants were all laymen and tenaciously preserved their movement's lay character.[200] They maintained the self-government, organization, prayer forms, monthly Mass, and autonomy of the early conversi. Flagellant groups borrowed wholesale structures and provisions dating back to the "Memoriale."[201] Like the early penitenti, they placed special emphasis on cultivation of fraternal unity, civic peace, and love of neighbor.[202] The flagellants fa-

196. Meersseman, *Ordo*, 1:457–58; on the flagellants, see John Henderson, "The Flagellant Movement and the Flagellant Confraternities in Central Italy, 1260–1400," *Religious Motivation: Biographical and Sociological Problems for the Church Historian*, ed. Derek Baker, Ecclesiastical History Society, 15 (Oxford: Blackwell, 1978), 147–60, and Gary Dickson, "The Flagellants of 1260 and the Crusades," *Journal of Medieval History* 15 (1989): 227–67, esp. 261–66, for bibliography.

197. For the rituals of flagellation, consult Lucca, Biblioteca Statale, MS 1310, fols. 10ᵛ–11ᵛ (Lucca, 1299); Piacenza, Biblioteca Comunale, MS Pallestrelli 323, fols. 8ᵛ–11ᵛ (Piacenza, 1317); Milan, Biblioteca Nazionale Braidense, MS AC.VIII.2, fols. 9ᵛ–10ʳ (Pavia, 1332, discipline in the house of the society); ibid., fols. 21ʳ–25ᵛ (Pavia, 1332, public procession). On indulgences for self-flagellation, see Meersseman, *Ordo*, 2:1059.

198. Milan, Biblioteca Nazionale Braidense, MS AC.VIII.2, fol. 1ʳ; the robes and blessing are given on fols. 13ᵛ–14ʳ. See Weissman, "From Brotherhood," 76, on modern stereotypes of the flagellants.

199. Lucca, Biblioteca Statale, MS 1310, fol. 2ʳ, promulgated on 5 March 1299.

200. See Casagrande, "I veri laici: I disciplinati," *Religiosità*, 353–438, esp. 388–90.

201. E.g., the table of contents of the 1332 Pavia flagellant statutes, Milan, Biblioteca Nazionale Braidense, MS AC.VIII.2, fols. 1ᵛ–3ᵛ, lists admissions, daily prayers and Mass, fasts, Communion and confession, Sunday flagellation, processions, elections, obedience to superiors, sick care, suffrages, funerals, poor assistance, officials, and provision for hearing sermons.

202. The 1317 statutes of the Piacenza flagellants, Piacenza, Biblioteca Comunale, MS Pallestrelli 323, fol. 2ᵛ, lift that triad from the Rule of Saint Augustine. Cf. Lucca, Biblioteca Statale, MS 1310, fols. 10ʳ–ᵛ (Lucca flagellants, 1299); Milan, Biblioteca Nazionale Braidense, MS AC.VIII.2, fols. 7ʳ–ᵛ (Pavia flagellants, 1332).

vored the same civic and neighborly purposes as the early penitents. They made special provision for their poor, and for the material and spiritual needs of sick members.[203] Only in their tendency toward a more centralized government, with a single "prior" instead of a pair of ministers, did they depart from older forms of organization.[204] Even when a group of flagellants received statutes from a Dominican bishop, as at Mantua in 1308, they preserved their freedom to choose any priest as their chaplain.[205]

In origin and development, the conversi were a lay creation. And until the late 1200s, they managed to avoid subordination to the clergy and direct clerical control.[206] For their governance, they invented new forms of organization, not based on clerical models. Only in their piety did they draw on monastic asceticism, but even this they adapted to their life in the world. They bequeathed their genius for participatory and democratic organization to the communes themselves. The "Propositum" answered the laity's desire for a more ordered penitential life, and they adopted it voluntarily, not because ecclesiastical authorities imposed conformity. The "Memoriale" of 1221 shows no sign of clerical supervision; penitents adopted it spontaneously, as they had the "Propositum." Only the provision making the rule bind, not under pain of sin, but under an imposed penalty, hints at Dominican influence, since this principle was typical of that order's discipline. It was a very minor contribution. The rest of their rule is the product of the lay ethos. In 1280, Bolognese jurists, themselves laymen, not clerics, compiled the most important commentary on the rule.[207] Until the last decade of the century, the blessing and imposition of the penitent habit could be done by a layman without priestly involvement.[208]

But by the 1270s, penitent autonomy began to suffer from the attentions of their most successful offshoot, the Franciscans. The rival Dominicans too sought to bring penitent groups under their supervision. So arose the schism between "Gray" and "Black" Penitents, perhaps at Florence in the 1270s.[209] Clerical domination of most penitent groups would be the result. By the late 1280s, the two mendicant orders vied with each other in subordinating penitents to their direction. On 18 August 1289, the Franciscan pope Nicholas IV, by the bull *Supra Montem*, subordinated all penitents to Franciscan

203. E.g., Lucca, Biblioteca Statale, MS 1310, fols. 6ᵛ–7ʳ (Lucca flagellants, 1299); Milan, Biblioteca Nazionale Braidense, MS AC.VIII.2, fols. 36ʳ⁻ᵛ (Pavia flagellants, 1332).

204. E.g., Lucca, Biblioteca Statale, MS 1310, fols. 2ʳ–3ᵛ, 8ᵛ–9r; Milan, Biblioteca Nazionale Braidense, MS AC.VIII.2, fols. 28ᵛ–30ᵛ.

205. For these statutes and a commentary on them, see Thompson, "New Light," esp. 155, 162.

206. *Pace* De Sandre Gasparini, "Laici devoti," 222, who emphasizes clerical control, which is certainly typical after our period: e.g., the "Statuti della Confraternita di s. Lucia" (Statuti L, 1334), 1–2, De Sandre Gasparini, *Statuti*, 68.

207. See Meersseman, *Dossier*, 11–17; on the Bolognese commentary, see "Expositiones Regule," ibid., 113–17.

208. Meersseman, *Ordo*, 1:420–22.

209. Meersseman, *Dossier*, 9; for the history of these schisms, see ibid., 28–37.

control, repeating as he did so the myth that Saint Francis had written the penitents' rule.[210] The non-Franciscan penitents of Florence got support from Bishop Mozzi in their struggle to save their independence.[211] They ultimately lost. At Vicenza in 1294, the Franciscan minister Fra Andrea di fu Federico of Marostica monopolized control of the penitents, rendering them lay auxiliaries to the Minorites.[212] Penitent confraternities began to admit clerics, and the tradition of lay membership and governance went the way of lay autonomy. Reformed as the Confraternity of the Holy Cross, under the direction of the Franciscans at Santa Croce, Florentine "penitents" might carry on the activities and devotions typical of their tradition, but leadership was now restricted to clerics.[213]

Penitents influenced by the Dominicans resisted Franciscan hegemony and sought legal recognition and statutes from the Preachers. In one case, the Dominican Master Munio of Zamora placed a group of women penitents at Orvieto under the direction of the local prior, approved their simple rule, and gave them permission to wear the Dominican habit. But it was not until the fifteenth century that such Black Penitents were formally constituted as the Dominican "Third Order of Penance." Male penitents abandoned Dominican groups for the flagellants, leaving only pious women.[214] The Gray Penitents did not surrender their autonomy easily. In spite of Pope Nicholas IV, the Lombard Penitents reasserted their right to choose any priest, even a secular, as visitator. They fought for their rights even after 1289, when the Franciscan pope ignored their appeal and refused to protect them.[215] The general chapter of the Lombard Penitents, meeting at Bologna in 1290, called on a secular priest, not a friar, as their advisor and then defied the new papal rule by choosing lay, not clerical, visitators.[216] Even the Marian confraternities, those most influenced by mendicant spirituality, cherished their lay autonomy right up to the Council of Trent.[217] Penitents mostly conformed to the requirement that they meet only in Franciscan churches,

210. "Bullarium," 50 (Nicholas IV, 18 August 1289), Meersseman, *Dossier*, 75; for which, see also *BF* 4:94–97; Potthast, *Regesta*, 23044.

211. See Casagrande, "Ordine," 250.

212. Mantese, "Fratres et sorores," 705.

213. Florence, Biblioteca Nazionale Centrale, MS II.IX.49, fols. 2ʳ–11ᵛ, stipulates that the *rettore* had to be a priest. The 1339 matricula of the Confraternity of the Holy Cross shows that thirty-five of the ninety-nine members were priests, including three Augustinians and one Dominican: ibid., fols. 11ᵛ–12ʳ. For mendicant-sponsored confraternities in the contado, see Charles M. De La Roncière, "La place des confréries dans l'encadrement religieux du contado florentin au XIVᵉ siècle," *Mélanges de l'École française de Rome: Moyen Âge–temps modernes* 85 (1973): 31–77, 633–71.

214. Maiju Lehmijoki-Gardner, "Writing Religious Rules as an Interactive Process: Dominican Penitent Women and the Making of Their *Regula*," *Speculum* 79 (2004): 660–87, shows conclusively that the "Dominican Third Order Rule" traditionally ascribed to the work of Munio of Zamora dates to the early 1400s; on the feminization of the third orders, see Vauchez, *Laity in the Middle Ages*, 115.

215. On the losing battle of the Lombard Penitents to maintain their autonomy, see Meersseman, "Il manuale dei penitenti di Brescia," Meersseman, *Ordo*, 1:416–17; for the appeal, see ibid., 445–56.

216. Ibid., 433.

217. Meersseman, *Ordo*, 2:996–1004.

but in Brescia, at least, they balked at this rule and continued to meet, as they always had, in their neighborhood chapels.[218]

The conversi were the fruit of a peculiarly lay piety dating from the earliest days of the communes. They became a fixture of communal life, their "lay" habit a visible witness to a more intensely spiritual, yet lay, life in the world. Their ranks numbered many lay communal saints, both female and male. But their slide to clericalization was far advanced by the end of the communal period.[219] The 1289 revision of the penitents' rule included a provision (§ 28) granting exemption from military service, but this right lapsed soon after 1300.[220] At Bologna in 1289, the city closed public offices and supervision of public works to the penitents.[221] In a crushing blow to lay autonomy, Bishop Arrigo of Lucca, by a ruling of 1308, forbade rectors of the city chapels to hear the vows of private conversi. Was he yielding to mendicant pressure? In any case, Bishop Arrigo "grandfathered in" those already professed and living in their houses, so long as they avoided secular affairs.[222] This marked the end of the old independent style of lay penance. By the 1300s the golden age of the communes was over, and with it that of the Brothers and Sisters of Penance.

218. Meersseman, "Il manuale dei penitenti di Brescia," ibid., 1:410–50.
219. See Benvenuti Papi, "I penitenti," 42–49, on clericalization at Florence.
220. Meersseman, *Ordo*, 1:424–45.
221. "Ordinatione Fratrum de Penitentia" (Bologna, 1289), 9, Meersseman, *Dossier,* 174; cf. Bologna Stat. 1 (1259/67), 8.97. Parma had already excluded them in 1266: Parma Stat. ii, 137, 239.
222. Lucca Synod (1308), 23, pp. 180–81.

Chapter Three
The Holy City

The Italian communes, like the Mother Church and the pious associations of the faithful, created their own sacred geography. Scholars have occasionally highlighted the Italian republics' profoundly religious nature, but as religious organisms in themselves, they remain largely unexplored.[1] Scholars prefer to study them, almost exclusively, as the earliest examples of nonimperially governed lay "states" in Italy.[2] Those governments underwent great change over time, and that affected their religious texture as well. Every commune's history was unique, but all shared similar stages of political development. When cities ended imperial rule, republican but oligarchic regimes arose. This happened in the early 1100s; at Bologna, for example, government by imperial counts ceased in 1113–14. The republican political structures that replaced the imperial government were discontinuous with it, new creations in themselves.[3] Commonly, two or more consuls presided over a city administration in which a small group of wealthy merchants and judges dominated the political life through a number of assemblies or councils. The German monarchs did not formally acknowledge the cities' de facto independence or legitimacy until the Peace of Costanza in 1183, and even then only grudg-

---

1. For study on the communes, see Edward Coleman, "Recent Work and Current Trends," *Journal of Medieval Studies* 25 (1999): 378–97, esp. 393–95, and "Un bilancio storiografico," *Forme di potere e struttura sociale in Italia nel Medioevo*, ed. G. Rossetti (Bologna: Il Mulino, 1977), 153–73. But cf. Maria Consiglia De Matteis, "Societas Christiana e funzionalità ideologica della città in Italia: Linee di uno sviluppo," *La città in Italia e in Germania nel Medioevo: Cultura, istituzioni, vita religiosa*, ed. Reinhard Elze and Gina Fasoli (Bologna: Mulino, 1981), 13–49, and Steven A. Epstein, *Wage Labor and Guilds in Medieval Europe* (Chapel Hill: University of North Carolina Press, 1991), 155–57, 164–65. On the religious influence, see Meersseman, *Ordo,* 1:205–8.

2. As, for Bologna, does E. Gualandi, "Podestà, consoli, legati pontifici, governatori e vice legati che hanno governato la città di Bologna (1141–1755)," *L'Archiginnasio* 55–56 (1960–61): 191–236; on the communes generally, see Hyde, *Society and Politics;* on the signori, see Pini, *Città, comuni e corporazioni,* 108–11.

3. Pini, *Città, comuni e corporazioni,* 221–43.

ingly.[4] Rampant factionalism eventually forced the cities to experiment with a single executive (*podestà*), usually a foreigner chosen for a short term of six months or a year. Bologna chose its first podesta in 1147 and made this system permanent in 1175. The podesta served as sole city manager, in the hope that his lack of local connections would isolate him from factionalism and favoritism. Popular participation in government remained very restricted until the so-called revolutions of the Popolo in the early 1200s. These brought a gradual expansion of participation through the inclusion of various civic corporations in the government. North Italians had long formed such corporations for both military and economic purposes. As a group, they formed the Popolo, which, with its own assemblies, took a place beside the city's older organs of government. At Bologna, the corporations of the Popolo elected a "Captain of the People" to head them for the first time in 1223.[5] There, as elsewhere, this official took a place beside the podesta as a kind of second executive. Like the commune itself, the corporations of the Popolo had little or no precedent in earlier political structures.[6]

Heaven and the Early Communes

But let us begin at the beginning. When the Italian cities threw off imperial control in the early 1100s, some bishops, appointees of the German emperors, resisted. But cities and bishops more commonly developed a working relationship.[7] Some, like Bishop Ubaldo of Gubbio, we remember, happily defended local freedom against "foreigners" like the emperor Frederick Barbarossa. The citizens of Gubbio expected their bishop, as a good citizen of the commune, to raise his spiritual sword and defend their city. Once, during a local conflict, Bishop Ubaldo refused to excommunicate the city's enemies at the commune's request, and the city fathers organized a boycott. Finding that he could not celebrate Mass, since no one came to serve him, the bishop, "with tranquil spirit," removed his vestments, mounted the pulpit, and preached a "hard sermon."[8] There was a limit to his identification with the city; the citizens remained unimpressed. Such conflict between bishop and commune could escalate into violence.[9] At Piacenza ecclesiastical and secular authorities clashed in 1204, and the Piacentine clergy abandoned their city for three years.[10] At Bologna in 1193, where Bishop Girardo di Ghisello Scannabecchi had been elected city executive, the four consuls of the commune fell out with the bishop-podesta. A faction developed around the

4. Milan, *Gli atti del comune di Milano fino all'anno* mccxvi, ed. Cesare Mamaresi (Milan: Capriolo, 1919), doc. 139 (25 June 1183), pp. 198–206.

5. Girolamo de' Borselli, *Cronica Gestorum* (1223), 21.

6. Something first noted by Vauchez, *Laity in the Middle Ages,* 110.

7. On the cooperation between bishops and communes, see Webb, *Patrons,* 60–92.

8. Giordano of Città di Castello, *Vita Beati Ubaldi Eugubini Episcopi,* 10.6, p. 99.

9. Pini, *Città, comuni e corporazioni,* 82–83.

10. Giovanni de' Mussi, *Chronicon Placentinum* (1204), *RIS* 16:457.

bishop. Soon communal and episcopal mobs fought in the streets, torching each other's houses. But the strife represented political factionalism, not a conflict between clergy and laity.[11]

Other bishops were less hesitant to cooperate. The bishop was the one leader who could represent the local society before both emperor and pope. If cooperative, he was the early commune's natural leader.[12] In the 1100s bishops remodeled their residences and began to call them *palazzi* (palaces). The first communal governments met in these new buildings rather than build their own.[13] So, communal governments developed in physical proximity to the bishop's court, or *curia*.[14] For the lay theologian and lawyer Albertano of Brescia, "sacred" and "secular," though distinguished in theory, were an integrated whole.[15] At the end of imperial rule, cathedral canons began to elect local men to the bishopric. These bishops-elect belonged to the same class that dominated the early communes; they were local men. The Bolognese election of bishop Girardo to the communal office was natural.[16] At Pisa and Milan arose a judicial interpenetration of ecclesiastical and civil functions that seems strange for a post-Gregorian age. Bishops heard civil cases, and city courts gave decisions on tithes—with little complaint about conflict of jurisdiction. Even in cities with less cooperation than Milan or Pisa, use of the ordeal in criminal courts, a practice only abolished in 1215 by the Lateran Council, demanded a bishop's presence to bless the hot iron or cold water.[17] The sorting out of ecclesiastical and civil functions would wait until the mid-1200s.[18]

Only after a riot burned the inquisition offices at Parma in 1278, resulting in a papal interdict, did that city enact truly punitive legislation against the clergy. Parma prohibited gifts of real property to clerics, seized the property of those who became clerics, and imposed penalties on those who dared to take civil cases to Church courts.[19] But such overt hostility was rare, and this was an unusual case. More commonly, secular and ecclesiastical authorities cooperated in communal governance throughout most of the mid–thirteenth century. In 1237, the Franciscan bishop of Milan, Leo de' Valvassori of Perego, represented the city in negotiations with the emperor Frederick at Lodi. At the same meeting, Piacenza was represented by its Cistercian bishop, Dom Egidio, and its Dominican prior, Fra Giacomo.[20] Cities regularly culti-

11. *CCB:* A, Bol., Vill. (1193), 56; Alfred Hessel, *Storia della città di Bologna, 1116–1280,* ed. Gina Fasoli (Bologna: ALFA, 1975), 74–77.

12. So Hyde, *Society and Politics,* 58.

13. Or in the cathedral complexes, as they did in Milan and Pisa: Gabriella Rossetti, "Le istituzioni comunali a Milano nel XII secolo," *Atti dell'11° Congresso,* 85.

14. Miller, *Bishop's Palace,* 96, 118–19.

15. Powell, *Albertanus,* 75.

16. *CCB:* A, B, Vill., Bol. (1187), 49.

17. For these rites, see *Manuale Ambrosianum,* 2:492–97.

18. On this unity, see Hyde, *Society and Politics,* 99.

19. Parma Stat. II (1282), 211–13, 220–22.

20. Muzio of Modena, *Annales Placentini Gibellini,* ed. Georg Heinrich Pertz (1237), *MGH.SS* 18:477–78.

vated alliances with important ecclesiastics by granting them citizenship, as Bologna did to Bishop Tommaso of Imola in 1254, and again to the powerful abbot of Nonantola in 1259.[21] In 1254 the bishop-elect of Ravenna, Filippo, served as podesta of his city, promulgating statutes to guarantee internal peace.[22] Filippo and his city also cooperated on defense: the bishop was responsible for the upkeep of the tower over the Porta San Mama.[23]

Unity was in the interest of both city and bishop. In the early 1200s, their mutual enemy Emperor Frederick II connived to divide communes and bishops. In 1219 he confirmed Parma's prerogative, granted at the Peace of Costanza, to abolish the temporal jurisdiction of its bishop, Obizzo Fieschi—who was then happily cooperating with the communal government. The podesta Negro di Mariano took up the challenge and dispossessed the bishop. In retaliation, on 25 November 1220, a papal legate excommunicated the commune—with the hearty approval of Emperor Frederick, now seeking a papal coronation. The following year, a new podesta, Torello of Strada, reached an agreement with the bishop that, among other provisions, re-turned episcopal properties, promised the bishop control over clergy and tithes, and confirmed his jurisdiction in disputed areas. The bishop agreed that the army would have free passage through his lands, the commune would get half of episcopal court fines, and he would refrain from meddling in wardship cases. Such a partition of jurisdictions became typical of the age of the later communes, but overlaps always remained.

In 1233, new Parma city statutes stipulated that the commune and the bishop would act together in mediating feuds.[24] Parma's was a typical condo-minium, reaffirmed by both parties as late as 1262.[25] Ever since the arrival of the Peace of God movement in Lombardy during 1042, peace possessed a sacral flavor. Throughout the communal period, ecclesiastics and penitents held a privileged place in peacemaking. In 1204 and in 1207, Fra Alberto of Mantua preached peace and reconciled factions at Bologna, a task taken up again in the 1230s by the Dominican Guala of Brescia.[26] In 1231, the Francis-can Anthony of Padua combined peacemaking with debt relief, emptying Paduan prisons of their paupers.[27] During the revival known as the Alleluia of 1233, Dominican and Franciscan preachers orchestrated peacemaking be-tween feuding factions and between warring cities. Bishops and communal governments supported the project, and the religious ritual for peacemaking, the "Kiss of Peace," entered city statutes.[28] The preachers prevailed on the

21. Bologna Stat. I, 5.22, 1:455–56.
22. E.g.: Ravenna Stat., 199, pp. 110–11 (stipulates the terms of a podesta's service); 334, pp. 154–55 (regulations and fines); 365b–368, pp. 175–77 (on peacekeeping).
23. Ibid., 335b, pp. 155–56.
24. See addition to podesta's oath: Parma Stat. I, 3.
25. See ibid. (10 July 1221), 194–97.
26. *CCB:* A, B, Vill., Bol. (1204 and 1207), 67, 69; *CCB:* B, 98.
27. Padua Stat. (1231), 2.9, p. 178, no. 551; (1258), 2.2, p. 162, no. 498.
28. E.g., Verona Stat. II (1276), 3.40, p. 415.

cities to enact laws against heresy, which both removed a cause of community division and protected orthodoxy.[29] Peacemaking in the late 1200s remained the prerogative of preachers like Fra Lorenzo at Bologna in 1287 and of lay religious movements like the flagellants in 1260.[30] Until the end of the communal period, cities called on their clergy to administer peace oaths to end internal conflicts.[31]

By the 1240s, civil governments had developed a more distinct identity, and bishops began to lose their direct role in communal governance. The spheres of jurisdiction were becoming separate. In the 1220s, the Veronese stopped enforcing summonses to the episcopal court, although they continued to respect clerical exemptions by sending cases of clerical truce breaking to the bishop.[32] After midcentury, at least in legal matters, the distinction between the civil administration and Church administration had become clear and explicit everywhere. In 1250, Bologna prohibited appeal to the bishop's court in secular matters.[33] But the commune continued to compel clerics summoned to the episcopal court for ecclesiastical matters.[34] Bologna's actions defined the different courts' spheres of authority; they did not reduce episcopal power per se. In theory, the communes vigorously rejected the ecclesiastical claim that criminal clerics were subject only to the church courts.[35] In practice, bishops yielded authority over such cases to the commune and worked out agreements. At Padua, the bishop agreed to defrock criminal clerics and hand them over.[36] Bishop Ottaviano of Bologna accommodated his city in the matter and handed over weapon-bearing clerics for civil trial. He also enforced civil law by excommunicating the clerics of any church or monastery who harbored criminals wanted by the commune. He gave permission to the podesta's men to enter convents and churches to arrest offending clergy.[37] Reciprocally, the late-thirteenth-century communes enacted legislation favoring the "liberties of the Church," promised to protect church property, and helped discipline (and execute) heretics.[38]

The growing division of civil and ecclesiastical jurisdictions paradoxically

29. On this movement, see Augustine Thompson, *Revival Preachers and Politics in Thirteenth-Century Italy* (Oxford: Oxford University Press, 1992).

30. For Lorenzo, see Matteo Griffoni, 23; for some peace statutes of 1260, see Bologna Stat. 1, 2.15, 1:268.

31. As at Brescia in 1313: Brescia Stat., Pax 98, col. 282.

32. Verona Stat. 1 (1228), 74, p. 60; 109, p. 84.

33. Bologna Stat. 1 (1250), 4.51, 1:421.

34. Ibid. (1250), 4.22, 1:404. Also, on property cases before the bishop, see ibid. (1252 and 1267), 4.51a, 1:422–23.

35. E.g., ibid. (1259, 1260, 1262), 11.6, 3:277.

36. Padua Stat. (1270), 3.10, p. 267, no. 812.

37. Bologna Stat. II (1288), 4.68, 1:228–29; (1288), 4.65, 1:221–23.

38. E.g., Parma stat. 1 (by 1255), p. 105; Verona Stat. II (1276), 1.249–57, pp. 197–202; Brescia Stat. (1313), 1.22, col. 11. For signs of growing tension after 1300, see Lucca Synod (1300), 44–48, pp. 226–30 (excommunicating officials who violate liberties of the Church); 37, p. 183 (disciplining clergy who draft instruments harmful to the commune; Parma Stat. III (1316), 110–11 (excluding clerics from communal offices).

led the commune to cultivate an ever more sacred ethos for itself. As bishops became less visible in government and cities constructed their own public buildings, the commune ceased to share the holy aura of the Mother Church. "Secularized" communes needed their own divine legitimacy. They sought it in heaven, invoking the protection of new patron saints, and on earth, saturating their laws, assemblies, and communal institutions with sacred rhetoric, symbolism, and ritual. They had little choice. They had banished their old sacred imperial overlord, and no one on earth remained to replace him as a source of legitimacy. When the communes constructed and elaborated their republican and democratic institutions, they could draw on neither imperial nor "secular" forms for legitimacy.[39]

Although born in war, the Italian republics had little enthusiasm for the crusading fervor sweeping Europe around the year 1200. Bolognese chroniclers claim that "two thousand" crusaders left Bologna to relieve Jerusalem in 1188 and that "many" went east after the fall of Damietta in 1219.[40] They exaggerate; perhaps two hundred crusaders left in 1188, and far fewer, a mere handful, in 1219.[41] But sacred war did stir communal hearts. Italians fought, not to defend the distant Holy Land, but their own cities. Throughout the north, the struggle against the emperor Frederick Barbarossa in the 1170s was a religious war, fought with intensity and determination. Piacenza fought pro-imperial Cremona in 1215 under "divine protection."[42] The Paduans spoke of the war against Ezzelino da Romano in 1259 in the language of First Samuel. Ezzelino was Goliath the Philistine; little Padua was David: God gave the weak victory over the mighty.[43] The rhetoric of divine favor and holy war implied that God and his saints led the commune in battle.[44] Heavenly powers granted favor, but the beneficiary might cease to merit it. Bishop Sicardo of Cremona observed that although Saint Mark the Evangelist had chosen to be buried in Alexandria, where he had preached, the city lost his favor when it fell into heresy. The evangelist chose Catholic Venice as his new resting place and allowed the Venetians to carry off his bones, supposedly in the ninth century.[45] The other Italian cities could also measure God's favor. Its proof was victory on the battlefield. Victory proved the special relation between heaven and earth, or, better, the part of the earth

39. Powell, *Albertanus*, 121.

40. *CCB:* Bol., 50; *CCB:* A, Vill. (1188); *CCB:* A (1220), 82.

41. Augusto Vasina, "Le crociate nel mondo emiliano-romagnolo," *AMDSPPR*, n.s., 23 (1972): 32–39. Communes did protect crusader property: e.g., at Verona: Verona Stat. I (1228), 49, pp. 43–44; Verona Stat. II (1276), 109, p. 347.

42. Miccoli, "La storia religiosa," 600–601.

43. *Annales Sanctae Iustinae Patavini* (1259), ed. Philip Jaffé, *MGH.SS* 19:174–75.

44. On communal patrons, see Hans Conrad Peyer, *Stadt und Stadtpatron im mittelalterlichen Italien* (Zurich: Europa, 1955); Alba Maria Orselli, *L'idea e il culto del santo patrono cittadino nella letteratura latina medievale* (Bologna: Zanichelli, 1965); and Golinelli, *Città e culto*.

45. Sicardo, *Mitrale*, 2.4, col. 70D; on saints' "allowing" their relics to be stolen, see Patrick Geary, *Furta Sacra: Theft of Relics in the Middle Ages*, 2d ed. (Princeton: Princeton University Press, 1990).

that was your own contado. According to Bishop Sicardo, Milanese devotion to the ancient martyrs Gervase and Protase arose, not because Saint Ambrose had miraculously discovered their bones, but because the city successfully concluded the Lombard Wars on their feast day. The saints had proved their intercessory power by crowning their day with victory. The Milanese knew what was expected. They changed the opening chant of the martyrs' Mass to commemorate the victory they had given the city.[46] Tuscan saints too manifested their favor by victories. The Florentines traced their special devotion to John the Baptist back to his feast in 401, when, through his intercession, the city defeated the invading Goths. Centuries later, after the Florentine victory at Campaldino on 11 June 1289, the commune adopted as one of its city patrons (there were almost always more than one) Saint Barnabas, the saint whose day marked the victory.[47] Defeat might imply disfavor, but this conclusion did not suggest itself easily. The Modenese were loath to go to war on Mondays and Tuesdays, since they had suffered humiliating defeats on those days.[48] In cases of misfortune, it was usually the weekday, not the saint, that got the blame.

Communes changed or added patrons after victories. Saint George, the warrior saint, became a patron of Siena after its great victory over Florence at Montaperti; at Faenza, Saint Cassian became a city patron after the Guelf victory that reestablished the commune in 1280. Female saints gave victory on their feasts, too—as the serving girl Saint Zita did for Lucca in 1278 and the lay penitent Saint Margherita did for Cortona in 1298. Examples could be multiplied endlessly.[49] In art, saints proclaimed their victories in war. Throughout Tuscany, especially in Florence, saints on altarpieces sometimes hold an olive branch, absent from their usual iconography. It means that the city where the image was painted had enjoyed victory on the saint's feast day.[50] No victory-giving saint compared to Saint Sixtus at Pisa. This second-century pope repeatedly saved Pisa's armies in pitched battles fought on 6 August, his feast day. By 1216, the commune had constructed a chapel in his honor. The citizenry annually honored him by bell ringing and candle offerings. Saint Sixtus became so identified with the commune that, by the 1280s, city assemblies met in his church rather than the cathedral.[51]

During the early to mid-1200s, there was no greater danger to northern republican liberties than the tyrant Ezzelino da Romano, vicar of the em-

---

46. Sicardo, *Mitrale*, 9.28, col. 415.

47. See Trexler, *Public Life*, 77; on Barnabas and Florence, see Webb, "Cities of God," 122–24.

48. Salimbene, *Cronica* (1284), 786, Baird trans., 547.

49. Vauchez, "Reliquie, santi e santuari," 461–62. On Margherita's cult, see Cannon and Vauchez, *Margherita of Cortona*.

50. George Kaftal, *Iconography of the Saints in Tuscan Painting* (Florence: Sansoni, 1952), 1:xx; see also Webb, "Cities of God," 121.

51. Pisa Stat. 1 (1286), 2.1, pp. 345–47, esp. pp. 345–46; on the assemblies of the Popolo: ibid., Popolo 94, p. 623, and Pisa Stat. 11 (1313), 2.1, pp. 269–70. On the mingling of ecclesiastical and civil identities, see Jones, *Italian City-State*, 437–38.

peror Frederick II. The holy war against Ezzelino and Frederick revealed new celestial friends of the communes. At Vicenza, the liberation of the commune came on 29 September 1264, obviously by the intercession of Saint Michael. The archangel became a patron of the city, and the commune gave £50 to the Augustinians to build a church in his honor. The city had his image added to those of other city patrons above the gates.[52] At Milan in the late 1200s, the city commissioned the workshop of Giovanni di Balduccio to decorate Porta Ticinese with the protectors of the commune Saint Lawrence, Saint Ambrose, Saint Eustorgius, Saint Peter of Verona, and, enthroned in the center, the Virgin Mary and child Jesus (fig. 36). At Bologna, where the commune captured Frederick's son Enzo in battle on the Translation of Saint Augustine, they appropriated five years of alms for construction of the Augustinian church, which they hoped would be rededicated under the title of Saint Augustine (it was not and remains San Giacomo Maggiore to this day). The city raised its offering of £40 bon. to £50 the following year; the war was going well.[53] During the early 1250s, Ezzelino entered Padua, expelled the republican government, and established personal rule. The army of the Lombard League commanded by the papal legate Filippo Fontana, archbishop of Ravenna, besieged the city, but without success. Fra Bartolomeo di Corradino, the sacristan, was keeping vigil on 19 June 1252 at the tomb of the Franciscan saint Anthony of Padua, praying for deliverance of his city. In a dream or vision—the source is unclear—Fra Bartolomeo heard a voice promising liberation of the city before the octave of Anthony's feast, that is, by the very next day. And so it came to pass. In recognition of the deliverance from Ezzelino, the Paduans translated his body and placed it in *arca* raised on columns in 1263. The saint confirmed this favor by a miracle—the great preacher's tongue was found miraculously incorrupt.[54] But on Anthony's feast in 1272, the combined pro-imperial forces of Faenza and the exiled Bolognese Lambertazzi faction defeated the Bolognese commune's army (led by the more pro-papal Geremei faction) at the Battle of Porta San Procolo.[55] Never again would the Bolognese "party of the Church" willingly hear the saint's name mentioned. Present at victory and defeat, saints could preside over peacemaking, too. In 1286 Cardinal Latino finally brought an end to a long war between Parma and Modena. The

52. Vicenza Stat. (1264), 3; on the cult of Saint Michael at Vicenza, see Webb, *Patrons*, 150–51.

53. Bologna Stat. I (1251), 5.21, 1:454–55.

54. The source for this story is late: *Chronica xxiv Generalium Ordinis Fratrum Minorum*, 157–58. On the translation of 1263, see the vita attributed to John Peckham, *Legendae Sancti Antonii Presbyteri et Confessoris "Benignitas,"* 21.1–5, *Vita del "Dialogus" e "Benignitas,"* ed. Virilio Gamboso (Padua: Messaggero, 1986), 562–66. For references to the arca on columns, see *Vita prima di S. Antonio o "Assidua" (c. 1232),* ed. Vergilio Gamboso (Padua: Messaggero, 1981), 136–37. For city recognition of Saint Anthony, see Padua Stat. (pre-1238), 2.28, p. 193, no. 599.

55. Salimbene, *Cronica* (1250), 573, Baird trans., 399; ibid. (1275), 716, trans., 501. The Lambertazzi and Geremei are often contrasted as "pro-imperial" and "pro-papal"; in fact, both factions were opportunistic.

treaty draft invoked the patrons of both cities, Saint Mary the Virgin and Saint John the Baptist. But those saints were not specific enough to identify the parties involved, so the communes had him add Saint Hilary for Parma and Saint Giminiano for Modena. Saint Peter was greater than them all, said the cardinal; he chose the feast of Saint Peter for signing the treaty. It was a good day on which to make peace.[56]

Everywhere, the Virgin Mary claimed a special place as protectress and patroness. She was an impartial giver of victory and universal protectress of peace. In the early 1200s the Sienese already had a special devotion to Mary, substituting Marian chants for the traditional Asperges Me during the sprinkling of holy water on Sundays in Lent. Outside Easter time, the sprinkling used the traditional chant, but the procession began at Mary's altar.[57] In 1260, the Virgin rewarded Sienese devotion. Visitors to the duomo of Siena can still see, attached to the columns of the crossing, what look like two massive telephone poles (fig. 37). They are the drawbars from the city's carroccio, its standard-bearing battle wagon, at the Battle of Montaperti, the last great Sienese defeat of Florence. The city placed them there as a votive offering to commemorate Mary's protection. Before going out to fight Florence and her Guelf allies, the Sienese had dedicated their city to the Virgin. When she gave them victory, the city fathers, at the request of Bishop Tommaso Balzetti, appropriated funds from the Opera del Duomo to tear down the old chapel of Saint James and replace it with one dedicated to the Virgin and "those saints on whose solemnity God gave victory to Siena over her enemies." The shrine stands to this day, the Cappella del Voto.[58] This "Chapel of the Vow" replaced the Virgin's old side altar. From 1260 on, the Sunday sprinkling of holy water began there. The sprinkling now recalled not only baptism but also the victory that had—much to Dante's chagrin— "made the water of the Arbia run red" with Florentine blood.[59] The Glorious Virgin's victory became part of Sienese identity, and they remember it with pleasure to this day.[60]

The Virgin also protected the troops of Parma. That city undertook the war against Frederick II as a communal act of penance. In 1248, on the first campaign, they took and sacked the imperial stronghold of Vittoria. In retaliation, the emperor besieged their city, intending to destroy it. While the city militia manned the walls, Parma's women gathered in the cathedral and beseeched the Virgin for deliverance. To the Parmese, the subsequent repulse of Frederick was the work, not of the militia, but of the women and

---

56. *Chronicon Parmense*, 50–51.

57. *Ordo Senensis*, 1.11, p. 12; 1.83, p. 74.

58. Siena Stat. 1 (1262), 1.14, p. 29.

59. Dante, *Inferno*, 10.85–87: "Lo strazio e 'l grande scempio | che fece l'Arbia colorata in rosso, | tal orazion fa far nel nostro tempio."

60. See, on the Virgin and Siena, Diana Norman, *Siena and the Virgin: Art and Politics in a Late Medieval City State* (New Haven: Yale University Press, 1999).

the Blessed Virgin. Mary had shown her special favor.[61] But in the 1260s, invocation of Saint John the Baptist and Saint Hilary of Poitiers came to replace that of the Virgin in Parma's statutes and decrees, reflecting new victories under their patronage. Nevertheless, the Virgin remained dear to the commune, now more a patron of peace than a patron of victory. When Guelf Parma and Ghibelline Cremona ended their long war in 1281, they returned each others' carrocci on 7 September, the vigil of the Virgin's nativity.[62] Cremona, like Siena, tended toward the imperial party, but devotion to the Glorious Virgin transcended mere political differences.

Survival of republican institutions became even more closely linked to heavenly intervention in the later 1200s, when princely domination threatened them with destruction. Patron saints presided over revolts against tyranny. On the night of 26 January 1306, the Modenese, in league with Parma, Mantua, Verona, and Bologna, finally threw off the yoke of Azzo VIII d'Este, lord of Ferrara. They drove out his garrison with shouts of "Death, death to the marquis!" The next day Reggio also threw off Este control. Modena ascribed the liberation to the ancient patron of their commune, San Giminiano. On 22 January 1307, the city, in the person of the podesta, Gilberto of Correggio, celebrated their freedom from slavery to Pharaoh by declaring Saint Giminiano's feast a civic holiday for all time. For a week, criers circulated through the streets, summoning all citizens to the duomo. There, on the steps, the city had erected an altar decorated with precious draperies and golden vessels. On the eighth day, Bishop Giacomo presided at a solemn Mass in honor of Saint Giminiano, chanted—loudly!—by the city clergy. The open-air location allowed attendance by the whole population, which would not have fit inside the cathedral. None would have missed the event, since the arm bone of Saint Giminiano was also offered for public veneration.[63] At the Mass, the restored societies of the commune presented offerings to construct a victory chapel in honor of God, the Blessed Virgin, and Saint Giminiano. At the city's request, the bishop blessed the event with an indulgence of forty days. He appointed a priest to serve the new chapel at city expense.[64] The city fathers soon expressed renewed faith in the patron. That spring, the podesta moved to launch a new campaign against the Este. The General Council of the Eighty approved it, again invoking Saint Giminiano and again calling "for the destruction and death of the marquis!"[65]

Saintly patronage became so much part of civic identity that would-be princes tried to appropriate it. At Mantua, after the Bonacolsi monopolized control of the commune in 1272, they preserved the old forms. Bardellone

---

61. *Chronicon Parmense* (1248), 18; on Saint Mary at Parma, see Miller, *Bishop's Palace,* 134.
62. Alberto Milioli, *Liber,* 555–56.
63. Modena Stat. (1306/7), 1:99–100; Webb, *Patrons,* 216–21.
64. Modena Stat. (1306/7), 2:157–59.
65. Ibid. (15 July 1306), 1:216.

de' Bonacolsi, under the title "captain of the people," had a vermilion banner created with an image of Saint Peter, and so co-opted the patron of the independent commune. Under this banner, he enrolled for his regime two thousand armed men from the "better people" of the city.[66] But in 1303, Reginaldo and Butirone expelled their cousin and his brother Guigino with help from the Scaligeri of Verona. It was merely a feud within the ruling family, but the victors wanted its date, the Feast of the Precious Blood, to be forever celebrated by a Mass and offerings in the church of Sant'Andrea. The republican-minded people were not impressed; the observances disappeared.[67] In contrast, when on 30 November 1323 the Guelfs of Cortona finally drove out the imperial party, which had ruled the city since 25 April 1261 (the feast of Saint Mark the Evangelist), the citizenry demanded a change of patron. Out went the imperialist-favored Saint Mark, and in came the republican-favored Saint Margherita. Her incorrupt body, preserved in her anchorhold at the church of San Basilio, became the focus of communal devotion. The cult at her tomb endures to this day. She had even chosen to die, the Cortonese remembered, on the Feast of the Chair of Saint Peter—an excellent Guelf saint![68]

PATRONS AND PATRIOTISM

From antiquity Christians dedicated their churches to saints, usually the Blessed Virgin, an apostle, or an ancient martyr. In the Italian cities the oldest cults often centered on the titular of the cathedral. The role of Saint Reparata as the patroness of the Florentine duomo gave birth to a cult, which generated miracles and finally led to the composition of a pious but wholly fictitious vita.[69] The development was typical. By the early communal period, cities celebrated the patrons of the duomo and other city churches with religious rituals. Secular observances honored them as well; markets occurred on their feast days.[70] The splendor of these observances fostered civic pride. The chronicler of Faenza, Maestro Tolosano, fondly remembered his hometown's celebration of its patron, Saint Peter the Apostle, in 1184.[71] On 29 June of that year Pope Lucius III presided at the apostle's vigil and at solemn Mass in the duomo. He granted an indulgence of twelve days, not only to those present, but in perpetuity to all who visited the cathedral on the feast. Their shared patron united little Faenza with mighty Rome, the center of the world.

66. *Annales Mantuani* (1293), ed. Philip Jaffé, *MGH.SS* 19:31.

67. Mantua Stat. (1303), 6.39, 2:152; on popular resistance to princely co-opting, see ibid., 168.

68. On these events, see Menestò and Rusconi, *Umbria*, 56–58.

69. On the cult of Saint Reparata at Florence, see Raffaello Morghen, "Vita religiosa e vita cittadina nella Firenze del duecento," *La coscienza cittadina nei comuni italiani nel duecento*.

70. For examples of such devotions at Bergamo, see Valsecchi, *Interrogatus*, 109–14. On the market of Saint Alexander, see ibid., 122.

71. Maestro Tolosano, *Chronicon Faventinum*, 99 (1184), p. 91.

A patron saint protected and personified his city, though personification of the city did not need to be the monopoly of a single saint. In 1187, Master Buono de' Mozzi called Saint Alexander "standard-bearer of the whole city of Bergamo."[72] Alexander was not the patron of the cathedral in the 1100s; that was Saint Vincent. Bergamo was under joint patronage.[73] Shared patronage was not uncommon: at Vicenza, the Virgin shared responsibilities with Saints Felix and Fortunatus; at Verona, with Saint Zeno.

As the thirteenth century progressed, intensity of devotion to civic patrons grew, if government documents are any indication. The earliest extant city statutes of Verona, those of 1228, invoked only God and the Blessed Virgin, and did so only in their preface. The rest of the laws have a distinctively nonreligious tone. Later in the century, holy protectors multiplied, and their invocation become almost obsessive. In the Veronese statutes of 1276, Saint Zeno had joined God and Saint Mary—with special mention made of his relics.[74] At Parma in the 1250s, the fathers invoked the Blessed Virgin not only in the prologue to their city statutes but repeatedly in routine enactments, even those concerning such projects as wall and bridge construction.[75] At Vicenza, after the expulsion of the da Romano family, the new republican oath of the podesta invoked God, the Virgin, Saints Felix and Fortunatus, and commemorated the greatest relic of the city, the Lord's Crown of Thorns at Santa Corona.[76] One could multiply examples endlessly. By 1325, the city fathers of Florence invoked by name not only God, the Virgin, Saint Michael, and John the Baptist ("patron and protector of the commune") but also Peter, Paul, Philip, James, Barnabas, Reparata, Cenobius, and Miniatus, and "all the saints of God."[77] The saints' legitimizing and protective functions intensified as the communes experimented with more democratic and imperially unsanctioned forms of government and when they suffered attacks from princes, the empire, or rival cities.

The cities found new patrons suitable to their new republican identity and untainted by connection with the old imperial regime. No cult more vividly exemplifies appearance of the patron as symbol of communal identity than the Sienese invention of Saint Ansano. This ancient martyr, perhaps a victim during the Diocletian persecution of 304, had no cult until the 1170s. According to the life written for his liturgical Office, Ansano had fled a persecution in Rome to become the apostle of Siena and so the "baptist" of the city.[78] The rediscovery of his tomb took place while Siena was building and embel-

---

72. "Instrumentum Litis" (September 1187), 3.25, p. 161: "vexillifer tocius civitatis pergamensis."
73. Ibid., p. 39.
74. Verona Stat. ii (1276), p. 21; on the lack of religious reference in earlier statutes, see Webb, *Patrons*, 111–12.
75. E.g., Parma Stat. i, 87, 106.
76. Vicenza Stat. (1264), 8.
77. Florence Stat. ii (1325), p. 1.
78. Preserved, e.g., in an early-fourteenth-century Sienese Franciscan breviary: Siena, Biblioteca Comunale degli Intronati, ms F.viii.12, fols. 573ʳ–581ᵛ.

lishing its first communal baptistery. News of the discovery evoked popular demands that the bones of their baptist be moved to a place of honor in the duomo.[79] Some Sienese knights scouted out the ancient site, sending back a report of success in the bone hunt. An unruly mob of citizens gathered at the tomb, and finally the cathedral clergy arrived in procession, late and out of breath. The canons hesitated to supervise the translation of such an obscure saint. Some laymen broke open the sepulcher, and the martyr's incorrupt body vindicated the laity's spiritual acuity. It gave off an odor of aromatic spices. With joyful songs and psalms the people and clergy carried his relics back to the city.[80]

Townspeople flocked to the new shrine, crying out to Ansano, "Come, come, Father Ansano, wait no longer to come and rule the city that you first instructed in the faith and preserve the place signed with the name and title of Jesus Christ!" Recalling that the name Ansano included the word "healthy" (sano), townspeople demanded healings.[81] Miracles followed, pilgrims converged from afar, and night vigils commenced.[82] The real test of patronage was, of course, whether the saint could protect his city. Indeed, outnumbered Sienese troops defeated their enemies while invoking the saint, and display of his arm bone quenched a fire threatening the city; thereafter, Bishop Gunteramo and the commune underwrote construction of a splendid marble shrine altar.[83] The saint's cult even spread to Lombardy, where a pieve in the diocese of Bologna took his name as titular and invited the bishop of Siena to perform the church's consecration.[84] Saint Ansano had claimed a bit of the Bolognese contado for Siena. Healings, victory, carrying Siena's fame abroad: Ansano had proved himself a true patron and a true, if naturalized, Sienese. Alas, he had not been born there. The most beloved saints of the period were more commonly homegrown. The identification of city and citizen-saint might become proverbial. Dante personified the city of Lucca in its most famous daughter, Saint Zita. In the Commedia, demons in hell greet one grafter from the Lucca city council with the shout "Here is one of Saint Zita's officials!"[85] When Dante wrote in 1300, Zita did not even have an ecclesiastically approved cult: her hometown had canonized the serving girl all on its own.

The heavenly patron became the overlord of the city, replacing the emperor. At Verona, over the west portal of Saint Zeno's great Romanesque church, that city's patron confers legitimacy and independence on his city (fig. 38). This is a political theology carved in stone. The bishop saint holds

79. Ibid., fol. 579ᵛ.
80. Ibid., fols. 579ᵛ–580ʳ.
81. Ibid., fol. 580ʳ.
82. Ibid., fols. 580ʳ⁻ᵛ.
83. Ibid., fol. 580ᵛ.
84. Ibid., fols. 581ʳ⁻ᵛ.
85. Dante, Inferno, 21.37b–38: "O Malebranche, | ecco un de li anzïan di Santa Zita!"

his pastoral staff and blesses the communal militia. Cavalry stand at his left, and foot soldiers on his right. The latter hold the banner of the commune. An inscription below reads: "The bishop with sincere heart grants to his people a standard worthy of defense." The sculpture commemorates nothing less than the end of imperial rule and the creation of the Veronese Commune in the 1130s, and it is the "people"—not the old knightly aristocracy with its imperial connections—to whom Zeno hands his banner.[86] The lord of the Commune is its heavenly patron, not the earthly emperor.

Other new communes resurrected forgotten bishop saints, reviving or inventing cults from the distant past.[87] These cults underwent a political transformation. At Bologna, the cult of the city's two earliest bishops, Saints Zama and Justinian, dates to the early communal period.[88] But neither Zama nor Justinian had obvious links to the new communal regime. The links had to be invented. When they were, they focused on another saint who soon eclipsed both Zama and Justinian, Saint Petronio. He is by far the best-studied example of this phenomenon, and, like Ansano, he was a "new" saint.

The historical Petronio, who was perhaps of Gallic origin, served as bishop of Bologna from about 432 to about 450. His contemporaries, Hilary of Arles and Eucher of Lyons, mention him but give next to nothing in the way of biographical information.[89] He enjoyed no cult and fell into centuries of obscurity. Petronio first appears in a Bolognese liturgical calendar of 1019, but his actual cult and first vita were both products of the communal period.[90] On 4 October 1141, Bishop Enrico I of Bologna (1130–45) preached a sermon announcing the discovery of his predecessor's relics in the Santo Stefano complex.[91] The bishop claimed that, thanks to a written record (*scriptura*) found during reconstruction of the altar of Saint Isidore of Seville, a workman had located a large collection of relics. The cache included a marble arca with the bones of Bishop Petronio. While preparing a shrine for

86. See Hyde, *Society and Politics*, pl. 2 and p. 61, esp. n. 15; M. B. Becker, *Medieval Italy: Constraints and Creativity* (Bloomington: Indiana University Press, 1981), 40; Webb, "Cities of God," 116; and, on this image of Zeno, ead., *Patrons*, 62–63.

87. A phenomenon studied for Modena, Reggio Emilia, Mantua, and Verona by Paolo Golinelli, *Indiscreta Sanctitas: Studi sui rapporti tra culti, poteri e società nel pieno Medioevo*, Studi storici, 197–98 (Rome: Istituto Storico Italiano per il Medio Evo, 1988), esp. 55–101. On patron saints and legitimacy generally, see Webb, *Patrons*, 5–7.

88. See inscriptions concerning their relics, originally in the monastery of Ss. Narborre e Felice, now at Santo Stefano: *Iscrizioni medievali bolognesi*, 114, no. 1. On bishop saints and early communal identity, see Golinelli, *Città e culto*, 70–72.

89. Lanzoni, *San Petronio*, 19–34. For bibliography from the Middle Ages to the twentieth century, see Alba Maria Orselli, "Spirito cittadino e temi politico-culturali nel culto di san Patronio," *La coscienza cittadina nei comuni italiani nel duecento*, 285–87 n. 1; for modern scientific studies, see ibid., "Excursus," 331–43.

90. Lanzoni, *San Petronio*, 35.

91. Bologna, Biblioteca Universitaria, MS 1473 (ca. 1180), fols. 265ʳ–268ᵛ; printed editions: *Sermone de Inventione Reliquiarum [S. Petronii]*, ed. Francisco Lanzoni, *San Petronio vescovo di Bologna nella storia e nella legenda* (Rome: Pustet, 1907), 240–50; *AS* 50 (Oct. II), 466–70. On this text, see Orselli, "Spirito," 294.

the ancient bishop in the San Sepolcro, or "Golgotha" chapel, workmen found other relics, mostly connected with Christ's Passion. Those relics were a godsend to Santo Stefano, with its chapels modeled on the Holy Sepulcher. This gave the complex a physical connection with the holy places in Jerusalem. Petronio remained of secondary interest. By the 1180s, a Santo Stefano monk had provided Petronio with his first Latin vita, which is preserved in the martyrology of the monastery (fig. 39).[92] The codex was for refectory use, and the long life of Petronio was its centerpiece. Soiling and marginal notes show that the life was the most heavily used section of the codex. The author focused on Petronio's connection to the monastery, especially his role in its reconstruction.[93] But Petronio's episcopacy is not ignored. His appointment as bishop, the author reports, resulted from a revelation to Pope Celestine.[94] The life tells how the ancient bishop played a central role in the rebuilding of the city after Theodosius I had destroyed it in retaliation for the murder of an imperial legate.[95] For this act and no other, the author says, Saint Ambrose of Milan excommunicated the emperor.[96] The life focuses on Petronio's relic hunting in the Holy Land and Italy—a project that explained the great hoard discovered in 1141.[97] The stories are fictions, but suggestive of things to come.

In the late 1100s, Petronio's cult was still restricted to the monastery. As late as the 1240s, Saint Peter, the titular of the duomo, remained the sole patron of the city and alone appeared on the seal of the Popolo.[98] Even after Petronio was adopted as a city patron at midcentury, few Bolognese were named after him. Pietro, Domenico, and Francesco were the most common Bolognese names. These were the names of the patron of the duomo and the two mendicant founders.[99] The city was slow to adopt Petronio. Jurists of the university did not cancel classes on his feast day.[100] But sometime between 1257 and 1267, indifference turned to adoration. In that period, the city fathers ordered the offering of forty candles at Saint Petronio's shrine altar each year on his feast.[101] The old Latin life inspired the forgery of

92. Bologna, Biblioteca Universitaria, MS 1473, *Vitae Sanctorum et Vita S. Petronii*; printed editions in *AS* 50 (Oct. II), 454–64, and Lanzoni, *San Petronio*, 219–40. Ibid., 39–49, describes the life. On a possible earlier Latin life, see Antonio Ivan Pini, "Origine e testimonianze del sentimento civico bolognese," *La coscienza cittadina nei comuni italiani nel duecento*, 150–51.

93. Bologna, Biblioteca Universitaria, MS 1473, fol. 259ʳ; *Vita S. Petronii*, 2.12, *AS* 50 (Oct. II), 458–59; Lanzoni, *San Petronio*, 231.

94. Bologna, Biblioteca Universitaria, MS 1473, fols. 257ʳ⁻ᵛ; *Vita S. Petronii*, 1.6, *AS* 50 (Oct. II), 455–56; Lanzoni, *San Petronio*, 227–28.

95. Bologna, Biblioteca Universitaria, MS 1473, fols. 262ʳ–263ʳ; *Vita S. Petronii*, 2.19–20, *AS* 50 (Oct. II), 460–61, Lanzoni, *San Petronio*, 235–36.

96. Bologna, Biblioteca Universitaria, MS 1473, fols. 260ᵛ–262ʳ; *Vita S. Petronii*, 2.15–18, *AS* 50 (Oct. II), 459–60; Lanzoni, *San Petronio*, 233–35.

97. Bologna, Biblioteca Universitaria, MS 1473, fols. 264ᵛ–265ʳ; *Vita S. Petronii*, 3.24–25, *AS* 50 (Oct. II), 462–63; Lanzoni, *San Petronio*, 239–40.

98. Bol. Pop. Stat. (1248), 2.12, 1:510.

99. Pini, "Origine," 186.

100. Orselli, "Spirito," 329.

101. Bologna Stat. 1 (1257–67), 1:441.

imperial charters—ascribed to the emperor Theodosius—defining the city boundaries and granting privileges to the university. The *Registrum Novum* of the commune enshrined these privileges in law.[102] After 1279, under Bologna's anti-imperial Guelf-dominated government, Saint Petronio first joined the "anti-imperial" Saint Ambrose on the seal of the Popolo and then replaced him entirely.[103] Petronio reached the height of his popularity in the years after 1284, when, under the leadership of Rolandino Passaggeri, the city again asserted its independence from imperial control. The manuscript of new vernacular vita produced in this period includes a miniature showing the saint holding the city in his hands.[104] By 1295, the city honored Saint Petronio and Saint Procolo, another newly discovered saint, by processions and candle offerings at their respective shrines.[105] Images of Saint Ambrose and Saint Petronio decorated the Bolognese carroccio and its military banner.[106] Central to the later diffusion of Petronio's cult was a miracle-producing well (still visible today) in the San Sepolcro chapel of Santo Stefano. The faithful came to drink and wash there. On Pentecost Sunday of 1307, miraculous healings began.[107] The commune had eagerly adopted the formerly monastic cult, but the clergy of the Mother Church lagged behind. Perhaps they were jealous for their cathedral's titular, Saint Peter, who was slowly lapsing from public recognition. Not until 1310 did the canons adopt Petronio's feast and institute a procession to his tomb on 4 October, the now traditional feast day.[108]

The rationale for the city's devotion to Petronio is found in his vernacular vita, dated about 1257.[109] The life is by an anonymous Bolognese, probably a layman.[110] Drawing on the Latin vita, the author invented or embellished narratives reporting how Petronio secured rights and privileges for the city, defended its independence, and laid out its sacred spaces and shrines.[111] The vita is an expression—perhaps the first literary expression—of Bolognese communal identity.[112] The Saint Petronio of the vita never ceases to speak

102. On these forgeries and the life, see Lanzoni, *San Petronio*, 125–34, and Pini, "Origine," 166–67.

103. Lanzoni, *San Petronio*, 151–53; Orselli, "Spirito," 285–86.

104. Orselli, "Spirito," 324.

105. Lino Sighinolfi, "Il culto di s. Procolo nella storia di Bologna," *Atti e memorie della Deputazione di storia patria per l'Emilia e la Romagna* 8 (1942/43): 305–30, esp. 307–8.

106. Orselli, "Spirito," 320–21, quoting C. Ghirardacci, *Della historia di Bologna* (Bologna, 1597), 1:429.

107. Matteo Griffoni (1307), 31; Girolamo de' Borselli, *Cronica Gestorum* (1307), 36; *CCB:* A, Vill., 280, 282; and *CCB:* B, Bol., 282.

108. See cathedral statutes of 1310 in *Studia Gratiana* 8 (1962): 447–552, and Orselli, "Spirito," 300.

109. Because it uses a forgery dated to that year: Lanzoni, *San Petronio*, 143–44; but cf. Orselli, "Spirito," 341–42, who suggests a later date.

110. Bologna, Biblioteca Universitaria, MS 2060 (XIV cent.), *Vita e li meriti del glorioso messer s. Petronio.* Later copies are found in Biblioteca Universitaria, MSS 696 and 1680; fragments in Bologna, Archivio di Stato, Cod. cartaceo 31/1883. MS 2060 is edited by Maria Corti in *Vita,* 1–50; on which edition, see the review in *Analecta Bollandiana* 82 (1964): 464–65, and B. Terracini, "Intorno alla vita di San Petronio (Testo bolognese del secolo XIII)," *Archivio glottologico italiano* 48 (1963): 27–51.

111. See Orselli, "Spirito," 331–43.

112. So Pini, "Origine," 148; see also Lanzoni, *San Petronio*, 137–76.

of his love and concern for "la mia citade di Bologna." The life turns Petronio into the primary author of the civic rights that the Theodosian forgeries of the 1250s enshrined.[113] Petronio founds both the independent
commune and its university.[114] The life claims that the "evil emperor Theodosius" had destroyed Bologna because its citizens had—with justice—killed
his tyrannical vicar. The author did not invent this incident out of whole
cloth: he modeled it on the emperor Frederick Barbarossa's leveling of the
city walls as punishment for the murder of his legate Boso during the Lombard Wars for communal independence.[115] In the life, Petronio—the busy
communal patron doing his civic duty—intercedes with the new "good emperor," Theodosius II. He boldly remonstrates with the emperor, convinces
him to enlarge Bologna's contado, and prevails upon him to grant the city
perpetual independence from imperial control.[116] His political work at home
complete, Petronio voyages to the Holy Land, Constantinople, and Rome,
and then returns to Bologna with a great haul of relics. He enshrines them
in the Santo Stefano complex, which he has redesigned and reconstructed
after the model of the holy places in Jerusalem.[117] Later, with the help of
Saint Ambrose, the good bishop maps out the city center by erecting four
monumental crosses to indicate the quarters of the medieval city. He dedicates the crosses to apostles, virgins, martyrs, and confessors, placing suitable
relics in each.[118] Petronio is not only Bologna's patron but its chief architect
and urban planner.[119] Before returning to Milan, Saint Ambrose joins Petronio in excommunicating all, emperors included, who might harm the city.
Worn out by his labors, Petronio dies and is buried at Santo Stefano. In
conclusion, the vita laments, using the words of Jeremiah, that the city had
for so long forgotten so great a father. The Bolognese commune had itself
reasserted its independence, thrown off imperial tyranny, nurtured its university, rebuilt its walls, and modeled its shrines on the earthly Jerusalem.
Bologna became the image of the heavenly city. It came to possess all the
relics necessary to become an "urban reliquary." The vernacular vita presents Petronio as the sole actor in all these endeavors. He is the celestial
validation for the accomplishments of the republican regime.

Cities and their patrons had a reciprocal relationship. The saints in
heaven protected their cities by intercession with God; the cities on earth

113. Bologna, Biblioteca Universitaria, MS 2060, cc. 29–31, fols. 11ʳ–12ᵛ; Corti, *Vita*, 26–29.

114. Bologna, Biblioteca Universitaria, MS 2060, c. 30, fol. 12ʳ; Corti, *Vita*, 27–28.

115. Bologna, Biblioteca Universitaria, MS 2060, cc. 19–24, fols. 7ᵛ–9ᵛ; Corti, *Vita*, 17–21. Cf. Bologna,
Biblioteca Universitaria, MS 1437, fols. 260ᵛ–262ʳ; *Vita S. Petronii*, 2.15–18, *AS* 50 (Oct. II), 459–60; Lanzoni,
San Petronio, 233–35. *CCB:* B (1163), 34, records the historical murder and Barbarossa's revenge. On the
vitae and this incident, see Pini, "Origine," 153, and Lanzoni, *San Petronio*, 46–48, 57–70. On the anti-
imperial flavor of the Petronio cult, see Golinelli, *Città e culto*, 79–81.

116. Bologna, Biblioteca Universitaria, MS 2060, c. 29, fols. 11ʳ⁻ᵛ; Corti, *Vita*, 26–27.

117. Bologna, Biblioteca Universitaria, MS 2060, cc. 31–39, fols. 12ʳ–17ʳ; Corti, *Vita*, 28–41.

118. Bologna, Biblioteca Universitaria, MS 2060, cc. 41–45, fols. 17ʳ⁻ᵛ; Corti, *Vita*, 42–43.

119. See Lanzoni, *San Petronio*, 149–50, on how this changes the focus of the Latin life.

celebrated their patrons with acts of devotion and homage. At San Gimignano, the podesta had the responsibility to ensure that the people celebrated
the feast of the titular saint with all due solemnity.[120] At Parma, the city
treasurer provided a banner, to be safely kept in the sacristy of the duomo,
for the city to offer at the altar of the Blessed Virgin on the vigil of her
Assumption, that by her intercession she might procure peace and security
for the commune.[121] Mantua constructed an altar to the "victorious Saint
Michael" in the church of San Zeno, where the podesta and people paid
him fitting honor.[122] As cities adopted new patrons, these were incorporated
into public life. At Florence, where by the early fourteenth century Saint
Zenobius had joined John the Baptist and Reparata in the civic cult, the
podesta, captain of the people, priors, standard-bearer, judges, knights, notaries, and the captains of the twenty-one arts each offered a candle at each
saint's altar on the vigil of the titular feasts. Monetary offerings on the feast
of Saint Reparata went to construction of the new cathedral.[123] When foreigners venerated a city's patron, this gave honor to the city. In 1262, Bolognese flagellant confraternities went to offer candles and a purple altar cloth
to the shrine of San Giminiano, the patron of Modena. The bishop, government officials, and the civic corporations of Modena came in procession to
meet them at the border settlement of Castelleone and escort them to the
duomo. The Modenese populace greeted the procession with honor. Bishop
Alberto Boschetti produced Saint Giminiano's arm for veneration, and it
freed a possessed Bolognese woman of her demons.[124] What did the city
fathers of Bologna think of all this? And how did Saint Petronio feel about
his children's homage to a foreign saint? Perhaps he felt episcopal solidarity
with Saint Giminiano rather than jealousy.

SACRED IMAGES AND SACRED SPACES

Early communal assemblies met in the duomo or in other city churches. At
Florence, before the construction of the civic palazzo began in 1298, the
priors met before the altars of the various saints in city churches, according
to a rotation. Even after the commune had its own palazzo, the tradition
of a religiously consecrated meeting space continued: the fathers dedicated
communal altars in the new civic buildings.[125] At Ferrara, where city officials
still met in the duomo, they carved the communal statutes of 1173 into the
church's south wall, facing the main piazza (fig. 40).[126] Not for a hundred

120. San Gimignano Stat. (1255), 4.29, p. 725.
121. Parma Stat. II (1266), 100.
122. Mantua Stat. (1303), 5.12, 3:96.
123. Florence Stat. II (1325), 5.20, p. 378.
124. Matteo Griffoni (1262), 15.
125. Trexler, *Public Life*, 49.
126. Adriano Franceschini, *I frammenti epigrafici degli statuti di Ferrara del 1173 venuti in luce nella cattedrale*
(Ferrara: Deputazione Provinciale Ferrarese di Storia Patria, 1969), 5–12. Fragments of the statutes can
best be seen in the shop at Piazza Trento Trieste, 21.

years did these carvings of the civic laws into the cathedral fabric become obsolete. Market construction finally covered them in the late 1280s.[127] Other cities did not follow Ferrara's example, but many inserted municipal units of measure into the walls of major churches (see fig. 41 for such an installation in a palazzo wall).[128] Communal governors appropriated a space for themselves within the duomo. At Brescia, the commune erected a "good and beautiful bench" for its rectors between the nave columns in San Pietro and arranged a clean and spacious area around it for city assemblies.[129] Even after civic bodies had moved to their own palazzi, the sacristies of the duomos and larger churches remained favorite places to deposit municipal records.[130] Some cities deposited unexpended funds in these sacristies and allowed diversion of fines to church maintenance.[131] As with space, so with time. The early republics lived by the religious calendar, observing its seasons as well as its feasts. In early-thirteenth-century Parma, city courts sat from the ringing of Prime until Terce and from the ringing of None until Vespers. Parma curtailed court hours not only on feast days but also on fast days, as in Lent, when empty stomachs might impair judgment. During fasts, Paduan judges stopped hearing cases at the ringing of Sext.[132]

While sacred place and time hedged the organs of government around with a holy aura, the government sanctified the city itself through religious painting and sculpture. Like Saint Petronio at Bologna, the ancient Florentine Bishop Saint Zenobio had, according to legend, set up the crosses that marked the four quarters of his city.[133] Communes preserved and protected such symbols of civic and pious responsibility. At Modena, after the restoration of the republic in 1306, the commune immediately restored, at the cost of £3 mut., the great city cross dedicated to Saint Mary and Saint Giminiano. The act especially honored the latter, through whose prayers the city now enjoyed the restoration of its liberties.[134] When the republic published its new statute book several months later, it decorated the manuscript with a monumental picture of its heavenly protector, Saint Giminiano, blessing his city from horseback.[135] The city fathers commissioned other civic-religious art that year. By a commission of 26 March 1306, the magistrates, with advice from the bishop and cathedral clergy, had carved of "beautiful stone" an image of Saint Giminiano with a standard and erected it on the wall of the duomo facing the Piazza Comunale. Angels flanked the patron, and, as

127. Ferrara Stat. (1287), 5:38, pp. 5–12.
128. As in Ravenna Stat., 273 and 297, pp. 121–22, 138.
129. Brescia Stat. (before 1277), col. (106).
130. Padua Stat. (1265), 4.9, p. 344, no. 1133; Brescia Stat. (before 1277), cols. (132)–(133); "Capitoli inediti di una redazione statutaria pavese del secolo XIII," 1.387, p. 14.
131. Ravenna Stat., 7, p. 17; 354, p. 167.
132. Parma Stat. 1 (1241), p. 6; (before 1233), 1, pp. 110–11.
133. Lanzoni, *San Petronio*, 159.
134. Modena Stat. (1306/7), 1:128.
135. On this image, see Golinelli, *Città e culto*, 93.

was fitting for celestial defenders of the republic, one held a cross and the other the communal banner. The image carried the inscription "Justice, Mercy, Truth, and Peace."[136] As for the Mother Church, so for the city's nonecclesiastical buildings. On 20 May of the same year, the fathers commissioned a painting of the Virgin and San Giminiano for the Palazzo del Popolo, "that they might protect and extend the liberty of the people of Modena." Oil lamps illuminated the new images at night.[137]

Such artistic embellishments made a doctrinal statement. Cities placed images over their gates to proclaim communal orthodoxy. "Let images be placed over the five major gates of the city in honor of the Blessed Virgin, Saint Michael the Archangel, Saint Christopher, Saint Peter, and the blessed martyrs Felix and Fortunatus; and let this be completed between Easter and the first of August," ordered the commune of Vicenza in 1262—a visible declaration of orthodoxy after the expulsion of the impious and heretical da Romano tyranny.[138] Attitude toward cultic images of the saints could, in fact, be a litmus test of orthodoxy. The notary Ugonetto de' Molari was walking one day with two acquaintances. He suggested that they drop into a church and pray there before the images of the saints. His friends agreed to come and pray, but refused to venerate the images. Such images were made "more for worldly use than out of devotion." They certainly were "worldly" in the sense of "communal" and "civic." But they were holy objects of devotion as well. The inquisitor who took down Ugonetto's words concluded the men were heretics, under the influence of some Waldensian preacher.[139] Perhaps they were from another city as well. Honoring images of the saints proved both Catholic and communal identity.

Bologna commissioned marble images of Saints Peter and Paul to embellish the major portal of the duomo, a sign of fidelity to the Roman See.[140] At Pisa in 1275, the new podesta pledged himself to assure, in cooperation with the officials of the city, that images of the Virgin, Saint Peter, and Saint Mark be painted over the principal gates. He became responsible for their preservation.[141] Sacred images embellished city palaces—sometimes flanked by paintings of condemned criminals. Heaven might mix with hell in scenes worthy of Dante. Padua ordered counterfeiters to be depicted on the communal palace walls, with bags of false money around their necks. The Paduan damned took their place beside the city's saints. The city's *Liber Falsariorum* lists the names of some one hundred counterfeiters for the period

136. Modena Stat. (1306/7), 1:99; on this sculpture, see Webb, *Patrons*, 124–25.

137. Modena Stat. (1306/7), 1:158–59.

138. Vicenza Stat. (1264), 3–7.

139. Alberto of Castellario, "Inquisicio que fit et fieri intenditur per fratrem Albertum de Castelario de Cuneo inquisitorem (1335)," ed. Grado G. Merlo, (13), Merlo, *Eretici e inquisitori*, 166.

140. *CCB:* Vill. (1223), 87; later further embellished with columns: *CCB:* A, B, Vill. (1252), 131.

141. Pisa Stat. 1 (1275), pp. 46 and 52; repairs were ordered a decade later: ibid. (1286), 1.154, pp. 264–65.

1217 to 1277.[142] It must have gotten crowded on the palazzo walls. The city could become an icon itself. In 1247 the women of Parma offered a silver model of their city to the Blessed Virgin in thanksgiving for her protection. The model showed the walls, the duomo, and the notable public buildings.[143] The Virgin had protected Parma, and now the city itself became a votive gift to her.

The early communes concentrated their resources on the cathedral complex, then the seat of both ecclesiastical and civil government. Only at Florence, the one city that had not constructed a truly monumental cathedral before 1250, did a regime have to undertake new construction of the Ecclesia Matrix in the later 1200s. The city then replaced the small temple of Santa Reparata with one what would become today's Santa Maria del Fiore. The great new cathedral was an expression of civic identity.[144] Three times the size of the older church, construction required the demolition of the old Spedale di San Giovanni.

In the thirteenth century, the communes began building structures for their particular use as well. At Florence and elsewhere, the thirteenth century saw a building boom of *palazzi comunali*. These buildings provided new public spaces for city government, but removal of government from the cathedral did not bring secularization. Rather, the separation from the duomo focused greater attention on the city's other religious institutions. Lesser churches now became sources of civic pride.[145] At Bologna, by 1253, the city granted annual funds reaching £100 bon. for construction and maintenance of the church of San Giacomo di Sevena in Strà Sam Donato.[146] In 1284, the city wholly reconstructed it, creating today's San Giacomo Maggiore of the Augustinians.[147] They placed a memorial inscription under the portico on its north flank to record their good work.[148] At the same time, smaller edifices, like Santa Cristina, between Strada Maggiore and Strada Santo Stefano, received annual appropriations.[149] Similar building campaigns and repristinations occurred in other cities.[150]

After the defeat of the da Romano, the republics began a "reconquest of the civic centers of worship."[151] At Vicenza, independence inspired the construction of three enormous churches, Santa Corona for the Dominicans,

142. Padua Stat. (1265), 1.4, p. 26, no. 59; for the *Liber Falsariorum*, see Padua Stat., pp. 385–422, nos. 1263–363; on such paintings, see Jones, *Italian City-State*, 379–80.

143. Webb, "Cities of God," 126–27.

144. So Morghen, "Vita religiosa," 201.

145. Pini, "Origine," 182.

146. Bologna Stat. 1 (1250), 5.12, 1:449–50.

147. *CCB*: A (1284), 225; Matteo Griffoni (1284), 24.

148. *Iscrizioni medievali bolognesi*, 310, no. 9 (1315).

149. Bologna Stat. 1 (1252/53), 5.17, 1:453: £15 bon.

150. E.g., Ravenna, where the podestà Tommaso of Folliano appropriated £50 rav. for work on Santo Stefano: Ravenna Stat., 348, p. 163.

151. Lomastro, *Spazio urbano*, 21–22: "riconquista dei centri di culto cittadini."

San Lorenzo for the Franciscans, and San Michele, named for the saint on whose feast the tyrant was defeated. The city later entrusted that church to the Augustinians. Precisely in the center of this triangle of monumental churches, the city placed two *palazzi del comune,* one replacing an 1195 construction leveled by Frederick II in 1236, and the other an enlargement of the palazzo of 1221/22, which had itself been built in defiance of the da Romano. Demolition of the da Romano towers provided stone for the new construction and symbolically purged the city center of heresy and tyranny. A zone of holiness defended the seat of the reestablished republic.[152] Vicenza's conception of the civic center as a consecrated jewel set in civic religious space has reminiscences elsewhere. When Piacenza began construction of its palazzo at sunrise on 12 May 1281, the rector of the city, Brusciato of Brescia, and the captain of the Popolo, Girardino de' Boschetti of Modena, had the Franciscan friars on hand to consecrate the site by singing the opening of John's Gospel.[153]

New civic buildings inevitably absorbed older landmarks. Piacenza took down the ancient church of San Bartolomeo to construct its new Palazzo Comunale. But that palazzo included a public chapel that incorporated the sacred functions of the old church.[154] At Bologna, the communally expanded church of Sant'Appolinare and Sant'Ambrogio became itself part of the curia, the government complex. City statutes reserved to the city the presentation of chaplain.[155] Where city palaces could not incorporate preexisting churches, they included new municipal chapels. The Bolognese Palazzo Nuovo included such a chapel, for use of the podesta himself, under the tall tower of the Arenga (fig. 42).[156] At Modena, the city chapel, dedicated to Saint Giminiano of course, provided Mass for the podesta and his judges; consultations among experts treating city needs also occurred there.[157] After 1268, at Parma, the podesta's stipend included money specifically earmarked for oil and candles to illuminate the "chiesa del palazzo." Maintaining votive lights before the image of the Virgin was a sacred responsibility, imposed upon the executive under oath.[158] City leaders' desire to embellish the Treviso chapel may lie behind the vows extracted from their podesta in 1230 (and again in 1260), by which he promised not to confiscate any relics, in particular the body of Saint Ticino, from churches of the dependent commune of Ceneda. Other Treviso officials took the same oath.[159]

152. Ibid., 30–31; on these building projects, see also A. Morsoletto, "Città e chiesa a Vicenza nel secolo XIII (1200–1260)," Laurea thesis, Facultà di Lettere e Filosofia, Università di Padova, 1967–68.

153. Muzio of Modena, *Annales* (1281), 572.

154. On city chapels, see Mauro Ronzani, "Le 'chiese del comune' nelle città dell'Italia centrosettentrionale (secoli XII–XIV)," *Società e storia* 6 (1983): 499–534, esp. 525–30, on the chapels in city palazzi.

155. Bologna Stat. 1 (1250), 9.194, 2:445; Matteo Griffoni (1250), 12.

156. Matteo Griffoni (1255), 13; (1256), 13.

157. Modena Stat. (1327), 1.226, p. 208.

158. Padua Stat. (1268), 1.20, p. 78, no. 224; Parma Stat. III (1316), 105.

159. Treviso Stat. (1230), 77, 2:31; for the rubric of a lost reenactment, see ibid. (1260), 2:297.

Like the duomo, municipal chapels provided tempting space for profane meetings, detentions, storage, and secular business. The heightened religious sensibilities of the thirteenth-century communes demanded protection for these holy places, much as they did for the duomo. Concern for the purity of the communal chapel seemed, if anything, greater than that for the cathedral. At Bologna, three years after the palazzo chapel's completion, the commune forbade all secular business there, specifically mentioning detention of prisoners.[160] A Franciscan or Dominican friar was to be engaged for daily Mass. Like Bologna, Reggio enlisted mendicants to say Mass at the communal chapel. Dominican, Franciscan, Augustinian, and Saccati friars served on a rotation for Mass each week. The city provided the priests with twenty-four loaves of bread a week as Mass alms—to be baked at a bakery of the friars' choosing.[161] The Bolognese treasurer (*massarius*) had responsibility for equipping the city chapel. He maintained the votive lamp (a sketch in city statutes showed the style the fathers preferred [fig. 43]—the anticipated cost was £5 bon.) and provided the two Mass candles and, on solemnities, incense for the Divine Offices. Each February, on the Feast of the Purification, the treasurer provided the podesta with three pounds of wax for chapel use and made certain that the altar linens had been washed, Mass Hosts provided, vestments furnished, and palms procured for Palm Sunday.[162] By 1288, the chapel was so well supplied with vestments, altar cloths, books, and fine silver chalices that the fathers enacted special measures to provide security.[163] Nor did the city ignore the ministry of the Word. The year the chapel opened, the city arranged for a preacher to edify the public at least once a month at city expense.[164]

Erection of the communal palazzi did not end city presence in the cathedral complex. That most potent civic talisman, the carroccio, stayed there. No city moved its war wagon to the new Palazzo Comunale. More than any other object, it reflected the union of sacred and civic in communal life. The first known carroccio appeared at Milan in 1039, when Archbishop Ariberto devised a chariot bearing a crucifix and the standards of the city to serve as a rallying point for troops in the war against the emperor Conrad.[165] From the beginning it was a simultaneously religious and republican emblem. Whether kept in the duomo itself, as at Brescia, Bologna, or Siena, or in the baptistery, as at Parma, this wagon was the center of a religious cult.[166] At

---

160. Bologna Stat. 1 (1252–53, 1259, 1260–67), 7.146, 2:159–60; the temptation to hold prisoners in city chapels seems to have been widespread: Modena Stat. (1327), 4.196, p. 494; Parma Stat. 1 (1242), pp. 76–77; see also the provision for a city-jail chaplain in Florence Stat. II (1325) 5.III, p. 438.

161. Reggio Stat. (1265), 1.48, p. 141.

162. Bologna Stat. 1 (1259, 1260–67), 7.146, 1:160–61—Bologna, Archivio di Stato, MS Comune Governo, vol. 4, fol. 36ᵛ (1259).

163. Bologna Stat. II (1288), 2.18, 1:94.

164. Bologna Stat. 1 (1250), 5.5, 1:443.

165. Webb, "Cities of God," 115.

166. Brescia Stat. (before 1277), col. (185); for Bologna, see Pietro Cantinelli, *Chronicon*, ed. Francesco Torraca (1272), *RIS²* 28:2:11; *Chronicon Parmense* (1282); on the carroccio, see Hannelore Zug Tucci, "Il

Siena, after the Blessed Virgin had crushed the Florentines at Montaperti, the city enshrined its carroccio before her altar in the duomo. On that altar, two candles burned day and night at city expense, and a perpetual vigil lamp hung above the carroccio itself.[167] Like Siena's battle wagon, that of Parma was a shrine to Saint Mary. The Parmese decorated their cart with images of patron saints and mounted above it a banner bearing the image of the Glorious Virgin.[168] The wagon concentrated municipal pride, religious devotion, and hometown affection. Cities had pet names for their wagons: the Parmese called theirs Agrola; at Cremona, the people named it Gargiardo; at Vicenza, Martinello.[169] The chronicler Rolandino of Padua puts the following story into the mouth of a communal representative welcoming the city militia and the papal legate after the defeat of the da Romano in 1256:

> If you would ask where [our carroccio] had its ancient origin, look above the high altar of the cathedral of Padua; there you will see in beautiful and finely wrought images Milone, then bishop of Padua [1083–95], King Conrad, and his queen, Bertha by name. This queen interceded before the king for the people of Padua, that he grant them the grace of reconstructing their carroccio, which the tyrant Attila once destroyed. . . . When this favor had been granted to them—for through the queen's intercession they received that grace—they made a magnificent carroccio and, in memory and honor of the queen, gave it the name Bertha, by which it is called today and shall be called for all eternity.[170]

For Salimbene, the loss of Parma's carroccio to Cremona was the greatest disgrace his commune could suffer.[171] When captured in battle, the enemy

---

carroccio nella vita comunale," *Quellen und Forschungen aus italienischen Archiven und Bibliotheken* 65 (1985): 1–104, esp. 80–81, on the sacral nature of the wagon.

167. Siena Stat. 1 (1262), 1.2, p. 26. In contrast with northern European practice, Italians never carried the consecrated Host on their battle wagons: Tucci, "Carroccio," 78. Perhaps the carroccio was already holy enough. On the religious significance of Montaperti to the Sienese, see Webb, "Cities of God," 119–21. On the myths and realities of Montaperti, see ead., *Patrons*, 251–75, esp. chap. 6, "The Virgin of Montaperti."

168. *Chronicon Parmense* (1303), 85.

169. *Mem. Pot. Reg.* (1250), col. 1117 (for Parma); *Chronicon Parmense* (1281), 38 (for Cremona); *Liber Regiminum Padue*, ed. Antonio Bonardi (1198), *RIS²* 8:1:298 (for Vicenza).

170. Rolandino of Padua, *Cronica in Factis et circa Facta Marchie Trivixiane*, ed. Antonio Bonardi (1256), *RIS²* 8:1:124: "Si vero forte quereres, unde primitus originem habuit, respicies supra altari maiore ecclesie paduane; ibi namque videre poteris in picturis pulcre et artificose protractis Milonem, tunc episcopum paduanum, regem Conradum et reginam uxorem eius, Bertam nomine, que regina peciit pro populo paduano a rege, ut Paduanis graciam faceret, ut hedificarent carrocium, quod eis olim Athilla tyranpus destruxerat. . . . Hoc igitur munere eis dato, quoniam intercedente regina istam graciam habuerunt, fulgentissimum fecerunt carrocium et ad ipsius regine memoriam et honorem imposuerunt carrocio nomen Berta, quo quidem nomine vocatur hodie et vocabitur in eternam." This story is somewhat off—Bertha was the wife of Henry IV, not Conrad, but the altar painting did exist: ibid., 124 n. 3. On this story, see Tucci, "Carroccio," 97–98.

171. Salimbene, *Cronica* (1247), 305, Baird trans., 203.

carroccio, taken in triumph to the victors' cathedral, became a votive offering to God for the enemy's defeat. Parma captured the carroccio of Cremona after defeating the Cremonese and Frederick II at Vittoria. They lodged it in their baptistery—but only after allowing the citizenry to strip it for souvenirs. To the undying shame of Cremona, nothing remained but the wheels, frame, and mast, leaning against the baptistery wall.[172] When Bologna captured the carroccio of Modena in 1272, it became a votive offering in San Pietro, after public display in the Piazza Maggiore.[173] The Paduans kept the captured Vicentine carroccio in the Curia Episcopalis.[174] After a rout in 1213, the Milanese abandoned their carroccio on the field, where the victorious Cremonese seized it. They entrusted it to the keeping of their Piacentine allies. But on Pentecost Sunday, the Milanese drove off the Piacentines and captured the Cremonese carroccio. Cremona resumed the war the following year, we are told, simply to get back their lost battle wagon.[175] The carroccio figured in processions of triumph as well. When the Bolognese captured Frederick's son Enzo at Fossalta, their carroccio carried the royal prisoner to jail in the Palazzo Nuovo.[176]

The republican army was consecrated by sacred rites. The communes, bourgeois in their ethos, preserved the practices of knighthood but transformed its ceremonies to conform to republican sensibilities. Each city created its own knights, usually on Pentecost Sunday, the Sunday of the Knights (*Pasqua Militum*).[177] Nevertheless, in cities under special patronage of the Virgin, such as Siena, the Assumption was the favored date for knighting.[178] The bishop, as pastor of the city, presided at the ceremony. Only on the most exceptional—irregular—occasions did Italians have recourse to a mere layman, however noble, to knight a citizen of their republics. Such an event occurred at Forlì on All Saints' Day, 1285, when Count Alberto of Gorizia knighted two citizens in the field. Raimondo, the patriarch of Aquileia, had refused to preside, because one candidate was under excommunication for homicide.[179] Servants of the city participated in its sacred character. The lay theologian Albertano of Brescia spoke of city lawyers as the priests of the commune. They purified the mouths of citizens with the salt of justice, as the Church's priests did those of neophytes with the blessed salt at baptism.[180] God's judgment was invoked in communal courts. Even after prohi-

---

172. Ibid. (1247), 292–93, trans., 193. The papal legate, Gregorio of Monte Longo, put Frederick's relic collection, also captured at Vittoria, on view in the duomo sacristy: ibid. (1247), 293, Baird trans., 194.

173. *Annales Veteres Mutinenses* (1272), col. 71.

174. *Liber Regiminum Padue* (1198), 298.

175. Galvano Fiamma, *Manipulus Florum* (1213), 246, *RIS* 11:665.

176. Tucci, "Carroccio," 31.

177. E.g., as at Reggio in 1270; see Alberto Milioli, *Liber*, 536.

178. Stefano Gasparri, "I rituali della cavalleria," *Riti e rituali nelle società medievali*, ed. Chiffoleau, Martines, and Paravicini Bagliani, 111.

179. *Annales Foroiulienses*, ed. Wilhelm Arndt (1285), *MGH.SS* 19:202–3.

180. See Powell, *Albertanus*, 58.

bition of trial by battle in 1215, the communes continued to practice it, inviting divine intervention into their legal processes.[181] In a ritual book that once belonged to the Benedictine nuns of Sant'Alessandro at Parma, the Mass and rituals for trial by battle are pasted onto the flyleaf (fig. 44).[182] The paste-in is thirteenth-century and well used. Litigants heard the Mass of the Trinity and the litany of the saints. They confessed and received Communion or blessed bread. Their shields and weapons were anointed in the sign of the cross with the oil of the sick, as were the combatants' heads and hands. As in battle between cities, let God and the saints defend the right!

GOD AND THE POPOLO

To this point I have spoken of the communes generally; I now focus more narrowly on the later republican regime itself, the "popular" commune. The popular communes provide a glimpse of grassroots civic life that the less-documented earlier communes do not. The "revolutions of the Popolo" occurred in the period from 1200 to 1230, after approximately fifty years of political instability. I do not intend to trace the political and economic events that led to these revolutions, since others have treated them exhaustively.[183] I focus on one particular aspect of these new regimes, their heightened religious identity. The Popolo brought more men into communal government, although this citizenship was exercised in a corporate, not individualistic, manner.[184] The institutions of the new regimes rendered the commune more clearly distinct from the bishopric.[185] Bishops did not become podestas after the rise of the Popolo. The earliest popular regime was at Milan, where an association called the Credenza di Sant'Ambrogio appeared alongside the older communal organs in 1198. City statutes finally recognized the Credenza's political dominance in 1216.[186] In having a single organ for popular participation, Milan was unique. Nonetheless, the Credenza was similar to the typical smaller corporations that made up the Popolo elsewhere. In all cases, there were strong organizational and devotional similarities to the religious confraternities of the last chapter, although the Credenza (at least) did not evolve directly out of an earlier religious association.

181. Hyde, *Society and Politics*, 85, records a traditional judicial duel in 1225 at Siena; on such practices, see Robert Bartlett, *Trial by Fire and Water: The Medieval Judicial Ordeal* (Oxford: Clarendon Press, 1986).

182. Parma, Biblioteca Palatina, MS Par. 44 (paste-in is XIII cent.), *Rituale delle monache benedettine di Sant'Alessandro in Parma*.

183. For bibliography in English, see Hyde, *Society and Politics*, 201–7; for major works in other languages, see ibid., 207–16, and Jones, *Italian City-State*, 651–73.

184. Powell, *Albertanus*, 16; on the nonpassive nature of communal citizenship, see Pini, *Città, comuni e corporazioni*, 148.

185. See François Menant, "La transformation des institutions et de la vie politique milanaises au dernier âge consulaire (1186–1216)," *Atti dell'11° Congresso*, 128–29, and Gina Fasoli, "Ricerche sulla legislazione antimagnatizia nei comuni dell'alta e media Italia," *Rivista del diritto italiano* 12 (1939): 88–90, on the increasingly democratic nature of communal government in the early 1200s.

186. The source for the origins of the Credenza is Galvano Fiamma, *Cronica Maior*, 745–46; on it, see Menant, "Transformation," 113–44, esp. 116–17,

The usual vehicles for the popular revolution were small neighborhood or craft associations. After claiming political space by military uprisings, these collectively organized to form a larger corporation, the Popolo itself.[187] Some of these corporations had an overtly religious quality; craft guilds were commonly pious associations in origin. At Ferrara, early-twelfth-century records of the shoemakers' guild show that it was originally a purely religious association and only later a craft guild, and then later a corporation of the Popolo.[188] By 1233, at Padua, the Popolo consisted of *fratalie*, the local word for such societies, based on craft.[189] These probably had origins similar to those of the shoemaker's guild at Ferrara. At Parma the most important organs of the Popolo were the neighborhood militia associations: the *vicinia, rua*, or *contrada* (all three meaning neighborhood, the last, *contrada*—plural: *contrade*—commonly used everywhere). The *fratalie* elected their consuls in the neighborhood chapel (*ecclesia viciniae*) and met there at the ringing of the church bell.[190] At Cremona parishes (*parrochie*) themselves formed the Popolo. They were grouped into quarter associations, and each owed a quota of soldiers to the city. Of the fifty-seven cappelle of Cremona, the largest, San Michele in Porta San Lorenzo (which was itself divided into districts), owed 759 soldiers, while smaller chapels like San Martino in Porta Portuzzi (Porta Portusii) owed as few as ten. The total number of soldiers owed by the four quarters was 5,826.[191] If Cremona had something like twenty-five thousand people, the military component represented a large percentage of the adult male population, perhaps over half. Verona assessed local cappelle for units of the militia in the same way.[192] Such grassroots organizations of the Popolo seem voluntary and local, which makes sense in light of the dictum, formulated by the theorist of communal polity Albertano of Brescia, that nothing could be more "absurd" than a "free" city whose government was feared instead of loved.[193] It could be loved because it was made up of neighbors. Sadly, neither of these cities has preserved documents revealing the internal organization of these neighborhood societies. Bologna has the best documented neighborhood societies. There, the backbone of the Popolo was the Società delle Armi.[194] Under the popular regime, these societies (along with the craft guilds known as the Società delle Arti) elected the city councils and

187. Menant, "Transformation," p. 127–28.
188. See Hyde, *Society and Politics*, 80.
189. *Liber Regiminum Padue* (1223), 306; Padua Stat., 1.31, pp. 129–30; the commune eventually suppressed any *fratalia* that was not subordinate to the commune: "Statuti extravaganti [padovani]," ed. Maria Antonietta Zorzi, *L'ordinamento comunale padovano nella seconda metà del secolo XIII: Studio storico con documenti inediti*, Miscellanea di storia veneta 5:3 (Venice: Deputazione di Storia Patria per le Venezie, 1931), doc. 5 (1293), p. 205.
190. Parma Stat. I (1233), p. 99; (1241), p. 12.
191. Cremona Stat. (1270), 101–2.
192. Verona Stat. II (1276), 5.32, pp. 688–90.
193. Powell, *Albertanus*, 59.
194. Hyde, *Society and Politics*, 110–12.

provided the grassroots political organization. They formed the units of the militia. The "Societies of Arms" were in origin temporary and probably evolved to provide police services. Evidence from the late communal period shows that similar associations existed not only at Cremona but also at Florence, Mantua, Brescia, and Biella.[195] In those cities, unfortunately, evidence on these neighborhood societies dates after 1300, after the societies had become permanent, mandatory organizations, closely controlled by a centralized city administration.[196]

Bolognese records show the societies in their earlier incarnation and to some extent reveal their original organization and life.[197] Although every Popolo was unique, the Bologna corporations seem typical. When founded, the societies of the Bolognese Popolo found their forms of organization ready to hand. The rhetorician Boncompagno of Signa, probably during his first year of teaching at Bologna (1194), drafted a set of model statutes for a *società* and included it in his famous *Cedrus*.[198] He noted that these societies were multiplying in Italy, and characterized them as private and usually religious in character—like the earlier penitent associations. That early quasi-religious groups might form a part of government is not wholly surprising. Later religious associations also received such roles. At Bologna, again, the flagellant confraternities became equals of the Armi and the Arti and came to be incorporated into the Popolo.[199] Unfortunately, none of the Bologna statutes show us a society in formation. We can, however, observe citizens in midcentury using Boncompagno's forms to organize themselves, as members of the Popolo corporations had in the generation before. On 20 September 1258, a group of forty-four Bolognese, including the priest of San Cristoforo in Porta Saragossa, created the Società di Sant'Eustachio.[200] It was a corporation to manage some vineyards outside the city walls.[201] The group approved and

195. Florence Stat. 1 (1322–25), 5.83–113, pp. 292–312; Mantua Stat. (1303), 1.64, 2:109–11; Brescia Stat. (1313), 2.148, cols. 104–5; ibid. (1245) 3.18 (78).

196. As in Lucca Stat. (1308), 3.29, pp. 152–53, and 3.142–48, pp. 234–40; Pisa Stat. 1 (1286), Popolo 102, pp. 632–35. Archbishop Federico Visconti mentioned the Fraternitas Sancte Lucie in his famous sermon describing Saint Francis of Assisi as a merchant: *Les sermons et la visite pastorale de Federico Visconti archevêque di Pise (1253–1277)*, ed. Nicole Bériou (Rome: École Française de Rome, 2001), Sermo 57.12, p. 778–79.

197. On the *società* at Bologna, see Gina Fasoli, "Le compagnie delle armi a Bologna," *L'Archiginnasio* 28 (1933): 158–83, 323–40, and ead., "Le compagnie delle arti a Bologna fino al principio del secolo xv," *L'Archiginnasio* 30 (1935): 237–80. See also Epstein, *Wage Labor*, 82–83, on the composition of the Arti statutes.

198. Boncompagno of Signa, *Cedrus*, *Briefsteller und Formelbücher des elften bis vierzehnten Jahrhunderts*, ed. Ludwig Rockinger (Munich, 1863; rpt., New York: Franklin, 1961), 121–26; on which, see Meersseman, *Ordo*, 1:18.

199. Meersseman, *Ordo*, 1:509–10.

200. Bologna, Biblioteca dell'Archiginnasio, ms Gozz. 210, vol. 8, fols. 123ʳ–152ᵛ, *Statuta Anni 1258 et matricula [Annorum 1258–1310] Societatis S. Eustachii*: 1258 statutes, fols. 123ʳ–126ʳ; matricula, fols. 126ᵛ–128ʳ. For comparison, statutes of a later society with a secular purpose, in this case management of family property, may be found in Lucca, Biblioteca Statale, ms 333.

201. Bologna, Biblioteca dell'Archiginnasio, ms Gozz. 210, vol. 8, fol. 124ᵛ (repeated in the later revision of the statutes: fols. 142ʳ⁻ᵛ); the financial management is treated in ibid., fols. 123ᵛ–124ʳ (repeated: fols. 141ʳ⁻ᵛ).

inducted new members in the chapel of San Cristoforo before the group's own altar, that of Saint Eustace. That altar was also their usual place of meeting.[202] On the feast of their patron, the society elected as leaders eight ministers. These received an annual compensation of 10s. bon.[203] Given its worldly purpose, the group's statutes come as something of a shock to modern readers. This commercial entity is structurally and devotionally identical to the early penitent confraternities. Its statutes first provided for devotion to the patron saint. The treasurer (*massarius*) was to assure that an oil lamp burned perpetually before the patronal altar. He procured "the two large wax candles" that burned during the Masses of the society. At the vigil Mass of Saint Eustace, each member personally presented a candle, to be valued at least 18d. bon., to the patron—failure to do so resulted in expulsion from the society.[204] The society met each month on the last Sunday for a votive Mass of Saint Eustace, for which the statutes provided a 6d. bon. stipend to the priest engaged to chant the service.[205] The Mass ended with a *benedizione*, that is, a loaf of fine white bread, which was blessed and shared by the members as a nonsacramental communion. After the service, the members met to conduct society business if there was any. The major social affair of the year was the annual banquet in honor of Saint Eustace.[206] The statutes appropriated a sum of 15s. bon., which paid for the dinner and allowed the priest of the chapel to hire a suitable choir to chant the solemn Mass that preceded it. A smaller dinner was held in the fall, in preparation for the annual candle offering. The society members were obliged to say five Paters and Aves daily in honor of the blessed martyr Saint Eustace. One might easily mistake this vineyard society for a religious confraternity. That would not be wholly mistaken. It would be a worse mistake to see it as a business corporation with some pious trappings.

In the Society of Saint Eustace, sacred and worldly elements formed a seamless whole, and they did so from its very foundation. The societies of the Popolo should be understood in the same way. The statutes of the Bolognese Società delle Armi present the same merging of secular purpose (military and police functions) with religious forms. Their organization is identical to that of the later vineyard society and earlier penitent associations. The founders used the religious forms that were ready to hand. For only one society, the Lombardi, does the group's origin by itself explain its religious character. The "Lombards" were localized in the university district toward Porta Ravenna and limited to those of north Italian family origin. The society was in origin a true religious confraternity, formed by the students of the

202. Ibid., fol. 123^r.
203. Ibid., fol. 123^r (repeated: fols. 140$^{r\ v}$).
204. Ibid., fols. 123^v–124^v (repeated: fols. 140^v–141^r).
205. Ibid., fols. 124^{r-v} (repeated: fols. 141^v–142^r).
206. Ibid., fol. 125^r (repeated: fols. 142^v–143^r).

university for their spiritual needs.[207] All other societies of the Bolognese
Popolo were created for military, political, or craft purposes; they were voluntary, local, and temporary.[208] The use of religious forms to organize the
corporations, through which a much increased percentage of the adult male
population found a role in city government, reflects the Popolo's understanding of itself.[209] In the period of these societies' foundation, the early 1200s,
the communes cultivated an ever more pronounced religious ethos. They
sacralized their offices and functions as these became distinct from the
Mother Church. New patron saints gave legitimacy as the cities broke away
from the authority of the empire. The societies' mass political base is suggestive: the popular communes were not merely a new political order; rather,
they were a reconception of the city as a new organism—permeated with
religious flavor from the ground up. The Bologna societies were grassroots
organizations. Analysis of the Bolognese matricula for 1274 shows approximately 7,025 men enrolled; in 1310 the figure was 8,032.[210] Bologna's population in 1290 was about fifty thousand .[211] If we cut that figure in half and so
exclude women, we have twenty-five thousand; eliminating roughly half of
that figure, as foreign students and minor children, leaves a native adult
male population of perhaps twelve thousand. Dividing this by the average
matricula figure yields 60 percent of adult males as society members. This
may be a bit high, since a man might belong to more than one society, but
membership of more than 50 percent is not at all unlikely. The suggestion
that one third of Bolognese citizens held some city office in a given year is
reasonable.[212] They held such office by membership in their *società*. This does
not, of course, mean they were democratic in the modern sense: certainly
some members counted more than others, and the less wealthy certainly had
less leisure for political involvement. Nevertheless, Albertano of Brescia, the
thirteenth-century lay theologian, considered these associations the backbone of the citizens' liberty.[213]

Like that of Saint Eustace, each society of the Bolognese Popolo met for

207. Bol. Pop. Stat., 1 (Lombardi, 1255, c. 36), 1:15. See Meersseman, *Ordo*, 1:190, remarking on
Gaudenzi's analysis of statutes 14–16 of the Società della Armi. They alone among the Bologna societies
had specific moral requirements, expelling those who kept prostitutes at home: Bol. Pop. Stat., 1 (Lombardi, 1255, c. 50), 1:18.

208. Some societies preserved their ancient temporary character: see, e.g., Bol. Pop. Stat., 1 (Aquila,
1255, c. 28), 1:246 (oaths binding for ten years); (Chiavi, 1255, c. 1), 1:181 (oaths binding for five years).

209. Meersseman, *Ordo*, 1:8.

210. Pini, "Problemi di demografia," 189.

211. Ibid., 216–18.

212. Pini, *Città, comuni e corporazioni*, 152, quoting Waley: "si può calcolare a circa ¹⁄₃ i cittadini ogni
anno impegnati nel governo e nell'amministrazione." Pini considers this estimate low. Jones, *Italian City-
State*, 589, and esp. 573 n. 541, is much more pessimistic (5–10 percent).

213. Powell, *Albertanus*, 32. Antonio Ivan Pini, "Le arti in processione: Professioni, prestigio e potere
nelle città-stato dell'Italia padana medievale," *Lavorare nel Medio Evo: Rappresentazioni ed esempi dall'Italia dei
sec. X–XVI, 12–15 ottobre 1980*, Convegni del Centro di studi sulla spiritualità medievale, 21 (Todi: Accademia Tudertina, 1983), 91–95, notes that popular involvement in government reached a peak in the communal period and fell to nearly nothing under the signorie.

Mass in a church of the district from which it drew its members.[214] The
Quartieri, who met at Sant'Ambrogio, even had benches installed there for
the members.[215] The group's standard-bearer, as the military leader of the
society, called out and rallied the members in front of the society's chapel
or, less commonly, at the neighborhood cross.[216] Chanting of Mass preceded
business meetings, elections, and discussion of whatever "touched the honor
of the society and the city of Bologna," including financial reports.[217] A few
societies also joined Mass with the distribution of poor alms, but that does
not seem universal.[218] Mass alone was essential. The societies sometimes
chose their church because of their patron, as did the Balzani. This group
came from the area around Santo Stefano but decided to meet in the church
of San Giovanni in Monte because they preferred Saint John's patronage.[219]
Other societies too chose patrons different from those of their home chapels.
The Aquila, whose church was San Salvatore, chose Saints Peter and Paul.[220]
As an associative principle, the place and patron were secondary to the act
of worship. One of the oldest Bologna societies, that of the Traverse di Porta
San Procolo, was not originally localized in any particular church. Meetings
moved monthly from chapel to chapel. The Traverse later adopted Saint
Proculus as their particular patron. Only then did they meet exclusively in
his church. The members' monthly Mass and their annual candle offering
established the society's corporate identity.[221] In extant Bologna society statutes, the monthly Mass, held on the first or second Sunday of the month,
was constitutive of membership; all provided a stipend for the priest, usually
stipulated at 6d. bon.[222] If necessary, because of the numbers present, Mass
could be sung outdoors using society tents.[223] Societies fined those who failed

214. Lombardi at S. Stefano; Tusci at S. Giovanni di S. Stefano; Balzani at S. Giovanni in Monte;
Traverse di Porta S. Procolo at S. Procolo; Delfini at S. Salvatore; Castelli at S. Damiano; Schise at S.
Caterina delle Muratelle; Chiavi at S. Pietro; Sbarre at S. Sismondo (other than for Mass, at S. Cecilia);
Traverse di Barberia at S. Barbaziano and S. Isaia; Cervi at S. Leonardo; Aquila at S. Salvatore; Branca
at S. Maria Maggiore; Leoni at S. Felice; Quartiere at S. Ambrogio; Spade at S. Giovanni Battista and
S. Tommaso; Vari at S. Martino dell Aposa. At Biella, the churches of the societies were protected against
vandalism by special fines: Biella Stat. (1245), 1.3.10 (69); but I find nothing like that for Bologna.
215. Bol. Pop. Stat., 1 (Quartieri, 1256), 1:295.
216. Ibid. (Branca, 1270, c. 1); (Castelli, 1255, c. 29), 1:165–66; (Schise, 1254, c. 24), 1:177; (Lombardi,
1255, cc. 25–27), 1:11–12.
217. Ibid. (Schise, 1254, c. 6), 1:171. For elections after the Mass, see ibid. (Sbarre, 1255, c. 28),
1:195–96; (Branca, 1255, c. 21), 1:270. For finances, see ibid. (Balzani, 1230, c. 43), 1:130.
218. Ibid. (Toschi, 1256, c. 13), 1:95–96.
219. Ibid. (Balzani, 1230), 1:121–31.
220. Ibid. (Aquila, 1255, c. 3), 1:237 (the Aquila later added Saint Francis of Assisi as patron, p. 253).
221. Ibid. (San Procolo, 1231), 1:135–45.
222. Ibid. (Aquila, 1255, c. 3), 1:237; (Barberia, 1255, c. 3), 1:204; (Delfini, 1255, c. 1), 1:149; (Spade,
1262, c. 14), 1:329–30; (Castelli, 1255, c. 4–6), 1:159; (Quartieri, 1256, c. 8), 1:298; (San Procolo, 1231, c. 2),
1:135; (Schise, 1254, c. 6), 1:171; (Vari, 1288, c. 11), 1:351; (Quartieri, 1256, c. 8), 1:298. Lack of documents
makes it difficult to say if a monthly Mass for societies of the civic militia was normative in other communes. Nevertheless, that was the case when the Florentines expelled the Medici in 1527; the most important
public ritual of the new republican militia was the Communion Mass of the young soldiers. On this, see
Trexler, *Public Life,* 541.
223. Bol. Pop. Stat., 1 (Toschi, 1256, c. 24), 1:99.

to attend the Mass (12d. bon. was typical) and even expelled regular absen-tees.[224] Society policing of attendance at religious exercises was not unique to Bologna. At Florence in the 1280s, during processions by the Society of Saint Mary of the Carmine, its captain stood on a raised dais and checked off those present on the society roll.[225] Bolognese statutes usually specified that the priest chant a particular votive Mass, commonly that of the society patron or the Blessed Virgin, a common copatron.[226] Like the society of Saint Eustace, all societies shared blessed bread at the monthly Mass. Their statutes carefully specified its quality and value (usually between 7d. and 15d. bon.).[227]

The event that defined the society as a corporate entity was the annual candle offering. The Bologna Popolo as a whole observed this practice. Gov-ernment officials (*anziani*) came as a group, and each offered a one-pound wax candle to Saint John the Baptist in the church of San Giovanni in Monte on 24 June, the saint's nativity.[228] The Popolo was a neighborhood society writ large. The societies typically offered four one-pound candles of "fine wax," two for use at the society Mass and two as a votive gift to the chapel. Some societies offered as few as two candles and some as many as six.[229] The Barberia, which met in two different churches, had two annual candle ceremonies, one offering of two tapers to Saint Isaiah at his church and another offering of two to Saint Barbatianus at his.[230] The society's officials, the ministers, treasurer, and standard-bearer—as representative of the mem-bership—presented the candles during the Mass of the patron saint.[231] In others, such as the Lombardi, each member offered an individual candle once a year. The Lombardi's ministers organized the ritual on Pentecost—total candle costs were 20s. bon.—and then provided a banquet dinner. Societies added other devotions according to their own tastes. Typical was an offering of oil to light the vigil lamp before the patron's altar.[232] Social functions were important for creating fraternity in the societies, but they did

224. E.g., ibid. (Matteo Griffoni, 1258), 1:307–24; (Aquila, 1255, c. 3), 1:237; (Balzani, 1230, c. 1), 1:121; (Sbarre, 1255, cc. 1–4), 1:191; and outside Bologna: Biella Stat. (1245) 3.24–25 (85–85).

225. *Libro degli Ordinamenti della Compagnia di S. Maria del Carmine scritto nel 1280*, ed. G. Piccini (Bologna: Romagnoli, 1867), 39; on this text, see Trexler, *Public Life*, 268, and 507–10 on the ways the Medici purged their city of republican rituals and symbols.

226. E.g., Bol. Pop. Stat., 1 (Delfini, 1255, c. 1), 1:149; (Cervo, 1255, c. 7), 1:216.

227. Ibid. (Aquila, 1255, c. 3), 1:237; (Branca, 1255, c. 1), 1:261; (Balzani, 1230, c. 1), 1:121; (Castelli, 1255, cc. 4–6), 1:159; (Cervo, 1255, c. 7), 1:216; (Branca, 1255, c. 1), 1:258. The flagellants had mandatory monthly Masses: Meersseman, "Statuto dei Disciplinati di Bologna (1260)" 11, Meersseman, *Ordo*, 1:480–82; id., "Statuto dei Disciplinati di Vicenza (1263)" 7, 22, ibid., 482–83; Novara Battuti Stat. (XIV), 281.

228. Bol. Pop. Stat., 2 (General Stat. 1248, c. 5), 1:507.

229. E.g., ibid., 1 (Vari, 1256, cc. 16, 43), 1:340, 345; (Branca, 1255, c. 1), 1:261; (Cervo, 1255, c. 8), 1:217; (Sbarre, 1255, cc. 1–4), 1:191; (Quartieri, 1256, c. 7), 1:297; (Delfini, 1255, c. 3), 1:149; (San Procolo, 1231, c. 47), 1:143–44; (Sbarre, 1255, cc. 1–4), 1:191; (Aquila, 1255, c. 4), 1:237.

230. Ibid. (Barberia, 1255, c. 10), 1:205.

231. Ibid. (Branca, 1270, c. 1), 1:458.

232. Ibid. (Lombardi, 1291, c. 2), 1:47; (Toschi, 1256, c. 15), 1:96.

not create a group's corporate identity; the statutes of only two societies mandated annual dinners.[233] When the members broke bread together, they normally did so in the sacramentalized sharing of the *benedizione*, the blessed bread, at Mass. Typically, corporate meals were linked to members' funerals. Societies paid for poorer brothers' obsequies, lest any lack suffrages, prayers, and the dignity of Christian burial. Summoned by the society messenger, members attended the deceased's Requiem Mass at the society chapel. The ministers then assigned pallbearers for the procession to the cemetery. Afterward, pious duties completed, the society retired for their common dinner.[234]

The religious ethos of the Bologna Armi statutes stands in strange contrast to that of the city's professional guilds, the Società delle Arti. Their legislation shares the same external forms as that of the Armi. It stipulates chapels, monthly Masses, blessed bread, candle offerings, and funeral provisions.[235] But no fines punish absences, even at funerals. When the Arti legislate on the *benedizioni*, their concerns seem almost profane. The carpenters carefully specified "two focaccias made with saffron and cumin, valued at 2s. 14d. bon."[236] Perhaps a tasty snack brought out better attendance than fines. The Arti's statutes did prohibit work on holy days. But days of closure are so numerous—and include nonreligious observances like May Day—that religious purpose seems lost or much demoted.[237] What are we to make of this difference? It cannot be mere accident. The guilds did not reflect a more "secularized" segment of the population in any measurable sense. These organizations were hardly restricted to the well-to-do, even if the rich were less pious than the poor—a dubious assumption. Their matricula show membership numbers equaling or exceeding those of the Armi societies.[238] Nor does their economic nature as professional or craft associations suffice to explain this. The wine-making corporation of Saint Eustace was just as religious in flavor as the Armi and probably more a business contrivance than any arts society. If we turn to Pisa, where professional guilds alone composed the Popolo, the late fragments of their statutes have the same intensely religious flavor as those of the Bologna Armi.[239] At Padua, where the *fratalie* were again craft oriented and again the sole corporations of the

233. Ibid. (Balzani, 1230, c. 19), 1:126; (Branca, 1255, c. 18), 1:269.

234. E.g., ibid. (Balzani, 1230, c. 31), 1:128; (Delfini, 1255, c. 10), 1:151; (Cervo, 1255, cc. 30–31), 1:223. Only one society had a regular Mass for the dead: ibid. (Lombardi, 1255, cc. 7–8), 1:7.

235. E.g., for monthly Mass and meeting: ibid., 2 (Bambagina, 1288, c. 4), 2:399; (Fabbri, 1252, c. 18), 2:228; (Formaggiari, 1242, cc. 5–6), 2:167; (Coltelli, 1294, cc. 3–4), 2:412. On candle offerings: ibid. (Cambiatori, 1245, c. 79), 2:95; (Formaggiari, 1242, c. 37), 2:176. On funerals, e.g.: ibid., 1 (Beccai, c. 44), 2:374–75.

236. Ibid., 2 (Falegnami, 1264, c. 48), 2:213. The ironworkers, ibid. (Ferratori, 1248, c. 22), 2:185, specified "duas pulcras focacias" for their annual Mass on the Feast of the Purification of Mary.

237. E.g., ibid. (Mercanti XIII, c. 17), 2:127–28; (Lana 1256, c. 100), 2:309; (Spadai, 1283, c. 34), 2:343.

238. Pini, "Problemi di demografia," 197.

239. For what remains, see the statutes of the Guardia della Beata Vergine Madonna Santa Lucia of 1322: Pisa Stat. 1, pp. 703–10. These treat almsgiving (ibid., pp. 704–5), suffrages (pp. 705–6), monthly Mass (pp. 706–7), the society chapel (pp. 707–8), and candle offerings (p. 708).

Popolo, the feel of a religious confraternity is again marked.[240] Could the explanation lie in the Armi's particular role in Bolognese communal life? They formed the militia. The militia was the city's strong arm but also its spiritual heart. The Armi, not the Arti, defended the Ecclesia Matrix, the carroccio, Saint Petronio, and his city. The craft guilds at Padua and Pisa had the same defensive task. They formed the militia. They, with the help of the city's patrons, defended the city in battle and so shared the city's sacred character. Their statutes reflect their simultaneously religious and civic nature.

The Holy City Legislates

At no time were the communes secular in the modern sense. But before the rise of the Popolo, Italian city statutes are oddly lacking in religious references. The early commune at Ferrara sanctified its city statutes by carving them into the wall of the cathedral, but those laws lack religious content. The same is true elsewhere. At Pisa, the only overtly religious passage in the statutes of 1162 comes in the consuls' oath, where these officers swear to protect the honor of the Mother Church and other religious institutions.[241] The 1162 statutes are fragments, but those of 1233, for which we have more complete texts, are equally lacking in religious references.[242] God intrudes into the early-thirteenth-century statutes of Treviso only in the requirement that city officials take their oaths on the Gospels; the saints appear only in the use of their feasts for dating.[243] Milan's earliest extant statutes are wholly nonreligious, tithes being the only ecclesiastical matter mentioned.[244] But religion was not alien to the early communes. They were formed within the episcopal curia; they met in sacred spaces; they replaced the emperor with new patron saints. The fathers felt no need to proclaim their faith when legislating on roads, drains, taxes, and court procedure. The rise of the popular communes brought a sea change in legal rhetoric. This was the age when the cities built their palazzi and established civil courts and administration consciously distinct from that of the bishop and the Mother Church.[245] As communes developed a more purely "lay" government and housed it in new

240. See the notaries' statutes in Padua, Biblioteca Universitaria, MS 1359, *Ordinamenta [Fratalie Notariorum Vicentinorum, 1272–1304]*. They treat candle offerings (fols. 3ʳ⁻ᵛ); vigil lamps (fol. 3ᵛ); monthly and annual meetings—called *capitolo* and *capitolo generale* (fols. 3ᵛ–4ʳ); funerals (fol. 17ᵛ). The group had about five hundred members, according to the matricula, fols. 58ʳ–68ᵛ. These statutes are also found in Vicenza, Biblioteca Civica Bertoliana, MSS 533–34.

241. Pisa Stat. I (1162), p. 3; Pisa Stat. II (1313), 1.1, p. 11.

242. Pisa Stat. I (1233–81), pp. 643–1026.

243. Treviso Stat. (1207–18), 1:3–147; (1207), 50, 1:42–52; (1211), 199, 1:121–22 (dating by saints' feasts). Early Volterra statutes mention only God and the Virgin: Volterra Stat., 233–37, pp. 224–32.

244. Milan, *Liber Consuetudinum Mediolani Anni MCCXVI*, ed. Giulio Porro Labertenghi, Historiae Patriae Monumenta 16: Leges Municipales 2:1 (Turin: Regius, 1876), cols. 859–960; cols. 926–36 on tithes. This text is also edited in Enrico Besta and Gianluigi Barni, *Liber Consuetudinum Mediolani Anni MCCXVI* (Milan: Zappa, 1945).

245. On these building projects, see Jones, *Italian City-State*, 442.

communal palazzi, however, they steeped the city's "secular" legislation in heavily religious language and imagery. This was also the age of politically loaded hagiography like the vita of Saint Petronio. For the first time, the cities explicitly legislated on the moral and religious life. The communes now made large-scale investments in city churches and communal chapels besides the cathedral. By the late communal period, city statutes open with endless invocations of the saints, and their opening enactment, the podesta's oath, always commits him to defend the orthodox Church and suppress heresy.[246]

The statutory language of the popular communes was not pious rhetoric; religious identity and republicanism went hand in hand. The commune's religious base became visible whenever its republican independence was endangered. God and the saints most dominated a city's laws when it had to throw off imperial control or resist local tyranny. The prologue of Vicenza's 1264 statutes expresses that commune's fundamental theology with bracing clarity. The statutes open with the podestarial oath of Rolando de' Inglesci of Padua, who took office that year on the feast of Saint Michael the Archangel—the anniversary of the expulsion of the da Romano.[247] The oath outlines God's rule over the angelic choirs, the eight cosmic spheres, and the earth's four climatic zones. It recalls his creation of animals and how he gave them instinct as their guide. Finally, it celebrates God's creation of humanity, which shares existence with stones, life with plants, sensation with beasts, and understanding with angels. God did not leave humanity without a guide. The human race, from the beginning, lived in "cities, villages, and towns," and God established justice "in the provinces, by dukes, marquises, and counts, and, in the cities, by podestas," who promoted the good and repressed the wicked.[248] The oath majestically maps God's creation, with the commune highest in rank, implicitly an advance on the old nobility "of the provinces." Markedly absent is any reference to the old empire. As podesta, Rolando says he will promulgate statutes unto the honor of the Lord Jesus Christ, the Glorious Virgin Mary, Saints Felix and Fortunatus (whose bodies lie in the city of Vicenza), and Saint Michael, "on whose feast the city of Vicenza was recently liberated from the bloody oppression and rule of the perfidious Ezzelino."[249] The authority of the popular commune came from heaven, and the commune lived in communion with it.

In their religious concerns, the popular communal laws contrast markedly with those from before 1250.[250] Late-thirteenth-century communes legislated on religious matters that earlier would have been left to the Mother Church. Bologna took it upon itself to supervise the admission of young people to

246. E.g., Modena Stat. (1327), p. 3; Siena Stat. II (1310), 1.1–5, 1:29–48.
247. Vicenza Stat. (1264), 1–2.
248. Ibid., 1.
249. Ibid., 1–2: "festo cuius civitas Vicentie a cruenta clade ac dominio perfidi Ecelini fuit denuo liberata."
250. The lone exception is Volterra Stat. (1210–22), 21, p. 13, which protects ecclesiastical property.

religious life and protect parental rights. Parents' permission was required for girls under twelve and boys under fourteen to take religious vows, just as stipulated in canon law.[251] Cities now regularly provided protection and financial support for hospitals, leprosaria, and religious houses, some of which—like the house of Gerardo Segarelli's Apostolici at Parma—lacked official ecclesiastical approbation.[252] The funds involved were large enough to occasion anxiety about fraud. At Bologna, on 3 June 1257, the city forbade correctors of city statutes to introduce new grants to charitable institutions.[253] Elsewhere, the trend toward ever larger religious expenditures and increased legislation on sacred and moral matters continued to the end of the communal period.[254] The union of Church and city, which marked the early communes, persisted in new forms, and the mutual support between them intensified. On the ecclesiastical side, the Mother Church helped fund the nonreligious needs of the city. At Siena and Parma, the bishop and clergy paid for paving the city's streets.[255] Everywhere, the communes made the Church's old responsibility for "miserable persons" their own. At Parma, Bologna, and Reggio, for example, the city reestablished legal and special courts to protect the poor, widows, orphans, and religious.[256] One senses that the clerical-lay condominium still extended to the whole fabric of the city and to all its residents.

The cities legislated as never before on morality. At Ravenna, the podesta explicitly censured loans usurious according to Church teaching.[257] Virtually every popular commune issued laws against blasphemy, particularly that defaming its patron saint.[258] Ferrara and Vicenza dunked blasphemers in a tub in the piazza.[259] Parma whipped them across town.[260] Siena cut out the offending tongues. Bologna, in a show of chivalry, singled out for that punishment any man who slandered the Virgin Mary or any other female saint.[261] Punishable moral offenses multiplied during the period of the popular regimes, coming to include gambling (especially near churches), sexual

251. Bologna Stat. II (1288), 12.34, 2:224.

252. Parma Stat. I (by 1255), pp. 115–16. See also the public support of religious foundations in Bologna Stat. I (1250), 5.1, 1:435–38; Siena Stat. I (1262), 1.21–39, pp. 31–36 (the hospital of La Scala), and 1.96–118, pp. 48–53; Modena Stat. (1327), 2.50–54, pp. 266–68; and Bologna Stat. I (1252/53), 5.18, 1:453–54.

253. Bologna Stat. I (1259–62), 11.109, 3:358–59.

254. E.g., Lucca Stat. (1308), 1.2–5, p. 8–12; Pisa Stat. II (1313), 3.7, pp. 288–89; Florence Stat. I (1322), 2.9, p. 98, and 3.5, pp. 146–47.

255. Siena Stat. I (1262), 1.191, p. 79; Padua Stat. (1274?), 4.5, p. 316, no. 979.

256. Parma Stat. I (1233), p. 5, and Parma Stat. II (1266), 9; Bologna Stat. I (1243, 1259–64), 1.24, 1:214–15; Reggio Stat. (1242), p. 7, and (1265), 1.16, p. 85.

257. Ravenna Stat., 139b, p. 78.

258. Brescia Stat. (1253), cols. (179)–(180); San Gimignano Stat. (1255), 3.47, p. 712; Mantua Stat. (1303), 1.23, 2:77; Lucca Stat. (1308), 3.91, p. 199; Pisa Stat. II (1313), 3.34, p. 311; Modena Stat. (1327), 4.41, p. 407; Ravenna Stat., 157, pp. 87–88. For the only pre-1250 examples, see Verona Stat. I (1228), 171, p. 130, and Biella Stat. (1245), 3.11 (71); neither is as savage as later law.

259. Vicenza Stat. (1264), 186–87; Ferrara Stat. (1287), 4.68, p. 274–75.

260. Parma Stat. I (by 1255), p. 319.

261. Bologna Stat. II (1288), 4.23, 1:191; Siena Stat. II (1310), 5.266, 2:345.

infractions, and cross-dressing.[262] In contrast, the only moral issue regularly addressed in pre-1250 statutes was prostitution. But these laws seem mostly ad hoc affairs, enacted during religious revivals and then forgotten.[263] The legislation of the popular regimes against prostitution was on a wholly different scale. Their antiprostitution statutes protected the sacred spaces of the city: the city center, the cathedral complex, the piazzas of churches, and the neighborhoods of monasteries and convents.[264] These were perpetual laws, not ad hoc evictions. But even the popular regimes made no attempt to outlaw prostitution itself.[265] Their legislation did not police morals. Rather, it protected the dignity of the city's holy places and shrines. Vice in such places was sacrilege, offensive not only to God but to the city as a religious organism. This expulsion of the unrighteous from sacred spaces did not, as far as one can see, yet affect the Jews. Not until 1311 did a north Italian synod legislate on the Jewish badge. Among cities, only Pisa tried to establish a Jewish quarter, and that two years after the synod. The project failed. Internal exile for north Italian Jews would wait for nearly two hundred years, until the age of the Renaissance tyrants.[266]

Little communal legislation focused on heretic hunting. Legislation against heresy itself was common enough in statutes throughout the period, but its practical implications seem oddly obscure. When it occurs, communal legislation against heresy seems a by-product of episodes of religious fervor, like the revivals of 1233.[267] This was true even in a city like Orvieto in the Papal States, where the popular regime "effectively tolerated" Catharism.[268] Until the 1290s, no city legislation mentioned papal inquisitions, although heretics were "relaxed to the secular arm" for execution well before that. Perhaps before the 1290s, communes preferred to deal with heresy in their own way, without recourse to ecclesiastical courts.[269] Extant communal legislation against heretics often looks pro forma. Cities inserted Fredrick II's antiheresy decree into their statutes verbatim or pledged to obey it—without

---

262. Bologna Stat. I (1259–62), 3.21, 1:278–79; Siena Stat. II (1310), 5.24–32, 2:243–47, and 5.40–49, 2:251–53; Florence Stat. II (1325), 5.88, p. 416; Ravenna Stat., 326b–327, pp. 150–51.

263. Treviso Stat. (1233), 615, 2:242; Parma Stat. I (1233), pp. 42–43; Padua Stat. (1233?), 3.7, p. 262.

264. E.g., Bologna Stat. I (1250), 5.15, 1:450–53; (after 1250), 2.52, 1:309–13; (1259), 5.24, 1:457–58; Pisa Stat. I (1286), 3.33, p. 396; Bologna Stat. II (1288), 4.34, 1:197–98; Florence Stat. II (1325), 3.115, pp. 270–72. Only Pisa Stat. II (1313), 3.40, pp. 315–17, expels prostitutes from the city.

265. Bologna, in fact, provided help to reformed prostitutes: Bologna Stat. I, 5.7, 1:444–46.

266. Ravenna Council (1311), 23, p. 462; Pisa Stat. II (1313), 3.89, pp. 377–78. The first Jewish ghetto in Italy was established in Venice in 1516. Bologna, Biblioteca dell'Archiginnasio, MS B.3695, doc. 36 (Nicholas III, original of 4 August 1278, Viterbo), commissions friars to preach to Jews in Bologna.

267. Verona Stat. I (1228), 156, pp. 116–17; *Memoriae Mediolanenses*, ed. Philip Jaffé (1233), *MGH.SS* 18:402; Parma Stat. I (1233), pp. 10–11, and (1233?), 269–71; Treviso Stat. (1233) 734, 2:250–52; Vercelli Stat., 370–92 (1234), cols. 1231–38. Jones, *Italian City-State*, 428–29, remarks on the late and unsystematic nature of communal heresy repression.

268. Lansing, *Power and Purity*, 57–59; the phrase is hers. Before the age of the Popolo, Orvieto experienced only short periods of repression during visits by inquisitors.

269. As suggested by Gabriele Zanella, "Malessere ereticale in valle padana (1260–1308)," *Hereticalia*, 23–27, who evaluates statutes from Aquileia (ca. 1220), Verona (1270–1300), Treviso (1270), Ferrara (1287), and Cividale del Friuli (1307–9).

any provisions for enforcement.[270] Pope Innocent IV reprimanded the Bolognese for ignoring the local inquisition in 1254; three years later Alexander IV complained to the bishop of Modena that the commune was not helping root out heresy.[271] The Franciscan inquisitor Fra Bartolomeo Mascara complained about the negligence of the bishop and commune of Treviso in 1263, and Fra Alessio of Mantua made similar complaints against the podesta and bishop of Padua in 1279.[272] The impression is one of general laxity. Reggio, Siena, and Vicenza did enact antiheresy statutes with bite in the early 1260s.[273] But in Vicenza, at least, the legislation seems to express communal rejection of the perfidious and heretical da Romano more than the will to persecute. Serious communal legislation supporting papal inquisitors had to wait until the last years of the thirteenth century, a period that also saw increased episcopal vigilance against heresy.[274] Why this lack of concern for heresy? I suggest that in the holy cities of communal Italy private theological error posed little perceived threat to the commonwealth. So long as people frequented the sacraments, avoided profaning sacred places, and showed respect for the names of God, the Virgin, and the saints, repression seemed unnecessary.[275] The religion of the cities was a practical religion, best expressed in the common worship, processions, and civic rites by which the city expressed its order and identity. Orthodoxy, like citizenship, meant participation in them.

270. Bergamo, *Antiquae Collationes Statuti Veteris Civitatis Pergami,* 9.29 (1238), ed. Giovanni Finarzi, Historiae Patriae Monumenta 16: Leges Municipales 2:2 (Turin: Regius, 1876), cols. 1943–46; Padua Stat., p. 423, no. 1364; Vercelli Stat. 31 (1241), col. 1107; Bologna Stat. 1 (1250), 5.8, 1:446; Brescia Stat. (before 1277), cols. (125)–(128); Pisa Stat. 1 (1286), 3.4, p. 364; Ferrara Stat. (1287), 6.1–8, pp. 349–63. Although Bologna did include a pledge to suppress heresy in the podesta's oath (Bologna Stat. 1 [1250], 1.1, 1:67), as did Ravenna (Ravenna Stat., 1, p. 13). San Gimignano Stat. (1255), 4.22, p. 724, expelled heretics from the city.

271. Bologna, Biblioteca dell'Archiginnasio, ms B.3695, doc. 22 (*BOP* 1:251) and doc. 28 (*BOP* 1:357), both originals of 1257.

272. Zanella, "Malessere ereticale," 32–33.

273. Siena Stat. 1 (1262), 1.119–22, pp. 53–54 (expels heretics); Reggio Stat. (1265), 1.37, pp. 107–8 (jails heretics, imposes death penalty); Vicenza Stat. (1264), 11–12, 131–32 (fines neighborhoods with heretics).

274. For statutes with practical import, see Pisa Stat. 1 (1286), 1.4, p. 63; Padua, "Statuti extravaganti [padovani]," doc. 8 (1297), pp. 209–10; Lucca Stat. (1308), 3.230, p. 230; Florence Stat. 11 (1325), 3.3, pp. 183–84. On episcopal repression of heresy, see Grado G. Merlo, "'Cura Animarum' ed eretici," *Pievi e parrocchie,* ed. Erba et al., 1:555 n. 49.

275. On this I agree with Lansing, *Power and Purity,* 15–16 and esp. 83–84, who finds that Orvietan "Cathars" regularly served as godparents, went to confession, and attended Mass.

Chapter Four
Ordering Families, Neighborhoods, and Cities

As political entities, the communes lacked the ancient roots and dignity that made for civil legitimacy.[1] They invoked their new patron saints as a replacement for the emperor. They organized their corporations using religious forms and so borrowed a sacred authority. In ceremonies the community experienced itself as a corporate reality. Through its rituals, the city came alive, claimed a place in the world, and united its citizens into an ordered society. By their rituals, medieval Italian cities created an integrated religious geography for those who lived in them. Through participation in public rituals, individuals created families, families created neighborhoods, and neighborhoods created the city.

Making Families

Near the beginning of the communal period, the French bishop Hildebert of Lavardin said to the bishops assembled for the Council of Chartres: "In the city of God there are three sacraments that precede all the others by the time of their institution and that are the most important for the redemption of the children of God: baptism, the Eucharist, and marriage. Of these three the first is marriage."[2] Although he lived in France, Hildebert spoke for the Italians of the age of the communes. Marriage was not only a sacramental act, it was a civic act, which created the smallest unit of society, the family.[3]

---

1. As noted by Trexler, *Public Life*, 43, and Thompson, *Revival Preachers*, 1–9. See also Quentin Skinner, *The Foundations of Modern Political Thought, 1: The Renaissance* (Cambridge: Cambridge University Press, 1978), 3–22, on the communes' de facto, but not de jure, freedom from imperial rule.

2. Council of Chartres (1124), Mansi 21:307; on this text, see Francesco Chiovaro, "Le mariage chrétien en occident," *Histoire vécue du peuple chrétien* (Toulouse: Pivat, 1979), 1:245.

3. On marriage in the communal period, see Gabriella Airaldi, "Il matrimonio nell'Italia medievale," *Atti dell'Accademia ligure di scienze e lettere* 34 (1977): esp. 228–35. On the medieval period generally, see Chiovaro, "Mariage," 225–55. Christopher Brooke, *The Medieval Idea of Marriage* (Oxford: Oxford University Press, 1991), has an excellent bibliography, pp. 287–312.

Its rituals laid the foundation of the civic order. Over the family was the father, its head and patriarch. Those related by blood composed webs of relations, extended families or clans, but these webs were not the domestic unit. That unit was the couple, a husband and wife, along with their children and the unattached relations, servants, and others who lived under the same roof. Subordination to the patriarchal father affected the newly married, or even long married, as long as they shared space with their parents. Creating a new family was the father's responsibility or, should he be dead or absent, that of older brothers or uncles. Marriage of children was a family project, and, as such, the fathers of both future spouses arranged it. If they were wise, the fathers took their children's desires into account; Church law explicitly required free consent of the parties, and without it, no marriage was valid.

The bride's and the groom's status changed once they had married; they formed a family. In the case of the woman, the change was visible. An unmarried woman wore her hair uncovered; the married woman veiled it. Francesco Piperino, looking back from the 1300s at what he perceived as a golden age of female modesty in the 1230s and 1240s, described the proper garb for a virgin. She wore a plain tunic, the *sotano*, of simple cloth. Over it, she threw a mantle of linen, the *socca*. Piperino claimed that in the old days young women wore their hair plainly dressed, not elaborately decorated and "styled" as in his own day.[4] Perhaps it was wishful thinking. Exposed hair was the mark of the virgin, a sign of availability for marriage. Certainly women looking for husbands tried to make themselves attractive. If a woman did not wish to marry, she might do just the opposite. In the 1350s, the young Saint Catherine of Siena announced her rejection of marriage by cutting off her hair. Unveiled hair attracted male attention. In the 1270s, Verona forbade women to comb their hair in doorways or under porticoes. The city also forbade them to spin thread in public. At Vercelli, a generation earlier, the city fathers complained that some young women had taken to walking through the streets spinning. They fined such 2d. and awarded the fine to any man who threw the maid's distaff and thread in the mud.[5] Perhaps the women were looking for suitors, advertising their availability. Such public appearances had the effect of short-circuiting the "correct" way of finding a husband: negotiations between the patriarchs.

Propriety required that new families be created with decency and with attention to civic needs and order. Marriage to a foreigner meant that the wealth of the woman's dowry might be lost to the city. Vicenza legislated to prevent such losses.[6] Fathers' rights might also be thwarted. Catherine of Siena was not the only woman to rebel against family marriage planning. When the pious Oringa Christiana reached marriageable age, her brothers

4. Francesco Pipino, *Chronicon ab Anno* MCLXXVI *usque ad Annum circiter* MCCXIV, 2.49, *RIS* 9:669–70.
5. Verona Stat. II (1276), 4.113–15, pp. 582–83; Vercelli Stat., 348 (1241), col. 1223.
6. Vicenza Stat. (1264), 141–42.

wanted to marry her off. She threw herself into the river Guisciana, "out of laudable zeal, but without reflection" (*ex bono zelo, licet non secundum scientiam*). Water plants miraculously formed themselves into a mat so that she passed over to the other side and escaped without getting wet. Or so the story went.[7] Early-thirteenth-century Milanese laws, among the earliest communal legislation on marriage extant, protected the father's decision in matches.[8]

It would have been unthinkable that a "decent" woman, that is, a suitable future wife, not be under her father's control. Dutiful sons also respected their fathers. Parental power extended to sons, as well as daughters, at least until they were sixteen. Parma fined any male reckless enough to marry a woman without his own father's consent £300 parm. Admittedly, the city could not control those who lacked fathers and brothers, but they did forbid independent women from contracting marriage until they were twelve years of age, a rather tender age to be independent.[9] One way around uncooperative fathers was abduction (*raptus*). The Church defined abduction as "carrying a woman off by force for the sake of marriage." Canon law stipulated that abduction impeded marriage vows and rendered the union void. It also specified that the "force" need not be physical and that it might be against the woman, her father, or both. Abduction with force used only against the father was nothing but elopement, and cities made this subversion of paternal authority a civil crime. They divided abduction fines between the city and the offended father; Bologna punished abduction of males—suggesting that some women who eloped got help from their own male relatives if their beloved's father was not cooperative.[10]

Assuming that civil and ecclesiastical proprieties were observed, the process of marrying off a daughter began when her father settled on her the sum that would become her dowry. By Roman, canon, and Italian statute law, this money became and remained the property of the daughter, not her husband.[11] In a few rural and smaller communes, some marriages were still conducted without dowries, following the Lombard law. By that law, a wife got her personal property as a gift from her husband on the morning after the wedding (*morgengab*).[12] But the communes were slowly ending this prac-

7. *Legenda Beatae Christianae Virginis de Castro S. Crucis Vallis Arni Lucanae Dioecesis*, ed. Giovanni Lami, 5, *Vita della b. Oringa Cristiana fondatrice del venerabile convento di S. Maria Navello e di S. Michele Arcangelo dell'Ordine Agostiniano nella terra di Santa Croce in Toscana* (Florence: Albiziniani, 1769), 193–94.

8. Milan, *Liber Consuetudinum Mediolani Anni MCCXVI*, ed. Labertenghi, 18, cols. 897–900.

9. Parma Stat. I (1229, 1255), p. 289.

10. For communal abduction laws, see Treviso Stat. (1233), 436, 2:165 (divides fine of £1,000 between city and father); Pisa Stat. I (1286), 3.3, pp. 361–63; Pisa Stat. II (1313), 3.2, pp. 281–85; Bologna Stat. II (1288), 4.30–31, 1:194 (punishes abduction of males); Lucca Stat. (1308), 1.4, pp. 8–9 (punishes churches where such unions occur), and 3.4–7, pp. 136–39 (a rare reference to the possibility that the women might be unwilling); Florence Stat. II (1325), 3.69, p. 229.

11. Although male relatives did try to challenge women's dowry rights in court: see Duane Osheim, "Countrymen and the Law in Late Medieval Tuscany," *Speculum* 64 (1989): 329.

12. Treviso Stat. (1233), 654, 2:257; San Gimignano Stat. (1255), 2.19, p. 692; Brescia Stat. (1313), 151–52, col. 175. On the Lombard law of marriage, see Airaldi, "Matrimonio," 222–24.

tice. Dowry in the Roman manner replaced it. Dowry was given for the sake of a marriage, and fathers expected that it be so used. When the widowed Umiliana dei Cerchi chose not to remarry, her father demanded her dowry back. In theory, he had no claim. She did return it to him, although she refused to sign a notarial instrument forfeiting her legal claim to it. She considered oaths about temporal matters unsuitable to one who had become a Sister of Penance. Her father seems to have been satisfied with the cash; he let her move back into the family tower, where the conversa refitted her room as an "oratory," a quasi-monastic cell.[13] After marriage, use of the dowry passed to the husband, but it remained the woman's property (*iure peculii*); she could sue to get it back from creditors if her husband had disappeared for ten years.[14]

A woman of good character and repute, provided with a suitable dowry, was what the father of a potential groom sought for his son's marriage. When two fathers had determined on a match, arrangement of espousals could begin. Elaborate regulations of canon law governed unions. These included times when contracting was forbidden, permissible degrees of affinity and consanguinity, and prohibitions against marrying godparents and even the children or parents of godparents.[15] After Lateran Council IV (1215), the parish priest had to announce upcoming espousals in the parish church to ensure the absence of impediments. Nearly everyone (except priests, monks, and nuns) got married, and this had to be done in conformity with Church requirements. Even the illiterate knew, at least in general outline, the Church's marriage regulations. Fra Salveto of Cesena reported that Don Leto, a canon of Cesena with a degree in canon law, used to visit the penitent Giovanni Buono of Mantua at his hermitage. Giovanni was a former minstrel with no Latin to speak of. The two men liked to argue marriage law, and the canon brought a codex of papal decretals to prove his points. Try as he might, he could not find the text he wanted to cite. After some page flipping, Giovanni found the right section for him—it turned out the pious layman had the marriage law right; the learned canonist was wrong.[16] Ordinary parish priests felt themselves competent to judge marriage cases, a practice both synods and cities tried to prohibit.[17] Cities were as concerned as the Church about the sanctity of marriage, touching as it did the honor of citizens and their families. They punished adultery, bigamy, and incest,

---

13. Vito of Cortona, *Vita [B. Humilianae]*, 1.8, p. 387.

14. "Capitoli inediti di una redazione statutaria pavese del secolo XIII," 1.396, pp. 18–19; for more on dowries, see the extensive treatment in Pisa Stat. II (1233), Leges 25–30, pp. 750–56; on women's dowry rights, see also Airaldi, "Matrimonio," 230.

15. Gratian, *Decretum*, CC. 23–34, and in X 4. For local canons, see Novara Synod II (1298), 1.2–7, pp. 190–92; Ravenna Council (1311), 19, pp. 459–60; and Grado Council (1296), 29, p. 1170. On the marriage canons, see Brooke, *Medieval Idea*, 128–43.

16. *Processus Apostolici Auctoritate Innocentii Papae IV Annis 1251, 1253, et 1254 Constructi de Vita, Viritutibus et Miraculis B. Joannis Boni Mantuani*, 1.1.14, AS 57 (Oct. IX), 779.

17. Lucca Synod (1308), 61, p. 191; Padua Stat. (pre-1238), 2.16, p. 190, no. 588.

sometimes making it explicit that the "gender-neutral" language of their laws also applied to men.[18] Marriage made families; it founded the society; it was everyone's business.

The first public step to marriage was betrothal. When Ezzelino da Romano betrothed Salvaza, the daughter of the emperor Frederick II, in 1238, the ceremony was conducted on Pentecost Sunday before the doors of the great church of San Zeno at Verona.[19] More commonly, the ceremony was held, and the promises to marry sealed, at the house of the bride. The groom came in procession with his father, brothers, male relatives, and retainers. The principals, father and son, came on horseback in all their finery; the others walked. Powerful and wealthy families demonstrated their importance by the size and splendor of the procession. At the woman's house, her female friends and relatives assembled in equally impressive numbers to welcome her future husband. In the later 1200s, cities restricted these displays, usually limiting the men's and women's parties to twenty members each, a rule that probably applied only to guests who were not blood relatives.[20] The betrothal might last for years, but sometimes only months, before the marriage itself occurred. Some parents betrothed their children under the legal age of marriage. Some even betrothed infants in the cradle. Ecclesiastical law prohibited infant betrothals, but parents replaced the "betrothal" with a contract to betroth their children at some future date, usually when the children had both reached the age of seven, the legal age for betrothals.

The canons required that those betrothed before puberty be given freedom to ratify or reject the union when they reached maturity (twelve for a girl, fourteen for a boy), but fathers and mothers had their own means of persuasion.[21] At least in theory, the actual wedding had to wait until the couple were old enough to act for themselves. This ceremony, like the betrothal, included a grand procession, but now the focus of attention was on the bride, not the groom. Marriage was the one occasion when thirteenth-century Italians delighted in having their women make a public show of themselves. The bride's elegance and manner reflected on the family's status.[22] At least until sumptuary legislation tried to put a stop to it, the bride's hair was elaborately dressed on this day, the last time it would be

18. Verona Stat. I (1228), 115, p. 89; Vicenza Stat. (1264), 196 (specifically applies to men); Verona Stat. II (1276), 3.57–59, pp. 425–28; Bologna Stat. II (1288), 4.30, 1:195; Mantua Stat. (1303), 1.24–25, 2:78–79; Brescia Stat. (1313), 2.77, col. 86; Lucca Synod (1308), 43, pp. 184–85 (contraceptive magic and abortion); Modena Stat. (1327), 4.27, pp. 397–98.

19. Parisio di Cerea, *Annales*, ed. Philippus Jaffé (1238), *MGH.SS* 19:10–11. On marriage "at the church door" in France and England, see Brooke, *Medieval Idea*, 248–57.

20. Reggio Stat. (1242), 55, p. 34 (imposes a limit of ten); Ferrara Stat. (1287), 6.76, p. 399; Bologna Stat. II (1288), 4.94–95, 1:251–51 (also fines "uninvited" guests); Modena Stat. (1327), 4.28, p. 399 (imposes a limit of twelve). On sumptuary legislation for weddings at Bologna, see Lodovico Frati, *La vita privata di Bologna nel sec. XIII al XVIII con appendice di documenti inediti* (Bologna: Zanichelli, 1900), 49–50.

21. Gratian, *Decretum*, C. 30 q. 2; *X* 4.2.

22. On weddings and sumptuary law, see Catherine Kovesi Killerby, *Sumptuary Law in Italy, 1200–1500* (Oxford: Clarendon Press, 2002), 66–71.

seen in public. This was an occasion when other women, even the married, displayed their finery, at least if preachers' exempla are to be taken seriously. The vain wedding-goer whose beauty led men into sin was something of a homiletic stereotype. In one version, the temptress (unknowingly) engaged a demon to do the makeup but, finding that the cosmetics had ruined her looks, died in anguish. Her stinking corpse became an embarrassment to her husband, her family, and her serving maid—not to mention the delight of gossips.[23] Preachers were more indulgent about the bride herself. The bride symbolized her family's wealth and reflected honor on both her husband-to-be and her father.[24] She wore a crown decorated with jewels or pearls.[25] Her gown was as sumptuous as the family could afford, preferably with a long train carried by pages. Fur trim was especially popular. A richly embroidered purse, studded with pearls, symbolic of her dowry, was a nice touch. Suitably attired, the bride and her escort come in procession through the streets to the house of the groom. If possible, she, her parents, and the maids of honor rode on horseback; retainers walked alongside.[26] As many as twenty-five men might accompany the bride as an escort of honor. When Pisa in the 1310s tried to control such processions and displays, they limited the men in the bride's procession to two. Popular objections later forced the city to double the size of the cortege.[27] Old habits died hard, or not at all.

Although by medieval Church law a simple exchange of vows between a man and a woman, even without witnesses, sufficed to make a marriage, a proper wedding was a public event. "Clandestine marriages" were, in the end, no better than elopements. Papal canon law condemned them, while admitting their validity. Local synods punished them by excommunication, sometimes reserving absolution to the bishop himself.[28] The earliest communal legislation prohibited clandestine marriages.[29] A proper exchange of marriage vows happened in public, and not during times of penance like Lent, Advent, or Rogation Days.[30] The couple took their vows in the morning, so that the ceremony might be followed by Mass. The actual marriage, the vows themselves, did not take place in the church. While marriages on the church steps were possible, the usual venue was the house to which the

---

23. E.g., in Siena, Biblioteca Comunale degli Intronati, ms I.v.10 (early xiv cent.), fols. 2ʳ⁻ᵛ.

24. For attempts to control display, see esp. Florence Stat. 1 (1322), 5.13, pp. 227–31; Modena Stat. (1327), 4.177, pp. 479–80.

25. Attempts, however, were made to stop the practice: Pisa Stat. 1 (1286), 3.65, pp. 452–54; Mantua Stat. (1303), 1.72, 2:121–23. The Pisans even tried to get their bishop to excommunicate women who insisted on wearing their crowns!

26. Except, perhaps, in Florence, which tried to prohibit this: Florence Stat. 1 (1322), 5.7, p. 222.

27. Pisa Stat. 1 (1286), 3.50, pp. 435–36; Pisa Stat. ii (1313), 3.59, pp. 352–53. See also Treviso Stat. (1233), 610, 2:240; Ferrara Stat. (1287), 6.78, p. 399; Mantua Stat. (1303), 6.35, 3:146–47 (limits the procession to twelve serving maids).

28. Ravenna Council (1286), 8, p. 623; see also Bologna Synod (1310), 493–94.

29. Verona Stat. 1 (1228), 119, p. 91, imposed a £50 fine; San Gimignano Stat. (1255), 4.77, pp. 735–36, required twelve witnesses.

30. Bologna Synod (1310), 493; Grado Council (1296), 30, p. 1171.

bride had come in procession, that of her spouse. Couples took vows in their temporary or future home, the place where they would rear their children—or perhaps before a notary, if there was some money involved, since marriage was very much a legal transaction. This kind of informal ceremony was probably typical of all but the most wealthy.[31] A nuptial Mass might be added, said by the priest, whose presence to witness the vows was prescribed by the canons, even if the marriage was still considered valid were he absent.[32] It might conclude with an exchange of rings, the veiling of the bride, and the ceremony of tying the couple together with a red-and-white pleated cord, which symbolized their union of body and spirit.[33] In the rare cases when the Lombard law was followed, the wife gave her husband a sword as a sign of submission, instead of participating in the Roman mutual exchange of rings.[34] In the case of families with extraordinary prestige or influence, the bishop himself might witness the vows. Lottieri della Tosa, bishop of Faenza, did so for Maurino di fu Domenico of Bologna and Giacomina di fu Alberto Cavini of Trentola on 6 May 1291.[35] But such solemnity was rare; Bishop Lottieri records only three such marriages in his daybook.[36] In any case, along with the parents, crowds of invited friends and relatives came to witness the profession of vows.[37] But now we are in the world of the socially prominent and politically powerful.

When Donna Mabilia, daughter of Count Lodovico of San Bonifacio, married in Reggio on the Friday before Septuagesima Sunday in 1283, the couple professed their vows at the count's house. They immediately went to hear the Mass of the Blessed Virgin Mary at the Franciscan church.[38] A luncheon banquet followed on the grounds of the church of San Giacomo. This marriage was typical, if more sumptuous than usual. After the vows the typical couple went, in procession, to the church. This procession, in which the families of both bride and groom partook, manifested even greater pomp than the earlier one of the bride. Twelve horsemen and four footmen might accompany the couple to church.[39] Although the pair might request some other votive Mass according to their personal devotion, the liturgical books

---

31. I thank Prof. Katherine Jansen for reminding me of this.

32. The question whether Lateran IV required a priest to witness the vows has now been resolved in the negative by David d'Avray, "Marriage Ceremonies and the Church in Italy After 1215," *Marriage in Italy, 1300–1650*, ed. Trevor Dean and K. J. P. Lowe (Cambridge: Cambridge University Press, 1998), 107–15.

33. Gratian, *Decretum*, C. 3 q. 5 c. 7; for Spain, see Attilio Carpin, *Il sacramento del matrimonio nella teologia medievale: Ad Isidoro di Siviglia a Tommaso d'Aquino* (Bologna: Studio Domenicano, 1991), 14, 40. I find no evidence for or against such ceremonies in the Italian communes.

34. Airaldi, "Matrimonio," 224.

35. Lottieri della Tosa, *Il codice di Lottieri della Tosa*, ed. Giovanni Lucchesi (Faenza: Banca Popolare di Faenza, 1979), doc. 159 (6 May 1291), p. 134.

36. Ibid., doc. 169, pp. 140–41; doc. 176, pp. 144–45.

37. Pisa Stat. II (1313), 3.59, pp. 352–53, limits the witnesses to twelve from each family.

38. Salimbene, *Cronica*, 750–51, Baird trans., 523; Alberto Milioli, *Liber*, 561.

39. Pisa Stat. II (1313), 3.59, pp. 352–53; Ferrara Stat. (1287), 6, p. 400, allows twelve to accompany the bride, thirty the groom.

did include a nuptial Mass (*Missa pro sponso et sponsa*). This Mass inserted special prayers for the couple into the Canon, the most sacred prayer of the Mass.[40] If it had not been given at the time of the vows, the priest imparted the nuptial blessing to the couple during Mass, after the recitation of the Lord's Prayer. This blessing invoked God's care for the couple and asked that they be conformed to all the holy married couples of Scripture. Following the ancient and Pauline preference that a Christian marry only once, the blessing was given only at a first marriage, even when a subsequent marriage occurred after the death of a spouse.[41]

After the chanting of Mass, the procession returned to the home of the groom for the wedding banquet. To this day, in Italy, the banquet overshadows the solemnities at the church. Oddly, in the Middle Ages, the couple departed before the banquet, leaving the festivities to the families and invited guests.[42] The spouses presumably had other things on their minds. At this midday feast, one course followed another, and wine flowed freely. Those who could afford it hired mimes and minstrels to entertain at the party.[43] There was dancing, and when the crowds grew large and boisterous, there might be problems. After Don Scanabecco de' Ramponi of Bologna had married the daughter of Don Scappo de' Scappi, his faithful retainer Gurono of Sala drew blood from a guest of the bride's family, Bartolomeo de' Beccadelli, because the latter had performed a lewd dance with a certain "woman of low character" (*domicella minus honesta*). This had dishonored the family and the couple. Bartolomeo probably meant it as a joke, but relatives on both sides unsheathed their swords. The podesta himself had to come and reconcile the parties.[44] Weddings could make families, but wedding parties could cause feuds. Both were a public matter. Many concerns led late-thirteenth-century communes to limit the numbers present at wedding banquets. But even they excepted men of rank, such as doctors, lawyers, and university professors, from limits on the number of wedding guests.[45]

Communities in Procession

Like families, the larger communities of neighborhood and city created and expressed their order and unity by public rituals. As for families at weddings, processions provided a finely tuned expression for corporate identity. Any-

---

40. For the Roman rite, see Pont. Rom. (xii), 37.1–15, pp. 260–61. On this pontifical, see Cyrille Vogel, *Introduction aux sources de l'histoire du culte chrétien au Moyen Âge* (Spoleto: Centro Italiano di Studi sull'Alto Medioevo, n.d.), 206–8. For a local Italian version, see Gabriella Airaldi, *Le carte di Santa Maria delle Vigne di Genova (1103–1392)*, Collana storia di fonti e studi, 3 (Genoa: Bozzi, 1969), docs. 113–15; even monastic rituals included this Mass, as in Bologna, Biblioteca Universitaria, ms 1767, fol. 114ᵛ.

41. *X* 4.21.1 and 3; Pont. Rom. (xii), App. 8.1–23, pp. 300–302.

42. As is implied in Florence Stat. 1 (1322), 5.12, pp. 226–27.

43. See Ravenna Council (1286), 1, p. 615.

44. Girolamo de' Borselli, *Cronica Gestorum* (1269), 29.

45. Ferrara Stat. (1287), 77, p. 399 (six women, ten men); Florence Stat. 1 (1322), 5.7, p. 222 (ten of each sex—exceptions for professionals); Pisa Stat. ii (1313), 3.59, pp. 352–53 (ten of each sex); Modena Stat. (1327), 4.176, p. 478 (no more than twelve total).

one could take part in processions, laity and clergy, men and women. A procession was one rite where laity and clergy were on equal footing, if not in positions of equal honor. One did not need to be ordained or know Latin to march in procession. From the 1100s forward, processions proliferated until the streets of the communes suffered from liturgical congestion. In Florence on feasts of the Virgin, confraternity processions were rerouted through Piazza Santa Maria Novella to avoid traffic jams with the communal processions going past the duomo.[46] Processions, by their order of march, made social order visible. When formed by particular groups—neighborhood associations or cappelle—they made these intentional communities visible. Corporate participation in a procession expressed the group's identity to onlookers; an individual's presence indicated membership. A successful procession not only claimed social place, it ordered those who occupied the place. It expressed a living order.[47]

To those whose spiritual senses could pierce the heavens, the other world presented itself in similar ordered motion. The blessed Benvenuta Bonjani saw the saints entering the heavenly sanctuary. They came in procession. As in the earthly rite, the women came first, followed, in place of honor, by the Blessed Virgin. Then came the male saints, according to their rank and dignity. Finally, Christ himself. Like a celebrant at High Mass, he entered after two angelic acolytes, a subdeacon, and a deacon. Arriving two by two before the altar of heaven, each celestial pair made a profound bow and filed into the choir stalls. Having reached the throne, Christ intoned the Mass *Rorate Caeli,* which all sang melodiously.[48] High Mass, whether in the duomo or the court of heaven, followed the same rubrics.

The procession before solemn Mass was the origin and model of all other processions. Bishop Sicardo of Cremona commented on this procession; he must have participated in it countless times.[49] His text fills the gaps in Benvenuta's vision. At Cremona, the bishop entered his cathedral to the sounding of all the church bells. Before him went all the others in the procession: Seven acolytes with lighted candles led. Next came seven subdeacons, seven deacons, and seven priests, representing the ranks of the ecclesiastical hierarchy. Preceded by three acolytes with lighted censers came the priors of the city's twelve collegiate churches. Last, in the place of honor, came the bishop. Before him a subdeacon carried the sacred Scriptures; to his left walked the deacon for Mass, and to his right the archpriest of the cathedral. The numerology of the procession provided Sicardo the allegorist with food for thought: seven gifts of the Holy Spirit, seven virtues, twelve apostles. The

---

46. See, on processions, Meersseman, *Ordo,* 2:950, and Webb, *Patrons,* 16–17.

47. On use of rituals to create order, see Mary Douglas, *Natural Symbols: Explorations in Cosmology* (London: Routledge, 1996), and Victor Turner, *The Ritual Process: Structure and Anti-Structure* (Chicago: Aldine, 1969).

48. Corrado of Cividale, *Vita Devotissimae Benevenutae,* 3.28, p. 157.

49. Sicardo, *Mitrale,* 3.2, cols. 92–93.

bishop and his escort were the image of the Trinity. Like Christ, he was received by the Gentiles (the three incense-bearing acolytes are the Magi) and proclaimed by the Old Testament (the subdeacon carrying the Bible).

At Pisa, on the feast of the Holy Cross, a procession carried a relic of the True Cross from the sacristy to the altar; other holy days also had their own special processions.[50] The procession was too powerful a symbol to relegate to the interior of the duomo. At Pisa again, on the feast of the dedication of the duomo, the bishop arrived for High Mass on horseback from his residence. The city clergy, present already for the night Office, welcomed him at the cathedral's great western doors.[51] In cities of the so-called Ambrosian Rite, such as Milan, morning Lauds and evening Vespers both ended with a procession out of the cathedral for a circumambulation of the baptistery.[52] In late-twelfth-century Bergamo, custom dictated a procession of cathedral clergy each Sunday to a different cloister of nuns. The canons arrived chanting the praises of the Blessed Virgin, whose handmaids the nuns were. Each Sunday was a symbolic little Easter, and the virgin nuns symbolized the Holy Virgin. As good medieval Catholics knew, even if the Bible did not mention it, the resurrected Christ appeared first to the Virgin Mary before showing himself to the Magdalene. These processions reenacted the Lord's appearance to his mother on Easter morning.[53]

The clergy of Pisa had a procession each Friday to the Camposanto, the cemetery of the cathedral complex, to recall Christ's death on Good Friday for the sins of humanity. In this procession, a litany for the dead suitably replaced Verona's Sunday chants to the Virgin. The processional used in this rite was written in large letters for myopic bishops—and the edges of the pages are black with grease from centuries of episcopal thumbs.[54] Clerical processions like these focused on the clergy and the bishop. The primary readers of their symbols were the city priests who came to participate, and read them they must. At Bergamo in 1135, Bishop Gregorio, a Cistercian who had taken office the previous year, requested from Pope Innocent a letter commanding the city clergy to be present for the major processions of the cathedral clergy.[55] Every time they participated, they reaffirmed their subordination to their new monk bishop. Participation was a sign of submission to the Ecclesia Matrix.

Processions did more than express subordination and hierarchy. They validated the identity and dignity of the neighborhood chapels. Sometimes

---

50. Bologna, Biblioteca Universitaria, ms 1785 (late xii cent.), Rolando the Deacon, *Liber de Ordine Officiorum*, fol. 45r; for the saints' days, see ibid., fols. 36ᵛ–37ʳ.

51. Ibid., fols. 51ʳ⁻ᵛ.

52. Enrico Cattaneo, "Il battistero in Italia dopo il Mille," *Miscellanea Gilles Gérard Meersseman*, ed. Maccarrone et al., 1:181.

53. Verona, Biblioteca Capitolare, ms lxxxiv (xii cent.), fol. 107ʳ.

54. Verona, Biblioteca Capitolare, ms dccxxxvi (xiii cent.), *Ordo Benedicendi seu Rituale ad Usum Ecclesie Pisane*, "Ordo Processionis," fols. 55ᵛ–57ᵛ.

55. Valsecchi, *Interrogatus*, 68.

the cathedral chapter itself paid respect, coming in procession to honor the titular saints of individual cappelle on their patronal feasts. In the communal period, titular processions proliferated everywhere.[56] At Siena, the canons went in procession to San Lorenzo on its patronal feast.[57] Were there other processions there? We do not know. But at Bologna, with more than fifty urban chapels, they were a weekly event. The processions had social as well as religious dimensions. The patronal feast not only brought a more splendid liturgy than usual, it included a parish party. In Bergamo, Don Galdo of San Vincenzo explained, the canons of the duomo went in procession to the city chapels on the vigil of their patronal feasts. They helped chant Vespers, as on the morrow they would help chant Mass. After Vespers, there was a supper, with wine, fruit, and "clouds" (*nebule*)—fine white rolls of special quality.[58] The canons of San Vincenzo made processions to the city's other major church, Sant'Alessandro, each Friday and Sunday during certain times of the year. The cappellani of the city joined these processions, and the duomo rang its bells.[59]

We should not overemphasize the role of the cathedral clergy in these patronal festivities. They provided the music and gave dignity to the occasion, but the real festival belonged to the chapel priests and their laity, to the parish itself. These feasts multiplied without hierarchical direction during the communal period. In early-fourteenth-century Verona, the confraternity of the lower clergy had already instituted and organized their own version of the rite. They made Friday processions to the chapel of each confraternity priest in rotation. On the day of the capella's festival, the priests of the surrounding neighborhoods came in procession with their people for the celebration. Activities included a sermon as well as food and drink. The confraternity requested and received an indulgence for those attending.[60] Even with music, spiritual benefits, and abundant food and drink, such events could not have succeeded without being popular with the laity. And so they were. Saint Bona of Pisa, a lay penitent, intervened to end a squabble among the clergy of San Michele de Orticaria so that the parish procession could leave for the feast of San Giacomo in Podio. The procession from San Michele arrived on time. Saint Bona, it is said, herself arrived early—by levitating and flying the distance.[61] Even saints did not risk arriving late for a parish party.

Clerical processions were theology in motion; when the whole city itself marched, this was political theory on the move. Towering in importance

56. See Cattaneo, "Spazio ecclesiale," *Pievi e parrocchie*, ed. Erba et al, 1:473, on the popularity of such rites during the 1200s.

57. *Ordo Senensis*, 1.384, p. 346.

58. "Instrumentum Litis" (September 1187), 3.28, p. 173; on the *nebule*, see ibid., 111 n. 331.

59. Ibid. (September 1187—Galdo, primicerio of S. Vincenzo), 3.28, p. 170; 5, p. 201.

60. Rigon, "Congregazioni," 16.

61. *Vita [Sanctae Bonae Virginis Pisanae]*, 3.32, p. 150.

above all the lesser processions were the two great processions of the spring-
time. Unlike other processions of the year, these involved the entire city,
clergy and laity. They traversed not a single neighborhood but the entire
city. Medieval Christians knew these as the Major Litanies on the feast of
Saint Mark the Apostle (25 April) and the Minor Litanies on the three days
before Ascension Thursday (forty days after Easter). Neither of these events
was "minor," and the Minor Litanies were the more impressive and important. The Major Litanies were very ancient, predating even the feast of Saint
Mark with which they coincided. From the eight century, at least, writers
linked this ceremony to the *Robigalia,* the ancient pagan procession to ward
off crop blight.[62] Saint Claudius Mamertus of Vienne supposedly instituted
the Minor Litanies, or Rogation Days, after a great fire in 469. Pope Leo III
(795–816) introduced them into Roman practice, and from there they spread
throughout Europe.[63] Both observances were old by the age of the communes, and the cities happily observed them, creating a fitting expression of
unity and order.[64]

The processions of both litanies were identical in form. First came the
city clergy. They had a processional order among themselves: Leading were
acolytes with candles and incense, then the processional cross and banners
of the city. Next came deacons and subdeacons carrying the city's major
relics, then the bishop carrying his pastoral staff, followed by a priest sprinkling holy water. As the parade moved, the city churches pealed their bells.
To the symbolist, the clergy represented an image of the leaders of the holy
people of Israel. The candles and incense were the pillar of fire and the pillar
of cloud of Exodus. The reliquaries represented the ark of the covenant; the
bishop with his crosier, Moses with his staff. The sprinkling of holy water
recalled the rites of the Passover Lamb in Egypt. The bell ringing during the
procession evoked the memory of the trumpets that threw down the walls of
Jericho.[65]

The symbols evoked sacred power, and the processional order did not
reflect mere allegorical fancy. Popular attention focused especially on the
city's relics. The right to carry them and their order in procession could
generate contention. Resolution of disputes over this privilege might even
require intervention from Rome.[66] Each city had a different order. Prior
Galdo of San Vincenzo explained the practices at Bergamo. There the arch-

62. So Sicardo, *Mitrale,* 7.6, col. 368.

63. On these rituals, see John Baptist Mueller, *Handbook of Ceremonies* (St. Louis, Mo.: Herder, 1956),
341–42.

64. For north Italian practice generally, see Sicardo, *Mitrale,* 7.6, cols. 367–70.

65. See commentaries on symbolism in ibid., col. 370; *Ordo Senensis,* 2.39, p. 439; Verona, Biblioteca
Capitolare, MS LXXXIV, fol. 114ʳ. The Minor Litanies also recalled the journey of the apostles to Mount
Olivet, as in Sicardo, *Mitrale,* 7.8, col. 373.

66. For examples of this, see Valsecchi, *Interrogatus,* 68–73, 118–22. On use of relics in processions, see
Nicole Herrmann-Mascard, *Les reliques des saints: Formation coutumière d'un droit* (Paris: Klincksieck, 1975),
197–200. I thank Paul Flemer for referring me to this book.

priest of Sant'Alessandro had the privilege of carrying the casket with the bones of Saint Cassian during the Litanies of Saint Mark, but he wore the relics of Saint Vincent around his neck, showing deference to the major church of the city.[67] In Siena, where the image of the Madonna of the Vow recalled her aid in the defeat of the Florentines at Montaperti, her votive images and icons took precedence even over the city relics.[68] The new people of God, like the Israelites of old, set out in procession overshadowed by divine presence and power.

The commune was the new people of God, and in the spring processions, one could see its proper order. Following the bishop came the people, not in a promiscuous mass, but according to their states of life. After the city clergy came the monks and canons regular; third, the nuns; fourth, the children; fifth, the unmarried; sixth, widows; and finally, the married, all two by two.[69] The rogations were a civic celebration. All work was suspended, and shops closed so that even servants and housemaids might also attend.[70] At Verona and Siena, a folkloric element—almost certainly used elsewhere but undocumented—dramatized the defeat of evil. During the three Rogation Days, an effigy of a dragon, symbolizing the Devil, was carried before the cross and candles. During the first two days, the dragon came before the cross and city banners, with his long powerful tail inflated and erect, showing his power during the ages before and under the Old Law. But on the third day, the dragon's head and tail drooped down, and he followed behind the processional cross, as a captive prisoner of Christ Crucified. In this, the third age, that of Grace, Christ had defeated the Devil and robbed death of its sting.[71]

As befitting a procession begging God's mercy on the city, the city observed a Lenten fast during the rogations.[72] As the clergy chanted the penitential psalms and the litany of the saints, the procession moved with a slow and solemn tread. Dante alluded to the possibility that those participating shed tears of sorrow and repentance.[73] The rogation procession began with the chanting of the rogation Mass in the cathedral church. Siena added an additional votive Mass, "for help in any affliction," at the church where the procession terminated.[74] The processional chants of the clergy expressed the religious meaning of the rite. First the clergy sang the seven penitential psalms, which they would have known from memory. Then the cantors began the Litany of the Saints in responsorial form. This was especially

67. "Instrumentum Litis," 1.1, p. 129.

68. Kempers, "Icons," 97.

69. Sicardo, *Mitrale*, 7.6, col. 368C.

70. Ibid., col. 369B.

71. Verona, Biblioteca Capitolare, MS LXXXIV, fols. 113ʳ–114ᵛ; *Ordo Senensis*, 1.222–28, pp. 204–19. On the customary use of the dragon, see Sicardo, *Mitrale*, 7.6, col. 368D.

72. Ibid., col. 369; *Ordo Senensis*, 1.224, p. 206.

73. Dante, *Inferno*, 20.7–9, describing the diviners: "E vidi gente per lo vallon tondo | venir, tacendo e lagrimando, al passo | che fanno le letane in questo mondo."

74. See *Ordo Senensis*, 1.343–44, pp. 315–18.

adapted to processional use by the laity. The cantors invoked each saint by name, and all answered with the simple chant "Ora pro nobis" (Pray for us). The litany, one of the most popular of Catholic lay devotions in the communal age, remained this popular until the Vatican Council of the 1960s. In the manuscript of the Pisan ritual at the University of Bologna library, the litany of saints is the most worn and soiled part, evidence of heavy use—some leaves have even fallen loose and been pasted back in.[75] In the late Middle Ages the Milanese produced a marvelous scroll, with ever-growing numbers of Lombard saints, for use by the cantors on Rogation Days.[76] As the processions grew longer, even the seemingly endless list of saints was not enough. The psalms and litany might be repeated as many times as necessary to provide suitable "traveling music."

In their original agricultural use, the rogation processions circled the fields of the village and returned for final prayers at the village church. This was not practical in an urban environment like that of the communes. So the Italians adapted the ritual, each city mapping out routes to the sacred sites of the city. Rogations in Italy sanctified the city itself and mapped its sacred geography. The procession circled minor churches along the route, to the sound of their bells. On the way, the clergy entered particular "stational" churches through their great western doors, singing a chant to honor each patron. At the conclusion of the chant, the bishop intoned a collect invoking the protection of the church's saint.[77] Bishop Sicardo of Cremona said of the rite: "As we approach any church, it is as if we were entering the Promised Land. So we enter the church singing, as though we were joyfully returning to our homeland. When we carry the reliquaries around the church to the sound of bell ringing, it is as if we have circled Jericho with the sound of trumpets and the shouts of the people."[78] The peculiarities of streets and the size of the churches determined the selection of stational churches, but sacred numbers gave an overall symbolism. At Milan during the Minor Litanies, the processions of the first and third days stopped at twelve stational churches, in honor of the Twelve Apostles. The middle procession stopped at nine: the square of the Trinity, the principal article of faith. Each procession passed through a different third of the city.[79] Even in small communes,

75. Bologna, Biblioteca Universitaria, MS 1785, Rolando the Deacon, *Liber de Ordine Officiorum*, has these pasted in out of order; the proper order would be fols. 56ʳ⁻ᵛ, 54ʳ⁻ᵛ, 61ʳ⁻ᵛ.

76. Milan, Biblioteca Ambrosiana, MS Z 256 Sup., *Rotulus Letaniarum in Letaniis Minoribus Ambrosianis* (XIV–XV cent.).

77. See "Instrumentum Litis," 3.28, p. 172, for Verona practice in 1187. For a late example, see Giuseppe Ferraris, "Le chiese 'stazionali' delle rogazioni minori a Vercelli dal sec. X al sec. XIV," *Bollettino storico vercellese* 4/5 (1975): 9–92.

78. Sicardo, *Mitrale,* 7.6, col. 370C: "Cum ad aliquam ecclesiam tendimus, tunc quasi ad terram promissionis accedimus. Cum ecclesiam cantantes introimus, quasi gaudentes ad patriam pervenimus. Cum circa ecclesias feretrum campanarum compulsione portamus, quasi cum arca, cum sono tubarum, cum cangore populi, Jericho circuimus."

79. *Manuale Ambrosianum*, 2:245–69. Day 1 (ibid., 245–54): From the main gate to (1) S. Simpliciano, (2) S. Carpoforo, (3) S. Protesio in Campo, (4) S. Vittore ad Ulmo, (5) S. Vittore a Corpo, (6) S. Martino, (7) S. Vincenzo, (8) S. Ambrosio, (9) S. Vitale, (10) S. Valerio, (11) S. Naborre, (12) S. Vittore a Refugio.

routes carefully included all parts of the city. San Gimignano had its processions, imitating the rituals of its diocesan center, Volterra. This small hill town managed to find enough churches, shrines, and chapels to provide stational points for elaborate rogation processions. But sometimes the people had to sing the litanies outside a church door, as at chapels like San Pietro in Salice, which were too tiny to enter.[80] Outside the walls, the contado received its holiness by association. Florence forbade processions to leave the city for the countryside; the contado got its blessing by its dependence on the city.[81]

In a hilly city like Siena, numerological multiplication of stational churches proved impractical. The Sienese cut their stational churches to a minimum.[82] Instead, they elaborated the rites along the way, preserving, of course, the circumambulation of the reduced number of stational churches. On the first rogation, the procession went to San Lorenzo to hear a sermon from the bishop, passing three stations along the way (San Peregrino, San Cristoforo, San Donato). Mass was celebrated at Santa Petronilla, and the clergy returned to the duomo chanting Terce and Sext along the way.[83] The next day, they made four stops: stations at San Desiderio and San Martino, a sermon at San Giorgio, and Mass at Sant'Eugenia.[84] On the third rogation, after a circumambulation of San Quirico they chanted Terce and Sext at San Matteo. The last rogation ended with Mass and a sermon at the Arco di Castrovecchio.[85] Perhaps to compensate for the lack of stations, the Sienese added a fourth procession on Ascension Day itself. After the construction of the new baptistery under the duomo, the entire city assembled there and then climbed up the hill—in imitation of the Apostles' assent of Mount Olivet—to enter the duomo in procession through the great west door.[86]

In rural areas throughout Europe, chanting the opening verses of the Gospels while crossing the fields was a common rogation practice. Siena's four processions suggest that the clergy recited the openings of a Gospel during each procession, a practice known elsewhere. At Verona, during circumambulation of stational churches, a deacon chanted one Gospel while

Day 2 (ibid., 254–60): (1) S. Fidele, (2) S. Dionisio, (3) S. Romano, (4) S. Stefano, (5) S. Calimero, (6) S. Agata, (7) S. Nazario, (8) S. Alessandro, (9) S. Giovanni. Day 3 (ibid., 260–69): (1) S. Eufimia, (2) S. Cleso, (3) S. Nazario, (4) S. Eustorgio, (5) S. Laurenzo, (6) S. Sisto, (7) S. Genesio, (8) S. Maria a Circulo, (9) S. Quirico, (10) S. Giorgio, (11) S. Sebastiano, (12) S. Maria di Bertrada.

80. *Ordo Officiorum della cattedrale [volterrana] (anno 1161), De Sancti Hugonis Actis Liturgicis*, ed. Mario Bocci, Documenti della Chiesa volterrana 1 (Florence: Olschki, 1984), 139–43, editing Volterra, Biblioteca Comunale Guarnacci, MS 273, fols. 57r–59r, and San Gimignano, Biblioteca Comunale, MS 3, fols. 66r–69v.

81. As noted by Trexler, *Public Life*, 6; cf. later practices in Spain: William A. Christian Jr., *Local Religion in Sixteenth-Century Spain* (Princeton: Princeton University Press, 1981), 115.

82. See *Ordo Senensis*, 1.226, pp. 208–9.

83. Ibid., 1.226, pp. 208–16.

84. Ibid., 1.227, p. 217.

85. Ibid., 1.228, pp. 217–18.

86. Ibid., 1.232, p. 221.

facing each of the four points of the compass.[87] These texts were especially pregnant with sacred power, symbolically containing the whole of the Gospel that followed. Their mere recitation could bring healing and fend off demons. When Palmaria, a matron of Viterbo, jostled an old woman during the consecration of Santa Maria di Orçanse by Pope Gregory IX, the crone cursed her. She miscarried and fell deathly sick. Only after a priest chanted Gospel verses over her at the tomb of Saint Ambrogio of Massa did she regain her health.[88] Saint Agnese of Montepulciano witnessed the exorcism of a possessed woman from Aquapendente performed by reading Gospel verses over her.[89] As with human bodies, so with civic spaces. Chanting the four Gospels toward the cardinal directions could cleanse and protect a sacred building. At Bologna during the Litanies of Saint Mark, the procession circled the city walls, stopping at the four principal gates, San Matteo, San Pietro, San Niccolò, and San Vitale. At each gate, the bishop himself chanted a Gospel incipit toward the respective cardinal direction.[90] Pisa blessed the gates and countryside using a similar rite.[91] In the ancient statute books of both Volterra and Verona, verses of the four Gospels appear in an appendix.[92] The texts of Volterra are especially interesting, for they incorporate, not the opening words of the four Gospels, but pericopes focusing on Christ's miraculous powers and dignity. During the Saint Mark processions in these two cities, it seems, the bishop chanted the words of power out of the very law book of the city.

Although the origin of processions was ecclesiastical, they came naturally to reflect the civil order. Communal governments adopted the procession to their own use. In later medieval Florence, city processions became a central administrative concern and left their mark on city documents and laws—their expense had grown heavy, the closing of shops burdensome.[93] In the golden age of the Italian republics, civic processions were never as elaborate as ecclesiastical ones. The earliest examples were ad hoc, assembled to welcome dignitaries. Cities modeled these on the reception of monarchs, the royal entry. They used the same form for church dignitaries. Don Pietro Pace, canon of San Vincenzo, described how Bergamo welcomed a cardinal, emperor, or imperial representative in the late 1100s. The clergy came to meet the dignitary at the city gate and led him first to the duomo and then

87. Valsecchi, *Interrogatus,* 70.

88. *Processus Canonizationis B. Ambrosii Massani,* 49, *AS* 68 (Nov. IV), 594–95; on this saint, see Lansing, *Power and Purity,* 129–33.

89. Raimondo of Capua, *Legenda Beate Agnetis de Monte Policiano,* ed. Silvia Nocentini (Florence: Galluzzo, 2001), I.11., p. 26.

90. Bologna, Biblioteca Universitaria, MS 1785, Rolando the Deacon, *Liber de Ordine Officiorum,* fols. 44^{r-v}.

91. Ibid., fols. 32^{v}–33^{v}.

92. Volterra Stat. (1210 and 1224), pp. 103 and 107; Verona Stat. 1 (1228), pp. 209–12.

93. As noted by Trexler, *Public Life,* 213.

to greet the bishop.[94] The Bolognese so welcomed Pope Gregory IX in 1227 and Pope Innocent IV in 1250.[95] The Milanese clergy and people all turned out to meet the cavalcade of the emperor Otto in 1209, providing a choir of virgins and young boys to serenade him.[96] But on these occasions the true procession was that of the dignitary's cortege, not the people. The city clergy and laity were spectators, a backdrop for princely splendor, at best an escort.

Reception of outsiders was more the exception than the rule in the communal period. The most important receptions happened once or twice a year, when the city received a new podesta. In that ritual, the ordered society welcomed and incorporated into itself a new administrative and judicial head. The Bolognese included rubrics for the procession among their municipal laws.[97] There the new podesta entered on horseback by the main gate. Joined by the Bolognese judges and other administrators, he went in procession to the cathedral of San Pietro, where he entered and prayed. Next the procession marched the short distance to the Palazzo del Comune. There the new podesta dismounted and, taking in his hands the four Gospels, swore his oath of office in the name of God the Father, Jesus Christ, the Holy Spirit, the Virgin Mary, and the Holy Angels Michael and Gabriel. The ceremony proclaimed the union of the Mother Church and the commune under their heavenly protectors. Only after completing this rite could the podesta enter and take control of the palazzo.

As acts of the whole society, such rites of welcome and incorporation, like the Litanies, ordered the parts of the civic body. On 28 October 1253, the feast of Saints Simon and Jude, the commune of Reggio in Emilia turned out to welcome their bishop-elect, Guglielmo of Foliano. He arrived accompanied by Gilberto de Gente, podesta of Parma, and officials (*anziani*) of that city. A procession of city corporations with their banners and ecclesiastical colleges with their crosses welcomed him at the city gates. All entered the city to the sounding of trumpets and the pealing of church bells.[98] A procession like this had its own order. The standard-bearer and trumpeters of the commune led the procession. Behind them came the neighborhood and craft associations, and finally the chief city magistrate.[99] The associations had their own order of precedence, usually in order of the "dignity" of the craft or the date of the group's foundation.[100]

94. "Instrumentum Litis," 3.27, p. 177.

95. *CCB:* A (1227), 94; (1250), 129.

96. Galvano Fiamma, *Manipulus Florum* (1209), 242, col. 663. Similar popular acclamations greeted the entry of Archbishop Otto Visconti in 1277, an arrival that effectively ended the popular commune in Milan: ibid. (1277), 313, col. 705.

97. Bologna Stat. II (1288), 1.3, 1:7; cf. the forms of 1282: ibid., 1:284–85 n. 1; on the ordering of corporations in processions, see Pini, *Città, comuni e corporazioni*, 264–65, 273–76.

98. *Mem. Pot. Reg.* (1253), col. 1119.

99. Pini, "Le arti in processione," 82–83, summarizes the procession at the election of the doge Lorenzo Tiepolo in 1268.

100. See ibid., 84–89, for summaries of the order of precedence at Padua (1287), Cremona (1313), Regio (1318), Ferrara (1322), Modena (1327), Milan (1385), and Brescia (1385).

On 22 March 1291, when his hometown of Parma welcomed back Gerardo Bianchi, now cardinal bishop of Santa Sabina, they modeled the procession on that for a new podesta.[101] The Popolo of the city marshaled under
the banners of the neighborhoods. Followed by the Arti and the religious
houses, they met him at the gate. They placed him, like a new podesta, on a
horse to enter the city. As in a rogation procession, Cardinal Gerardo came
last, in the place of honor, riding under a scarlet canopy. All marched to the
episcopal palace, where he was to lodge. Cardinal Gerardo was a good guest.
During the days that followed he presented great gifts (*magna dona*) to the
podesta, Ungaro degli Oddi of Perugia, and to the captain of the people,
Lapo degli Ughi of Pistoia, as well as made offerings to the religious houses
of the city. When he left, a similar procession escorted him to the gates. Only
with the end of communal independence did government processions revert
to spectator events, in which the prince rode in pomp and his subjects
watched from the sidelines.[102]

Processions imploring divine help during adversity were even more an
expression of civic unity and identity than those to welcome dignitaries.
These processions took their form from the rogations rather than royal en-
tries. As with the original rogations, natural disasters, especially drought,
demanded such observances. At Parma, at the beginning of May in 1303,
during the height of a dry spell, the city organized processions throughout
the city. They chanted the litanies and carried the relics of the saints. The
observance had effect, and a torrential downpour arrived on the feast of
Saint John before the Latin Gate (6 May), sparking universal rejoicing.[103]
Such observances usually included a vow to commemorate any help received, often by repeating the procession annually in perpetuity, or at least,
as at Parma, by recording it in city chronicles.[104] Perhaps because war threatened the very independence of the commune, it was the calamity most likely
to spark processions. War and defeat resulted from sin. When the twelfth-
century city of Gubbio underwent a terrible siege, its bishop, Saint Ubaldo,
organized processions to ask for forgiveness. According to their ranks and
orders, the clergy, laymen, and laywomen went barefoot chanting the litanies. Mass and Communion were celebrated. Bishop Ubaldo fortified the
city with a special episcopal blessing. The citizenry was the image of the
people of Israel in the desert. Their leader, like Moses, extended his hand of
blessing over them. Ubaldo stood on the city walls, invoked the God of
Battles, and prayed for liberation from the new Egyptians and Philistines. At

101. *Chronicon Parmense,* 60–61.
102. As can be seen at Bologna in *CCB:* A, Vill. (5 February 1327), 276–79, which describes the
reception of the papal governor Cardinal Bertrando Del Pogetto.
103. *Chronicon Parmense* (1303), 84.
104. A practice that outlived the Middle Ages: Christian, *Local Religion,* 185.

the sight of the bishop, the enemy fled in terror. The army of Gubbio fell upon them; there was great slaughter and, afterward, great rejoicing.[105]

For efficacy, processions did not require episcopal blessings or leadership. In May of 1233, the itinerant Dominican preacher Fra Giovanni of Vicenza organized penitential processions at Bologna to invoke divine help in ending a general war in Emilia. Peace, or at least a temporary truce, followed.[106] Podestas organized penance processions, as Manfredo of Coranzano did at Parma on 3 June 1239. The clergy and people carried the relic of the True Cross, and God showed his favor by an eclipse during the very ceremony.[107] Peace was restored. Marshaling of the city could have a natural as well as supernatural effect. On 19 April 1287, ambassadors of Cremona arrived at Modena to negotiate an end to hostilities. They encountered fierce resistance from the Modenese authorities. With negotiations deadlocked in the Palazzo Comunale, the archpriest of the duomo organized a procession of the clergy and people. Led by the usual incense, cross, and candles, the people marched according to their ranks and orders. In the place of honor came the ark bearing the arm of Saint Giminiano, patron of Modena. As the people chanted the litanies, divine grace moved the city fathers. They concluded a perpetual truce with Cremona "to the honor of Saint Geminiano and the whole court of heaven."[108] Even worldly governors had to yield when faced with such a display of earthly and heavenly unity.

The most famous intercessory ceremony of the entire communal period took place at Siena in 1261, before the Battle of Montaperti. On that occasion, while organizing prayers for deliverance, the city made vows to the Virgin. After the victory, they fulfilled them by building a chapel to commemorate the victory. Today, this Cappella del Voto enshrines a votive image of the Virgin, the *Madonna del Voto,* properly called the *Madonna delle Grazie,* the "thank-offering" presented to Saint Mary in gratitude for the victory.[109] Popular piety identifies that image with the vow of 1261, but the actual image before which the vows were made was the *Madonna di Mezo Rilievo,* or *Madonna dei Occhi Grossi,* an early-thirteenth-century local production, stylistically primitive and rigidly frontal, which resides today in the Opera del Duomo. The Sienese moved this *Madonna with the Large Eyes* from the high altar to a little tabernacle by the side door of the duomo to allow the people immediate access to such a great victory-bringing talisman. The

105. Giordano of Città di Castello, *Vita Beati Ubaldi Eugubini Episcopi,* 14.6–15, p. 101.

106. Girolamo de' Borselli, *Cronica Gestorum* (1233), 22; see also Thompson, *Revival Preachers,* 52–62.

107. Salimbene, *Cronica* (1239), 240, Baird trans., 156.

108. *Chronicon Parmense* (1287), 52.

109. On the Madonnas discussed here, see Henk W. Van Os, *Sienese Altarpieces, 1215–1460: Form, Content, Function* (Groningen: Bouma, 1984), 11–20; supplemented by Kempers, "Icons," 89–136, and Norman, *Siena and the Virgin,* esp. 21–34. For the fifteenth-century legend, see Van Os, *Sienese Altarpieces,* 11.

new image known today as *Madonna del Voto* replaced it on the high altar. There it remained, far from popular devotion, until the Sienese moved it to the new Chapel of the Vow to make space on the high altar for the installation of Duccio's great *Maestà* in 1311.[110]

After 1261, the *Madonna with the Large Eyes* took the place of the relics usually carried at Siena in the Major and Minor Litanies.[111] Victory and rogations would always be linked at Siena. In a law drawn up after the battle, the city was to make an annual commemoration of the divine help at the church of San Giorgio, the "great and powerful standard-bearer and protector" of the city.[112] Each year the podesta, the captain of the people, the chamberlain, the standard-bearer, and the priors of the city were to offer two candles in gratitude for a long list of victories by Siena over its neighbors. As a perpetual memory, they included the list in the city statutes. Processions were made to implore help, but, as at Siena, candles were given to celebrate the city's victories and deliverance. It was wax, not images, that fueled the most intense moments of communal celebration.

CANDLES AND THE COMMUNE

Among Catholics candle lighting was and remains an archetypically lay devotion.[113] Even in their law books, the cities displayed a careful, by modern standards obsessive, attention to wax, wicks, candles, and the rituals involved in their use. Like processions, medieval candle piety appropriated a liturgical practice. The Feast of the Presentation (2 February) was the great candle feast of the liturgical year, Candlemas. On that day, a priest blessed all the liturgical candles to be used in the coming year.[114] As with the Litanies of Saint Mark, the February candle ceremony was a Christianization of an ancient pagan rite that predated the liturgical feast.[115] But here the union of the feast and the rite, unlike that of Saint Mark and the Major Litanies, made some sense. Medieval Catholics knew that the Virgin Mary, like all women, came on this date—precisely forty days after her son's birth at Christmas—to offer candles at the Temple in thanksgiving for her safe delivery. This day, the church celebrated the feast of her Purification. When people carried and offered candles on this day, the city became a collective representation of Mary rejoicing in Christ, born in their midst through

110. On Duccio's image, see Van Os, *Sienese Altarpieces*, 39–61.

111. On these images, see Kempers, "Icons," 98–110, who notes the use of the Madonna with the Large Eyes in "Ascension Processions." E. B. Garrison has subjected narratives concerning the votive images of the Virgin of Montaperti to extensive critique; see Webb, *Patrons*, 253–55, who takes a middle position similar to my own. On the confusion of the two Madonnas in popular piety, see ibid., 265–66.

112. Siena Stat. 1 (1262), 1.123–26, pp. 54–56.

113. For a general study of candles in the Christian cult, see D. R. Dendy, *The Use of Lights in Christian Worship* (London: SPCK, 1959).

114. For a Candlemas blessing of the 1180s, see *Rituale di Hugo [di Volterra]*, 322–23.

115. This origin was known in the Middle Ages: *Ordo Officiorum della cattedrale [volterrana]*, 69 (San Gimignano, Biblioteca Comunale, MS 3, fol. 19ᵛ; Volterra, Biblioteca Comunale Guarnacci, MS 273, fol. 19ʳ).

preaching and the sacraments. The commune itself represented the priest Simeon and the prophetess Anna, who held Jesus, the Light of the World, in their arms when Mary presented him in the temple.[116] Mary's Purification, her "churching," involving as it did the offering of candles, was a fitting time also to bless candles.

On the Purification at Siena, the canons chanted Terce as they came into the duomo in procession. The celebrant, usually the archpriest, blessed and mixed salt and water, creating holy water. He then handed a lighted candle to each present, clergy and laity, as they kissed his hand.[117] Then, as the canons chanted Simeon's Song from Lk 2:29–32, the "Nunc Dimittis," he sprinkled the tapers with holy water. The candles carried in procession that day were alight.[118] Each of the faithful carried a living flame, not a dead candle, and so bore a fitting symbol of the living Christ—as the Dominican preacher Bartolomeo of Braganze explained in his sermon for the day.[119] Then the bishop and clergy, followed by the laity, went in procession, carrying their candles, to an altar erected outside the church, where the clergy sang chants in honor of the Virgin. The procession returned to the duomo for the Mass, entering the church singing the chant "Cum Induceret Puerum Iesum" (When they brought the boy Jesus into the Temple).[120] The worshipers came forward to offer their candles at the altar. After Mass, the people received blessed tapers for devotional use at home, thereby allowing them to extend the festival throughout the year. The cathedral canons of Siena recalled this special day by a candle-lighting ceremony on the vigils of major feasts.[121] In some cities, magistrates gave public banquets on that day, Saint Mary of the Candlemakers, to celebrate entry into office.[122]

The candle-offering ritual recommended itself to lay piety. Zita of Lucca offered a candle to Saint Mary Magdalene each year on her feast. What Zita did privately, offering a candle on a day special to her, the communes did corporately. Candle offerings punctuated the civic year. They accompanied municipal elections. At Padua, according to an enactment of 1267, the forty members of the Paduan Great Council, which elected the three rectors of the subject city of Vicenza, began their consultation by going two by two to the altar of the Palazzo Comunale and offering a lighted candle. This ritual

116. Sicardo, *Mitrale*, 5.11, cols. 243–44.

117. *Ordo Senensis*, 1.322, pp. 298–99.

118. Bologna, Biblioteca Universitaria, MS 1785, Rolando the Deacon, *Liber de Ordine Officiorum*, fols. 41^{r–v}.

119. Bartolomeo of Vicenza, *Sermones de Beata Virgine (1266)*, Sermo 111.3, p. 739: "Candela sine lumine dicitur mortua." *Ordo Officiorum della cattedrale [volterrana]*, 68–70 (San Gimignano, Biblioteca Comunale, MS 3, fols. 19r–20^r; Volterra, Biblioteca Comunale Guarnacci, MS 273, fols. 19^v–21^r), places special emphasis on each individual's carrying a lighted candle, so as to imitate Mary when the procession enters the church.

120. See Pont. Rom. (XII), 27.1–11, pp. 206–8. A sermon by the bishop sometimes followed, e.g., *Ordo Senensis*, 1.319–25, pp. 297–301.

121. See Kempers, "Icons," 95.

122. E.g., Biella Stat. (1245), 1.1.5 (5).

had a practical element; the council members had to complete the election before the candles burned out.[123]

At Bologna, the officials (*anziani*) of the city inaugurated their term by offering (at their own expense) a one-pound candle of fine wax in the church of San Giovanni in Monte. Those of the autumn term offered candles on the feast of Saint John the Baptist (24 June), those of the spring term on the feast of Saint John the Evangelist (27 December).[124] The Sienese captain of the people offered candles on titular feasts in the different churches where courts met.[125] At Bologna, the city fathers expressed thanks to churches, like Santa Maria in Porta Ravennate, where they conducted city business, by having city officials attend the church's patronal feast—when the largest number of parishioners would be present—and make a candle offering.[126] The Bolognese societies of the Popolo imposed obligatory attendance at candle offerings when the city made them an official gesture of respect. If a society made a devotional offering to a church or religious house on its own, none could be forced to attend.[127] In some cities, candle offering became so distinctive a public rite that city law forbade it on private occasions, such as a priest's first public Mass or a nun's profession.[128]

Offerings marked days of particular importance to city history. The Bolognese marked their victory at Castro Bassano on 6 July 1247, the feast day of Saint Isaiah the Prophet, by a candle offering. On the anniversary, the podesta and his officials carried forty candles to the church of Sant'Isaia and offered them to God, the Virgin, and the victory-granting prophet.[129] Annual candle offerings to city patrons were universal by the mid-1200s. In Bologna, the two oldest patronal offerings each consisted of forty pounds in wax candles. The city made one at the duomo on the vigil of its patron, Saint Peter, the other at the chapel of the commune on the vigil of its titular, Saint Apollinaris of Ravenna.[130] The podesta carried his candle personally, as did each member of the smaller and greater city councils. The podesta or one of his judges weighed the candles and tested their wax quality in the church itself as they were presented at the altar. At Padua, the day set aside for the cult of Saint Anthony brought the closing of shops and expulsion of women of ill fame (but just for the day). A procession of representatives from the associations (*fratalie*) of the Popolo offered candles at his shrine.[131]

123. Padua Stat. (1267), 1.29, p. 108, no. 335.
124. Bologna Stat. 1 (1245–50), 1.10.
125. Siena Stat. 1 (1262), 1.315, p. 120.
126. Bologna Stat. 1 (1262–67), 7.146, 2:168–69.
127. Bol. Pop. Stat., 1 (Vari, 1265, c. 34), 356.
128. Bologna Stat. II (1288), 4.92, 1:248; Mantua Stat. (1303), 1.45, 2:94; Florence Stat. 1 (1322), 5.6, p. 221.
129. Bologna Stat. 1 (1250), 5.3, 1:441–42.
130. Ibid. (1250), 5.2, 1:439–41.
131. Padua Stat. (1257), 2.10, p. 181, no. 558; (1269), 2.10, p. 181, no. 557.

Unlike processions, which always carried marks of their churchly origins because of the necessary presence of the clergy, communal candle offering was a lay ceremony, and its forms bespoke the sensibilities of lay piety. Responsibility for candle offerings fell to the rectors of the city, not the bishop. At Ravenna, city statutes put the podesta under oath to organize the biannual candle offerings at the church of San Vitale.[132] At the commune's determination and expense, he organized the offerings of his knights, judges, notaries, and officials. They assembled with their candles at the monastery of San Vitale the night before, so as to be ready to lead the city on the morning of the feast. That morning messengers summoned both the men and the women of Ravenna (*mares et mulieres ravenne*), under penalty of a 5s. rav. fine for failure to appear. In Ravenna, government leaders alone made the actual offering; elsewhere more people participated. At Mantua, the city as a whole made one candle offering yearly, at the duomo on the feast of Saint Peter (29 June). Organized as at Ravenna, the rite differed in that representatives of the societies of the commune joined city officials in the offering.[133] Mantua later added a second offering on the feast of Saints Philip and James (3 May) at the Augustinian monastery of Sant'Agnese. This was truly a mass offering. Heralds and trumpeters circulated throughout the city two days before, reminding all men of the city (*omnes milites et pedites et omnes boni viri*) to be present for Mass on the feast. At this Mass, each citizen offered his candle.[134]

By the 1260s, Parma had systematized its annual offerings. On vigils of the Assumption and Saint Lucy's day, that city sent criers to announce the events.[135] The next day, all presented themselves with candles in hand. It fell to the podesta to check attendance and punish any "enormity." Along with the people's individual candles, the commune offered two one-pound candles for altar use. Each city chapel and baptismal church presented a five-pound candle inscribed with its name.[136] The candles remained on display in the church—doubtless the labels on the large ones did something to discourage theft, an abuse Lucca had to enact laws to control.[137] The rites of candle offering acquired popular touches. At Gubbio, for example, the traditional candle offering became an athletic spectacle. The candle offering on Saint Ubaldo's feast there remains to this day a major holiday. During its festivities, the *ceri*, huge, heavy candles, are carried up the hill to the town—in a contest to see who can carry the biggest candle up the fastest.

132. Ravenna Stat., 356–61, pp. 169–72.
133. Mantua Stat. (1303), 5.1, 3:93.
134. Ibid., 5.2, 3:93.
135. Eventually offerings were added on the feast of Saint Hilary as well: Parma Stat. II (1266), 158.
136. Ibid., 155–58.
137. For these laws, see Domenico Barsocchini, *Dissertazioni sopra la storia ecclesiastica lucchese*, 2.1, Memorie e documenti per servire all'istoria del ducato di Lucca (Lucca: Bertini, 1844), 5:1:11 n. 3.

The first up makes the first offering. This aspect of the cult may not actually be medieval, but it certainly captures the lay ethos of candle offering.[138]

We catch glimpses of the crowd dynamics as people made their offerings. In early-fourteenth-century Perugia, members of the large Confraternity of the Virgin had an annual offering.[139] At the sounding of the church bells, people formed up, women and men separately, to receive candles from those in charge, giving them in return a money offering (2d.). The people heard a sermon while holding their candles, the sexes on separate sides of the church. This finished, the men went in procession with lighted candles, singing a vernacular *lauda,* around the nave and cloister before depositing their candles. The women, however, remained, with their lighted candles, "devoutly and quietly" in the church. Men as well as women were to show proper devotion at candle offerings. At Parma, the population made mass candle offerings on the feasts of the Assumption of Mary (15 August) and of Saint Lucy (13 December). On one occasion, pushing and shoving in the line of candle offerers got out of hand. In response, the city rectors, Giovanni Nessi and Giovanni Arlotti, joined the council of "ancients" (*anziani*) in leveying a £300 parm. fine for jostling or shouting.[140] This may have stopped the pushing, but some impatient citizens resorted to throwing their candles over others' heads toward the altar. The city enacted a fine for that too.[141]

As the century wore on, offerings multiplied. By the 1260s, the Bolognese podesta, knights, judges, notaries, and other officials were obliged to make processions and candle offerings at the churches of the Dominicans, Franciscans, and Augustinians, as well as an offering at the tomb of the new city patron, Saint Petronio, in Santo Stefano.[142] By the end of the century, this multiplication of offerings threatened to turn devotion into routine. As traffic in candles increased, so did occasions for abuse. The merchant guild at Piacenza once discovered adulterated candles on sale in their town. They ordered them publicly burned in the Piazza Santa Brigida and imposed a 3s. placen. fine on adulterators.[143] Bologna and Parma were plagued by inferior votive candles. They legislated on wick quality (fine linen to be used), wax purity (beeswax only), and appointed a commission to examine the candle molds and oversee production.[144] Such legislation affected candles for religious use only, not those for simple illumination. Votive wax quality affected the integrity of a corporate act of worship and devotion. Inferior wax shamed the commune. Some cities directly supervised the production of candles for

---

138. I am obliged to Fr. Eugenio Marino, O.P., of Santa Maria Novella in Florence for describing the feast at Gubbio to me.

139. "Statuto della Congregazione della Vergine di Perugia (1312)" 1, Meersseman, *Ordo,* 2:1063.

140. Parma Stat. 1 (1232), p. 282.

141. Ibid. (1228–55), 202.

142. Bologna Stat. 1 (1262), 5.2, 1:441.

143. Piacenza, *Statuta Antiqua Mercatorum Placentiae, Statuta Varia Civitatis Placentiae,* Monumenta Historica ad Provincias Parmensem et Placentinam Pertinentia, 1 (Parma: Fiaccadori, 1855), 108.

144. Parma Stat. 1 (1228–55), p. 202; Bologna Stat. II (1294), 5.153, 1:572–75.

offering at feasts. Parma appointed an official votive-candle maker in each quarter to assure size and quality; at Pisa, the podesta contracted out candle production to trustworthy artisans.[145] At Florence and Modena, too, the communes eventually passed laws to protect the quality of votive candles.[146]

By the end of the communal period, candle offering had undergone a not-too-subtle change in character. The first offerings were individual devotional acts. By the 1280s, Pisa, not atypically, simply delivered so many pounds of candle wax to the various city churches and religious institutions along with other alms.[147] Early-fourteenth-century Modena diverted fines for fraud in weights and measures to keep the vigil candles alight in the churches of San Gimignano and San Giovanni of Cantono.[148] Bologna statutes confirm a shift from devotional oblation to corporate almsgiving, although they still stipulated that city officials hand over the wax in person after procession to the church on its patronal feast. Eventually, wax alms were converted to cash.[149] At Ravenna and Imola by the early 1300s, the reduction of candle offerings to alms in wax seems complete. Their statutes simply listed city churches and their annual gift.[150] The linkage of wax and devotion was lost. In 1306, the city of Bologna determined (by a council vote of 264 to 104) that the podesta would arrange for the standard-bearer and the ministers of the popular societies to go to San Domenico on its patronal feast and offer £100 cash, not wax, at the altar. They went in procession, carrying large candles and with flags flying, to show honor to the founder of the Preachers.[151] Ten years later, the Bolognese Società dell'Aquila gave £4 14s. 4d., and that of the notaries £10 4s., at the altar of San Francesco on his feast.[152] No longer was there mention of a procession. Monetary offerings like this were rare or nonexistent earlier.[153] As the communal period ended, candle offering became less a work of piety and more a compulsory assessment to support religious institutions. City corporations sought to limit their "tax rate." The Lombards in Bologna had to make a candle offering on Pentecost to the abbot of the monastery where they met. They limited by statute the amount that would be spent on trumpeters and drummers (30s. bon.) and the value

145. Parma Stat. II (1266), 157 (candles for the Assumption); Pisa Stat. I (1275), p. 48; Pisa Stat. II (1313), 1.207, p. 224.

146. Modena Stat. (1327), 2.31, p. 248; Florence Stat. II (1325), 3.13, p. 187, where the statute comes in the midst of legislation against blasphemy!

147. Pisa Stat. I (1286), 1.57, p. 142.

148. Modena Stat. (1327), 2.33, p. 249.

149. Bologna Stat. II (1288), 11.5, 2:193–94. Modena Stat. (1327), 6.1, p. 682, mixes wax and money alms as a matter of course.

150. Ravenna Stat., 358, p. 170; Imola, *Statuti di Imola del secolo XIV I: Statuti della città (1334)*, ed. Serafino Gaddoni, Corpus Statutorum Italicorum, 13 (1334), 4.50 (Milan: Hoepli, 1931), 299–302.

151. Bologna, Biblioteca Universitaria, MS 89.XI.1, fols. 2ʳ⁻ᵛ.

152. As we know from the Franciscan financial records in Bologna, Biblioteca dell'Archiginnasio, MS B.490 (1769, from XIV cent. original), p. 110; other alms are given for 1331, in ibid., p. 154: Societas Specialorum, £6; Societas de Lignanis, £14 5s. The manuscript is paginated, not foliated.

153. Bol. Pop. Stat., I (Lombardi, 1291, c. 16), 66; see revision in ibid. (Lombardi, 1255, c. 59), 20.

of the candles (3s. bon.).[154] But they still went in procession and offered real beeswax. And Florence, at least, continued to institute new candle offerings well into the fourteenth century.[155]

Honoring the Virgin and the City

That some wax offerings became routine did not rob the candles of their popularity and symbolic power. By the late 1200s, in nearly every city, one candle offering took on a new life, that on the Assumption of the Blessed Virgin into heaven, the feast of Saint Mary in August. The doctrine that Christ's mother was taken up—assumed—bodily into heaven at the end of her life, and its celebration on 15 August, were both very ancient by the thirteenth century. The Church liturgy of the day was innocent of any candle rituals. The August offering was distinctly civic, a fusion of two lay devotions: communal candle offering and petition to the Mother of God in times of distress. As a celebration of Mary the intercessor in heaven, this feast rivaled, even overshadowed, the other great feast of the Virgin, Saint Mary in Lent (25 March), when the archangel Gabriel made the Annunciation of the birth of Christ. As the feast of Mary's entry into heaven, the Assumption recommended itself as the time for ritualizing homage to Mary as intercessor at God's side. On this date, the cities paid republican homage to their heavenly queen. Only cities that early lost their republican government, for example, Mantua under the Bonacolsi or Ferrara under the Este, failed to establish the Assumption offering. They too developed Marian candle offerings but avoided the image of Mary as the city's *domina* by having them on some other feast.[156]

The August offering was nearly universal, and its rites were remarkably similar everywhere. Publicity for the event began as much as two months ahead.[157] It peaked a week before, when the commune dispatched heralds and trumpeters to the city and countryside.[158] Messengers received new livery for the occasion, that they might fulfill their task with decorous splendor.[159] During preparation week, the militia suspended exercises. Proper observance demanded a time of peace during which each citizen could be on hand to offer his candle, even if this meant recalling the army from the field. Only in the most dire circumstances might troops make their offerings while on campaign.[160] Within the walls, the podesta hired street cleaners to remove trash and obstructions from the streets and squares where proces-

---

154. Ibid. (Lombardi, 1291, c. 18), 67.
155. E.g., at Florence in 1325: Florence Stat. II, 5.48, p. 395.
156. Ferrara Stat. (1287), 2.116, p. 93, on candles for Saint George; Mantua Stat., 3:93, on offering and palio for Saint Peter. On the palio, see Golinelli, "Dal santo," 22–23.
157. E.g., Pisa Stat. II (1313), 1.207, pp. 222–24.
158. As in Brescia Stat. (1273), col. (121).
159. As in Parma Stat. II (1266), 164; Parma Stat. III (1316), 114, 144–45.
160. See Parma Stat. I (1248), p. 203, on the purpose of the feast, and ibid. (by 1255), 84, on the suspension of military actions. See also Parma Stat. III (1316), 113–14.

sions would take place. Crews scrubbed the cathedral inside and out.[161] The government suspended the tolls and fees imposed on those coming from the countryside.[162] Cities themselves took charge of candle production, enlisting trustworthy men, such as the Brothers of Penance, to make candles or supervise their quality. Those in charge erected booths in the main piazza to sell "official" candles. Anyone who dared smuggle in "alien" or adulterated candles faced severe penalties.[163]

Although ceremonies took place in the ecclesiastical center, the cathedral, the rites themselves created a special link between the civic community and its heavenly protectress. As the day of the feast approached, cities further sanctified the already sacred time. Brescia suspended treasury functions (*rationes*) for the three days preceding the feast. Severe fines punished those who would dared defile the occasion by riot or breaking the peace. With the striking of Terce on the vigil, all shops closed, except those authorized to sell candles.[164] Horseback riding within the walls was prohibited after None of the vigil.[165] By that hour, citizens were to be assembling at the duomo, not gadding about. In the square outside the duomo, an assembly ground was set up. The Pisa Council of Ancients festooned their loggia with vermilion drapery; and in the Piazza dei Miracoli, workmen erected the "tent of the city," also of vermilion stuff, as a reviewing stand for the marshaling of citizens before the procession to the cathedral.[166]

The candle offering in August had two parts. One was the people's offering of homage to Mary, the other the city's candle offering. Homage took place at Vespers of the vigil, chanted by the bishop and his cathedral clergy. The candle offering took place on the feast-day morning. Unlike Vespers, this rite did not require the clergy or bishop, although the cities hoped for their presence. The podesta and magistrates of Pisa sent an invitation two weeks before the feast, asking the bishop to grace the ceremonies with his presence and bring his canons and clergy along to offer candles with the magistrates.[167] For civil magistrates attendance was obligatory. At Piacenza, the offering to Saint Mary in August was the magistrates' only obligatory ceremony of the year—no exceptions were allowed (*sine tenore*).[168] As a corporate act of the commune, the presence of the citizens was essential to both

161. Parma Stat. I (1228–55), p. 203, with a 6s parm. fine for those who dirtied it up afterward.

162. As in Pisa Stat. I (1275), pp. 46–48, 51.

163. As in Parma Stat. I (1228–55), p. 203, where the fine for alien candles is 100s. parm.

164. Brescia Stat. (1273), col. (121); (1313), 1.118, cols. 35–36. On special fines, see Vicenza Stat. (1264), 201.

165. Pisa Stat. I (1275), pp. 46–48; (1286), 1.154, p. 265.

166. On the feast of the Assumption at Pisa, see ibid. (1286), 1.154, pp. 263–84; Pisa Stat. II (1313), 1.207, pp. 219–25.

167. Pisa Stat. I (1275), p. 45; repeated in ibid. (1286), 1.154, p. 263, and Pisa Stat. II (1313) 1.207, p. 219. Ravenna similarly requested the presence of the bishop and chapter for their large candle offering on Pentecost: Ravenna Stat., 353, p. 167.

168. Piacenza, *Statuta Antiqua Mercatorum Placentiae*, 164–65.

rituals. In practice, not every adult male had to come, but only householders and heads of families. The podesta imposed attendance on them under oath.[169] At Pisa, the director of the Opera Sanctae Mariae, the cathedral building fund, stood in a prominent place on the reviewing stand, holding the city Gospel book on which officials took their oath of office.[170] Next to him, the officials of each contrada checked attendance and rigorously excluded anyone suspect as a "forger, traitor, or rebel" against the city.[171]

The citizenry arrived for Vespers just as the great bells of the duomo sounded. Absence from Vespers or failure to bring one's candle resulted in a fine.[172] Assembled in the church, each citizen attentively listened to the service, holding in his hand the candle he would offer the following day. At their head stood communal officials, the podesta, and the captain of the people.[173] During Vespers focus was on the Glorious Virgin in heaven; the city would be the center of attention the following day. At this evening rite, leaders were not to call attention to themselves. Gilberto de Gente, podesta of Parma, showed singular bad taste in 1252 when he showed up for the vigil amid great pomp—and armed no less! He came in for bitter criticism. Did he have ambitions for princely status? Such was the suspicion of Fra Salimbene of Parma.[174]

The feast-day offering began with a grand marshaling of the city.[175] Standard-bearers led each district in procession to the piazza before the church where the offering would be made. Neighborhoods and municipal associations formed committees by quarters to assure the dignity and order of the assembly.[176] Once all had arrived, the citizens, each holding his candle, fell into formation by companies. Before each company stood its captain, holding a larger, decorated candle inscribed with the name of their chapel, to represent the group as a whole.[177] At the sounding of trumpets, each company, led by a standard-bearer or by cross and candles, marched past the reviewing stand and, under the watchful eyes of the city fathers and (perhaps) the bishop, approached the sacristy door or the commune's ceremonial door in the side of the cathedral.[178] There they offered their candles to an official

---

169. Pisa Stat. I (1275), p. 45; Pisa Stat. II (1313) 1.207; Brescia Stat. (1313), 1.118, cols. 35–36; Parma Stat. III (1316), 114.

170. Pisa Stat. I (1275), pp. 48, 51.

171. Siena Stat. II (1310), 1.64, on "falsatori et traditori et ribelli."

172. Parma Stat. I (1228), p. 201 (20s. parm.)

173. Pisa Stat. I (1286), 1.154, p. 265; Pisa Stat. II (1313), Popolo 128, p. 566. Florence had the standard-bearers of the districts present at this service: Florence Stat. II (1325), 4.1, p. 304.

174. Salimbene, *Cronica* (1252), 654, Baird trans., 549.

175. On this kind of offering, see esp. Florence Stat. II (1325), 4.1, pp. 303–5.

176. E.g., the fifteen-member committee for the *corredo* in Bol. Pop. Stat., 1 (Lombardi, 1291, c. 19), 67–68.

177. Parma Stat. I (1248), p. 203; Pisa Stat. I (1275), p. 46; repeated in Pisa Stat. II (1313), 1.207, pp. 222–24.

178. Siena Stat. II (1310), 1.36, 1:66 (which legislation actually dates to 1200); Parma Stat. III (1316), 115. On the ceremonial door and use of crosses instead of standards, see Vicenza Stat. (1264), 202. At Modena, this was one of the rare times when the Porta Regia was used: Modena Stat. (1327), 6.1–2, pp. 680–85.

of the Opera del Duomo. At Modena in the 1260s, the districts of the city entered the duomo by the Porta Regia and approached the altar itself to make their offering. The corporate banners along with the candles remained on display throughout the octave of the feast.[179] Sworn representatives of the commune usually witnessed the offerings. At Siena, a notary carefully recorded each candle as the one offering handed it over.[180] Brescia, not satisfied with mere witnesses and notetakers, conducted a candle audit after the ceremony.[181] When the officials were satisfied that everything had been done with honesty and order, sacristans placed the candles of the various districts on display in the great church as a sign of the city's self-oblation to the Queen of Heaven.[182] The candles remained on view until the next year's offering, after which they were dedicated to altar use. Surplus candles were then sold and the proceeds dedicated to the fabric of the Mother Church.[183]

Candle offering was no mere sign of devotion and piety. It was a display of civic identity and political order.[184] Political identity became visible as the companies of each district marched into the piazza for the marshaling that preceded the offering. Political order manifested itself as they queued up to make their offerings. The political nature of the ritual dictated that citizens and no others—be they foreigners, women, or children—march with the corporations of the commune. The noncitizens acknowledged the city by their presence as observers, looking on from upper windows or street corners. As a company passed through its own district to the city center, it became a representative of those left at home. Passing through other districts of the city, it claimed its space in the political fabric. Whether the march was orderly or disorderly, the claim was made. Unlike Vespers, which the canons began whether everyone had arrived or not, the offering could not begin until every neighborhood was present. Arrival in the piazza followed a prescribed order, for nothing is more divisive than waiting for late groups to make their appearance. The podesta and officials ensured that protocol was followed, lest the unity of the city be compromised.

In candle offering size mattered. The greater gave greater offerings according to a careful hierarchy; the powerful came first. The candle offering at Pisa had a precise order of precedence for the four quarters, and a hierarchy of districts within each quarter. In each delegation's offering, quarter officials offered first, followed by the individual cappelle.[185] Candles showed the importance of their bearers by size and design. At Vicenza, the podesta

179. This thirteenth-century legislation is included in a 1326 law in Modena Stat., 6.1–2, pp. 680–85.
180. Siena Stat. II (1310), 1:66 (again in legislation dating to 1200); Brescia Stat. (1273), col. (121).
181. Brescia Stat. (1313), 1.118, cols. 35–36.
182. Parma Stat. I (1248), p. 203; Siena Stat. II (1310), 1:67–68; Lucca Stat. (1308), 1.42, p. 46.
183. Florence Stat. II (1325), 4.1, p. 303.
184. A reality captured nicely by Paolo Nardi, "I borghi di San Donato e di San Pietro a Ovile: 'Populi,' contrade e compagnie d'armi nella società senese dei secoli XI–XIII," *Bullettino senese di storia patria* 73–75 (1966–68): 41–42.
185. Pisa Stat. II (1313), Popolo 131–33, pp. 571–87; Pisa Stat. II (1324), pp. 1226–28.

offered a large candle of "at least" ten pounds; city councilors each gave three small candles, while other officials presented only one.[186] Lucca carefully codified the offerings by number and weight in a law of 1304.[187] That city's great offering took place on the Illumination of the Holy Cross (7 May). The rector of the city and his knights and judges carried two lighted *duplones* (three pounds of wax each) and eight lighted ordinary candles (two pounds of wax each). The captain of the people, with his knights and judges, presented two duplones but only four ordinary candles. The members of the council of ancients, the chancellor, and the city notaries each presented a one-pound candle. After them came representatives of the twenty-two urban cappelle, each of whom presented a flower-decorated candle weighing from six to twenty-five pounds, according to the size and dignity of their parish church. The chapels marshaled by quarters, according to the gates of the city. The citizens of each chapel, men between seventeen and seventy years of age, came behind their chapel's corporate candle. They stood waiting as the director of the Opera Sanctae Crucis checked wax quality and tested candle weight.[188] Next came the suburban communes of Controne, Lulliano, Montesubmano, and Montefegatese, each offering a twelve-pound candle. Behind them were the twenty-one pievi of the vicariate districts, each with a candle of twelve pounds; next, the nineteen dependent communes, each offering a four-pound candle. Last came a variety of subject towns and villages, offering twelve-, eight-, or four-pound candles.[189] The hierarchy of power reflected in wax weight and precedence would not have been lost on observers.

Subject towns and villages were not truly citizens of the republic, and their offerings exposed their subordination in a naked manner. The little town of Baccagnano recognized the overlordship of Faenza in 1192, after the podesta of that city, Antonio di Andito of Piacenza, had seized it from Count Guido Guerra IV of Modigliana. This was a great victory in Faenza's war to free its contado from the count's control. As proof of subordination, Baccagnano annually offered eight to ten pounds of wax to the Mother Church of Faenza.[190] At Parma, where the podesta appointed governors to outlying towns and villages, delegations from those towns brought candles to the city to express their subordination.[191] For outsiders, participation in a city candle offering signaled their dependence on the city making the offering. Some towns, especially small ones, fined their citizens who participated in other

---

186. Vicenza Stat. (1264), 201.

187. Lucca Stat. (1308), 1.42, pp. 35–46.

188. See the candle statute from the lost 1261 statutes of Lucca in Domenico Barsocchini, *Dissertazioni sopra la storia ecclesiastica lucchese*, 2.1, pp. 11–14, n. 4; for a later version, see Lucca Stat. (1308), 1.42, pp. 44–46.

189. For a similar hierarchy of candles, see Florence Stat. II (1325), 4.13, p. 310.

190. Maestro Tolosano, *Chronicon Faventinum*, 118, p. 113.

191. Parma Stat. I (by 1243), pp. 162–63.

towns' vigils or offerings, since this implied subjection.[192] At Pisa, the subject lords of Sardinia and the communes of the contado offered candles along with the city officials, chapels, and societies in the August ceremonies, but they did not deliver them to the sacristy. As a mark of their subjection to Pisa, they brought them directly to the city office (*curia*). Their wax acknowledged, not the overlordship of Saint Mary, but that of the commune of Pisa. They surrendered candles, and these were to be big ones too (*candeli grossi*).[193] Size did not represent power here; this was tribute. There were candles offered to the Virgin and candles offered to the city; no one forgot the difference.

Candle offerings at the end of a parade—for what is a procession but a parade?—provided a suitable ritual for patronal and Marian feasts, but they did not make the feast a festival. Suspension of work, the presence of people from the contado inside the walls, and even operation of the market gave license for other entertainments.[194] The clergy of Novara in 1210 complained that people were dancing and singing "lascivious" songs in the streets after Mass on feast days. If they did not desist, the clergy would bar them from entering the church for services.[195] Much as the city fathers loved a festival themselves, disorder had to be kept within bounds, lest the piety of the commonwealth come into question. The Vicentines did not outlaw dancing, chatting, littering, and children's games on their festival of the Crown of Thorns, the city's chief relic. They removed such goings-on from the church of Santa Corona, its piazza, and cemetery to other parts of the city, lest they disrupt candle offerings or interrupt the sermon. Prostitutes relocated to another neighborhood for the day too.[196] Cities struggled to control the rock fights between teams of youths (*battaglie dei giovani*) that happened during festivals. "Youth battles" continued, with teams representing the various neighborhoods, but outside the walls.[197] If left unsupervised, the festival fun could become rowdy. At Lucca, the consuls dispatched police to the contrade, the neighborhoods, of San Martino and San Regolo on their patronal feasts. On Holy Cross Day, they stationed armed men around the church of San Frediano, where that relic was enshrined. Exuberance still got out of hand. The Lucchese fretted over immodest acts (*turpitudines*) and assaults on women (*rapina*) during patronal festivities. Consuls of contrade who failed to control such disorders were fined £10.[198] Feasts drew both the pious and the profane.

192. E.g., Biella Stat. (1245), 3.14 (74).
193. Pisa Stat. 1 (1286), 1.154, p. 265.
194. On feast-day markets, see Ravenna Stat., 290, p. 133, and 294–95, pp. 136–37; Modena Stat. (1306/7), 2:143.
195. Novara Synod 1 (1210), 29.
196. Vicenza Stat. (1264), 201–2; on the prostitutes, see ibid., 203.
197. On such games in Florence, see Giovanni Ciappelli, "Carnevale e quaresima: Rituali e spazio urbano a Firenze (secc. XIII–XVI)," *Riti e rituali nelle società medievali*, ed. Chiffoleau, Martines, and Paravicini Bagliani, 163–65.
198. Lucca Stat. (1308), 1.7, p. 12.

Processions, candle offerings, dancing, singing, and rock fights were "popular," insofar as they were open to all, or at least all male, members of the commonwealth. These were participatory activities. One group seems absent from communal celebrations, the military aristocracy, whose position the communes had subverted from their very inception in the twelfth century. The knightly class did not cease to exist; it remained an essential part of the communal army. Nevertheless, when present for the republican ceremonies of the Assumption, the knights were part of a "bourgeois" crowd. At Parma by midcentury, even the making of knights had been subsumed in the republican Assumption festivities. Church ritual blessed the sword and shield.[199] But the city made the Parmese knights; any citizen with sufficient money to buy a horse and arms might present himself, with communal approval, to get them blessed.[200] The early communes had tolerated greater aristocratic visibility. In 1198 Spinello de' Carbonesi was killed in the piazza of Bologna when he fell off his horse while *bagurdando* (tourneying).[201] Under the Popolo, with its antiaristocratic prejudices, cities excluded chivalric games, at least for a while. But the republics had to make a public place for their aristocrats. Florence grudgingly turned its "boys' battles" into "chivalric games"—jousts.[202] But it did so only after the knights had recommenced tournaments themselves—to compete with communal processions on the feast of Saint John the Baptist.[203]

Chivalric games underwent a republican transformation. The joust on horseback became a horse race, the palio, so called from the cloth banner (*pallio*) that usually formed the prize. The palio retained something of a military flavor. When Cremona defeated the army of the emperor Henry VII on the feast of Saint Bartholomew, the city ordered an annual palio in honor of the saint.[204] During the war with Arezzo in 1288, the knights of Florence ran a palio around its besieged city's walls. They mocked their exiled bishop, who had taken refuge there, by displaying mitered asses' heads below the walls.[205] The Florentines forced subject cities to supply palios, in this case precious cloth, as a sign of subordination.[206] Verona had two palios, one a foot race, the other a horse race. The Veronese made merry with the contestants who came in last. They tied a *baffa* around the neck of the jockey who

199. Pont. Rom. (xii), App. 9.1–3, p. 302.

200. Parma Stat. 1 (by 1255), p. 200.

201. Matteo Griffoni, 7. In the fourteenth century, jousts and aristocratic games reappear; e.g., the joust of Saint Leonard in Parma Stat. iii (1316), 114.

202. See Ciappelli, "Carnevale," *Riti e rituali nelle società medievali*, ed. Chiffoleau, Martines, and Paravicini Bagliani, 163–65, and Stefano Gasparri, "I rituali della cavalleria," ibid., 101.

203. On this, see Trexler, *Public Life*, 218.

204. Cremona Stat. (1313), 105. On the mixture of civic, spiritual, and merely recreational elements in the palio, see Webb, *Patrons*, 211–12.

205. Giovanni Villani, *Cronica*, 7:120. On this event, see also Trexler, *Public Life*, 4 n. 9.

206. See Trexler, *Public Life*, 262.

placed last in the horse race. The last contestant in the foot race got a hen as consolation prize, which he had to carry through the city to general amusement.[207] Imola ran a palio to honor their patron, Saint Cassian—with prizes of a scarlet cloth (the palio), a piglet, a falcon, and a pair of falconer's gloves. The city provided £25 for the prizes and commissioned a trustworthy agent to buy the cloth at the Bologna markets.[208] In contrast, the Bolognese ran one of their palios on 29 June, the feast of their cathedral's titular, Saint Peter. The race recalled the Bolognese defeat of Imola on that date in 1153 and may have been a survival of chivalric games of an early date. After Bologna later subjugated Imola, that city had to supply the palio cloth as a sign of its subordination.[209] The palio of Saint Peter was open to any rider who registered within three days of the race, and its prize was a scarlet cloth worth £20 bon. and a chicken. The prize and date may be stereotypical and have no symbolic meaning. At Mantua, on the same feast of Saint Peter, contestants raced below the city walls, also for a scarlet cloth and a chicken.[210] Before 1250, when Bologna passed laws to keep spectators off the course, the Saint Peter's palio was run along the road to San Giovanni in Persiceto. In the 1260s, the city moved it to a better location and expanded it to three races, the *scarlatus*, the *spaverius*, and the *roncinus*. The last two they later transferred to the feast of Saint Bartholomew (24 August).[211]

The chronicler Girolamo de' Borselli recounted the supposed 1281 origin of the Saint Bartholomew palio. Tibaldello de' Zambracci of Faenza had a grudge against seven members of the exiled Bolognese Lambertazzi faction then living in his city. They had killed one of his pigs and then threatened his life when he demanded reparation. In revenge, he sent the key of Faenza's city gates to Bologna so that the Lambertazzi's enemies, the Geremei, could make a copy. That faction used the duplicate to enter Faenza by night. They killed the Lambertazzi while they were at morning Mass in the church of San Francesco. After this Tibaldello fled to Bologna and was made a Bolognese citizen by public decree. In memory of this they instituted on the feast of Saint Bartholomew at the gate of Strada Maggiore the "race of the horse, falcon, two dogs, and the cooked pigs."[212] The prizes for first place

---

207. Verona Stat. II (1276), 1.47, pp. 61–62. Such prizes were common in other cities: see, e.g., Ferrara Stat. (1287), 2.116–17, p. 93, on the feast of Saint George; Modena Stat. (1327), 2.27–28, pp. 246–47, which offered a scarlet cloth, a pig, and a chicken for the palio; and Lucca Stat. (1308), 1.41, p. 35, for two palios on the feast of Saint Regulus.

208. Imola, *Statuti di Imola del secolo XIV I* (1334), 4.52, p. 303. By the time of this enactment, the palio was already traditional.

209. Orselli, "Spirito," 291 n. 7, citing the 1153 document edited in Ludovico Savioli, *Annali Bolognesi* (Bassano, 1784), 1:2:228.

210. Mantua Stat. (1303), 5.1, 3.93.

211. Bologna Stat. I, 7.118, 2:128–29.

212. Girolamo de' Borselli, *Cronica Gestorum* (1281), 32. On these palios at Bologna, see Frati, *Vita privata*, 148–49, 162–64.

were a horse (*rocinus*) and a hawk, both rather aristocratic in tone. There were two pigs for second place, one live and one roasted. There is no record of who got the dogs.[213]

Originally an aristocratic recreation, equestrian exercises became a potent symbol of communal pride, pious devotion, and republican military prowess. That combination marked the festivities in Padua on 19 June, the feast of Saint Anthony. On that date in 1256, the Paduans had expelled the tyrant Ezzelino da Romano and reestablished republican institutions. In memory of the liberation, the podesta, his curia, and the associations of the commune went in procession to the saint's basilica and attended Vespers in honor of God, the Virgin, Saint Anthony, and the other patrons of the commune. The following day, they returned in procession for a candle offering at Mass. During Mass they displayed the three prizes of the palio to be run afterward: a scarlet cloth eight meters in length, a hawk, and two gloves.[214] Padua's allied city of Vicenza instituted an identical festival to honor Saint Anthony.[215] The most famous union of Marian devotion, civic identity, and racing is, of course, the Palio of Siena, still run on the feast of the Assumption. True to its republican ethos, Siena, however, long resisted adding the race, with its flavor of knights and horses, to the candle offerings and processions of its August feast. When the race finally appeared in Sienese statutes, it took a back seat to religious rites, processions, and candle offerings.[216] Candle wax and religious processions, not horse races, remained the essence of communal self-celebration until the fall of the republics.

Sounds of Urban Order

As visible processions and candles ordered the neighborhood and city, so did sounds. Anyone who has spent a night in the historical center of Florence, Bologna, or Siena knows that even today morning differs from that in an American town. The narrow streets of the center discourage the noisy traffic that fills our cities. Morning silence in Italy is filled by bells. Thanks to the imperfection of even the best automated systems, one church always sounds before the others. As other bells join, a web of music washes over the city. The effect is powerfully suggestive, more numinous than nostalgic. Bells, consecrated by sacred rites, wrote the church fathers of Ravenna, are "useful and necessary, for by their sound the faithful are inspired to divine worship and devils are driven off."[217] Anointed with oil and named in a ceremony

213. Bologna Stat. II (1288), 12.25, 2:220–21.
214. Padua Stat. (1256), 2.10, pp. 181–82, no. 559.
215. Vicenza Stat. (1264), 7–8 n. 2; cf. Padua Stat. (1275), 2.10, p. 182, no. 560.
216. On the offerings and devotions, see Siena Stat. II (1310), 1.212, 1:178; 1.583, 1:360–62; 6.84, 2:533. On the palio, see ibid., 1.586, 1:366. On the palio of Saint Ambrose Sansedoni, instituted in 1306, see ibid., 1.56, 1:189.
217. Ravenna Council (1311), 8, p. 454: "utilis et necessaria, ad cujus sonum maxime fideles excitantur ad Divinum cultum, et daemones propelluntur."

nicknamed the "baptism of bells," each bell had a living personality that acknowledged saints and terrified devils. When Saint Torello died, the bells of his parish church rang without a hand laid to their ropes. The priest and townspeople ran to his cell. They knew that a consecrated bell rang miraculously only at the death of saints or the approach of danger.[218] The bell recognized a holy man, even when people did not. While on pilgrimage to Santiago of Compostella, Saint Contardo arrived at Bruni, near Piacenza, in 1242. He died that night in a peasant's hut—the town's innkeeper had thrown the unknown vagrant into the street. The town's bells rang in jubilation to welcome the holy man into heaven, and the locals repented of their blindness. They turned their old baptismal font into a reliquary for his body. The pilgrim vagabond was a saint.[219]

The first bell of a city belonged to the cathedral. Bologna chroniclers recorded the casting in 1227 of the duomo bell, the work of Master Ventura.[220] As Don Giovanni di Bolgare, dean of Sant'Alessandro in Bergamo, explained in 1187, bells rang each day during the opening chants of the solemn Mass, that the townspeople would know the city's principal act of worship had begun. The duomo bell rang before all other bells of the city. That his church rang first proved it to be the Mother Church of Bergamo, Don Giovanni of Sant'Alessandro explained.[221] The bells of the duomo spoke an intelligible language. At Siena, the order of peals of cathedral's two great bells—"San Ansano" and "Santa Maria"—along with a rank of smaller bells, told the liturgical rank of the feast day and which Office the canons were to chant.[222] Morning and evening peals were the pivots of the day, their order most carefully regulated.[223] Don Alberto di Scanzo, Giovanni's fellow priest in Bergamo, explained that San Vincenzo rang first for morning Lauds, evening Vespers, and Masses of the dead, sharing, in part, the privileges of Sant'Alessandro. Proper hierarchy had to be preserved. The cathedral clergy jealously guarded their bell-ringing privileges. The first peal came from the duomo, and the other churches followed in order of their rank and age. The cathedral not only rang first; other churches of the city followed its cadences. But on the feast of a chapel patron, his little church rang first, even before the duomo.[224] To deviate from this order was criminal: in Piacenza the local synod punished deviant bell ringing by excommunication.

Only orders exempted from episcopal jurisdiction by the papacy, the

<hr />

218. *Acta [B. Torelli Puppiensis]*, 2.15, *AS* 8 (Mar. 11), 497.
219. *Acta [S. Contardi Peregrini]*, *AS* 11 (Apr. 11), pp. 444–48; on the baptismal font, see ibid., 2.12, p. 447.
220. Matteo Griffoni (1227), 9.
221. "Instrumentum Litis," 6, p. 216. On bell ringing's legal status, see Valsecchi, *Interrogatus*, 94–95.
222. *Ordo Senensis*, 1.439, pp. 393–94.
223. The ringing of the Angelus at morning, noon, and night is late: Piacenza Stat. Cler. (1337), 50, pp. 554–55.
224. "Instrumentum Litis," 1.7, p. 141.

Dominicans, Franciscans, and Augustinians, could ring outside of the usual order.[225] Some grumbled against the din. At Gubbio, a traveling Franciscan, Fra Ricardo, labeled the ostentatious Dominican bell ringing that announced the vigil of Saint Peter of Verona offensive and a vanity. The Dominican Saint Peter appeared that night to Fra Ricardo in a dream and disabused him of the misconception.[226] God, his saints, and true Catholics rejoiced in bell ringing; only demons objected. No, some Catholics did have occasional problems. Fra Salimbene of Parma tells us that in Genoa the bells of morning Mass at Sant'Onorato near the Franciscan convent annoyed the friars engaged in silent meditations after their night Office. The friars turned to Pope Alexander IV. The pontiff obliged by giving them the church.[227] In the future, its bells rang in tandem with those of the Minorite convent. Perhaps the noise bothered the friars less than the order in which the bells rang.

The secular day ran by ecclesiastical time.[228] At Ravenna, the evening bells of the duomo marked the hours of the civil day and signaled the curfew.[229] San Gimignano in Tuscany was subject to Florence and had no bishop or duomo, but it had a baptismal church, and its bells regulated the communal day. The town had a special cadence for curfew. The pieve gave three distinct tolls of its bell. The pause between each stroke lasted as long as it took to walk from porta San Giovanni to Porta Nova San Matteo. Sangimignanese who threw out night soil before that bell risked a fine.[230] In most places, a church bell was also the commune bell. Modena did not buy its own bell to announce secular events until well into the fourteenth century.[231] At Bologna, where exceptionally the Palazzo Comunale already had a bell in the 1200s, the labors of bell ringing were apportioned between palazzo and duomo. Curfew began when the palazzo rang its bell for night guard duty. The duomo bell of San Pietro sounded the arrival of dawn.[232] The two custodians of the duomo, Savorotto Cavalieri and Nasimbene de' Nasimbeni, had the duty and privilege of opening the Bolognese workday. They did so by twenty distinct and solemn strokes, followed by five quick taps. That signal at other times of day or night meant there was a fire.[233]

The Church put its loudest bell in a city at the disposal of the commune

225. Piacenza Stat. Cler., 532; the Carmelites were later granted a similar exemption: ibid., 17, p. 541.

226. *Vita S[ancti] Petri Martyris Ordinis Praedicatorum*, ed. Ambrogio Taegio, 8.62, *AS* 12 (Apr. III), 713 (text from "Miracula Berenguerii," dated to 1310s). On the text of Taegio's vita and its components, see Antoine Dondaine, "Saint-Pierre-Martyr: Études," *AFP* 23 (1953): 67–73.

227. Salimbene, *Cronica* (1248), 460, Baird trans., 316.

228. I find no evidence for the dichotomy between religious time and secular time detected by Jacques Le Goff in "Au Moyen Âge: Temps de l'Église et temps du marchand," *Annales: Économies—sociétés—civilisations* 15 (1960): 417–33.

229. Ravenna Stat., 156, p. 87.

230. San Gimignano Stat. (1255), 3.46, p. 711; 3.64, p. 716, on night soil.

231. Modena Stat. (1327), 1.180, p. 171.

232. Bologna Stat. II (1288), 4.7, 1:175; (1288), 2.20, 1:95–96.

233. Ibid. (1288), 2.20, 1:95–96.

for important events. Bolognese officials rang Master Ventura's great bell to announce the daily opening of their courts to hear pleas—but not from Good Friday to Easter. During that penitential time the great bell, like all other bells, was silent. So the canons let the commune bang the big wooden clapper that replaced it.[234] The bell for the canons' solemn Mass signaled the opening of the city hall for the day's business. The ringing of Nones in the afternoon announced its reopening after lunch. Lest judges linger at table or siesta, the city reinforced the signal from the duomo by a "continuous" sounding of the palazzo bell.[235] The duomo's great bell rang to announce the execution of criminals. On the following day, it again tolled its fearful message, that the citizens might pray for the criminal's soul. And certainly he had need of prayers. Good Catholics, like Saint Zita of Lucca, prayed for those executed, not only on the day when the execution bell rang, but every day afterward for a week.[236] Fortified by sacred rites and prayers, the ordered commune extended from citizens on earth to patron saints in heaven, and from there to its wayward souls in purgatory.

234. Ibid. (1288), 6.1, 2:5.
235. Bologna Stat. 1 (1262–67), 4.8a, 1:393.
236. *Vita [Sanctae Zitae Virginis Lucencis]*, 4.30, *AS* 12 (Apr. III), 512.

Chapter Five
Holy Persons and Holy Places

A Christian society produces saints after its own image of holiness. Communal Italy was no exception. The city made the saints. Citizens found their saints, not in the monastic or clerical world of churchmen, but among themselves, the lay faithful. Recognizing holiness, they canonized it themselves, calling on the pope or hierarchy only rarely to ratify their perception. The religiosity of the period's holy persons—its saints—was really that of the city and Mother Church, albeit lived more intensely.[1] Although not wholly typical of ordinary lay piety by their very exceptional behavior and styles of life, the saints and their cults were a fixture of communal cities. Our spiritual geography of the Italian republics would be incomplete without them.

The twelfth-century cities found their saints among the spiritual fathers of the Mother Church, but these were bishops with a difference. They defended both true religion and the independence of their cities. Bishop Ubaldo of Gubbio (d. 1160) uttered prayers from the walls of his besieged city and set enemy armies to flight. This, with his many works of charity, inspired outpourings of devotion. Soon after Ubaldo's death, his successor, Bishop Teobaldo, and another contemporary, Giordano of Città di Castello, celebrated the good bishop in Latin and vernacular lives.[2] Northern communes also chose bishops as city patrons, as the Mantuans did with Anselm of Lucca, who was not their bishop but merely spent some time there while in exile.[3] The good communal bishop supported communal independence

---

1. So Richard Kieckhefer, "Holiness and the Culture of Devotion: Remarks on Some Late Medieval Male Saints," *Images of Sainthood in Medieval Europe*, ed. Renate Blumenfeld-Kosinski and Timea Szell (Ithaca: Cornell University Press, 1991), 288–305; and on the "ordinariness" of the communal saints, see Golinelli, *Città e culto*, 84–87.

2. François Bolbeau, "La vita di sant'Ubaldo," *Bollettino della Deputazione di storia patria per l'Umbria* 74 (1977): 81–82. For Teobaldo's vita, see *AS* 16 (May III), 630–37.

3. On early Mantuan communal cults, see Golinelli, "Dal santo," 12–24.

from imperial tyranny. In Lombardy, Giovanni Cacciaforte (1125–83), first prior of San Vittore at Cremona, then abbot of San Lorenzo, and finally bishop of Mantua and Vicenza, rallied Cremona to the aid of the Lombard communes in their struggle with Frederick Barbarossa. Through his sermons, he supported Cremona's own struggle for communal independence, an activity for which he paid with his life. He was also famous for his protection of citizens against the magnates of the countryside. His cleric Enrico explained that the holy bishop's murder happened because he refused to abandon a poor man while Enrico went off to buy the pauper a cloak.[4] During Giovanni Cacciaforte's canonization investigation by Bishop Omobono Medalberti of Cremona, citizens of Cremona and Vicenza testified to the holiness of their spiritual father, not only as a defender of the Mother Church but also as a pastor who took his greatest delight in celebrating the liturgy for his people.[5] More important, the good bishop saint brought internal reconciliation to his city. During one feud, Bishop Ubaldo walked out into the piazza where the factions stood ready to do battle. He lay down between the two groups as the swordplay began. The men stopped fighting, in panic that someone had struck the bishop down. This allowed the women to pour into the square, assaulting their hotheaded men and crying to high heaven for help. Ubaldo got up and slowly walked away. Contrite, factions swore to patch up the quarrel.[6] Lanfranco of Pavia (d. 1194), a member of the Beccaria family of Grupella, a village near Pavia, promoted peace between his city and its neighbors.[7] He retired to a Vallombrosan monastery soon before his death, just as an independent lay government was replacing the early communal union of city and bishop. He continued working reconciliations after death. When Pavia was to hang a delinquent, Alberto of Novara, the man prayed aloud to Saint Lanfranco for a pardon. The bishop did what the city would not. Three attempts to hang the malefactor, including one in which strong men yanked his feet, failed to kill him. So the hangmen let Alberto go, and all sang the praises of the merciful Lanfranco, the new patron of Pavia.[8]

Early communal holiness combined identification with one's city, pious orthodoxy, forgiveness, and neighborliness, virtues accessible to any devout Christian. One did not have to be a bishop to manifest these qualities. Characteristically, holiness was found among one's neighbors. The communal

4. *Inquisitio Facta Cremonae per d. Homobonum Episcopum Cremonensem de Vita et Moribus b. Joannis Cazefronte Abbatis Sancti Laurentii de Cremona postea Episcopi Vicentini,* ed. Alessandro Schiavo, *Della vita e dei tempi del b. Giovanni Cacciafronte cremonese, vescovo di Mantova poi di Vicenza* (Vicenza: Paroni, 1866), 245.

5. Ibid., 239–43.

6. Giordano di Città di Castello, *Vita Beati Ubaldi Eugubini Episcopi,* 13.3, p. 100.

7. For his life, see Bernardo Balbi, *Vita [S. Lanfranci],* pp. 533–42. For a bibliography of modern scholarship, see Alban Butler, *Lives of the Saints,* complete ed., ed. Herbert Thurston and Donald Attwater (Westminister, Md.: Christian Classics, 1991), 2:622–23.

8. Bernardo Balbi, *Vita [S. Lanfranci],* 4.42, p. 540.

period was the great age of the neighborhood saint.[9] Before 1200, the triangular region framed by Verona, Milan, and western Tuscany venerated a
legion of pious laymen.[10] Born in the cities of their later cults, they grew up
there, practiced trades, married, and exhibited a prayerful charity toward
their neighbors.[11] Throughout the thirteenth century, the cities continued
to produce homegrown saints. In contrast to the bishop saints of the early
communes, those of the thirteenth century included many laywomen, often
of humble background, like the serving girl Zita of Lucca.[12] The popular
communes added new requisites to the earlier formula of holiness: pilgrimage, personal asceticism, and social work.[13] These later saints came from
the culture of the Brothers and Sisters of Penance, and they remained lay
freelancers. Their clerical patronage came from the secular clergy, not mendicants.[14] Only at the end of the thirteenth century did the late medieval
model of holiness—clerical orders for men, ascetical and mystical seclusion
for women—begin to eclipse the neighborly style of holiness.[15]

THE CONVERSION TO PENANCE

Penance implied a turning from sin, a conversion, followed by a life of self-
denial. The pursuit of holiness through asceticism was a congenial theme for
the clerical biographers of communal saints. For clerics, "conversion" meant
leaving the "world," that is, the lay state. Consequently, saints' lives written
by clerics exaggerate the contrast between a lay saint's habits before and
after conversion. But clerical authors could not hide the reality: the communal saints continued to live in the same world after their conversion. Only
among female saints of aristocratic background, like the Este abbesses Beatrice (d. 1226), daughter of Azzo VI, and Beatrice II (d. 1263), daughter of
Azzo VII, did cloistered holiness find exemplars in communal Italy.[16] But

9. As remarked by André Vauchez, "Lay People's Sanctity in Western Europe: Evolution of a
Pattern (Twelfth and Thirteenth Centuries)," *Images of Sainthood in Medieval Europe*, ed. Blumenfeld-
Kosinski and Szell, 21–32. Vauchez, *Laity in the Middle Ages*, 59, reflects on their generally humble status.
On the shift from episcopal patron saints to lay saints, see Golinelli, *Città e culto*, 65–86, esp. 86.

10. André Vauchez, "Une nouveauté du XIIe siècle: Les saints laïcs de l'Italie communale," *L'Europa
dei secoli XI e XII fra novità e tradizione: Sviluppi di una cultura: Atti della decima Settimana internazionale di studio,
Mendola, 25–29 agosto 1986* (Milan: Vita e Pensiero, 1989), 65–66; trans. as "A Twelfth-Century Novelty:
Lay Saints of Urban Italy," *Laity in the Middle Ages*, 51–72.

11. On the social dimensions of this piety, see Vauchez, "Lay People's Sanctity," 27–28.

12. On the late appearance of female lay saints, see Vauchez, *Laity in the Middle Ages*, 58. On holy
women in Florence, see Benvenuti Papi, "Donne religiose nella Firenze del due-trecento," *In Castro
Poenitentiae*, 593–634.

13. Noted by Vauchez, "Nouveauté," 67–69, and by Antonio Rigon, "Dévotion et patriotisme communal dan la genèse et la diffusion d'un culte: Le bienheureux Antoine de Padoue surnommé le 'Pellegrino' (+1267)," *Faire croire: Modalités de la diffusion et de la réception des messages religieux du XIIe au XVe siècle*,
Collection de l'École française de Rome, 51 (Rome: L'École Française, 1981), 263–64.

14. So Miccoli, "La storia religiosa," 807–8, agreeing with André Vauchez, "Sainteté laïque au XIIIe
siècle: La vie du bienheureux Facio de Crémone (v. 1196–1272)," *Mélanges de l'École française de Rome: Moyen
Âge–temps modernes* 84 (1972): 37.

15. On this, see Vauchez, "Nouveauté," 79–80.

16. On these two women, see *Chronicon Marchiae Trevisinae et Lombardiae* (1226), 51–52, and *Annales
Sanctae Iustinae Patavini* (1263), 184–85.

theirs was not the piety of the city. Inside the walls, even *inclusae*—anchoresses—interacted with the world on a daily basis. For male saints, such an urban "hermitage" was not an option. Penitents lived at home and labored at their crafts just like their neighbors. They simply changed their clothing and abandoned a "worldly" style of life. When Pietro Crisci of Foligno "converted" around the year 1273, he sold his property and donned a simple sacklike garment, without cuffs or buttons. He had made himself a "penitent."[17]

Laypeople who took up a life of asceticism after conversion had already appeared in the twelfth century. Galgano (1148–81), patron and protector of the commune of Siena, was a rather unexceptional son in a knightly family of rather moderate wealth. Saint Michael appeared to him as he rode in the countryside. The archangel told him to dismount and build himself a hermitage at the place called Montesiepi. Galgano did so and gave away all he had to the poor.[18] His poverty did not prevent him from going on pilgrimage to Rome, however, nor did his hermitage isolate him from townspeople. He died within the year, on 30 November 1181, and immediately became the object of a cult. Four years later, during the week following 4 August 1185, a commission investigated his sanctity and examined witnesses, perhaps the first example of a "canonization inquest."[19] Galgano gave up a moderately comfortable life, went on pilgrimage, and had visions, but his sanctity lay in taking up the life of penance. The thirteenth-century communes produced similar convert saints. Giovanni Buono of Mantua (ca. 1168–1249) spent the first forty years of his life as a dissolute minstrel, wandering about northern Italy. During a severe illness, fear of death led him to petition Bishop Enrico of Mantua for permission to become a penitent. He practiced fearful mortifications and sought seclusion, first in a hermitage near Cesena and later near Mantua. But he could not escape devotees and admirers.[20] At his death, a spontaneous cult developed, and another early canonization commission investigated his life.[21]

Conversion implied a previous life of sin, but what counted as rejection of sin covered a wide spectrum. Occasionally the break was dramatic. When Pietro Crisci of Foligno (1243?–1323) repented after thirty years of wealth

17. On his way of life, see Giovanni Gorini, *[Legenda de Vita et Obitu Beati Petri de Fulgineo]*, 1.6, *AS* 31 (Jul. IV), 666.

18. *Vita Sancti Galgani*, ed. Eugenio Susi, 2–4, 6, and 10, *L'eremita cortese: San Galgano fra mito e storia nell'agiografia toscana del XII secolo* (Spoleto: Centro Italiano di Studi sull'Alto Medioevo, 1993), 189–90, 192–93, and 196–97. For Saint Galgano's earliest vita (ca. 1220), by Rolando of Pisa, see Siena, Biblioteca Comunale degli Intronati, MS G.I.2, fols. 195ʳ–196ᵛ.

19. The inquest is found in Siena, Biblioteca Comunale degli Intronati, MS K.VII.24, fols. 399ʳ–404ʳ.

20. Golinelli, "Dal santo," 24–26, which possibly exaggerates the novelty of Giovanni Buono's style of holiness. On this saint and his order, see Salimbene, *Cronica* (1248), 367–68, Baird trans., 248–49.

21. His canonization acta are extant in Mantua, Archivio di Stato, Fondo Gonzaga, Busta 3305, *Processus et Alie Scripture Pertinentes ad Canonizationem Sancti Iohannis Boni*, edited as *Processus Apostolici Auctoritate Innocentii Papae IV Annis 1251, 1253, et 1254 Constructi de Vita, Virtutibus et Miraculis B. Joannis Boni Mantuani*, *AS* 57 (Oct. IX), 778–885.

and comfort, he sold his goods to benefit the poor and sold himself into slavery. Only when redeemed from servitude by a buyer who asked nothing from him but prayers did he take up the more conventional life of a penitent.[22] Conversion usually happened in the most common of places, most ordinary of situations, and to the most ordinary of people. It did not need deadly illness, visits from archangels, or notorious bad living. Ranieri of Pisa (d. 1160), still that city's patron saint, with a splendid shrine in the south transept of the duomo, underwent two conversions, one from a frivolous youth to mercantile industry, and a second from mercantile industry to self-mortification and social service.[23] The young Ranieri had sat playing the lyre in a female relative's house. She happened to notice the reformed knight Alberto Leccapecore of San Vito passing by the window. "Do you know an angel of God is passing by?" she remarked to Ranieri. "Where?" he asked. "It's Alberto Leccapecore, run and catch him!" Ranieri ran out and caught up to him at the church of San Vito. That encounter convinced Ranieri to give up his unfocused way of life; the holy man promised to pray for him.[24] Perhaps those prayers later caused him to abandon his career as a merchant and take up asceticism.

Pellegrino Laziosi of Forlì (ca. 1265–1345) was converted through an especially moving sermon. He listened to the admonitions of the Servite preacher Filippo Benizzi (himself later a popular saint) and immediately "left the world."[25] The decision to take up penance might require no external suasion at all. Penitents made the choice alone, without clerical or miraculous direction. Giovanni Pelingotto (1240–1304) converted during a lavish feast-day dinner. He suddenly felt the call of God and sneaked out. He absconded with some meat, sat down in the square, and passed the food out to the beggars.[26] A penitent might find her calling through rejection. Umiltà of Faenza (1226–1310) lived a more or less ordinary married life for nine years, until the death of her husband. Accepted by the nuns at Santa Perpetua, she managed to survive in cloister for fourteen years—until the nuns expelled her "because she was too pretty." She then found her true vocation. Umiltà

22. See his life by his Dominican contemporary Giovanni Gorini, *[Legenda de Vita et Obitu Beati Petri de Fulgineo]*, 1–2 (i.e., 1–9a), *AS* 31 (Jul. IV), 665–68; for chapters 9b–11, see *Analecta Bollandiana* 8 (1889): 365–69.

23. On Ranieri, see Vauchez, *Laity in the Middle Ages*, 55, and Colin Morris, "San Ranieri of Pisa: The Power and Limitations of Sanctity in Twelfth-Century Italy," *Journal of Ecclesiastical History* 45 (1994): 588–99, esp. 589 and 599, on the two editions of his vita. I have used the *AS* edition, since the other, *San Ranieri di Pisa in un ritratto agiografico inedito del secolo XIII*, ed. Réginald Grégoire (Pisa: Pacini, 1990), was not available to me.

24. Benincasa of Pisa, *Vita [S. Raynerii Pisani]*, 1.7, p. 348: "Praedicta autem matrona eum intuens, sic B. Raynerio ait: Nonne vides Angelum Dei transire. B. Raynerius hoc audiens dixit: Et ubi est ille dei Angelus? Et illa: En, inquit, prope est homo Dei, qui dicitur Albertus Lingens-pecus: Curre, eumque sequere."

25. See the vita by his contemporary Vitale de' Avanzi of Bologna, *Leggenda del beato Pellegrino*, ed. Benedetto Angelo Maria Canali, *Vita del beato Pellegrino Laziosi da Forlì* (Lucca: Marescandoli, 1725), 165–67.

26. *Vita [Sancti Pilingotti Urbinatis]*, 1.10, *AS* 21 (Jun. 1), 147.

set up as an anchoress at the house of a relative. Only later did observers recognize her freelance holiness; the Vallombrosan nuns at Florence invited the conversa to become their abbess.[27] Umiliana dei Cerchi (1219–41) faced similar problems when she tried to convert. Having entered an arranged marriage to a usurer at the age of sixteen, she gave the man two children in five years of marriage. After his death, relatives took in the children because she wanted to enter monastic life. After rejection by the Poor Clares, she devoted her life to social service and did penance at home, thereby becoming the first *pinzochera* of Florence.[28] Communal piety flowered in town; it was not at home in a monastery.

Nevolone of Faenza (d. 1280) practiced the trade of a cobbler until he was twenty-four, when he felt the call to penance. But he remained married and devoted to his wife. He expressed his new life by occasional retreats in a hermitage and regular good works. He still had family responsibilities. His exercise of full-time mortification had to wait until his wife died. He then set off on the first of ten pilgrimages to Rome and Santiago de Compostella, flagellating himself as he walked the roads. At home, he organized the first flagellant confraternity at Faenza.[29] Otherwise, he spent his days in the piazza among the down-and-out, begging bread for himself and the poor.[30] Nevolone was an independent operator; his decisions and activities betray no sign of clerical direction or influence.

Sometimes only God could provide laypeople with the freedom to take up the ascetic life—that is, if they wanted to be penitents and adopt a style of life patterned in part on a monastic asceticism. Lucchese of Poggibonsi (d. 1260) wandered one day by himself in a quiet place. "He fell to thinking about the great power, wisdom, and mercy of God in creation, and how kindly he guides, puts up with, and accepts back sinners; and lest his [Lucchese's] children would impede him, he, like the similarly encumbered Angela of Foligno, began to hope they would die."[31] He explained all this to his wife. It moved her to pray with him for a solution. The children promptly died, the couple sold their superfluous goods, and both entered the state of penance together. The death of his mother allowed Gerardo of Cagnoli (1267–1347) to take up the penitent's garb and go on pilgrimage to Rome.[32]

---

27. See her life by Biagio of Faenza, *Vita [S. Humilitatis Abbatissae]*, AS 18 (May v), 207–23.

28. Vito of Cortona composed her vita three years after her death: *Vita [B. Humilianae]*, pp. 385–402. For her cult, see Anna Benvenuti Papi, "Una santa vedova," *In Castro Poenitentiae*, 59–98.

29. *Vita Beati Nevoloni*, ed. Francesco Lanzoni, 7, in "Una vita del beato Nevolone faentino, terziario francescano," *AFH* 6 (1913): 647.

30. Ibid., 4, p. 646.

31. *Vita Sancti Lucensis Confessoris*, ed. Martino Bertagna, in "Note e documenti intorno a s. Lucchese," *AFH* 62 (1969): 453: "cogitare cepit Dei summam potentiam, sapientiam et clementiam in creatione, gubernatione et benigna peccatorum toleratione et receptione. Et ne vita filiorum ullum foret impedimentum, contra naturam ipsorum mortem cepit appetere."

32. Bartolomeo Albizzi, *Legenda Sancti Gerardi Ordinis Fratrum Minorum*, ed. Filippo Rotolo, 1.6, in "La Leggenda del b. Gerardo Cagnoli, O. Min. (1267–1342) di Fra' Bartolomeo Albizzi, O. Min. (+1351)," *Miscellanea Francescana* 57 (1957): 398.

Raimondo Palmerio of Piacenza (ca. 1140–1200) was able to initiate his life of penance and the first of his many pilgrimages only after God had freed him from his wife.[33]

For lay men and women, penance often began with pilgrimage. One might choose the career of a holy person, but convention required that God accept the choice. So many took to the road, seeking ratification of their conversion. No extravagant portent was required. God might respond to prayer by unlocking the door so a pilgrim could visit the catacombs while in Rome. Or he might provide an unexpected opportunity to hear Mass at the altar containing the relics of Peter and Paul in the Vatican. He did both for Giacomo Salomone, and that was enough.[34] The father of Bona of Pisa (1156–1207) abandoned her at the age of three to go on pilgrimage to the Holy Land. When she came of age, Bona went to Jerusalem herself, inspired by a vision. Jesus Christ ratified her conversion to penance by appearing to her in a dream, breathing into her mouth, and saying, "Receive the Holy Spirit."[35] Although a woman, she made pilgrimages throughout the world for the rest of her life.[36] In the church of the Holy Sepulcher, Ranieri stripped himself of his clothing as a sign of conversion, a gesture that prefigured the later conversion of Francis of Assisi.[37] Pisa adopted both as patrons, which counted as canonization in the maritime republic. Lay saints enjoyed similar freedom and mobility after conversion. Gualtiero of Lodi (d. 1223/24) locked himself up as an anchorite at the hospital of San Bartolomeo, but he continued to leave and go on pilgrimage when the urge hit him.[38] For lay saints, pilgrimage decisively separated them from their past sins, much as entry into a religious order signaled a new life for clerics. Bona and Ranieri's travels, facilitated by Pisa's commercial links to the Levant, replaced the monastic novitiate.[39]

Pilgrimage marked conversion, not sanctity. Saint Gualfardo of Verona (d. 1127) was the earliest communal lay saint.[40] He arrived in Italy as a German pilgrim; his name is probably an Italianization of the German *Wallfahrer*—"pilgrim." He earned his reputation for holiness only after settling

---

33. Rufino of Piacenza, *Vita et Miracula B. Raymundi Palmarii*, 1.7, *AS* 33 (Jul. VI), 646; 5.20 [i.e., 2.20], p. 648; on Raimondo Palmerio and his vita, see Luigi Canetti, *Gloriosa Civitas: Culto dei santi e società cittadina a Piacenza nel Medioevo* (Bologna: Pàtron, 1993), 167–227. Vauchez, "Nouveauté," 72–73, suggests that the frequency with which deaths of family members cleared the way for entrance into a life of penance shows a tension between sanctity and married life.

34. *Vita [Beati Jacobi Veneti Ordinis Praedicatorum]*, 3.16–17, *AS* 20 (May VII), 457.

35. *Vita [Sanctae Bonae Virginis Pisanae]*, 1.9, p. 145.

36. Contrary to later tradition, Bona was never a Franciscan nun or affiliated with the mendicants, although it is recorded that she prophesied the coming of the Dominicans: *Vitae Fratrum Ordinis Praedicatorum*, 1.2, ed. Benedict Maria Reichart, MOPH I (Louvain: Charpentier & Schoonjans, 1896), 12–13.

37. On Ranieri's conversion, see Morris, "San Ranieri of Pisa," 592.

38. Bongiovanni of Lodi, *Vita Beati Gualterii Confessoris*, ed. and trans. Alessandro Caretta, 7, in "La vita di s. Gualtiero di Lodi," *Archivio storico lodigiano* 88 (1968): 20; on Saint Gualtiero, see Vauchez, *Laity in the Middle Ages*, 57–58.

39. On their pilgrimages, see Vauchez, "Reliquie, santi e santuari," 478–79.

40. On Gualfardo, see Vauchez, *Laity in the Middle Ages*, 54.

down in Verona and taking up the trade of a harness maker in a shop near the monastery of San Salvatore. His piety and humility impressed the neighbors. When he finally decided to become a hermit, just before death, the Veronese flocked to him for miracles and healings. The cleric Benincasa of Pisa, in his life of Ranieri of Pisa, declared that the saint became a priest "by the mortification of his body." By this he meant not a quasi-clerical status but an intensification of the "chrism on his crown and forehead"—that is, the grace of his baptismal and confirmation anointings. Good women, who crucified Christ in their bodies, could also be called "priests of God," in the opinion of the hagiographer Benincasa of Pisa.[41] By their way of life, lay saints were a rebuke to some clerics. Giovanni Buono of Mantua, after his conversion, built for himself a hermitage outside the city walls, under the protection of the Virgin, Santa Maria di Botriolo. He spatially distanced himself from the squares and streets where he had plied his trade as a minstrel. As his reputation spread and admirers arrived, he adopted greater asceticism to protect himself against backsliding. He had three different beds, each of increasing discomfort, so that he could choose a degree of mortification proportionate to the temptations of the day. Some thought such conversi should have entered a regular religious order or submitted themselves to more direct control of the clergy. Giovanni of Mantua, a lay follower of Giovanni Buono, explained to the holy man's canonization commission: "I saw the said brother Giovanni Buono suffer tribulations and persecutions from the Friars Minor, luring away the said Giovanni Buono's brothers and convincing them to accept their rule, which persecution and tribulation he endured patiently."[42] Giovanni Buono simply went on competing with the followers of Saint Francis. Perhaps the satisfaction was worth the occasional loss of a follower.

Holiness flowered among the human refuse of the contrada. Fina of San Gimignano (d. 1253) was the lovely child of a poor family. She lived at home until the age of twelve, quietly doing domestic work and helping her family. Then her father suddenly died, and she herself fell sick, ending up as a cripple covered with festering sores. Until she died five years later, at the age of seventeen, she lived in continuous pain, strapped to a board. Her disgusted relatives left her to live in squalor, an object of contempt. Miraculous bell ringing at her Requiem announced her overlooked holiness. Miracles of healing began during her funeral, and the town of San Gimignano soon adopted her as its patron saint.[43] Not all professional religious recognized

41. Benincasa of Pisa, *Vita [S. Raynerii Pisani]*, 3.43, p. 355; see also Vauchez, *Laity in the Middle Ages*, 63.

42. *Processus . . . B. Joannis Boni*, 4.5.294, p. 846: "Vidi dictum fratrem Joannem Bonum pati tribulationes et persecutiones a fratribus Minoribus, auferentibus fratres dicti Joannis Boni, et ducentibus eos ad regulam suam, quam persecutionem et tribulationem sustenuit patienter."

43. Giovanni of San Gimignano, *Vita [S. Finae Virginis]*, AS 8 (Mar. II), 232–38. On another unpublished vita of Fina, see Antonella Degl'Innocenti, "Agiografia toscana del XIV secolo: Il leggendario del ms. Laurenziano Plut. XX, 6 e un'inedita vita di Fina da San Gimignano," *Immagini del Medioevo: Saggi di cultura mediolatino* (Spoleto: Centro Italiano di Studi sull'Alto Medioevo, 1994), 125.

this kind of holiness immediately. The daughter of Parisio and Emilia of Metula, near Massa San Pietro, who would later become Saint Margherita of Città di Castello (1287–1320), was born blind and deformed. After first shutting the child up at home "as a penitent for her father's sins," the parents later took her, at the age of seven, to the tomb of a local saintly Franciscan— perhaps Fra Giacomo of Città di Castello. When nothing happened, they abandoned her in the church.[44] The priests there disposed of her in a local convent. But the nuns found her fervent piety a burden and expelled her. A neighborhood family finally took her in. She set herself up as a lay penitent, loosely affiliated with the Dominicans. Her real support came from the neighbors who provided her with odd jobs, mostly teaching their children. Her legenda, composed by a lay admirer, took the nuns and clerics to task for failing to recognize the saint in their midst.[45] In contrast, Benvenuta Bojani of Cividale in Friuli (1252–92) was fortunate enough to be born to a pious family. Having taken up the life of penance at home under the direction of some local Dominicans, she too became incapacitated by ill health. She bore this patiently until her death at the age of forty, occasionally enjoying visions and fighting off temptations of the Devil. Her own brother wrote the vita celebrating her life.[46]

Mystical gifts or miracles were not essential to these saints' holiness—their patience and single-minded piety marked them out.[47] Physical afflictions set Fina, Benvenuta, and Margherita apart from other conventionally pious women and provided an asceticism ready to hand. Female penitents who enjoyed good health found the road to heroic sanctity hedged about by convention. In the later 1200s, pious women experienced growing pressure to enter monastic orders. Oringa Cristiana of Lucca (1240?–1310), born to poverty, refused marriage and became a conversa.[48] After a pilgrimage, she gathered a group of followers in the town of Castro Santa Croce. Local mendicants gave her support and convinced the group to "regularize" their life. Oringa and her followers obediently learned to read and chant the Office, settling into a more or less normal cloistered life in the monastery she founded, Santa Maria Novella at Castelfiorentino.[49] Many chose to escape conventual life by becoming inclusae—anchoresses. Sibyllina Biscossi (1287–1367) went blind at the age of ten, but unlike Benvenuta, she found no family to take her in. Instead, she entered an anchorhold and lived there for sixty-

44. Legenda B. Margaritae de Castello, 9, p. 120; 14, p. 122.
45. Ibid., pp. 115–28.
46. Corrado of Cividale, Vita Devotissimae Benevenutae, pp. 152–85; Butler, Lives of the Saints, 4:223–24.
47. Cf. Kieckhefer, "Holiness and Culture," 291, who perhaps overemphasizes mystical experience.
48. On Oringa Cristiana, see Anna Benvenuti Papi, "Santità femminile nel territorio fiorentino e lucchese: Considerazioni intorno al caso di Verdiana da Castelfiorentino," Religiosità e società in Valdelsa nel basso Medioevo (Florence: Società Storica della Valdelsa, 1980), 113–44. Her life is edited in Legenda Beatae Christianae, pp. 189–258.
49. Legenda Beatae Christianae, 12, pp. 197–98.

four years.[50] Bricked into a room attached to the local church, she became an urban hermitess. The arrangement allowed her contact with Mass and Office through a peephole into the church and contact with neighbors through a window in the door. Most *inclusae* received no cult after their deaths—and thus no vitae. But they were visible saints, a living part of the religious geography of their cities.[51] For their neighbors, they become spiritual counselors, and for the city, vehicles of prophetic insight into political or ecclesiastical problems. Florence provides a fine example of such a freelance holy woman. Verdiana (d. ca. 1240) came from a poor family. She refused marriage and took up a life of penance after a rich relative paid for her pilgrimage to Santiago.[52] In 1202, Verdiana convinced the commune of Castelfiorentino to construct an anchorhold for her at the church of San Antonio at Florence. During the construction she took off again, on a pilgrimage to Rome. Verdiana then settled down in the anchorhold back in Florence. Under a vow of obedience to her local pastor, she lived on her own. The priest merely heard her confession and brought her Communion. During her thirty-two years as a hermitess, Verdiana befriended two snakes from the garden, who came daily to eat with her. She asked and received special permission from Bishop Ardingo of Florence to keep them. When a local castellan accidentally killed her pets, she knew she would die, which she promptly did. Thanks to prophetic insight, she did so fortified by the last rites.[53] The locals renamed the parish church in her honor. Hers was a homely sort of piety.

Identifying the Saint

In its very ordinariness or oddness, lay holiness could remain invisible to those closest to it. Penance could be mistaken for eccentricity or even dementia. Giovanni Pilingotto, with his weird homemade habit of rags and his predilection for giving away his food and clothing to beggars, received more contempt than admiration in his hometown. Only on pilgrimage to Rome at the time of Boniface VIII's Jubilee Indulgence did a stranger single him out of the crowd as "that saint from Urbino."[54] His neighbors were never so sure. Conversely, experiences on pilgrimage might convince a holy man to seek sanctity at home. Meditation on the Romans' disrespect for the Vicar

50. Tomasso of Bossolasco, *Vita [B. Sibyllinae]*, pp. 68–71.

51. On this phenomena, see Casagrande, *Religiosità*; Mario Sensi, *Storie di bizzoche: Tra Umbria e Marche* (Rome: Edizioni di Storia e Letteratura, 1995); and Benvenuti Papi, "Donne religiose," 595–97. For the subordination of these penitents to the mendicants after 1300, see ibid., 597–98.

52. See *Vita Sancte Viridiane*, ed. Olinto Pogni, *Vita di S. Verdianan d'incognito autore estratta dal codice latino trecentesco esistente nella Biblioteca Mediceo Laurentiana di Firenze dal fiorentino monaco Biagio* (Empoli: Lambruschini, 1936), 7–13; there is also a late life by Giocomini of Florence (d. 1420), edited in *AS* 4 (Feb. 1), 257–61.

53. *Vita Sancte Viridiane*, 8–10. She seems to have had a special relationship with snakes; one of her posthumous miracles (ibid., 12) includes helping a man vomit up a snake he had swallowed while asleep!

54. *Vita [Sancti Pilingotti Urbinatis]*, 2.18, p. 148. On the crowds in 1300, see *Annales Veteres Mutinenses*, col. 75, and *Chronicon Parmense* (1300), 80–81.

of Christ, which Ranieri of Pisa witnessed while on pilgrimage to Saint Peter's, made him doubt they were worthy of the pope's presence (and his own). The voice of God came to him in prayer: "Follow your thoughts, my ways are your ways, I, the Lord, am speaking."[55] He promptly left Rome and went home to Pisa.

The laity recognized a good death as the surest sign of holiness, the ultimate "conversion." Michele Delceti was a convicted criminal. At his execution in 1225, he made a very good death, repenting of his sins, calling for a priest to hear his confession, taking Communion with devotion, and invoking the help of God and the saints, and the Bolognese honored him with a cult.[56] The clerics had to work hard to suppress it—which they finally did. One Pisan preacher of the late 1200s spoke to popular belief. He recounted the story of a rather ordinary lustful man who depended on the Blessed Virgin to avoid his sin. But smitten with a beautiful woman, he managed to get her to bed. Eventually he got around to asking her name and found out that it was Maria. His contrition and remorse were such that he died on the spot, leaving the woman stuck with his body. Miraculously, the bells of the city churches began to ring. Summoned by the sound, the bishop, clergy and "whole people" (totus populus) arrived at the cathedral. The woman joined them and recounted her sad story. Touched by pity, the clergy agreed to bury the body. Arriving at the woman's house, they found the body strewn with flowers and surrounded by candles, each inscribed with the words "Ave Maria." After the man's burial in the duomo, candles miraculously lighted themselves around his tomb. Healings multiplied. The city had found an unexpected saint in its midst.[57] If the Pisan preacher recounting this story knew the town where this cult flourished, he failed, unfortunately, to mention it.

Prophetic gifts might reveal the vocation to sanctity, although they were not at all essential to it. Ranieri of Pisa was famous for his visions and prophecies. God appeared to him in the church of the Holy Sepulcher and told him to take up a life of penance to expiate the immoral life of his hometown clergy. "I have given the priests over to the hands of Satan," God declared. The pious layman made atonement for them.[58] People consulted the *mantellata* Mita of Siena on the eternal condition of the Servite Francesco Patrizzi. He was in heaven, crowned by the Virgin, she informed the inquirers.[59] His neighbors knew Gerardo of Cagnoli best for his prophecies and healings.[60]

55. Benincasa of Pisa, *Vita [S. Raynerii Pisani]*, 4.56, p. 357: "Factae sunt cogitationes tuae, viae meae, viae tuae, aio ego Dominus."

56. *CCB:* Vill. (1225), 90.

57. Pisa, Biblioteca Cateriniana del Seminario Arcivescovile, MS 139, "Miracula de Beata Virgine," fol. 149ʳ.

58. On this rather anticlerical story, see Morris, "San Ranieri of Pisa," 594.

59. Cristoforo of Parma, *Legenda Beati Francisci de Senis Ordinis Servorum B. M. V.*, ed. Peregrine Soulier, 36, *Analecta Bollandiana* 14 (1895): 189.

60. Bartolomeo Albizzi, *Legenda Sancti Gerardi*, pp. 384–88.

Lay prophecy need not deal with grand events. The pious goldsmith Saint
Facio of Cremona was staying in Modena and intended to return to Cremona after two weeks. He mentioned in passing that he expected no rain
before his return. So it happened. The hearers ascribed this weather report
to divine illumination and recorded it in his vita.[61] No local prophet took
second place to the illiterate cobbler Asdente of Parma.[62] He was a simple
craftsman whose large teeth caused a speech impediment. The chronicler
Salimbene insisted that he could predict the future "like Abbot Joachim,
Merlin, Methodius, the Sibyls, Isaiah, Jeremiah, Hosea, Daniel, the Apoca-
lypse, and Michael the Scot." In 1282, Asdente predicted the August death
of Nicholas III and the election of Martin IV.[63] He predicted the destruction
of Parma's rival Modena and on another occasion the defeat of the Pisan
navy by Genoa. Salimbene admired his hometown prophet because Asdente
was unpretentious and humble. Bishop Obizzo of Parma agreed. He used to
invite the cobbler to dinner at the episcopal palace to hear his views on
ecclesiastical and secular politics. Asdente obligingly predicted tribulations
for Reggio and Parma after the death of Martin IV and then added that
Martin would be followed by three popes, two of which would be illegiti-
mate.[64] Such prophecies might amuse, but later observers of more refined
taste, like Dante, thought Parma's prophet was a fraud. He placed him in
hell.[65] Did he have a cult in Parma after his death? Sadly, we do not know.

Christianity has produced convert saints since the days of Saint Paul.
What distinguished the conversi of communal Italy was their independent
practice of asceticism without entering a religious order, their predilection
for lay devotions such as pilgrimage, and their focus on charity and service
to the poor. Hagiographers emphasized just these features of their lives: asceticism, pilgrimage, and charity; they were forms of piety intelligible to
clerics. But none of these activities required a dramatic conversion experience. If one reads the vitae of lay saints, paying attention to their encounters
with other laypeople, a different constellation of traits presents itself: neighborliness, orthodox devotional practice, and civic responsibility.[66] Perhaps

61. See *Vita Beati Facii*, ed. André Vauchez, in "Sainteté laïque," 36–49. For this incident, see ibid.,
46 (Miraculum 10); on Facio generally, see "Sainteté laïque," 13–36.

62. *Mem. Pot. Reg.* (1282), cols. 1152–53, describes Asdente and gives his trade, although no name is
given.

63. Salimbene, *Cronica* (1282), 749–50, Baird trans., 522–23.

64. Ibid. (1284), 777–78, trans., 541.

65. *Inferno*, 20.118–20.

66. Zucchero Bencivenni, *La sposizione di questa santa orazione del paternostro*, ed. Luigi Rigoli, *Volgarizzamento dell'esposizione del paternostro* (Florence: Piazzini, 1828), 23, commenting on the Lord's Prayer, paid
special attention to humility. Zucchero Bencivenni (fl. 1300–1313) translated Laurent of Orleans, *Somme
du roi* (1294) into Italian; only these sections are published. On a Sicilian version, see Ettore Li Gotti in
Repertorio storico-critico dei testi in antico siciliano dei sec. XIV–XV (Palermo: Editrice Siciliana, 1949), 2:39–48.
Vauchez, *Laity in the Middle Ages*, 60–67, perhaps allows the clerical voice too great a role in defining lay
communal sanctity. He is more on target (ibid., 65) when he notes traits the clerics have discounted (e.g.,
work, family, marriage).

the most important traits of sanctity were patience and humility in the company of family and neighbors. Extravagance might even bring suspicion. A band of youths (*brigata di fanciuli*) once took to harassing Pietro Pettinaio (d. 1289), the combmaker saint of Siena, chanting songs about his being a sorcerer. The marvelous, after all, could have diabolical origins. When Pietro tamed the boys by his mildness, they started praising him as a saint. Now, that was really bad. He ran off in horror—better to be maligned than to be singled out as the object of a cult.[67]

The surest holiness was ordinary and useful. Raimondo Palmerio of Piacenza, the pilgrim and penitent, was married and had five children. His reputation for sanctity came from his humility and from his founding a poor house (*xenodochia*) near the church of the Dodici Apostoli at Piacenza.[68] Omobono of Cremona (1117?–1197), born into a family of merchants, married and practiced the trade of a tailor. Only the intensity of his prayer life and occasional extravagant almsgiving—for which his wife regularly chastised him—marked him out from his neighbors. Like Pietro Pettinaio, he won admiration and respect for his humility. So trusted was he that the city of Cremona called on him to mediate between feuding factions. After Omobono's death, his bishop, Sicardo of Cremona, went to Rome in person as a representative of the city to request that Pope Innocent III canonize the holy tailor.[69] Innocent emphasized three elements of Omobono's holiness in his bull of canonization: his devotion to Mass and Office, his almsgiving, and his work for peace among his fellow citizens. The pope did not try to hide Omobono's distinctively lay and civic-minded piety. His late-thirteenth-century biographer also praised Omobono's honesty in business, thereby recapturing an aspect of his piety missed by the pontiff but prized in the workaday world of the communes.[70]

Biographers of the communal saints emphasized their subjects' orthodoxy, perhaps because they often came from trades, like textiles and leatherworking, with a reputation for heresy.[71] Omobono's biographer contrasted his orthodoxy with general practice in the "heretical city" of Cremona in his

---

67. Pietro of Monterone, *Vita del beato Pietro Pettinajo*, 10, pp. 114–15.

68. Rufino of Piacenza, *Vita et Miracula B. Raymundi*.

69. As he tells us in his chronicle: Sicardo of Cremona, *Chronica*, *MGH.SS* 31:176.

70. *Vita Sancti Homoboni*, ed. Francesco Saverio Gatta, in Francesco Saverio Gatta, "Un antico codice reggiano su Omobono il 'santo popolare' di Cremona," *Bollettino storico cremonese* 7 (1942): 111. His charity earned him the nickname "pater pauperum": ibid., 112. On his mediating role, see F. S. Gatta, "Un antico codice," 108; he was never a member of the Humiliati: *Vita di s. Omobono,* ed. Giuseppe Bertoni, in "Di una vita di s. Omobono del secolo XIV," *Bollettino storico cremonese* 3 (1938): 174–75. On the ways he was portrayed by his medieval hagiographers, see André Vauchez, "Le 'trafiquant céleste': Saint Homebon de Crémone (+1197), marchand et 'père des pauvres,'" *Mentalités et sociétés*, vol. 1 of *Horizons marins, itinéraires spirituels (V^e–XVIIIe)*, ed. Henri Dudois, Jean-Claude Hocquet, and André Vauchez (Paris: Sorbonne, 1987), 115–22, who notes this life's bourgeois quality, in comparison to the earlier (unpublished) vita, which emphasizes asceticism: ibid., 118. On Saint Omobono, see Vauchez, *Laity in the Middle Ages*, 55–56.

71. As suggested by Vauchez, *Laity in the Middle Ages*, 59.

very first sentence. Omobono was a "rose among thorns."[72] The witnesses at Giovanni Buono's canonization inquest emphasized his dislike of heretics. He worked suitably edifying and orthodox miracles: on Easter, the day of new birth, he planted a stick cut from an apple tree. It put forth buds within an hour.[73] For learned clerical observers, an *idiota et illiteratus* like Giovanni Buono presented difficulties. He could not formulate theologically sophisticated statements of belief.[74] But for lay neighbors, the communal saint's orthodoxy was less problematic. It manifested itself in reverence for the name of God and the sacraments. As a child, Oringa Cristiana miraculously vomited whenever anyone uttered blasphemies or obscenities (*verba turpia*) in her presence. As an adult, she got sick whenever a priest in mortal sin came to give her Communion or anointing.[75] Sibyllina Biscossi counted Communion one of the rare justifications for leaving her anchorhold.[76]

But extravagances raised eyebrows. Sibyllina, the fiercest of ascetics, moderated her self-flagellation when friends criticized it as excessive and bad for her health. But her genuflections and prostrations were not extreme, she protested; they kept her warm in cold weather.[77] No affectation caused Pietro Pettinaio to call his wife his *patrona*. He came straight home after work rather than hang out with the boys.[78] His marital devotion proved, in spite of the combmaker's proclivity for self-mortification, that he held the duties of marriage in high regard. Layman that he was, Pietro honored monasticism: he named one of his sons Monacho—"Monk."[79] Armanno Pungilupo (d. 1269), the holy man of Ferrara whose cult would attract the attention of inquisitors in 1301, was known for his prayers and vigils in church.[80] He was "devoted to God and to the glorious Virgin, as is pleasing to the Lord."[81] Saints also respected the clergy. When Pietro Pettinaio wanted to go on retreat, he took a cell in the infirmary of the Franciscan monastery and placed himself under the tutelage of the priests.[82] But mostly Pietro wandered out to various shrines of the Sienese contado to pray. There the locals could catch glimpses of him rapt in ecstasy.[83] Raptures aside, shrine visiting was a devotion accessible to everyone.

72. *Vita Sancti Homoboni*, 111.

73. *Processus . . . B. Joannis Boni*, 1.10.79, p. 792; 1.11.89, p. 794; on the importance of orthodoxy in the saint's canonization process, see Golinelli, *Città e culto*, 65–66.

74. Golinelli, "Dal santo," 33–34, thinks that anxiety over orthodoxy caused the shelving of Giovanni Buono's case.

75. *Legenda Beatae Christianae*, 1–2, p. 192.

76. Tomasso of Bossolasco, *Vita [B. Sibyllinae]*, 2.7, p. 69.

77. Ibid., 2.8–10, p. 69.

78. Pietro of Monterone, *Vita del beato Pietro Pettinajo*, 1, p. 8–9.

79. *Vita di s. Omobono*, ed. Giuseppe Bertoni, in "Una vita di s. Omobono," 169.

80. On his cult, see "Acta contra Armanum [Punzilupum]," ed. Gabriele Zanella, *Itinerari ereticali: Patari e catari tra Rimini e Verona*, Studi storici, 153 (Rome: Istituto Storico Italiano per il Medio Evo, 1986), 48, 67.

81. So said one of the witnesses in his favor during the posthumous inquisition into his orthodoxy: ibid., 72.

82. Pietro of Monterone, *Vita del beato Pietro Pettinajo*, 4, p. 22.

83. Ibid., 4, pp. 23–27.

SERVICE, CITIZENSHIP, AND SANCTITY

Asceticism was ultimately second to service. When Giovanni of Chiusi visited Galgano's hermitage, he found the ex-knight not performing acts of mortification but preparing loaves of bread for the poor. Galgano asked the visitor to take them to town and distribute them to the needy.[84] Lay saints also proved their holiness in the work they did to earn a living.[85] The pious domestic Zita of Lucca found her real penance in the abuse she received from her master and other domestics; she used her free time to serve the poor and won over her detractors by her patience and humility. The illiterate Enrico of Treviso (d. 1310) daily visited every church in his city and practiced mortification by night, but his neighbors knew him as a day laborer who gave away all he acquired.[86] Pietro Pettinaio was selling combs from his bench in the Siena Piazza del Campo when a man rushed by and knocked it over. Rather than get angry, the combmaker blessed God and patiently set it up again. Mortified, the man came back and asked pardon. Pietro cheerfully granted it, recalling Jesus' recommendation of forgiveness.[87]

It was consistency in small acts of charity that made the saint. Miracles, when they came, confirmed little acts of kindness. Omobono's wife left him at home with a cake (*torta*)—he gave it to some beggars. When she returned home and wanted the cake to serve at dinner, Omobono prayed and God miraculously replaced it. On the way to deliver lunch wine to vineyard workers, Omobono weakened and gave it away to some beggars. He filled the bottles with water in desperation. God changed it to wine. "Per Dio, meior vino'n may noy gustassemo più de questo," said the workers—"By God, we've never tasted wine better than this."[88] Omobono refrained from criticizing their use of the Lord's name in vain. Charity included overlooking the peccadilloes of others. God could work miracles in spite of saintly humility. Maria Bella of Modena brought her son Vivaldino to Giovanni Buono and asked him to heal an ulcer on the boy's leg. Giovanni refused to come out of his hut, insisting, "Ego non sum Deus" (I'm not God). The boy was healed anyway.[89]

No saint matched Pietro Pettinaio as a model of day-to-day holiness. When a butcher offered him a good deal on soup bones, he insisted on paying the "just price" of 24s.—refusing the 12s. bargain.[90] On arrival in

84. *De Vita et Actibus Galgani*, ed. Fedor Schneider, 3, in "Der Einsiedler Galgan von Chiusdino und die Anfänge von S. Galgano," *Quellen und Forschungen aus italienischen Archiven und Bibliotheken* 17 (1914–24): 73.

85. A point well taken by Sophia Boesch Gaiano, "Lavoro, povertà, santità fra nuove realtà sociali e luoghi comuni agiografici," *Cultura e società nell'Italia medievale: Studi per Paolo Brezzi*, Studi Storici, 184–87 (Rome: Istituto Storico Italiano per il Medio Evo, 1988), 117–29, esp. 121–25.

86. *Miracula [B. Henrici Baucenensis]*, AS 22 (Jun. II), 369–88. See also Butler, *Lives of the Saints*, 2:520.

87. Pietro of Monterone, *Vita del beato Pietro Pettinajo*, 10, pp. 113–14.

88. *Vita di s. Omobono*, 168–69.

89. *Processus . . . B. Joannis Boni*, 1.8.73–74, p. 791.

90. Pietro of Monterone, *Vita del beato Pietro Pettinajo*, p. 7; Pietro's willingness to forgo profit has special significance, since in the 1200s greed overtook pride as the most serious of the deadly sins; see

Pisa to purchase material for making combs, the locals tried to cheat the naive Sienese bumpkin with defective merchandise. He paid their price but tossed the worthless horn into the Arno, thus showing he was not deceived.[91] Pietro's reputation for honesty did help sales. On Saturdays, when he sold in the Piazza del Campo, people came from the whole district to buy, and no other combmaker got any business. Mortified, since he respected the business of his fellow combmakers, Pietro took down his stand and reopened only after Vespers, when the other vendors had closed for the day.[92] Moderns would have called the saint a good union man. But Pietro made no claim to moral superiority. Youths once accosted him in the street and posed a sordid question: "Tell us, Pietro, if by chance you found yourself in a locked room with a beautiful woman and no one would ever know, what would you do?" The saint replied, "If I were in that position, I know what I should do, but I do not know what I would do; I tell you, I guard myself from sins when no one knows, just as if the whole world were watching." The boys took off, disarmed by Pietro's honesty.[93] The key to holiness was to live a good life at work and home, avoid sin, and not seek worldly attention and honor.[94]

Communal holiness flourished in community; it was social. Even a recluse, like Umiliana dei Cerchi of Florence, lived surrounded by friends and neighbors. So important were they to her life that her hagiographer had to include their names: her companion Gisla, Donna Luciana di Ranieri from the parish of San Procolo, Donna Dialta di Ugalotto from the parish of Santa Margherita, and Donna Bene di Ricco from the parish of San Lorenzo.[95] Not even an anchoress could find holiness in isolation. Siena once levied a tax to reduce a brigand's stronghold in the contado. When Pietro heard the news, he immediately asked the rate, gathered the money, and paid it. No pacifist he, but a good citizen. The commune refused his money and asked only that he pray for victory. Pietro insisted on paying: "My dearest governors, I always desire to walk in peace, but this money belongs to my commune. I will not take it away, since it is the commune's, not mine." He left the cash on the tax counter and departed.[96] The communal saint was a model of civic rectitude. Returning late one night from prayers,

Lester K. Little, "Pride Goes Before Avarice: Social Change and the Vices in Latin Christendom," *American Historical Review* 76 (1971): 16–49.

91. Pietro of Monterone, *Vita del beato Pietro Pettinajo*, 1, pp. 6–8.

92. Ibid., 1, p. 8.

93. Ibid., 6, p. 72: "Dì a noi o Pietro se per caso tu ti trovassi in una camera riserrato solo con una bellissima donna e nessuno nè allora, nè mai il sapesse: or che faresti tu? . . . Se io fossi posto in tal caso so ben quello che dovrei fare, ma non so quel che fecessi: questo ben vi dico che così mi guarderai dal peccato se nessuno il sapesse: come se tutto il mondo apertamente mi vedesse."

94. Pietro warned his fellow Sienese, the Dominican Ambrogio Sansedoni, to turn down a bishopric: ibid., 9, pp. 95–97.

95. On Umiliana's friends, see Benvenuti Papi, "Una santa vedova," 93–95.

96. Pietro of Monterone, *Vita del beato Pietro Pettinajo*, 8, pp. 82–83: "Carissimi miei Maggiori sempre desidero andare nella pace di Dio, ma pure questa pecunia quale è del mio Comune non la porterò, imperciochè è sua, e non mia, e lassatala, prestamente si partì."

Pietro ran into the members of the Bargello family who were responsible for night guard. Although he had technically broken curfew, they let him off. The next day Pietro turned himself in to the podesta and insisted on paying the fine for his infraction. The chagrined podesta assured him that "the law was not made for you, but for transgressors and other bad livers"; Pietro did not need to pay. The city offered him exemption from the curfew and city taxes. Much to the podesta's astonishment, Pietro declined the curfew exemption and insisted on paying not only his fine but also the upcoming taxes.[97] No tax audit ever found this Sienese in arrears; he was a man of his city.

Writing of the saints of communal Italy, André Vauchez remarked, "These saints were not at all fictional or mysterious beings but well-known people, nearby in time and place, who brought themselves to the attention of their contemporaries while still alive."[98] Riccobaldo of Ferrara, when asked by an inquisitor what locals thought about Armanno Pungilupo, replied that they called him a "friend of God" (*amicus Dei*) because he consoled the sick, visited those imprisoned, and encouraged his friends. His was a compassionate and generous piety. People liked that. Unlike the inquisitor, they did not ask what Armanno thought about Cathars and heretics.[99] Albertano of Brescia, the thirteenth-century lay theologian, emphasized that true piety showed itself in practical fruits. Gherardo dei Tintori of Monza, Gualtiero of Lodi, Raimondo Palmerio of Piacenza, Facio of Cremona, and other communal holy men founded or ran hospitals.[100] God gave Raimondo Palmerio, the most famous of the hospital founders, his mission. As Raimondo was returning from pilgrimage to Rome, God appeared to him and told him to found a house for "indigents and pilgrims" back home at Piacenza. God also warned him that the Piacentines were factious, stiff-necked, and unlikely to honor their hometown prophet. God designed the habit Raimondo was to wear: sky blue (*coloris aetheriei*), falling below the knees, with large sleeves, a cross on the shoulder, and no capuche. So dressed, Raimondo presented his plan to his bishop, who was delighted to approve it.[101] At least the bishop could recognize a good thing when he saw it. By the time of his death, in 1202, Raimondo had won over the entire city by his service. They took to

97. Ibid., 8, p. 81.

98. Vauchez, "Sainteté laïque," 35–36: "Ces saints ne sont pas en effet des êtres fictifs ou mystérieux mais bien des personnages connus, proches dans l'espace et le temps, qui se sont imposés de leur vivant déjà à l'attention de leurs contemporains."

99. Gabriele Zanella, "Armanno Pungilupo, eretico quotidiano," *Hereticalia*, 12. Zanella seems surprised that the inquisition would be interested in such a harmless person. Perhaps such interest reflected the inquisitors' belief that doctrine mattered as much to holiness as did social service. See also Lansing, *Power and Purity*, 83–84, on Armanno's "orthopraxis."

100. André Vauchez, "Comparsa e affermazione di una religiosità laica (XII secolo–inizio XIV secolo)," *Storia dell'Italia religiosa I: L'antichità e il Medioevo*, ed. André Vauchez (Rome: Laterza, 1993), 404–8; on Albertano, see ibid., 415–17.

101. Rufino of Piacenza, *Vita et Miracula B. Raymundi*, 3.31, pp. 650–51; Canetti, *Gloriosa*, 198–204.

invoking their new saint in rhyming verse.[102] Raimondo's hospital became a training ground for other social workers. Gualtiero of Lodi (1084–1224) became a hospital brother in Raimondo's hospital at the age of fifteen. After suitable experience, he returned to Lodi to work at the hospital of San Bartolomeo. Finally, he founded his own hospital, the Misericordia. The bishop and commune of Lodi both funded the project. Pietro Pettinaio, although not a hospital founder, visited and nursed the sick at the Ospedale della Scala. He inspired a circle of wealthy and influential Sienese to dedicate themselves to hospital work. By 1277, these men had become the hospital's administrators, and Bishop Bernardo granted them permission to found a confraternity to assist the poor.[103]

Hospital work was not restricted to men. Margherita of Cortona (d. 1297) had been the mistress of a local nobleman. After his murder in a feud, her family disowned her, and she entered a life of severe penance. With time, she recast her penance into a useful mold, worked as a midwife, did charitable work, and founded both a hospital and a charitable confraternity.[104] Her life spent in service caused the people of Cortona to declare the former kept woman a saint immediately after her death.[105] In Cortona, visitors can see her with the nimbus of a saint in a fourteenth-century stained-glass window—although her papal canonization had to wait until 1728.

Siena viewed hospital service as a suitable expiation for crime, as well as a way to holiness. The city banished Andrea de' Gallerani (d. 1251), a successful soldier, after he killed a blasphemer in a fit of rage. They later let him return to found a hospital and devote himself to serving the sick. Again, a cult sprang up immediately after his death.

The carpenter Giacobino di Bonifacino—who admitted at Giovanni Buono's canonization that he had been a heretic and the son of a heretic—used to visit the Mantuan holy man. He dropped nuts and nutshells at the foot of Giovanni's bed so people would think the hermit was secretly breaking his fast. Giovanni caught him out and tried to argue theology with him. But, Giacobino admitted, he only began to doubt his heresies because a hawk flew in the window, landed at Giovanni's feet, hopped on the holy man's knee, and obeyed him when he told it to leave. That merely made Giacobino a regular at Giovanni's hermitage. Full conversion came later, in a more homely incident. Giovanni saved the ex-heretic's life and house by appearing

---

102. Giovanni de' Mussi, *Chronicon Placentinum* (1202), col. 457.

103. Pietro of Monterone, *Vita del beato Pietro Pettinajo*, 3, pp. 16–19.

104. As noted by Bornstein, "Uses of the Body," 165, who, following the lead of her clerical (Franciscan) biographer, emphasizes her asceticism.

105. For her vita, see Giunta Bevegnati, *Legenda de Vita et Miraculis Beatae Margaritae de Cortona*, ed. Fortunato Iozzelli (Grottaferrata: Collegium Bonaventurae ad Claras Aquas, 1997), pp. 178–478. Giunta Bevegnati was one of the custodians at her shrine and witnessed miracle depositions: ibid., 11.1, p. 455. On her life, see Menestò and Rusconi, *Umbria*, 56–73; for her vita in Italian translation, see *Leggenda della vita e dei miracoli di Santa Margherita da Cortona*, trans. Eliodoro Mariani (Vicenza: Santuario di S. Margherita, 1978).

to him in a dream and telling him to wake up because the building was on fire.[106] Saints cared about households as well as houses. Sor Maria Bella of Modena, the widow of Fra Bonacursio, told how her husband had become a member of Giovanni's order without revealing that he was married. When Giovanni found out, he ordered Bonacursio to go home and live with his wife. He replied that he could not, because Modena had exiled him for debt. Giovanni arranged for Maria Bella to move to Cesena so the couple could reestablish their family. Eventually, both spouses became penitents dedicated to the pious ex-minstrel.[107] True charity concerned home and family.

Enclosure in an anchorhold did not prevent service to neighbor. Oringa Cristiana built up her reputation for visions by conferences with those who daily spoke to her at her enclosure's consultation window.[108] Umiltà of Faenza had her cell at Sant'Apollinare fitted with a window into the church for Communion and one to the outside for receiving alms and dispensing advice.[109] Such women's legendae give glimpses of those who visited them and of their requests. Donna Grigia asked Margherita of Città di Castello to be godmother for her granddaughter, and she agreed.[110] Dionisio of Modena, master general of the Augustinians, visited Sibyllina Biscossi at the window of her anchorhold to consult on his leadership of the order. Giovanni di Taddeo de' Pepoli consulted the elderly Sibyllina on politics while traveling to Avignon in 1353 as agent of the Visconti during negotiations with Pope Urban V.[111] Sibyllina's favorite place to meditate and pray was at her little window to the world. That it was open showed she was on call to give advice or receive little gifts of cherries from her friends.[112] The message from the anchorhold could be frightening as well as convivial. In May of 1288, Margherita of Cortona prophesied that the Antichrist was near at hand and that many would fall away. She twice warned her clerical admirers to repent, reform, and prepare to endure tribulations.[113] Umiliana dei Cerchi foresaw severe tribulations at the hands of the podesta of Florence when she denounced the city's anti-papal policies. This persecution, she knew, would make her one with Christ.[114]

Male saints generally practiced temporal works of mercy and left spiritual

---

106. *Processus . . . B. Joannis Boni*, 3.7.228, pp. 828–29.

107. Ibid., 1.8.69, p. 790.

108. *Legenda Beatae Christianae*, pp. 189–97. Hermit monks also gave advice and counsel, e.g., Saint Odo the Carthusian (d. 1189): see *Apographum Processus Informationis circa Vitam, Mortem, Translationem et Miracula B. Odonis*, in "Documenta de B. Odone Novariensi Ordinis Carthusiani," *Analecta Bollandiana* 1 (1882): testes 33–34, p. 346.

109. Biagio of Faenza, *Vita [S. Humilitatis Abbatissae]*, 1.10, p. 208.

110. *Vita Beatae Margaritae Virginis de Civitate Castelli*, ed. A. Poncelet, 12, *Analecta Bollandiana* 19 (1900): 32–33.

111. Tomasso of Bossolasco, *Vita [B. Sibyllinae]*, 3.19–20, p. 70.

112. Ibid., 2.12, p. 69.

113. Giunta Bevegnati, *Legenda . . . Margaritae de Cortona*, 9.23, pp. 384–85; 9.26, pp. 387–88.

114. Vito of Cortona, *Vita [B. Humilianae]*, 3.36, p. 395; on Umiliana's Guelf political activities, see Benvenuti Papi, "Una santa vedova," 76–88, esp. 84.

works to the women, but even a craftsman could serve as physician of the soul. Pietro Pettinaio, on the way to Florence for combmaking supplies, stopped at the water fountain at Castellina in Chianti to snack on fresh figs with some of the locals. The figs' quality inspired him to give a little sermon on the sweetness of the God who made them.[115] The men were properly edified. Gerardo of Cagnoli received consoling messages from God for important personages, such as Enrico de' Abbati, the justiciar of the king of Naples (a promise that he would recover his health), and King Robert of Sicily (notice that he would succeed in war).[116] But mostly, male saints performed the spiritual work of "correcting the erring" by helping confute heresy. Omobono of Cremona regularly unmasked and rebuked heretics who came to visit him.[117] When messengers from Enzo, the son of Frederick II, arrived at his cell, attracted by his holy reputation, Giovanni chided them and their master as excommunicates.[118] They went away offended rather than reformed. Even the power of sanctity had limits.

The saint worked for peace among neighbors. In 1199, Pope Innocent III sent Pietro Parenzo from Rome to Orvieto as podesta. He was to suppress Catharism and loose living. It appears that the "Catharism" there was the result of divisions in the city between pro-papal and anti-papal factions, rather than actual heresy. A conspiracy kidnapped and murdered him that very year because he punished factional brawling during carnival. Afterward, the Orvietans remembered Pietro more as civic peacemaker than lay inquisitor. His cult became popular because he had restored unity to the commune.[119] Margherita of Cortona not only joined a confraternity dedicated to putting down riots and feuds, she facilitated the process by her visions. In them, God supplied information for her confessor Fra Giunta Bevegnati to use in internal peacemaking at Cortona. God told her that it was his will that Arezzo grant independence to Cortona and that Guglielmo degli Ubertini (1248–89), bishop of Arezzo, stop aiding the commune's Arettine enemies.[120] Conflict might be resolved in less dramatic ways. After a sermon by Ranieri of Pisa, one woman walked off by accident with another's mantle. She returned only to meet the other woman in a huff on the way. The women agreed that God had arranged their meeting as an opportunity to show the forgiveness praised in Ranieri's sermon. A possible rift between neighbors had been averted.[121] Even after the age of the communes, lay saints continued their work. Peace negotiators credited the prayers of Ge-

115. Pietro of Monterone, *Vita del beato Pietro Pettinajo*, 4, p. 29.
116. Bartolomeo Albizzi, *Legenda Sancti Gerardi*, 5.80–90, pp. 421–24.
117. *Vita Sancti Homoboni*, 113–14.
118. *Processus . . . B. Joannis Boni*, 4.5.293, p. 846.
119. Giovanni of Orvieto, *Vita [S. Petri Parentii]*, 1.6, p. 88; see Lansing, *Power and Purity*, 23–42, on Pietro's murder and the rise of his cult.
120. Menestò and Rusconi, *Umbria*, 64–65, 68.
121. Benincasa of Pisa, *Vita [S. Raynerii Pisani]*, 11.112, p. 368.

rardo of Cagnoli with ending civil strife at Castro dei Marti in the contado of Pisa as late as the 1340s.[122]

Citizens and cities called on the recognized holy people in their midst to deal with sensitive aspects of public life. Outsiders sought out the local saints as points of contact. Ambassadors from Reggio approached Asdente at Parma in 1284, asking that his city take in exiles from Reggio. The big-toothed prophet told them to undertake their own work for internal peace by Christmas, lest Reggio be destroyed by civil war, as had happened to Modena. The ambassadors promised that they would arrange peace by marriage alliances, but then ignored the prophet's advice. They should have listened. Asdente predicted that any agreements they set up would be fraudulent. The peacemaking failed.[123] In the 1280s, Pietro Pettinaio acted as a go-between for Siena's Guelf government and the Sienese Ghibellines exiled at Arezzo. The commune named him to select prisoners for release on Easter in 1282 and 1284.[124] Oringa Cristiana left her anchorhold to warn the council of Castelfiorentino that disaster would follow if they became involved in a dispute between two neighboring towns. But one council member convinced the city to ignore any advice from that *muliercula*—"little old lady." The man died in the subsequent battle.[125] One ignored the saint at one's peril.

Pietro Pettinaio always exercised restraint in politics, even when he acted by invitation. A podesta from the March of Ancona requested political advice, but Pietro gave only the injunction not to offend God.[126] But the right kind of political association, one with clear Guelf sympathies, pro-communal and anti-imperial, was fully compatible with sanctity. Support for hometown independence and the rights of the Mother Church caused no misgivings among citizens of the communes. The goldsmith Facio of Cremona had to leave his native Verona after loss of its independence to the da Romano in June 1226. After the fall of the tyrant, Facio returned to his native city. Alas, the republican saint fell afoul of the new tyranny of Mastino and Alberto della Scala in 1259. He remained in prison until a Guelf army under the command of Azzo d'Este freed him in 1262.[127] Saint Facio sanctified a "worldly" trade like goldsmithing and active involvement in politics by personal asceticism, remarkable honesty, and charitable service. After a period of pilgrimage, Facio founded a hospital, an order of lay penitents (the Società dello Spirito Santo), and ministered to the sick and possessed. Conversion did not inhibit an active life. He healed the sick with blessed bread, person-

122. Bartolomeo Albizzi, *Legenda Sancti Gerardi*, 7.147, p. 442.
123. Salimbene, *Cronica* (1284), 774, Baird trans., 539.
124. Pietro of Monterone, *Vita del beato Pietro Pettinajo*, 9, pp. 97–98; for Easter amnesties, see the city records in ibid., p. 84, n. 1.
125. *Legenda Beatae Christianae*, 49–50, pp. 226–28.
126. Pietro of Monterone, *Vita del beato Pietro Pettinajo*, 9, p. 84.
127. Following Vauchez, "Sainteté laïque," 21–23.

ally exorcized demoniacs (even nuns, at the bishop's request), and practiced his trade for the glory of God.[128]

The City Makes a Saint

Good relations between holy person and city brought mutual benefits; cities competed to recruit possible saints. It took an apparition of the Blessed Virgin and an intervention from the bishop of Lucca to end the quarrel between Castelfranco and Castel Santa Croce over the right to construct a monastery for Oringa Cristiana. Castel Santa Croce got the honor.[129] The communes knew that any holy person might become a protector in heaven. After death, the commune and neighbors promoted the cults and erected the tombs of their divinely favored children. The parish or cathedral clergy wrote their lives, at least until later in the thirteenth century, when mendicants came to dominate hagiography.[130] In contrast with practice in the communal period, however, modern canonization is a centralized process, and the making of a saint can take decades, if not centuries.[131] The modern procedure has distinct steps: an initiation of the process for the "servant of God," approval of a restricted cult under the title of "blessed," and finally the papal canonization itself, which declares the blessed a "saint" of the universal Church. The people of communal Italy knew none of this.[132] Today public veneration of an uncanonized saint will block a papal canonization. The people of the communes created their saints by acclamation. The public cult came first, and it made the saint.

When the Dominicans buried Margherita of Città di Castello, they could not do so in the cloister, because the people demanded that her tomb be accessible in the church—they already considered her a saint and treated her as such.[133] When Francesco Patrizzi's Servite brothers intoned the opening chant of his funeral Mass, the congregation shouted down the choir and demanded instead the chants for the feast of a confessor. The friars obliged and sang the introit "Gaudemus in Domino" instead of "Requiem Aeternam." From that day forward, Francesco was a saint.[134] Not all clerics were so cooperative. When the founder of the Dominicans died at Bologna, the friars buried him in an unmarked grave. Within days, the laity starting showing up to honor "Saint" Dominic's tomb with flowers and candles and to

---

128. Ibid., 29–31; for his exorcism by blessed bread, see *Vita Beati Facii*, 44–45 (Miraculum 5).

129. *Legenda Beatae Christianae*, 22, pp. 205; see also the deed for the house: ibid., pp. 285–89.

130. Vauchez, "Nouveauté," 76.

131. On the shift from episcopal to papal control of canonizations, see Herrmann-Mascard, *Reliques des saints*, 87–105.

132. On saints' cults, see Sofia Boesch Gajano, *Agiografia altomedievale* (Bologna: Il Mulino, 1976), and the bibliographical and methodological update in ead., "Il culto dei santi," 119–36; and Golinelli, *Città e culto*. On the "canonization" of lay saints, see, above all, Vauchez, "Between Church and City," *Laity in the Middle Ages*, 67–72.

133. *Legenda B. Margaritae de Castello*, 24, p. 126.

134. Cristoforo of Parma, *Legenda Beati Francisci*, 32, p. 187.

pray for cures. The disgusted friars kicked the offerings over and threw the devotees out, but the laity kept coming. Finally, in 1233, Pope Gregory IX himself ordered the friars to erect a suitable shrine for Dominic's relics.[135] The commune of Gubbio constructed a worthy shrine for bishop Ubaldo just in time for his funeral and appointed a notary to record the expected miracles. At the bishop's funeral, people from the countryside insisted on singing Alleluias instead of the usual somber chants of the Requiem.[136] The Dominicans of Siena did manage to chant a Requiem for Ambrogio Sansedoni (d. 1286) inside their church, but his body had to lie in state outside because of the crowds of people who already considered him an intercessor in heaven. Donna Ghiluccia, wife of Masso of San Cristoforo, was trampled while trying to kiss the dead friar's hand. She lay on the pavement spitting up blood. She was healed by invoking the holy Dominican, after futile petitions to several other saints. God had directly validated Ambrogio's cult.[137] People said that when Alberto of Villa d'Ogna, known as the Brentatore ("wine porter"), died at Cremona on 6 May 1279, the ground itself refused to receive his body; so dense were the roots and rocks that the funeral party had to bury him in the choir of the church, where he was accustomed to pray. It was a fine spot for a shrine. This was only the first of the miracles that proved his holiness.[138]

When the canonist pope Gregory IX opened an inquest for the canonization of Ambrogio of Massa (1225–40), he recognized that the locals were often the best judges of holiness. He began his investigation in the very year of the holy man's death, responding to the pleas of the "people and council" of Orvieto.[139] In the people's mind, miracles, not papal commissions, made saints. Miracles attracted the devotees.[140] Saint Omobono of Cremona's biographer observed that miracles not only confirmed faith in God, they proved the holiness of his servants, "for a good tree cannot bring forth bad fruit."[141] The "fruit" did not need to be of cosmic dimensions. The miracle that initiated the cult of Oringa Cristiana occurred a couple of days after her death. A cleric named Don Tommaso was suffering from a bad headache and offered a candle at her new tomb. The headache suddenly left him—and

135. *Processus Canonizationis S. Dominici*, ed. M.-H. Laurent, Bologna Process 9, MOPH 16 (Rome: Institutum Historicum Fratrum Praedicatorum, 1935), 130–31.

136. Giordano of Città di Castello, *Vita Beati Ubaldi Eugubini Episcopi*, 21–29, pp. 106–12; see esp. 23.12–15, p. 108.

137. For her deposition notarized by Giacomo di fu Rustico, see *Miracula [B. Ambrosii Senensis]*, doc. 2 (12 March 1287), *AS* 9 (Mar. III), 201; recorded a second time (6 April 1287), in Recupero of Arezzo, *Summarium Virtutum et Miracula [B. Ambrosii Senensis]*, 10.III, *AS* 9 (Mar. III), 224.

138. Muzio of Modena, *Annales* (1279), 571–72.

139. *Processus Canonizationis B. Ambrosii Massani*, 2, p. 572 (letter of Gregory IX); note also the city involvement in the "canonization" of Raimondo Palmerio: Canetti, *Gloriosa*, 215–16.

140. As noted in *Inquisitio de vita Joannis Cazefronte* (shrine section), 254–55.

141. *Vita di s. Omobono*, 166: on saints miracles: "miraculi fortificha noy nella fede del nostro signiore. . . . Non potest arbor bona fructus malos facere."

the candle remained lighted in spite of the wind.[142] The miracles that followed were more substantial, including healings, restoration of sight to the blind, liberation of a paralytic, exorcism, and rescue from drowning. At Oringa's shrine the miracles seem to have come during waves of devotion every other year.[143] Great cults were made of little miracles. A poor woman's chicken had gone off its food. She invoked Gerardo of Cagnoli, and it regained its appetite.[144] And devotees, even pious ones, did expect results from their saints. When Sibyllina Biscossi got no results from her prayers to Saint Dominic to restore her eyesight, she berated the saint: "Give me back those prayers and praises I offered to you for no purpose!"[145] The saint got the message and restored Sibyllina's sight posthaste.

Saints did not demand special holiness before granting help. A toper in a Sienese tavern bit his wineglass and swallowed a shard. Invoking Saint Ambrogio Sansedoni, he escaped unharmed and became a devotee.[146] Cerubino de' Francheri had a Mass said in honor of Saint Ambrogio before fighting a duel with Salimbergo de' Roselli of Arezzo. During the fight, he was downed and invoked the saint's help. Salimbergo suddenly backed off, claiming later that he had seen the saint next to his adversary.[147] Dueling was a mortal sin, but Ambrogio was from an aristocratic family himself and understood the temptations of young knights. Saints saved their most impressive miracles for fellow citizens. Twenty knights from Gubbio were captured by Saracens in the Holy Land and thrown into a dark dungeon. They invoked their city's patron, Saint Ubaldo. He appeared in a flash of light: " 'Peace be to you, I am Ubaldo, the bishop of Gubbio, whom you have called upon.' Breaking their fetters, he led them from the prison." They got home safely and recorded the miracle at his shrine.[148]

The saints who specialized in particular problems built up the most constant followings. The ex-knight of Siena, Saint Galgano, was partial to helping his fellow knights, especially when jailed or punished by their lords.[149] Considering her own difficult life, it is no surprise that Saint Margherita of Cortona helped mistreated children, once resuscitating a baby beaten to death by her abusive father.[150] Three such resuscitations triggered her formal canonization process. Ranieri, the citizen of maritime Pisa, specialized in

---

142. *Legenda Beatae Christianae*, 71, pp. 250–51.

143. See ibid., pp. 250–58, for the years 1310–45.

144. Bartolomeo Albizzi, *Legenda Sancti Gerardi*, 6.108, p. 430.

145. Tomasso of Bossolasco, *Vita [B. Sibyllinae]*, 1.3, p. 68: "Resitue mihi orationes meas et laudes aliaque quae tibi obtuli frusta!"

146. Recupero of Arezzo, *Summarium Virtutum*, 247, p. 238.

147. Gisberto of Alessandria et al., *Vita [B. Ambrosii Senensis]*, 10.102, *AS* 9 (Mar. iii), 198.

148. Giordano of Città di Castello, *Vita Beati Ubaldi Eugubini Episcopi*, 29.1–4, pp. 111–12: " 'Pax vobis, ego sum Ubaldus quem invocastis eugubinus episcopus' et confractis vinculis omnes de custodia eiecit."

149. *De Vita et Actibus Galgani*, 5–7, p. 74. The other patron of Siena, Saint Ansano, seems to have been known for similar liberations; see Siena, Biblioteca Comunale degli Intronati, ms F.viii.12 (early xiv cent.), fols. 580ᵛ–581ʳ.

150. Giunta Bevegnati, *Legenda . . . Margaritae de Cortona*, 11.7.46, p. 466.

water-related miracles: safety during storms at sea, aid for dropsy, and cures for jaundice.[151] Clavello the fisherman reported Ranieri's first miracle, a catch of fish. In the later 1200s, when hierarchical involvement had become more common in making saints, the papal commissions were very interested in saints' "virtues" while still alive. Nevertheless, a glance at the 1253 canonization-commission report of Saint Simone of Collazone, who died in 1250, reveals drab and stereotyped depositions on virtue. When reporting the miracles, the witnesses came alive.[152]

The good records for the shrine of Saint Zita at Lucca show how miracle working established the cult and canonized the saint. Zita died on 27 April 1272. A handful of miracles were reported at her tomb over the next five years. The cult might have died. But in 1278, the family who had employed Zita as a domestic hired the notary Fatinello de' Fatinelli to keep track of her miracles and publicize them. In his first year he notarized, catalogued, and publicized some 150 miracles at her tomb. Fatinello recorded sixty-eight of the miracles in the period from 1 to 5 May 1278, and eighty by the end of May. His good record keeping got Zita the recognition she deserved. With such statistics, none could question the serving girl's heavenly power.[153] Almost all the vitae of communal saints, especially the women, include collections of notarized shrine miracles as appendixes.[154] After miracles, publicity came next in importance. Domenico of Capodistria was in jail for homicide, awaiting execution, when he heard a blind man outside his window praising the miracles of Armanno Pungilupo of Ferrara. He vowed a week's fast and a pilgrimage to Armanno's tomb if he were freed. On the night before his execution, a pale man appeared to him and said, "Arise and leave this place." Domenico then found himself outside in the piazza. In accord with his vow, on 21 February 1270, he submitted a deposition to Don Giacobo de' Azani, the bishop of Ferrara's vicar. Word had traveled fast; it was hardly a month since Armanno's death.[155] At Ferrara, Armanno's cult was already a fixture, but the formal collection of miracles for his official canonization did not begin until 1286.[156]

151. Benincasa of Pisa, *Vita [S. Raynerii Pisani]*, 12.131, p. 371; 13, pp. 372–73; 15.154, p. 375.

152. In *Summarium Processus Vitae et Miraculorum B. Simonis a Collazzone Discipuli S. Francesci Fabricatum A. 1252 et 1253*, ed. D. M. Faloci Pulignani, in "Il b. Simone da Collazzone e il suo processo nel 1254," *Miscellanea Francescana* 12 (1910), compare the "virtutes," on pp. 117–20, with the "miracula," on pp. 120–32.

153. *Vita [Sanctae Zitae Virginis Lucencis]*, 5.33, pp. 512, 515–32.

154. E.g., for Saint Bona of Pisa, *Vita [Sanctae Bonae Virginis Pisanae]*, 6, pp. 156–60; for Saint Margherita of Città di Castello, *Vita Beatae Margaritae Virginis de Civitate Castelli*, 10–15, pp. 29–36; for Agnese of Montepulciano, Raimondo di Capua, *Legenda Beate Agnetis de Monte Policiano*, 3.1–12, pp. 68–102; for Saint Margherita of Cortona, Giunta Bevegnati, *Legenda . . . Margaritae de Cortona*, 11, pp. 453–78; for Saint Umiliana, Hippolito of Florence, *Miracula intra Triennium ab Obitu Patrata [B. Humilianae de Cerchis]*, AS 17 (May IV), 402–7 (first three years of the cult); and, finally, for Saint Ambrogio Sansedoni, *Miracula [B. Ambrosii]*, 200–207 (for the first two months of the cult). For another male example, see the records of Saint Antonio "the Pilgrim" of Padua in the 1270s, described in Rigon, "Dévotion et patriotisme," 270–71.

155. "Acta contra Armanum [Punzilupum]," 78.

156. On this incomplete process, dated 15 April 1300, see ibid., 72.

Any publicity was good publicity. The bishop of Mantua was preaching a sermon in honor of Saint Giovanni Buono when suddenly Armellina of Descanzano interrupted it to announce that Saint Giovanni had healed her from dropsy the night before. Witnesses described her running and jumping down the nave of the cathedral, calling attention to her cure.[157] One wonders what the bishop thought. Perhaps he was pleased to have his message confirmed from heaven. The notary Ser Guglielmo di Francesco, who had an unhealed broken leg, came to the tomb of Saint Margherita in the choir of the Dominican church at Città di Castello. He prayed, shed tears of repentance, and swore on the Gospels that "as much as human frailty permitted," he would avoid sexual sin. He was immediately healed and made it his special vocation to spread the saint's cult, repeating "with tears" the story of his healing to all and sundry. He filed a deposition regarding his cure (notarized by Giovanni di Francesco) at Margherita's shrine.[158] Armellina and Guglielmo were individual devotees. The establishment of a recognized cult demanded a dedicated, preferably local, group of admirers. This was easy for those belonging to a religious order, even an unofficial one. Saint Galgano, genuine hermit that he was, had attracted a group of *socii*, who attended him in his last illness. They promoted the cult after his death.[159] Saint Peter of Verona, the Dominican preacher martyred by the Cathars in 1252, had his order to organize protests after his murderer escaped and then to promote his shrine and cult.[160] Members of Saint Giovanni Buono's lay-hermit congregation testified at his canonization inquest, and eventually the Augustinians adopted the cause.[161] But canonization process or not, the ex-minstrel's cult, like that of other lay saints, was spread the old-fashioned way—by the people who had known him and for whom he had worked miracles. The canonization acta of his never-completed process show that it was artisans, workmen, and paupers who testified. There were no merchants, no nobles, and very few clerics.[162] Saint Giovanni was a man of the people.

The Franciscan Salimbene and an anonymous chronicler of Parma both provide vivid descriptions of the growth and establishment of the popular cult of Alberto of Villa d'Ogna "the wine porter" in the 1280s.[163] Alberto, a humble and pious laborer, had died at Cremona in 1279. Reports of the multiplying miracles at his tomb threw his hometown into religious exaltation. The reports reached Piacenza, where a chronicler recorded the death of "Saint Alberto, a man splendid for his miracles."[164] Throughout Lom-

157. *Processus . . . B. Joannis Boni*, 2.6.140–42, p. 807.
158. *Vita Beatae Margaritae Virginis de Civitate Castelli*, 10, p. 30.
159. *Vita Sancti Galgani*, 16–18, pp. 203–4.
160. Galvano Fiamma, *Manipulus Florum* (1252), 286, col. 684.
161. On the activities of these groups in his cult, see Golinelli, "Dal santo," 26–29.
162. See ibid., 29–31.
163. On Alberto, see the negative reports in Salimbene, *Cronica* (1279), 733–34, Baird trans., 512, and the positive one in *Chronicon Parmense* (1279), 34–35. The facts reported complement each other perfectly.
164. Giovanni de' Mussi, *Chronicon Placentinum* (1278), col. 481.

bardy, people made pilgrimage to the shrine at Cremona. Among these was a group of wine carriers from Parma, several of whom reported cures. They returned to Parma with relics of Alberto. Some of these the porters carried to nearby cities. At Parma itself, they got permission to display the relics in San Pietro near Piazza Nuova. At Reggio, that city's wine carriers' society displayed relics in the churches of San Giorgio and San Giovanni Battista. In both places, wine carriers began to congregate and venerate the relics. Soon the clergy joined the laity in flocking to Alberto's new shrine at Parma. The commune and the clergy erected pavilions and stretchers for the sick in the Piazza del Comune, facing the duomo of San Giminiano. The cathedral clergy offered solemn Masses daily. Cures multiplied. The ministers of the city, the wine carriers, and other devotees decorated Alberto's shrine in San Pietro with purple drapes, damask hangings, and a baldachino. Offerings estimated at the extraordinary sum of £300 imp. were collected. These permitted the commune to purchase the Malabranchi family's house in Strada Claudia, near the church of Santo Stefano, and establish there a hospital for the sick and poor, the Hospital of Saint Alberto. On his festival, the societies of the city processed through town with the reliquaries, carrying crosses and banners and singing. Priests erected images of him in their churches at popular request, and the city had his image painted on porticoes and city walls. From there, images and devotions spread to the villages and castles of the Parmese contado.

Lay devotion powered the canonization of Saint Alberto, the spread of his cult, and its subsequent patronage by the commune. The supervision of the cult was the work of the city government, which collected the offerings and oversaw expenditures. Clerical involvement began with the clergy of the chapels where the cult was located. It spread to the duomo after the people and commune demanded more splendid and public veneration. Cities played a role in the making of other saints. When the beggar penitent Saint Nevolone of Faenza died in 1280, the podesta, city officials, consuls, and the whole council attended the funeral with lighted candles. The first postmortem miracles were recorded at the deposition of his body on 18 July of that year.[165] When Saint Margherita of Città di Castello began to work miracles from her tomb, the city fathers paid for the balsam to embalm the body.[166] When Bishop Sicardo of Cremona made the first petition to Rome for a papal canonization, that of Saint Omobono, he acted in the name of his city.[167] It was at the request of the commune, as Pope Gregory IX admitted, that he granted approval to the cult of Saint Ambrogio of Massa.[168] During the canonization inquest for Saint Giovanni Buono, it was Mantua's city

---

165. Pietro Cantinelli, *Chronicon* (1280), 42.
166. *Legenda B. Margaritae de Castello*, 25–26, pp. 126–27.
167. *Vita Sancti Homoboni*, 115; see also Gatta, "Un antico codice," 108.
168. *Processus Ambrosii Massani*, 2, p. 572 (letter of Gregory IX).

herald Michelino who summoned the witnesses.[169] When Giovanni's canonization commission asked Domenica of Guastalla if she had come to testify of her free will, she replied that she had come "at the order of the commune."[170]

The cities had the power to ensure the continued observance of a cult. In 1286, at Pisa, the podesta and the captain of the people ordered all citizens to attend the ceremonies at the shrine of the new city patron Saint Ranieri (under fine of 20s pis.) and dispatched the criers to announce the festival.[171] Since Ranieri was both miracle working and popular, they probably need not have imposed a fine. But to insult the saint by absence would have insulted his city, so the fathers were determined to ensure a good turnout. After 1250, cities began to lobby Rome for recognition of the saints they had created. Padua appealed to Rome to protect the cult of their local hero, Saint Antonio the Pilgrim, in the face of Franciscan opposition. It seems that the Pilgrim, whose claim to holiness rested on his practice of penance, his fondness for pilgrimage, and his posthumous miracles, was giving competition to the Franciscan saint of the same name. The friars had more "pull" in Rome. The pope replied that "one Anthony is enough for you," and suppressed the Pilgrim's cult.[172] Times were changing. By the end of the century, the prerogative for promoting saints was becoming the property of the mendicant orders.[173]

Saints and Their Places

Each Italian city had a place, sometimes several places, to which people went on pilgrimage. Unlike the pilgrimage sites of Rome, these were not sites of events from biblical or ancient Christian times.[174] With few exceptions, such as the Jerusalem complex at Santo Stefano in Bologna, the shrines were depositories of relics of local saints. When one visited the churches of Ravenna, Fra Salimbene noted, the relics carried the indulgences, not the churches.[175] Even at Bologna's Santo Stefano, the relics of Saints Vitalis and Agricola became the major attraction by the late thirteenth century.[176] Although certainly not unknown there, the countryside outside Umbria and

169. *Processus . . . B. Joannis Boni*, pt. 2, pp. 797–814.

170. Ibid., 2.5.134, p. 805: "Interrogata si sponte venit ad hoc testimonium, respondit quod sibi praeceptum fecit per missum communis."

171. Pisa Stat. I (1286), 1.185, p. 339; Pisa Stat. II (1313), 1.233, p. 245.

172. See Rigon, "Dévotion et patriotisme," 271–73.

173. As evinced by the activity to get Saint Filippo Benizzi canonized at Todi in the 1280s; see *Processus Miraculorum B. Philippi [Benitii]*, ed. Arcangelo Giani, 1.1, *Annales Sacri Ordinis Fratrum Servorum Beatae Mariae Virginis* (Florence: Giunta, 1618), vol. 1, fol. 51ʳ.

174. Richard C. Trexler, "The Construction of Regional Solidarities in Traditional Europe," *Riti e rituali nelle società medievali*, ed. Chiffoleau, Martines, and Paravicini Bagliani, 263.

175. Salimbene, *Cronica* (1240), 245, Baird trans., 160.

176. Bologna, Biblioteca Universitaria, MS 1473, fol. 327ʳ, notes that the relics made the place holy, not vice versa.

the south lacked shrines of this type.[177] The best-known Tuscan exceptions are both Sienese. One was the shrine of Saint Ansano, the ancient martyr adopted as a communal patron.[178] The other was the shrine of Saint Galgano, but that shrine originated during the saint's lifetime because of relics that Galgano himself collected.[179] There were very few recorded healings or interventions linked to images—it was the saints' bones and the places touched by them that worked the cures.[180] When Umiliana visited the holy places of Florence, she visited the *loca sanctorum*, the places where relics resided. Beggars came, too. They knew where to go to find the crowds.[181] Saints themselves hallowed places. When the canons of the city of Cremona decided to erect a shrine for Saint Facio, they positioned his tomb on the very spot where he was accustomed to pray in the cathedral.[182] Saint Bona of Pisa appeared in a vision to a woman with a broken arm and identified herself as "Bona of San Martino," the saint whose shrine was in that particular parish. The woman understood and found the right church. In the shrine record, the largest block of miracles worked by Saint Bona were for people of her chapel.[183] The saint was local; the devotees were her neighbors.

Relics were a tangible sign of orthodoxy. The Cathars, who represented the major dissent from the Catholicism of the communes, rejected miracles (even if actual cures occurred) as religiously insignificant events. The physical world was under control of an evil god. For believers, devotion to the relics of the saints, along with reverence for the sacraments, was the truest sign of orthodoxy.[184] While perhaps more theologically sophisticated than most, the clergy and the city fathers understood this. They paid special attention to the shrines and relics in their churches. The clergy of Ravenna required that all relics not sealed within an altar stone be regularly examined for authenticity.[185] When a chronicler of Piacenza set out to list the podestas and consuls who had ruled his city, he appended a list of the major relics in his city's churches.[186] The monks of Santo Stefano in Bologna proudly claimed that their relics of Saints Vitalis and Agricola had been brought to Bologna by Saint Ambrose of Milan himself.[187] Bishops might patronize the relics of

177. As noted by Trexler, *Public Life*, 4.

178. On this shrine's replacing a pagan site, see Siena, Biblioteca Comunale degli Intronati, MS F.VIII.12, fols. 579^{r-v}.

179. See *Vita Sancti Galgani*, 13–14, pp. 199–202.

180. For two examples of images working cures, see the life of Saint Gerardo of Cagnoli: Bartolomeo Albizzi, *Legenda Sancti Gerardi*, 1.30, p. 406; 7.143, p. 441.

181. Vito of Cortona, *Vita [B. Humilianae]*, 1.5, p. 386.

182. *Vita Beati Facii*, 44–43, 49 (an extract from the necrology of the cathedral, Cremona, Archivio Capitolare, MS 1181, p. 335).

183. *Vita [Santae Bonae Virginis Pisanae]*, 6.62, p. 157; for the parishioners: ibid., 6.66–73, 75–76, pp. 158–59.

184. As noted by Raoul Manselli, "Il miracolo e i catari," *Bollettino della Società di studi valdesi* 140 (December 1976): 15–19.

185. Ravenna Council (1311), 5, p. 453.

186. *Chronica Rectorum Civitatis Placentiae*, RIS 16:611–26.

187. Bologna, Biblioteca Universitaria, MS 1473, fols. 325^{v}–326^{r}.

a particular saint. The Dominican bishop of Brescia, Bartolomeo di Breganza, gave special indulgences to those who venerated the relics of Saint Peter of Verona in the sacristy of his cathedral on the saint's feast day.[188]

We should not be deceived by monastic boasts or episcopal patronage. Not all shrines were equal: some shrines provided miracles, others did not.[189] People knew where to go when they were in need—usually. If not, they had to find out. In the mid-1200s, Donna Pametta of Reggio was demon obsessed, seeing scorpions attacking her head. After worthless visits to many shrines, she wasted her money on doctors. Finally, a male relative was going to Bologna, and she went along. She was not getting better. At the river Reno she fell in, and when her relative tried to save her, she tried to drown him. Other travelers had to pull them out. The party got to Bologna and lodged with a local woman. She tried to get Pametta to church on Sunday for Mass. Pametta tried to kill the woman with a sword. The neighbors tied the demoniac up and took her to church. There the demons shouted that only Saints Vitalis and Agricola could defeat them. The relatives and friends finally got the woman to the right tomb in Santo Stefano. She was healed as they kept vigil at the shrine through the night.[190] Accessibility was important. When the cathedral clergy of Treviso erected a shrine to their holy beggar Saint Enrico, they projected an arca in the center of the nave, raised on columns and decorated with statues of angels. On completion—after the delays occasioned by the war against Cane della Scala—the shrine included an altar to provide daily Mass for pilgrims.[191] A raised arca on six columns was the universal favorite: we also know of such tombs at the famous shrines of Saint Dominic at Bologna (no longer on its columns), Saint Anthony at Padua (only the columns remain, now in a portico, fig. 45), and Saint Peter of Verona at Milan (gloriously intact, fig. 46). In the first year after erection of the shrine of Saint Enrico, the numbers visiting the shrine were staggering, about a hundred a day, if the figure of thirty thousand a year given by his hagiographer is at all accurate.[192] Considering that his was a minor shrine in an out-of-the-way city, the crowds at the more popular pilgrimage sites must have been even greater.

With the greater crowds on the saint's day and on major feasts of the Church year, the possibility of miracles increased—as evident from the dates of miracles recorded at the shrine of Saint Giovanni Cacciaforte. Easter Week leads the entire year as a time for cures.[193] On Passion Sunday, just before Easter, at the shrine of Saint Pietro Parenzo in Orvieto, the crowds

188. See the decree in Meersseman, *Ordo*, 2:1037. The church also had special blessings for pilgrims: e.g., Pont. Rom. (XII), 47.1–3, p. 265.

189. As Trexler, *Public Life*, 83, notes.

190. Bologna, Biblioteca Universitaria, MS 1473, fol. 329ʳ.

191. Pierdomenico of Baone, *Vita B. Henrici Baucenensis*, 2.24, *AS* 22 (Jun. II), 369.

192. Ibid., 2.23, p. 369.

193. *Inquisitio de vita Joannis Cazefronte*, 246, 247, 255, 256, etc.

present at Mass—the hagiographer Giovanni among them—saw the lamps around his tomb miraculously lighted during the offertory. In the enthusiasm, several blind received their sight again.[194] Similar marvels happened at the tomb of Saint Peter of Verona in Milan.[195] At the tomb of Saint Pellegrino Laziosi in Forlì, the custodian, Vitale de' Avanzi, observed that people came as much to see miracles as to honor the saint. He had placards describing the cures made up and posted near the shine.[196] At Bologna and Siena, city statutes assured the safety of pilgrims to the local shrines and guarded the inviolability of wills drawn up in those holy places.[197] Local clergy provided encouragement and publicity in their shrine sermons.[198] The vernacular life of Saint Omobono of Cremona was probably originally such a panegyric.[199] The devout included aristocrats as well as commoners. At the shrine of Saint Ambrogio Sansedoni, Ser Giunta of Sant'Egidio, one of the Nine who governed the commune of Siena, was cured of his sore throat as he stood along with the plebeians.[200] The saints were great levelers.[201]

As diverse as the lives of the communal saints were the local rituals and practices at their shrines. The blessed Bona of Pisa was especially receptive to petitions made by locals with bare feet and dressed in sackcloth—recalling her own garb as a serving girl.[202] At the tomb of Saint Simone of Collazone, the best results came from kneeling and rubbing the afflicted part of the body on the tomb.[203] Healing power was physical and tangible. Brusca of Giano came to Saint Simone for a cure of her paralyzed hand. She put it through the opening in the shrine that allowed pilgrims to touch the reliquary inside. On touching it, she felt a "wind" pass through her hand; drawing it out, she found it healed.[204] Bishop Riccardo of Trivento, the guardian of the tomb of Saint Odo of Novara, was obliging. In serious cases he had the tomb opened and applied the saint's incorrupt hand to the afflicted part. Berarduccia di Oderisco di Pietro received such a ministration on the feast of Saint Nazarius in June of 1240. She was cured of a fistula on her jaw.[205] Contact could be more indirect. Friends brought a demoniac from Poggicavallo, in the contado of Bologna, to the feast of the new city patron, Saint

---

194. Giovanni of Orvieto, *Vita [S. Petri Parentii]*, cc. 4–5, esp. 5.39, p. 97.

195. *Vita S[ancti] Petri Martyris Ordinis Praedicatorum*, 5.42, p. 706 (from Tommaso of Agni's thirteenth-century vita).

196. Vitale de' Avanzi, *Leggenda del beato Pellegrino*, 167.

197. Bologna Stat. II (1288), 6.35, 2:31; Siena Stat. I (1262), 2.47–48, pp. 218–19.

198. I find little evidence for sacramental confessions at the shrines. The acta of Saint Giovanni Buono include two rare examples: *Processus . . . B. Joannis Boni*, 2.9.157, p. 811.

199. See, e.g., the closing exhortation, in *Vita di s. Omobono*, 169; on which, see Bertoni, "Una vita di S. Omobono," 170–71.

200. Recupero of Arezzo, *Summarium Virtutum*, 14.165, p. 229.

201. As remarked by Golinelli, "Dal santo," 33.

202. E.g., *Vita [Sanctae Bonae Virginis Pisanae]*, 6.68–71, p. 158.

203. E.g., *Summarium Processus . . . B. Simonis*, 2.5, p. 122; 2:14, p. 126.

204. Ibid., 2.6, p. 123.

205. *Apographum Processus . . . B. Odonis*, testis 24, pp. 344–45; for another opening, see ibid., testis 63, p. 349.

Petronio. She found freedom when the custodians covered her with the altar linens from the shrine containing the relics of Saint Vitalis and Agricola. The woman went away praising all three Bolognese saints and their power.[206]

While the tomb provided the most direct access to the saint, custodians provided portable objects of devotion. At the shrine of Saint Enrico in Treviso, Bartolomeo of Castagnolo, Antonio of Baone, and Girardo di Narlo, the three lawyers paid by the commune to record miracle depositions, supervised a stall distributing blessed bread and wine to pilgrims.[207] At the tomb of Saint Gerardo of Cagnoli, the custodian Bartolomeo wrote out cards with hymns and collects in honor of his saint. These could be taken away and used like relics for curing the sick—one touched them to the affliction.[208] The perfectly orthodox practice of leaving unconsecrated hosts on a saint's tomb overnight and keeping them as relics was not restricted to the shrine of the somewhat dubious Saint Guglielma at Milan.[209] The royal saint Elizabeth of Hungary's body famously exuded a trickle of miraculous oil. In this, she was outdone by the poor serving girl of Lucca: streams of oil gushed from the tomb of Saint Zita. Clergy and laity mopped it up and carried it away.[210] What the saint did not provide, the shrine custodians could. At the shrine of Saint Giovanni Buono, the custodians dipped his relics in water and distributed that to the faithful. At the shrine of Saint Gerardo of Cagnoli, they added rose essence to the infusion. At the tomb of Saint Simone of Collazone, Catarinuccia of Spoleto received a cure for cataracts by rinsing her eyes with water used to wash the tomb.[211] No saint's water was more celebrated in communal Italy than that of Saint Ranieri of Pisa. Saint Ranieri's Water originated when someone noticed that water used to wash his tomb had become perfumed with an aroma of wine.[212] His relic-infused water was available to all who visited. His hagiographer reminded readers that the saint himself had, while alive, blessed water for the sick.[213] Ranieri's

206. Bologna, Biblioteca Universitaria, ms 1473, fol. 328[r].

207. Pierdomenico of Baone, *Vita B. Henrici*, 2.20–22, pp. 368–69.

208. Bartolomeo Albizzi, *Legenda Sancti Gerardi*, 1.18–20, pp. 403–4, which includes one of the hymns.

209. Known from the trial of her followers for heresy: *Atti inquisitoriali [contro i Guglielmiti], Milano 1300: I processi inquisitoriali contro le devote e i devoti di santa Guglielma*, ed. Marina Benedetti (Milan: Scheiwiller, 1999), esp. 1.5, pp. 64–65. On this heresy, see Marina Benedetti, *Io non sono Dio: Guglielma di Milano e i figli dello Spirito Santo* (Milan: Biblioteca Francescana, 1998), and, more briefly, Stephen E. Wessley, "The Thirteenth-Century Guglielmites: Salvation Through Women," *Medieval Women*, ed. Derek Baker (Oxford: Blackwell, 1987), 289–303; the trial is partly translated by Trevor Dean in *The Towns of Italy in the Later Middle Ages* (Manchester: Manchester University Press, 2000), 88–94.

210. Salimbene, *Cronica* (1228), 50–51, Baird trans., 11, on Elizabeth of Hungary; and *Vita [Sanctae Zitae Virginis Lucencis]*, 5.36, p. 513, on Saint Zita. On this kind of miraculous secretion, technically called manna, see Charles M. Jones, *Saint Nicholas of Myra, Bari, and Manhattan: Biography of a Legend* (Chicago: University of Chicago Press, 1978), 66–73. I thank Fr. Michael Morris, O.P., of the Graduate Theological Union, Berkeley, Calif., for this reference.

211. *Processus . . . B. Joannis Boni*, 6.16.450, p. 884; Bartolomeo Albizzi, *Legenda Sancti Gerardi*, 2.48, p. 412; *Summarium Processus . . . B. Simonis*, 2.1, p. 120.

212. Benincasa of Pisa, *Vita [S. Raynerii Pisani]*, 14.143, p. 374; see Morris, "San Ranieri of Pisa," 595–97, on the miracle cult at this shrine.

213. Benincasa of Pisa, *Vita [S. Raynerii Pisani]*, 14, pp. 373–74.

vita includes the prayers to bless his water, so that readers could make more if they ran out.[214] These prayers are filled with biblical images, like those in the blessing of baptismal water at Easter. There is also a blessing of Saint Ranieri's bread, which could be taken to the sick. But it was the water that worked the greatest miracles. It gave the saint his nickname, "Saint Ranieri of the Water" (S. Raynerius de Aqua). One paralytic cured by use of Saint Ranieri Water donated his crutches to the church and became a shrine custodian. He rang the bells for daily Mass, and afterward people could find him on duty, dispensing Saint Ranieri Water to those who needed it.[215] The devout took Ranieri Water away for anointing and drinking. Sometimes it miraculously became wine. The hagiographer Benincasa of Pisa recorded two such miracles: once it became a light white; on the other, a fine rosé.[216]

CREATING A SPECIAL RELATIONSHIP

In 1240, Donna Orvetana obtained a cure for her crippled son, Belbruno, by laying him on top of the sarcophagus of Saint Ambrogio of Massa.[217] We find full body contact with saints throughout central and north Italy.[218] One petitioner at the shrine of Saint Benvenuta Bojani in Forlì made a prostration on top of the tomb and promised a Mass if she were cured.[219] At Cortona, Nuta, wife of Acorsuccio of Lucignano, placed her three-month-old son, Angiolo, on the altar containing relics of Saint Margherita. His older brother had accidentally suffocated the boy by tossing a pile of bedclothes on him while rushing to get his weapons for a street fight. Contact with the saint revived the infant.[220] At Saint Margherita of Città di Castello's shrine— which like many others was raised on pillars—the sick regularly slept under the arca, hoping for cures.[221] Whole families kept vigil together. Tofania di Giovanni of Vicenza had given birth to a paralyzed infant. She took him to the shrine of Saint Giovanni Cacciaforte for the vigil on the Purification of the Virgin. She spent the night in prayer with her husband and her sister-in-law. Her child was well in the morning.[222]

When immediate relief was not forthcoming, devotees extended contact with the tomb for a night or even several nights. On 21 December 1269, one week after the death of Saint Armanno Pungilupo, Gisla di Lendenaria, wife of Stefano of Villanova, spent the night in vigil at his tomb. At dawn, when

214. Ibid., 7.82–85, pp. 363–64.
215. Ibid., 13.133, p. 372; the shrine record includes numerous examples of Saint Ranieri Water, e.g., ibid., 9–10.95–111, pp. 366–68.
216. Ibid., 11.116–20, p. 369 (esp. 11.118, p. 369).
217. *Processus Ambrosii Massani*, 73, p. 601.
218. For examples at just one shrine, see *Summarium Processus . . . B. Simonis*, 2.3, p. 121; 2.4, p. 121; 2.18, p. 128.
219. Corrado of Cividale, *Vita Devotissimae Benevenutae*, 14.112, p. 180.
220. Giunta Bevegnati, *Legenda . . . Margaritae de Cortona*, 11.7.38, p. 454.
221. E.g, ibid., 12.12, p. 320.
222. *Inquisitio de vita Joannis Cazefronte*, 253.

the priest raised the Host at Mass on his altar, she was cured of paralysis in her arms. She gave in thanksgiving a wax arm and a candle as long as herself. Her husband confirmed her testimony concerning the miracle.[223] Bertoldo di Pietro spent four days and nights at Saint Armanno's tomb, beginning on the very day of his burial. His paralyzed arm was healed.[224] In Vicenza, Nicola de' Pianecci, a paralytic, had himself carried to the tomb of Saint Giovanni Cacciaforte, where he spent two nights before he was cured. He stayed on for another week giving thanks.[225] Perhaps the record for long-term petition is held by Palmeria di Gerardo de' Fontanivi of Vicenza, who prayed twenty-two days and nights at the shrine of Saint Giovanni Caccia-forte before the saint cured her limp.[226]

Such extended vigils can only be described as "incubation," the ancient practice of sleeping in a temple in hope for a cure, as at the famous shrine of Asclepias at Epidaurus in the Peloponnese.[227] The practice of sleeping in shrines was known elsewhere in Christian Europe. Fra Salimbene of Parma spent a night in the cave of Saint Mary Magdalen near Marseilles.[228] The Dominican preacher Bartolomeo of Braganze, bishop of Brescia, recorded that while sleeping overnight at the tomb of Saint Peter in Rome, a hermit learned the birth date of the Blessed Virgin.[229] But these are isolated examples. In communal Italy, examples of incubation multiply everywhere. In antiquity, the devotees hoped for advice from the healing deity in dreams, and dreams do sometimes figure in Italian miracle stories. Nicola of Tolentino's parents heard the prediction of their son's birth from Saint Nicholas of Myra while sleeping in his shrine at Bari.[230] But the incubators of the communal shrines hoped for healing from extended contact with the relics.[231] At the shrine of Saint Giovanni Buono in Mantua, canonization records provide striking examples. One woman vowed to sleep five nights at Giovanni's tomb and, having done so, was cured of blindness.[232] At that shrine, incubation usually took place in the *fossa*, the empty grave from which the saint's body had been translated, rather than at the shrine proper. This

223. "Acta contra Armanum [Punzilupum]," 73. For another successful all-night vigil, see *Processus Miraculorum B. Philippi [Benitii]*, 1.10, fol. 51ᵛ.
224. "Acta contra Armanum [Punzilupum]," 79–89.
225. *Inquisitio de vita Joannis Cazefronte*, 246–47.
226. Ibid., 258.
227. On ancient incubation, see Hans-Joseph Klauck, *The Religious Context of Early Christianity: A Guide to Graeco-Roman Religions*, trans. Brian McNeil (Edinburgh: Clark, 2000), 154–68, which includes bibliography. On incubation in the Italian communes, see Golinelli, *Città e culto*, 63–65.
228. Salimbene, *Cronica* (1283), 762, Baird trans., 531.
229. Bartolomeo of Vicenza, *Sermones de Beata Virgine (1266)*, Sermo 34.2, p. 207; also reported in Giacomo of Varazze's *Golden Legend*, trans. Granger Ryan and Helmut Ripperger (New York: Arno, 1969), 524–25.
230. Pietro of Monte Rubiano, *Vita [S. Nicolai Tolentinatis]*, 1.1, *AS* 43 (Sept. III), 645.
231. See examples in Bernardo Balbi, *Vita [S. Lanfranci]*, 4.40, p. 540; Recupero of Arezzo, *Summarium Virtutum*, 12.129, p. 226; *Processus Ambrosii Massani*, 33, p. 587–88, and 90, p. 606; *Processus . . . B. Joannis Boni*, 2.1.101–2, p. 798.
232. *Processus . . . B. Joannis Boni*, 2.4.123, p. 803.

practice originated with Tommasina di Allegro de' Fassani, who came to the shrine on the day of the translation. Tommasina suffered from a pustulating fistula in her left cheek. She climbed down into the open grave, where she saw other devotees praying, and spent the night in it. She woke in the morning to find herself cured "on account of the reverence shown to the man of God." She was too poor to make an offering, so she went and gleaned some grain—probably to be made into Hosts for Mass—and gave it to the brothers at the shrine. They returned it to her "for the love of God."[233]

Incubators at Giovanni's tomb heard Mass or Office at the shrine the following morning, and some miracles happened then rather than during the night.[234] One devotee, Marta, wife of Don Falchetto of Mantua, from the contrada of San Simone, who suffered from gout, came to sleep in the cloister of the shrine church so that she could hear Matins on the morning of the translation. After Matins, as the saint's body was raised, she found herself freed of her affliction.[235] The crippled Massarola, daughter of Lanfranco de' Bagatini of Desenzano, near Brescia, vowed to incubate five nights at the tomb of Saint Giovanni, but when she arrived, the crowds were so great that she could not approach the tomb. She had to be satisfied with sleeping in the cloister, promising to fast a day a week if cured.[236] She went home restored to health. Giovanni could work his cures at a distance if the petitioner showed proper devotion.

Sometimes the petitioner might strike a bargain with the saint. Donna Riccadonna of Ruga Mattiera, near Mantua, had a beautiful fat pig that became sick and went off its feed for a week. She vowed a candle "with a wick the same length as her pig" to Saint Giovanni Buono and promised to pray before his tomb as long as the candle burned if Giovanni helped her stricken animal. The pig ate; her candle burned all night.[237] Giovanni had done his duty. The sight of Riccadonna in prayer with her candle must have made an impression on those visiting the tomb. A devotee of Saint Pietro Parenzi vowed in return for a healing that he would have a deposition describing the cure notarized and entered in the shrine records at Orvieto.[238] At the shrines of the mendicant saints, parents of sick children vowed to have their children wear a miniature version of the order's habit, should a cure be granted. Such a child, wearing the Augustinian habit, can be seen today in an altarpiece of Saint Agostino Novello by Simoni Martini in Siena, a witness to the saint's intercession (fig. 47). Nicoluzzo di Giunta fulfilled such a vow after the Servite saint Francesco Patrizzi cured his son Guntino of

---

233. Ibid., 2.3.112, p. 801.
234. Ibid., 2.4.120, p. 803.
235. Ibid., 2.3.115–19, pp. 802–3.
236. Ibid., 2.6.135, p. 806.
237. Ibid., 6.7.372–74, p. 867.
238. Giovanni of Orvieto, *Vita [S. Petri Parentii]*, 6.47, pp. 98–99.

dropsy.[239] A vow might be the only remedy for the misfortunes inflicted on those who failed to recognize the saint's holiness. Maria di fu Albertino of Padua dragged her husband, Albertino, to visit the shrine of Saint Giovanni Cacciaforte in Vicenza. As she stood paying her respects at the tomb, with a crowd of other women, Albertino lost his patience. He blurted out, "Silly women, what are you doing praying to that saint?" He left and went down-town to the Palazzo Comunale to buy fish for Wednesday lunch. His wife returned to find him deathly ill from eating the fish. He lay sick until Friday, when he finally pledged a candle to Saint Giovanni. His friends Triviso and Albrigetto carried him to the tomb and, after a sweat during Vespers, he was healed.[240] Giovanni got his candle.

A candle like Albertino's—or, better, one with particular specifications, like Riccadonna's—was by far the most common votive offering to the com-munal saints. Such offerings by private devotees mirrored the city oblations during their great candle-offering ceremonies. Some individuals vowed not merely a single candle but sets of them representing sacred numbers, seven for the sacraments, twelve for the apostles, or three for the Trinity—as devo-tees of Saint Benvenuta Bojani did at the church of San Domenico in Forlì.[241] In Mantua, Giovanni di Ugo de' Vitali promised Saint Giovanni Buono a candle every year on his feast day, if the saint would heal his daugh-ter of paralysis—which he did.[242] At the shrine of Saint Ranieri of Pisa, the faithful commonly vowed candles as tall as themselves or of their specific weight.[243] Such candles symbolically represented the person of the donor. In desperate cases, they even vowed to circle the entire shrine with candles.[244] Sometimes the candles were so tall that it was impossible to relight them when they blew out. Saint Giovanni Buono understood the problem and intervened, rekindling candles at his tomb when drafts extinguished them.[245] One knew better than to remove such consecrated votive offerings. Or one learned. Liutefredo, a novice of Santo Stefano in Bologna, walked off one night with a very beautiful candle from the shrine of Saint Bononio. An angel not only struck him with illness but revealed his crime to the abbot in a dream.[246]

While the lighted candle was always the most popular offering, many preferred more permanent memorials, albeit also in wax. These represented

239. Cristoforo of Parma, *Legenda Beati Francisci*, 49, p. 193; for similar practices at the shrine of Saint Ambrogio Sansedoni, see Gisberto of Alessandria et al., *Vita [B. Ambrosii]*, 10.91, p. 197; and at the Servite shrine of Saint Filippo Benizzi, *Processus Miraculorum B. Philippi [Benitii]*, 1.23, fol. 52ʳ.

240. *Inquisitio de vita Joannis Cazefronte*, 248.

241. Corrado of Cividale, *Vita Devotissimae Benevenutae*, 15.124, p. 183.

242. *Processus . . . B. Joannis Boni*, 2.7.145, p. 808.

243. E.g., Benincasa of Pisa, *Vita [S. Raynerii Pisani]*, 18.183, p. 380 (height); 13.135–36, p. 372; 16.160, p. 376.

244. E.g., ibid., 15.149, p. 374.

245. *Processus . . . B. Joannis Boni*, 6.16.450, p. 884.

246. Bologna, Biblioteca Universitaria, MS 1473, fols. 164ᵛ–165ʳ.

the part of the body healed or even the whole body. We find records of such "ex-voto" wax images in the twelfth century at Cremona, where Bishop Sicardo witnessed a document promising one to the shrine of Saint Raimondo at Piacenza in return for a cure from jaundice.[247] The practice is certainly much older, possibly in continuity with similar practices at the healing shrines of antiquity.[248] But the practice seems a revival of pagan practice without having any direct link thereto. When a woman brought a wax ex-voto of her once deformed hand to the shrine of Saint Galgano in 1185, Bishop Ugo of Volterra, who was also visiting the tomb, asked her what she meant by the offering. Perhaps he was merely curious, but he seems not to have been acquainted with the practice.[249] By the 1200s, wax ex-votos were ubiquitous.[250] At the tomb of Saint Umiliana in Santa Croce at Florence, one man not only left an ex-voto, he had the notary trace in the shrine record the size and shape of the bone in his throat that the saint had helped him cough up.[251] Occasionally, records report other offerings, such as a silver cord long enough to go around the tomb.[252] But the traditional offering remained wax. Devotees of Saint Margherita of Cortona regularly vowed to circle her shrine, not with silver, but with candles, often including in their vows the monetary value of the wax promised.[253]

A late medieval chronicle for Todi records that in 1313, after a knight of the podesta was saved from ambush through the intercession of Saint Fortunatus, the man made a magnificent offering to that saint's church. This included twenty-nine pounds of silver and four hundred gold florins, enough to build the saint a new chapel and furnish it.[254] Such a lavish offering was truly exceptional in the communal period. Vows of money were rare and usually for small amounts: 5s. for a cure by Saint Simone of Collazone or 10s. (with some lime) for a cure by Saint Ambrogio of Massa.[255] The candles offered came mostly from local shops rather than the sacristy of the shrine. Offerings for Masses, such as those supervised by the commune at the altar of Saint Fina in San Gimignano, were a bit more profitable than candles,

247. "Miraculorum S. Raymundi ex ms. Archivi Monialium Ejusdem Sancti Placentiae," *AS* 33 (Jul. VI), 657–58; for more on Raimondo's miracles, see Canetti, *Gloriosa*, 216–27.

248. See Klauck, *Religious Context*, 165.

249. *De Vita et Actibus Galgani*, 18–19, pp. 76–77.

250. A few of the many examples of the practice: *Summarium Processus . . . B. Simonis*, 2.11, p. 25; *Processus Miraculorum B. Philippi [Benitii]*, 1.32, fol. 53ᵛ; Bartolomeo Albizzi, *Legenda Sancti Gerardi*, 7.144, p. 441; Benincasa of Pisa, *Vita [S. Raynerii Pisani]*, 16.164–65, p. 376–77; *Vita S[ancti] Petri Martyris Ordinis Praedicatorum*, 13.99, p. 722 (Tommaso of Agni's thirteenth-century vita); Recupero of Arezzo, *Summarium Virtutum*, 9.103, p. 223.

251. Hippolito of Florence. *Miracula intra Triennium*, 404.

252. *Miracula [B. Ambrosii]*, doc. 17, p. 205.

253. E.g., Giunta Bevegnati, *Legenda . . . Margaritae de Cortona*, 11.1.1, p. 454; 11.2.10, p. 456; 11.9.56, p. 469.

254. Ioan Fabrizio degli Atti, *Cronicha de la egregia città de Tode*, ed. Franco Mancini, *Le cronache di Todi (secoli XIII–XVI)* (Florence: Nuova Italia, 1979), 163–64.

255. *Summarium Processus . . . B. Simonis*, 2.16, p. 127; *Processus Canonizationis B. Ambrosii Massani*, pp. 571–608.

but these fees did not come from pilgrims or because of vows.[256] Where the income at the shrine of a communal saint can actually be calculated—as Daniel Bornstein has done for that of Saint Margherita of Cortona in the period 1369–84—the yearly "take" averaged a mere £30, a quarter of the yearly earnings of a day laborer in Florence.[257] Granted the local hostels and taverns got some business from pilgrims, but one is left with the conclusion that the communes did not promote their saints as a source of cash. Devotion to the local shrine was synonymous with civic patriotism.[258] The shrine reflected the honor of the city that produced the saint; it made the city holy.

256. San Gimignano Stat. (1255), 4.101, pp. 741–42.
257. Bornstein, "Uses of the Body," 174; on the Franciscan appropriation of her cult, see ibid., 169–77.
258. As noted by Rigon, "Dévotion et patriotisme," esp. 267.

fig. 34 Altarpiece showing Margherita of Cortona, a lay penitent, in her homemade habit, late thirteenth century. Cortona, Museo Diocesano. (photo: Soprintendenza per i Beni Artistici e Storici)

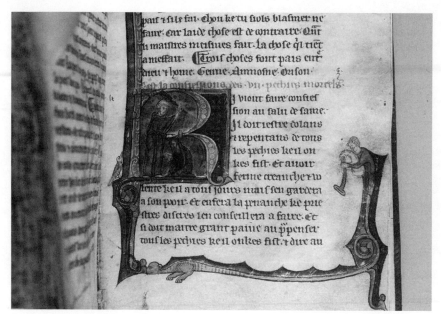

fig. 35 Monk receiving penance, miniature, fourteenth century. Modena, Biblioteca Estense Universitaria, MS a.P.9.1, fol. 114ʳ.

fig. 36 Porta Ticinese, Milan, showing Saint Lawrence, Saint Ambrose, Virgin and Child, Saint Eustorgius, and Saint Peter Martyr, from the workshop of Giovanni di Balduccio, thirteenth century.

fig. 37 The duomo at Siena, crossing column, incorporating a drawbar from the Sienese carroccio at the Battle of Montaperti, 1260. (photo: Christine Sundt)

fig. 38 Saint Zeno gives his blessing to the communal army of Verona,
church of San Zeno, west tympanum.

fig. 39 The life of Saint Petronio in
the martyrology of Santo Stefano.
Bologna, Biblioteca Universitaria, MS
1473, fol. 254ʳ, ca. 1180. (photo:
Gianni Roncaglia; permission granted
by Biblioteca Universitaria, Bologna)

fig. 40 City statutes of 1187 carved on the cathedral of Ferrara, as seen today in a shop at Piazza Trento Trieste, 21.

fig. 41 Units of measure built into the wall of the Palazzo Comunale, Bologna.

fig. 42 Palazzo del Podestà, Bologna, city chapel, thirteenth century.

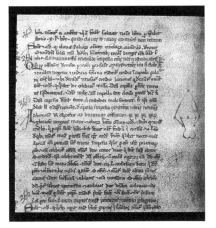

fig. 43 Bolognese statutes of 1259 showing the lamp designed by the city fathers for their chapel. Bologna, Archivio di Stato, MS Comune Governo, vol. 4, fol. 36ᵛ. (photo: Ministero per i Beni e le Attività Culturali, Archivio di Stato, Bologna)

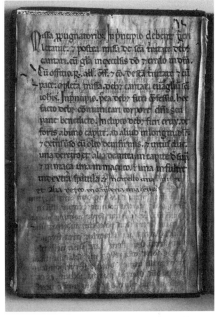

fig. 44 Ritual for trial by battle pasted onto a manuscript flyleaf, thirteenth century. Parma, Biblioteca Palatina, MS Par. 44, fol. 0ᵛ.

fig. 45 Santa Maria dei Servi, Padua, porch columns from the old shrine of Saint Anthony of Padua, demolished 1372.

fig. 46 Sant'Eustorgio, Cappella Portinari, Milan, tomb of Saint Peter of Verona, 1338.

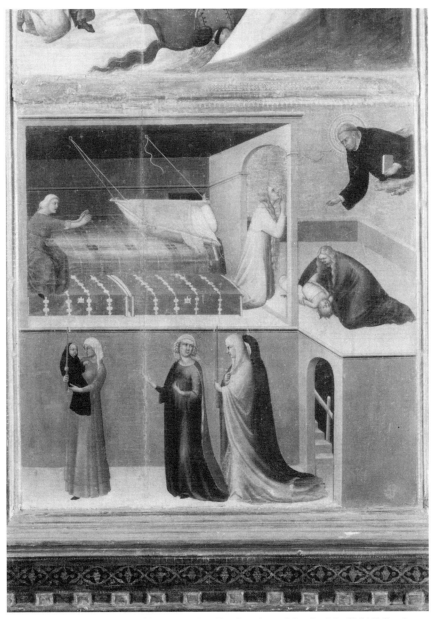

fig. 47 Simoni Martini, Sant'Agostino Novello altarpiece, *Miracle of the Child Fallen from the Cradle*. Siena, Pinacoteca Nazionale. (photo: Art Resource, New York)

fig. 48 A layman at prayer, kneeling before an image of the Virgin, from Peter the Chanter of Paris, *De Oratione et Speciebus Illius*. Padua, Biblioteca Antoniana, MS 532, fol. 47ᵛ, thirteenth century.

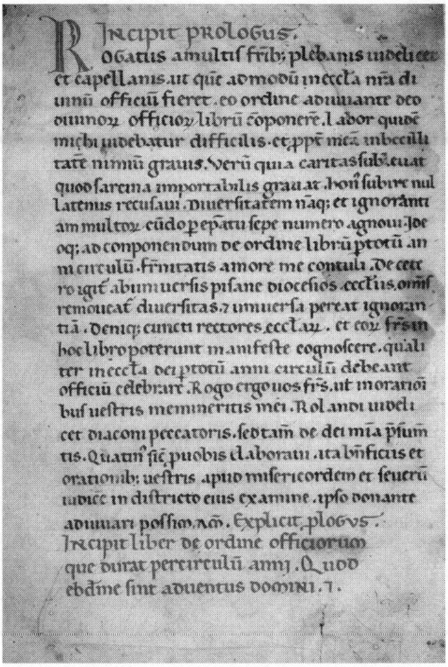

fig. 49 Rolando the Deacon, *Liber de Ordine Officiorum*. Bologna, Biblioteca Universitaria, MS 1785, fol. 1ᵛ, late 1100s. (photo: Gianni Roncaglia; permission granted by Biblioteca Universitaria, Bologna)

fig. 50 A typical low chancel screen, in the pieve church of San Giorgio in Brancoli, near Lucca, ca. 1194.

fig. 51 The Palm Sunday procession entrance at Verona, Pons Fractus, twelfth century.

fig. 52 Laymen use their bodies in prayer, from Peter the Chanter of Paris, *De Oratione et Speciebus Illius*. Padua, Biblioteca Antoniana, MS 532, fol. 45ʳ, thirteenth century.

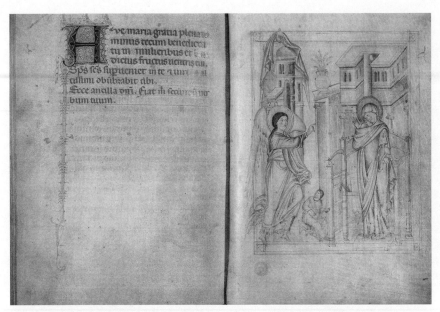

fig. 53 Words of prayer before an image, from a Florentine book of devotion. Florence, Biblioteca Medicea Laurenziana, MS Pl. xxv 3, fol. 365ᵛ–366ʳ, late thirteenth century. (photo: Micofoto; permission granted by Biblioteca Medicea Laurenziana, Florence)

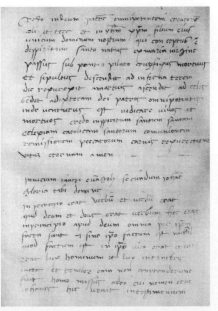

fig. 54 Omobono of Cremona and Raimondo of Piacenza follow Bernard and Columban in the litany from a Paduan book of devotion. Padua, Biblioteca Universitaria, MS 469, fol. 113ʳ, ca. 1300. (photo: Biblioteca Universitaria, Padua)

fig. 55 The Credo in Latin in a vernacular book of devotion. Modena, Biblioteca Estense Universitaria, MS γ.W.2.40, fol. 4ʳ, early fourteenth century. (permission granted from Biblioteca Estense Universitaria, Modena)

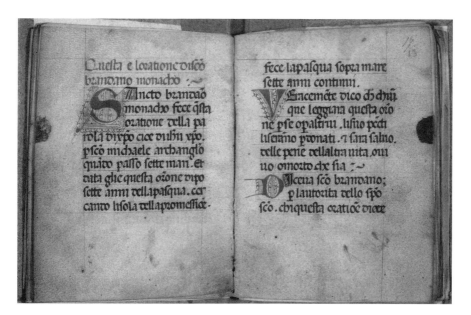

fig. 56 Prayer to Saint Brendan in a Sienese book of devotion. Siena, Biblioteca Comunale degli Intronati, MS I.VIII.21, fols. 16ᵛ–17ʳ, fourteenth century. (photo: Renzo Pepi, permission granted by Biblioteca Comunale degli Intronati, Siena, 20 October 2003)

fig. 57 Christ with a ground line to calculate his height, in a Florentine book of devotion. Florence, Biblioteca Medicea Laurenziana, MS Pl. XXV 3, fol. 15ᵛ, late thirteenth century. (photo: MicoFoto; permission granted by Biblioteca Medicea Laurenziana, Florence)

fig.58 Holy women (Mary of Cleophas and Mary Magdalene) raise the pianto, but Saint John maintains a priestly reserve, in Niccolò dell'Arca's *Compianto su Cristo morto*, Santa Maria della Vita, Bologna, 1463.

fig. 59 The tomb of Rolandino de' Passaggeri, Piazza San Domenico, Bologna, fourteenth century.

fig. 60 Site of the protests of 1299: Piazza Maggiore, from the Asinelli tower, Bologna.

fig. 61 Site of Fra Guido's condemnations, May 1299: Arenga tower, Palazzo del Podestà, from the Piazza del Nettuno, Bologna, thirteenth century.

PART TWO

Buoni Cattolici

RELIGIOUS OBSERVANCE

Chapter Six
The City Worships

To be a citizen of the commune was to take part in its corporate life. This was both an obligation and a right. To belong to the city meant to be part of a quarter, a neighborhood, and a chapel. Medieval Italians belonged to the place where they worshiped, where they experienced the sacred rituals that made them Christians. In the records of the collegiate church of Santa Maria delle Vigne of Genoa from the 1170s, *parrocchiani*, parishioners, belonged to the church where they "heard Mass and Vespers," confessed and took Communion, and, at marriage, received the nuptial blessing. By the early 1300s, participation in the Church's rites and reception of the sacraments were not simply marks of a parishioner, they were the parishioner's *diritti*, rights. People considered a family a true "neighbor" if their involvement in the local church's rituals had lasted at least a generation.[1] Only in 1324 do documents at Santa Maria delle Vigne begin to define the parish geographically.[2] It is notable what rites the documents do not include: baptism and confirmation. Reception of those sacraments joined one to the Mother Church itself; all received them at the cathedral and its baptistery. A heretic, the nonneighbor, became so by not participating in worship, by avoiding the Catholic clergy, and, after Lateran IV, by refusing Easter Communion.[3]

This practical understanding of orthodoxy explains the exceeding oddity of the inquisition penances imposed on convicted heretics in the thirteenth century. The inquisitor Guido of Vicenza sentenced Zaccaria di Sant'Agata

---

1. A. Boldorini, "Aspetti e momenti della *Cura Animarum* nel basso Medioevo ligure (secc. XIII–XV) con appendice documentaria," *Archivum Ecclesiae Ianuensis* 1 (1981): 7, 33–46, and Geo Pistarino, "Diocesi, pievi, e parrocchie nella Liguria medievale (secoli XII–XV)," *Pievi e parrocchie*, ed. Erba et al., 2:656–57.

2. Boldorini, "Aspetti," 46–50.

3. On this, see Grado G. Merlo, "'Cura Animarum' ed eretici," *Pievi e parrocchie*, ed. Erba et al., 1:551.

of Bologna, who had fallen afoul of the Bolognese inquisition, to the "penance" of confessing once a year and going to Mass on feast days (but not Sundays?). The Bolognese inquisition sentenced a Paterine of Vicenza to visit the Franciscan church there, to genuflect three times, and to say an Ave Maria and a Pater Noster.[4] Orthodoxy followed from participation in the religious life of the Catholic community and in the practice of its devotions. Even an intellectual like Fra Guido, with his sometimes painfully doctrinal understanding of orthodoxy, knew that reforming dissenters meant reimmersing them into the community of believers and that community's devotional life.

The House of Prayer

Every church or chapel, whether public or private, was part of the greater religious entity of the diocese. In theory, at least, no individual, clerical or lay, could erect an altar, chapel, or oratory without the permission of the bishop.[5] Whatever the law about permission, the local chapel was the collective property of those who worshiped there. The people built it, and they paid for it. Provision of the vestments, Mass books, and other paraphernalia was a responsibility shared half-and-half by priests and people. Clergy and people owned the altar goods in common.[6] But some vestments belonged to the laity alone, such as those made from the gifts of their dress clothing. The emperor Henry VII gave his cloth-of-gold gown to the church of Sant'Eustorgio in Milan to make paraments and a cope. Donna Berirama from the parish of Oppreno did the same, in a more modest way, when she gave a silk dress to her church.[7] Donors could see their benefactions in use on any given Sunday or feast. Attachment to the chapel and its rights was intense. Bishop Lanfranco Civolla of Bergamo announced from the cathedral pulpit in 1187 that the priests and people of San Giovanni, San Salvatore, Sant' Agata, and Santa Grata delle Vigne were henceforth to go to the collegiate church of Sant'Alessandro for Mass on Sundays and feasts. This was an abridgment of local autonomy and caused an outburst of murmuring. The bishop explained in self-defense that he acted on order of Pope Urban III himself.[8] Throughout a diocese or ecclesiastical province, the same rituals and celebrations created unified liturgical culture, but the place of prayer, its equipment, and the organization of worship there were always a local matter.[9]

4. *ASOB*, 1:147. On these examples, see Gabriele Zanella, "Malessere ereticale in valle padana (1260–1308)," *Hereticalia*, 64–65.

5. Milan Council (1287), 24, pp. 879–80.

6. Ravenna Council (1311), 8, p. 454.

7. Galvano Fiamma, *Cronica Maior* (1311), 338–39.

8. "Instrumentum Litis" (September 1187—Alberto Vacca, priest), 1.8, p. 141.

9. On the unifying effects of shared rites, see Antonio Rigon, "Organizzazione ecclesiastica e cura d'anime nelle Venezie: Ricerche in corso e problemi da risolvere," *Pievi e parrocchie*, ed. Erba et al., 2:706–7.

All churches, except perhaps private chapels, had some sort of barrier or physical demarcation separating the choir of the clergy from the nave of the laity. This division reflected the clergy and people's condominium of ownership. The people stood or knelt to pray outside in the nave, which was free of the modern clutter of pews. Medieval screens provided more than visual access to the choir; the central door allowed processions to leave and enter (fig. 30). The clergy came to the people's side for rites like the blessing of candles on Candlemas, and the people entered the choir for the marriage blessing.[10] In the nave, the parishioners had great freedom of movement and expression, in part because they literally owned it. Much to the irritation of clerics, people wandered onto the clergy's side of the screen to venerate altars and relics or simply to gawk.[11] The screen was not an impassible barrier; its door did not have a lock. Benvenuta Bojani once received Communion at a Dominican church on the feast of the order's founder. As she made her thanksgiving, Saint Dominic himself appeared and healed her of a disability in her legs. He then led her and two other pious women through the door of the screen into the choir, much to the displeasure of the sacristan (who could not see the saint). Benvenuta went directly to the high altar, where she professed a vow of chastity to God. Other women in the church, inspired by her example, crowded into the choir after her. After giving thanks there at the side altars of the Blessed Virgin and Saint Dominic, Benvenuta cast away her staff and walked home. Her hagiographer complained that her presence in the choir was "contrary to custom," but it was hardly unusual.[12]

Nearly every church of the communal period was built with its apse toward the east. When a bishop blessed a church, he pronounced the consecratory prayers toward the east and the rising sun, positioning himself along the west-east axis of the building.[13] When they assembled, the people and clergy faced toward the east, toward the high altar. When Christians turned to the east in western Europe, they also turned toward the Holy Land and the city of Jerusalem, the place where the Savior died, rose, and would return.[14] Their posture showed that they expected the completion of salvation history and the end of time. The assembly was a people on the march in time and space; they did not pray turned in on themselves. So universal and normative was this positioning in cosmic space and sacred time, even during private prayer, that during the inquisition investigation of the popularly canonized Saint Armanno Pungilupo, the witness Bonfandino wondered

---

10. See Verona, Biblioteca Capitolare, MS LXXXIV (XII cent.), fols. 73ᵛ–74ᵛ.

11. Cremona Cath. Stat. (1247), 40, p. 458.

12. Corrado of Cividale, *Vita Devotissimae Benevenutae*, 3.29, p. 157.

13. Sicardo, *Mitrale*, 1.2, col. 17. On Sicardo's views on the Mass, see Mary M. Schaefer, "Twelfth-Century Latin Commentaries on the Mass: Christological and Ecclesiological Dimensions" (Ph.D. diss., University of Notre Dame, 1983).

14. Richard C. Trexler, *The Christian at Prayer: An Illustrated Prayer Manual Attributed to Peter the Chanter (d. 1197)* (Binghamton, N.Y.: Medieval and Renaissance Texts and Studies, 1987), 38.

whether the holy man's occasional failure to pray facing east might indicate heresy.[15] As the 1200s progressed, the laity became ever more sensitive to the division of sacred and profane space and activity. They made their own part of the church, the nave, as sacred a place as the choir, to be used for prayer, not for secular business. One lay writer emphasized that in the nave one paid reverence to God and the saints quietly: no laughing, games, jokes, or nonsense.[16] Cities soon looked with horror on the older uses of the nave for drinking, assignations with women, or, even worse, violence or insult.[17]

Peter the Chanter, in a manual of prayer circulated in communal Italy, explained how to enter the church. "Catholic men and women" first knelt or bowed toward the altar in the east, reciting a Gloria Patri to greet the Trinity. That prayer was also a suitable greeting for the Savior after the Consecration at Mass.[18] Kneeling to pray or express reverence was relatively new in the thirteenth century, and it was a lay habit (see fig. 48).[19] The clergy chanted their prayers sitting or standing. Priests still made a deep bow to the cross as a gesture of respect; the lay faithful preferred to kneel. The Franciscan Salimbene of Parma noted that thirteenth-century layfolk not only knelt to pray, they were rapidly adopting the single-knee genuflection—especially at the elevation of the Host.[20] Salimbene's remarks suggest that not all priests liked laypeople's freedom of bodily expression. Better that the laity conform to clerical styles, like standing for prayer. Popes, however, showed themselves more open to lay piety. Starting with the reign of Gregory IX (1227–41), the friend of Saint Francis, images of popes at prayer invariably show them kneeling with hands folded, the lay posture, in place of the older iconography showing the pope standing with arms extended, the clerical mode.[21] The laity eventually won over the clerics: priests adopted the lay genuflection beginning in the early 1300s, but it did not become the normal priestly form of reverence at Mass until the end of the fifteenth century. For the laity, action and gesture expressed inner prayers and dispositions better than spoken words. After four of his children suddenly died, Raimondo of Piacenza took his fifth child to the church of Santa Brigitta, where he was accustomed to hear the Mass and Office. He stood before the great cross on the choir screen and silently held the child aloft, thereby promising Christ that he

15. "Acta contra Armanum [Punzilupum]," 55.

16. Zucchero Bencivenni, *Sposizione*, 84.

17. Mantua Stat., 5.12, 2:96; Parma Stat. 1 (by 1255), p. 275.

18. Peter the Chanter, *De Oratione et Speciebus Illius, The Christian at Prayer*, ed. Trexler, 190.

19. On the lay love of kneeling, see Pietro Browne, "L'attegiamento del corpo durante la Messa," *Ephemerides Liturgicae* 50 (1936): 404–5.

20. Salimbene, *Cronica* (1248), 444, Baird trans., 304. See Trexler, *Christian at Prayer*, 86, on the lay origins of the genuflection. For Peter the Chanter's views on adoration of the Host, see V. L. Kennedy, "The Moment of Consecration and the Elevation of the Host," *Medieval Studies* 6 (1944): 139–42.

21. See, on this shift, Gerhart B. Ladner, "The Gestures of Prayer in Papal Iconography of the Thirteenth and Early Fourteenth Centuries," *Didascaliae: Studies in Honor of Anselm M. Albareda, Prefect of the Vatican Library*, ed. Sesto Prete (New York: Rosenthal, 1961), 245–75.

would devote the infant to a life of chastity. Raimondo kept the oblation a secret for the rest of his life. When, on his deathbed, he revealed the oblation to his son, the young man promised to keep the vow. At his father's funeral, he asked the bishop to make him a frater in the *canonica* founded by his father, so that he might serve at Raimondo's tomb.[22]

THE PEOPLE'S SHARE IN WORSHIP

Medieval Catholics did not share the view that unreflective believers were semipagans whose ignorance barred them from true Christianity. The medieval Church was composed of "doing Christians as well as comprehending Christians."[23] That the lay faithful might not fully understand or mouth the language of the liturgy did not mean that they somehow failed to participate in the rite. There is a temptation to see bald incomprehension as the condition of simple people with no Latin. Waldensian heretics, described by Peronetta de Bruna to the inquisitor Fra Alberto of Castellario in 1335, reflect this prejudice. The heretics had told her that after Christ's death the twelve apostles divided into two groups. A group of four "sang the books of Christ so all could understand," meaning "in the common tongue," and a group of eight sang "from other books no one could understand," meaning "in Latin." Out of envy and viciousness, the eight drove out the four and forced them to go underground. These four apostles were the first Waldensians.[24] Was the singing of the other eight, the priests of the Catholic Church, really an elitist religion thought to be superior to that of the simple faithful? Jacques of Vitry, that very pastoral bishop of Genoa, writing of the early Humiliati, put on par the literate laymen who recited the Divine Office in Latin from a book and their unlettered brothers who joined by reciting quietly their Pater Nosters.[25] Both gave suitable worship to God. They did not need to do so in exactly the same way.

The evidence is that the lay faithful understood the rites enacted before them quite well, if not the words themselves, at least the meaning conveyed thereby. The heretics were exaggerating to make a point. Italians got the drift of the lessons at Mass when they took the trouble to listen carefully, as admittedly some failed to do.[26] But the pious who did try could get the basic message. The layman Francis of Assisi's conversion came while hearing the commission of the apostles in Matthew sung at Mass. Latin had enough in common with his Italian to be broadly understandable, even if Francis had

22. Rufino of Piacenza, *Vita et Miracula B. Raymundi*, 5.24 [i.e., 2.24], p. 649; 4.50, p. 654; 5.54, p. 655.

23. As Christopher Haigh, *English Reformations: Religion, Politics, and Society Under the Tudors* (Oxford: Clarendon, 1993), 286, said of their sixteenth-century descendants.

24. Alberto of Castellario, "Inquisicio" (136), p. 220.

25. Jacques of Vitry, *Historia Occidentalis*, 28, pp. 144–43, and Andrews, *Early Humiliati*, 125.

26. Alexander Murray, however, in his study of six clerical preachers' criticism of lay piety, "Piety and Impiety in Thirteenth-Century Italy," finds that the preachers attacked moral failures and (p. 92) minimal church attendance, not deportment at services.

to get some clarifications on particulars from the celebrating priest after the service.[27] With relatively little instruction and effort, decent comprehension was possible. Even writing simple Latin prose was not beyond the capacity of laypeople with a modest education. Throughout the communal period lay Italians composed hymns, prayers, and saints' lives in Latin "as if it were a spoken language."[28] The council fathers meeting at Grado in 1296 ordered that deacons use no fancy or melismatic intonations in their reading of the Gospel, because "these impeded the understanding of the hearers and so the devotion in the minds of the faithful is reduced."[29] Note that it is the faithful's attention, not the clergy's, that concerns the council. The fathers restricted elaborate tones to the chanting of the genealogies of Christ on Christmas and Epiphany and "to the first Gospel chanted by a newly ordained deacon."

At least some of the simple faithful considered it worth their while to achieve a working comprehension of the sacred language of the cult. Although a mature woman of secular life at the time she first tried a monastic vocation, Umiltà of Faenza managed to learn enough Latin to read the table lessons after she entered the convent of Santa Perpetua at Faenza. Nevertheless, the choir nuns still considered her an *illitterata*, unlettered. When she left Santa Perpetua to lead the life of a penitent, she took a Psalter with her.[30] The Church expected even illiterate believers to say their daily prayers in Latin, and they seem to have accomplished this feat. A group of imprisoned paupers vowed to honor Saint Ranieri of Pisa if he helped them escape. After chanting the Pater Noster three times in Latin, they fell asleep. Ranieri appeared to one in a dream and explained how to break out of the prison. They were to use iron bars from the window to dig through the wall. The hagiographer considered the dream a miracle; he took it for granted that the poor wretches could chant their prayers in Latin.[31] In any case, this was an age of increasing literacy. The father of Saint Venturino of Bergamo (1304–46) personally taught his son to read his Latin devotions, although a hope that the boy might become a friar may have lain behind the lessons.[32] Paolo of Certaldo, writing in the later 1300s, considered it normal that boys learn to read, and read Latin, by the age of seven. He fulminated against all the women who were learning to read; they should have been learning to

27. Tommaso of Celano, "First Life of St. Francis," 9, *St. Francis of Assisi: Writings and Early Biographies*, ed. Marion A. Habig (Chicago: Franciscan Herald, 1972), 246–47.

28. As the liturgist Enrico Cattaneo, "La partecipazione dei laici alla liturgia," *I laici nella Societas Christiana*, 406, marvels incredulously.

29. Grado Council (1296), 7, p. 1166: "intellectum audientium impediant vel perturbent, et propter hoc in mentibus fidelium devotio minuatur."

30. Biagio of Faenza, *Vita [S. Humilitatis Abbatissae]*, 1.5, p. 208; her biographer notes she preached in Latin: ibid., 3.30, p. 213. Literacy as an orthodox religious phenomenon awaits a study: J. K. Hyde, *Literacy and Its Uses: Studies on Late Medieval Italy*, ed. Daniel Waley (Manchester: Manchester University Press, 1993), treats only secular literacy; Peter Biller and Anne Hudson, *Heresy and Literacy, 1000–1530* (Cambridge: Cambridge University Press, 1994), only the topic of their title.

31. Benincasa of Pisa, *Vita [S. Raynerii Pisani]*, 18.180, p. 379.

32. *Legenda Beati Fratris Venturini Ordinis Praedicatorum*, ed. A. Grion, *Bergomum* 30 (1956): 40–41.

sew instead. If a girl was to be a nun when she grew up, then let her learn her Latin letters in the convent.[33] Communal Italy's women were not all literate, but they were well on the way.

Hagiographic asides suggest that such precocious Latinity already existed in the communal period, at least among men. Saint Giovanni of Alverna learned to read Latin by the age of seven, "as [was] typical of boys."[34] By the same age, Peter of Verona had already learned enough Latin in school to argue with his uncle about theology, quoting biblical texts from the Vulgate.[35] The father of Ambrogio Sansedoni, knight that he was, hired a man to teach his son the Latin Psalter, the Office of the Blessed Virgin, and other prayers. Peter's father had noticed that the boy constantly interrupted his mother's reading of the Psalter, demanding to see what her book contained.[36] So Ambrogio's mother was literate, if her husband was not. And it is gratuitous to assume that he could not read. The pious grandmother of the future Dominican saint Giacomo Salomone bribed him to practice reading. She offered him money to read her the Office of the Blessed Virgin for a hundred days running. She must have already known the text by heart herself—and at the end of the contract, so did Giacomo.[37] Laypeople who could not hold ordinary jobs found work teaching children to read. The chronicler Salimbene of Parma mentions a Brescian living in Reggio who lost his wits, became convinced that a famine was coming, and began stockpiling food. That was the oddity. Salimbene considered it quite unremarkable that the man supported himself by teaching children to read Latin. He sang quite nicely, too, and gave chant lessons to laypeople.[38] The city of Siena considered the teaching of letters important enough to exempt instructors from service in the municipal militia.[39]

The Church's liturgical Office was the primary duty of the parish priest and his clerics. He sang it each day, chanting the major Offices of Matins (composed of Vigils and Lauds), Mass, and Vespers, as well as the minor hours of Prime, Terce, Sext, None, and Compline.[40] The hours were to be executed with dignity, without any "ruckus, movement, chatting, or dissension." At least until the hour of the solemn Mass, there was to be silence in the church, unless some civic business or crisis required that it be used for a meeting.[41] The clergy of Piacenza fined an unordained cleric or priest for absence from one of the hours: 2d. for members of collegiate churches and

33. Paolo of Certaldo, *Libro di buoni costumi*, ed. Alfredo Schiaffini (Florence: Vonnier, 1945), 155, pp. 127–28.

34. *Acta [B. Joannis Firmani sive Alvernae]*, 1.3, *AS* 36 (Aug. 11), 460.

35. *Vita S[ancti] Petri Martyris Ordinis Praedicatorum*, 1.2, p. 696.

36. Gisberto of Alessandria et al., *Vita [B. Ambrosii]*, 1.5–7, p. 182.

37. *Vita [Beati Jacobi Veneti Ordinis Praedicatorum]*, 1.1, p. 453.

38. Salimbene, *Cronica* (1286), 904, Baird trans., 627.

39. Siena Stat. II (1310), 4.18, 2:160.

40. Bologna Synod (1310), 495–96.

41. Ravenna Stat., 195, p. 108.

1d. for the staff of a chapel.[42] At Lucca, failure to chant the Office was a major clerical transgression. The city's synod also stipulated that every chapel, no matter how tiny, have at least one "scholar" trained in reading and singing to assist the priest in the celebration of the hours.[43] Daily worship continued throughout the year; only a papal interdict stopped it, and that by stripping the city of its clergy.[44] In larger churches, monasteries, and cathedrals, the clergy filled the intervals between the canonical hours with recitations of the Office of the dead and the little Office of the Virgin. These hours were chanted in a subdued tone, to distinguish them from the great hours that made up the official prayer of the Church.[45]

Matins, the first canonical hour of the day, was the longest and most elaborate. It was so essential to the daily round of prayer that a priest could not say Mass unless he had already recited this Office, at least privately.[46] The laity knew these clerical obligations and expected their clergy to obey. Matins began with the chanting of Vigils: twelve long psalms on ordinary days, or ferias, sixteen psalms on Sundays, or nine psalms divided into three "nocturns" on feasts. At the end of ferial Vigils came three readings from the Bible. The three nocturns of a feast each ended with a set of three readings. In most cases, the readings of the first nocturn were from Scripture, the second from a life of the saint, and the third from a treatise by a Church Father. After each lesson came an elaborate responsory. From reading to reading and day to day, the responsories formed narratives of events from the Scriptures, and each such narrative set was called a "history." For medieval listeners, this musical presentation of biblical stories overshadowed the lessons as the essential "message" of Matins. Attached to Vigils were the six psalms and canticles of Lauds, the twin of the evening Office, Vespers.[47]

Since the psalms of the minor hours were identical each day, the variable psalms of the long Office of Matins and the shorter Office of Vespers had to complete the recitation of all 150 psalms of the Psalter each week. For each psalm, the verses were chanted alternately by the clerics on the north and south sides of the choir. Today, the chanting of Matins before dawn is unique to monks and some other groups of religious clergy. In thirteenth-century Italy, Matins was the normal morning Office of every church and parish, even the smallest. Matins and Vespers, along with Mass, were the essential

---

42. On obligations, see Lucca Synod (1300) (repeating statute of 1252), 1, p. 214; Piacenza Stat. Cler. (1297), pp. 529–30; (1337), 1–2, pp. 537–38.

43. Lucca Synod (1253), 1–2, p. 54.

44. As happened in Forlì in 1282: *Chronicon Parmense*, 39.

45. On these lesser Offices, see Cremona Cath. Stat. (1247), 2, p. 453. On the canonical hours, see Sicardo, *Mitrale*, 4, cols. 147–90.

46. Grado Council (1296), 1, p. 1165.

47. See Sicardo, *Mitrale*, 4.1, cols. 151–54 (on ferial Matins), and 4.2, cols. 154–59 (on festival Matins). In the province of Milan, the "Ambrosian Rite" followed different arrangements; on which, see "Instrumentum Litis," 8, p. 269, and Valsecchi, *Interrogatus*, 110 n. 324, citing Enrico Cattaneo, *Il breviario ambrosiano* (Milan: n.p., 1943), 12, 27.

minimum. The other small hours might occasionally be omitted, especially in churches with a very small staff.[48] The great hours occurred daily in every church, and the church signaled the beginning of each with a special peal of its bell.[49]

Whether chanted by two large choirs or by one priest and his cleric, Matins was a clerical Office. Bishop Sicardo assumed that clerics would be present in the dark church for these hours, but he did not exclude the people's presence absolutely.[50] At Sicardo's own Cremona, Omobono rose every night when the cathedral bell sounded for the two-hour Matins service. He seems to have been a lone attender, since the canons detailed a priest of the duomo, Don Osberto, to make sure that the church door was open when he arrived.[51] Omobono lived in the late 1100s; by the mid-1200s, lay penitents commonly attended the night Office.[52] Anecdotal evidence suggests the practice became common also among pious laypeople, like the young Andrea de' Gallerani.[53] Margherita of Cortona used to get up to hear the Franciscans chant Matins. She then stayed praying in the conventual church until Terce in midmorning.[54] Ranieri of Pisa, during his visit to the Holy Land, spent his nights praying in the church of the Holy Sepulcher. He left the building during the chanting of the night Office by the Armenians only "because he could not understand the Office." He did stay for Latin Matins, which suggests that he could follow at least some of the psalms and chants.[55]

In 1299, on the feast of Saint John the Baptist, when lightning struck the cathedral of Cassis during the chanting of Matins, two of the laypeople present in the nave were killed—the canons chanting in the choir, however, were spared. "Many" of the canons who had "anticipated" Matins the evening before and stayed in bed were also killed.[56] Matins became even more popular with the laity as the thirteenth century wore on. There was a growing consensus that the obligation to attend church on feast days and Sundays included attendance at Matins and Vespers as well as Mass.[57] The presence of the laity at Mass and Vespers presented no extra work for the clergy, for these were at a convenient time. But clerics found the presence of laypeople at Matins something of a nuisance, since it meant having to open the doors in the middle of the night. The beggar saint Nevolone got into the habit of attending all the canonical hours after his conversion to the ascetic life. The priests found it impossible to keep him out of the church during Matins.

48. On the lesser hours and Vespers, see Sicardo, *Mitrale*, 4.3, cols. 159–62, and 4.8, cols. 181–86.
49. *Ordo Senensis*, 2.1, pp. 403–4; 2.5, p. 406.
50. Sicardo, *Mitrale*, 4.4, col. 165A.
51. *Vita Sancti Homoboni*, 112.
52. Bertoni, "Una vita di s. Omobono," 174–75.
53. *Vita [Beati Andreae de Galleranis]*, 1.8, *AS* 9 (Mar. III), 54.
54. Giunta Bevegnati, *Legenda . . . Margaritae de Cortona*, 2.1c, p. 188.
55. Benincasa of Pisa, *Vita [S. Raynerii Pisani]*, 2.30, p. 352.
56. *Annales Foroiuliensis*, 209.
57. Cattaneo, "Partecipazione," 415.

They locked the door, but he kept finding ways to get in.[58] He took up sleeping on the bare floor of the church to be sure he would not be locked out—no doubt provoking more clerical ire.

What was the spiritual experience of the pious who got up so early to hear Matins? Even more important, what was the experience of the ordinary people who came to hear Vespers and Mass? Peter the Chanter, in his little book on prayer, suggested that merely standing at devout attention was the limit of lay capacity for participation in the public cult.[59] This was a view congenial to the prejudices of a learned twelfth-century cleric. Other conclusions on lay participation are possible. At least for the pious, participation in worship was by no means so inert and passive. Ranieri of Pisa, layman that he was, had learned to read. During Matins, it was his practice to read his Psalter and recite a special litany of the saints that he had composed himself.[60] He may not have been reading the same psalms that the clerics chanted, but he did get through the entire Psalter in a week, just as they did. While in Jerusalem, he stayed on after the chanting was completed, reading his prayers—at least until a demon (or was it a tired cleric?) extinguished his candle.[61] Pietro Pettinaio of Siena was famous for listening so attentively to the Office and Mass that he committed much of the liturgy to memory.[62] When he attended Matins at the Dominican church in Siena, he quietly recited his "customary prayers." These he addressed most likely to the Blessed Virgin—his favorite place during services was next to her altar. Pietro's behavior seems more typical of the laity than Raimondo's. The comb-maker's habits were well enough known to the Dominicans and the canons of the Siena duomo that they made special provision to admit him when he came for private midnight devotions.[63]

For Pietro, reciting his many Ave Marias near the Virgin's altar, the experience of the Divine Office certainly was otherwise than for Ranieri, who read his Psalter very much like a cleric. But they had this in common: each sought in his own way to make the Church's public cult his own. Each performed a free act of devotion. Unlike the clerics of Piacenza, they incurred no fine if they failed to show up. Unless it was a day of obligation, when the laity (like the clergy) had to attend Mass, feelings about worship could be quite different on the two sides of the choir screen. The cleric, Fra Salimbene of Parma, wrote of the thirteenth-century Office:

> Up to the present day, some flaws remain, as many men say, and it is indeed true. For the liturgy contains much that is superfluous,

58. *Vita Beati Nevoloni*, 7, p. 648.
59. Peter the Chanter, *De Oratione*, 185.
60. Benincasa of Pisa, *Vita [S. Raynerii Pisani]*, 3.44, p. 355.
61. Ibid., 3.38–39, p. 354.
62. Pietro of Monterone, *Vita del beato Pietro Pettinajo*, 1, pp. 5–6.
63. Ibid., 4–5, pp. 32–45.

which causes boredom rather than devotion, both to the congregation and to the celebrants. Take, for example, the hour of prime on
Sunday: priests are required to say their own private Masses, forcing
the laity to wait impatiently. There is no celebrant, for he is still
occupied. The same is true with the recitation of the eighteen psalms
in the office of nocturns on Sunday before the *Te Deum Laudamus*,
both in the winter and in the summertime, with its short nights,
intense heat, and pestiferous flies: only weariness comes forth from
such an ordeal. Even now, there are many things in the service that
could be changed for the better, and rightly so, since, though not
recognized by everyone, it is full of crudities.[64]

Nevolone, Pietro, and Ranieri, who were constantly after the clergy to let
them in for Matins, would probably have been a bit shocked by such clerical
carping. Some of the clergy considered the presence of the pious laity at the
night Office something of a nuisance. One cleric found Ranieri's night visits
a burden and kicked him out of the church. God took the layman's side.
The priest was punished by a horrible nightmare in which a vicious dog
ripped out his entrails. He woke up with stomach problems that lasted for
months.[65] Ranieri had no more trouble getting into Vigils. When a young
Franciscan complained to Pietro Pettinaio about the tedium of Office, the
combmaker remarked that people should not focus on the "pain" but think
about celestial rewards. The layman then returned to reciting his own devotions.[66] After a while, Pietro approached the same cleric and asked what was
being chanted. The friar replied that it was the canticle "Benedicite omnia
opera Domini Domino" (Dan. 3:57–88 in the Vulgate). Pietro knew that this
was part of festive Lauds and called on all living creatures of land, sea, and
sky to praise God. The layman shook his head and remarked how odd it was
that irrational animals were being called on to praise God and yet a rational
friar was merely wandering about the church. The friar went back to choir.[67]

The Sacrifice of the Mass

The Office was only the setting for that jewel of medieval worship, the sacrifice of the Mass. Throughout the day, the chants and prayers of the Divine
Office recalled those of that day's Mass. The calendar recorded what saving
event or saint would be celebrated at Mass. No festival, civic or religious,
was complete without the solemn chanting of Mass. The Mass made heaven
present on earth. "In the time of the celebration of the holy Mass, who

64. Salimbene, *Cronica* (1215), 43, Baird trans., 4–5.
65. Benincasa of Pisa, *Vita [S. Raynerii Pisani]*, 3.46, pp. 356–67.
66. Pietro of Monterone, *Vita del beato Pietro Pettinajo*, 5, pp. 58–59.
67. Ibid., 5, pp. 59–60. Italian synods blamed the clergy more than the laity for irreverence in
church: e.g., Ravenna Council (1317), 12, pp. 611–12. This contrasts with the clerical sermons studied by
Murray, "Piety and Impiety in Thirteenth-Century Italy," 83–106, which emphasize lay defects.

among the faithful can doubt that the heavens open at the voice of the priest, that a chorus of angels is present at that mystery of Jesus Christ, that the depths are joined to the heights, that heaven and earth are joined, that invisible things are made visible," wrote Friar Salimbene, paraphrasing a passage from Saint Gregory the Great.[68] So awesome was the celebration of the Mass that priests were not to celebrate more than once a day without necessity—except on the great feast of Christmas, with its three Masses—lest they acquire a sacrilegious familiarity with such a great mystery.[69] Presence at Mass was the most powerful catechetical tool of the medieval Church.[70] Celebration of Mass, especially Sunday Mass, sealed the unity of a community or neighborhood. One early-fourteenth-century Italian copied into his collection of devotions a hymn whose first verse united the transcendent and communal dimensions of the Mass by focusing on Christ as offered there:

> Hail living Host, the truth and life,
> In which all sacrifices are complete;
> Through you infinite glory is given the Father,
> So that, through you, the Church stands united.[71]

Absence from Mass by choice implied a rejection of one's fellows, and so of Christianity itself. This ritual created and vivified the community. The Mass was its very life, as the midday meal was the life of the family.[72]

By ecclesiastical statute, Divine Office and Mass were celebrated for the people daily and without charge in every chapel and collegiate church.[73] In churches or religious houses with several priests, the priest who chanted Mass for the people did so *voce alta,* with due solemnity. The other priests and clerics of the church attended this Mass, clad in surplices or, for the major feasts, in copes.[74] Bishop Sicardo, commenting on the use of the word "feria"—which means "feast"—as the name for an ordinary weekday, explained that this word was used because the principal daily Mass was always celebrated with festive solemnity.[75] Should it be necessary for another priest to celebrate a "private" Mass during the people's celebration, it was done

---

68. Salimbene, *Cronica* (1250), 490—"Quis enim fidelium habere dubium possit in ipsa immolationis hora ad sacerdotis vocem celos aperiri, in illo Iesu Christi misterio angelorum choros adesse, summis ima sociari, terram celestibus iungi, unum quid ex visibilibus et invisibilibus fieri?"—Baird trans., 337. Cf. Gregory the Great, *Dialogi,* 4.58, *Dialogues,* ed. and trans. Adalbert de Vogüé (Paris: Cerf, 1978), 3:194.

69. Piacenza Stat. Cler. (1337), 43, p. 548.

70. See Giovanni Cherubini, "Parroco, parrocchie e popolo nelle campagne dell'Italia centro-settentrionale alla fine del Medioevo," *Pievi e parrocchie,* ed. Erba et al., 1:362.

71. Bologna, Biblioteca Universitaria, MS 1563 (XIV cent.), fol. 53ᵛ: "Ave vivens hostia, veritas et vita; | in qua sacrificia cuncta sunt finita; | per te patri gloria datur infinita, | per te stat ecclesia igitur unita."

72. As observed by Trexler, *Public Life,* 85.

73. E.g., Ravenna Council (1317), 2, p. 604.

74. Milan (ecclesiastical province), *Synodus Provincialis Pergami habita in Castono sive Cassono Mediolani Archiepiscopo anno MCCCXI, RIS²* 9:3:6.

75. Sicardo, *Mitrale,* 5.7, cols. 231–32.

silently, so as not to distract from the main service. And he was not to begin until the deacon of the people's Mass had chanted the Gospel.[76] To replace the people's Mass with some other celebration so as to convenience the clergy was a serious abuse. The saintly minister general of the Franciscans, Fra Giovanni of Parma, put an immediate stop to the practice in some Franciscan houses of replacing the people's Mass with a Requiem when one had to be said.[77] The time for solemn Mass was early to mid morning. Mostly, the proper hour fell after Matins but before Terce, but a later time, just after Terce, was common on Sundays and feasts. Then the canons at Siena chanted Sext immediately following Mass as a thanksgiving. Because the Mass celebrated both Christ's Passion on Good Friday and his Resurrection on Easter morning, it was almost never said after None, lest the connection with that Resurrection morn be lost.[78] People frequented Masses other than the solemn Mass when these were available. These Masses had the attraction of being more intimate, especially when celebrated at nave altars or in small side chapels, and of being briefer, since they were celebrated with lesser solemnity, although still sung.

In a practice probably nearly universal, the canons of Siena celebrated a "Mary Mass" a little after the solemn Mass of the day during most of the year. It complemented their recitation of the daily Office of the Virgin. They omitted this devotional Mass only from Advent to Epiphany, Palm Sunday to Pentecost Octave, and on a few of the most solemn feasts. It attracted so many laypeople that the clerics called it the "popular," or "people's," Mass (*Missa popularis*), although that title really belonged to the Mass of the day or the Mass during which there was a general Communion.[79] The ancient Roman practice had been to repeat the Sunday Mass each day of the following week, but in a shorter version (without the Gloria and Credo), unless the week included a feast or saint's day. The clerics of the communes broke this monotony by celebrating a "votive Mass," that is, a Mass with a special theme, on each weekday. On Monday, this was usually the Mass of the Holy Trinity; on Tuesday, that of Charity; on Wednesday, that of the Holy Spirit; on Thursday, that of the Angels; on Friday, that of the Holy Cross; and on Saturday, that of the Blessed Virgin Mary. Everywhere, the choir added a Gloria to the votive Mass of the Blessed Virgin on Saturday as a way of giving her special honor. Local churches, however, in other ways enjoyed freedom to establish their own customs. Bishop Sicardo knew of some Italian churches that sang a Requiem Mass on Tuesday, a Mass for Peace on Wednesday, and a Mass against Tribulations on Thursday.[80] Since choice of

76. Grado Council (1296), 4, p. 1166, and Bologna, Biblioteca Universitaria, MS 1785 (late XII cent.), Rolando the Deacon, *Liber de Ordine Officiorum*, fol. 35ᵛ.
77. Salimbene, *Cronica* (1248), 439, Baird trans., 301.
78. See ibid. (1250), 608, trans., 425; *Ordo Senensis*, 1.14, p. 14.
79. *Ordo Senensis*, 2.12–15, pp. 413–15.
80. Sicardo, *Mitrale*, 8.1, cols. 388–89.

votive Mass was free, the laity had a say in it. When the Franciscan Fra Corrado asked Margherita of Cortona's advice on what votive Masses to say, she replied that Jesus himself had told her to have the Mass of the Dead on Monday, that of the Passion on Friday, and that of the "Glorious Virgin Mary" on Saturday.[81] Saint Bona of Pisa and her friends came one day to request a votive Mass from her parish priest at San Martino. He demurred, dissembling a sore throat that prevented him from singing that morning. The real problem was a secret but minor hidden fault. Bona, with her spiritual insight, called him aside, revealed the fault, and chastised him for his scrupulosity.[82] The women got the votive Mass of their choice.

Priests existed to say Mass for the people, living and dead. This was the priest's unique privilege and his most serious obligation. Failure to celebrate was to deny the living their rights and the dead their succor. So essential was Mass to priestly service that the canons stripped a non–parish priest of his benefice or living if he failed to say Mass at least once a year.[83] Canons of collegiate churches and cathedrals received their stipends prorated according to the number of times they celebrated Mass or were present to help chant the Mass and Office.[84] The synod of Lucca excommunicated any new priest who did not chant his first Mass within three months of ordination.[85] To ensure that new priests celebrated correctly and with proper reverence, each had an older, pious priest assigned to teach the chants and motions. Fra Guglielmo of Piedmont did this for the Franciscan priest Salimbene of Parma, who never forgot the help.[86] Some future priests began to practice early. The young Ambrogio Sansedoni, a future Dominican, erected and decorated sand altars while his knightly playmates built sand castles.[87] Giacomo Salomone, a future Dominican, learned the priestly chants while a child and organized a choir of his friends to sing the Mass parts while he celebrated at a tiny altar. It was the only "game" (*ludus*) he really enjoyed.[88] People paid attention to the celebrant's demeanor. The Franciscan minister general Giovanni of Parma was famous among the clergy for celebrating Mass every day, and among the laity for the devotion with which he chanted it.[89]

81. Giunta Bevegnati, *Legenda . . . Margaritae de Cortona*, 9.24 and 9.72, pp. 385, 424–45.

82. *Vita [Sanctae Bonae Virginis Pisanae]*, 4.42, p. 152.

83. Ravenna Council (1314), 13, p. 546.

84. Mantua (cathedral chapter), "Constitutiones Antiquae Aecclesiae Mantuanae," ed. Petro Torelli, *L'archivio capitolare della cattedrale di Mantova fino alla caduta dei Bonacolsi*, Pubblicazioni della R. Accademia virgiliana di Mantova, serie 1: Monumenti 3 (Verona: Mondadori, 1924), 231–32.

85. Lucca Synod (1300), 32, p. 223.

86. Salimbene, *Cronica* (1248), 459, Baird trans., 315.

87. Gisberto of Alessandria et al., *Vita [B. Ambrosii]*, 1.6, p. 182; on the growing sacramentality of high medieval piety, see André Vauchez, "La valorisation de la pratique sacramentelle," *Histoire du christianisme des origines à nos jours*, ed Jean-Marie Mayeur et al. (Paris: Desclée-Fayard, 1990), 5:745–48.

88. *Vita [Beati Jacobi Veneti Ordinis Praedicatorum]*, 1.1, p. 453.

89. Salimbene, *Cronica* (1248), 433, Baird trans., 297.

Not all clerics were scrupulous in the discharge of their most sacred duty.[90] Christ appeared in vision to Margherita of Cortona and praised a priest of her acquaintance for saying Mass with tranquillity of mind, avoiding curiosities in preaching, not rushing the service, and preparing piously rather than chatting with other clerics.[91] Christ merely voiced Margherita's own sentiments and those of other pious layfolk. Devotion to the Mass appears so often in the lives of the communal lay saints that it must have been typical of lay conventions of holiness, but, as it appears in the lives, the level of intensity is certainly exceptional. The serving girl Zita of Lucca tried to attend Mass at every city church on its patronal feast, and she especially loved the first Masses chanted by new priests.[92] Pietro of Foligno never missed the daily Mass in his parish church of San Feliciano. Afterward he cleaned the church and lit candles before the images of the Blessed Virgin and saints. He also washed the statues on a regular basis. When he could find time, he did the same in the other churches of Foligno.[93] Sibyllina Biscossi had no fewer than five priests on call to celebrate Mass at her anchorhold when she felt a special need.[94] Such extremes of devotion marked only the professionally pious, but Don Burigardo, captain of the army of Sassuolo, had a chaplain on call to say Mass and Office daily in his house.[95]

The material aspect of high lay devotion to the Mass surfaces in an 1143 lawsuit at the collegiate church of Sant'Ambrogio in Milan. The church was home to both a monastery of monks and a house of canons. The two groups came to court over the laity's free-will Mass offerings at one of the altars. The offerings were so substantial that the canons considered them sufficient to construct a new residence (*canonica*) and put in a drain (*cloaca*). The monks and canons finally split the offerings half-and-half.[96] Heretics could not escape the lure of the Mass. Gherardino, mixed up with the anticlerical and apocalyptic Dulcinite heresy, explained the group's habits. They went to Mass to hear the chants and the Gospel but left when the priest prepared to recite the Consecration.[97] Andrea Seramita, explaining the habits of the Guglielmite sect, explained and itemized the vast array of liturgical paraphernalia and vestments the group had collected for their future female pope. They also had plenty of candles to burn at the tombs of their saints.[98] Heretics might reject the Catholic priesthood, but they could not imagine life without the Mass, or at least without some part of it. Only the Cathar

---

90. Ibid., 615, trans., 430.

91. Giunta Bevegnati, *Legenda . . . Margaritae de Cortona*, 9.12, pp. 377–78.

92. *Vita [Sanctae Zitae Virginis Lucencis]*, 3.19, p. 509.

93. Giovanni Gorini, *[Legenda de Vita et Obitu Beati Petri de Fulgineo]*, 10, *Analecta Bollandiana* 8 (1889): 365–66.

94. Tomasso of Bossolasco, *Vita [B. Sibyllinae]*, 3.15, p. 69.

95. Salimbene, *Cronica* (1285), 856, Baird trans., 594.

96. Milan, *Gli atti del comune di Milano fino all'anno MCCXVI*, doc. 9 (June 1143), pp. 16–18.

97. *Historia Fratris Dulcini Heresiarche*, ed. Arnaldo Segarizzi, *RIS²* 9:5:55–56.

98. *Atti inquisitoriali [contro i Guglielmiti]*, 2.4, 3.13, 3.15, pp. 133–34, 230, 236.

dualists were willing to go entirely without, but theirs was the most extreme dissenting option available in high medieval Italy.

The Mass, in its basic structure and parts, has changed little since the earliest days of the Western Church, although each age has added unique flourishes or emphasized different aspects of the rite. The churches of communal Italy, with the exception of Milan, where the distinctive Ambrosian Rite held sway, followed a north Italian variant of the liturgy of the city of Rome. This local Italian usage has characteristics that distinguish it from the modern Roman rite, as well as from the old "Tridentine" rite that was used by nearly all Roman Catholics from the sixteenth to the mid–twentieth century. So recovering the experience of worship in the communes demands first an overview of this Mass's rituals and peculiarities. The following sketch assumes Mass in a cathedral or larger church, one with the staff necessary to provide the fullest solemnity. Smaller churches did what they could.

Before Mass, men and women entered the church, not by the great western door, but by separate, smaller doors in the north and south aisles. The women took their place on the "Gospel side," in the northern part of the nave; the men stood on the "Epistle side," on the south. A rite known as the Asperges preceded the solemn Mass of Sunday. In it, the priest, in surplice and stole, walked through the church sprinkling the people with holy water. As he did so, the choir chanted an antiphon, normally "You Sprinkle Me" (Asperges) but during Easter season "I Saw Water" (Vidi Aquam). This rite recalled the congregation's common baptism. Even more, it expelled demons and by its very power forgave venial sins.[99] In cathedral churches, the prayers and psalms that accompanied the entrance of the canons and bishop also preceded Mass. These chants continued as the clergy kissed the altar, which represented Christ, and the book of the Gospels held by the deacon, which represented his word.[100] During the opening chant of the Mass itself, the Introit, the celebrant incensed the altar, going around it counterclockwise, imitating the movement of the heavens. The chanting of the ninefold litany called the Kyrie followed, joined in nonpenitential seasons by the Gloria, a hymn of praise. These chants completed, the celebrant greeted the congregation and sang the opening prayer, or "collect," at the altar. If the celebrant was the bishop, he then went to his throne in the east; a priest sat on the south side of the choir.

The subdeacon, standing in the middle of the choir and facing east, then sang the Epistle. The choir responded to this with a chant taken from the psalms, the Gradual, from which the book of Mass music, the Graduale,

99. It was obligatory every Sunday: Ravenna Council (1311), 9, p. 455. On its power to forgive venial sins, see Thomas Aquinas, *Summa Theologiae*, III, Q. 87, a. 3.

100. E.g., at Modena, as seen in the great altar missal of the duomo: Parma, Biblioteca Palatina, MS Par. 996 (late XII cent.), fols. 83ᵛ–89ᵛ. For psalms before Mass in a noncathedral liturgy, see Sicardo, *Mitrale*, 4, col. 149.

took its name. As the priest blessed incense and a procession with censer and candles left to accompany the deacon to the great pulpit in the screen, the choir sang the Alleluia or, in penitential seasons, another scriptural chant composition called the Tract. Unlike the modern Roman liturgy, the medieval Italians chanted the Nicene Creed (the Credo) immediately after the Gospel. It provided "traveling music" as the deacon and his procession returned to the choir so that the celebrant could kiss the sacred text. During the Credo, both clergy and laity genuflected at the verse recalling Christ's Incarnation, "Et homo factus est."[101] An almost universal practice in north Italy had the people express their acceptance of the Creed by singing the Kyrie a second time.[102] If there was a sermon, as stipulated by synodal law for Sundays and feasts, it usually came at this point. But a "solemn sermon" by a famous preacher might be delayed until after Mass, lest it overly extend the service.[103]

After the Credo, the celebrant led the congregation in a rite acknowledging their sins. The people knelt, and the clerics chanted the Confiteor, a liturgical general confession of sin, in the name of the people. The Confiteor confessed the people's sinfulness before God and the Virgin by "thought, word, and deed." The priest or bishop then chanted the absolution, to which the response was "Amen." In many places, the priest then led the whole congregation in a spoken recitation of the Pater Noster and Ave Maria, prayers known to all good lay faithful. Since Christ had told those coming to the altar to be reconciled first to their brothers and sisters, and since sin was the foundational cause of dissension, this rite prepared all for presentation of their offerings. The celebrant then came out through the door of the screen to accept these, whether in coin or in produce, from each member of the congregation individually. The gifts were dedicated to the support of the church and the poor. More than at any other point in the Mass, this gave laypeople an individual and direct role in the Mass. One troubled student at Bologna about the year 1219 made his offering along with the people at the Dominican church. The celebrating priest was the founder of the order, Dominic himself. As the man gave his gift and kissed the saint's hand, he received the grace to avoid sins of the flesh.[104] Coming forward with one's offering was a moment charged with sacred power. Meanwhile, the ministers prepared the bread and wine at the altar.[105] The celebrant then performed the offertory, placing the chalice and Host on the altar and incensing them.

101. Florence, Biblioteca Nazionale Centrale, MS Magl. XXXVI.81bis, fol. 36^v.

102. *Ordo Senensis*, 2.56, pp. 458–59; Sicardo, *Mitrale*, 3.4, col. 113D.

103. Siena placed the sermon after the Sanctus on nonfeast days. *Ordo Senensis*, 2.54, p. 454, objects strongly to it; see Jean-Baptiste Molin, "Le prières du prône en Italie," *Ephemerides Liturgicae* 76 (1962): 41.

104. *Vitae Fratrum Ordinis Praedicatorum*, 2.26, p. 82, trans. Placid Conway as *Lives of the Brethren of the Order of Preachers, 1206–1259* (New York: Benziger, 1924), 69–70.

105. *Ordo Senensis*, 2.55–57, pp. 457–60. Some Italian churches prepared the bread and wine earlier, during the chants between the Epistle and Gospel; Sicardo, *Mitrale*, 3.6, col. 116C, rejects this practice.

As an acolyte went to incense the people, the priest quietly asked the clerics to pray for him. This incense represented the Church's prayers as its smoke drifted upward. Its odor recalled Christ's merits; the burning coals, the fire of charity in the hearts of the faithful.[106] In a loud voice, the priest sang the short dialogue that opened the Preface; the choir then chanted the Sanctus, a hymn glorifying God and Christ, while the faithful "listened attentively."[107]

At this point, the Italian liturgy introduced a distinctively medieval rite, the "Common Prayer of the Faithful," or, as it was known in England, the "Bidding of the Bedes."[108] This rite was common in most of western Christendom, but outside of north Italy it usually occurred earlier, during the offertory.[109] The priest turned from the altar, came to the door in the screen, and addressed the people in the vernacular. First, he announced the major feasts of the week. He then bid them pray silently for each of four general intentions, first for peace, next for the clergy, then for the sick, and finally for all of the dead. Next, he announced the names of all who had died or whose anniversary of death had occurred in the previous week. He also requested prayers for the local clergy, for the dead buried in the church's cemetery, and for the parents of all present. Then the priest asked the congregation to gather all these prayers into one by chanting with him the Latin Pater Noster. This completed, the clerics chanted a psalm for the dead. The priest concluded the rite by singing a collect, also in Latin.[110] So popular were these bidding prayers that lay penitent groups adopted them into their own corporate devotions.[111]

The priest now returned to the altar, facing the same direction as the people, toward the east. He began, in their name, the great consecratory prayer over the bread and wine, the Canon. This prayer—in particular, the words of Jesus, "This is my Body" and "This is my Blood"—changed the offering of bread and wine into the true body of Christ, the *Corpus Domini*, and united heaven and earth. Out of reverence and to prevent profanation,

---

106. So explained in Florence, Biblioteca Nazionale Centrale, MS Magl. XXXVI.81[bis], fol. 36[v].

107. Ibid.

108. Placement after the Agnus Dei was known, but after the Sanctus was nearly universal: *Ordo Senensis*, 2.54, pp 454. For the Sienese rite, see *Ordo Senensis*, 2.54, pp 454–56; for that of Volterra, see Marchetti, *Liturgia e storia della chiesa di Siena nel XII secolo*, 109–11. On these prayers, see Landotti, "Preghiera dei fedeli," 98–100. On use of Italian, see Jean-Baptiste Molin, "L'Oratio Communis Fidelium' au Moyen-Âge en Occident du xe au xve siècle," *Miscellanea liturgica in onore di sua eminenza il Cardinale Giacomo Lercaro*, 2 (Rome: Desclée, 1967), 321–22.

109. Originally this "Common Prayer" probably came after the offertory *Dominus vobiscum* and is found in that position elsewhere in Europe: Molin, "Oratio Communis Fidelium," 315–20, 330–455. On these prayers in late medieval England, see Duffy, *Stripping of the Altars*, 124–25. Cf. T. Maertens, *Pour un renouveau des prières du prône* (Bruges: Apostolat Liturgique, 1961), 13, and Molin, "Prières du prône," 39–42, on the prayers. Italy was the last to drop the "Common Prayer": id., "Oratio Communis Fidelium," 318.

110. Siena, Biblioteca Comunale degli Intronati, MS G.v.8, fols. 178[r–v]; edited in Molin, "Oratio Communis Fidelium," 351–52 (no. 14). Molin (ibid., 352 n. 1) thinks the clergy's psalm and people's Pater were simultaneous, but both were sung (see the MS version cited above). For other examples, see Landotti, "Preghiera dei fedeli," 116–31.

111. E.g., Piacenza Battuti Stat. (1317), 67–69; on bidding prayers in confraternities, see Landotti, "Preghiera dei fedeli," 101–9.

the priest recited this prayer in a hushed voice, audible only to those, like the deacon, who knelt next to him at the altar. So essential was this prayer to the Mass that an aging or distracted priest, who could not remember whether he had recited it, was to stop the Mass and repeat it again.[112] The people in the nave joined their own prayers to the celebrant's by reciting the Pater Noster slowly and quietly several times or, if they were literate, by reciting a psalm.[113] In the early communal period, the people knew that the Consecration had been completed only when the priest raised his voice to chant the closing doxology of the Canon.[114] Around 1200, growing demands by the laity to view the newly consecrated Body of Christ led priests to raise the Host over their heads for the faithful's adoration. What was originally a private and local practice first became obligatory in Paris in 1208.[115] Within a year or two, this elevation, along with the ringing of a bell to alert the laity to it, had already appeared in Italian synodal statutes.[116] The focus on showing brought with it new synodal legislation on the whiteness of the Communion bread, not only because of the symbolic purity, but to increase visibility.[117] Elevation torches, multiwick candles held by acolytes, to illuminate the sacred bread also became popular at this time.[118] Somewhat later, an elevation of the chalice balanced that of the Host.[119] By midcentury, unless poverty prevented it, deacons incensed the Host and the chalice continually during the elevations, giving honor to Christ's presence and symbolizing the people's prayers of praise.[120]

After the doxology and its amen, the priest chanted (alone) the Pater Noster and prayed for peace in the world. He then turned to greet the people with the words "Pax Domini sit semper vobiscum" (The Peace of the Lord be always with you). Then followed one of the most distinctive rites of the medieval Mass. After first kissing the chalice containing the precious blood and a small fragment of the Host, the celebrant then kissed a small instrument, the Pax, usually an object of glass, wood, or metal decorated with an image of the Lamb of God, Jesus Christ, or the Crucifixion. The subdeacon took this instrument, which symbolized the Peace of Christ flowing from his

112. See J. Pohle, "Eucharist," *The Catholic Encyclopedia* 5 (1909): 585; cf. Trexler, *Christian at Prayer*, 33 and 124 n. 23.

113. Florence, Biblioteca Nazionale Centrale, MS Magl. xxxvi.81bis, fol. 36^v.

114. This is the only "elevation" known to Sicardo, *Mitrale*, 3.6, cols. 128–29, and *Ordo Senensis*, 2.64, p. 467, both of which predate 1210.

115. Hans Caspary, "Kult und Aufbewahrung der Eucharistie in Italien vor dem Tridentinum," *Archiv für Liturgiewissenschaft* 9 (1965): 102, and Lett, *Enfant*, 85; cf. a later date in V. L. Kennedy, "The Date of the Parisian Decree on the Elevation of the Host," *Medieval Studies* 8 (1946): 87–96.

116. For a 1210 example at Novara, see Michele Maccarrone, "'Cura animarum' e 'parochialis sacerdos' nelle costituzioni del IV Concilio Lateranense (1215): Applicazioni in Italia nel sec. XIII," *Pievi e parrocchie*, ed. Erba et al., 1:88 n. 20.

117. See Salimbene, *Cronica* (1250), 496, Baird trans., 342.

118. See, e.g., Recupero of Arezzo, *Summarium Virtutum*, 12.125, p. 225.

119. It appears in Guillelmus Durandus, *Rationale Divinorum Officiorum*, ed. A. Davril and T. M. Thibodeau (Turnout: Brepols, 1995), 5.41.47–52, 1:264–65, which is after 1250.

120. For an early statute on this, see Lucca Synod (1253), 8, p. 55.

precious Body and Blood, to the clergy, who kissed it in order of rank and seniority. At the popular Mass on Sunday, the Pax then passed to the laity. The subdeacon carried it out the door of the screen and presented it to be kissed, first by the men, on their side, and then by the women, on theirs.[121] At Siena, city officials kissed it first, followed by the other men according to their social rank. Observance of this order was probably a near-universal practice. Women also kissed it in order of their social precedence.[122] As the subdeacon presented the image to each of the faithful, he greeted them with the words "Peace be with you" (*Pax tecum*). The subdeacon was to make special provision to ensure that all the aged, the infirm, and paupers also received the Pax. Christ's love encompassed all.[123] The Pax rite substituted for the Sunday sacramental Communions of the early Church. It was a true, if nonsacramental, Communion, symbolizing the unity of the community through the power of Christ present on the altar. It made visible the gift of his grace to the assembly in all its members and parts. By the time the Pax instrument had finished its journey through the congregation, the priest's Communion was finished, and he was ready to chant the closing collect. Unless it was one of the three Sundays a year with a general Communion, the people did not communicate. The deacon then dismissed the faithful with the words "Ite Missa Est," and the clergy filed out.

After Mass on Sundays and feasts, a special ceremony followed the dismissal, the distribution of blessed bread. To the faithful, this rite held a centrality near to that of the elevation. At weekday Masses, when bread was not blessed, many laypeople simply left after the Canon.[124] At the end of Mass, the celebrating priest came out from behind the screen for the Eulogia, the blessed bread. The people presented baskets of *nuvole* (white rolls) and *focacce* (spiced buns), and the priest blessed them with a prayer recalling the graces of sacramental Communion.[125] Making such breads was the special work of the parish's women, their particular contribution to worship. Umiliana dei Cerchi and other women of her chapel collected grain to make the Hosts for Mass, also a near-universal women's duty.[126] But women's most visible contribution to the cult was not the priest's Host but the Eulogia. Neighborhood chapels rotated responsibility for making it through the housewives of the contrada. Statutes of the civic societies at Bologna reveal the kinds of bread the women prepared. They were more cake than bread, and they were substantial. The Toschi, in their 1256 statutes, prescribed for their Mass

121. Sicardo, *Mitrale*, 3.8, col. 140.

122. *Ordo Senensis*, 2.10, pp. 410–11.

123. Bonvesin de la Riva, *Vita Scholastica*, ed. Anežka Vidmanová-Schmidtová, *Liber Quinque Clavium Sapientiae* (Leipzig: Teubner, 1969), 67, lines 350–52.

124. Synods regularly castigated this bad habit: e.g., Ravenna Council (1311), 9, p. 455.

125. For the blessing of Eulogia, see *Rituale di Hugo [di Volterra]*, 325; on its symbolism, see *Ordo Senensis*, 2.70, pp. 474–75.

126. Vito of Cortona, *Vita [B. Humilianae]*, 1.4, p. 386.

a twenty-four-pound focaccia made with saffron and cumin (*aromata groci et cumini*). The swordmakers preferred a white loaf made of fine flour, valued at 18d. bon. The societies enacted more legislation on their Eulogia's quality, size, and production than that on the Mass itself.[127] This was natural. The priest chanted the Mass; the blessed bread was a distinctive work of the laity. All partook of it together. They took it home for the sick and the elderly. People kept pieces as a divine protection in times of distress. In emergencies, it might have to replace the sacramental Communion of the dying. The Eulogia extended the fruits of the Mass to all who believed but could not be present.[128]

THE FAITHFUL AT CHURCH

Instructions emanating from the medieval Church hierarchy instructed the faithful to be silent and still during Mass. The impression is one of imposed passivity. Since the people were quite active when presenting their offerings, kissing the Pax, and sharing the Eulogia, the image of passivity is certainly deceptive. How silent were they? Not very. Well-known strictures against noise and motion concern, not the adults, but the children they brought with them.[129] Italian devotional literature expected not passive presence but attentive engagement, and stipulated that this be signaled by bodily gestures. The thirteenth-century writer Bonvesin de la Riva, after advising readers to attend Mass as frequently as possible, urged them to arrive at church in time for the sprinkling of holy water, the Asperges. Entering the building, the faithful first directed their eyes to the image of Christ Crucified above the screen and, after coming forward, knelt in view of the altar. They made the sign of the cross as the priest sprinkled them.[130] While hearing Mass, they stayed in one place and avoided unseemly acts, such as spitting. Bonvesin told them to direct their ears to what was chanted and to greet the singing of the Gospel by making a small cross on their foreheads. Whenever the priest or deacon chanted the name of Jesus or Mary, all bowed their heads.[131]

To catch audible cues like the holy names and respond with a gesture asks a level of attention uncommon at modern church services. These instructions flatly contradict the notion that the Italians of the communes paid, or were expected to pay, little attention to Mass except at the offertory and the Consecration.[132] One anonymous treatise on the Mass dating to the mid-1200s focused on the words of Mass as of the greatest importance. The author compared negligence in listening to the Gospel to allowing the Body of

127. Bol. Pop. Stat., 1 (Toschi, 1256, c. 16), 96; 2 (Spadai, 1283, c. 33), 342.
128. On the fruits of Mass, see Florence, Biblioteca Medicea Laurenziana, MS Pl. XIX 29 (XIV cent.), fol. 257ᵛ.
129. E.g., Grado Council (1296), 3, p. 1166.
130. Bonvesin de la Riva, *Vita Scholastica*, 62–63, lines 321–326, 331–36.
131. Ibid., 65, lines 381–94.
132. E.g., Cattaneo, "Partecipazione," 411.

Christ to fall on the ground at Communion. Which was greater in the faith, the author asked his brothers and sisters, the Word of God or the Body of Christ? The Word was no less important than the Body.[133] Peter the Chanter, in his little booklet on prayer, prescribed that those present should "think of nothing at Mass except God." This might suggest a certain distraction from the liturgical action. But his directive was addressed to the priest rather than to the laity. "Thinking of God" meant attention to both prayers and the God to whom they were offered.[134]

The laity punctuated every part of the Mass by physical gestures. Children learned these gestures by watching and imitating adults.[135] They became second nature. Medieval churches, free as they were of pews, gave worshipers considerable liberty of physical expression. During penitential seasons like Lent, people listened for the deacon's command to kneel at the collects, and all knelt.[136] The author of the treatise on the Mass recommended a short biblical verse (Eph. 3:15) to say, which recalled why one knelt: "I bend my knee to the Father of Our Lord Jesus Christ, from which all fatherhood in earth or heaven takes its name."[137] Kneeling was the proper posture of devotion when the deacon commanded it, when the priest elevated the Host, and when the choir sang the Agnus Dei. Different postures distinguished the grade of feast. People stood when the priest chanted the Pater Noster on feasts, but they knelt on ordinary days.[138] Otherwise all were free to kneel or stand as they chose. Although some stood when the rubrics permitted it, the humility of kneeling suggested it to layfolk generally as the most suitable posture of prayer. After all, the Pharisee of the Gospel stood, and the publican knelt; the former was not heard, the latter was.[139] Everyone knew the story.

The congregation imitated the deacon as he made a large sign of the cross at the beginning and end of the Gospel. As he chanted it, all stood out of reverence for the proclamation of the Word of God. "Let none sit for the Gospel," said Bishop Sicardo.[140] As it began, men removed their hats and put aside their staffs. The first gesture showed respect for Christ's teaching; the second, acceptance of his command never to return evil for evil, even if that meant accepting physical blows without striking back.[141] The faithful also expressed their piety and responded to the service as they wished. The treatise on the Mass also suggested a fitting response to the Gloria—the

---

133. Florence, Biblioteca Nazionale Centrale, ms Magl. xxxvi.81bis, fol. 35^v.
134. Peter the Chanter, *De Oratione*, 204–5.
135. Bonvesin de la Riva, *Vita Scholastica*, 68, lines 415–19.
136. Florence, Biblioteca Medicea Laurenziana, ms Conv. Soppr. 137 (late xii cent.), fols. 59^r–60^r.
137. Florence, Biblioteca Nazionale Centrale, ms Magl. xxxvi.81bis, fol. 35^v: "Flecto ienua mea ad Patrem Domini nostri Iesu Christi, ex quo omnis paternitas in celo et in terra nominatur."
138. Sicardo, *Mitrale*, 3.5, col. 134D.
139. Florence, Biblioteca Medicea Laurenziana, ms Conv. Soppr. 137, fols. 59^r–65^v.
140. *Ordo Senensis*, 1.13, p. 14; Sicardo, *Mitrale*, 3.4, col. 111A.
141. So Florence, Biblioteca Nazionale Centrale, ms Magl. xxxvi.81bis, fol. 36^r.

hymn whose first verse was composed by angels (Luke 2:14). The devout might bow profoundly at the intonation and recite to themselves its second verse, "and peace to men of good will." Human beings and angels might thus join in giving glory to God.[142] Saint Omobono prostrated himself before the crucifix on the choir screen as the priest intoned the Gloria, extending his arms in the form of a cross, "as a knight imitating his Lord." While he often remained prostrate, Omobono never failed to rise for the Gospel. When he died, right in the middle of Mass, everyone knew something was wrong, because he remained on the floor during the chanting of the Gospel.[143] Outside of the general Communions at Christmas, Easter, and Pentecost, the priest alone received Communion. Nonetheless, any prayer said at Communion time had a special power. Christ was truly present on the altar. Many layfolk prostrated themselves at this time, a less theatrical gesture than it might appear, because nearly all would already have knelt for the Agnus Dei. At Communion, the devout prayed for the living and the dead, that the merits of the sacrifice might also be theirs. The anonymous Mass treatise suggested two prayers for this time, one for the living, the other for the dead. Since these prayers were too long to memorize, the author meant them for a literate readership. Most simply repeated a Pater and an Ave.[144]

In 1427, confraternity members in the Veneto were found serving the priest at the altar. "Artisans and mere laymen" (*artifices et meri seculares*) were singing along with the priest; they moved the missal for him, carried the Pax, ministered the incense and water. They even joined in the responses, saying: "Kirieleison, Christeleison, etc., Spiritu tuo, Sanctus sanctus, Credo in Deum Patrem, Agnus Dei qui tollis peccata mundi."[145] The priest who had observed all this was scandalized. This was a job for clerics, not the laity, at least in the fifteenth century. But those pious men had probably not introduced anything new. In the late eleventh century, Bishop Sicardo of Cremona took it for granted that the people would chant the Kyrie and respond at the Agnus Dei; they replied to the Pax and its prayer (which should be sung *alta voce*, "so that the people who wish can respond," said the bishop). Layfolk sang "Amen" to the opening collect, responded "Et cum spiritu tuo" to the "Dominus vobiscum," and "Deo gratias" to the "Ite missa est." In short, they made all the easy responses.[146] In the case of the Credo, which was long and difficult but essential to the faith, the people showed assent by singing the Kyrie after it. That chant everyone could master.[147] The only short response that Sicardo gave to the *chorus* rather than the *populus* was the

142. Ibid.

143. *Vita Sancti Homoboni*, 114, 166.

144. Florence, Biblioteca Nazionale Centrale, MS Magl. XXXVI.81bis, fol. 37^r.

145. Rigon, "Organizzazione," 723.

146. Sicardo, *Mitrale*, 3.2, col. 101A; 3.4, col. 107D; 3.5, col. 114B; 3.6, col. 134B; 3.6, col. 138B; 3.8, col. 143B; 3.8, col. 139.

147. Ibid., 3.4, col. 113D; see Cattaneo, "Partecipazione," 411.

"Et cum spiritu tuo" at the beginning of Mass, but he wrote nothing to suggest that the people might not join in there as well.[148] The church of Siena in about 1210 also expected the people to make the short responses, such as the reply to the greeting, the dialogue before the Gospel (where they also crossed their foreheads), the reply to the Agnus Dei, and the "Deo Gratias" at the dismissal.[149] One might dismiss these rubricians' directions as wishful thinking, but a document produced by the laity themselves, the commentary on the 1221 Rule of the Penitents, mentioned the laity's giving these responses at the Mass and Office.[150] During the flagellant processions of 1260, the people had no trouble singing the simple responses to the litanies: "Kyrie eleison," "Miserere nostri," and "Te rogamus audi nos."[151] Any idea that the Italians of the communes could only stand mute and passive at their Masses begins to look a bit absurd.

In addition, there is no reason to exclude participation by some of the laity in the choir's chants of the Ordinary—those texts that did not change from day to day, the Kyrie, Gloria, Credo, Sanctus, and Agnus Dei—although there is also no evidence to support such a practice. The other music, the biblically based chants of the Propers, which changed daily, demanded trained singers or at least a cantor with a Graduale containing the music. Diocesan synods legislated to assure the presence of trained clerics in each church to execute these chants.[152] The Propers included complex choir pieces: the Officium or Introit at the beginning, the Gradual Psalm with the Tract or Alleluia between the readings, and the elaborate, if shorter, chants of the Offertory and Communion. Churches with fine choirs had a competitive edge over those without; most people preferred well-executed music to bad. The superior of the Franciscan house in Pisa, Fra Enrico, was famous for singing plain chant and harmony during Mass. He composed hymns and sequences in honor of the patron saints of the churches where he was stationed. On one occasion, a nun who heard him singing in the street fell out the window of her convent and broke her leg.[153] Saint Giacomo Salomone's mother arranged for him lessons in the chant from a Cistercian monk of a local monastery. This training gave the future Dominican an ear for the music and helped him avoid the errors typical of those who got their training as adults.[154] At Siena, the canons installed a great organ in the duomo. They were so proud of it that it was used almost every day to support their singing. They could not resist using it—even in Lent!—to lend splendor to trium-

148. Sicardo, *Mitrale*, 3.2, col. 98D.
149. *Ordo Senensis*, 2.40, pp. 440–41; 2.52, p. 454; 2.67, p. 472.
150. "Expositiones Regule," 12, Meersseman, *Dossier*, 115.
151. Meersseman, *Ordo*, 1:504–5.
152. Lucca Synod (1300), 2, p. 214 (repeating a statute of 1254); on legislation in Bologna and Milan, see Zelina Zafarana, "Cura pastorale, predicazione, aspetti devozionali nella parrocchia del basso Medioevo," *Pievi e parrocchie*, ed. Erba et al., 1:516.
153. Salimbene, *Cronica* (1247), 262–63, Baird trans., 172; ibid., 266, trans., 175.
154. *Vita [Beati Jacobi Veneti Ordinis Praedicatorum]*, 1.2, p. 453; 2.12, p. 456.

phant hymns like the "Vexilli Regis" of Passiontide.[155] When Bona of Pisa
went to Sunday Mass at the collegiate church of San Giacomo in Podio, she
heard a choir of seven Pisan clerics. The music was so exquisite that she
was certain she could hear Christ and his apostles singing with the choir.[156]
Laywomen were also connoisseurs of good chant.

Execution of the cult with elegance, solemnity, and attention was always
a crowd pleaser. Collegiate churches, with their larger staffs and resources,
were magnets. So was the duomo, the Mother Church of the city, where one
might even find the bishop himself "pontificating" when he was in town.[157]
Secular priests went complaining to Pope Innocent IV about the laity's de-
serting their proper chapels to go to the churches of the mendicants: "these
two orders celebrate Mass so well that the people turn to them." Fra Salimbene of Parma, who reported this incident, could not resist suggesting that
the secular clergy's real complaint was loss of money rather than people.[158]
That the laity's taste for finer and more edifying liturgy led them to the friars
may reflect Salimbene's Franciscan ego more than the reality, but synods of
diocesan clergy inveighed against laypeople's going from church to church
in search of more spiritually satisfying Masses.[159] They responded in more
constructive ways, too, requiring that candles be properly lit during parish
services and, in particular, that the Host be properly illuminated at the elevation.[160] If parish priests could not outsing the friars, they could at least show
greater reverence for the Blessed Sacrament.

Churches did not attract the laity merely by the quality of their music, the
devotion of their ministers, or the splendor of their ceremonies. The worship
of a small cappella, with its intimate community of friends, had an immediacy that monastic churches and cathedrals lacked. In small churches, clerics
bent the rules and even invited the laity to come within the choir screen for
the Consecration.[161] This not only permitted closer visual contact with the
consecrated Host but even allowed the people to hear the whispering of that
most sacred of prayers, the Canon, by which Christ's body and divinity were
made present under the forms of bread and wine. The canons of the cathedral at Siena surely understood the lay desire for immediacy when they
allowed the great solemn Mass to be moved from the high altar in the choir
to altars in the nave on the feasts of the saints to whom the altars were
dedicated.[162] But there always remained reasons for keeping the laity out of
the choir and at a reverential distance. Fra Nicola of Tolentino celebrated

155. *Ordo Senensis*, 1.11, p. 12; 1.126, p. 112.

156. *Vita [Sanctae Bonae Virginis Pisanae]*, 3.28, p. 150.

157. As at Bologna, where an earthquake struck in 1222 during the bishop's Mass: *CCB*, 85–87.

158. Salimbene, *Cronica* (1250), 607–8, 610–11, Baird trans., 425, 427.

159. See, e.g., Piacenza Stat. Cler. (1297), p. 532; (1337), 22, p. 542.

160. Lucca Synod (1308), 7, p. 215; 4, p. 177.

161. Trexler, *Christian at Prayer*, 125 n. 28; on the popularity of viewing, see Kennedy, "Moment of
Consecration," 125–42.

162. *Ordo Senensis*, 1.58, p. 55.

Mass one day at a nave altar. From nowhere, a woman, Viridiana of Tolentino, arrived and interrupted him. She demanded that he say a Pater Noster over her head. She had a splitting headache. Nicola did so, blessed the woman, and recommenced his Mass. God could not have been too displeased; the headache vanished.[163]

THE MOST HOLY SACRAMENT

The elevation of the Host, illumination torches, and incense after the Consecration all came on the heels of the laity's growing devotion to the Blessed Sacrament.[164] Although the layfolk of the communes might receive sacramental Communion three times—or perhaps only once—a year, Christ's sacramental presence played an ever more central role in their piety. At the Consecration, all knelt, if they were not already kneeling; the men uncovered their heads and, after viewing the Host, bowed in homage. Clerics tried to respond to the people's needs. Peter the Chanter's manual, in the short version known in Italy, suggested a prayer for lay use at the Consecration and elevation. That there is only one prayer suggests the period before the institution of an elevation of the chalice: "May the consecration, receiving, and accepting of your Flesh and Blood, Lord Jesus Christ, not bring me and all the faithful, living and dead, into judgment or condemnation, but by your mercy let it be for us protection of mind, soul, and body, and let it bring us true salvation and the reward of eternal life. Who live and reign for ever and ever. Amen."[165] This prayer is stiff, rather formal, and, by its reference to the reception of the Host, a sacerdotal, rather than lay, prayer. Peter adapted it from the priest's private preparation for Communion found in most medieval missals. One wonders if any of the laity ever used it. The layman Bonvesin de la Riva, writing directly for an Italian audience, suggested forms less clerical, more warmly emotional, the kind that became so beloved of the laity. He gives two, indicating that his audience already knew the elevation of both the Host and chalice. At the elevation of the Host: "Hail, O Body of Christ, born of the Holy Virgin! Living Flesh, wholly God yet very Man! True Salvation, Way, Life, and Redemption of the world, free us by your arm from all our sins!" And at the elevation of the chalice: "Hail Blood of Christ, most holy drink from heaven, Flood of Salvation, washing away our sins. Hail Blood flowing from the wound of Christ's side; O saving flood

---

163. Pietro of Monte Rubiano, *Vita [S. Nicolai Tolentinatis]*, 5.40, p. 654.

164. On Eucharistic devotion, especially in northern Europe after 1300, see Miri Rubin, *Corpus Christi: The Eucharist in Late Medieval Culture* (Cambridge: Cambridge University Press, 1991).

165. Peter the Chanter, *De Oratione*, 190: "Confectio, suscepio, susceptio carnis et sanguinis tui, domine Jesu Christi, non proveniat mihi et cunctis fidelibus tuis, tam vivis quam defunctis, in iudicium et condempnationem, sed ex tua pietate sit nobis tuta mentium, animarum, et corporum, et prosit nobis ad veram salutem, atque premia vite eterne recipienda. Qui vivis et regnas." (Doxology expanded in the translation.)

from him hanging on the cross, hail!"[166] These prayers beautifully capture lay Eucharistic devotion, with its link to Christ's Passion so typical of the thirteenth century. One pious Italian summed up this Christocentric piety with an elevation prayer he copied onto the last page of his manuscript of Giacomo of Varazze's *Golden Legend:*

> Hail Jesus Christ, Word of the Father, Son of the Virgin, Lamb of God, Salvation of the World, Sacred Host, Word made Flesh, Font of Mercy.
>
> Hail Jesus Christ, Splendor of the Father, Prince of Peace, Gate of Heaven, Living Bread, Vessel of the Godhead born of the Virgin.
>
> Hail Jesus Christ, Praise of the Angels, Glory of the Saints, Vision of Peace, Perfect Godhead, True Man, Flower and Fruit of the Virgin Mother.
>
> Hail Jesus Christ, Praise of Heaven, Ransom of the World, Joy of the Martyrs, Bread of Angels, Joy of the Heart, Virginity's King and Spouse.
>
> Hail Jesus Christ, Sweet Way, True Strength, and Eternal Life of all.[167]

A dramatic unmediated contact between believer and Savior marks this little poem. Versions of it are found in many manuscripts.[168] Its litanic aspect has clear links to Bonvesin's elevation prayer. Multiplying the titles of Christ of the earlier devotion by adding attributes drawn from the Scriptures and the liturgy, its repetitions paint an image of the merciful Savior who is the food of the Christian soul. The closing phrases of the three middle verses subtly associate Christ's work with that of his Virgin Mother, yet without sacrificing the prayer's Christocentricity. Such staccato litanies of devotion had a spe-

---

166. Bonvesin de la Riva, *Vita Scholastica*, 67, lines 337–48: "'Christi corpus, ave, sancta de Virgine natum, viva caro, deitas integra, verus homo. Salve, vera salus, via, vita, redempcio mundi, liberet a cunctis nos tua dextra malis.' Quando levat calicem manibus, cor surrige, iunctis ac infra totidem carmina scripta feras: 'Christi sanguis, ave, celi sanctissime potus, unda salutaris crimina nostra lavans. Sanguis, ave, lateris Christi de vulnere sparse, in cruce pendentis unda salubris, ave.'"

167. Milan, Biblioteca Ambrosiana, MS A 98 Sup., fol. 297ᵛ: "Ave Iesu Christe, verbum Patris, filius virginis, agnus Dei, salus mundi, hostia sacra, verbum caro, fons pietatis. | Ave Iesu Christe, splendor Patris, princeps pacis, ianua celi, panis vivus, virginis partus vas deitatis. | Ave Iesu Christe, laus angelorum, gloria sanctorum, visio pacis, deitas integra, homo verus, flos et fructus virginis matris. | Ave Iesu Christe, laus celi, pretium mundi, gaudium martirum, angelorum panis, cordis iubilus, rex et sponsus virginitatis. | Ave Iesu Christe, via dulcis, virtus vera, vita perhennis omnium." Dated approximately 1310.

168. E.g., a thirteenth-century elevation prayer in Florence, Biblioteca Nazionale Centrale, MS Magl. XXXVI.81ᵇⁱˢ, fol. 263ʳ: "Ecce salus mundi, verbum Patris, hostia vera, viva caro, Deitas integra, verus homo. Ave principium nostre creationis. Ave precium nostre salvationis. Ave viaticum nostre peregrinationis. Ave premium nostre retributionis." And, about 1300, in Italian, alongside the "Ave Verum" and the "Anima Christi," in Bologna, Biblioteca Universitaria, MS 2530 (1308), fol. 32ʳ. The much loved "Anima" also appears in Italian, as in Modena, Biblioteca Estense Universitaria, MS γ.W.2.40 (XIV cent.), fols. 1ʳ⁻ᵛ. Cf. these elevation prayers with the English ones in Rubin, *Corpus Christi*, 155–63.

cial appeal to the laity.[169] They appealed to layfolk perhaps even more than elegant learned devotions like the "Anima Christi" or the "Ave Verum Corpus," although both of these found lay devotees.

To communal Italians, the Mass was a place of power. The French Franciscan Jean de La Rochelle captured this perception perfectly when, in the midst of an otherwise dry scholastic treatise, he suddenly rhapsodized: "This whole sacrament exceeds human understanding, for it is so completely filled with miracles; it is best, as Augustine says, simply to believe in it piously."[170] One Italian preacher wrote that when the believer approached the Sacrament, he approached the very blood of Christ shed on the cross. To approach it was to be submerged in his Passion, to be washed with his blood, to have a new baptism.[171] From it flowed the power to perform the fourteen Spiritual and Corporal Works of Mercy and all other acts of piety. These were the "Fruits of the Mass."[172] Although set in Egypt, a miracle story in the popular collection of Giovanni Italo captured the nearly physical presence of Christ in the Eucharist as understood by the Italians of the communes. According to Abba Daniel, a pious but ignorant disciple of Abba Arsenius expressed doubts about the real presence. His abbot explained that this presence was "true" (veritas), not "symbolic" (figura). Nevertheless, the man continued to doubt. The disciple prayed that Jesus himself would reveal the truth to him. God opened his intellectual eyes. At Mass, when the bread was placed on the altar, it turned into a little child. An angel descended with knife in hand and sacrificed the child, pouring his blood into the chalice. As the priest broke the Host, the angel divided the boy's body into three parts. At Communion, the disciple was given a piece of bloody flesh to eat. But since human nature cannot bear to eat raw meat (crudam carnem), it miraculously turned back into bread. The old monk believed and gave thanks.[173] In communal Italy, visible miracles testified to the invisible miracle of the Host. Both Omobono of Cremona and Giovanni Buono worked miracles changing water to wine to show that God could easily change the Host into Christ's body.[174] The first report of a bleeding Host comes from Ferrara, dated 1170. But this story, like the bleeding Host of Bolsena, is probably an early-fourteenth-century fabrication.[175] Nevertheless, by the end of the communal pe-

169. One early-fourteenth-century owner of a text of Bonaventure's *Arbor Vitae* copied a splendid example into his codex: Milan, Biblioteca Ambrosiana, MS Y 5 Sup., fols. 44ʳ–45ʳ.

170. Florence, Biblioteca Medicea Laurenziana, MS Conv. Soppr. 145 (XIV cent.), [Jean of La Rochelle, *Summa de Vitiis et Virtutibus*], fol. 146ʳ: "super omnem intelligentiam omnium hominum quia sacramentum totum plenum est miraculis, unde melius est in hoc sacramento pie credere sicut dicit Augustinus."

171. Zucchero Bencivenni, *Sposizione*, 8.

172. See Florence, Biblioteca Medicea Laurenziana, MS Pl. xx 17, fols. 176ʳ–178ᵛ.

173. Bologna, Biblioteca Universitaria, MS 1767, fols. 139ᵛ–141ʳ.

174. *Processus . . . B. Joannis Boni*, 1.1.7, p. 773; *Vita Sancti Homoboni*, 113.

175. Dante Balboni, "Il miracolo eucaristico di Ferrara: 28 marzo 1171," *Atti del convegno di Ferrara (1971)*, Ravennatensia 4 (Cesena: Santa Maria del Monte, 1974), 23–53, holds for an eleventh-century date. On the cult of the Host at Bolsena, see Dominique Nicole Surh, "Corpus Christi and the Cappella del Corporale at Orvieto" (Ph.D. diss., University of Virginia, 2000).

riod, during Ascensiontide of 1298, in the church of Sant'Andrea at Mantua, the Precious Blood began to work miracles. A chronicler reported that the Precious Blood of Mantua soon began to cure many: the mute, the paralyzed, the lame, the blind, and the deformed.[176] One could cite numerous other examples.

An early-fourteenth-century Italian who owned a sumptuous book of Latin devotions over one hundred years old added to his precious text only one new prayer. He inscribed on the back of the first blank leaf a salutation that focused on Christ's Body and its power:

> Hail Word Incarnate
>   on the altar consecrated,
> Living Bread of Angels,
>   only hope of Christians;
> Greetings, Body of Jesus Christ,
>   who for us descended,
> World's Health for salvation,
>   free us by your power. Amen.[177]

The Body of Christ was the key that opened heaven to believers at Mass and ushered them into heaven at the hour of death. When the heretics struck down Pietro Parenzi by a blow to the head, he marshaled all his dying strength and placed a small bit of earth in his mouth, thereby showing he died longing for the Blessed Sacrament.[178] He longed for what his Cathar killers despised. The heretic was the one blind to the hidden realities of Christ's presence. More than any doctrinal deviation from the articles of the Creed, this defined the heretic. The heretic rejected as impossible the substantial presence of Christ to his people and so lost both holiness and understanding.[179] The Dominican preacher Fra Bartolomeo of Vicenza conceived of heresy almost solely as rejection of the Eucharistic Presence.[180] Fra Megliorino of Piadena testified to Giovanni Buono's love of the Eucharist in the same sentence in which he reported his hate for heretics. Saint Giovanni would cry with joy when the priest brought him Communion or when the subdeacon brought its symbolic substitute, the Pax.[181] By the late communal

176. *Breve Chronicon Mantuanum*, ed. Carlo d'Arco, in "Cronichette di Mantova di autore anonimo dal 1095 al 1299," *Archivio storico italiano*, n.s., 1:2 (1855), 57.

177. Florence, Biblioteca Nazionale Centrale, MS II.IV.III (XIII cent.), fol. I'': "Ave verbum incarnatum in altare consecratum, | panis vivus angelorum, sola spes Christianorum; | salve corpus Iesu Christi, qui pro nobis descendisti, | salus mundi pro salute, libera nos cum virtute. Amen."

178. Giovanni of Orvieto, *Vita [S. Petri Parentii]*, 2.89, p. 89.

179. Zanella, "Malessere ereticale," 52–57.

180. E.g., in his sermon at Christmas, Bartolomeo of Vicenza, *Sermones de Beata Virgine (1266)*, Sermo 9.2, p. 58.

181. *Processus . . . B. Joannis Boni*, 4.4.282, p. 844.

period, laypeople left benefactions to erect altars in honor of the Body of Christ.[182]

After the institution of the elevation, both men and women in communal Italy cultivated a visual mysticism focused on the elevated Host.[183] The lay practice of genuflecting instead of bowing at the elevation was partially motivated by the desire to keep visual contact. Oringa Cristina had visions of Christ before the altar at the time of the elevation, as did Giovanni Buono, who often shed tears as he gazed at the Host.[184] Giovanni of Alverna saw Christ become present at the altar during the Consecration or the Canon.[185] The elevation itself was a privileged time, a powerful time, for petition. Donna Neze, the prioress of the Franciscan sisters at Empoli, prayed to Saint Gerardo of Cagnoli for help in ending the factions that plagued her convent. The saint spoke to her during the elevation and told her that the nuns should kneel and say a Pater and an Ave, that the "King and Queen of heaven might grant them peace." They did as instructed, holding candles and wax votive hearts. Peace was restored.[186] Not all encouraged visual contact. When asked why his face was so radiant during the Canon, the Servite priest Francesco Patrizzi chastised the inquirer. During the Consecration, the priest was in Christ's presence, as Moses was in God's presence on Mount Sinai. Moses had veiled his radiant face lest the Israelites see it, so the laity should avert their eyes at the sacred moment and not look at the Host.[187] Francesco was in the minority.

Saint Francis of Assisi's deathbed testament expressed the lay Eucharistic piety of his age. He placed reverence for the Sacrament at the head of his instructions to his followers: the Little Poor Man ordered them to provide rich receptacles for the Blessed Sacrament. Francis returned time and again to the Real Presence in his short letters and writings.[188] One senses in Francis of Assisi's typically lay concerns a rebuke of routinized clerical piety. The visions and miracles of the communal saints reveal less veiled criticisms. Jesus himself assured Margherita of Cortona, after one of her most fervent Communions, that although her long thanksgivings after Mass might bother the clerics, they delighted him.[189] Let Margherita express her feelings in her own words, or rather in the words of Christ she recorded on another occasion: "My daughter, I complain to you about the irreverence of priests who, in such great number, handle me daily and yet neither love nor recognize me. If they truly recognized me, they would know that nothing among all

182. As at Bologna in San Giacomo Maggiore: *Iscrizioni medievali bolognesi*, 313–14, nos. 14–15.

183. Cf. Kieckhefer, "Holiness and the Culture," 290.

184. *Legenda Beatae Christianae*, 63, p. 238; *Processus . . . B. Joannis Boni*, 3.9.240, p. 832.

185. *Acta [B. Joannis Firmani sive Alvernae]*, 4.36, p. 466; *Acta Alia [B. Joannis Firmani]*, 3.24–26, AS 36 (Aug. II), 474.

186. Bartolomeo Albizzi, *Legenda Sancti Gerardi*, 7.148, p. 443.

187. Cristoforo of Parma, *Legenda Beati Francisci*, 9, p. 178.

188. See citations in Maccarrone, "Cura animarum," 157–59.

189. Giunta Bevegnati, *Legenda . . . Margaritae de Cortona*, 2.1f, pp. 193–94.

the created things anyone might find matches in beauty a priest celebrating Mass. Nevertheless, they dare to touch me with polluted hands; even more, they make no more of me than they do mud from the piazza."[190]

But the clergy were coming along. Already in the 1100s, Bishop Sicardo of Cremona prescribed that chalices to hold the Precious Blood be of unbreakable, nonporous metal, preferably silver or gold. Early-thirteenth-century councils reiterated his concerns.[191] To spill the Precious Blood was clearly a fault, if not a crime. In 1210, Bishop Guglielmo della Torre of Como named it one of the major faults a priest could commit, one worthy of excommunication if deliberate. He specified how to clean the floor where the Precious Blood had fallen. The priest washed and scraped the stone lest any of the Blood soak into it. He then burned the scrapings and washed them down a special sink in the sacristy.[192] Mid-thirteenth-century legislation at Lucca reflected this growing reverence for the Sacrament. The synod prescribed that the corporal on which the Host rested during Mass be clean and perfect, that special candles be lit on the altar after the Consecration, and that incense be used in all churches during the elevation of the Host and chalice—poverty was no excuse for nonobservance of the last requirement![193] In 1257, Bishop Sigeberto of Novara introduced the ringing of the great cathedral bell at the Consecration and commanded special marks of respect as the Host was carried through the streets to the sick.[194]

Salimbene of Parma gave three arguments for reservation of the Sacrament in churches. It allowed convenience in taking Communion to the sick, it allowed the faithful to show devout and due reverence to Christ's Body, and it was a tangible sign of Christ's promise to stay with us always.[195] The Novara synod mandated reservation for the first time in 1210. This legislation directly served the people's growing desire for access to the reserved Sacrament in the church. Clerical convenience as much as lay devotion encouraged reserving the Sacrament. Fra Salimbene noticed that easy access to the reserved Sacrament freed the priest on days of general Communion from having to count out the proper number of Hosts for those communicating. He needed only to consecrate a few, or only one, and then use the reserved sacrament for the rest. Likewise, adding Hosts to the pyx was an easy solu-

190. Ibid., 7.179, p. 340: "Filia, inquit, conqueror tibi multum de irreverentia sacerdotum, qui me in tam magna multitudine quotidie tangunt, nec me diligunt, nec agnoscunt. Sit enim me veraciter agnoscerent, scirent quod nulla posset in rebus creatis similitudo, pulchritudo, reperiri per aliquem, cui debet Sacerdos celebrans comparari. Et tamen me pollutis manibus tangere non verentur: sed majus faciunt de me forum, quam de luto facerent platearum."

191. Sicardo, *Mitrale*, 1.13, col. 55D; Novara Synod 1 (1210), 29.

192. Milan, Biblioteca Trivulziana, MS 1335 (copied 1272), Guglielmo della Torre, *Costituzioni date ai canonici di S. Maria di Torello* (1217), fol. 15ᵛ.

193. Lucca Synod (1253), 3–6, pp. 54–55.

194. Novara Synod 1 (1257), 32.

195. Salimbene, *Cronica*, 493–94, Baird trans., 339. On reservation legislation, see Maccarrone, "Cura animarum," 32 and 88 n. 20.

tion if too many were consecrated. With disgust, Salimbene watched a sacristan climb up to put extra Hosts in a hanging pyx during the middle of a general Communion of the friars. Like the manna in the desert, the Hosts should be used the day they are consecrated, Salimbene complained, and not "kept until the next day." Nor was there any excuse for interrupting Mass to get Communion for the sick from the pyx; a priest should say a private Mass and consecrate the Hosts needed.[196] Reservation served the devotional needs of the laity, but it also allowed the clergy to detach sacramental Communion from the Eucharistic sacrifice.

As popular veneration of the Eucharist, with its awesome power, grew, so did temptations to use it for practical, even sinful, ends. The hanging pyx over the altar had become nearly universal in Italy by the later 1200s.[197] But it was an easy target for theft. The clergy recognized the need for greater security. At Lucca in 1253, the synod required that the pyx containing the Blessed Sacrament above the altar have a strong lock. In the early 1300s, enactments to prevent theft of the Sacrament for use in sorcery multiplied in Italian synodal statutes.[198] A theft of Hosts from his church, probably for use in spell casting, caused a parish priest to keep consecrated Hosts in his house and an unconsecrated Host in the pyx in the church. When the unconsecrated Host was mistakenly used for her Communion, Saint Margherita of Cortona recognized immediately that something was wrong, since the reception did not give her the usual spiritual delight.[199] Margherita would have seconded Salimbene's warnings about Communion from the reserved Sacrament. Benvenuta Bojani never failed to recognize Christ's presence in Communion. One day the Blessed Virgin appeared to her in prayer and told her to go to church. There she found her confessor going to the Virgin's altar to say Mass and give Communion to a small group of the faithful. Saint Mary appeared at the altar during the Mass and bowed in homage to the Host as the priest gave each person Communion. Then, following the usual practice, the priest gave the communicants each a sip of unconsecrated wine to cleanse their mouths. The Virgin Mary herself came down and helped the priest hold the unconsecrated chalice when he ministered it to Benvenuta. The Blessed Virgin followed the priest in procession to the sacristy after the Mass.[200] During Communion, heaven joined with earth.

The visual mysticism of the elevated Host in the thirteenth century is a well-known phenomenon. Less well known is the increase in mystical experi-

---

196. Salimbene, *Cronica* (1250), 494–95, Baird trans., 340.
197. E.g., Lombardy (ecclesiastical province), *Constitutiones Domini Coelestini Legati in Lombardia* (1287), Mansi 24:884; Lucca Synod (1300), 4, p. 214; Lucca Synod (1308), 4, p. 177.
198. Ravenna Council (1311), 7, pp. 453–54; Padua Synod (1339), 11, pp. 1136–37; Perugia (diocese), *Synodus Perusina sub Episcopo Fr. Francisco circa Annum 1320 Habita* (1312–30), 1, Mansi 25:639; Padua Synod (1339), 21, p. 1141.
199. Giunta Bevegnati, *Legenda . . . Margaritae de Cortona*, 7.26, pp. 338–39.
200. Corrado of Cividale, *Vita Devotissimae Benevenutae*, 6.51, p. 163.

ences connected to sacramental Communion. Writing about 1140, the canonist Gratian observed that lay Christians made three Communions a year, at Easter, Pentecost, and Christmas, "unless impeded by grave crime."[201] Bishop Sicardo lamented this three-times-a-year Communion as too infrequent. He compared it unfavorably to the ancient practice of Communion at every Mass. But he considered infrequent Communion an unavoidable given and suggested that more frequent lay Communion was spiritually dangerous at best. But he did consider infrequent reception "defective" and counted on three remedies to compensate for the missing Communions: the Pax, the blessed bread, and the prayers over the people at the end of Mass during Lent. Remarkably, he saw nothing wrong with a devoutly prepared layperson's taking Communion several times a day.[202] Although Lateran Council IV in 1215 reduced the mandatory lay Communions to one, Gratian's three annual Communions remained a standard for even the mildly devout laity. Most Italian confraternities of the communal period required three or four Communions a year, and penitents in Umbria had monthly Communions.[203] Bishop Guglielmo della Torre of Como prescribed the traditional three Communions in his rule for canons of 1217.[204] Admittedly, various expectations militated against even triannual lay Communion—in particular, the requirement that those receiving fast not just from food and water but also from sexual relations.[205] Italian devotional writers of the period did not interpret the "daily bread" of the Pater Noster as sacramental Communion the way the Fathers of the Church had.[206]

Nonetheless, it would be a mistake to read legal minimums as actual practice. Bishop Jacques of Vitry, writing in the early 1200s, repeated Sicardo's remarks about the decline to thrice-yearly Communion, and the further reduction to once a year "because of the growth of sin." Nevertheless, he refused to condemn daily Communion and strongly urged weekly Communion.[207] Fra Salimbene, expressing what was probably the conventional wisdom at midcentury, thought it suitable to communicate whenever the recipient felt free of mortal sin—although he did recommend abstaining occasionally, out of recognition that no one is ever truly worthy of so great a gift.[208] An anonymous Italian instruction on Communion written in the

---

201. Gratian, *Decretum*, De cons. D. 2 c. 16.

202. Sicardo, *Mitrale*, 3.8, col. 148.

203. See the tabulations in Guiseppina De Sandre Gasparini, "Movimento dei disciplinati, confraternite e ordini mendicanti," *I frati minori e il terzo ordine*, 95–97: Caro's rule for Franciscan Penitents: three to four times a year; flagellant rule: three times a year. On the Umbria penitents, see ibid., 111 n. 98. "Propositum," 15, Meersseman, *Dossier*, 89, prescribed three times a year.

204. Milan, Biblioteca Trivulziana, MS 1335, Guglielmo della Torre, *Costituzioni date ai canonici di S. Maria di Torello*, fol. 11ᵛ.

205. See Gratian, *Decretum*, De cons. D. 2 c. 19.

206. E.g., Zucchero Bencivenni, *Sposizione*, 10–12.

207. Jacques of Vitry, *Historia Occidentalis*, 38, p. 244.

208. Salimbene, *Cronica* (1250), 492, Baird trans., 338.

later 1200s took a similarly permissive line. That author claimed that Saint Thomas Aquinas himself had said that only two things were necessary for a worthy daily Communion—freedom from serious sin and a desire for Christ. But he acknowledged that many devout laypeople communicated only three times a year and abstained otherwise.[209] Nevertheless, that was still more than the once-a-year minimum of Lateran IV.

These authors actually discussed daily lay Communion. That suggests that attitudes had changed since the time of Sicardo. Anecdotal evidence confirms the impression of more frequent reception, at least among the devout. Pietro Pettinaio was known for his frequent Communions, and people did not find this very unusual, at least in comparison with his daily attendance at Matins.[210] Fra Vitale, a witness at the canonization of Giovanni Buono, thought it laudable that the holy man communicated every Sunday, although he admitted that some considered this excessive.[211] When Margherita of Cortona began to skip Communions out of reverence for the Sacrament (the Salimbene principle), Jesus appeared and told her to receive as often as she could, provided that she had first gone to confession.[212] This link of Communion and confession was a conventional and important limiting factor. In practice, the required confession before every sacramental Communion inhibited frequent reception. If the laity of the communes were making increasingly frequent use of confession, as I will suggest in the next chapter, the vogue of more frequent Communions becomes more intelligible. Confessing more frequently had the side effect of allowing more frequent Communion. And a desire to communicate never seemed lacking.

One early-fourteenth-century devotional book contains a vernacular treatise on how to receive Christ's body in the Eucharist.[213] It suggests how the devout prepared for Communion. Preparation began a week before, with meditations on the great gift to sinners of the true Body and Blood of Christ. The communicant called this to mind as often as possible during the week. A day or two before the Communion, he either set aside time for meditation and devotional reading conducive to a proper disposition or, at least, recited some preparatory prayers. The book gave, for use at Matins on the day of the Communion, a long prayer on personal unworthiness and the grandeur of the Sacrament. After many protests of unworthiness and petitions for forgiveness and mercy, the prayer ended with a declaration of faith in the Sacrament:

---

209. This treatise is preserved in a fourteenth-century French codex: Florence, Biblioteca Medicea Laurenziana, MS Pl. XX 17, fols. 176ʳ⁻ᵛ.

210. Pietro of Monterone, *Vita del beato Pietro Pettinajo*, 5, p. 59.

211. *Processus . . . B. Joannis Boni*, 1.4.66, p. 789; Antonino of Florence, "De Joanne Bono Cive Mantuano" (*Chronicae*, 24:13:3), p. 747.

212. Giunta Bevegnati, *Legenda . . . Margaritae de Cortona*, 7.4, p. 321.

213. Florence, Biblioteca Riccardiana, MS 1419, fols. 70ᵛ⁻71ʳ.

What is it that I should receive? This is the body and the blood of my Creator. This is Jesus Christ in flesh and bone, made no more and no less than he was, when he was in the body of his Mother, when he came forth, when he was nailed to the wood of the cross, when he was raised, and when he went gloriously to heaven. Who is this? This is Jesus Christ, the son of God, the king of eternal life, savior of heaven and earth, the creator of the world, God omnipotent, the food of angels, the consolation of the saints. Who is this? This is the Son of God, who is one with the Father and with the Holy Spirit.[214]

The prayer adopts the same litanic recitation of messianic titles found in the earlier elevation prayers. Meditating on it before sacramental Communion, the believer stood in awe that such a great God and Savior might come to dwell within him, a wretched sinner. No wonder Salimbene and others remarked on the many who abstained from Communion out of humility. Yet when the author considered the condition of one who has just received Communion, new perspectives opened. After the briefest acknowledgment of personal sin and unworthiness, this prayer moves to rapturous exaltation in the sweetness and bliss of the gift, picking up the litanic form of the preparation prayer:

O what a matchless gift is this that I, a miserable and vile sinner, have received in my soul? How could I approach to receive such a boon and so great a gift? With what devotion and with how many tears, with how much fear, how much spirit, how much fervor to receive the highest love, the delight of Our Lady, the food of angels, the consolation of the saints, the glory of the blessed, the true light, the true sweetness, the true hope, the true delight, the highest glory, and the highest consolation. Now then enjoy, and be glad! Now do not delay! Rejoice now and burn with devotion and fervor! Be inebriated with love, and with pleasure and sweetness, thinking well on these most sweet, pleasant, and lovely things![215]

214. Ibid.: "Che chosa e questa chio debbo ricevere? Questo e lo corpo el sangue del mio creatore. Questi e Gesu Cristo in carne et in ossa, ne piu ne meno, fatto come egli era quando fu nel corpo della madre, et come era poiche fu uscito, et come era quando fu confitto nelegno della croce, et quando fu risuscitato, et quando nando in cielo glorioso. Chi e questi? Questi e Gesu Cristo, figliuolo di Dio, re di vita eterna, signore del cielo et della terra, creatore del mondo, Idio omnipotente, cibo delli angeli, consolatione de santi. Chi e questi? Questi e figliuolo di Dio, il quale e una cosa col Padre e collo Spirito Santo."

215. Ibid., fol. 71ʳ: "O che dono smisurato e questo, chio, misero et vilissimo peccatore, ricevo nella anima mia. Chome mi douvrei apparrechiare a ricevere cosi fatto benificio et grande dono? Con quanta devotione, con quante lacrime, con quanto timore, con quanto spirito, con quanto fervore, a ricevere il sommo amore, il diletto della Donna, lo cibo delli angeli, la consolatione de santi, la gloria de beati, il vero lume, la vera dolcezza, la vera speranza, vero diletto, soma gloria, et somma consolatione. Ora adunque godi et ti ralegra! Ora ti non mora. Et ti diletta ora, ardi per divotione, et per fervore. Ora tinebria damore, et di soavita, et di doleza, pensando bene in queste cose dolicissime, soavissime, et amorose."

This text beautifully expresses the sacramental mysticism that complemented the visual mysticism of the Eucharist in the piety of communal Italy.

These examples focus on sacramental Communion as a private devotional act. For most of the laity, Communion, however mystical and sacred, was a corporate event. In Siena, after the general Communions on each of the three great feasts, the cathedral canons and clergy led the people in a thanksgiving procession through the city to the ringing of bells.[216] General Communion was a citywide celebration. As a sign of membership in the society, these rites could not exclude even secret sinners; they were not to be denied Communion if they approached on the day of a general Communion.[217] Communion was the sacrament of unity. In 1266, a general Communion was held to seal the making of peace among factions at Piacenza. Mass was chanted before the relics of Saint Justina at the duomo for the people and clergy of the city. Some sixty leading men, after exchanging the kiss of peace, received Communion. Then, reconciled to each other, they took an oath on the relics of the saints to keep the peace.[218]

The ordo of Siena described the general Communions of Christmas and Epiphany. The general Communion occurred at a "popular Mass," before the solemn Mass, so as to make the fasting less burdensome. The celebrating priest gave a brief instruction to the people. He invited all to communicate, save those with unconfessed sins requiring penance. He reminded the assembly that those receiving Communion should also attend the solemn Mass and hear the bishop's sermon. He led the people in the Confiteor and gave the absolution.[219] The people approached, men first, then women. Kneeling, they received the sacred Host on the tongue—to touch it with profane hands smacked of irreverence. A minister followed the priest and gave each a sip from a chalice of unconsecrated wine. This assured that all particles of the Host had been swallowed, and it recalled the cup of wine Christ had promised to drink with his followers in the kingdom.[220] The Sienese ordo commenting on the rite urged that during Communion each recipient recall Christ's promises to the church, pray for its present unity, and look forward to the descent of the celestial Jerusalem at the end of time.

Reception of the sacred Host as part of a general Communion proved one's place in the city. To abstain was to set oneself apart. It was to be a heretic, not a citizen. When Armanno Pungilupo was posthumously accused of heresy, the most powerful evidence in his defense came in the testimony

---

216. Kempers, "Icons," 95.

217. Novara Synod II (1298), 1.2.1.4, pp. 184–86.

218. Muzio of Modena, *Annales* (1266), 520; unfortunately, the peace later failed. For another example (between the Lombard cities and the Palavicino in 1269), see ibid., 532.

219. *Ordo Senensis*, 1.46, p. 42; 1.71, p. 65.

220. Florence, Biblioteca Nazionale Centrale, MS Magl. XIV. 49, fol. 58ᵛ; perhaps distribution of consecrated wine continued even into the thirteenth century. At Milan in the late 1100s, the two were still given together by dipping the Host in the chalice; see *Manuale Ambrosianum*, 1:152, 147.

of Don Bonaventura, priest of San Salvatore in Ferrara. Bonaventura vowed that he had, on numerous occasions, heard Armanno's confessions and that he gave him Communion on Christmas and Easter during each of his three years at San Salvatore.[221] Fra Bonaventura, prior of the collegiate church of San Nicolò, agreed that these confessions and Communions proved Armanno's orthodoxy. He declared that Armanno also confessed at San Nicolò during Lent, Advent, and on the feast of Saint Lucy. Just before his death, Armanno made his confession in a "suitable" part of the church. "When he had confessed to him, the same Armanno seemed contrite in his confession, and he immediately asked that I give him the Body of Christ. But I responded that I could not give him the Body of Christ without permission of his own priest but that, when I got permission, I would give it to him. He went away and did not return, for on the following Monday he marvelously completed his last day."[222] That was a Catholic man and a good member of his community.

221. "Acta contra Armanum [Punzilupum]," 87–88.

222. Ibid., 88: "Facta vero confessione per eum ipse idem Armanus vere contritus et confessus ut videbatur instanter petiit a me corpus Christi, sed ego respondi ei quod non darem sibi corpus Christi nisi super hoc haberem licentiam a presbitero suo parochiali, sed ea recepta tradderem illud eidem, qui recessit, nec post reddiit, quia die lune sequenti mirifice diem clausit extremum."

Chapter Seven
Feasting, Fasting, and Doing Penance

The liturgical calendar of the medieval Church molded religious sensibilities and gave believers a living sense of contact with Christ and his saints. It was one of the most effective forms of popular catechesis.[1] The cycle of feasts and fasts expressed the realities of repentance and forgiveness. The great festivals of Christmas, Epiphany, Holy Week, Ascension, and Pentecost not only commemorated events in the Savior's life but made them present to the faithful. Saints' days punctuated the liturgical and civic calendars, displaying the varieties of holiness and honoring the city's glorious intercessors in heaven. In Bergamo, Vespers of the patronal feasts brought community banquets, sometimes outside under pavilions, sometimes in the church cloister. All partook of fruit, wine, and fine white bread.[2] The calendar shaped private religious experience to an extent hard to imagine today. Margherita of Cortona's mystical visions and locutions, usually after sacramental Communion, almost always correlated with the feast celebrated at Mass.[3] Oringa Cristiana had a vision of the Passion every Friday, the weekly day of fast that recalled that saving event. Oringa's other visions of episodes from Jesus' life came with remarkable regularity on their proper liturgical days.[4] Benvenuta Bojani enjoyed uncounted visits from the saints, who invariably chose to appear on their feast days. The Blessed Virgin came to visit, along with Saint John the Baptist, Saint Catherine of Alexandria, and Saint Agnes, on the Assumption; Saint Dominic arrived with the Virgin, Saint Catherine, and Saint Margaret on the feast of the translation of his relics.[5] The saints in heaven knew and observed this calendar.

1. Enrico Cattaneo, "La partecipazione dei laici alla liturgia," *I laici nella Societas Christiana*, 420.
2. Valsecchi, *Interrogatus*, 112–14.
3. See Giunta Bevegnati, *Legenda . . . Margaritae de Cortona*, 5–6, pp. 241–318.
4. *Legenda Beatae Christianae*, 39, p. 218.
5. Corrado of Cividale, *Vita Devotissimae Benevenutae*, 8.68–69, p. 168.

The City Feasts

Feasts had a social as well as a religious role. Cities fixed their court sessions according to the liturgical calendar. Padua and Mantua courts scheduled recess from Christmas to Epiphany and during the week of Michaelmas (29 September). In the spring, courts closed from Palm to Low Sunday, the time of Holy Week and Easter Week—unless some delinquent dared violate that holy season by rioting. Courts always closed on Sunday.[6] Christmas and Easter were the very minimum for days of rest. Cities suspended sessions on feasts of the Virgin, the apostles, and their local patron saints, including the titulars of every city chapel.[7] From calculations based on festivals in rural areas, we know that medieval farmers typically enjoyed a number of vacation days unequaled in later ages until the postindustrial society of the twentieth century. The communes, with their closings for chapel patrons, certainly had even more. Bologna in 1288 observed closings for Sundays and all major solemnities of the calendar. The latter included the octaves (eight days) following Christmas and Easter, Holy Week itself, the two days before Christmas, the major Marian feasts, the Ascension, all feasts of apostles, the solemnity of Saints Peter and Paul, and the feast of Saint Michael. Bologna thus enjoyed at least ninety-five days of rest a year. The number of closings due to patron feasts varied from city to city, depending on the number of chapel and city patrons. In 1288, Bologna observed twenty-two days for chapel titulars and added more as the century waned.[8] The large city of Florence and smaller Lucca were among the highest in the number of titular closings, each adding approximately twenty-five local saints to the major festivals of the calendar. Ferrara required the least, only two. Brescia was probably typical, with about ten.[9] On all feasts, Lucca forbade such noisome activities as leatherworking in the Piazza San Pietro, lest the stink spoil the decorum.[10] But Florence exempted barbers from festival closing, so that all participating in the ceremonies of the day could look presentable.[11] Most cities did not observe what Bishop Sicardo considered New Year's Day, the pagan 1 January.[12] The communes preferred 25 March, the date of the Annunciation to the Virgin, thereby linking the new civil year with Christ's Incarnation in the body of his mother. City officials received their biannual

6. Padua Stat., 2.10, p. 180, nn. 554–56; Mantua Stat., 2.25, pp. 191–92. On saints' days, see Webb, *Patrons*, 96–111; and on saints in municipal statutes, ibid., 95–134.

7. E.g., Verona Stat. II (1276), 4.158, p. 617; Modena Stat. (1327), 3.1, pp. 282–83; Biella Stat. (1245), 1.3.12 (72); Vicenza Stat. (1264), 181.

8. Bologna Stat. I (1250–67), 4.18, 1:400–402; Bologna Stat. II (1288), 6.51, 2:41–42.

9. Florence Stat. II (1325), 2.13, pp. 95–96; Lucca Stat. (1308), 4.1, pp. 249–50; Ferrara Stat. (1287), 2.396–97, p. 199; Brescia Stat. (before 1277), cols. (149)–(150). Treviso only added All Saints and the feast of Saints Peter and Paul: Treviso Stat. (1230), 150, 2:57, and 168, 2:63. See also the closing for patrons' feasts in Parma Stat. II (1266), 158.

10. Lucca Stat. (1308), 3.141, p. 221.

11. Florence Stat. II (1325), 5.21, p. 379.

12. See Sicardo, *Mitrale*, 5.6, col. 218C, and 8.25, col. 404.

stipends on Christmas and Easter, the days on which craft associations gave a bonus to their familiars.[13]

Charitable works were suitable on feasts. Florence celebrated Christmas, Easter, and the feast of its principal patron, Saint John the Baptist, by granting pardons to the most wretched among those detained for debt in the city prison. Those freed by this grace went in thanksgiving procession to the baptistery church of San Giovanni, carrying candles and wearing special hats inscribed with their names. There they made an oblation of the candles and hats, which remained on display for a year to remind all of the mercy of God, Saint John, and the commune of Florence. Compassion did have a limit; a debtor could only receive this pardon once in a lifetime.[14] Modena freed its debtors on Christmas, Easter, and the feast of its principal patron, Saint Giminiano. That city appointed commissions of friars to decide which paupers most deserved a pardon.[15] Communes made festivals the occasion for other forms of public relief. At Siena, the podesta canceled the *casaticum* (a food tax) on Sundays, Holy Thursday, Christmas, and the feast of the Assumption, lest the burden hinder anyone from enjoying the day.[16]

City fathers did their part to make the festivals of the year joyous. The Church could do no less. Ecclesiastical legislation mandated the presence of the canons in the cathedral on feasts so that the cult could be performed with its full splendor.[17] Ecclesiastics began their year near the beginning of December, with the first Sunday of Advent. Advent was a penitential season of preparation for Christmas. But the canons did no more than add Wednesday to the weekly fasts on Friday and Saturday. Choirs stopped singing the joyful Gloria at the beginning of the Mass. Popular tradition claimed that the opening verse of this hymn could not be sung again until the angels sang it anew to the shepherds on Christmas morn.[18] But mostly the Advent season went on with little fanfare until its last day, Christmas eve. Special observances began on Christmas eve, with the first Vespers of Christmas and the supper that followed. Christmas eve, as a solemn vigil, was a strict fast day, but tradition dictated that the fish dishes served be unusually sumptuous. The clergy embellished the meal with solemn chanted blessings.[19] Among the laity, the eve was a day for charity. In the early 1200s, the rhetorician Filippo of Ferrara explained that on this day the wealthy commonly invited a group of carefully selected paupers to their dinner.[20]

13. For Christmas stipends, see Parma Stat. II (1266), 191; Piacenza, *Statuta Antiqua Mercatorum Placentiae* (ca. 1200), 127.

14. Florence Stat. I (1322), 5.1, pp. 217–18.

15. Modena Stat. (1306/7), 2:103.

16. Siena Stat. I (1262), 4.46, p. 416.

17. E.g., Cremona Cath. Stat. (1247), 10, pp. 454–55.

18. Florence, Biblioteca Nazionale Centrale, MS Magl. XIV. 49, fol. 26r.

19. E.g., *Ordo Senensis*, 1.38, pp. 32–33.

20. Bologna, Biblioteca Universitaria, MS 1552 (XV cent. copy of text dated between 1323 and 1347), Filippo of Ferrara, *Liber de Introductione Loquendi*, 7.23, fol. 8r. See Raymond Creytens, "Le manuel de conversation de Philippe de Ferrare, O.P. (+1350?)," *AFP* 16 (1946): 112 n. 23, on this manuscript.

Christmas itself began with predawn Matins, announced by the pealing
of the church bells. After Matins, the three Masses of Christmas, of night,
dawn, and day, immediately followed.[21] This once, the laity came in force
for Matins and kept vigil for the whole service, including the three Masses.
Bishop Sicardo, commenting on the presence of the laity, explained that
they were the reason why the deacon did not sing the dismissal, the "Ite
Missa Est," until the end of the third Mass.[22] At Cremona, the parts of this
service formed a seamless whole. When the clerics had finished Matins, with
its nine psalms and three sets of readings, the night Mass began immediately
with the Gloria. At Communion, the clerics sang the psalms of Lauds and
the deacon mounted the great pulpit for the genealogy of Christ from Matthew, chanted in an especially solemn tone. All responded by singing the Te
Deum Laudamus, that hymn of praise reserved for festive Vigils.[23] Bishop
Sicardo noted that a few north Italian churches followed a different order,
singing the Te Deum in its usual place at the end of Vigils and then intoning
the Gloria.

At Siena, the service followed Sicardo's order, but the Sienese kissed the
Pax before Matins, and the deacon proclaimed the lessons of Vigils from the
great pulpit, not from the usual small lectern in the choir. Night Mass there
ended with Matthew's genealogy. The Sienese also paused between the three
Masses, to ensure that the second would be precisely at dawn and that the
third would be in full daylight after Terce.[24] The night Mass at Pisa began
with the Pax and Matins as at Siena, but the second Mass began immediately
after, its Gloria taking the place of the Benedictus of the Office of Lauds,
which was chanted at the Communion of the night Mass.[25] The church of
San Gimignano followed yet another order, that of its Mother Church at
Volterra. There, Matins consisted of Vigils and Lauds together in their usual
form, and the night Mass began with the Gloria, which replaced the Benedictus of Lauds.[26] Everywhere, Christmas was one of the times for a general
Communion.[27] Mostly this happened at the day Mass. But at Siena it occurred at a fourth "popular" Mass preceding that of the day. The Sienese
day Mass featured the bishop's Christmas sermon and an extended pealing
of the duomo bells.[28]

The great festival of Christmas called for rejoicing; it even canceled the

---

21. On rising time, see Bologna, Biblioteca Universitaria, MS 1785 (late XII cent.), Rolando the Deacon, *Liber de Ordine Officiorum*, fol. 7r.

22. Sicardo, *Mitrale*, 5.1, col. 204C.

23. Ibid., 5.6, col. 222.

24. *Ordo Senensis*, 1.40–44, pp. 33–41.

25. Bologna, Biblioteca Universitaria, MS 1785, Rolando the Deacon, *Liber de Ordine Officiorum*, fols.
7v–8r.

26. *Ordo Officiorum della cattedrale [volterrana]*, 51–55 (Volterra, Biblioteca Comunale Guarnacci, MS 273,
fols. 10r–13r; San Gimignano, Biblioteca Comunale, MS 3, fols. 7r–10r).

27. Bologna, Biblioteca Universitaria, MS 1785, Rolando the Deacon, *Liber de Ordine Officiorum*, fol. 8v.

28. *Ordo Senensis*, 1.47, pp. 44–46.

Friday fast if it fell on that day.[29] Students at Bologna gathered for dinner parties on Christmas day, as they did on Epiphany and Easter. They traditionally partook of a common dish of tortellini at the local tavern.[30] Tommaso Musolini, from the cappella of San Salvatore, participant at a similar *festa* on Epiphany, fondly recalled how his friends sang well (*bene cantabimus*), danced, and cast dice to see who would pick up the tab. Such innocuous gambling was a usual part of the festivities among the students. The commune never enforced the gaming laws on the three great festivals—or, at least, that was what Tommaso told the court after city police raided the dinner at Lago di Gipso's tavern in 1289.[31] We do not know whether Tommaso and his five friends got off.

In the contrade, the neighborhoods, Christmas celebrations continued throughout the octave. Weather permitting, this was a time for street parties. At Bologna, from the monastery of Santo Stefano to the church of San Giovanni in Monte, neighbors banqueted nightly on tables and benches under the porticoes and built bonfires in the street for warmth. The commune tried to end these gatherings in the mid-1260s, claiming that they had gotten too rowdy, but the parties just moved elsewhere. City fathers finally satisfied themselves by forbidding the octave parties from being held in churches.[32] People could not be denied their good cheer. Christmas was a time for indulgence all around, something even the Christ Child approved, at least in popular preaching. One mid- to late-thirteenth-century collector of exempla recounted the story of a nun who had escaped and became a prostitute. After years outside the convent, on a fine Christmas morn, she began to worry about her salvation. Recalling the kindness with which mothers enjoy their infant children, she prayed before an image of the Christmas Madonna. She praised Mary's tender love for the infant Jesus and begged a share of it for herself. Mary and Jesus heard her prayer. The child's voice told her that all her sins were forgiven. The story is undated, but the tender devotion to Mary fits well in the communal period.[33]

The feast of Holy Innocents, December 28, commemorated the children murdered by King Herod, as recounted in Matthew's Gospel. In north Italy this was a time of another special Christmas frolic, the Feast of the Boy Bishop. At Mass, the celebrant wore dark vestments, and the choir did not chant the Gloria, out of respect for the children's sorrowing parents, even though the babes were already rejoicing in heaven.[34] At Office and table, young choir boys and adolescent clerics replaced the senior clergy, so as to

29. Ibid., 1.49, p. 46.
30. Hermann Kantorowicz, "Una festa studentesca bolognese per l'Epifania del 1289," *AMDSPPR*, 3d ser., 24 (1905/6): 321–22, and "Documenti," ibid., 323–26.
31. "Documenti," 325.
32. Bologna Stat. 1 (1262/67), 7.146ᵛ, 2:170–71.
33. Milan, Biblioteca Ambrosiana, MS N 43 Sup., fols. 23ᵛ–24ʳ.
34. Florence, Biblioteca Nazionale Centrale, MS Magl. XIV. 49, fols. 26ᵛ–27ʳ.

honor the tiny martyr saints of the day. They not only sat in their elders' stalls; one even took the bishop's throne and presided over the liturgy. Fra Salimbene, who usually had little good to say about popular customs, liked this feast—especially if the boy bishop was a Franciscan novice of good breeding instead of a vulgar secular cleric. Such a mendicant boy bishop added suitable dignity to the liturgy and had the graces to preside with style over the party that followed.[35] And youth had to have its fling. At Bologna, on the feast of John the Evangelist (27 December), custom allowed boys to tease any girl seen going to church. The more rowdy even found sport in knocking off her father's hat. One podesta tried to stop the fun, probably in vain.[36] Nativitytide ended on Epiphany with yet another celebration on the model of the boy bishop. That day was the Feast of Subdeacons, when the most junior of the ordained clergy for once presided at Office and meals.[37]

City patron saints provided good reason for celebration. Their feasts fell with striking regularity in the good weather of summer. Saint Prosper's feast, on 25 June, at his hometown of Reggio was a day of obligatory attendance for residents of the city and district, announced by criers for two weeks running.[38] Padua, too, loved her festivals. The Paduans held a *nundina*, or "tenting," of Saint Prosdocimo and Saint Justina in the Prato della Valle, and yet another tenting for All Saints on the isle of Montesalice.[39] The festivals' name seems to come from the pavilions erected on them. The religious calendar accommodated without strain the popular love of feasting for its own sake.

No saint inspired greater festivity and devotion than the Blessed Virgin, the mother of the Savior. She enjoyed a feast day every week on Saturday. Umiliana dei Cerchi went to Communion every week on that day and prayed that she might also die on Saturday.[40] The hermit Odo of Novara, who almost never left his cell, never failed to go out on Saturday to celebrate Mass at the altar of the Virgin.[41] Italian legendaries exalted the dignity of the Virgin's feast on Saturday. The celebration's origin is recounted in one of the Marian miracles from a fourteenth-century manuscript at Pisa. The Virgin alone had remained faithful on Holy Saturday, when all the apostles doubted; she healed her devotee Theophilus on a Saturday; and an image of her had been miraculously revealed on that day.[42] Devotion to Mary and her feasts brought rewards in this life and the next. The Pisa legendary tells of a thief who fasted on bread and water on vigils of the four principal Marian feasts, Annunciation, Assumption, Nativity, and Conception. The

35. Salimbene, *Cronica* (1248), 387, Baird trans., 262.
36. Bologna Stat. 1 (1262/67), 7.146ˣ, 2:169–70.
37. Sicardo, *Mitrale*, 5.7, col. 227D.
38. Reggio Stat. (1242), 59, p. 35.
39. Padua Stat. (1275), 2.10, p. 183, no. 566.
40. Vito of Cortona, *Vita [B. Humilianae]*, 3.32, p. 393; 3.52, p. 398.
41. *Apographum Processus . . . B. Odonis*, testis 77, p. 350.
42. Pisa, Biblioteca Cateriniana del Seminario Arcivescovile, MS 139, "Miracula de Beata Virgine," fol. 137ᵛ.

man escaped death by hanging because the Virgin came and supported his feet. When the thief revealed the miracle, the podesta pardoned him, and both gave thanks to God and his Blessed Mother.[43]

Sicardo of Cremona, as a theologian, might emphasize the Christological dimension of the five Marian feasts celebrated at Cremona: Immaculate Conception, Christmas, Annunciation, Assumption, and the Virgin's Nativity. And he ruefully observed that among these two, Annunciation and Christmas, were not Marian at all and that the Immaculate Conception was nonbiblical and boasted only a vision to authenticate it.[44] For the laity, the four feasts other than Christmas were the pivots of the year, marking the seasons—and they were the preserve of the Virgin. Two stood above all the rest, Mary's Assumption and her Nativity. In Padua and its contado, Mary's birthday, on 8 September, was the Marian center of the year. They honored her with yet another *nundina* in the Piazza Este.[45] For that feast in 1208, the podesta Viscontino of Piacenza organized pageants, singing, and parades in the Prato della Valle. The companies of the *contrade* marched, dressed in splendid outfits made especially for the occasion. The events ranged from the singing of psalms and hymns to feats of arms and included "the great game of the wild man"'(*magnus ludus de quodam homine salvatico*).[46]

But no feast matched the Assumption as a time of devotion and festivity.[47] This, the feast of Saint Mary in August, was the great civic festival of summer. Parma detailed the municipal trumpeters, Santo di Ugolino de' Vegatuli and Vetulo of Palanzano, to play at the festivities of that day and provided each with a stipend of £3 parm. and a new suit of clothing.[48] A document of 1273 records Brescia's August celebration of the Virgin.[49] The general council of the city publicized it in city and countryside. Heralds went through the whole district for the eight to ten days previous, summoning all to come and bring their offerings. Courts closed three days before the feast, and at Terce on the vigil all shops, except the candle sellers, closed. The captain of the people assembled the officials of the corporations (*antiani paraticorum*) with their offerings to honor the Virgin and to support work on the church of Santa Maria e San Pietro. Corporations and guilds suspended business during the feast.[50]

From the Annunciation, on 25 March, whose Lenten and winter date precluded festivities, to the Assumption, on 15 August, not a single Marian

43. Ibid., fols. 138[r–v].
44. Sicardo, *Mitrale*, 9.40, col. 420.
45. Padua Stat. (1275), 2.10, p. 182, no. 565.
46. Rolandino of Padua, *Cronica in Factis et circa Facta Marchie Trivixiane* (1208), 232; *Liber Regiminum Padue* (1208), 300–301.
47. Sicardo, *Mitrale*, 9.40–43, cols. 420–21.
48. Parma Stat. 1, 436, 470.
49. *Statuti bresciani del secolo XIII*, ed. Federico Odorici (Turin: Reale Tipografica, 1876), col. 1584; see also Pini, "Le arti in processione," 72–73, on this text.
50. E.g., the knife makers at Bologna: Bol. Pop. Stat., 2:412.

feast of importance marked the calendar. But May was traditionally the Virgin's month, and the crowning of "May queens" on 1 May to some extent satisfied the lack of festivity during this long dry period. But even when examined in haste, the merrymaking looks secular, if not pagan, in inspiration. Treating of Bologna in the 1260s, the chronicler Matteo Griffoni writes of May queens and their courts as already traditional. On May Day of 1267, a youth named Giovanni Tarafocolo and his friends snatched an expensive purse from the daughter of Pietro of Masimilla, who was presiding as queen under the portico of Paolo the shoemaker in Porta Saragossa. Pietro chased the boys down and wounded one of them in a scuffle.[51] In 1288, the city outlawed the rites and fined those who crowned May queens.[52] By then, the festivals had lost any religious element they might once have possessed.

The rites of May were famous at Florence.[53] Their observance dates to 1283, when, according to Giovanni Villani, the festivities extended for nearly two months, from May Day to the feast of John the Baptist (24 June).[54] During the first of these celebrations, the Rossi family and its neighbors crossed the Arno into the city to celebrate with "companies and brigades of a thousand men or more, all dressed in white robes, presided over by a Lord of Love." The brigades occupied themselves with games, amusements, and dances for women and knights. The party of the Popolo paraded through town with trumpets and other instruments and gathered for dinners and suppers. The festival was connected to 1 May after the Florentine victory at Campaldino on that date in 1289. In the new version, brigades of genteel youth dressed in new clothes, constructed "courts" throughout the city, and displayed queens on platforms decorated with drapes and banners. Women and young girls paraded through the city, playing musical instruments and dancing with garlands of flowers on their heads. Citizens spent their time in games and enjoyments, in dinners and suppers. Any excuse is probably good enough for a party, and spring, the Virgin, and victory are better than most.

The City Fasts

In the calendar of medieval Christianity, feast alternated with fast. The traditional fasts were the Advent fast, during the four weeks before Christmas, and the Lenten fast, from Ash Wednesday to Holy Week. The Lenten fast was the most solemn; at its start, men stopped cutting their hair and let it grow until Easter. This symbolically recalled Lent as a time for Christians to prolong their meditations and grow in good works.[55] Advent was always of secondary importance; its addition of a Wednesday fast to those of Friday

---

51. Matteo Griffoni, 18.
52. Bologna Stat. II (1288), 4.93, 1:249.
53. On these celebrations, see Trexler, *Public Life*, 217–18.
54. Giovanni Villani, *Cronica*, 7:84, 7:132.
55. Florence, Biblioteca Nazionale Centrale, MS Magl. XIV. 49, fol. 43ʳ.

and Saturday was sometimes not observed. Medieval piety knew two other fasts. In the spring came Saint John's Fast, lasting from Pentecost Octave to the birth of John the Baptist (24 June) or for six weeks, whichever was shorter. Some considered this fast optional, but many observed it as obligatory. Commentators considered Saint John's Fast a twin of Advent. It prepared for the birth of John, the herald of Christ, as Advent prepared for Christ's birth.[56] Saint Martin's Fast came in the fall and was well known, although its observance was always optional. At Siena, it lasted from the feast of the Holy Cross (14 September) to Saint Martin's day (11 November). During the fasts of Saint John and Saint Martin, the pious, like Benvenuta Bojani, ate only one meal a day.[57] That same regimen ruled canonically during Lent, when the faithful also abstained from dairy products, eggs, and meat, even on Sundays. At Siena, which was probably typical, the vigil fasts before major feasts, each with a Lenten-style fast, numbered eleven.[58] During both Advent and Lent, the traditional discipline also prescribed abstinence from sexual relations; marriages were not celebrated in those seasons.[59]

The Ember Days of the Four Seasons occurred, as the name suggests, four times a year, once in each season. They imposed a full Lenten fast on the Wednesday, Friday, and Saturday of the third week of Advent, the first full week of Lent, the octave of Pentecost, and the week after the Holy Cross.[60] In communal Italy, priestly and deaconal ordinations were held almost exclusively on the Ember Days.[61] Bishop Guercio of Lucca, for one, held ordinations only during the "four seasons." He also required the priests of the city chapels to present their clerics at the cathedral for reception of the tonsure and the "minor orders" of acolyte, lector, exorcist, and doorkeeper on these days.[62] Some bishops were more casual about minor orders, bestowing them on an ad hoc basis, sometimes in the privacy of the episcopal palace chapel.[63] Major orders were always linked to Ember Days. At Pisa, examination of ordination candidates took place on the Ember Saturday of Lent. In the late 1100s, the archdeacon examined candidates on the quality of their lives, literacy, orthodoxy, knowledge of liturgical books, canon law,

---

56. Sicardo, *Mitrale*, 5.1, col. 265D; 7.11, col. 383.

57. Corrado of Cividale, *Vita Devotissimae Benevenutae*, 1.7, p. 153.

58. *Ordo Senensis*, 2.74, p. 478.

59. Sicardo, *Mitrale*, 9.1, col. 405; on sexual fasts, see Chiovaro, "Mariage," 240–44.

60. *Carpsum, L'orazionale dell'archidiacono Pacifico e il Carpsum del cantore Stefano: Studi e testi sulla liturgia del duomo di Verona*, ed. G. G. Meersseman, E. Adda, and J. Deshusses (Fribourg: Edizioni Universitarie, 1974), 216; Verona, Biblioteca Capitolare, MS XCIV (late XI cent.), fols. 7ᵛ–8ʳ, describes these days in Verona.

61. *Ordo Senensis*, 1.29, p. 25; 1.113, p. 100; 1.255, p. 243; 1.286, p. 268.

62. Lucca Synod (1253), 11, p. 56; Piacenza Stat. Cler. (1297), p. 532; *Ordo Officiorum della cattedrale [volterrana]*, 84–86 (San Gimignano MS 3, fols. 29ᵛ–30ᵛ; Volterra MS 273, fols. 28ʳ⁻ᵛ).

63. As did, e.g., the bishop of Como: see Lottieri della Tosa, *Il codice di Lottieri della Tosa*, ed. Giovanni Lucchesi (Faenza: Banca Popolare di Faenza, 1979), doc. 43, p. 54 (tonsure on 13 April 1289); doc. 63, p. 68 (minor orders on 27 May 1290); doc. 76, p. 78 (tonsure on 17 July 1290); doc. 78, p. 80 (tonsure on 20 July 1290); docs. 140–41, pp. 122–23 (minor orders on 18 May 1291); doc. 175, pp. 144–45 (minor orders on 15 July 1291).

confessional practice, and the calculation of the date of Easter. If they passed, he set their ordination for Advent Ember Days of the following year.[64] Sicardo of Cremona followed the traditional practice of ordaining priests, deacons, and subdeacons on the Advent Ember Saturday, but he also foresaw the possibility of ordinations on the Ember Days of the other three seasons.[65] Siena celebrated the Advent ordinations by having the Gospel of the Ember Days chanted in both Greek and Latin so that the new deacons could show off their vocal and linguistic skills to the assembled citizenry.[66]

There were also local fasts, such as the first week of September at Pisa, when a Lenten-style fast was observed from Thursday to Saturday.[67] The pious added their own private mortifications to these times of self-denial. Nevolone of Faenza and Nicola of Tolentino fasted on bread and water on Mondays, Wednesdays, and Fridays in honor of the Blessed Virgin.[68] Some, like Omobono of Cremona, simply intensified the restrictions on meat and dairy by subsisting on bread and water. Omobono observed that regimen during the four seasonal fasts, the vigils of solemnities, the Ember Days, and the weekday fasts of Wednesday, Friday, and Saturday.[69] Pietro Pettinaio fasted only from All Saints to Christmas (thus combining the fasts of Saint Martin and Advent) and on vigils, Fridays, and Saturdays.[70] Occasionally we meet virtuoso fasters. One peasant from Piacenza went without food for seventy days. This so amazed some Piacentines that they spread the word about him. At Cremona, always at odds with Piacenza, some citizens put the man under guard to make sure he ate nothing during a fasting demonstration. On another occasion, he went forty days without food. This sort of behavior looked odd to contemporaries. It mystified Filippo of Ferrara, who commented on the fellow in his rhetorical manual.[71]

The days and seasons of fasting, punctuated by days and seasons of feasting, gave the devotional life of the communes an almost bipolar swing. Feasts at family meals gave a domestic aspect to celebrations that might have stopped at the great western doors of the duomo. Popular sensibility, if anything, exaggerated the swing from abstinence to indulgence. Lent was the great season of self-denial that led up to the feasting of Easter, but common attitudes focused as much on the feasting given up as that yet to come. The communes bid a raucous farewell to meat during the days before Ash Wednesday—carnival. The canonist Gratian begrudgingly admitted that

64. Bologna, Biblioteca Universitaria, MS 1785, Rolando the Deacon, *Liber de Ordine Officiorum*, fol. 18ᵛ.
65. Sicardo, *Mitrale*, 5.3, col. 208C; 8.14, col. 366–98.
66. *Ordo Senensis*, 1.25, p. 22.
67. Bologna, Biblioteca Universitaria, MS 1785, Rolando the Deacon, *Liber de Ordine Officiorum*, fol. 36ᵛ.
68. Pietro of Monte Rubiano, *Vita [S. Nicolai Tolentinatis]*, 3.19, p. 649; 3.23, p. 650; *Vita Beati Nevoloni*, 3, p. 646.
69. *Vita di s. Omobono*, 164.
70. Pietro of Monterone, *Vita del beato Pietro Pettinajo*, 7, p. 79.
71. Bologna, Biblioteca Universitaria, MS 1552, Filippo of Ferrara, *Liber de Introductione Loquendi* (ca. 1323–47), fol. 7ʳ.

there was no way to convince people not to stuff themselves with meat and wine until the stroke of midnight ushered in Ash Wednesday. This was immemorial custom and could not be broken.[72]

In Shrovetide—the time to be "shriven," to go to confession—just before Ash Wednesday, some acted wildly and foolishly; such was the custom of Christian cities, remarked Fra Salimbene. Men paraded around in women's clothing, wearing pale masks to hide their gender, oblivious of scriptural condemnations of cross-dressing. At Reggio, the millers once tricked the Franciscans into giving them their old habits, which they wore while dancing and singing in the streets. In the countryside, the rustics burned their sheds and huts.[73] At Padua, this was the season for tournaments in the Prato Sant' Ercolano.[74] Parma also had its war games. These activities so often got out of hand that the city council required those who put them on to apply for a permit.[75] The mock wars of Shrovetide sometimes brought serious injury or death to the participants and provoked condemnations from the moralists. Most people turned a deaf ear. Pietro Parenzi tried to stamp out carnival tournaments at Orvieto because of the homicides. He failed, even after he resorted to leveling the houses and towers of those who fought with swords and pikes in the piazza on Shrove Tuesday. These delinquents must have been heretics, Pietro's biographer opined.[76] More likely they were good Catholics enjoying immemorial custom.

Shrovetide put the ascetic piety of the communes in conflict with their love of celebration. A well-wisher presented the Tuscan penitent Torello a basket of meat for carnival. Torello accepted it with gratitude, only to be struck by a crisis of conscience. The holy man prayed for guidance, and suddenly out of nowhere a wolf showed up to eat the meat. The donor went away edified.[77] A blind man, Martino of Agello, had been healed at the tomb of Saint Pietro Parenzi, whose dim view of carnival was notorious. The man expressed his gratitude by keeping vigil before the tomb with a lighted candle. When melting wax flowed down and burned his hand, Don Matteo, the prior of the church, suggested he put the taper in the candelabrum. Martino explained he would happily undergo a little pain to show appreciation, especially because it was carnival, "the time when irreligious people [*homines seculares*] are accustomed to eat in excess."[78]

With the arrival of the fast on Ash Wednesday, the cities themselves took on a somber air. In the churches, on the night before Ash Wednesday, the great Lenten curtain was hung between the choir and the nave, where it

72. Gratian, *Decretum*, D. 4 c. 6.
73. Salimbene, *Cronica*, 913–15, Baird trans., 632–35; ibid., 931, trans., 645.
74. Ibid. (1283), 759, trans., 529.
75. Parma Stat. III (1316), 106.
76. Giovanni of Orvieto, *Vita [S. Petri Parentii]*, 1.5, p. 87.
77. *Acta [B. Torelli Puppiensis]*, 2.8, p. 496.
78. Giovanni of Orvieto, *Vita [S. Petri Parentii]*, 5.34, p. 96.

would remain until Good Friday. On the evening before the first Sunday of Lent, clerics covered the images and crosses in the churches.[79] Even the buildings symbolically donned their sackcloth and ashes. Padua forbade her citizens the pleasure of hunting rabbits.[80] Lent was the time to put an end to animosities. At Parma in Lent, the bishop and city fathers jointly held court sessions once a week to end feuds and contract reconciliations "in good faith and without deceit."[81] The more devout entered into the spirit of the time with gusto. Margherita of Cortona redoubled her fasting and works of penance on the first Sunday of Lent, when the Gospel recounted Christ's victory over the Evil One's temptation to break his fast. But even penance had to have a limit. Christ himself appeared to her and told her not to overdo her mortifications.[82] The Savior must have sympathized somewhat with the more indulgent tradition.

Lenten fasting was an external sign; the season demanded more, repentance from sin. Each year anew, Lent demanded a change of heart. Contemporary observers recognized that the best penance provoked tears; this was an age that cried easily. The common view was the more tears, the better. When Ranieri of Pisa repented of his frivolous life, the saintly Alberto, to whom he had unburdened himself, sent the would-be penitent to confess to the prior of the church of San Giacomo dell'Orticaria. Ranieri's confession brought on a crying jag that lasted several days. The convert took to sleeping on the ground in the piazza, and his family thought him insane. His teacher, Enrico, interceded for Ranieri, but his family locked him in his room. The poor man went blind from crying, but Christ restored his sight so that he could take up a life of service.[83] Such stories captured the attention of hagiographers and historians, but authentic penance, so long as the sinner was contrite, required only simple acts with a humble heart. The preacher Giordano of Pisa said as much in a Lenten sermon at Santa Maria Novella on 23 February 1306: "Merely alms given to the poor, merely kneeling before God or the Virgin Mary, these are worthy of eternal life. Just striking your breast merits eternal life. And not only these works. Just say an Ave Maria with a good heart, if you are repentant. Just say 'Blessed be God' and nothing more, and you are worthy of eternal life. I do not want you reading books or lots of psalms. No, and not to go to Rome or far away. No, just do the littlest work."[84] Pietro Pettinaio would have agreed. When a priest asked him

79. Sicardo, *Mitrale*, 6.5, col. 260; *Ordo Senensis*, 1.108, p. 96.

80. Padua Stat. (pre-1236), 3.25, p. 289, no. 589.

81. Parma Stat. 1, 3.

82. Giunta Bevegnati, *Legenda . . . Margaritae de Cortona*, 3.6, p. 214.

83. Benincasa of Pisa, *Vita [S. Raynerii Pisani]*, 1.15–21, p. 350; 1.17, p. 350.

84. Giordano of Pisa, *Quaresimale fiorentino 1305–1306*, ed. Carlo Delcorno (Florence: Sansoni, 1974), 16, p. 84: "Solo un danio chettu dei al povero, solo uno ingnocchiare dinanzi a Dio, a la Vergine Maria, è degna di vita eterna; solo uno picchiare di petto merita vita eterna. E non solamente opere attuali, ma eziandio pur una avemaria chettu dichi di buon cuore, essendo in istato di penitenzia, o dichi pur 'Benedetto Idio', non più, e se' degno di vita eterna. Non ti pongo leggere libri o molti salmi, no, né ire a Roma o a la lunga, no, ma pur la minima opera."

whether it was best to give heavy penances or light ones, Pietro replied that if the penitent was truly sorrowful, then light penances were the best—"since Christ our Savior asked of the sinner only contrition for the sin, and the intention not to commit it again."[85] This was not because Pietro undervalued confession and penance in the Christian life. He once wrote to two Florentine friends, Bartolomeo and Cerrino, that if they wanted to progress in holiness, the first thing they needed was a good confessor from a "proven" religious order.[86] Pietro put good confession ahead of frequent church attendance.

Versions of this message made their way into devotional tracts for the laity, often with odd twists. A set of edifying stories from early-fourteenth-century Italy focuses almost entirely on the power of contrition to forgive horrible sins.[87] No sin is too grave for repentance, especially if the sinner has cultivated a devotion to Christ's mother, Mary. An abbess sinned with the cook and was with child. Envious nuns reported the signs of pregnancy to the bishop. The abbess repented and implored Mary's help. Mary sent an angel to tell the abbess that the Virgin's *figliuolo*, Jesus, had two pieces of good news. First, her sin was forgiven because of her sorrow; second, the incriminating evidence would be invisible to the bishop. When the bishop arrived, he could find no sign of pregnancy. The abbess could not help recounting the vision and its result. The bishop was so impressed that he adopted the abbess's child, who grew up to be the next bishop. The bishop must have procured for the boy a dispensation for his canonical "defect of birth," his illegitimacy. The worst sins, even repeated shamelessly, were no reason to despair. Christ's Passion was so powerful that it canceled any sin so long as the sinner asked forgiveness "willing rightly."[88] "Willing rightly" meant intending to go to confession with contrition in the heart.

CONFESSION OF SINS

One thirteenth-century Italian preacher told the story of a great sinner who went to confession to a holy hermit priest. The man confessed his sins, but the priest could not convince him "to do satisfaction." Finally, the man agreed to bring the priest some water from a nearby fountain. When the man arrived there, he found the well was dry. One single drop came out;

85. Pietro of Monterone, *Vita del beato Pietro Pettinajo*, 9, pp. 85–86: "imperciocchè il Salvatore nostro Cristo cercò dal peccatore solo la contrizione del peccato e vero proposito in futuro di astenersi." For criticism of heavy penances in a confession manual, see Florence, Biblioteca Medicea Laurenziana, MS Aed. 37 (early XIII cent.), fol. 107ᵛ.

86. Pietro of Monterone, *Vita del beato Pietro Pettinajo*, 9, pp. 104–6; Pietro also urged frequent church attendance: ibid., pp. 107–8.

87. Bologna, Biblioteca Universitaria, MS 158 (XIV cent.), fols. 14ʳ–24ʳ; see fol. 20ᵛ for the story of the abbess.

88. To give up on forgiveness was the unforgivable sin. One early-fourteenth-century priest copied at the end of his copy of Berengario Fredelli's *Summa Confessionis* a little treatise on despair: Padua, Biblioteca Antoniana, MS 217, fol. 98ʳ.

this the man brought to the hermit. That was enough, the holy man said. It was as if Jesus shed a single tear for the sinner, for the Lord said: "If anyone drinks from the water I give him, that will be in him a fountain of water welling up to eternal life." The man burst into copious tears and was freed of his sins.[89] When Anthony of Padua preached his last Lenten series in 1231, those confessing were so many that all the friars and priests of Padua were not enough to hear them.[90] When Nicola of Tolentino heard confessions, he never imposed heavy penances; rather, he reassured the sinner that the humiliation of confessing was enough.[91] This was not confession as spiritual direction, catechetical formation, or admission to communion—this use of the sacrament was devotional. It was for the sinner an act of penance and mortification in itself. Francis of Assisi spoke for his age: when he used the words "doing penance," he usually meant "going to confession."[92]

Modern confession conjures up images of a darkened box with an opaque grill, the form instituted by the Council of Trent to prevent scandal by separating the priest from the penitent. The box gave a sense of privacy to the sacrament that it lacked in medieval Italy, when confession took place in more exposed surroundings. One woman came to confess at the friars' church in Milan and found Peter of Verona seated in the nave. She went over, knelt at his feet, and made her confession.[93] Salimbene gave his penitents a bit more privacy by hearing their sins behind the high altar, a common practice.[94] Synods commanded priests to hear a woman's confession out in the open, in a church or public space, unless she was gravely ill. Ecclesiastical legislators were not happy with the dark corners in the church—women's confessions belonged in a well-lighted place.[95] Men's confessions might be heard anywhere. Like the woman who came to Peter of Verona, the pious showed their humility by kneeling to recite their sins. Peter the Chanter's devotional book, in its Italian version, declared kneeling the best expression of repentance. It castigated lazy kneeling practices, too, such as leaning to one side and propping oneself up.[96] But even Armanno Pungilupo, who had a reputation for holiness with his priest, did not always kneel. Sometimes he stood while reciting his sins, but he always confessed with tears and other signs of contrition.[97]

89. Milan, Biblioteca Ambrosiana, ms N 43 Sup., fol. 55ᵛ.

90. See Roberto Rusconi, "I francescani e la confessione nel secolo XIII," *Francescanesimo e vita religiosa dei laici nel '200: Atti dell'VIII Convegno internazionale, Assisi, 16–18 ottobre 1980* (Assisi: Università di Perugia, 1981), 262, commenting on the passage edited in *Vita prima di S. Antonio, o, "Assidua,"* ed. Vergilio Gamboso (Padua: Messaggero, 1981), 13.13, pp. 344–46.

91. *Vita Altera [S. Nicolai Tolentinatis]*, 8, AS 43 (Sept. III), 665.

92. Rusconi, "Francescani e la confessione," 257.

93. *Vita S[ancti] Petri Martyris Ordinis Praedicatorum*, 4.28, p. 702 (text from "Miracula Berenguerii," 1310s).

94. Salimbene, *Cronica* (1250), 582, Baird trans., 405; ibid. (1250), 592–93, trans., 412.

95. Novara Synod II (1298), 1.2.1.3, pp. 180–84; Aquileia Constitutiones (1339), 18, p. 1123; Padua Synod (1339), 9, p. 1136.

96. Peter the Chanter, *De Oratione*, 233–34.

97. "Acta contra Armanum [Punzilupum]," 68, 87–88.

The ritual books of Bishop Ugo of Volterra and the church of Verona, both dating to the mid to late 1100s, give the forms for private confession typical of the early communal period.[98] The penitent knelt, and the priest recited a litany, including prayers for the sinner. The priest also requested prayers from others present, that the sinner make a good confession. In Verona, the priest then asked whether the penitent accepted each article of the Creed. He then interrogated the sinner concerning a list of sins (for each of which there was a specified penance) and about general violations against charity. The Verona rite included whole passages lifted from early medieval penitentials, in particular the "Roman Penitential" sections on homicide.[99] The ceremony ended with the imposition of a fast, or a commutation of that to almsgiving, and then a deprecatory absolution. The rite shows its roots in the ancient penitentials, with their tariffed sins. The confession envisioned is "general": it assumes that the penitent will confess all the sins of his entire life up to the present. As devotional confession proliferated, forms became simpler and more personalized. This is not to say that penitents in the later communal period did not make "general confessions." Don Zambono, arch-priest of Santa Gabiana in Cremona, explained how Armanno Pungilupo, on at least five or six occasions, had confessed all the sins he had committed since his youth.[100]

In contrast, the rites for private confession found in thirteenth-century manuscripts were based on the generic confession of sins made at Prime and Compline in the daily Office. Sinners recited the Confiteor formula, doubt-less to the best of their ability, and then listed their sins.[101] The priest gave absolution and imposed a penance—fasts or repetitions of the Pater and Ave seem the most common.[102] As the old interrogation model disappeared from use, ever greater responsibility fell on penitents to prepare what they intended to say. This could cause anxiety. Saint Anthony of Padua suggested to a nervous penitent that he prepare by compiling a written list of his sins.[103] Giovanni Pilingotto, the "saint from Urbino," kept a list of the sins he committed during the week and brought it with him to use at his regular Friday confession.[104] Pietro Pettinaio of Siena did not use paper and ink for his routine confessions, but when he decided to make a general confession for his entire life, he did.[105] A manuscript of Latin classics from northern Italy

98. *Rituale di Hugo [di Volterra]*, 290–300, and Verona, Biblioteca Capitolare, MS MCIX, fols. 15ʳ–20ᵛ.

99. Verona, Biblioteca Capitolare, MS MCIX, fols. 20ᵛ–23ᵛ. Pont. Rom. (XII), 48.1–2, p. 265 (text = Edmund Martène, *De Antiquis Ecclesiae Ritibus*, 2d ed. [Antwerp, 1736; rpt., Hildesheim: Olms, 1967], 1:818–20, Ordo 17), gives formulas for absolution of private penitents taken from the rites for public penitents on Holy Thursday in Pont. Rom. (XII), 30ᵃ.17–18.

100. "Acta contra Armanum [Punzilupum]," 68.

101. For a thirteenth-century Milanese example, see *Manuale Ambrosianum*, 1:167.

102. *Ordo Officiorum della cattedrale [volterrana]*, 210–13.

103. *Chronica XXIV Generalium Ordinis Fratrum Minorum*, 154.

104. *Vita [Sancti Pilingotti Urbinatis]*, 1.17, p. 148.

105. Pietro of Monterone, *Vita del beato Pietro Pettinajo*, 6, pp. 75–78.

in our period reveals just this kind of conscience keeping. There, on the blank verso of the last folio, the owner has jotted down vices and virtues. After each, he placed stroke marks, counting his temptations and good intentions.[106] Compiling lists of sins was a practice of the nervous and hyperdevout, but all believers were supposed to know how to make a "good confession." Bonvesin de la Riva explained what was expected of the penitent in the discipline of confession.

> Confess your sins often to a priest; condemn yourself, that the judge's anger may cease. Consider what you will say to him when you come with complete and heartfelt contrition. Come, meekly, as an offender, ask God's forgiveness with sorrowful heart. Bow, uncovering your head, but if he so commands, cover it again, lest you lose face. Sit not on a bench if your sins are evident, lest humiliated you find the earth is your grave. When you confess your sins to him, the priest is no man, but God. Speaking in circles as you show your sins besmirches your revelation with another fault. The more horrible the crime, the more need to express it; making it known cures it, hiding it compounds it. The demon harms those who hide things from the priest out of shame. Whenever you feel weighed down by sin, confess right away. A wise man avoids danger carefully, otherwise sudden death awaits. When you have confessed your sins to the priest, fulfill his commands, taking care not to return again to your vomit.[107]

Three aspects of a good confession are paramount in this rhetorical exercise: humility, complete disclosure, and the intention not to sin again. The rhetorician encapsulated nicely the teaching of the preachers and theologians. By the 1300s, the qualities of a good confession had become stereotyped. Many devotional collections from that period contained versions of this verse:

Let confession be simple, humble, pure, faithful, and true,

---

106. Milan, Biblioteca Ambrosiana, MS E 15 Sup., fol. 84ᵛ.

107. Bonvesin de la Riva, *Vita Scholastica*, 68–70: "Sepe sacerdoti proprios fateare reatus, ipsum te damna, iudicis ira cadet. Ad quem cum vadis contritus pectore toto, que dicturus eris, premeditatus eas. Vade, Deum, tamquam timidus, reverenter ad illum, offensor veniam corde dolente petas. Flectaris, dempto capitis velamine, sed si precipiat, retegas, ne paciare caput. Non equidem banco sedeas tua crimina pandens, ast humili pocius sit tibi terra quies. Non homo, sed Deus est hoc casu quisque sacerdos, crimina secure confitearis ei. Ambages linguas, tantum tua crimina pandas, alterius culpe pandere facta nocet. Quo scelus horridius, plus est fateare necesse, visa medens curat, vulnera tecta nocent. Ne sis, quem necuit demon, qui cetera fassus presbytero tacuit turpe rubore scelus. Quam cito peccati sentis gravitate gravari, tucior ut vivas, confitear citus. Est sapientis enim vitare pericula caute, nam multos subita morte perisse patet. Presbyteri post hec confessus perfice iussa, ad vomitum rursus velle redire cave." His recommendations were especially tailored for students: warning against sodomy (ibid., 49–51), prostitutes (48–49), overeating and drinking (50, 52), and bad company (58); but mostly (72–102) he dealt with problems of student life.

Frequent, open, discrete, willing, contrite, whole as due,
Holy, willed with tears, and repeated as per need,
Bold, self-blaming, and prepared to reveal the deed.
What confession ought to be is given in these verses.[108]

Thirteenth-century Italians learned to examine their consciences, not by reviewing the Ten Commandments, but by matching their behavior against the seven capital sins: pride, envy, anger, sloth, avarice, gluttony, and lust.[109] In fact, confessional expositions of the Ten Commandments are quite rare. A handful are in the vernacular. One Bergamascan poet produced a versed expansion of the commandments about 1253.[110] The poet used biblical exempla to elaborate each commandment. Susanna and the elders illustrate false witness, while Cain and Abel serve, not for murder, but for coveting a neighbor's goods.[111] The more common system of the vices was an old one; by the early communal period this was already a model, if not the practical norm. Contemporary theologians normally divided the lay aspects of confession—the priest handled absolution—into three: sorrow for sins, confession of sins, and doing penance for sins.[112] Confessional aids first diagnosed the disposition of the penitent. Such an aid might be by a story showing the proper (and improper) ways to approach the sacrament.[113] Or formulaic prayer might sum up what was needful. A small twelfth-century prayer book in Bologna includes two prayers for making a good confession.[114] The second and longer of these prayers rehearses each of the capital sins in turn, thus helping the penitent who uses it to make a complete confession. Confession was to be complete and candid. Devotional texts addressed this requirement by providing formulaic confessions, sin lists. Some general confession prayers were themselves sin lists, litanies of particular sins rather than expressions of proper dispositions.[115] Occasionally, particular sins might be organized according to the five senses, a practice that came into greater vogue in the late Middle Ages.[116]

An explosion of confessional literature followed the Lateran Council of

108. Milan, Biblioteca Ambrosiana, ms Y 5 Sup., fol. 107ʳ: "Sit simplex, humilis, confexio, pura, fidelis, vera, | frequens, nuda, discreta, libens, verecunda, integra, | sancta, lacrimalis, accellerata, | fortis, accusans, et sit parere parata. | Qualis debeat esse confessio in hiis versibus notatur."

109. On this practice, see Roberto Rusconi, "Ordinate Confiteri: La confessione dei peccati nelle 'Summae de Casibus,'" *L'aveu: Antiquité et Moyen Âge* (Rome: EFR, 1986), 297–313.

110. "Il decàlogo," *Poesie lombarde del secolo XIII*, ed. Bernardino Biondelli (Milan: Bernardoni, 1856), 195–210.

111. Ibid., 209.

112. E.g., the Franciscan Jean of La Rochelle, *Summa de Vitiis et Virtutibus*, Florence, Biblioteca Medicea Laurenziana, ms Conv. Soppr. 145 (XIV cent.), fol. 146ᵛ.

113. Milan, Biblioteca Ambrosiana, ms N 43 Sup., fol. 55ᵛ.

114. Bologna, Biblioteca Universitaria, ms 2858, fols. 8ᵛ–10ʳ, and 14ᵛ–18ʳ.

115. As in Cesena, Biblioteca Comunale Malatestiana, ms D.XVI.3 (early XIV cent.), fol. 342ᵛ.

116. For a vernacular example, see Bologna, Biblioteca Universitaria, ms 2530 (1308), fols. 31ʳ–32ʳ.

1215.[117] Casuistic theory predates our period, but council decrees encouraged its pastoral application.[118] This was to be a moral theology for practical use. Most early manuals combined schemes for analyzing sin, commonly the Ten Commandments, the stages of willing and acting, the five senses, the seven virtues, the fourteen works of mercy, the seven sacraments, and the twelve articles of the Creed. The most widely diffused of these manuals was that of Guillaume Perault (Peraldus), although that of Jean Rigaud was also important as the first attempt to produce a manual for lay use.[119] Among the mendicants, the *Summa* of the Dominican Raymond of Penyafort prevailed. These moral summae were massive, scholastic, and ultimately impractical. The elaboration of sin lists, intended to give a structure to all the phenomena a confessor might encounter, ended up being overly baroque.[120] Within a few decades of Lateran Council IV, shorter practical treatises would supplement, if not replace, the manuals.[121] Perhaps because they seemed all-encompassing, the seven capital sins became the formula of choice in these shorter works.[122] Oddly for modern Christian mentality, the Ten Commandments did not become popular for the examination of conscience until the late Middle Ages.[123]

Originally, authors paralleled the seven sins with the seven virtues, but later short forms for confession omitted the virtues.[124] As in Perault's manual, the seven sins became an outline for the faults thought typical of laypeople. Gluttony, for example, included not only rich banquets but love of overly

117. On these manuals, see Carla Casagrande, "La moltiplicazione dei peccati: I cataloghi dei peccati nella letteratura pastorale dei secc. XIII–XV," *La peste nera: Dati di una realtà ed elementi di una interpretazione: Atti del XXX Convegno storico internazionale dell'Accademia tudertina* (Spoleto: Centro Italiano di Studi sul Basso Medioevo, 1994), 253–84; for an introduction to confessional summae, see Leonard E. Boyle, "Summae Confessorum," *Les genres littéraires dans les sources théologique et philosophique médiévale* (Louvain: Institut d'Études Médiévales, 1982).

118. Ovidio Capitani, "Verso un diritto del quotidiano," *Dalla penitenza all'ascolto delle confessioni,* 22–24. For examples, see Florence, Biblioteca Nazionale Centrale, MS Magl. XXXV. 224 (Latin, early 1300s = Francesco of Perugia, *Tractatus de Septem Vitiis Capitalibus et Decem Preceptis*); Bologna, Biblioteca Universitaria, MS 1563, fols. 37r–44r (vernacular, XIV cent.); Milan, Biblioteca Ambrosiana, MS Trotti 541 (XIV cent.), fols. 135v–141v (vernacular, 1316). A search of Morton W. Bloomfield et al., *Incipits of Works on the Virtues and Vices* (Cambridge: Medieval Academy of America, 1979), would reveal others.

119. Guillaume Perault, *Summa de Virtutibus et Vitiis* (Venice: Paganinis, 1497), is the only printed version. Jean Rigaud is unpublished, but A. Teertaert, "La 'Formula Confessionis' du Frère Mineur Jean Rigaud (+1323)," *Miscellanea Historica in Honore Alberti de Meyer* (Louvain: Bibliothèque de l'Université, 1944), 2:662, outlines its contents; on it, see also Rusconi, "Francescani e la confessione," 299.

120. Casagrande, "Moltiplicazione," 281, seconding a remark by Pierre Michaud-Quantin, *Sommes de casuistique et manuels de confession au Moyen Âge (XII–XVI siècles)* (Louvain: Nauwelaerts, 1962), 87–88.

121. On this transition, see Muzzarelli, *Penitenze,* 63–64.

122. On the seven sins, see Morton W. Bloomfield, *The Seven Deadly Sins: An Introduction to the History of a Religious Concept, with Special Reference to Medieval English Literature* (East Lansing: Michigan State College Press, 1952); Casagrande, "Moltiplicazione," 271; Sigfried Wenzel, "The Seven Deadly Sins: Some Problems of Research," *Speculum* 43 (1968): 1–22, esp. 13–14; and Little, "Pride Goes Before Avarice."

123. See John Bossy, *Christianity in the West, 1400–1700* (Oxford: Oxford University Press, 1985), 42–46; and on the shift from the seven vices to the Ten Commandments, see Carla Casagrande and Silvana Vecchio, *La classificazione dei peccati tra settenario dei vizi e decalogo: Teologia e pastorale (sec. XIII–XV),* Documenti e studi sulla tradizione filosofica medievale (forthcoming).

124. Bloomfield, *Seven Deadly Sins,* 93.

refined food; envy included political sins, like plotting and flattery.[125] The
system of the seven sins meant that the sinners could not confess merely by
listing infractions of a set of rules like the Decalogue. Penitents had to identify
their sins and fit them into the structure of vices.[126] One anonymous Italian
layman, who seemingly had served in positions of major responsibility for at
least one northern commune,[127] struggled to use this method for a written
confession, probably just after 1327.[128] The purpose was almost certainly for
public penance. This was a general confession; that is, it covered the man's
entire life. The document is in a fine, clear professional hand, with red initial
letters, on good-quality parchment. This penitent (doubtless with assistance
from his priest) made his work easier by using the very popular "formula
for confession" devised by the canonist Johannes Teutonicus.[129] Johannes's
formula listed various infractions under each vice, giving concrete reality to
the abstract capital sins. Before preparing his text, this penitent listed the
qualities of a good confession. Addressed to a priest, it was to be simple,
humble, voluntary, pure and faithful, true, regular, shamefaced, complete,
secret, tearful, self-accusatory, and fully prepared.[130] As he prepared his confession, this man copied, adapted, or omitted from his model to fit his particular needs. In the process, the abstract Latin formulas became actual
personal sins in the Italian vernacular.

The man's sins of gluttony (gula) may serve as an example.[131] First, he
admitted that he took too much delight in food and drink, just as his formula
suggested. He did not try to decide whether he would have been willing to
break divine law to satisfy his hunger, thus committing mortal sin, or
whether he would have avoided breaking the law, and thus have sinned only
venially. He jumped over the seven grades of gluttony (borrowed by Johannes from Pope Gregory the Great) and focused on the most concrete sections
of the formula. Johannes listed actual sins, giving concrete specifics for each.
The man's responses track the formula. Yes, he stayed too long at table. Yes,

125. Casagrande, "Moltiplicazione," 265–66.
126. Very occasionally, however, owners of devotional books did supplement the vices system with
other schemata for organizing their sins. For an example, a user of Bologna, Biblioteca Universitaria, MS
2530, added a list of sins through the five senses to those of the vices, on fols. 31ʳ–32ʳ, and a user of
Bologna, Biblioteca Universitaria, MS 158, wrote the Ten Commandments on fol. 56ᵛ, after the vices, but
his control of the commandments seems vague. He got the first four right, but the rest are somewhat
original: "Ama il prossimo come te stesso. Non togliere laltrui. La donna altrui non disiderare. Non fare
usura. Non rendere falsa testimonanza. Non fare homicidio."
127. Most likely this man was one of the "podestrie," the podestates terrae, who governed outlying districts
for the communes; see Bologna Stat. II, 2.5, 1:54–56; 2.6, 1:56–67.
128. Bologna, Biblioteca Universitaria, MS 158, fols. 54ᵛ–56ᵛ. This document is found with lists of
virtues and elements of a good confession on fols. 52ʳ–54ᵛ. The text is in an Italian typical of Emilia or
the Veneto and datable paleographically to the early 1300s. Frati's cataloguing of the codex omits it:
Lodovico Frati and Albano Sorbelli, Indice dei codici italiani conservati nella R. Biblioteca Universitaria di Bologna,
Inventari dei manoscritti delle biblioteche d'Italia (Forlì: Bordandini; Florence: Olschki, 1909), 15:155–57.
129. Iohannes Teutonicus's Confessionale has never been edited. In the following, I have consulted the
version in Mantua, Biblioteca Comunale Centrale Teresiana, MS 399 (XV cent.), fols. 2ʳ–17ᵛ.
130. Bologna, Biblioteca Universitaria, MS 158, fol. 53ʳ.
131. Ibid., fol. 56ᵛ; cf. Mantua, Biblioteca Comunale Centrale Teresiana, MS 399, fols. 15ʳ⁻ᵛ.

he ate more than he had need for and so overburdened his stomach. Yes, he drank too much.[132] Since the formula had no other place to put them, the man also listed other sins he had committed with his mouth: vulgar language and gossip.[133] He then returned to Johannes and wrote down that he had violated church fasts—this does not seem to have been a major fault, since he merely stated the sin generally, not using the formula's list of fasts and the ways of breaking them. Finally, he confessed his general failure in his own words: "I am a pig, filling my mouth with every good thing *nimis lauta.*"[134] Probably because he or his priest could not translate the Latin phrase, which means "excessively lavish," the man left it in the original Latin. And so the penitent went on for the other six capital sins. He repeated some of his actual sins several times. He excessively enjoyed holding public office. Thus he committed the sins of pride (he liked people to admire him), avarice (he liked the money involved), and sloth (officers had servants to wait on them). So many sins; so many possibilities.

What this man did in preparation for public penance other penitents did for private confessions. In the early 1300s, the owner of a codex of Saint Augustine's *On the Truth of the Catholic Faith,* perhaps a Bolognese Augustinian, wrote out his confession on the back flyleaf. From its generality and scope, it seems to be a general confession, preceded and followed by elaborate Confiteor sections. Perhaps it was a penitential exercise rather than notes for an actual confession. Like the previous official, this man used conventional formularies and adapted the sections pertinent to him. The result is a litany of generic sins, mostly involving failures in chastity. The result was so vague that the draft might have helped the penitent organize his sins, but a conscientious confessor would have wanted details on the exact nature of the sins listed, in particular those of usury and theft.[135] The penitential self-discipline of examination of conscience, and the need to prepare for confession, suggested this kind of written exercise to the pious laity, especially with the increased literacy of the late communal period. One fourteenth-century nun wrote out her confession in a book of prayers and devotions.[136] Like the government official, the sister used a formula, but this one was already in vernacular. She adapted—omitting the many sins inapplicable to a nun—as she went. She included sins of the five senses and the violations of her monas-

---

132. "Descintomi a tavla per mangiare asai. . . . Abbo mangiato più che non è stato bizogno, stomacho n'era gravato a ritenello. . . . Item, bevuto espesse volte intanto che fummi m'anno facto male, e la lingua ingrossare, e dormire."

133. "In immunditia, scurilità, favellare, troppo usatomi."

134. "Son porcino empiere la bocha d'ogni cosa nimis lauta."

135. Josephus Maria Mucciolus, *Catalogus Codicum Manuscriptorum Malatestinae Caesenatis Bibliothecae Fratrum Minorum Conventualium* (Cesena: Blasinus, 1780–84), 1:66, has (inaccurately) edited this text, which is found in Cesena, Biblioteca Comunale Malatestiana, ms D.xvi.3 (early xiv cent.), fol. 342ᵛ.

136. Florence, Biblioteca Riccardiana, ms 1422 (late xiv cent.), fols. 143ᵛ–144ᵛ, contains the confession. The truncated confessional formula found in the more or less contemporary Florence, Biblioteca Riccardiana, ms 1316, fols. 22ʳ–24ᵛ, seems to represent her model, or one very close to it.

tic rule, such as willfulness against her abbess. Even without "worldly" sins to confess, her list grew to be long and searching. One can see why Giovanni Pilingotto and others decided to write down what they intended to say.

Confession was a penance in itself—especially if the priest did not pose questions and the penitents had to discover their sins for themselves. Jesus once appeared to Margherita of Cortona and told her to correct a priest who was either too unlettered or too shy or too lazy to quiz his penitents on their sins. Had he done so, he would have saved them considerable anxiety and labor. The good confessor gave his penitents some help and treated them in a gentle way.[137] Confessional manuals produced in the 1200s drove this point home. Johannes de Deo, in his *Summa,* reminded confessors that their first task was to comfort their penitents. They should listen to them, not argue with them about sins. And, of course, the confessor should not accept gifts from them.[138] A short anonymous treatise, which perhaps belonged to an Augustinian friar, told the confessor how to treat his penitents:

> Now something should be said about how the confessor should treat the one confessing. First, it is necessary that the confessor show a mild face to an honest sinner coming to confession and exhort him to confess all his sins honestly and completely, using perhaps words something like this: I myself am a sinner who could have done anything you have done, had God not helped me. I am ready to offer advice, sympathy, mercy, and prayers for you. I will impose a merciful penance because that pleases God, who is the Father of mercy.[139]

This friar's codex, like many ad hoc compilations to aid confessors, included a wide range of catechetical tools.[140] The good confessor was to detect and give penance for sins, but also help aid the spiritual formation of his penitents. Compilers adapted outlines of vices and commandments so that they became directly applicable to ordinary people's daily lives. One anonymous early-thirteenth-century cleric composed a little treatise on how to question sinners. It had a remarkable immediacy and specificity. He questioned peni-

137. Giunta Bevegnati, *Legenda . . . Margaritae de Cortona,* 8.16, pp. 362–63.

138. Florence, Biblioteca Nazionale Centrale, MS Magl. XXXIII. 13, fols. 18ᵛ–22ʳ. The owner of this codex had another penitential manual, Johannes Cappellanus's *Tractatus de Penitentia* (on fols. 35ʳ–143ᵛ), bound with it.

139. Milan, Biblioteca Ambrosiana, MS Q 38 Sup. (late XIII cent.?), fol. 70ᵛ: "Quomodo autem confessor se debet habere confessor erga confitentem sic nunc dicendum est. Debet ut puro confessor peccatori ad confessionem venienti primo faciem benignam ostendere et exortari ut confiteatur pure et integre et omnia peccata sua dicat, addens si videatur expediens: Ego ipse peccator sum, qui forsan fecissem que tu fecisti nisi me Deus invisset, et ideo paratus sum tibi consulere, compatri, et misereri, et orare per te. Et penitentiam misericorditer imponam, quia ita placet Deo, qui est Pater misericordiarum." The full treatise is on fols. 70ʳ–75ᵛ.

140. See Milan, Biblioteca Ambrosiana, MS Q 38 Sup.: on the cardinal virtues, fols. 52ʳ–53ᵛ; the gifts of the Holy Spirit, fols. 61ᵛ–62ᵛ; the laws of the Church, fols. 62ᵛ–66ʳ; the articles of the creed and the seven virtues, fols. 66ʳ–67ʳ; and the seven sacraments, fols. 67ʳ–70ʳ.

tents on the use of magic and usury, on visiting prostitutes, and on leading the innocent into sin by corrupting stepdaughters. This author then focused on gluttony and drunkenness, in particular the vices associated with the latter, such as listening to jongleurs and gossips. The last section of his treatise is a list of the typical sins of various professions. That inventory would later be perfected by the great canonist Hostiensis.[141]

CONFESSION AND LAY PIETY

Understanding the place of confession in lay piety entails, first, discovering how the laity made use of it. Illuminations in manuscripts of the section *De Penitentia* of Gratian's *Decretum* are suggestive. The earliest manuscripts never illustrate confession with images of a penitent whispering in the priest's ear or of the priest imparting absolution. No, the universal image is that of a priest scourging the penitent with a rod (see, e.g., fig. 35). Only in the late communal period do images of confessional self-accusation, like the penitent reciting sins, and ecclesiastical authority, like the act of absolution, appear.[142] The ethos of the earlier image makes confession principally an act of penance, a way of humbling the self before God and accepting the consequent mortification.[143] When Ranieri Fasani of Perugia, the founder of the flagellant movement, gave himself the discipline privately, he invariably linked it to making confession.[144] Flagellant confraternity statutes link the discipline to confession.[145] The statutes of the lay penitents, likewise, list confession among penances, along with fasting, almsgiving, and prayers.[146] When Alberto the priest gave his deposition about the ascetic practices of Armanno Pungilupo, he mentioned his frequent confessions, not his apparently annual Communion.[147] Even heretics paid homage to the discipline of confession. Ugonetto Gobaudi went to a Waldensian preacher, Martino Pastre, for confession. The "good man" not only heard his confession but assigned Ugonetto a forty-day fast on bread and water and recitations of the Pater Noster. Giovanni di Martino got a similar penance from the Waldensian preacher Francesco Marengo. He was to perform it every Friday from the feast of Saint Michael to Christmas.[148] Waldensian heretics distinguished themselves

---

141. Florence, Biblioteca Medicea Laurenziana, MS Aed. 37 (XIII cent.), fols. 107ʳ–109ᵛ.

142. On this suggestive change, see Roberto Rusconi, "Immagine della confessione sacramentale (secoli XII–XVI)," *Dalla penitenza all'ascolto delle confessioni*, 272–74, commenting on the images in Anthony Melnikas, *The Corpus of the Miniatures in the Manuscripts of "Decretum Gratiani"* (Rome: Studia Gratiani, 1975), 3:1069–84.

143. A point made by De Sandre Gasparini, "Laici devoti," 226.

144. See E. Ardu, "Frater Raynerius Faxanus de Perusia," *Il movimento dei disciplinati nel settimo centenario dal suo inizio (Perugia, 1260)*, ed. Lodovico Scaramucci (Perugia: Deputazione di Storia Patria per l'Umbria, 1965), 95, and, on this text, De Sandre Gasparini, "Laici devoti," 226.

145. So De Sandre Gasparini, "Laici devoti," 228, commenting on Meersseman, *Ordo* 1:482 (chap. 14).

146. On confession in confraternity statutes, see De Sandre Gasparini, "Laici devoti," 212–14.

147. "Acta contra Armanum [Punzilupum]," 87.

148. Alberto of Castellario, "Inquisicio" (126), p. 216; (175), p. 232; (102), p. 204.

from Catholics by the rigor of the penances they imposed in confession. Only a Cathar dualist despised confession and penance.

Statutes of lay confraternities invariably required far more confessions than canon law required. As the thirteenth century progressed, the number of confessions prescribed by confraternity statutes increased from two or three a year to monthly or even twice monthly.[149] The Bologna flagellant statutes of 1298 expected, at a minimum, monthly confession, but still required only the three traditional Communions a year—on Christmas, Easter, and Pentecost.[150] This combination of monthly confession with triannual Communion became the norm by the 1290s.[151] Was the clerical influence of the mendicants pushing more frequent confession?[152] I think not. Independent lay penitents, especially those outside the tutelage of the orders, show some of the highest rates of confession. Giovanni Buono confessed to his parish priest "daily, once, twice, or several times, as often as his conscience bit him."[153] Lucchese of Pogibonsi confessed twice a week, shedding copious tears as he pondered Christ's death on the cross.[154] It was Umiltà of Faenza who grilled a woman about a sin she had omitted from her general confession, not the priest who heard it.[155] After her death, Saint Benvenuta Bojani appeared to a sinner in a dream and reminded him to go to confession.[156] Verdiana of Florence confessed at minimum once a week. She also desired to receive Communion "often," but never without confession.[157] This reminds us of a peculiarity of lay status: the laity needed a confessor's permission to go to Communion; they could confess their sins as often as they liked. To the pious laity, confession was not merely a penitential act; it was the one moment when an ordinary person could hope to get spiritual advice or direction—and demands for such guidance increased as the communal period wore on.[158] The medieval Italian clergy, like their modern descendants, found confessional practices like those of Giovanni Buono a nuisance. By the fourteenth century, the confessor making light of a devout penitent's desire for confession had become a literary topos.[159] The story goes that a peasant went to church one day for confession. He found the parish priest working

---

149. De Sandre Gasparini, "Laici devoti," 235–38.

150. See the statutes edited by De Sandre Gasparini, *Statuti*, 3–7, 10–59; see also her remarks, ibid., 234–35.

151. See, e.g., "Chapitre de Pénitents" (Umbria, 1290), 3, Meersseman, *Dossier*, 177; "Statuti della Confraternita dei Servi di Dio e della S. Madre del Duomo" (Statuti D, 1298), 5, De Sandre Gasparini, *Statuti*, 12.

152. As suggested by De Sandre Gasparini, "Laici devoti," 240 n. 84.

153. *Processus . . . B. Joannis Boni*, 3.9.240^bis, p. 832: "confitebatur in die, semel, vel bis, vel pluries, secundum quod conscientia sua remordebat eum."

154. *Vita Sancti Lucensis Confessoris*, 454.

155. Biagio of Faenza, *Vita [S. Humilitatis Abbatissae]*, 3.27, p. 213.

156. Corrado of Cividale, *Vita Devotissimae Benevenutae*, 14.105, p. 178.

157. *Vita Sancte Viridiane*, 9.

158. As Muzzarelli, *Penitenze*, 34, notes.

159. E.g., the priest in *Novellino*, 87, pp. 872–73.

in the garden. "Sir," said the peasant, "I want to go to confession." "When did you last go," asked the priest. "At Easter," came the reply. "Well then," said the priest, "put something in the alms box and do the same penance this year."[160]

The pious laity probably drifted toward the mendicants in the late thirteenth century in part because confessors were more available and cooperative at Dominican and Franciscan monasteries. Margherita of Città di Castello went to services daily at the Dominican church, where she could find a priest to hear her daily confession.[161] Did these clerics favor frequent devotional confession? The master of the Dominican order Humbert of Romans spoke for them when he directed that a confessor should "dissuade those who want to confess frequently from such excessive and nearly worthless repetition; let him assign them a time to confess and refuse to hear them otherwise. Nor should he make himself available to them for other conversation, and let him always use hard and strict words with them rather than mild ones."[162] Humbert's words resonated with parish priests facing the growing lay demand for devotional confessions. The secular clergy were probably happy to see such people go to the mendicants, unless there was a risk of losing donations.[163]

The devout who might confess often, even weekly, were certainly a minority among the Catholics of the Italian cities. More commonly, confession was the first step to reception of sacramental Communion. This was, no doubt, the role it played in most people's piety. Confession was obligatory before every sacramental Communion.[164] Even the clergy, many of whom celebrated Mass daily, were expected to confess all "major" sins before doing so.[165] This rule applied to bishops, too, as the preacher Bartolomeo of Branganze reminded his hearers.[166] When Vito of Cortona remarked of Umiliana dei Cerchi that she only went to Communion after confessing her sins, he was reporting nothing extraordinary. It was the regularity of her Communions that was remarkable.[167] Miracles could make observance of the rule possible. Imiglia di fu Benencasa of Monte Molino could not go to Commu-

---

160. Ibid., 93, p. 875: "Qui conta d'uno villano che s'andò a confessare. Uno villano se andò a un giorno a confessare. E pigliò de l'acqua benedetta, e vide il prete che lavorava nel colto. Chiamollo, e disse:—Sere, io mi vorrei confessare.—Rispouse il prete:—Confessastiti tu anno?—E que' rispuose:—Sì.—Or metti un danaio nel colombaio, e a quella medesima ragione ti fo uguanno, ch'anno."

161. *Legenda B. Margaritae de Castello*, 21, p. 125.

162. Humbert of Romans, *De Officiis Ordinis*, ed. J. Berthier, Opera de Vita Regulari (Rome: Befani, 1889), 46, 2:368: "frequenter volunt confiteri, temperet ab huiusmodi nimia et quasi inutili frequentatione, et certum tempus eis assignet ad confitendum, extra quod ipsas non audiat, nec in aliis collocutionibus frequentibus se eis exponat umquam, et semper potius duris et rigidis verbis utatur ad eas quam mollis." On Humbert's confessional theory, see ibid., pp. 479–81, 360–69, and Rusconi, "Francescani e la confessione," 294.

163. Milan Council (1287), 25–26, p. 880.

164. Rusconi, "Francescani e la confessione," 254.

165. Novara Synod I (1210), 29.

166. Bartolomeo of Vicenza, *Sermones de Beata Virgine (1266)*, Sermo 21.2, p. 134.

167. Vito of Cortona, *Vita [B. Humilianae]*, 1.5, p. 387.

nion, because an illness had rendered her mute and unable to confess. Saint Filippo Benizzi answered her prayers and cured her. She went to confession.[168] So, around 1200, the "practicing" Catholic went to confession about three times a year, once for each of the general Communions of the three great feasts. The pious might go to confession much more regularly, even when only communicating three times. Preparation for a worthy Communion required much more than confession and so was always rarer than confession.[169]

The obligation of confession before all Communions and the prevalence of devotional confession without intention to communicate help explain the significance of the decree *Utriusque Sexus* promulgated by Innocent III at the Lateran Council of 1215. This decree introduced only two new obligations: first, that the confession for Easter Communion be to one's parish priest, and second, that failure to confess at that time brought automatic excommunication.[170] This excommunication did not bar one from Communion— failure to confess already did that—it prevented the delinquent from receiving the other ministries of the Church, such as the blessing of marriage or a proper funeral. The enactment did not mean that the old rule of three annual Communions fell by the wayside. Italian synods, like Innocent III himself, assumed that the old three-Communions-a-year rule remained in force and was still the common practice, even if the overall number of Communions declined.[171] Besides the juridical penalty for not confessing, Italian synodal legislation on *Utriusque Sexus* focused mostly on how to observe (or escape) the requirement that this annual confession be to "one's own priest."[172] Mendicants were not so happy with the rule. Saint Bonaventure, in his commentary on the Lombard, did try to explain the logic of the restriction, but Fra Salimbene quoted the rule only to attack it: Franciscans were better trained theologically, so people should be allowed to use them as

168. *Processus Miraculorum B. Philippi [Benitii]*, 1.33, fol. 53ʳ.

169. As noted by De Sandre Gasparini, "Laici devoti," 227.

170. See text in Heinrich Denzinger and Adolfus Schönmetzer, eds., *Enchiridion Symbolorum, Definitionum, et Declarationum*, 36th ed. (Barcelona; Herder, 1976), 264, no. 812. The rule applied to those over fourteen years: see Lucca Synod (1308), 57, p. 189, and Trexler, *Public Life*, 175 n. 86. Pierre-Marie Gy, "Le précepte de la confession annuelle e la nécessité de la confession," *Revue des sciences philosophiques et théologiques* 63 (1979): 532–38, correctly explains the juridical effects of the decree, often badly misunderstood.

171. So Michele Maccarrone, "'Cura animarum' e 'parochialis sacerdos' nelle costituzioni del IV Concilio Lateranense (1215): Applicazioni in Italia nel sec. XIII," *Pievi e parrocchie*, ed. Erba et al., 1:164; see also Innocent III's letter of 4 January 1216, edited in *Acta Innocentii Papae III*, ed. Theodosius Haluscynskyi (Rome: Vatican, 1944), 459. Miri Rubin, *Corpus Christi: The Eucharist in Late Medieval Culture* (Cambridge: Cambridge University Press, 1991), 70, also notes the persistence of the three-Communions rule. Cf., however, Pierre-Marie Gy, "Le précepte de la confession annuelle (Latran IV, c. 21) et la détection des hérétiques: S. Bonaventure et S. Thomas contre S. Raymond de Peñafort," *Revue des sciences philosophique et théologiques*, 58 (1974): 445.

172. E.g., Lucca Synod (1300), 57, p. 233; Lucca Synod (1308), 57, p. 189; Ravenna Council (1311), 15, pp. 457–58; Padua Synod (1339), 15, p. 1138. On the dissemination of the decree, see Maccarrone, "Cura animarum," 81–195.

confessors for Easter.[173] The Dominicans, however, warned their preachers not to circumvent the law.[174] Even after Pope Martin IV liberalized the rule by allowing people to make their annual confession to mendicants, the Dominicans hesitated to put this privilege to use.[175]

The Lateran decree certainly affected the parish clergy. For the first time, in many cases, priests became spiritual physicians for all their parishioners, even if this happened only once a year.[176] This new task partly explains the multiplication of confessional manuals during the mid-1200s. Confession became the task of every priest holding a pastoral cure, and not all were ready for it.[177] The experience of the English Franciscan Hymo of Haversham in the mid-1220s shows what this new rule meant for the laity. Hymo was present at a parish church in Canterbury during Lent, and his lay companion, Fra Benevent, preached on the "Easter Duty." The people were so convicted that they lined up to go to confession. It took three days to hear them all.[178] For the laity, the novelty brought by *Utriusque Sexus* was not obligatory confession; it was waiting in line to do so. It turned the more or less private event of confessing before Communion to any priest one liked into an annual public ritual of confession to the pastor.[179] One stood waiting, with others of the same parish, while each parishioner went up to the seated priest, knelt, confessed, received penance, and departed. Nor could the parishioners fail to notice the others in line, as they fidgeted, chatted, and generally made noise. But this long, drawn-out process, standing in line for confession, could never match other rituals as a mark of parish belonging.[180] Catholic Italians had always been able to see who absented themselves from Mass, rogation processions, and the great feasts.[181]

173. Bonaventure, *Commentaria in Quatuor Libros Sententiarum Magistri Petri Lombardi*, 4.17 and 4.21, *Opera Omnia* (Quaracchi: Collegium S. Bonaventurae, 1882–1902), vol. 4; and, on this, see Salimbene, *Cronica* (1250), 591–94, Baird trans., 410–11.

174. *ACGOP* (1282), 218.

175. See Rusconi, "Franciscani e la confessione," 283–84, on Martin IV's decree *Ad Fructus Uberes* (13 December 1281), and the Dominican hesitation in *ACGOP*, 218.

176. See Maccarrone, "Cura animarum," 161–62, citing Anthony of Padua, *Sermones Dominicales et Festivi*, ed. Beniamino Costa et al. (Padua: Messaggero, 1979), 1:304, 2:587–88, for examples of this new view of the parish clergy.

177. So in the 1300s the incompetent parish-priest confessor became the butt of jokes: *Novellino*, 91, p. 874. But confession did not become a major comic theme until later: see Emilio Pasquini, "Confessione e penitenza nella novellistica tardo-medievale (secoli XIII–XV): Fra Stilizzazione e parodia," *Dalla penitenza all'ascolto delle confessioni*, 179.

178. Thomas of Eccleston, *Tractatus de Adventu Fratrum Minorum in Anglia*, ed. A. G. Little (Manchester: Manchester University Press, 1951), 6, p. 28; see, on this passage, Rusconi, "Franciscani e la confessione," 260.

179. I dare to make this suggestion, even if De Sandre Gasparini, "Laici devoti," 211, correctly notes: "È assai difficile valutare il modo con cui i fedeli recepirono il sacramento della confessione."

180. As noted by Zelina Zafarana, "Cura pastorale, predicazione, aspetti devozionali nella parrocchia del basso Medioevo," *Pievi e parrocchie*, ed. Erba et al., 1:523.

181. My treatment of confession in the preceding section might shed a different light on the famous exchange between Thomas Tentler and Leonard Boyle over the "social-control" function of confession, which is conveniently reprinted in *The Pursuit of Holiness in Late Medieval and Renaissance Religion*, ed. Charles Trinkaus and Heiko A. Oberman (Leiden: Brill, 1974), 103–37.

THE CITY DOES PENANCE

So Lenten confession took its modest place in the annual round of corporate piety that united the Christian community. I say modest because Lent was above all the time to reconcile those alienated from city and Church, that is, those guilty of public crimes or laboring under excommunication. In Italy public penance and the solemn rites for reconciling penitents did not disappear in the early Middle Ages.[182] A mid-thirteenth-century Florentine priests' manual explains the difference between private and solemn public penance: "Penance is either solemn, public, or private. Solemn penance begins on Ash Wednesday when the penitents are expelled in ashes and sackcloth; it is also called public because it is done publicly. Public penance that is not solemn, such as a pilgrimage, is imposed before the church without the aforesaid solemnity. Private penance is done individually, at home or before a priest."[183] Public or solemn penance required the presence of the bishop and could only be undertaken once. The author of this manual especially noted, in addition to the usual crimes, that sins impeding marriage required public penance: incest, abduction, spousal homicide, murder of blood relatives. Public penance was never imposed for secret sins.

A communal Italian could be excommunicated deliberately by a judicial sentence (ferenda sententia) or automatically by statutory penalty (lata sententia).[184] Once excommunicated, at least for more serious offenses, the delinquent had to receive penance from the bishop, do that penance, and secure formal permission, in order to be readmitted to communion. Some excommunications were of a special sort. After the institution of papal inquisitions during the 1230s, bishops no longer handled those excommunicated for heresy.[185] The inquisitors, usually Franciscan or Dominican friars, imposed pen-

182. Public penance persisted into the 1200s in northern France as well: see Mary C. Mansfield, *The Humiliation of Sinners: Public Penance in Thirteenth-Century France* (Ithaca: Cornell University Press, 1994), which confirmed the suspicions of Cyrille Vogel, "Les rites de la pénitence publique au xe et xie siècles," *Mélanges offerts à René Crozet à l'occasionne de son soixante-dixième anniversaire*, ed. Pierre Gallais and Yves-Jean Riou (Poitiers: Société d'Études Médiévales, 1966), 1:137–44.

183. Florence, Biblioteca Medicea Laurenziana, MS Aed. 37, fol. 108^r: "Penitentia alia sollempnis alia publica alia privata. Sollempnis est que fit in capite ieiunii quando cum sollempnitate in cinere et cilitio eiciuntur, publica dicitur etiam quia fit publice. Publica non sollempnis est que fit in fatie ecclesia sine predicta sollempnitate, ut peregrinatio. Privata que fit singulariter in domo vel coram sacerdote." See also, on public penance, Florence, Biblioteca Medicea Laurenziana, MS Aed. 214 (ca. 1200), fol. 51^r.

184. For an example of a judicial excommunication, see Matteo Griffoni (1255), 13; for the list of statutory excommunications, see Innocent IV, *Apparatus super Libros Decretalium*, X 5.39.1, v. *Super eo* (Lyons: Moylin, 1525); Hostiensis (Enrico di Susa), *Summa Aurea* (Venice: Sessa, 1570), 5.59.3, col. 1880–84. On these texts, see Elisabeth Vodola, *Excommunication in the Middle Ages* (Berkeley and Los Angeles: University of California Press, 1986), 34 n. 27. Bishops could add other statutory excommunications subject to *Liber Sextus*, 5.11.5 (available, e.g., in vol. 2 of *Corpus Iuris Canonici*, 2d ed., ed. E. Friedberg [Leipzig: Tauchnitz, 1881]); for an example, see Lucca Synod (1308), 32, p. 182.

185. Parish priests, however, were expected to report suspected heretics among their people. For the procedures for doing so at Bologna, see Bologna, Biblioteca Universitaria, MS 1515 (XIV cent.): Documenta Officialium Ss. Inquisitionis (XIV Cent): fols. 18^{r-v}, ed. Lorenzo Paolini, *Il De Officio Inquisitonis: La procedura inquisitoriale a Bologna e a Ferrara nel trecento* (Bologna: Editrice Universitaria Bologna, 1976). *Utriusque Sexus* was *not* a heresy-detection device: Gy, "Précepte de la confession annuelle (Latran IV, c. 21)," 444–50, esp. 444–45, and Vodola, *Excommunication*, 32–33.

ances on these delinquents. These ranged from private fasts to wearing crosses, to fines, and ultimately to "relaxation to the secular arm"— execution by the communal government. Not all excommunications required public ceremonies. For those sins not reserved to the bishop, the confessor priest might absolve the penitent privately. And the bishop himself could decide to handle a matter in private. But an ordinary excommunication could be compounded if the delinquent remained contumacious for over a year. After that, other penalties, including civil disabilities, might be imposed.[186] Excommunications that demanded public punishment and reconciliation involved crimes that disturbed public order or decency and those that brought *infamia* (loss of legal rights)—in short, crimes against the community. Such sinners could only be reconciled and readmitted to Communion by a public absolution.[187]

Secular and ecclesiastical legislation from communal Italy reveals the crimes that brought public excommunication. One common way to become a public sinner was by open adultery. As early as 1210, the diocese of Novara excommunicated such sinners if they did not reform after an admonition.[188] Other churches enacted similar statutes, especially if the adulterers were thought to have used sorcery to achieve their aims.[189] But sorcery itself was a civil, not ecclesiastical, crime, punishable sometimes by death.[190] One might be excommunicated for perjury or other sinful oaths—such as those used to organize a cabal to rig the election of a parish priest.[191] In the later Middle Ages, the most common reason for excommunication was debt.[192] That excommunication was routine and administrative, not public or solemn. Crimes did not usually result in public discipline if they did not directly threaten the religious order. For example, merely defaulting on tithes was, at least initially, a matter between the delinquent and his priest. But tithe violations could become more serious if they became chronic or systematic. How such disputes could escalate can be seen at Reggio in 1280. There the bishop and clergy clashed with the captain of the people over tithe rates. The captain, with twenty-four other officials, enacted statutes preventing lay proctors from collecting tithes. This effectively stopped collection. The bishop excommunicated the captain, the officials, and the general council of

---

186. Milan Council (1287), 28, pp. 880–81; Ravenna Council (1311), 28, p. 472. See Siena Stat. 1 (1262), 2.63, pp. 223–24, for civil disabilities.

187. Novara Synod II (1298), 1.2.4.3, pp. 211–13. Such crimes barred membership in confraternities: see De Sandre Gasparini, "Laici devoti," 231, commenting on statutes in Little, *Liberty, Charity, Fraternity,* 112.

188. Novara Synod II (1210), p. 30.

189. Grado Council (1296), 23, p. 1170; Ravenna Council (1311), 29, p. 473.

190. See, e.g., Matteo Griffoni (1255), 13.

191. Pisa Stat. 1 (1286), 3.17, pp. 379–80 (which imposed as punishment cutting out the offender's tongue); Grado Council (1296), 25, p. 1170. In Milan priests were obliged to preach yearly on punishments consequent to this sin: Milan Council (1287), 18, p. 878.

192. Vodola, *Excommunication,* 38–40.

the city, placing Reggio under interdict. The city passed new laws, forbidding merchants from eating with or talking to the clergy, from baking bread for them or cutting their hair. We do not know exactly how this conflict was resolved, but by the next year the bishop was doing business as normal with the commune.[193] A church council in Ravenna put systematic resistance to tithes on par with invading church property or enacting laws limiting the liberties of the Church. Those guilty of such crimes, if they proved contumacious, were excommunicated by name at Mass on Christmas, Easter, and All Saints in all the major churches of the province.[194]

Violence was the most dramatic way to rupture the fabric of communal society. The lay theologian Albertano of Brescia considered violence the besetting evil of communal Italy and speculated on ways to prevent it.[195] In spirit, any antisocial act was like blood violence. The story was told of a Cremonese woman who could not forgive the murder of her son. She took some kind of unspecified but nonlethal revenge. From then on, whenever she ate, she saw the food filled with blood. When a poor neighbor who had relied on a Florentine man for food came begging alms during his dinner, he drove her away. He then saw his own food covered with blood.[196] Both sinners, it is said, repented and sought reconciliation. Savage sins generated savage punishments. A Bolognese man murdered his nephew and threw the boy's body down the well of Sant'Agnese. When captured, the city had him placed naked in a barrel studded with nails and rolled him to his decapitation in the city square.[197] Murder and crimes of blood demanded public expiation.

More serious yet was laying hands on a cleric, even if he himself was guilty of a crime. In theory, the punishment of clerics belonged to ecclesiastical courts alone. In 1313, the podesta of Bologna, Giovanni of Sassoferrato, incurred excommunication when he suspended a criminal monk of Santo Stefano, Dom Ugolino de' Rigucci, in a cage on the wall of the Palazzo Comunale and let him die there.[198] City officials might lose their patience with ecclesiastical malefactors and refuse to punish those who harmed them. At Padua in 1282, the commune, having had enough of criminal clergy, reduced the punishment for murdering clerics to 1d. ven. gros. Citizens took vengeance, killing "many priests, clerics, and monks" before the bishop agreed to turn criminal clergy over to the city for justice.[199] Murders of clerics fill the chronicles of communal Italy. In 1173, for example, two members of

193. *Mem. Pot. Reg.* (1280), cols. 1147–49.

194. Ravenna Council (1286), 9, p. 623.

195. See Powell, *Albertanus*, 115.

196. Padua, Biblioteca Universitaria, MS 717 (early XIV cent. section), [*Speculum Exemplorum*], fol. 5ʳ.

197. Matteo Griffoni (1253), 13; *CCB*, 134.

198. Girolamo de' Borselli, *Cronica Gestorum* (1313), 37. Similar rough justice was meted out to a clerical murderer in Padua: *Liber Regiminum Padue* (1331), 346.

199. *Liber Regiminum Padue* (1282), 336; (1308), 349. See also the law prohibiting city enforcement of excommunications in Padua Stat. (1258), 2.1, p. 158, no. 481.

the d'Andolò family struck down the priest Alberto de' Gifoni as he celebrated Mass in the church of Santa Margherita at Bologna.[200] In a notorious
case of 1235, assassins murdered Bishop Guidotto of Mantua during the rogation processions. They escaped punishment by fleeing to the protection of
the warlord Ezellino da Romano.[201] All these crimes against the clergy required public penance. Other sins, not punished by excommunication,
might also require public penance if they were publicly known. At Milan,
the list of sins requiring "major penance" included homicide, theft, adultery,
perjury, bestiality, and sodomy.[202]

Chance survival of the already mentioned manuscript of a public confession by an anonymous government official shows some of the crimes against
the Church that brought public penance.[203] Around 1327, in northeastern
Italy, this official underwent solemn penance because he had been excommunicated by an ecclesiastical judge. In the confession, prepared as part of
his process, he listed the crimes for which he had been excommunicated.
These included support for the Franciscan antipope Nicholas V, doubts
about transubstantiation, striking a cleric, breaking into a church, forging
papal letters, and passing enactments contrary to the clergy. He omitted
other offenses worthy of excommunication given in the formulary he was
using: setting fire to churches, obtaining an absolution or an excommunication by force, and trafficking in ecclesiastical property.[204] The earlier example of Church-commune conflict at Reggio sounds similar. Although this
man was of higher political stature than the usual public penitent, his infractions are no doubt typical.

Pope Celestine II laid down procedures for imposing solemn penance in
1143.[205] Since the tenth century, entrance into public penance had happened
on Ash Wednesday, at the beginning of Lent.[206] In early-thirteenth-century
England, at Winchester, when penitents assembled on Ash Wednesday, the
bishop sorted them out by asking: "Who are the homicides?" "Who are the
parricides?" "Who are publicly scandalous sinners?" The archdeacon then
accordingly presented each group to the bishop for the imposition of penances.[207] This ritual was unnecessary in Italy. There the penitents themselves

200. Girolamo de' Borselli, *Cronica Gestorum*, 15.

201. *Annales Sanctae Iustinae Patavini*, 154; *Annales Veteres Veronenses*, ed. Carlo Cipolla, *Archivio Veneto* 9
(1875): 92.

202. *Manuale Ambrosianum*, 2:474–78.

203. Bologna, Biblioteca Universitaria, ms 158, fols. 54ᵛ–56ᵛ. After I found this text, in the summer of
1998, Prof. Carlo Delcorno of the University of Bologna kindly examined it. He agreed with my conclusion that it is a written confession from a public penance and that it is, to his knowledge, the only example
of such from the period.

204. Ibid., fol. 54ᵛ. Cf. Mantua, Biblioteca Comunale Centrale Teresiana, ms 399, fol. 2ᵛ, the formula
being adapted.

205. Valsecchi, *Interrogatus*, 100.

206. Cf. Vogel, "Rites de la pénitence," 139, 141, who mistakenly thought that the Ash Wednesday
enrollment was gone by 1200.

207. Ibid., 140.

compiled, with the help of their priest, a written general confession and sometime before Ash Wednesday presented it to the archdeacon. In Bergamo during the 1180s, Don Giovanni di Bolgare of Sant'Alessandro explained that the parish priest summoned the sinner and presented him to a canon of either Sant'Alessandro or San Vincenzo. The canon had the archpriest of his church enroll the malefactor in the penitential state and determined the proper penance. Don Giovanni remarked that he had been present for this process *multociens*—many times—showing the frequency of solemn penance in north Italy in the late 1100s.[208]

The sharing of responsibility by the clergy of two churches at Bergamo was unusual. Elsewhere, the cathedral canons jealously guarded their right to enroll penitents. At Siena, the city clergy imposed the penances on public sinners under the direction of the bishop and canons. Just before Terce on Ash Wednesday, parish priests received from the bishop during a ceremony at the duomo the commission to impose penances. The clergy first chanted the seven penitential psalms, and the bishop then gave a sermon on how to impose penances. All prostrated themselves for the singing of Psalms 50 and 129, the "Miserere Mei Deus" and the "De Profundis." The bishop led the clergy in a general confession of sin, and all returned to their parishes to prepare their parishioners and public penitents for the rite later in the day.[209] Bishop Sicardo sketched the public rites of Ash Wednesday at Cremona. These included the Mass of the day (chanted just before None, as usual in Lent), the procession of barefooted penitents, the general imposition of ashes on the penitents and the faithful, the expulsion of the penitents from the cathedral, and their incarceration.[210]

Deacon Rolando explains in detail actual rites of Ash Wednesday at Pisa a little before 1200 (see fig. 49 for the preface of this treatise).[211] At Sext, the bishop blessed ashes made by burning the previous year's palms in the choir. He then went to the center of the nave. Meanwhile, the archpriest and a deacon stood on the steps outside the great western door of the church. These two clerics took the barefooted penitents, each holding a lighted candle, by the hand and let them into the nave. The penitents prostrated themselves between the archbishop and the choir screen. When all had entered and prostrated themselves, the archbishop went among them, sprinkling

---

208. "Instrumentum Litis," 6, p. 212; 1.1, p. 132. The Aquileia Constitutiones (1339), 10, p. 1119A, required that each cathedral have trained penitentiaries.

209. *Ordo Senensis*, 1.99, pp. 88–89.

210. Sicardo, *Mitrale*, 6.4, cols. 255–56.

211. Bologna, Biblioteca Universitaria, MS 1785, Rolando the Deacon, *Liber de Ordine Officiorum*, fol. 15ᵛ. The rite follows that described in Pont. Rom. (Durandus), 3.1.1–25, pp. 552–57 (text = Martène, *De Antiquis*, 1:821–23, Ordo 19), which I have used for missing details. On this pontifical, see Vogel, *Introduction aux sources*, 208–10. For Italian practice, see Zafarana, "Cura pastorale," 520–21. A briefer form of these rites is found in Pont. Rom. (XIII), App. 3.1–3, p. 578, and Pont. Rom. (XII), 28.1–7, pp. 209–10 (text = Martène, *De Antiquis*, 1:818–20, Ordo 17). Milan is again the exception; ashes were distributed there on the Saturday before the second Sunday of Lent: *Manuale Ambrosianum*, 2:142–43.

ashes on their heads. As he did this, each penitent's candle was extinguished. The bishop then either prostrated himself (the Pisan practice) or knelt (the practice elsewhere). The clergy sang the seven penitential psalms and the litany of the saints. The bishop rose and preached a sermon on how Adam and Eve were expelled from paradise because of their sins. He urged the penitents to make good use of their Lenten penances. The archpriest and the deacon then took each penitent by the hand and put him out of the church. As the choir sang the chant "In Sudore," recalling how Adam earned his food by the sweat of his brow after expulsion from paradise, the bishop went out to the penitents, who now knelt on the church steps. He urged the sinners to undertake their penances and promised, if they did so, that he would readmit them to the church on Holy Thursday. The prelate then reentered the church to begin Mass. The great western door was solemnly closed behind him and remained so for the rest of Lent. At Pisa, the bishop gave ashes to the rest of the faithful at this Mass. He used the famous formula "Remember you are ashes and to ashes you will return."[212] The Mass ended with a barefooted procession of the faithful around the duomo, singing penitential psalms and the litany.[213] Public penitents and ordinary sinners began the discipline of Lent together.

Some communes revived the ancient practice of "imprisoning" public penitents during Lent.[214] At Siena, only homicides were imprisoned. The priest penitentiary took them to the bishop's prison, stripped them of their clothing, and dressed each in a rough habit and capuce. As he did this, he asked each if he freely and wholeheartedly accepted his penance. When they said yes, he instructed each to prostrate himself before the door of his cell. The sinner cried out three times, "Through my fault I have sinned, Lord, have mercy on me." After the clergy present recited the penitential psalms and the litany again, the penitentiary incensed the penitents and sprinkled them with holy water. Giving each a little holy water and some blessed incense, he shut them in their cells, praying over each: "We commend to you in the present life, O Lord, your servant, that you might free him from every evil and, by the intercession of Blessed Mary Ever Virgin, lead him to eternal life. Through Christ our Lord. Amen."[215] The prayer is reminiscent of the collects in the Office for the dead. The penitents at Siena entered a more earthly purgatory. Until Holy Thursday, the Sienese penitents fasted on bread and water except on Sunday. But they did have the indulgence of

212. For this rite, see *Ordo Senensis,* 1.100, pp. 89–90; Parma, Biblioteca Palatina, ms Par. 996 (late XII cent.), fols. 20ᵛ–22ᵛ; Verona, Biblioteca Capitolare, ms mcix, fols. 70ʳ–71ᵛ; *Rituale di Hugo [di Volterra],* 323–24.

213. Best described in *Ordo Officiorum della cattedrale [volterrana],* 81 (Volterra ms 273, fols. 26ʳ–27ʳ; San Gimignano ms 3, fols. 24ᵛ–25ʳ).

214. Vogel, "Rites de la pénitence," 142.

215. *Ordo Senensis,* 1.89, pp. 87–88: "Commendamus tibi Domine Famulum tuum in vita praesenti, ut ab omni malo eum eripias, et intercedente B. Maria semper Virgine cum omnibus Sanctis, ipsum ad vitam perducas aeternam. Per etc."

a glass of wine on Tuesdays, Thursdays, and Sundays. Each day they made a hundred genuflections and recited an equal number of Pater Nosters. They could not wash and kept a solemn silence from Compline at night to Terce in the morning. If other cities imprisoned public penitents, we do not know; no rituals and regulations have survived.

Public penance and the Lenten fast culminated three days before Easter, on the morning of Holy Thursday. The ordo of Siena summarizes the many kinds of reconciliation and pardon celebrated on that day:

> On this day, in the whole world the Holy Chrism is blessed; on this day, also, aid is given to penitents through mercy, and discords are reduced to concord; on this day, the angry are pacified, princes give amnesty to criminals, lords forgive delinquent servants, judges spare malefactors, jails are thrown open, and in the whole world those who have been imprisoned in austerity for their sins come forth to the delight of the feast. . . . Today the penitents cast out of the church on Ash Wednesday are absolved, and the Mother Church takes them to her bosom. . . . Today's washing of the feet symbolizes the forgiveness of sin.[216]

This linking of the washing of feet (a ceremony performed among the clergy in private) to the absolution of public penitents is a clerical commonplace. Holy Thursday, one author wrote, was the fifth day of the week—paralleling the fifth day of creation, when the freest of animals, birds and fish, were created. This was the day when Jesus was arrested and bound, that we might be freed and have our sins unbound. This was the day when the great western doors of the cathedral stood open, that all who wished might enter through them.[217] On this day, criminals and sinners could hope for mercy. Ultramontano, a criminal bound to hard labor in the stone quarry of Orvieto, on the Saturday before Palm Sunday, sent a message begging indulgence from Bishop Riccardo. His cry was urgent; the quarry walls were on the verge of collapse. The bishop failed to come. Ultramontano invoked the aid of Saint Pietro Parenzi to protect him and the other prisoners from danger. The saint moved Bishop Riccardo's heart. He arrived to hear the man's confession on Holy Thursday. After he and several other prisoners had confessed, the bishop gave the "canonical admonition." The quarry did

216. Ibid., 1.142, pp. 124–25: "Hac die in toto Orbe sacrum Chrisma conficitur, hac die etiam Poenitenitibus per Indulgentiam subvenitur, discordes ad concordiam redeunt, hac die pacificantur irati, dant Indulgentiam Principes criminosis, Servis malis indulgent Domini, Judices autem Latronibus parcunt, patescant Carceres, et in toto Orbe hac die ad laetitiam festivitatis exeunt, qui clauserunt se pro austeritate culparum. . . . Hodie namque Poenitentes absolvuntur, et qui fuerant in capite jejunii ejecti ab Ecclesia, hodie in gremium Matris Ecclesiae recipiuntur . . . nam lotio pedum remissionem denotat peccatorum." For Verona, see Valsecchi, *Interrogatus*, 99–103.

217. On this symbolism, see Florence, Biblioteca Nazionale Centrale, MS Magl. XIV. 49, fol. 59ʳ; Verona, Biblioteca Capitolare, MS LXXXIV (XII cent.), fols. 91ᵛ–92ʳ.

collapse later, but all who had been absolved escaped—only the one man who had refused to confess was killed.[218]

For the people, the absolution of public penitents was the major rite of Holy Thursday, the most important liturgical ceremony of the day.[219] During the afternoon and evening, the great western doors of the duomo were thrown open for devotional visits, enriched with indulgences. At Siena, those of the city and district who passed through the great doors received a one-year indulgence for all confessed mortal sins and an indulgence of three months for their venial sins.[220] The rites of Holy Thursday appealed to lay penitent saints. Verdiana of Florence decided to become a penitent after Holy Thursday rites at which the entire population of Castelfiorentino was present.[221] The awesome ritual by which the bishop absolved penitents made its way into visions and miracle stories. A Roman visiting Pavia sinned by scoffing at the cult of Saint Lanfranco. He suddenly fell sick. The woman caring for him despaired of his life and begged the saint to forgive him. Saint Lanfranco promptly appeared to the sick man in a dream. The saintly bishop approached the prostrate sinner and tapped him with the end of his pastoral staff, the gesture of forgiveness in public reconciliation. The man arose, freed of his sin and of his illness.[222]

Preparations for reconciliation began in early morning.[223] The priests of the cappelle brought the parishioners doing penance to the cathedral canons, who confirmed that their penances were complete and authentic.[224] The bells of the duomo rang at noon to summon the people; the clergy chanted the combined Offices of Sext and None.[225] The ceremonies of reconciliation began after this Office, before the "evening" Mass with its Gospel describing Christ's washing his apostles' feet. The church was decorated with its most festive decorations, and candles burned everywhere. The penitents assembled with the whole people outside the great western doors. The bishop, dressed in pontificals and cope, took his seat on a chair before the doors,

218. Giovanni of Orvieto, *Vita [S. Petri Parentii]*, 5.38, p. 97.

219. See, e.g., Verona, Biblioteca Capitolare, MS LXXXIV, fols. 91ᵛ–92ʳ, which speaks as if the reconciliation of penitents were the only ceremony of Holy Thursday.

220. *Ordo Senensis*, 1.145, p. 127.

221. *Vita di Santa Verdiana, La gloriosa vergine di Castelfiorentino: Vita, chiesa, spedale di Santa Verdiana*, ed. Olinto Pogni (Castelfiorentino: Carpitelli, 1932–34), 8–9; on which, see Anna Benvenuti Papi, "La serva-patrona," *In Castro Poenitentiae*, 268.

222. Bernardo Balbi, *Vita [S. Lanfranci]*, 3.30, p. 538.

223. This reconstruction is based on the practice at Pisa, in Bologna, Biblioteca Universitaria, MS 1785, Rolando the Deacon, *Liber de Ordine Officiorum;* Verona, in Verona, Biblioteca Capitolare, MS XCIV, Stefano of Verona, *Carpsum sive Ordo Veronensis Ecclesie*, fols. 88ʳ–94ᵛ; and Padua, in Padua, Biblioteca Antoniana, MS 109 (XI cent.), fols. 148ᵛ–154ᵛ. These rites are variants of Pont. Rom. (XII), 30ᵃ.1–30, pp. 214–19 (Martène, *De Antiquis*, 1:818–20, Ordo 17), the pontifical of Christian I, bishop of Mayence, 1167–83. A briefer version is found in Pont. Rom. (XIII), App. 3.4, p. 579. This rite may be compared with that of the latter Middle Ages: Pont. Rom. (Durandus), 3.2.7–44, pp. 559–69 (Martène, *De Antiquis*, 1:821–23, Ordo 19).

224. *Ordo Officiorum della cattedrale [volterrana]*, 104 (Volterra MS 273, fols. 38ᵛ–39ʳ; San Gimignano MS 3, fol. 41ᵛ); Pont. Rom. (Durandus), 3.2.9–10, p. 560.

225. *Ordo Senensis*, 1.143, p. 125.

with a deacon at his side. His clergy assembled in silence around him. The bishop rose and chanted "Venite, venite, venite!"—"Come, come, come!" At each "Venite," the penitents prostrated themselves, prayed, and rose as the deacon directed. The Pisans elaborated the rite: the bishop chanted "Venite" once, then twice, and then three times, and each time the penitents prostrated themselves. At the last "Venite," the deacon brought the penitents forward to prostrate themselves at the bishop's feet. The clergy chanted a psalm, and the deacon addressed the bishop, asking him to accept the sinners' penances. At Padua, the bishop then preached a sermon, explaining the nature of penance and warning the penitents that they could only undergo solemn penance once in their lives. At Siena and most other cities, the sermon came at the end of the service.[226] The clergy chanted psalms and prayers over the penitents, who remained prostrate on the ground.

Then the deacon formally requested that the bishop accept the penitents back into the bosom of the church.[227] The bishop went to the great door, and the archdeacon raised each penitent by the hand and presented him to the bishop, who passed him through the great door to a priest, normally the pastor of his own chapel. The rite dramatically reversed the expulsions of Ash Wednesday and could not but be deeply affecting. Don Giovanni di Bolgare of Sant'Alessandro in Bergamo fondly recalled the very many times (*sepissime*) when he had helped Bishop Ghirardo and Bishop Guala reconcile penitents by passing them through the doors of the duomo.[228] The reconciled penitent's parish priest placed him within the congregation in the nave and indicated that he was again to prostrate himself. The clergy entered the church in procession and took their place in the choir. Led by the choir, all sang the litany. The bishop then chanted five collects, each imploring God's mercy and forgiveness. At Verona, the last of these celebrated Christ's victory over sins from which the penitents were now free: "pride, anger, envy, impatience, disobedience, lust, avarice, discord, vainglory, sloth, false witness, bitterness, the spirit of fornication, and all the machinations of the ancient foe." Then, using a long and solemn prayer, the bishop absolved each penitent individually, addressing him by name. The choir intoned the antiphon "Surge qui Dormis"—"Arise O Sleeper!" As ministers sprinkled the penitents with holy water and incensed them, the bishop touched each with his pastoral staff, signaling him to arise. As they did so, their candles, snuffed out on Ash Wednesday, were relighted.[229]

---

226. Ibid., 1.145, pp. 126–27; Pont. Rom. (XII), 30ᵃ.26, p. 219.

227. In Verona, the sermon was delayed until this point: Verona, Biblioteca Capitolare, MS XCIV, 88ʳ–89ʳ.

228. "Instrumentum Litis," 3.27, p. 175; 3.29, p. 177.

229. No manuscript source includes the relighting of the candles, found in Pont. Rom. (Durandus), 3.2.13–18, pp. 560–61. But since all the Italian rites included a snuffing of the candles on Ash Wednesday, it is reasonable to assume that the reconciliation rite included their relighting. On the use of the staff, see Martène, *De Antiquis*, 1:820 (Ordo 17).

The reconciled were now fully restored to the bosom of the church. All present recited the Confiteor in preparation for the Mass, at which Hosts would be consecrated for use over the next three days. There would be no general Communion this day. And no other Mass would be celebrated from now until the Easter vigil on Holy Saturday. Only at the morning Mass of Easter Sunday would the reconciled take their place beside their neighbors at Communion, receiving again their "rights" as Catholics and citizens of the commune.[230]

---

230. But in Volterra, they received with the newly baptized at the vigil: *Ordo Officiorum della cattedrale [volterrana]*, 120–21.

Chapter Eight
Resurrection and Renewal

Thirteenth-century Christians were made, not born. They were made when, as children, they were reborn from the womb of the city, the font of the baptistery in the Mother Church. When the children passed through the water of the font, they became, like the Israelites passing through the Red Sea, participants in a covenant with God. As one anonymous commentary copied about 1200 put it, the Christian's baptismal renunciation of Satan and acceptance of the faith of the Church was the Christian equivalent of the covenant contract between God and the Jewish people at Sinai.[1] Moralists often presented sin—be it personal, such as gluttony, or public, as in vanity of dress—as a kind of perjury, a violation of the baptismal covenant.[2] In communal Italy, as in most of pre-Reformation Europe, baptism was performed by immersion.[3] In baptism, the child went down into the tomb with Christ and rose again, united to the Savior's death and burial, and so became part of his living body, the Church, to await his return in glory.[4] The anonymous Italian commentator made little of baptism as the forgiveness of sin. He focused on the corporate aspect of the rite, its creation of a people, the Church. Baptism was a familial and community event—more so than Mass, Communion, or confession—since it associated the newly baptized with other Christians.[5] It populated the city and its church. The heresiarch Fra Dolcino and his followers' greatest crime, in the mind of the chronicler of his movement, was not his burning of churches or murder of clergy but

1. Florence, Biblioteca Medicea Laurenziana, MS Aed. 214, fols. 49ᵛ–50ʳ.
2. E.g., Francesco Pipino, *Chronicon*, 2.49, cols. 669–70.
3. As taken for granted in Jacques of Vitry, *Historia Occidentalis*, 36, p. 196, and Florence, Biblioteca Medicea Laurenziana, MS Conv. Soppr. 145 (XIV cent.), Jean of La Rochelle, *Summa de Vitiis et Virtutibus*, fol. 145ᵛ.
4. Florence, Biblioteca Medicea Laurenziana, MS Aed. 214, fol. 51ʳ.
5. As noted by Hay, *The Church in Italy in the Fifteenth Century*, 25.

his killing of pregnant women to prevent the baptism of their unborn children.[6] Merely to neglect baptism was a sin, close to heresy.

Baptism was essential for participation in the sacraments and rites of the Church. A Franciscan novice was unable to look at the Host when the priest raised it at Mass. His superiors investigated the matter and found that he had been born among the Saracens and never baptized. After they baptized him, the young man was finally able to gaze upon his Maker with the rest of the community. A Tuscan novice could never recite the Office or Pater Noster without stuttering. When priests blessed him, the boy would throw himself down and pound his head on the floor. Investigations showed that he was an *expositus*—a foundling—who had never been baptized.[7] Again, the sacrament allowed him to join in the Office and receive its blessings. God might work miracles to provide baptism. In 1240, Donna Montanaria, wife of Ugolino, a saddlemaker from San Cristoforo, near Orvieto, gave birth to a stillborn child. She invoked Saint Ambrogio of Massa, through whose intercession the child revived. After emergency baptism, the child lived four weeks before rejoining his Maker.[8]

Any layman or woman could perform emergency baptism if the child was in danger and no priest was available. Church councils repeatedly reminded the clergy that they were to explain to the people the Latin formula (in the name of the Trinity) and the manner (immersion preferred, pouring or sprinkling allowed) in sermons three times a year, on Holy Saturday, the Pentecost vigil, and the octave of Epiphany.[9] If illiterate, the baptizer could perform the rite in the vernacular.[10] If a priest was available for emergency baptism, he included as many of the other rites as possible, such as the exorcisms that preceded the baptism and the sacramental Communion that at this time still followed it, even for infants. As he was not a bishop, he omitted the anointing of confirmation.[11] The Verona ritual provided for "private" baptisms with a shortened form of the ceremonies of public baptisms.[12] Such rituals also allowed priests later to supply rituals omitted when, in truly desperate cases, a layperson baptized the child immediately after birth and the child survived.

All orthodox Christians knew that baptism remitted sin, both original and

6. *Historia Fratris Dulcinae Heresiarche*, ed. Arnaldo Segarizzi, *RIS²* 9:5:9.

7. *Chronica* XXIV Generalium Ordinis Fratrum Minorum, 310–11.

8. *Processus Canonizationis B. Ambrosii Massani*, 21, p. 581; cf. Thomas of Pavia, *Dialogus de Gestis Sanctorum Fratrum Minorum*, ed. Ferdinand M. Delorme (Quaracchi: Collegium S. Bonaventurae, 1923), 50, p. 180. See also a similar miracle by Saint Ambrogio Sansedoni in Gisberto of Alessandria et al., *Vita [B. Ambrosii]*, 11.110, p. 199.

9. Ravenna Council (1311), 9 and 11, pp. 455–56; Ravenna Council (1314), 14, p. 547.

10. Bologna Synod (1310), 488.

11. See *Manuale Ambrosianum*, 2:472–73; Milan, Biblioteca Ambrosiana, MS A 189 Inf., fols. 70ᵛ–72ᵛ.

12. Verona, Biblioteca Capitolare, MS MCIX (late XII cent.), fols. 4ᵛ–15ʳ.

actual.[13] Especially for children in danger of death, baptism was not to be deferred. When, as a priest, Uberto of Terzago, the future bishop of Milan, had a ritual prepared for his own use in the late 1100s, he included a blessing of water for emergency baptisms.[14] As the communal period was coming to a close, the concern that infants might lose their salvation by dying before baptism became more and more intense.[15] By the 1320s, in the district of Siena, parents might be excommunicated for the same number of days that they delayed the baptism of their children. When Benedetto, a newborn, seemed mortally ill, his family rushed to their parish priest for baptism, only to be warned they were excommunicated for the number of days they had delayed. They explained that the baby had been born that morning and that they had vowed a candle to Saint Francesco Patrizzi for each day he lived. Saint Francesco and the sacrament worked their saving power; Benedetto survived, grew up, and joined the saint's Servite order in 1341.[16]

BAPTISM AND CITIZENSHIP

By the thirteenth century, immersion in the font of the city baptistery made the baptized a citizen of the commune. It created a bond like siblinghood among all those baptized there. Dante, meeting Cacciaguida in heaven, heard his ancestor recall his rebirth at Florence's beloved San Giovanni; the baptismal bond had made them fellow citizens.

> To so restful and so true
>   a life as citizens, to such beautiful
> citizenship, to such a faithful household,
>   Mary, invoked with loud cries, gave me;
> and in your ancient baptistery,
>   at once I became both Christian and Cacciaguida.[17]

Lawyers such as Bartolus recognized the primacy of baptism as the way to citizenship: "Does baptism in a place make one a citizen of that city? So it seems, for through baptism one is freed from sin and the slavery in which one is held by Satan and his angels; therefore, like manumission, it seems as

---

13. Florence, Biblioteca Medicea Laurenziana, MS Aed. 214, fols. 42ʳ⁻ᵛ, takes this for granted. For a poem on the sin-removing power of baptism, see Modena, Biblioteca Estense Universitaria, MS α.R.2.3 (XIV cent.), fols. 1ʳᵇ⁻ᵛᵃ.

14. Milan, Biblioteca Ambrosiana, MS A 189 Inf., fols. 72ᵛ⁻73ᵛ.

15. J. D. C. Fisher, *Christian Initiation: Baptism in the Medieval West* (London: SPCK, 1965), 111–12, finds no Italian legislation before 1339 on baptism immediately after birth.

16. Cristoforo of Parma, *Legenda Beati Francisci*, 52, p. 194.

17. Dante, *Paradiso*, 15:131–36: "A così riposato, così bello | viver di cittadini, a così fida | cittadinanza, a così dolce ostello, | Maria mi diè, chiamata in alte grida; | e nell'antico vostro Batisteo | insieme fui cristiano e Cacciaguida."

a consequence one acquires citizenship through baptism."[18] There were other ways to become a citizen. At Volterra, one could receive protection as a citizen after ten years' residence, and the juridical status after that, if one petitioned the podesta. Siena required three years' residence before the citizenship petition, while Padua more stringently required forty years.[19] But such citizens remained in the end "naturalized," "adopted" members of the community. The natural-born Sienese, Volterran, or Paduan was one reborn in the city baptistery.

The rites of baptism created and ordered the community, and by participating in them the entire society experienced rebirth and renewal.[20] The baptisms of Easter on the afternoon of Holy Saturday were the great civic and religious events of the year. Only the baptisms of the Pentecost vigil, some fifty days later, could compare to them. For children not in danger of death, these two dates were the ordinary times of baptism, as Bishop Sicardo of Cremona explained in the late 1100s. On the two great feasts of redemption, the true baptizer of Christians was Christ himself, in whose death and Resurrection the redeemed shared. Sicardo rejected the mostly Greek practice of baptizing on the anniversary of Christ's baptism, on 6 January, Epiphany, since that baptism had been administered by John the Baptist, not Christ himself.[21] When in 1264 the city fathers of Vicenza spoke of Holy Saturday, they called it the "Saturday of Baptism."[22] Only grudgingly did Bishop Sicardo admit that risk of death might be a reason not to postpone a baptism until Easter. He admitted that bishops could, and perhaps should, grant an "indult" for such exceptions.[23] Sicardo's focus on Easter baptisms reflected the centralization of the cult in the Mother Church in the period of the early communes. Before the construction of the great monumental baptisteries in the 1100s, even a moderate-sized group baptism would have been impossible. The fonts were small, the chapels in which they were placed tiny.[24] The new baptisteries and their large fonts allowed for group baptisms

18. Bartolus, *Commentaria in Secundam Digesti Novi Partem*, vol. 6 of *Opera Omnia* (Venice, 1602), fol. 217[va]: "Secundo quaero, utrum baptizatus hic, efficatur civis huius civitatis? Quod videtur, nam tam per baptismum quis liberatur a peccato e servitute qua tenebatur satanae et angelis eius, ergo videtur quasi manumissio, per consequens videtur per baptismum contrahatur civilitas, quia certi sunt modi per quos civilitas contrahitur, ut hic et d. l. cives, C. de incol. li. X., in quos non est iste." On Bartolus, see Julius Kirshner, "Civitas Sibi Faciat Civem: Bartolus of Sassoferrato's Doctrine on the Making of a Citizen," *Speculum* 48 (1973): 694–713. On baptism's making citizens, see Enrico Cattaneo, "La *Basilica Baptisterii* segno di unità ecclesiale e civile," *Atti del convegno di Parma (1976)*, 26; on the bishop as "baptizer" of citizens, see Golinelli, *Città e culto*, 73–74.

19. Volterra Stat. (1210–22), 181, p. 93, and 149 (1224), pp. 184–85; Siena Stat. 1 (1262), 1.270, p. 108; Padua, "Statuti extravaganti [padovani]," doc. 3 (1281), p. 202.

20. As noted for Lyons by Jacques Rossiaud, "Les rituels de la fête civique à Lyon, XIIIe–XVIe siècles," *Riti e rituali nelle società medievali*, ed. Chiffoleau, Martines, and Paravicini Bagliani, 285.

21. Sicardo, *Mitrale*, 5.9, col. 236C.

22. Vicenza Stat. (1264), 168: "die sabbati de Baptismo."

23. Sicardo, *Mitrale*, 6.8, col. 277.

24. See pages 30–32 above.

on the two great feasts, and these became the days of the "solemn baptisms."[25]

Outlying communes and villages in the contado had their own baptismal fonts, if they were pievi.[26] In the country, the pievano, the "parish priest," was properly the archpriest who governed the clergy serving a baptismal church. That church had a stone font large enough for the immersion of children (fig. 28). The archpriest was to teach new godparents their Pater Noster and Credo if they did not know them. He sat on a throne in the apse of his church, the image of the bishop at his cathedral.[27] But he was emphatically not the bishop, and although he might baptize, he did so only as the bishop's delegate. That he had to come every year to the cathedral on Holy Thursday to get the holy oils for baptism and the sick showed his subordinate and delegated position.[28] Sacramentally, pievi were extensions of the Mother Church, the sole giver of spiritual life of citizens. The communal period slowly ended the independence of pievi close to the city. At Bergamo in 1197, the canons of the cathedral, led by the archdeacon Guasco, brought a suit against the priests Vifredo of Sant'Andrea, Lanfranco of San Salvatore, Alberico of San Michele dell'Arco, Guala of Sant'Eufemia, Lanfranco of San Lorenzo, Giovanni of Sant'Alessandro in Colonna, Alberto of Sant'Alessandro della Croce, and Giovanni of San Michele del Pozzo, to stop their independent baptizing on Easter and Pentecost. Bishop Lanfranco forbade those eight priests, and all other clergy of the district, to baptize anywhere but in the city font. Furthermore, there were to be no baptisms on the vigils of Easter and Pentecost save those performed at the Mother Church. The clergy were to come with their people to the "solemn baptisms" at the duomo. To justify these restrictions of time and place, Archdeacon Guasco had recourse to ancient patristic authorities, such as Tertullian of Carthage.[29]

Such a centralization process seems to have been successful throughout communal Italy—so successful that, at Siena, legislation stipulated that some of the "great multitude" of children needing baptism accumulated during the year might be baptized outside the two great feasts to make the ceremonies of the vigils more workable. But the indult for baptisms at other times did not apply to the two great feasts themselves. At those times, all baptisms were to be at the duomo.[30] So persistent was the tradition of solemn baptisms on Easter and Pentecost vigils that, even after the sixteenth-century liturgical reforms of the Council of Trent, the liturgical books required that no bap-

25. *Ordo Senensis*, 1.175, pp. 155–56; 185, pp. 168–69.

26. For bibliography on this topic, see L. Mascanzoni, *Pievi e parrocchie in Italia: Saggio di bibliografia storica*, 2 vols. (Bologna: n.p., 1988–89).

27. Brentano, *Two Churches*, 68–73.

28. Enrico Cattaneo, "Il battistero in Italia dopo il Mille," *Miscellanea Gilles Gérard Meersseman*, ed. Maccarrone et al., 1:186.

29. Giuseppe Ronchetti, *Memorie istoriche della città e chiesa di Bergamo* (Bergamo: Natali, 1805), 3:207–8.

30. *Ordo Senensis*, 1.119, p. 105.

tisms be done during Holy Week, at least in cathedral churches, so that there would be at least a small group to baptize at the vigil.[31] The Easter baptisms became ever more a civic, as well as an ecclesiastical, ceremony. Providing water for the great immersion pool of the baptistery became a communal responsibility. At Verona, the communal official responsible for water, on entering office, took an oath that he would provide a good supply of fresh water to the cathedral for baptisms and making holy water.[32] Modena pledged that the city itself would provide the water needed for Holy Saturday.[33] Mass Easter baptisms and their civic significance seem distinctively communal Italian, symbolic of that epoch's particular union of Church and city.

Making Catechumens

The making of new Christians began with the solemn announcement of the Easter date soon after Christmas. Easter was, and still is, a mobile feast, and only those with Easter tables and a good grasp of mathematics could determine the date themselves. Most people heard the date of the spring feast at this ceremony. At Siena, a procession with candles and incense wound its way to Giovanni of Pisa's great pulpit in the choir screen just after the pontifical Mass of Epiphany. From there the deacon proclaimed in song the dates of Lent and Easter to the assembled congregation.[34] On the fourth Sunday of Lent, another solemn announcement occurred at the end of the solemn Mass. One of the priests of the cathedral mounted the pulpit and announced that on the following Saturday the church would hold the first of the seven "scrutinies," the rites during which the children to be baptized were prepared by prayers and exorcisms. The scrutinies and the other rites for preparing catechumens, the candidates for baptism, originated in the ancient Church. At that time most new Christians were adult converts, who had to be examined—"scrutinized"—regarding their morals and beliefs. The Church combined these examinations with prayers and exorcisms intended to erase the clouds of their former paganism. For baptizing infants, the medieval Church knew no ritual distinct from the ancient rite for adults, but their ritual books called these ceremonies the "Rite for Making Children Catechumens."[35] In the communes, on the occasion when there was an adult

---

31. *Caeremoniale Episcoporum: Editio Princeps, 1600,* ed. Achille Maria Triacca et al. (Vatican City: Libreria Editrice Vaticana, 2000), 2.27, no. 8.
32. Verona Stat. II (1276), 4.181, p. 640.
33. Modena Stat. (1327), 5.41–42, p. 554.
34. *Ordo Senensis,* 1.76–77, p. 65.
35. See, e.g., Florence, Biblioteca Medicea Laurenziana, MS Aed. 214, fols. 42ʳ–59ʳ: "Quomodo Infantes Catechumeni Efficiantur" (a twelfth-century ritual); Mantua, Biblioteca Comunale Centrale Teresiana, MS 331 (XII cent.), fols. 34ʳ–25ᵛ; and Milan, Biblioteca Ambrosiana, MS A 189 Inf. (ca. 1200), fols. 70ᵛ–72ᵛ.

convert, perhaps rarely from Judaism or more rarely from Islam, this candidate was still examined as part of these ceremonies.[36]

In the communal period, parish priests gathered the children to be baptized, along with their parents and godparents, to attend the service at None on the Saturday before the fifth Sunday of Lent.[37] In the countryside, the rites occurred at the pieve, the baptismal church, but within the city walls, the scrutinies were the special prerogative of the Mother Church. Although he was anxious to preserve his own church's special role in the baptismal rites, Giovanni di Bolgare, the prior of Sant'Alessandro of Bergamo, admitted in 1187 that scrutinies had to be performed at the cathedral.[38] Each city handled the scrutinies in a slightly different way. At Siena, where the scrutinies began on the third Saturday rather than fourth Saturday of Lent, the great bell of the duomo announced the first scrutiny by pealing after the chanting of Sext.[39] It rang continuously until None, summoning the citizens, especially those with children to be baptized, to the duomo. Then, before the great west doors, a priest took down the names of the "pagan infants," writing those of the girls and the boys in separate registers. To Bishop Sicardo, this ceremony recalled Ezra's investigation of the Israelite genealogies after the Exile, the inquest by which he separated the true members of the chosen people from the Gentiles who had accompanied them back from Babylon.[40]

After the children had been enrolled, acolytes called each of the "elect" by name, and their parents took them in their arms into the nave of the church, the girls on the north side, the boys on the south. The choir intoned the Mass, which proceeded as usual until the collect, the opening prayer. At this point, when the chanting of the Epistle would normally have taken place, priests ascended the two flanking pulpits of the choir screen, one on the right and the other on the left. A deacon called on all to kneel. As each priest chanted the prayer of exorcism over his group of infants, priests fanned out throughout the church. They breathed on the face of each pagan boy or girl, invoking the Holy Spirit and claiming the children for Christ by inscribing the sign of the cross on their foreheads, a gesture repeated three times for each.[41] The signing on the forehead reminded those present that Christians

---

36. Florence, Biblioteca Medicea Laurenziana, MS Aed. 214, fols. 46ʳ⁻ᵛ; on voluntary converts from Judaism in our period, see Joseph Shatzmiller, "Jewish Converts to Christianity in Medieval Europe, 1200–1500," *Cross Cultural Convergences in the Crusader Period: Essays Presented to Aryeh Grabois on His Sixty-Fifth Birthday*, ed. Michael Goodich, Sophia Menache, and Sylvia Schein (New York: Lang, 1995), 297–318, esp. 310–12, his one Italian example. A Hebrew letter records that this man, a Master Andrea, converted in order to eat ritually unclean food rather than for religious reasons.

37. Sicardo, *Mitrale*, 6.8, cols. 283–84.

38. "Instrumentum Litis" (September 1187), 6, p. 216.

39. Third-week scrutinies were also the rule in Brescia: ibid., p. 107.

40. Sicardo, *Mitrale*, 6.8, col. 277.

41. *Ordo Senensis*, 1.120, p. 106, explains this rite in detail. See Florence, Biblioteca Medicea Laurenziana, MS Aed. 214, fol. 42ʳ, and the discussion in Sicardo, *Mitrale*, 6.8, col. 277.

should wear their faith publicly and not hide it. Popular sentiment considered this signing and breathing to be as powerful as the exorcism prayers themselves. These gestures drove off any demons that hovered around the unbaptized.[42] After the prayers and exorcisms, priests gave each catechumen a taste of salt, which Bishop Sicardo explained as a foretaste of the true doctrine in which the newly baptized were later to be instructed.[43] This taste of salt also recalled the cleansing of the prophet Jeremiah's mouth by God, which gave him the commission to "pull down and break down nations; to build and to plant."[44] The exorcisms were to be repeated five more times, usually on the Wednesdays and Saturdays of the next three weeks, but without the ceremonies of the signing and salt.[45]

On the Saturday before Palm Sunday (the sixth Sunday in Lent) came the last and most important of the scrutinies. This was also the seventh scrutiny. That these rituals totaled the perfect number seven made them, for allegorists, a symbol of the seven gifts of the Holy Spirit, which would be bestowed on the catechumens by their Easter baptism.[46] During the triple chanting of the solemn exorcism "Maledicte" over the infants at this Mass, priests approached each one and touched the child's ears and nostrils with his own saliva. As they did so, the priests said, using the ancient Aramaic language of Jesus, "Ephpheta, that is be opened." This rite paralleled Christ's action in John 13 and prepared the catechumens to hear the words of power that were now to be proclaimed to them. Their carnal ears were now spiritual.[47] In Cremona, one of the doorkeepers, a member of the minor order of *ostiarius*, selected two children, one male and one female, whom their parents then brought within the screen and over whom a deacon chanted passages from the Gospel.[48] In Siena and most other cities, deacons performed the rite over all the children, not just a representative couple in the choir. In the Sienese rite, the children, carried by their parents and accompanied by their godparents with lighted candles, assembled before the side altar of Saint Sevinus. Four deacons intoned the antiphon "Sitientes." Then deacons chanted the opening verses of one of the four Gospels over each child's head. The four Gospels used in this ceremony symbolized the calling of the Gentiles from the four corners of the earth. The reading of

42. Florence, Biblioteca Medicea Laurenziana, MS Aed. 214, fols. 42ᵛ–43ʳ.

43. Sicardo, *Mitrale*, 6.8, cols. 279–80. See also Mantua, Biblioteca Comunale, MS 331, fols. 32ᵛ–33ᵛ, and *Ordo Officiorum della cattedrale [volterrana]*, 93 (Volterra, Biblioteca Comunale Guarnacci, MS 222, fol. 32ʳ).

44. Jer. 1:9–10; so allegorized in Florence, Biblioteca Medicea Laurenziana, MS Aed. 214, fols. 43ʳ–44ʳ.

45. Bologna, Biblioteca Universitaria, MS 1785 (late XII cent.), Rolando the Deacon, *Liber de Ordine Officiorum*, fol. 19ᵛ; *Ordo Officiorum della cattedrale [volterrana]*, 92 (Volterra MS 222, fols. 31ᵛ–32ʳ); but compare *Ordo Senensis*, 1.118, p. 104. On Brescian practice, see Valsecchi, *Interrogatus*, 107–9.

46. *Ordo Senensis*, 1.118, p. 104; Sicardo, *Mitrale*, 6.8, cols. 286–87.

47. Florence, Biblioteca Medicea Laurenziana, MS Aed. 214, fols. 46ᵛ–47ʳ. On this rite, see Sicardo, *Mitrale*, 6.8, cols. 279–80, and Mantua, Biblioteca Comunale Centrale Teresiana, MS 331, fol. 33ᵛ.

48. Sicardo, *Mitrale*, 6.8, col. 279.

Christ's genealogy from Matthew, in particular, reminded the hearers that the names of the catechumens were now inscribed in heaven.[49]

Next came a mystical catechesis, symbolically completing the promise of the sacred Scriptures just chanted, the giving of the Credo and the Pater Noster. An acolyte presented a chosen boy at the chancel-screen door, and a priest read over him the Apostles' Creed in Latin. The same was then done for a girl, with the Creed this time read in Greek. The same ceremony was repeated for the Lord's Prayer, again in both sacred languages.[50] The reading of the Credo, with its twelve phrases, traditionally believed to have been composed by the twelve apostles, was the most important part of this rite, imparting as it did the essence of the faith. People knew this day as the Saturday for Giving the Credo. In Milan, at least, the catechumens' godparents made the children's baptismal vows renouncing Satan immediately before the giving of the Credo.[51] Mass continued with the Gospel of the day. The general practice was to "expel" the "neophytes" before the chanting of the Gospel and the sacrifice of the Eucharist. But Bishop Sicardo did not like the practice and, in Cremona, allowed his neophytes to stay for the reading of the Gospel and the Eucharist that followed.[52] The catechumens were now prepared to enter into the most holy week of the Christian year.

The rites of Holy Week, from Palm Sunday, with its great processions, to Easter, with its baptisms and general Communion, were the most splendid and important events of the year in communal Italy.[53] Palm Sunday reenacted the events of Christ's last days, and its Gospel was the entire narrative of the Passion according to Matthew. When the neophytes were baptized on Holy Saturday, they were sacramentally incorporated into Christ's death on the cross and his Resurrection. The whole city participated in these events, and the city became sacramentally what it was otherwise only metaphorically, the Holy City Jerusalem.[54] The communes forbade profane activities, such as gambling, in this sacred time.[55] For the participants, the Palm Sunday procession overshadowed all else. This procession had the same form everywhere. City chapels closed for the day so that the entire population could attend. As the clergy sang antiphons and hymns, the community went

49. *Ordo Senensis*, 1.120–21, pp. 107–8.

50. Sicardo, *Mitrale*, 6.8, cols. 279–80; *Ordo Senensis*, 1.120, p. 107; Florence, Biblioteca Medicea Laurenziana, MS Aed. 214, fols. 44ʳ–46ʳ; on the giving of the Pater, see Florence, Biblioteca Riccardiana, MS 256, fols. 137ᵛ–139ʳ.

51. *Manuale Ambrosianum*, 2:168–70 (Sabbato in Traditione Symboli). I do not find the baptismal vows at this point in churches outside Milan.

52. Sicardo, *Mitrale*, 6.8, col. 283.

53. Valsecchi, *Interrogatus*, 97 n. 259, quoting Enrico Cattaneo's pamphlet, *Città e religione nell'età dei comuni* (Milan: Vita e Pensiero, 1979), 53.

54. See, on these rites, Verona, Biblioteca Capitolare, MS LXXXIV (XII cent.), fols. 88ᵛ–90ʳ; Valsecchi, *Interrogatus*, 97–99; *Carpsum*, 254–65 (Verona, Biblioteca Capitolare, MS XCIV [late XI cent.], fols. 39ʳ–48ᵛ).

55. On gambling, see Modena Stat. (1327), 4.37, p. 405; on business closing, see ibid., 4.87, p. 433.

with the bishop to some point outside the walls. There, after a prayer, the deacon chanted from Matthew the Gospel of Christ's entry into Jerusalem. The bishop, with a solemn prayer and the chanting of the Sanctus, blessed olive branches and flowers (palms being rare in north Italy). For this reason, many people knew this feast as the Sunday of Olives. But it was the flowers carried in procession that gave this day its most popular title: *Pasqua Florita*— Flowery Sunday.[56]

After the blessing, the people reassembled, the bishop taking the place of Christ at the end of the procession. As the procession reached the closed city gates, cantors within broke out in the chant "Gloria, Laus, et Honor." The procession took up this hymn as the gates opened, and then entered the city, now symbolically Jerusalem. At the cathedral, the procession found the great western doors closed. After the bishop struck the doors with his cross, the choir intoned the responsory "Ingrediente," and doorkeepers threw the doors open. The procession entered the nave to the pealing of the great bells. Mass proceeded as on other days, save for the chanting of the Passion in dialogue form by three deacons.[57] The voice of Christ was sung in sonorous baritone, while the shouts of the crowd and the words of Judas were in a harsh tenor. The narrator pitched his reading in a middle register. This dramatic reading deeply impressed itself on the consciousness of the hearers, even if the Latin words were not wholly intelligible to Italian speakers. The story was well known, and the melodious voice of Christ was both mournful and reassuring. Whenever Saint Benvenuta Bojani heard the chanting of the Palm Sunday Passion, she went into ecstasy and saw in vision the whole story of the crucifixion of Christ. Each time, she saw herself kiss the dying Jesus.[58]

Bishop Sicardo lovingly recalled how the ceremonies of Palm Sunday at Cremona reenacted events from the history of the people of Israel.[59] As his city went out to the stational cross for the blessing of branches, they became the children of the Hebrews coming from Jerusalem to greet Christ, the Messiah. The procession's entrance into Cremona brought to his mind the image of the Israelites passing dry-shod over the Jordan and entering the Promised Land. The procession itself symbolized Christ's people's going forth to greet him at his return in glory on the last day. In the popular mind, the ritual's reminiscences of the past and the future were second to its present sacred power. The olive branches spoke their own language. At Volterra and other cities, unbroken tradition dictated that the people carry their olive branches upright only when the bishop was present to represent Christ; if a

---

56. Verona, Biblioteca Capitolare, MS LXXXIV, fol. 105ᵛ.
57. See Pont. Rom. (XII), 29.1–19, pp. 210–14. For an example from a parish, see Volterra, Biblioteca Comunale Guarnacci, MS 273, fols. 31ʳ–36ᵛ.
58. Corrado of Cividale, *Vita Devotissimae Benevenutae*, 8.63, p. 167.
59. Sicardo, *Mitrale*, 6.10, col. 293.

mere priest had to substitute, they carried them inverted.[60] People brought branches home; these extended the power of the feast to their families and to the sick. Priests brought the branches to those, such as anchoresses, who could not attend the procession in person. When a blind woman came to the cell of Saint Verdiana, the holy woman touched her eyes with the olive branch her confessor had brought from the procession in Florence. The woman was immediately healed.[61]

Each city added embellishments reflecting its own sacred history. In the late 1100s, at Bergamo, preparations began the Saturday before, when the bishop dispatched bundles of unblessed branches to the collegiate church of Sant'Alessandro and to the abbess of the nunnery of Santa Grata outside the walls. The blessings occurred at Sant'Alessandro, where the procession from the duomo of San Vincenzo arrived to the pealing of church bells.[62] The bishop deferred to the archpriest of the duomo and the prior of Sant'Alessandro for the blessing. This was a special privilege of the two chapters, as Canon Lanfranco Mazzocchi of San Vincenzo carefully pointed out.[63] The procession then left the city and returned by the gate near the nunnery of Santa Grata. The bishop stopped outside the walls, and the prioress showered him with flowers from her station above the city gate. The bishop preached a sermon, and the procession entered the city. Canon Arderico di Boffalmacco of Sant'Alessandro explained the origins of these rituals. When a procession had brought Saint Grata's relics to Bergamo, they suddenly became too heavy to carry at that very spot, showing that the saint wished to reside in the nunnery there and give it her name.[64] After the entrance, the procession passed through the city, pausing to venerate relics displayed before the major churches. Finally it arrived at the cathedral, San Vincenzo, for the solemn Mass and chanting of the Passion. The bishop's obligation to send branches to the canons and use their church for the blessing proved the privileged position of Sant'Alessandro as second church of the city, Don Margatto, the church's custodian, proudly recalled. He could not resist adding that the bishop only sent branches to the nuns as a courtesy.[65]

Cities adapted the ceremonies to their particular geography and holy places. At Siena, the blessing was conducted at the church of San Martino. After a simple morning Mass, the procession left the duomo to arrive at San Martino in time for Terce. The city clergy joined the canons of San Martino in chanting the Office. A lector then proclaimed the reading from Exodus in the piazza before the church, facing the rising sun in the east. A deacon, facing north, chanted the Gospel of Christ's entry, his words symbolically

60. *Ordo Officiorum della cattedrale [volterrana]*, 97–98 (Volterra MS 222, fols. 34ᵛ–35ᵛ).
61. *Vita Sancte Viridiane*, 13.
62. "Instrumentum Litis," 4, p. 186.
63. Ibid. (September 1187), 1.1, p. 129.
64. Ibid., 4, p. 189; on this miracle, see ibid., p. 98, citing *Biblioteca Sanctorum* 7 (1966): 152–55.
65. "Instrumentum Litis," 6, p. 226.

illuminating the arctic darkness. The choir sang, the bishop preached, and the procession returned to the cathedral.[66] Deacon Rolando, in his treatise on the particular rituals of the Church at Pisa, lovingly described Palm Sunday there. The Pisan ceremony focused on that city's magnificent cathedral complex, the Piazza dei Miracoli. The archbishop blessed the branches in the middle of the piazza, and the procession passed through the monumental cemetery, around the baptistery, and from there through the great west door of the duomo.[67] At Modena, out of respect for Saint Giminiano, the branches were blessed in the cathedral itself. The procession then circumambulated the duomo, with the people singing the litanies as on the rogations.[68]

One of the most touching additions to the usual ceremonies occurred at Verona. The cathedral canons left the cathedral and went in procession up a little hill to the church of San Pietro in Monte. There they chanted Mass, the bishop preached, a deacon declaimed the Gospel of Christ's entry, and priests distributed blessed branches. Meanwhile the clergy of the city waited at the duomo, singing Matins. The procession left San Pietro and crossed the Adige by a bridge near the point where the Ponte Nuovo now stands, at the foot of Via Stella. The triumphal procession reentered the city by a bridge upstream over the Adige at Castello (fig. 51). On this bridge, the Pons Fractus, so called because it had been constructed from a fallen Roman one, they were met by the children of the city singing "Gloria, Laus, et Honor." Verona's was a marvelous reenactment of the Gospel narrative, complete with a Mount of Olives, an entry into Jerusalem, a greeting by the Hebrew children, and so forth. Did the bishop ride a donkey? Perhaps. A figure of Christ riding a donkey followed the procession in the Baroque period.[69] Although liturgical books and clerical sensibilities dictated much of the Palm Sunday rite, we hear the voice of the whole city, not just its clergy, in matters like the processional routes, visits to relics, and other local practices. After the city of Vicenza received the relic of the Crown of Thorns in 1264, the city fathers petitioned for a rerouting of the Palm Sunday procession past its new shrine in the Dominican church of Santa Corona. The bishop obligingly changed the route, and the city pledged an offering of £20 each year at the shrine during the procession.[70]

THE PASCHAL TRIDUUM

While the whole week from Palm Sunday to Easter was known as Holy Week, the three days leading up to Holy Thursday were of far lesser religious

66. *Ordo Senensis*, 1.132–34, pp. 116–18.

67. Bologna, Biblioteca Universitaria, MS 1785, Rolando the Deacon, *Liber de Ordine Officiorum*, fols. 20ᵛ–21ʳ.

68. Parma, Biblioteca Palatina, MS Par. 996 (late XII cent.), fols. 37ᵛ–40ʳ.

69. *Carpsum*, 254 (Verona, Biblioteca Capitolare, MS XCIV, fols. 39ʳ–40ʳ). The Verona *Orazionale*, *L'orazionale dell'archidiacono Pacifico e il Carpsum del cantore Stefano*, ed. Meersseman, Adda, and Deshusses, 114, suggests the donkey. I am obliged to the *bibliotecario capitolare* of Verona, Don Giuseppe Zivelonghi, for information on the ancient rites of Verona.

70. Vicenza Stat., 200–203.

importance. Secular business resumed Monday to Wednesday, and only Wednesday's solemn fast had an impact on devotional consciousness. That fast, recalling Judas's betrayal of the Savior for thirty pieces of silver, was the prototype for the Wednesday fast throughout the year, just as the fast commemorating Christ's death on Good Friday was for that of the Fridays of the year.[71] The last three days of this week—the Paschal Triduum—were the culmination of the Church's year. On Palm Sunday, the cities celebrated Christ's entry into Jerusalem and his Passion. Now in this preparation period for Easter, they would meditate on that death. At Vespers on Thursday the bells of the city rang for the last time and then fell silent. In their place, wooden clappers announced the Offices and hours until Easter.

Popular piety focused on the combined Offices of Matins and Lauds, called Tenebrae ("Shadows"), on these three days. The readings of Matins were from the Lamentations of Jeremiah, adapted to mourning the death of Christ as recounted in the Passion Gospels of Palm Sunday, Monday, and Tuesday. The cantor sang these lessons in a tone peculiar to this Office, which some believed to date from the ancient synagogue. As the lessons progressed, Christ's slow death on the cross was manifested in the successive snuffing of candles fixed on a special, usually triangular, stand in the midst of the choir, called in English the hearse. Bishop Sicardo noted that the number of candles—12, 24, or 72—varied, but all had to be out by the chanting of the last canticle of Lauds, the song of Zachariah (Luke 1:68–79). The choir chanted this canticle in complete darkness, recalling the darkness of the tomb. All the music of the day was executed in a mournful and solemn tone, especially the litanies, with their Kyrie Eleisons, at the end of the rite.[72] But at Siena, a foretaste of Easter was added. As the litanies progressed, the candles were relighted, and at the end of the rite the custodian carried a candle to the people, who took tapers and relighted all the lamps of the duomo. On Holy Thursday morning, Siena celebrated a Requiem Mass for the dead.[73]

For pastors of the chapels and pievi, the most important ceremony was the bishop's Thursday-morning Mass at the cathedral, with its blessing of the holy oils, the Chrism Mass.[74] Only a bishop could consecrate the holy oils used to confirm the neophytes on Holy Saturday and anoint the sick throughout the year. Parish priests procured these oils anew each year, and as Bertramo Duramal, custodian of the duomo in Bergamo explained, the archpriests of all baptism churches in the outlying parts of the diocese were obligated (*ex precepto*) to come to the cathedral for the distribution.[75] At Ve-

71. Sicardo, *Mitrale*, 6.10, col. 295.

72. Ibid., 6.11, col. 297.

73. *Ordo Senensis*, 1.138–40, pp. 121–23.

74. On this rite, see Pont. Rom. (XII), 30ᵇ⁻ᶜ, pp. 227–34; *Ordo Senensis*, 1.141–52, pp. 124–34; Sicardo, *Mitrale*, 6.12, cols. 302–3.

75. "Instrumentum Litis" (September 1187), 2.15, p. 150; 7:3, p. 255.

rona, the unity of the clergy and their link with Christ and the apostles were symbolized by having twelve priests flank the bishop during the Canon of the Chrism Mass. There the bishop distributed the oils to the archpriests of baptismal churches at the Communion.[76] For the clergy, Holy Thursday included the greatest festive meal of the year. The gathered clergy enjoyed a banquet with the bishop, recalling Christ's Last Supper. At Bergamo, Pisa, and Siena, the bishop hosted the meal at his palace and invited prominent laymen.[77] During this private event, the bishop fulfilled the *Mandatum*, Christ's command that his disciples wash each other's feet. At Pisa, the archpriest of the duomo did the honors, washing twelve canons' feet while the archbishop watched. At Bergamo, the twelve "apostles" included six priests from the cathedral and six from the collegiate church of Sant'Alessandro.[78] Their meal ended with the bishop's gift of an Easter bonus of 12d. to each of the canons and smaller gifts to the lay domestics.[79] The modern evening Mass of Holy Thursday, with its public washing of parishioners' feet by the parish priest, is probably one of the best-known ceremonies of the contemporary Catholic Church. The parallel medieval Mass of Thursday, uniquely celebrated in the evening, lacked the *Mandatum*. It did have John's story of Christ's action as its Gospel and other peculiarities, such as the omission of the Pax ceremony—because Judas had profaned the kiss of peace in the betrayal of Jesus.[80] But this Mass had little place in the piety of the communes. It was performed principally to consecrate the Host for the bishop's Communion on Good Friday.[81] When the Dominican Giordano of Pisa preached on Holy Thursday, 31 March 1306, he captured the lay experience of the day by preaching on the Jews' journey in the desert. He ignored the rituals of the church.[82]

Along with the day's reconciliation of penitents, Holy Thursday's Vespers, with its stripping of the altars and washing of the church, captured some lay attention. In this ceremony, the sacristans removed the cloths and decorations from the altars of the church. The cathedral clergy then washed the altars and floors with a mixture of wine and water. For Bishop Sicardo, the washing of the floors was the more important, since it reminded observers of Christ's command to wash each other's feet and symbolized the cleansing

76. On these rites at Verona, see *Carpsum*, 256–59 (Verona, Biblioteca Capitolare, MS XCIV, fols. 41ʳ–44ᶠ).

77. For Brescia, see "Instrumentum Litis," 6.25, p. 229, and Valsecchi, *Interrogatus*, 103–5; for Pisa, see Bologna, Biblioteca Universitaria, MS 1785, Rolando the Deacon, *Liber de Ordine Officiorum*, fols. 23ʳ⁻ᵛ; for Siena, see *Ordo Senensis*, 1.149–53, pp. 131–33.

78. As Giovanni Occa, custodian of Sant'Alessandro, explained: "Instrumentum Litis," 6, p. 212; as did others: ibid., 3.28, p. 179; 4, p. 187; 1.6, p. 139.

79. Ibid., 6, p. 229; 7, p. 250.

80. Sicardo, *Mitrale*, 6.12, col. 310C.

81. In churches other than the cathedral, it was the only Mass of the day: Grado Council (1296), 31, p. 1171.

82. Giordano of Pisa, *Quaresimale*, 84, pp. 405–9.

of sin through baptism (water) and the Eucharist (wine).[83] At Siena, the stripping of altars was done with style. Two clerics and the custodian of the duomo came in procession with incense, chanting the Psalter. They stripped the altar of Saint Bartholomew and then the other altars in order, performing the ablutions with wine and water. The turnout for the stripping rite was certainly good at Siena; it included distribution of alms to the city poor. Almsgiving truly "washed the feet of the poor."[84] Bishop Guglielmo della Torre, the early-thirteenth-century bishop of Como, made the connection visible by having a *maior frater* wash twelve paupers' feet during the distribution of alms. All the paupers present got an alms of 1d. along with a free meal—and all had wine with their dinner.[85] In times of want, these distributions could be mobbed. On Holy Thursday at Bologna in 1227, during a famine, Bishop Enrico della Frata had alms and food distributed to the poor. So great was the rush that twenty-four paupers were trampled to death in the frenzy.[86]

No Mass was celebrated on Good Friday, the most somber day of the ecclesiastical year. Rather, Jesus' crucifixion was commemorated by the chanting of Saint John's Passion in a form like that of Palm Sunday. This service included one of the most emotionally charged ceremonies of the medieval Church, the veneration of the cross.[87] In the late Middle Ages, this day occasioned anti-Jewish incidents, and the Fourth Lateran Council did ban Jewish appearances during Holy Week, but disorders seem not yet to have been common in Italy.[88] At least for Christians, this day signaled forgiveness of crime. At Pisa, a commission consisting of four friars and two laymen from each quarter drew up amnesty lists of prisoners to be released. Only the most horrible crimes were excluded from mercy.[89] From morning until the solemn service at None, all kept reverential silence as for a funeral.[90] The actual service of the day began at that hour with the silent entry of the bishop and ministers in red vestments, recalling the blood of Christ shed this

83. Sicardo, *Mitrale*, 6.12, col. 309. For Pisa, see Bologna, Biblioteca Universitaria, MS 1785, Rolando the Deacon, *Liber de Ordine Officiorum*, fol. 21ᵛ.

84. *Ordo Senensis*, 1.152, pp. 132–33.

85. Milan, Biblioteca Trivulziana, MS 1335 (copied 1272), Guglielmo della Torre, *Costituzioni date ai canonici di S. Maria di Torello* (1217), fols. 11ʳ⁻ᵛ.

86. *CCB*: A, 92; B, 92; Vill., 93.

87. For these rites, see Sicardo, *Mitrale*, 6.13, cols. 311–21; *Ordo Senensis*, 1.154–65, pp. 134–45; Verona, Biblioteca Capitolare, MS LXXXIV, fols. 94ᵛ–98ʳ; *Carpsum*, 259–61 (Verona, Biblioteca Capitolare, MS XCIV, fols. 44ʳ–46ʳ). Cf. *Pont. Rom.* (XII), 31.1–12, pp. 234–37.

88. Ferrara Stat. (1287), 4.67, p. 274, enforces the Lateran seclusion of Jews on Good Friday by a fine of £10 fer. For other anti-Jewish legislation, see ibid., 3.42–43, pp. 246–48. Such legislation is lacking in the statutes of Bologna, Parma, and Piacenza. On the condition of Jews in high medieval Italy, see Kenneth R. Stow, *Alienated Minority: The Jews of Medieval Latin Europe* (Cambridge, Mass.: Harvard University Press, 1992), 64–88. Cecil Roth, *The History of the Jews of Italy* (Philadelphia: Jewish Publication Society, 1946), 74–117, remarks on the meager sources for Italy; perhaps publication of documents, such as Ariel Toaff's *Jews in Umbria* (Leiden: Brill, 1992), will yield more information. Prof. Daniel Bornstein has suggested to me that laws are lacking because Jewish settlements in central Italy mostly postdate 1300.

89. Pisa Stat. II (1313), Popolo 50, pp. 492–94; Popolo 144, pp. 594–605.

90. Sicardo, *Mitrale*, 6.13, cols. 312–13.

day. After a prostration and the opening collect came the scriptural readings and a sermon by the bishop. He usually preached on reconciliation and peace, themes that were a suitable preparation for the Easter general Communion that followed in two days.[91]

As three deacons chanted the Passion, other deacons removed two cloths covering a temporary altar below the pulpit—the "altar of the shroud"—and divided them, thus symbolizing the stripping of Christ for his execution and the division of his garments.[92] During Lent a veil blocked the view through the screen to the sanctuary. In some cities, as the story of Christ's crucifixion reached the climax of his death and the deacon chanted the words "the veil of the temple was torn in two," the Lenten veil was dramatically parted, revealing a great cross in the sanctuary. At least one canon of Siena, writing in that church's ordo, thought this rite "beautiful" (pulchre); it saddened him that his city omitted it.[93] The Passion completed, deacons announced intentions for prayer and bid the congregation kneel and pray. After each intention, subdeacons told them to stand for a collect sung by the bishop.[94] The intentions included the needs of the hierarchy and rulers, the conversion of Jews and pagans, and the needs of the various orders of the laity. In most cities, the cross was unveiled at this point, and not by parting the veil blocking the view through the screen, as described above. The usual rite, as at Cremona, had two priests and two deacons leave the choir, carrying a covered cross, and then, as the deacons chanted three times "Behold the wood of the cross," the priests progressively unveiled it. This was the signal to unveil all the crosses in the church and to part the Lenten veil of the choir.[95]

At the final "Behold," the priests raised the cross on high, and the congregation prostrated themselves.[96] This gesture recalled Moses' raising the healing bronze serpent in the desert.[97] At Pisa, the bishop himself went to the high altar and, using a long rod, removed the cloth that covered the crucifix above it. The clergy chanted the "Reproaches," or Improperia, at the end of which the people could come forward to venerate two crosses presented by kneeling priests at the door of the choir.[98] The people prostrated themselves, women before one cross, men before the other, and kissed the wood.[99]

91. As in Bologna, Biblioteca Universitaria, MS 1785, Rolando the Deacon, Liber de Ordine Officiorum, fols. 24ʳ⁻ᵛ, and Ordo Senensis, 1.163, pp. 143.

92. On the altare sindonae, see Sicardo, Mitrale, 6.13, col. 315; Verona, Biblioteca Capitolare, MS LXXXIV, fol. 96r; Parma, Biblioteca Palatina, MS Par. 996, fols. 42ᵛ⁻43ʳ; Ordo Senensis, 1.158, pp. 136–37.

93. Ordo Senensis, 1.162, p. 141.

94. Sicardo, Mitrale, 6.13, col. 317; Ordo Senensis, 1.159, pp. 138–39.

95. As in Volterra: Ordo Officiorum della cattedrale [volterrana], 113 (Volterra MS 222, fol. 43ᵛ).

96. Sicardo, Mitrale, 6.13, cols. 318–19.

97. Verona, Biblioteca Capitolare, MS LXXXIV, fol. 95ᵛ.

98. Bologna, Biblioteca Universitaria, MS 1785, Rolando the Deacon, Liber de Ordine Officiorum, fols. 24ᵛ⁻25ᵛ; as also in Ordo Senensis, 1.160–61, pp. 139–40.

99. For these rites, see Parma, Biblioteca Palatina, MS Par. 996, fol. 47ᵛ; Verona, Biblioteca Capitolare, MS LXXXIV, fol. 97ᵛ; Ordo Officiorum della cattedrale [volterrana], 107–13 (Volterra MS 222, fols. 40ᵛ⁻44ʳ).

Meanwhile, the clergy sang that great hymn of Venantius Fortunatus (530–604), the "Pange Lingua":

> Sing my tongue, the glorious battle
>> Sing the last, the dread affray;
> O'er the cross, the victors' trophy,
>> Sound the high triumphal lay:
> Tell how Christ, the world's Redeemer,
>> As a victim won the day.
>
> Bend thy boughs, O Tree of Glory!
>> Thy relaxing sinews bend;
> For a while the ancient rigor,
>> That thy birth bestowed, suspend;
> And the King of heavenly beauty
>> On thy bosom gently tend![100]

Within the choir, the clergy processed barefooted to kneel and venerate their own cross. Sometimes, as at Siena, the clergy kissed a relic of the True Cross itself.[101] Speaking of this rite around 1200, an anonymous Florentine commentator asked: "Why do we prostrate ourselves before the cross and kiss it? Just as Christ was humiliated and suffered death for us, we also ought to be imitators of his death; so it is fitting that we be humbled. We prostrate ourselves before the one cross so that the humility fixed in our minds be shown by the posture of our bodies."[102] The veneration of the cross, more than any other Holy Week ceremony, expressed the new emphasis on Christ's humanity and compassion typical of thirteenth-century piety. By the 1300s, it had inspired some of the earliest vernacular *laude*.[103] After the veneration, there remained for the clergy a brief ceremony in the choir at which the bishop received the Host consecrated at the evening Mass of Holy Thursday. So that his Communion would be "complete," he also took a sip of unconsecrated wine into which a particle of the Host had been dropped, a ritual that was probably a remnant of the ancient Christian belief that wine could be

---

100. Verses 1 and 9: "Pange lingua gloriosi | proelium certaminis, | et super crucis tropaeo | dic triumphum nobilem, | qualiter redemptor orbis | immolatus vicerit. ‖ Flecte ramos, arbor alta, | tensa laxa viscera, | et rigor lentescat ille | quem dedit nativitas, | ut superni membra regis | miti tendas stipite." English by John Mason Neale (1818–66), perhaps the better of the two common English translations.

101. *Ordo Senensis*, 1.165, p. 145.

102. Florence, Biblioteca Nazionale Centrale, MS Magl. XIV. 49, fols. 60ʳ⁻ᵛ: "Quare dum crux osculanda est prosternimus ante eam? Ideo qui Christus humiliatus est pati pro nobis usque ad mortem si huius mortis imitatore esse debemus. Humiliatos nos esse oportet, unum prosternimus ante crucem ut fixa humilitas mentis per habitum corporis demonstretur."

103. Such as the "Lauda del venerdì santo" from the *Laudario della Confraternita di S. Stefano d'Assisi*, edited in *Poeti minori del trecento*, ed. Nataino Sapegno (Milan: Riccardi, 1952), 1033–50.

consecrated by contract with a piece of the Host.[104] For the laity, Good Friday's rites culminated when they kissed the Lord's holy cross. At the cathedral of Aquileia, they added a suggestive rite unknown in the rest of north Italy, the "burial of Christ" in a replica of Jerusalem's Holy Sepulcher. The bishop carried a consecrated Host and an image of the crucified Christ to the "sepulcher" and sealed them in it. He then incensed the "grave" and departed. There the holy objects would lie, like Christ in the tomb, until Easter morning. On that day, the bishop returned, broke the seal, and showed the risen Christ to the people as the clergy chanted the antiphon "Venite et videte locum ubi positus est Dominus" (Come and see the place where the Lord was laid).[105]

THE EASTER VIGIL

The morning of Holy Saturday continued the somber penitential tone of Good Friday; Christ rested in the tomb.[106] The mournful chants of Tenebrae picked up the theme. At a quiet morning service, priests anointed the infant catechumens with holy oil on the shoulders and chest, the last of the preparatory rites before baptism. This anointing prepared their shoulders to carry the burden of Christ's cross, and that on the chest purified their hearts of evil inclinations.[107] Siena celebrated this rite just before the baptisms at the afternoon vigil.[108] In most churches, the babies' godparents professed baptismal vows for the children at the morning anointing. They vowed to accept the teachings of the Apostles' Creed. They renounced Satan and all his pomps and works. The vows were sevenfold, for Satan's works consisted of the seven capital sins: pride, envy, anger, sloth, avarice, gluttony, and lust. So the infants, vicariously, made the covenant vows of the new people of God. For thirteenth-century Christians, their baptismal rejection of the Devil included a rejection of the seven sins. Whenever medieval Italians prepared to go to confession by examining their consciences according to the seven capital sins, they recalled their seven baptismal promises.[109] After Terce, the clergy decorated the cathedral, dressing the choir, altars, nave, and walls

---

104. On this rite, see *Ordo Senensis*, 1.163–63, pp. 143–44; Parma, Biblioteca Palatina, MS Par. 996, fol. 46ᵛ; San Gimignano, Biblioteca Comunale, MS 3, fol. 47ʳ. Occasionally, the other ministers communicated with the bishop; see Bologna, Biblioteca Universitaria, MS 1785, Rolando the Deacon, *Liber de Ordine Officiorum*, fols. 25ᵛ–26ᵛ. Sicardo, *Mitrale*, 6.13, cols. 319–21, thought that all (*omnes*) should communicate at this service, but he probably meant "all the ministers."

105. Ousterhout, "Church of Santo Stefano," 317–18, suggests (without evidence) that the same rite was performed at Bologna. The Sarum Rite in England had a similar ceremony; see Duffy, *Stripping of the Altars*, 29–37.

106. Such was the theme of the Holy Saturday sermon in Giordano of Pisa, *Quaresimale*, 87, pp. 413–17, preached on 2 April 1306.

107. Sicardo, *Mitrale*, 6.14, col. 322; Florence, Biblioteca Nazionale Centrale, MS Magl. XIV. 49, fols. 58ʳ⁻ᵛ; Florence, Biblioteca Medicea Laurenziana, MS Aed. 214, fol. 47ᵛ: c. 10; *Ordo Officiorum della cattedrale [volterrana]*, 116–17 (Volterra MS 222, fols. 45ʳ–46ʳ).

108. *Ordo Senensis*, 1.176, p. 156.

109. Florence, Biblioteca Medicea Laurenziana, MS Aed. 214, fols. 48ʳ–49ʳ.

with the most precious and sumptuous hangings and adornments. The
Lenten veil was not only taken down but hidden out of sight, said Bishop
Sicardo. The clergy displayed banners and crosses all about and placed Gospel books and reliquaries, especially those resplendent with gold, silver, or
ivory ornamentation, on the altars.[110]

The Lenten fast continued in all its rigor on Holy Saturday; only the sick
and infants were excepted. It would not be broken until after the vigil.[111]
Today all bathed, and men shaved for the first time since the beginning of
Lent;[112] light-colored clothing replaced the somber hues of the fast. The
children's parents and godparents procured festive white garments and decorated candles for use in the ceremonies. Because this afforded an unseemly
opportunity for status competition between families, some communes carefully controlled extravagances.[113] Cities enforced peace pacts and truces with
special rigor during this sacred time.[114] Pisa expected large attendance from
both the city and the countryside, so the podesta dispatched his representatives and officers of the city militia for crowd control at the rites. They ringed
the great baptistery of San Giovanni, not only imposing order but reminding
all that this was simultaneously a civic and religious celebration.[115] To be
prevented from performing the Easter liturgy was among the greatest trage-
dies that might befall the commune, second only to the absence of the bishop
at the rites of the vigil.[116] Saint Ubaldo of Gubbio's last, and perhaps most
pastoral, miracle was to rise from his sickbed to preside at Easter. The people
had come to him in tears, lamenting that they would be deprived of his
presence at the vigil. Unable to resist their pleading, the bishop allowed
himself to be carried to the duomo. There he miraculously recovered his
strength and chanted the Mass with a fine and melodious voice. Only after
the service did he return to bed and, after mediating one last feud, relapse.
He died on the feast of Pentecost.[117] Would that every commune were
blessed with such a conscientious pastor!

The Easter vigil itself commenced at None, in the midafternoon. That
had been its time since at least Carolingian times, and it was suitable because

---

110. Sicardo, *Mitrale*, 6.15, col. 344; *Ordo Senensis*, 1.168, pp. 147–48; *Ordo Officiorum della cattedrale [volter-rana]*, 114 (San Gimignano, Biblioteca Comunale, MS 3, fol. 48ᵛ; Volterra MS 222, fols. 44ʳ⁻ᵛ).

111. *Ordo Officiorum della cattedrale [volterrana]*, 121 (San Gimignano MS 3, fols. 53ʳ⁻ᵛ; Volterra MS 222, fols. 47ᵛ–48ʳ).

112. Sicardo, *Mitrale*, 6.15, col. 344; Verona, Biblioteca Capitolare, MS LXXXIV, fols. 104ᵛ–111ᵛ, esp. fol. 106ʳ. Perhaps this is a remnant of the ancient bath of Holy Thursday or Palm Sunday; on which, see Attilio Carpin, *Il battesimo in Isidoro di Siviglia* (Rome: Gregoriana, 1984), 36–37.

113. E.g., Pisa Stat. I (1286), 3.50, pp. 435–36; Pisa Stat. II (1313), 3.59, p. 352.

114. E.g., Milan, *Gli atti del comune di Milano fino all'anno MCCXVI*, doc. 219 (28 March 1199), pp. 311–12.

115. Pisa Stat. I (1275), p. 48; (1286), 1.154, p. 266.

116. On the vigil, see Sicardo, *Mitrale*, 6.11–13, cols. 296–322; for local rites, see *Ordo Senensis*, 1.166–87, pp. 146–71; Valsecchi, *Interrogatus*, 106–7; *Carpsum*, 262 (Verona, Biblioteca Capitolare, MS XCIV, fols. 46ᵛ–47ʳ). Cf. Pont. Rom. (XII), 32.1–39, pp. 238–49; Pont. Rom. (XIII), App. 2.1–8, pp. 290–91.

117. Giordano of Città di Castello, *Vita Beati Ubaldi Eugubini Episcopi*, 20.1–5, p. 105.

Christ died at that hour and those baptized entered into his death.[118] The urban chapels, even those that enjoyed special exemptions, closed this day as the city clergy attended the vigil baptisms with their congregations.[119] On Holy Thursday, the church had extinguished all lamps and candles save those of the Tenebrae hearse; the vigil began with the kindling of the new fire of Easter. Most commonly, the archpriest struck it from flint and steel in the piazza before the duomo and blessed it. This rite was usually performed without solemnity, but at Modena the archpriest struck the new fire as the clergy chanted a litany of the saints, invoking the seven most important patrons of the city.[120] The people carried tapers, but these were not lighted until later, at the baptisms. People kept the Easter tapers and brought them home to light during storms and times of illness.[121] The vigil service itself was conducted in a darkness recalling that of Christ's tomb and of sin.[122] The archdeacon carrying the new fire led the people into the semidarkness of the cathedral, chanting three times "Lumen Christi"—"The Light of Christ." He then lighted the great towering Easter candle next to the pulpit and ascended to chant the Exultet, the solemn proclamation of Christ's Resurrection. During the Exultet, it was common to fix grains of incense into the candle and anoint it with holy chrism.[123]

At Siena, the new fire was struck in the confessional below the altar of Saint Crescentius. The cathedral clergy, who had gathered in the confessional, chanted None. A deacon took a clump of candles, lest a draft extinguish a single flame, lighted them from the new fire, and carried them along with a lighted wick (*arundinus*) to the bishop at his throne. The bishop blessed the new fire and sprinkled it with holy water. Then the canons, preceded by the cross, led the bishop and the deacon carrying a small Easter candle to the great western doors. There he showed the new fire to the people assembled outside, and all entered the church. The clergy returned to the choir before the high altar of the Blessed Virgin. The deacon lighted the great candle near the pulpit and chanted "Lumen Christi"—"Light of Christ." He then ascended the pulpit to chant the Exultet. The Exultet blessing traced the history of salvation and praised the bees who had produced the wax of which the candle was made. During this long prayer, the clergy came

118. Sicardo, *Mitrale*, 6.14, col. 337; Verona, Biblioteca Capitolare, MS LXXXIV, fol. 103ᵛ; for Carolingian witness to the hour, see Amalarius, *Liber Officialis*, 5.29.1, *Amalarii Episcopi Opera Liturgica Omnia*, ed. Jean Michel Hanssens (Rome: Biblioteca Vaticana, 1948), 1:499.

119. E.g., the exempt church of Santa Vita in Vicenza, whose clergy attended "sicut et alii Capellani nostri": Vicenza Stat., 168 n. 1; document edited in Francesco Barbarano dei Mironi, *Historia ecclesiastica della città, territorio e diocesi di Vicenza* (Vicenza: Cristoforo Rosio, 1649), 1:250.

120. Parma, Biblioteca Palatina, MS Par. 996, 47ʳ⁻ᵛ.

121. On these rites, see Sicardo, *Mitrale*, 6.14, cols. 322–23; "Instrumentum Litis," 1.1, p. 129; *Ordo Officiorum della cattedrale [volterrana]*, 113–26 (Volterra MS 222, fols. 44ʳ–50ᵛ). On the people's keeping the candles, see Sicardo, *Mitrale*, 6.14, col. 325.

122. Florence, Biblioteca Nazionale Centrale, MS Magl. XIV. 49, fols. 60ᵛ–61ʳ.

123. As at Modena; see Parma, Biblioteca Palatina, MS Par. 996, fols. 50ᵛ–51ʳ.

in procession to kiss the candle. No other candle was lighted.[124] At Verona, the fire and candle ceremonies all occurred in the baptistery, where that city's Easter candle was enthroned. There, after the blessings, the procession returned to the cathedral for the readings of the vigil.[125] Elsewhere, the readings simply followed the Exultet. In Bishop Sicardo's Cremona, the number of readings had already been reduced to the later Tridentine norm of four. But in Siena, Modena, Verona, and most probably elsewhere, the vigil preserved the ancient set of twelve readings.[126]

After the responsory to the last reading, cantors intoned the chant "Rex Sanctorum." As this was sung, the congregation and clergy left the cathedral in procession by the west doors and went to the baptistery, usually situated directly outside. The procession circumambulated the baptistery, singing the litany of the saints.[127] They entered the baptistery and stopped the litany at the invocation "Saint John the Baptist, pray for us." To the allegorists, the invoking of the saints during the procession around the baptistery evoked the image of the rainbow both as a glory circling the throne of God in Rev. 4 and as a sign of God's mercy after Noah's flood.[128] When all had assembled in the baptistery, the litany resumed and continued up to the invocation of "All saints of God, pray for us." The bishop then blessed the water of the font. Into it he plunged either a small lighted candle, symbolizing the pillar of fire in the desert of Exodus, or two candles, representing the burning love of God and of neighbor. Using the lighted wick, a cleric then lighted the catechumens' candles.[129] The Womb of the Church was now ready for its fruitful work.

At Siena, the bishop performed the first three baptisms; in most other places, the first two. Having removed his fine vestments, the bishop put on a cheaper set (*viliora paramenta*). He received a boy from his parents and baptized him with the name Giovanni, then a girl from her parents and baptized her with the name Maria. Last, he baptized a boy with the name Pietro. Elsewhere, the first two children were also baptized Giovanni and Maria, the names of Saint John the Baptist and the Blessed Virgin.[130] Baptism was done by a triple immersion, invoking the three persons of the Blessed Trinity.

124. *Ordo Senensis*, 1.166–87, pp. 146–71.

125. See Verona, Biblioteca Capitolare, MS LXXXIV, fol. 97ᵛ; "Instrumentum Litis," 3.28, p. 172.

126. Siena: Sicardo, *Mitrale*, 6.14, col. 228 (his readings were from Gen. 1, Exod. 14, Isa. 4, and Rom. 11); *Ordo Senensis*, 1.174, pp. 153–54. Modena: Parma, Biblioteca Palatina, MS Par. 996, 52ʳ–60ᵛ. Verona: Biblioteca Capitolare, MS LXXXIV, fols. 100ʳ⁻ᵛ; "Instrumentum Litis," 3.28, p. 172.

127. Sicardo, *Mitrale*, 6.14, col. 337; "Instrumentum Litis," 6, p. 213.

128. Florence, Biblioteca Nazionale Centrale, MS Magl. XIV. 49, fol. 63ᵛ; for the extended allegory of these ceremonies, see *Ordo Officiorum della cattedrale [volterrana]*, 117–18 (San Gimignano MS 3, fols. 51ʳ–53ᵛ; Volterra MS 222, fols. 46ʳ–47ʳ).

129. On these blessings, see Sicardo, *Mitrale*, 6.14, cols. 230–32; Verona, Biblioteca Capitolare, MS LXXXIV, fols. 101ʳ–102ʳ; *Ordo Officiorum della cattedrale [volterrana]*, 116 (Volterra MS 222, fol. 45ʳ).

130. *Ordo Senensis*, 1.177–86, pp. 157–68; Parma, Biblioteca Palatina, MS Par. 996, fols. 57ᵛ–58ʳ. For a sermon on such biblical names, see Bartolomeo of Vicenza, *Sermones de Beata Virgine (1266)*, Sermo 61.2, p. 403–4.

The bishop held the infant turned away from him, and first immersed the child while facing east, then while facing north, and finally south, thus forming a cross by the three motions.[131] Before passing the child to the godparents, the baptizer had them repeat the baptismal vows. Using the same ceremony, four delegated priests baptized, assembly-line fashion, the remaining children; the bishop stepped aside to begin the confirmations.

In contrast to the practice in northern Europe, newly baptized Italians immediately received the sacrament of confirmation. If there were adults who for some reason had never been confirmed, they could also receive the sacrament at this time.[132] After baptizing the first two children and handing them to the godparents, the bishop himself anointed them on the forehead with the holy chrism of confirmation. During the four priests' assembly-line baptisms, the baptizing priest merely anointed the crown of the child's head, as a pledge of the confirmation he would soon receive. The godparents then took the newly baptized to the bishop, who, after administering confirmation, gave each child the kiss of peace.[133] The holy anointing of confirmation was protected by a band, popularly known as the "crown" (*corona*), placed around the child's head. It symbolized that the child was now fit to be crowned with the saints in heaven (Rev. 4). Parents did not wash the child's head for the following eight days, lest the chrism be profaned.[134] When the week was over, a priest washed the child's head and gave the bands, after washing them, to the parents.[135] The pious kept this band as a sacred relic, just as new priests kept the cloth used to wipe the oil of ordination from their hands. After the confirmation, one godparent held the child's lighted candle, and the other brought the white garment to be blessed. The family then clothed the child. The white baptismal robe symbolized the good works that were the true garment of every Christian.[136] At Milan, the Ambrosian Rite added a final gesture to the ceremony. Before the newly baptized left the baptistery, the bishop washed the feet of each child.[137]

131. Sicardo, *Mitrale*, 6.14, cols. 332–34; Parma, Biblioteca Palatina, ms Par. 996, fols. 58ʳ⁻ᵛ; *Ordo Senensis*, 1.182, p. 166; Verona, Biblioteca Capitolare, ms LXXXIV, fol. 102ʳ.

132. On confirming infants at Easter, see Florence, Biblioteca Medicea Laurenziana, ms Aed. 214, fols. 53ᵛ–58ʳ; Florence, Biblioteca Nazionale Centrale, ms Magl. XIV. 49, fol. 58ʳ; *Ordo Officiorum della cattedrale [volterrana]*, 122–23 (Volterra ms 222, fols. 48ᵛ–49ʳ; San Gimignano ms 3, fols. 54ʳ–55ʳ). On confirmation of adults at the vigil, see Novara Synod II (1298), 1.2.1.2, pp. 178–79. Cf. Lett, *Enfant*, 112–14, which describes the delay of confirmation in France and England, with their huge dioceses and many baptismal churches.

133. Sicardo, *Mitrale*, 6.12, col. 308; for the formulas of both rites, see ibid., 6.14, col. 334. On chrismation and confirmation at the vigil, see also Verona, Biblioteca Capitolare, ms LXXXIV, fols. 102ʳ⁻ᵛ; Parma, Biblioteca Palatina, ms Par. 996, fol. 58ᵛ; Florence, Biblioteca Medicea Laurenziana, ms Aed. 214, fols. 52ᵛ–53ʳ (treats only chrismation); *Ordo Senensis*, 1.183, p. 167.

134. Sicardo, *Mitrale*, 6.14, col. 334; Verona, Biblioteca Capitolare, ms LXXXIV, fol. 102ᵛ; *Ordo Senensis*, 1.185, p. 169; Parma, Biblioteca Palatina, ms Par. 996, fol. 58ᵛ; Bologna Synod (1310), 489.

135. Jacques of Vitry, *Historia Occidentalis*, 37, p. 202.

136. Sicardo, *Mitrale* 6.14, col. 335; Florence, Biblioteca Medicea Laurenziana, ms Aed. 214, fols. 51ᵛ–52ᵛ.

137. *Manuale Ambrosianum*, 2:209–11.

Although many, if not most, children were privately baptized on account of the danger of death, the numbers baptized at the vigil were sizable. In 1500, when the city of Pisa had a lower population than in the communal period, the number of baptisms a year averaged about 1,155.[138] If only the babies born in Holy Week were baptized at the vigil (the later Tridentine rule), that meant a minimum of twenty baptisms. This number is certainly too small; the total of all the babies born in Lent, about a hundred, seems most likely. And Pisa was far smaller than Florence, Bologna, or Milan. The great communal baptisteries, with their large fonts allowing for simultaneous immersions, had ample space for the crowds. The assembly line must have worked, with only occasional confusion or mix-up.

When the priests had finished baptizing, cantors again intoned the litany, and all circumambulated the baptistery three times. As the bells pealed for the first time since Holy Thursday, this procession entered the cathedral by the great doors. After the clergy had lit all the candles and lamps, Easter Mass began with the singing of the Gloria.[139] The great bells pealed through-out this hymn; in Pisa, this gave the signal for the custodians of all the city churches to ring their church bells.[140] In many cities, the newly baptized infants received Communion at this Mass, thus completing their incorpora-tion into the Church.[141] Bishop Sicardo did not approve of this practice. In his opinion, the shortness of the vigil Mass, with its exceedingly brief Vespers service, was a concession to the fussy little neophytes. They were ready to go home for their evening feeding; it would not do to delay this by Commu-nions. Indeed, it would prove difficult to convince mothers not to breast-feed their cranky infants and so not break their Eucharistic fast. At Cremona, the newly baptized received their first Communion, their "rights," along with all the other citizens at the Mass of Easter Sunday morning.[142] Before the disappearance of Communion from the chalice in the early 1100s, infants received a drop of the Precious Blood from the priest's finger; in the later communal period, their Communion would have been a very tiny fragment of the Host. In the fourteenth century, anxiety over children's spitting out the Blessed Sacrament led to a decline in the practice of baptismal Commu-nion, although it was not officially abolished until the Council of Trent.[143] In Pisa, the vigil ended with a second festive singing of the Gloria. The clergy

138. M. Luzzati, "Primi dati sulla distribuzione della popolazione nelle parrocchie e nei sobborghi di Pisa fra 1457 e 1509 in base agli elenchi battesimali," *Pievi e parrocchie*, ed. Erba et al., 2:833–35.

139. On this Mass, see Sicardo, *Mitrale*, 6.14, col. 337.

140. *Ordo Senensis*, 1.186, pp. 169–70; Verona, Biblioteca Capitolare, MS LXXXIV, fol. 103ᵛ; Bologna, Biblioteca Universitaria, MS 1785, Rolando the Deacon, *Liber de Ordine Officiorum*, fol. 28ʳ.

141. Verona, Biblioteca Capitolare, MS LXXXIV, fol. 102ʳ; *Ordo Officiorum della cattedrale [volterrana]*, 124–25 (Volterra MS 222, fols. 50ʳ⁻ᵛ; San Gimignano MS 3, fols. 55ʳ⁻ᵛ); Mantua, Biblioteca Comunale Cen-trale Teresiana, MS 331, fol. 38ʳ; but cf. Sicardo, *Mitrale*, 6.14, col. 310C.

142. Sicardo, *Mitrale*, 6.14, col. 340.

143. On infant Communion in Milan up to Trent, see Fisher, *Christian Initiation*, 106–7.

then went in procession to purify the canons' dormitory by sprinkling the rooms with the new Easter water.[144]

Easter morning brought special adaptions to the liturgy, calling attention to the unique status of the day. From this day until Pentecost, seven weeks later, the night Office of Matins consisted of only three psalms and three short readings—a welcome respite after the interminable Vigils of Lent. On this morning, many churches added a Gloria Patri to each of the three responsories, in thanksgiving for the gift of baptism. In Bishop Sicardo's Cremona and elsewhere in north Italy, the Easter-morning Office concluded with a dramatization of the apostles' visit to the empty tomb. After the last responsory, a group in costume, representing Saint John, Saint Peter, and the holy women, entered the nave, where an image of Christ's empty tomb was displayed. A choir dressed as angels met them. The two groups sang a responsory, rehearsing the dialogue between the women and the angels. It ended with the proclamation: "Jesus, whom you seek, is not here; he is risen!" The "apostles" then intoned the Te Deum. Other churches performed this little rite before Matins—a practice Bishop Sicardo disliked because it did not put the Te Deum in its proper place at the end of Matins. Sicardo began Matins by having a priest incense the cross venerated on Good Friday, sprinkle it with holy water, and place it on the high altar. The priest then proclaimed three times that Christ was risen from the dead, to which the choir responded, "Deo gratias."[145]

A dramatic rite embellished the singing of the Matins' Gospel. Three precious cloths covered the high altar. The outer cover was black, the next off-white, and the last flaming red. As a deacon chanted the Gospel, ministers removed each of these veils, symbolically presenting salvation history's ages of nature, law, and grace. The red of the last veil was the fire of the holy grace-giving Spirit.[146] Later, during Prime, a procession, led by crosses and banners showing the resurrected Christ, left the cathedral. The canons, clothed in white albs, followed in procession throughout the city, sprinkling Easter baptismal water and chanting hymns in honor of the Resurrection. Sicardo said the people of the neighborhoods crowded to greet the procession.[147] When it returned to the duomo, the day Mass began. Verona, too, called attention to the solemn day Mass of Easter by having the bishop vest elsewhere and enter the duomo in procession with all his clergy, singing the antiphon "Salve Festa Dies."[148] At Siena, the Mass underlined the universal

144. Bologna, Biblioteca Universitaria, MS 1785, Rolando the Deacon, *Liber de Ordine Officiorum*, fol. 28ᵛ.

145. On these rites, see Sicardo, *Mitrale*, 6.15, col. 345–46.

146. Ibid., col. 344. The colors used in this rite are reminiscent of those of the three steps described by Dante in *Purgatorio*, 9:94–102, although the order is different. Perhaps Dante's order represents the practice in Florence.

147. Sicardo, *Mitrale*, 6.15, cols. 346–47.

148. *Carpsum*, 263 (Verona, Biblioteca Capitolare, MS XCIV, fol. 47ʳ).

effects of the Resurrection by a special chanting of the Gospel. Three deacons mounted Giovanni Pisano's pulpit. The first declaimed the opening verse of the Gospel in Hebrew, the next the second verse in Greek, and the third chanted his verse in Latin. The choir then chanted the rest of the Gospel, accompanied by the great organ.[149] At the end of the Mass, the bishop blessed lambs to be prepared for the Easter dinner.[150]

For the citizenry, these rites were secondary to the general Communion at the people's Mass that followed Prime. Even before the Lateran Council made the Easter Communion the sole obligatory Communion of the year, Easter was already the greatest of the three general Communions. The Sienese ordo (just before the council) described how, at morning Mass, sacristans in every church of the city filled ciboria with sufficient Hosts to communicate all those expected. They were to communicate worthily. Conscientious preachers, like the Dominican Bartolomeo of Vicenza, kept the need for confession before Easter Communion ever in the ears of their hearers.[151] Before the Communion itself, the celebrating priest warned sinners against profaning the Sacrament by irreligious Communion. He excluded from Communion those guilty of usury, withholding tithes, public crimes, and "harboring hate in their hearts toward their neighbors." While some of these sins might have demanded public penance, the last was known only to the individual. The priest warned those who fomented discord in the community that they could not approach the Sacrament without confession and restoration of harmony. If any parishioners were known troublemakers, the priest was to prevent their Communions "willy-nilly" and stop the service until a reconciliation had been achieved.[152] Sins against church, city, and neighbor profaned this rite, but abstaining from Communion was antisocial, if not heretical. Excluding the outcast sinners, all people approached the altar, and all received the Lord. The Easter Communion was, above all, a sacrament of the community's unity and identity. Not only Sicardo's desire for convenience urged moving the children's Communion from the vigil to Easter day. The newly baptized who received Communion at this Mass so demonstrated their full incorporation into the community of the city.[153] The children were now fully citizens and neighbors.[154]

Special observances prolonged Easter festivities. Easter Monday and

---

149. *Ordo Senensis*, 1.197, p. 181.

150. See Sicardo, *Mitrale*, 6.15, col. 350, for the blessing; for the menu of dinner, see *Ordo Senensis*, 1.198, p. 183.

151. E.g., Bartolomeo of Vicenza, *Sermones de Beata Virgine (1266)*, Sermo 55.6, p. 369.

152. *Ordo Senensis*, 1.194, pp. 177–78.

153. Although some churches did communicate the babies on Saturday: see, e.g., *Ordo Officiorum della cattedrale [volterrana]*, 127 (Volterra MS 222, fol. 51r; San Gimignano MS 3, fol. 58r).

154. Lett, *Enfant*, III, notes that Lateran IV, c. 21, which required children over the age of "reason" to receive Communion at Easter, triggered legislation in France that forbade giving Communion to those younger. I find no such prohibitions in Italian synods. Italian priests' rituals include Communion even at private baptisms of children: e.g., *Manuale Ambrosianum*, 1:143–47.

Tuesday were holidays, not to be profaned by secular work or business, a hiatus in the city that lasted until the following Sunday. But in the country-side, agricultural labor resumed on Wednesday, "since rural labor is more necessary."[155] The clergy urged the laity to pray standing during the Easter season, to symbolize Christ rising from the dead.[156] But the kneelers per-sisted; we can be sure of that. Throughout Easter week, the Pisans had a daily procession around the baptistery of San Giovanni before the solemn Mass at the duomo. At Cremona, processions took place after the chanting of the Magnificat at Vespers. During the procession, they chanted the psalm "Laudate, Pueri, Dominum" (Praise the Lord, you children) when they reached the font, to commemorate Saturday's infant baptisms. The proces-sion went then to the oratory of Sant'Andrea, chanting "In Exitu Israel de Egypto," linking baptism's cleansing power to the Israelites' liberation from bondage in Egypt.[157] At Siena, Volterra, and San Gimignano, godparents carried the white-robed newly baptized and their lighted baptismal candles during the Vespers processions. The children came first, right after the cross.[158] Not all cities had Easter processions. Verona lacked them, but the bishop celebrated stational Masses in two different churches on each day of the week. His presence spread the joy of Easter through the neighbor-hoods.[159] On the Sunday ending Easter week, neophytes removed their white robes and chrismation bands. As Christian infants, they remained under the particular care of the Virgin Mother Mary. One fourteenth-century Italian recalled the Virgin's special protection in one verse of a long poem celebrat-ing Mary and Jesus. He invoked her help for the newly baptized:

> Those receiving blessed baptism
>   clothed in white,
> let them be blessed,
>   so innocent in the state of grace;
> let us who rightly bear his name,
>   have your Son from whom we are called,
> lest the deceit of the Devil
>   draw those bearing it into sin.[160]

155. Sicardo, *Mitrale*, 6.15, col. 355: "autem licet viris ruralia opera exercere . . . quia ruralia magis sunt necessaria."

156. They seem to have had little success convincing the laity not to kneel. Sicardo was satisfied, however, that there was no genuflection during the opening Collect of the Mass: ibid., col. 351.

157. For Pisa, see Bologna, Biblioteca Universitaria, ms 1785, Rolando the Deacon, *Liber de Ordine Officiorum*, fol. 29v; for the north, Sicardo, *Mitrale*, 6.15, cols. 350–51.

158. *Ordo Senensis*, 1.201, p. 187; *Ordo Officiorum della cattedrale [volterrana]*, 130 (Volterra ms 222, fols. 52ᵛ–53ʳ; San Gimignano ms 3, fols. 61ᵛ–62ᵛ). Similar ceremonies occurred during Pentecost week: *Ordo Senensis*, 1.249, p. 238.

159. *Carpsum*, 263–65 (Verona, Biblioteca Capitolare, ms xciv, fols. 47ᵛ–49ʳ); similar stational Masses occurred on Sundays, Tuesdays, Wednesdays, and Thursdays of Lent: *Orazionale*, 111–12.

160. Bologna, Biblioteca Universitaria, ms 1563 (xiv cent.), fol. 17ᵛ: "Suscipientes baptismum beatum albis amicti, | sic innocentes per gracie statum fiant benedicti; | nomen habentes iuste tuum natum quo sumus dicti, | quos deferentes trahit in peccatum fraus maledicti."

Everyone danced. At Cremona, even staid Bishop Sicardo—with some misgiving—danced in the cloister with his canons. Their traditional dance had a cosmic dimension and perhaps, he admitted, a pagan origin. It once imitated the movements of the heavenly bodies, but the good bishop assured readers that it now commemorated the dance of Miriam and that of David before the Ark of the Covenant.[161] Sicardo's canons shared in the lay practice of the *Ludus Paschalis* (the "Easter Game") by playing practical jokes on each other. They missed out on the more rambunctious lay fun. Throughout the Veronese contado, Easter Monday was a day for role reversal: wives got to beat their husbands. But the men got their turn on Wednesday![162] The games and dances passed, but, at least liturgically, the city wore its white baptismal garb and lit extra candles for all fifty days until Pentecost. On the eve of that feast, the vigil duplicated Easter and included baptism for babies born in the Paschal season.[163] On that day, at Mass after the Credo, the deacon solemnly announced the dates of the Apostles' Fast; at the dismissal, he chanted the "Ite Missa Est" with alleluias for the last time.[164] Easter was over.

LEARNING THE FAITH

In 1201, Pope Innocent III wrote to the parish priest of San Gavino in Florence about the duties of a pastor. At their head was preaching to the people.[165] In 1211, the synod of Milan required the priest of every chapel to preach to his people every Sunday.[166] Canon lawyers like Enrico of Susa (Hostiensis) also beat the drum for regular preaching.[167] Physical evidence for preaching is mostly lost—great stone pulpits like those in the cathedrals of Siena or Modena were for liturgical proclamation of the Gospel rather than for preaching. The preaching pulpit stood on the north side of the nave, halfway down, so that the preacher could be heard by all.[168] Weekday preaching in the chapels was probably rare. Saint Giacomo Salomone's biographer thought it exceptional that this priest gave a short reflection on each day's saint or feast at Mass.[169] But then Giacomo was a member of the Order of Preachers. His Servite confrere, Saint Francesco Patrizzi, used to

---

161. Sicardo, *Mitrale*, 6.15, cols. 351–52.

162. Verona, Biblioteca Capitolare, MS LXXXIV, fol. 108ᵛ.

163. On the Pentecost vigil, see Sicardo, *Mitrale*, 7.10, cols. 375–76; *Ordo Senensis*, 1.241–43, pp. 229–31; Parma, Biblioteca Palatina, MS Par. 996, fols. 69ʳ–71ʳ; Bologna, Biblioteca Universitaria, MS 1785, Rolando the Deacon, *Liber de Ordine Officiorum*, fols. 33ᵛ–34ʳ; *Ordo Officiorum della cattedrale [volterrana]*, 146–47 (Volterra MS 222, fols. 60ᵛ–61ʳ). Pentecost was the occasion of one of the earliest Italian mystery plays, that at Forlì in 1298, described by an eyewitness in *Annales Foroiuliensis*, 208.

164. Bologna, Biblioteca Universitaria, MS 1785, Rolando the Deacon, *Liber de Ordine Officiorum*, fols. 34ᵛ–35ʳ.

165. *PL* 216:1256–57; and see, on this text, Michele Maccarrone, "'Cura animarum' e 'parochialis sacerdos' nelle costituzioni del IV Concilio Lateranense (1215): Applicazioni in Italia nel sec. XIII," *Pievi e parrocchie*, ed. Erba et al., 1:115.

166. On this legislation, see Maccarrone, "Cura animarum," 91.

167. Hostiensis (Enrico of Susa), *Summa Aurea* (Venice: Sessa, 1570), fols. 314ᵛᵇ–315ʳᵃ.

168. Sicardo, *Mitrale*, 1.4, cols. 21–22.

169. *Vita [Beati Jacobi Veneti Ordinis Praedicatorum]*, 2.15, p. 457.

preach at daily Mass "without any preparation."[170] He would get his superi-
or's blessing and recite the Ave Maria all the way to church. He invoked
God's help as he entered the pulpit. If Cristoforo of Parma is to be believed,
Francesco's sermons were "glorious." Francesco himself used to say, "Not
paper but love teaches theology."[171] But by Saint Francesco's time, in the
late 1200s, things had changed since the days of Bishop Sicardo, who spoke
of preaching only when treating the duties of a bishop.[172]

Busy city leaders considered themselves exempt from attending sermons.[173] Indeed, the ordinary Italian faithful were known for avoiding sermons, if the criticisms of moralizing preachers can be taken at face value.[174]
On the other hand, if we believe the hagiographers, the lay saints of the
communes were avid sermon-goers. Omobono was widely known for his
love of sermons, as well as his love for the poor.[175] Lucchese of Poggibonsi
happily heard the Office each day, and any preaching that might follow.[176]
Saint Ranieri of Pisa supposedly loved sermons, but the only actual sermon
mentioned in his vita was one by Bishop Fulcher of Chartres during the
pilgrim saint's journey to the Holy Land.[177] Serious preaching, a "solemn
sermon," was expected not of the parish clergy but of professionals, the
religious. Pope Innocent IV reminded the Dominicans and Franciscans of
Paris in the mid-1200s that just as parish priests had the task of celebrating
Mass for the people on Sundays, so it was the friars' duty to preach to
them.[178] In saints' lives, descriptions of preaching usually involve "solemn
sermons" by mendicants, the kind of preaching that the Dominican Giordano of Pisa called the "food of the soul."[179] In sermons, Jesus came knocking at the door of the soul.[180] Giordano could fill the piazza in front of Santa
Maria Novella in Florence with hearers twice in a single day.[181] Giordano's
were bravura performances, not routine preaching on elementary morals or
doctrine. Even the pious had to be reminded occasionally that they should
attend sermons. Margherita of Cortona intended to spend the feast of Saint
Thomas the Apostle begging for the poor. Jesus appeared to her in a vision
and recommended that she go to church and hear a sermon instead. She

170. Cristoforo of Parma, *Legenda Beati Francisci*, 10, p. 178.

171. Ibid.: "Non charta sed charitas docet theologiam."

172. E.g., Sicardo, *Mitrale*, 3.4, col. 112C.

173. Pisa Stat. II (1313), 3.92, p. 382, forbade clerical attempts to force city officials to attend sermons.

174. Murray, "Piety and Impiety in Thirteenth-Century Italy," 93–95.

175. *Vita di s. Omobono*, 164–65.

176. *Vita Sancti Lucensis Confessoris*, 454.

177. Benincasa of Pisa, *Vita [S. Raynerii Pisani]*, 2.26, p. 351.

178. Innocent IV, in *Chartularium Universitatis Parisiensis*, ed. Heinrich Denifle (1891; rpt., Brussels: Culture et Civilisation, 1964), 1:268; on this text, see Maccarrone, "Cura Animarum," 126.

179. Giordano of Pisa, *Quaresimale*, 10, p. 51.

180. See Zelina Zafarana, "Cura pastorale, predicazione, aspetti devozionali nella parrocchia del basso Medioevo," *Pievi e parrocchie*, ed. Erba et al., 1:469 n. 8, on this trope in Florence, Biblioteca Medicea Laurenziana, MS Pl. XXXIII Sin. 1, fol. 46ᵛ.

181. See Giordano of Pisa, *Quaresimale*, pp. 368–418.

heard preaching on "Sundays and major feasts," but Jesus did not think that enough.[182] Most churches probably had a preacher like Margherita's, who gave a paraphrase or reflection on the Gospel each Sunday.[183] Perhaps she did not go on other days because the weekly fare tended to be somewhat repetitive. Diocesan statutes directed the clergy to preach regularly on the twelve articles of the Apostles' Creed, the Ten Commandments, and the seven deadly sins—a routine that probably became stale in short order.

Repetition is the mother of memory, and so perhaps it had catechetical effect. Nevertheless, most catechesis of communal Catholics occurred not from the pulpit but in the home. All the newly baptized became the godchildren of those who received them from the font. Godparenthood had religious responsibilities, although from the lay point of view its primary utility was the creation of yet another web of social and familial alliances.[184] I emphasize the religious role here. When Bartolomeo of Vicenza preached on the Presentation of Jesus in the Temple, he paralleled the holy couple, Mary and Joseph, offering their two doves in the temple, with godparents. The two godparents presented a holy child, the newly baptized, in the temple, the Mother Church, and, by their profession of the child's baptismal vows, offered a Christian version of the two doves. In the vows, they renounced Satan and accepted the faith of the Creed, which they had to teach to their godchild.[185] The Sienese church expected godparents to know the Pater Noster in Latin, or at least in Italian, since they had to teach it to the godchild. Anyone who could not recite this prayer was not a true Christian.[186] In theory, the parish priest carefully examined godparents-to-be before allowing them to serve. Florentine synodal law acknowledged the importance of this task when, in limiting the multiplication of godparents to three, it stipulated that there be two godfathers for each boy and two godmothers for each girl. Males had to teach males, and females had to teach females—without a backup, one death could rob the child of proper religious education.[187] Everyone admitted that a heretical godparent (God forbid!) did not invalidate the power of the sacrament.[188] But heresy or ignorance ren-

182. Giunta Bevegnati, *Legenda . . . Margaritae de Cortona*, 2.1e, pp. 191–92.

183. See Maccarrone, "Cura animarum," 124, on the practice of paraphrasing the readings in the vernacular. I suspect most Italians could say of their parish priest what some Englishmen told Bishop Walter of Exeter, England, in the early 1300s: "He preaches in his own way"; quoted in Zafarana, "Cura pastorale," 503.

184. For the social (and religious) functions of godparenthood, see Joseph H. Lynch, *Godparents and Kinship in Early Medieval Europe* (Princeton: Princeton University Press, 1986), and, closer to our period, Christiane Klapisch-Zuber, "Parrains et filleuls: Une approche comparée de la France, l'Angleterre et l'Italie médiévales," *Medieval Prosopography* 6:2 (1985): 51–77.

185. Bartolomeo of Vicenza, *Sermones de Beata Virgine (1266)*, Sermo 107.3, p. 709.

186. *Ordo Senensis*, 1.184, p. 167.

187. See Sicardo, *Mitrale*, 6.14, col. 335; on the duties of godparents, see Richard Trexler, *Synodal Law in Florence and Fiesole, 1306–518* (Vatican City: Biblioteca Vaticana, 1971), 67–68, and Lett, *Enfant*, 228. In the postcommunal period, this concern seems to have disappeared. Aquileia Constitutiones (1339), 12, p. 1120A, limited each child to one godparent.

188. E.g., Florence, Biblioteca Nazionale Centrale, MS Magl. XIV. 49, fol. 64.

dered godparents incapable of fulfilling their office. Synodal legislation on ignorant godparents multiplied after 1300. Perhaps this merely acknowledged the universal tendency of parents to choose godparents because of respect or affection rather than theological literacy.[189] Saint Margherita of Cortona refused to stand as a godmother, because she found the obligation to provide education incompatible with her status as a penitent.[190] Pietro Pettinaio of Siena, living in the world, was very diligent in these duties. When his wife died, she asked him to take care of a woman with whom she was "co-mother." In medieval jargon, a godmother was "co-mother" with the natural mother. Pietro not only took over the spiritual formation of his wife's godson but provided materially for his mother. Eventually, he arranged for the boy's apprenticeship to a tailor.[191]

Pietro was an exceptionally conscientious foster godparent. Spiritual formation of children normally fell to their parents.[192] When Saint Venturino of Bergamo's biographer attempts to account for his precocious piety, he traces it to the boy's imitation of his parents in their devotions, especially in their frequent attendance at Mass and preaching.[193] Mothers certainly played a greater role in religious education than fathers. Although our knowledge of home life in communal Italy is very dim, it seems that at least some mothers took this responsibility seriously. The preacher Jacques of Vitry, remarking on parents' responsibility to teach their children the Pater Noster, Ave Maria, and Credo, spoke glowingly of the warmth and diligence with which mothers taught their children the "Mother's Prayer," the Ave.[194] He compared such mothers to Queen Blanche of Castile, who personally taught her son, Saint Louis of France, his Pater and Ave. Hagiography and art provided the child-care manuals of the High Middle Ages. Mothers could see themselves in the ubiquitous icons of Saint Anne teaching the Blessed Virgin to read her Psalter.[195] Mothers knew their responsibility, even if they discharged it imperfectly. And they were probably better at it than stereotypes suggest. In the inquisition registers of Jacques Fornier, bishop of Palmiers and later pope, illiterate peasants, as often as not, knew the three essential prayers, the Pater, Ave, and Credo. Their mothers had usually been the teachers.[196]

189. On this, see Zafarana, "Cura pastorale," 508.

190. Giunta Bevegnati, Legenda . . . Margaritae de Cortona, 2.10, p. 207.

191. Pietro of Monterone, Vita del beato Pietro Pettinajo, 1, p. 10.

192. So concludes Klapisch-Zuber, "Parrains et filleuls," regarding Italy, as well as France and England; on France, see also Lett, Enfant, 231–32.

193. Legenda Beati Fratris Venturini Ordinis Praedicatorum, 40.

194. Danièle Alexandre-Bidon, "Des femmes de bonne foi: La religion des mères au Moyen Âge," La religion de ma mère: Les femmes et la transmission de la foi, ed. Jean Delumeau (Paris: Cerf, 1992), 94. Now that the idea that premodern parents were indifferent to the physical life of their children has been exploded (e.g., Lett, "Le sentiment de l'enfance," Enfant, 144–49), their spiritual indifference should likewise be rejected.

195. See Lett, "Le sentiment de l'enfance," Enfant, 155–56; Alexandre-Bidon, "Des femmes," 92.

196. Nicole Bériou, "Femmes et prédicateurs: La transmission de la foi aux XIIe et XIIIe siècles," Religion de ma mère, ed. Delumeau, 60.

With their higher literacy rate and more formed religious society, the mothers of communal Italy would have scored higher, had Jacques queried them. Saint Galgano's mother suffered greatly from her perceived failure to form her son in religion and curb his wilder instincts.[197] That Saint Michael the Archangel supplied some help was unusual, but her conscientiousness was more universal. Saint Raimondo of Piacenza's mother, who apprenticed him out to a trade rather than have him taught to read, did teach him the three essential prayers.[198] Imparting this minimum was certainly not an insurmountable task. Italian was close enough to Latin so that regular repetition of the essential prayers within the child's hearing, in church and at home, could imprint them on the memory.[199] After the Lateran Council of 1215, all Christians approaching confession for a general Communion had to recite the Pater, the Ave, and the Credo, at least in the vernacular.[200] But learning by osmosis favored learning the prayers in the normative language, Latin. All three prayers were liturgical. The priest sang the Pater Noster at every Mass. The Ave and the Credo had their place at the beginning of every hour of the Office. When the average Italian recited the Credo, he, like Saint Giovanni Buono, knew the "Faith of the Roman Church," not as the catechetical Apostles' Creed, but as the liturgical Nicene Creed.[201] That was the creed people heard sung (to a simple and memorable tune) every Sunday.

Letters in thirteenth-century Italy were no monopoly of the clergy; lay theologians like Albertano of Brescia wrote sermons and discussed theology in a nonclerical environment. Thirteenth-century Italian Bibles occasionally included catechetical appendixes adapted to lay needs, such as expositions of the Creed.[202] These expositions focused on the topics attacked by heretics, such as the authority of the Church and the real presence in the Mass. Theology, like prayers, could also be learned by osmosis. Saint Raimondo of Piacenza, while a young shoemaker and still illiterate, sought out other spiritually minded laborers for theological conversation on feast days. When word of this got around, other laypeople gathered in his shop for pious conversation during free time. The discussions became so popular, and Raimondo's spiritual understanding so well known, that people asked him to give little spiritual talks (*conciones*) in his shop. Raimondo humbly refused, saying that this was the office of priests and doctors of theology. But the lay study group continued to meet. It was certainly not the only one in communal Italy.[203] I belabor this point since too sharp a distinction is often made between a "literate" piety of the clergy and the "popular" piety of the laity.[204]

---

197. *Vita Sancti Galgani*, 1, p. 188.
198. Rufino of Piacenza, *Vita et Miracula B. Raymundi*, 1.6, p. 646.
199. On such learning of prayers by osmosis, see Zafarana, "Cura pastorale," 511–12.
200. Lett, *Enfant*, 110.
201. *Processus . . . B. Joannis Boni*, 4.6.307, p. 849.
202. E.g., Pisa, Biblioteca Cateriniana del Seminario Arcivescovile, MS 177 (XIV cent.), fols. 3ʳ–6ʳ.
203. Rufino of Piacenza, *Vita et Miracula B. Raymundi*, 5.19–20 [i.e., 2.19–20], pp. 648–49.
204. *Pace* Cinzio Violante, "Sistemi organizzativi della cura d'anime in Italia tra Medioevo e Rinascimento: Discorso introduttivo," *Pievi e parrocchie*, ed. Erba et al., 1:29, who thinks the piety of the urban faithful was "parecchio diversa da quella ufficiale," meaning that represented by synodal legislation.

Before the Lateran Council, synods and bishops had drawn up outlines for a catechetical program adapted to lay needs. It highlighted the three prayers and a rudimentary moral theology based on the seven capital sins, the Ten Commandments, and the seven sacraments.[205] We do not have any examples of routine catechetical preaching by parish priests; whether mothers or godparents used such a program with their children and godchildren is hard to say. Nonetheless, by the late communal period, the program was familiar to some, perhaps many, of the laity. In the late 1200s, a wealthy Pisan or Luchesan commissioned a sumptuous manuscript of vernacular texts on moral and religious themes.[206] The most important of these was *Lo libro de l'amore et de la dilectione di Dio et del proximo,* a work by Albertano of Brescia translated into Italian. Along with Albertano, the translator included works by Seneca and stories of the Roman emperors. He included purely devotional items, too, such as the hymn "Ave Verum Incarnatum." This was pretty much standard fare. More important, he included an outline course in religious education, perhaps of his own devising. It began with a short summary of the Ten Commandments, which not only translated them into the vernacular but also briefly explained their meaning. Of the first commandment he wrote: "One commandment consists in this: You shall have only one God, who is creator and maker of all things, and you shall love and fear and serve him above all things."[207] He then rehearsed the twelve articles of the Apostles' Creed, translating them and identifying the apostle who, according to legend, had composed each. The program ended with a series of lists: the seven sacraments, the seven gifts of the Holy Spirit, the seven virtues, the seven capital sins, and the fourteen spiritual and temporal works of mercy. The compiler effectively produced, in the vernacular, an outline of the catechetical program found in the thirteenth-century pastoral treatises by clerics. It does seem that the program had become standardized and known.

By the fourteenth century, at the end of the communal period, vernacular versions of this catechetical outline became very common in manuscripts. They show some variety. One compiler, for example, included translations of the Gospels of the Church year, along with the articles of the Creed, the sacraments, the theological and cardinal virtues, the capital sins, the Ten Commandments, and the gifts of the Holy Spirit.[208] Did any parents and godparents use this kind of outline for their children and godchildren? And

205. Leonard Boyle, *Pastoral Care, Clerical Education, and Canon Law* (London: Variorum, 1981), 19–32.

206. Florence, Biblioteca Nazionale Centrale, MS II.IV.111 (XIII cent.), esp. fols. 74ʳ–75ʳ (the morals section). On this manuscript, see Michele Barbi, "D'un antico codice pisano lucchese di trattati morali," *Raccolta di studii critici dedicata ad Alessandro d'Ancona* (Florence: Barbèra, 1901), 241–59.

207. Florence, Biblioteca Nazionale Centrale, MS II.IV.111, fol. 74ʳᵃ: "Et in cio ee luno comandamento: Non auerai se non uno dio. Lo quale ee creatore et fattore di tutte le cose et lui amerai et temerai et seruirai sopra tutte le cose."

208. Florence, Biblioteca Nazionale Centrale, MS Palat. 4 (XIV cent.): the Gospels on fols. 1ʳ–50ʳ, catechetical materials on fol. 75ᵛ.

if so, was the practice common? One fourteenth-century pamphlet bound into a miscellany that once belonged to the Bolognese pope Benedict XIV suggests that, at least occasionally, godparents used such aids.[209] The pamphlet, entitled *Catacumina*, was composed by a godfather for future use by his godson. The man had a little theological training; perhaps he was a lawyer. The work consists of a treatise in the vernacular on the Nicene Creed, that sung at Mass. He introduces his work in this way: "It is written in the *Decretum*, De Cons. D. 4 c. 105, that the godparent, that is, he who receives another at baptism, is bound to explain the faith to the one baptized. And since you, my son, were not baptized by people who are going to teach you much, and I perhaps will not be around at the time when you are ready, you may confirm yourself in the faith into which you were baptized by reading this 'Catacumina,' that is, explanation of the faith."[210] This godparent was not only mindful of his duties, he was well informed. He quoted suitable scriptural authorities for his propositions and elaborated his points by citing Gratian, Thomas Aquinas, and Augustine. For example, of the Creed article "and in one holy catholic and apostolic Church" he writes: "The Catholic Church is the whole of all faithful Christians. Holy Scripture says that the apostles and disciples and those who believed in Christ were of one heart, one soul, and one will."[211] The quotation from Acts 5:32 may not be letter perfect, but the author's point was clear. Were there many other careful and learned lay catechists? Perhaps not in the early 1200s. But they certainly became more common as the communal period drew to its close and literacy spread.

209. Bologna, Biblioteca Universitaria, MS 158 (XIV cent.), fols. 47ᵛ–50ᵛ.
210. Ibid., fol. 47ᵛ: "Scrivesi nel Decreto de Consecratione, distinctione quarta, capitolo *Vos ante omnia* et cetera, che el santolo cioe colui che tene altri a baptismo e tenuto a mostare al baptismato la fede. Et perche tu figliuolo no se baptizato da persone intendenti che ti sapesseno de rozare e forse io non siro al tempo che tu asai intendimento perfetto. Acio che tu legendo ti confirmi in fede, ne la quale tu se batizato leggi questa Catacumina, cioe digrossatione de fede."
211. Ibid., fol. 50ᵛ: "La catholica chiesa e la universita dei fedeli cristiani. Dice la sancta scriptura che degli apostoli discipuli e da quelli che in Cristo credero era una core e una anima e uno desiderio."

Chapter Nine
Good Catholics at Prayer

Thirteenth-century Italians worshiped in a world of sacred spaces and sacred rites. Individual piety arose within those spaces and rites, not in competition with them. When Margherita of Cortona attended Matins, she stayed on in the church for private devotions. She turned her attention to Christ's Passion, visibly represented on the great cross above the choir screen. She recited ten Pater Nosters in honor of the Last Supper, ten more for Christ's arrest, and ten for his crowning with thorns. Focusing directly on the cross, she recited another ten for each of the five wounds, ten for each ear, ten for each eye, and ten each for the spitting and the veiling of Christ's eyes. Finally, she said ten for the gall and ten for the lance. Prayer was a physical exercise, a speaking of sacred words, and here it honored the most precious body of all, that of the Savior. That very body would become present on the altar at the solemn Mass later in the day, and Margherita would adore it.[1] Margherita's prayer grew out of and returned to the Church's liturgy.

Other laypeople attended the liturgy of the duomo and joined their prayers to it. Omobono of Cremona went for Matins and, like Margherita, extended the Office by his own devotions. He prayed lying prostrate on the ground before an ancient painted cross until the hour of Mass.[2] Each participant in the liturgy had a different office. The bishop presided, the clergy chanted, the lectors read, and the laity sang the simple responses and supported the cult with their own prayers. When Enrico of Treviso attended Office and Mass, he always carried his knotted "Pater Noster cord" in his hands. He joined his Paters, "according to his own understanding, for he was unlettered," to the community's corporate praise of the Creator. As for

---

1. Giunta Bevegnati, *Legenda . . . Margaritae de Cortona*, 6.12, p. 296.
2. *Vita Sancti Homoboni*, 113.

sermons at the cathedral, he never failed to attend them.[3] Offered in accord with each one's office and understanding, the web of prayer formed a seamless whole.

Words, Gestures, and Places

Never passive spectators, the laity engaged in the actions, the motions, of worship. Consolations and special divine favors—"mystical experiences"— occurred as often as not when the saint was at Office or Mass, rather than at home. Benvenuta Bojani attended Mass and Compline daily, arriving early enough for Vespers on feasts. Her favorite time for prayer was Compline, the night Office—it was then, during the chanting of the Salve Regina in honor of Mary, that she received the greatest spiritual gifts. Once, in 1290, while Benvenuta was present for the Salve in the Dominican church at Forlì, she had a vision of Saint Dominic. The holy man replaced the absent prior, Fra Girardo de' Barbara, and embraced each friar after sprinkling him with holy water.[4] The singing of the Salve in Dominican churches, which included a procession to the people's section, was a great favorite with the laity.[5] The Salve Regina became so much a part of lay piety that it came to rival the Ave Maria as the favorite way to greet the Blessed Virgin.[6] Even when the clergy were not chanting the Office or Mass, the church building remained a privileged place for lay prayer. When Pietro Pettinaio was not selling combs at his bench in the Piazza del Campo of Siena, he spent time in his favorite churches. Hearing his spoken prayers during a visit to San Domenico for his usual devotions, a pious woman who had fallen down the church steps, seemingly dead, was healed where she lay. On another occasion, when a local boy had fallen out a window, the neighbors found the pious combmaker praying in San Martino and brought him to pray and make the sign of the cross over the boy. He too recovered. Pietro prayed privately at home, but he preferred to pray in a church.[7]

When Ambrogio Sansedoni's Sienese wet nurse wanted to pray for a healing of his infantile deformities, she went to Santa Maria Magdalena near Porta Romana to pray before the relics. She knew this was the place to pray, because the baby would cry when she moved away from the shrine. It was the right place; the future Dominican was healed.[8] Visiting a church was an act of piety and devotion in itself. When the flagellant confraternity of Bolo-

3. Pierdomenico of Baone, *Vita B. Henrici,* 1.6, p. 366.

4. Corrado of Cividale, *Vita Devotissimae Benevenutae,* 1.10, p. 153; 3.26, p. 156; 7.59, p. 166.

5. On this rite, see *Vitae Fratrum Ordinis Praedicatorum,* 1.7, pp. 58–60, Conway trans., 44–49, and Jordan of Saxony, *Libellus de Principiis Ordinis,* ed. M.-H. Laurent (Rome: Institutum Historicum Fratrum Praedicatorum, 1935), 120, pp. 81–82.

6. As suggested by the introduction to one commentary on it: Florence, Biblioteca Nazionale Centrale, MS Palat. 1 (XIV cent.), fol. 12ʳ.

7. Pietro of Monterone, *Vita del beato Pietro Pettinajo,* 5, p. 65 (on events at San Domenico), pp. 66–68 (at San Martin), and p. 69 (on prayer at home).

8. Gisberto of Alessandria et al., *Vita [B. Ambrosii],* 1.3, p. 182.

gna drew up their statutes in 1260, they required that members visit a local church each day, before they commenced work. The requirement allowed no exemption. In contrast, members' attendance at daily Mass was obligatory only "if there was no impediment."[9] Enrico of Treviso daily visited each of the churches of his native city. When he found an open church, he entered and recited his prayers prostrate on the floor, "as was his custom." If the church happened to be closed, he knelt outside before the doors and "and prayed even longer."[10] After completing this daily round, he went to the cathedral. Under the portico, in the corner facing the episcopal palace, was a painting of the Blessed Virgin. There Enrico recited his prayers for the rest of the day, on his knees, leaning against the stone of the portico. His were not silent meditations but vigorous recited prayers. People next door, in the vestibule of the palace, could hear him quite clearly.[11]

Prayer implied both presence in a sacred place—the church, before an altar or image—and sacred gestures—bowing, kneeling, prostrating. I have previously mentioned Peter the Chanter's small treatise on prayer. Since it gives illustrations of gestures of prayer used by the laity, I now consider it directly. The Italian version is found in manuscripts at Venice and Padua and has recently been edited.[12] The text was popular and found imitators in clerical circles.[13] The text is particular, even revolutionary, in several ways. It focuses on physical gestures and motions and makes use of biblical authorities.[14] Drawings portray each "mode" or posture of prayer (fig. 52). Although the book's users were probably literate, the illustrations made it accessible to the unlettered.[15] The men portrayed in the Italian illustrations are clearly lay.[16] The text probably circulated in confraternity circles; its audience, if the images reflect the audience, consisted of young males. The book was equally applicable to women—so said Peter, and he praised Saint Mary Magdalene because she said the canonical hours with full attention of mind and heart.[17] Although stylized and idealized, the images present lay gestures of devotion described in other sources. Peter does not ignore the words. He emphasizes

9. "Statuto dei Disciplinati di Bologna" (1260), 7, Meersseman, *Ordo,* 1:480; for identical legislation in Vicenza, see "Statuto dei Disciplinati di Vicenza" (1263), 23, Meersseman, *Ordo,* 1:481.

10. Pierdomenico of Baone, *Vita B. Henrici,* 1.7, p. 366.

11. Ibid., 1.8, p. 366.

12. Peter the Chanter, *De Oratione,* 178–234, edited from Padua, Biblioteca Antoniana, MS 532 (XIII cent.), fols. 1ʳ–78ᵛ, and Venice, Archivio di Stato, S. Maria della Misericordia in Valverde MS B.1 (XIII cent.), which depends on the Paduan text.

13. E.g., *The Nine Ways of Prayer of St. Dominic,* ed. Simon Tugwell (Dublin: Dominican, 1978), a thirteenth-century Dominican product.

14. Trexler, *Christian at Prayer,* 119. On gesture in prayer, see Desmond Morris, *Gestures: Their Origin and Distribution* (New York: Stein & Day, 1979). For further bibliography, see Trexler, *Christian at Prayer,* 125 n. 31.

15. Although Trexler (*Christian at Prayer,* 50) suggests that the volume was so textually oriented that it was probably meant only for the literate.

16. Ibid., 59–60. The Venice text was owned by a confraternity, the Paduan by the Franciscan tertiaries: ibid., 68.

17. Peter the Chanter, *De Oratione,* 182.

the importance of proper pronunciation, along with correct use of gestures.[18] The need to combine gestures with words reflects the Italian scene. Donna Risa di Giacomo di Andrea was obsessed by a demon. Among its other baneful effects, she "could not raise her arms to heaven, place them on her head, make the sign of the cross, cry out to God or the Virgin Mary, or recite the Pater Noster or the Ave Maria." A visit to the tomb of Saint Filippo Benizzi in the church of San Marco on the first Wednesday of June 1287 allowed her to resume her earlier, more physically and verbally demonstrative, habits of prayer.[19]

Prayer began with movement. On entering a church, worshipers' actions placed them in harmony with its sacred space. A good Catholic entered the door and turned to the right, not the left—thus recalling that Christians should turn away from sin (left) and toward grace (right). The devout moved around the church counterclockwise, imitating the movement of the heavens, as the priest did while incensing the altar. On finding a place to pray, one saluted the altar, bowing three times and saying three Paters in honor of the Blessed Trinity.[20] The altar, though partly hidden by the choir screen, was the site of the miracle of the Mass. People directed their gaze to it, making God's mysterious presence there the focus of prayer.[21] Many began their devotions with a triple salutation to the altar. Peter's booklet assumed three genuflections; Sicardo's prescription, three bows. At each reverence, one recited a Pater.[22] The devout similarly reverenced crosses, since they too represented the presence of Christ, the second person of the Trinity. Genuflection here meant going down on both knees, rather than the later medieval single-kneed genuflection common to this day.[23] Peter describes the exuberant lay practice, Sicardo the habits of the more conservative clergy. Fra Salimbene of Parma commented on the habits of the saintly king Louis IX of France, whom he had seen at Auxerre. On entering a church, the monarch saluted the altar with genuflections and knelt before it for an extended period of prayer. The king knew the proper lay style. When servants brought benches out for the convenience of courtiers, Louis showed his humility by sitting on the ground.[24]

The good Catholic always saluted the cross, an image of Christ, or any painting of the saints, with at least some gesture, commonly a bow and suitable prayer.[25] In churches of the communal period, to greet the altar was also to greet the great crucifix above the door of the screen through which

18. Trexler, *Christian at Prayer*, 41–42.
19. *Processus Miraculorum B. Philippi [Benitii]*, 1.36, fol. 53ʳ.
20. Sicardo, *Mitrale*, 4.1, cols. 149–50.
21. Trexler, *Christian at Prayer*, 114.
22. Ibid., 46 (citing Peter the Chanter, lines 941–60).
23. Ibid., 86–87.
24. Salimbene, *Cronica* (1248), 323, Baird trans., 216.
25. Peter the Chanter, *De Oratione*, 191.

the altar was visible. Laypeople acknowledged Christ's image as they passed. Bona of Pisa, "after the manner of the laity," always bowed and crossed herself when passing a painting of Christ Crucified, whether that was above the screen door or merely painted on a wall. Once, the crucified Savior bowed back![26] Some laypeople added short invocations to the Paters used to salute the altar. In Piacenza, the flagellant confraternity members added, "I give thanks to you, O Christ, because you are my redeemer and savior."[27] They used the same prayer whenever they passed an image of Christ Crucified. Vernacular greetings appear in devotional manuscripts of the communal period, even before reservation of the Host above the main altar became a common practice. These often link the image of Christ with his real presence in the Eucharist. A well-worn early-fourteenth-century collection of devotions prescribed the famous "Anima Christi" in an Italian version as a suitable greeting for images of Christ Crucified.[28] The very pious, such as Pietro Pettinaio or Saint Clare of Assisi (according to Sora Pacifica de' Guelfuzzi of Assisi), reverenced the cross by prostrating themselves before it and reciting several prayers.[29]

In the nave, their part of the church, the laity adopted whatever stance they found conducive to prayer. Only the extremely devout were given to full prostrations or groveling on all fours as a regular posture, although Peter the Chanter included these as his fifth and seventh modes of prayer. He gave no indication that they were exceptional.[30] To stand praying was fully acceptable, even if it called to mind the negative image of the proud Pharisee of the Gospel (Luke 18:9–14). While standing, supplicants raised their arms over their heads toward God (first mode), extended them to form a cross (second mode), or joined their hands palm to palm on the chest (third mode).[31] Peter was emphatic that nothing should hinder use of the more dramatic extensions of the arms. Only the vice of pride discouraged this gesture, suggesting that it might be embarrassing.[32] This was a demonstrative age. Folding the hands before the breast was seemly and the least disruptive mark of respect in crowded churches during Mass. But even then most knelt to pray, with hands folded palm to palm.[33] Peter rounded on indolent clergy and monks, along with the rich and knights, who found this kneeling tiresome and uncomfortable. When the clerics and rich men did adopt a more becoming posture, they often committed the sin of "fraud in kneeling"— propping themselves up or leaning against walls or columns. Tellingly, Peter

26. *Vita [Sanctae Bonae Virginis Pisanae]*, 1.8, p. 145: "modo laico."
27. Piacenza Battuti Stat. (1317), 64: "Ago tibi Christe gratias, quia redemptor et salvator meus es."
28. Modena, Biblioteca Estense Universitaria, MS γ.W.2.40 (XIV cent.), fol. 1ᵛ. See "Anima Christi," *The Catholic Encyclopedia* 1 (1913), 515.
29. *El proceso della canoniçatione de sancta Chiara*, 1.9, p. 444.
30. Peter the Chanter, *De Oratione*, 152 (mode 5), 160 (mode 7).
31. Ibid., 134, 140, 144.
32. Ibid., 193.
33. The sixth mode: ibid., 156 (Padua manuscript).

never castigated the ordinary lay faithful for failing to kneel or for using fraudulent postures. The sick and aged properly sat down to pray, but for others to refuse to kneel or prostrate was to "pray badly." "Bodily gesture is aid and proof of interior devotion."[34] During long periods of prayer, it was best to change postures occasionally, to reflect different needs in prayer and to avoid tedium.[35] Pietro of Foligno took this strategy to heart. His prayer was vigorous; he used many different gestures and genuflected every time he heard or invoked the name of Jesus. Even a moderate session at prayer left him bathed in sweat.[36]

Prayer placed the Christian in an interior sacred space, in contact with Christ and the saints. Bodily gesture reflected interior disposition, and so the body claimed a space for prayer. Prayer could make any place a chapel. Umiliana dei Cerchi kept an image of Mary in the corner of her bedroom. She was accustomed, in the darkness of night, to recite there with careful devotion the words of the Pater Noster. She pondered each syllable with such care that one recitation seemed sufficient to last an entire night. The Holy Spirit rewarded her piety, appearing in the form of a white dove, holding a rosebud in its beak and hovering over the image of the Virgin.[37] Lacking visits of the Holy Spirit, the laity sanctified their oratories with holy water, a practice commended and encouraged by the Church hierarchy. Before Mass each Sunday and feast day, the priest sprinkled the people with a mixture of holy water and blessed salt or—even better—during Easter season, with water from the very font of the baptistery. Such a blessed mixture of salt and water went back, tradition had it, to the times of the prophet Elisha (2 Kings 2:20–21).[38] After Mass, the clergy filled vessels for the laity so they could take the water with them for use at home. One early-fourteenth-century Italian wrote out the virtues of holy water into his collection of private prayers. It cleansed venial sin, increased goodness, loosed the snares of the Devil, and protected against impure thoughts.[39] Miracles confirmed its power. In Franciscan legend, a crippled novice used to sprinkle the convent's dormitory with holy water. One night, in a dream, he saw the Devil prowling about the convent but unable to enter the sleeping areas. When the novice asked him why he could not enter, the Devil said it was because of the holy water.[40] The penitent Giovanni Buono of Mantua furnished his hermitage with a crucifix, an image of Our Lady, and a vessel of holy water. At his canonization, his private oratory and its embellishments evidenced his ortho-

---

34. Ibid., 208: "Gestus vero corporis est argumentum et probatio mentalis devotionis"; see Trexler, *Christian at Prayer*, 47.

35. Peter the Chanter, *De Oratione*, 218.

36. Giovanni Gorini, *[Legenda de Vita et Obitu Beati Petri de Fulgineo]*, 2.9, AS 31 (Jul. IV), 667.

37. Vito of Cortona, *Vita [B. Humilianae]*, 2.14, p. 389.

38. *Ordo Senensis*, 2.18, p. 419; for a rite to bless water and salt for use by the laity, see Pont. Rom. (XII), 46, p. 264.

39. Bologna, Biblioteca Universitaria, MS 158 (XIV cent.), fol. 45ᵛ.

40. *Chronica XXIV Generalium Ordinis Fratrum Minorum*, 381.

doxy. They made public and manifest that he was a good and Catholic man. Visitors often found him kneeling before his little altar.[41] No private chapel compared with that of the future Dominican Giacomo Salomone. As a youth, he secretly erected a small altar in his bedroom and went there to make his thanksgiving after Communion. He made sets of paraments for this altar, according to the liturgical colors of the year. On the mornings and evenings of duplex feasts he lighted four candles on it and incensed it "according to the norms of the ecclesiastical office" (*juxta ecclesiastici morem Officii*).[42]

Giacomo's clericalized piety was probably not typical of even the more devout laity. In their devotions, the people favored simplicity. When reciting their Aves and Paters, they contented themselves with simple shrines, usually enthroning the Virgin and Child. More than sprinkling with holy water, this sacred image sanctified a place of prayer and showed forth the sacred presence. While Ambrogio Sansedoni was still an infant, his love of the sacred images in books his father read to him portended his future holiness.[43] As a layman, Francisco Patrizzi, who entered the Servites in 1285, erected an image of the Blessed Virgin Mary in one room of his house. There he prayed morning and evening, genuflecting fifty times and reciting Aves and other praises of the Virgin. Then he would scourge himself.[44] The image did not need to be elaborate or valuable. When Umiliana dei Cerchi invoked God's help to escape a second marriage, she prayed before a rude image of the Virgin sketched on a piece of parchment.[45] Francesco Patrizzi sometimes prayed before an old and faded painting of the Virgin on a cemetery wall at Presciano, near Siena. He expressed his devotion by leaving flowers.[46] The flagellant confraternity of Bologna captured the lay link between devotion and image in their statutes of 1260. These stipulated that whenever members of the confraternity found themselves before an image of Christ or the Virgin, whether stationary or carried in procession, they bow their heads and say a prayer. Images made their subjects present in a mysterious way, but the images were not the reality that was worshiped. A story tells that "in Lombardy" ordinary people put up images of the Virgin Mary in their homes, and fathers led their families and servants in prayer before them. Once, a boy from one such family fell in the river—was it the Po?—and was feared drowned. But his mother, with joy, found him still alive on a sandbar. When asked how he was saved, the boy said it was by "Our Lady, the one

---

41. *Processus . . . B. Joannis Boni*, 3.1.173, p. 815; 3.3.183, p. 818: "quod publicum et manifestum erat, quod ipse erat religiosus et catholicus homo." See also ibid. 4.4.288, p. 845.

42. *Vita [Beati Jacobi Veneti Ordinis Praedicatorum]*, 1.2, p. 453; 2.14, p. 457.

43. Gisberto of Alessandria et al., *Vita [B. Ambrosii]*, 1.6, p. 182.

44. Cristoforo of Parma, *Legenda Beata Francisci*, 6, p. 176; he continued his devout repetition of Aves even after becoming a Servite: ibid., 13, p. 180.

45. Vito of Cortona, *Vita [B. Humilianae]*, 1.7, p. 387.

46. Cristoforo of Parma, *Legenda Beati Francisci*, 28, p. 186.

who is in our house." The moral: "And so, dearest brethren, let us bow, bending the knee and uncovering our heads, to greet her whenever we see the image or hear the name of the blessed Mary."[47]

Peter the Chanter's treatise divided prayer into two kinds, "vocal" and "real."[48] He never treated "real prayer" directly, but his comments describing acts of mercy as perfecting prayer suggest that real prayer consisted in works of charity.[49] For Peter, as for communal Italians, prayer was, above all, the words spoken to God. As a cleric, he read his prayers from a book, in particular the Divine Office, rather than recite memorized prayers like laypeople.[50] From Peter's own point of view, prayer was virtually impossible for the unlettered, since they could not decipher written texts.[51] The illiterate might use the postures his booklet portrayed, but they could not really pray. Italian lay piety rejected such elitism entirely; the God-given biblical prayers of the Ave Maria and Pater Noster were the finest possible prayers, and anyone could recite them.[52] Wiser clerics than Peter agreed. A layman approached the master of the Dominican order Jordan of Saxony, perhaps at Bologna, and asked him, "Is the Pater Noster worth as much in the mouths of simple folk who do not know its full meaning as in the mouths of learned clerics who understand all they are saying?" To which the friar replied that indeed it was, just as a gem's value did not depend on the possessor's knowing anything about gems.[53] Christ gave the prayer its power when he composed it. Zucchero Bencivenni (fl. 1300–1313), in his Italian adaption of the late-thirteenth-century French Dominican Laurent of Orleans's ethical and catechetical treatise *Somme le roi* (dated 1279), dispensed with the need for intellectual comprehension of set formulas entirely. Prayer was the "cry of the heart." Praying Christians just needed to "cry out" like the apostles in the boat with Jesus. What made prayer perfect was the union of intention with any vocal utterance. So David cried out, "Lord hear my voice when I cry out and pray to you from the depths of my heart."[54]

It was better to pray well briefly than at length badly. To pray badly was to pray without firm attention on God or with mangled words. Worse was to let the mind drift off to business or worldly distractions.[55] Prayer was

47. Pisa, Biblioteca Cateriniana del Seminario Arcivescovile, ms 139 (xiv cent.), fol. 136ᵛ: "Et nos, fratres karissimi, visa eius ymagine et audito nominis beate Marie, flexi genibus et pilleo remoto salutando, ipsam ei inclinamus."
48. Peter the Chanter, *De Oratione*, 181.
49. See ibid., 197–98.
50. See Trexler, *Christian at Prayer*, 35.
51. See Peter the Chanter, *De Oratione*, 179, where words and syllables are the "matter" of prayer, and, on this, Trexler, *Christian at Prayer*, 25–26.
52. Lay pious associations allowed that recitations of Paters and Aves discharged the obligation to recite the Latin Office even for the literate: Piacenza Battuti Stat. (1317), 61–63; Novara Battuti Stat. (xiv), 282.
53. *Vitae Fratrum Ordinis Praedicatorum*, 3.31, p. 125, Conway trans., 120 (slightly modified).
54. Zucchero Bencivenni, *Sposizione*, 81–87, esp. 83.
55. With this, Peter the Chanter, *De Oratione*, 206, 223, agrees.

addressed to the Father in heaven who had adopted us. So the perfect prayer was the Our Father; it was short and God empowered Christians to use it. Zucchero Bencivenni explained: "Adoption is a legal term. That is, according to the imperial law, when a man does not have a natural son, he can select the son of a poor man, if he wishes, and make him an adoptive son, just as if he was his own son. . . . This grace God the Father does for us through no merit of ours, as Saint Paul says. He brought us to baptism, though we were poor and vile, sons of wrath and hell."[56] The Our Father reminded those who said it of the baptism they had received as children, which made them children of the Father. The simple baptized could pray the Pater Noster with as much right as any cleric. By decree of the Lateran Council, children were to learn by heart, in the Church's Latin, the Pater Noster and the Apostles' Creed. The Apostles' Creed seems to have played little or no role in lay devotion, seldom if ever appearing among the prayers used by confraternities.[57] But Christ himself taught the words of the Pater to children, to whom belonged the kingdom of heaven (Matt. 19:14, Mark 10:14, Luke 18:16). It was the first prayer a teacher taught his pupils when parents engaged him to teach them to read. It contained the fullness of beauty and wisdom.[58] The authority of the Pater Noster was so great that even Cathar heretics could not abandon it. And they, like the Catholics, dared not translate the sacred words from Latin, at least in Italy.[59] Unlike examples from France, Italian devotional manuscripts of the communal period almost never have translations of the Pater, Ave, or Credo.[60] Only at the end of the communal period do vernacular Paters, composed for devotional purposes, appear. These use tropes and rhymes rather than literal translations of the sacred words. One fourteenth-century example, perhaps late, went:

> When saying, our Father who in the heavens be,
>   may we hallow always your holy name,
>   give grace and praise for all to thee;
> Make your kingdom come, as is ever meet,
>   and in all things your will be done,
>   that our earth heaven in union greet;
> Lord, give us this day the bread we need,

56. Zucchero Bencivenni, *Sposizione*, 5–6: "Adozione è un motto di legge, ch'è secondo la legge dello'mperadore, quando un uomo non ha veruno figliuolo, elli puote elegger un figliuolo d'un povero uomo, s'elli vuole, e farne suo figliuolo adottivo, si ch'egli è avuto per suo figliuolo, e porteranne il retaggio. . . . Questa grazia ci fece Dio padre sanza nostro merito, come dice san Paulo, quando elli ci fece sentire al battesimo ch'eravamo poveri e vili, e figliuoli d'ira e d'inferno."

57. As noted by De Sandre Gasparini, "Laici devoti," 256–58.

58. Zucchero Bencivenni, *Sposizione*, 3–4.

59. See Raniero Orioli, *Venit Perfidus Heresiarcha: Il movimento apostolico-dolciniano dal 1260 al 1307*, Studi storici, 193–96 (Rome: Istituto Storico Italiano per il Medio Evo, 1988), 131–33.

60. On this phenomenon in France, see Alexandre-Bidon, "Des femmes," 117. For an Italian example, see Modena, Biblioteca Estense Universitaria, MS γ.W.2.40, fol. 4ʳ.

and pardon us all the sins we do
that we displease you not by any deed;
And show us how to pardon grant,
and form so the virtues you impart,
that the enemy will not them supplant.[61]

Most felt no need of such elaborations when the original words were so
close to hand. Giovanni Buono, pious illiterate that he was, memorized the
Nicene Creed, the beloved "Miserere Mei Deus" (Psalm 50 of the Vulgate),
and several other standard Latin prayers. Fra Greco of Mantua remarked
on this unusual accomplishment of going beyond the Pater and the Ave.[62]
For most, the Lord's Prayer had an immediacy and urgency sometimes lost
on modern Christians. Italians knew to pray for deliverance "from evil,"
meaning from the great demon, Satan, who sought the ruin of souls and the
corruption of goodness, as the devotional version above said.[63] Christ's words
could put the Evil One to flight. So could the power of his cross. By no
more than the sign of that cross, the Pater, and the Creed, Saint Agnese of
Montepulciano exorcized the demons from a possessed man and restored
him to his senses. Agnese used her "Pater Noster cord" to count the Paters
she recited each day. When she died, the nuns placed the cord in her hands.
During the funeral, it gave off a miraculous fragrance.[64]

Next to the Pater, the Ave Maria was slowly becoming the "lay prayer"
par excellence, which it was already in France.[65] The Ave, too, had the
power to drive off temptations and demons.[66] Its brevity and simplicity also
commended it, especially to the illiterate. The "Angelic Salutation" of the
communal period included only the biblical words of Gabriel and Elizabeth.
It stopped at the words, "blessed is the fruit of your womb." Addition of
even the holy name of Jesus had to wait till the 1300s. Laywomen like Umiltà
of Faenza, Benvenuta Bojani, and Margherita of Cortona all recited the Ave
Maria in the short, purely biblical form.[67] Nevertheless, in devotional use,
the pious added other biblical phrases to the angelic salutation. One late-

61. Modena, Biblioteca Estense Universitaria, MS α.R.2.3 (early XIV cent.), fol. 2ʳᵃ: "Dicendo padre
che nel celo stai, | sanctificato sia il tuo sancto nome, | e gratie ellode di cio che ci sai. | Avegna nel tua
regno, come pone | questa ragione, tua volunta sia facta, | come in celo sia in terra unione. | Signore
daccj oggi pan che ci piaccia, | di perdonarci gli peccati nostri, | e cosa non facciam che ti dispiaccia. | E
chome perdonar tu si ci mostri, | exemplo di noi mondan di tua virtute, | accioche dal nemico ognun si
schosti."

62. Processus . . . B. Joannis Boni, 4.3.279, p. 843.

63. Zucchero Bencivenni, Sposizione, 15. See also Trexler, Christian at Prayer, 35.

64. Raimondo of Capua, Legenda Beate Agnetis de Monte Policiano, 3.1, pp. 68–69.

65. On its use in France, see Nicole Bériou, Prier au Moyen Âge: Pratiques et expériences (Vᵉ–XVᵉ siècles)
(Turnout: Brepols, 1991), 174–75.

66. Vitae Fratrum Ordinis Praedicatorum, 4.23, pp. 212–13, Conway trans., 194.

67. Corrado of Cividale, Vita Devotissimae Benevenutae, 4.50, p. 163; Umiltà of Faenza, "Sermo 3," ed.
and trans. Adele Simonetii, I sermoni di Umiltà da Faenza: Studio e edizione (Spoleto: Centro Italiano di Studi
sull'Alto Medioevo, 1995), 27–29; Giunta Bevegnati, Legenda . . . Margaritae de Cortona, 5.42, p. 282.

thirteenth-century example, perhaps from a Franciscan environment, went:

> Hail Mary, full of grace,
>> the Lord is with you.
> Blessed are you among women,
>> and blessed is the fruit of your womb.
> The Holy Spirit will come upon you;
>> the power of the Most High will overshadow you.
> Behold the handmaiden of the Lord;
>> be it done unto me according to your word.[68]

A splendid full-page image of the Annunciation flanks this prayer on the opposite page of the codex, giving inspiration for the mind as the text gave words for the voice (fig. 53). Filippo of Ferrara knew of an illiterate man who could not memorize the Pater Noster, something even children could do. But he did memorize the Ave Maria and used it as a blessing whenever he took a drink at the local tavern. Filippo also knew a knight who had entered a religious house in penance. The monks gave up trying to teach him the psalms. Trying the Pater, they found even that was too long for him. "So they taught him the Ave Maria."[69] This was the prayer for everyone. Miracles big and small confirmed the power of the angelic salutation. One woman was accustomed to regular, almost perpetual, recitation of the Ave. She had to take dinner to her husband in the garden one day. Before going, she invoked Mary's blessing on her sleeping child and said an Ave Maria over him. While she was outside, the untended fire spread and destroyed the house. But the child was found unharmed in the ashes, shielded by the Blessed Mother.[70] The Ave's miraculous reputation and its biblical, indeed heavenly, origin gained it, beside the Pater Noster, an unchallenged place in Catholic piety. Together, the Pater and the Ave were all the prayers anyone really needed.

With this small repertoire of formulas and the centrality of vocal prayer, desire for extended devotions turned naturally to repetition. Before 1201, the Humiliati created an "Office" for lay members consisting of sevenfold repetitions of the Pater for each of the seven clerical hours. To their Paters, they added recitation of the Credo at the hours of Prime and Compline.[71]

68. Florence, Biblioteca Medicea Laurenziana, MS Pl. xxv 3, fol. 363ᵛ: "Ave Maria, gratia plena, Dominus tecum. Benedicta tu in mulieribus et benedictus fructus ventris tui. Spiritus Sanctus superveniet in te; virtus Altissimi obumbrabit tibi. Ecce ancilla Domini; fiat michi secundum verbum tuum."

69. Bologna, Biblioteca Universitaria, MS 1552 (xv cent., original ca. 1330), Filippo di Ferrara, *Liber de Introductione Loquendi*, 1.2, fols. 1ᵛ–2ʳ.

70. Ibid., 2:18, fol. 6ʳ.

71. Meersseman, *Dossier*, App. 1.10 (Humiliati Rule of 1201). On the Humiliati Office, see John Wickstrom, "The Humiliati: Liturgy and Identity," *AFP* 62 (1992): 198–200. Repetition of Paters and Aves flourished, in spite of clerical concerns about "rote recitation": see Trexler, *Christian at Prayer*, 35.

The Poor Catholics, a lay penitent group converted from heresy, prescribed fifteen Paters for each of the hours by their rules of 1208 and 1212. To these they added, once a day, the recitation of the Credo, the "Miserere," and some other easily memorized prayers. There were some literates among these penitents: their 1212 rule stipulated that the "learned" could chant the canonical Office instead.[72] Repetition of Pater Nosters became the "lay office" of the thirteenth century. Marian confraternities added Ave Marias to it. In the 1260s, an Arezzo confraternity of the Virgin committed its members to the daily recitation of Paters and Aves for each canonical hour. Before bed, they added the verse "In manus tuas, Domine, commendo spiritum meum." And when they said Paters and Aves for the dead, they closed the recitation with "Requiem eternam dona eis, Domine."[73] These verses were well-known invocations from the public liturgy and reassociated the lay office with the public cult from which it was born. The truly unlettered could say these verses in the vernacular, but the Paters and Aves were always in the Church's holy language.

Peter the Chanter's manual records a version of the lay office that consisted in saying one hundred Paters for Matins, thirty each for Lauds and Vespers, fifty for Mass, and twenty for Prime.[74] Repetitions often reflected sacred numbers. A group of Piacenza flagellants of the late 1200s prescribed three Paters and three Aves, kneeling, each day to honor of the Blessed Trinity, followed by five Paters in honor of the five wounds of Christ. They said a Pater and an Ave before each meal as grace.[75] Andrea de' Gallerani of Siena used to recite fifty Paters and Aves each morning and evening. When possible, he extended the recitation to three sets of fifty each. Lest he nod and fall asleep during the recitation, he tied his hair to a nail in the wall above the place where he was kneeling.[76] Confraternities always tended toward a clericalized piety. But even as literacy increased, the lay office endured in the confraternities. Like the clergy, the literate might recite prayers from books, but the illiterate (and those who so preferred) stuck to the lay office and repeated their Paters quietly in the back of the room.[77] The multiplication of repetitions allowed lay prayer to match the length of liturgical services.

The bastion of the lay office was always the ordinary faithful themselves, especially the women. An elderly woman taught the young Sibyllina Biscossi to recite a certain number of Paters for each of the canonical hours of the

72. Meersseman, *Dossier*, App. 2.4 (1208 rule); App. 4.13 (1212 rule).

73. "Nuovo statuto della congregazione della Vergine di Arezzo" (1262), 15, Meersseman, *Ordo*, 2:1015–27.

74. Peter the Chanter, *De Oratione*, 185 (longer version of the text).

75. Piacenza Battuti Stat. (1317), 59–60. The group also compiled vernacular prayers for the members to recite: ibid., 66–69.

76. *Vita [Beati Andreae de Galleranis]*, 1.7, p. 54.

77. De Sandre Gasparini, *Statuti*, ciii–cv.

day. The young saint, much to her biographer's edification, counted it a serious sin for her to omit her lay office, just as it was a sin for the priest to neglect saying his clerical office.[78] Women's adaptions revealed the same devotional creativity that had given the lay office birth. Margherita of Cortona invented special devotions for the Church year. On the vigil of the Purification, one of her favorite feasts, she recited the Pater, the Ave, and a Gloria Patri forty times, once for each of the days since Jesus' birth at Christmas. She recited sets of one hundred Paters for various incidents in the life of Christ, the Virgin, and the saints.[79] But no one equaled Benvenuta Bojani in her elaboration of the lay office. From the age of seven to the age of twelve, she said a hundred Paters and Aves daily, doing a hundred prostrations in honor of the Lord's Nativity and a second hundred prostrations in honor of his Resurrection. To this she later added a thousand Aves in honor of the Blessed Virgin, except on Saturdays, Our Lady's special day, when she doubled the number. Benvenuta also had special offices for her favorite feasts. On the Annunciation, she celebrated by saying three thousand Aves and doing five hundred prostrations, something that even she had to admit wore her out. After entering religious life, she kept up the same lay regimen. She said a hundred Paters and Aves daily to honor the angels and then recited the same number for the apostles, the patriarchs, the martyrs, the confessors, and the holy virgins. No wonder the place in the garden where she liked to pray was denuded of vegetation, becoming like a blasted heath or a heavily trodden path.[80]

Saint Benvenuta recommended such practices to others. To a nun who came to her suffering some unknown illness, she prescribed a thousand Aves and a thousand prostrations—a prescription to be repeated daily until she was cured. One ailing but learned nun who hoped for healing vowed to imitate Benvenuta's simple form of prayer by reciting an Ave after each psalm when she read the Divine Office.[81] One suspects that the first sister had the more rapid cure. Benvenuta's daily Paters and Aves approached something like perpetual prayer, though her practice was not quite as peculiar as it sounds. Inspirational tales of pious individuals who recited Aves throughout the day were preachers' stock-in-trade. One preacher told of a man devoted to the Blessed Virgin who visited churches and shrines and tried to sanctify each hour by recitation of the Ave. When he died, a tree grew on his grave. It had the word "AVE" imprinted on each of its leaves.[82] Such stories and practices have an air of the fantastic, but they captured the popular imagination. When Saint Benvenuta Bojani died in 1292, the laity

---

78. Tomasso of Bossolasco, *Vita [B. Sibyllinae]*, 1.2, p. 68.
79. Giunta Bevegnati, *Legenda . . . Margaritae de Cortona*, 6.3 and 6.12–14, pp. 288–89, 296–300.
80. Corrado of Cividale, *Vita Devotissimae Benevenutae*, 1.2–3, pp. 152–53.
81. Ibid., 15:118, p. 182; on the learned nun, see ibid., 15:119, p. 182.
82. Pisa, Biblioteca Cateriniana del Seminario Arcivescovile, MS 139, fols. 140ᵛ–141ʳ.

of Forlì flocked to her funeral and crowded around the bier. They all wanted to touch their own Pater Noster cords to her body.[83] The spiritual appeal of these repeated prayers is perhaps also explained by their resemblance to a "mantra," a repeated formula that can induce states of profound contemplation. Even in modern America, Buddhist-inspired versions of the same kind of practice have an ever-increasing vogue, as the Rosary has had among young Catholics. The simple Italian laity with their Pater Noster cords may be the forgotten mystics of the Middle Ages.

According to their ability, Christians added other prayers to the Pater and Ave. The sign of the cross marked pivotal points of the day. Bonesvin de la Riva, writing for students, told them that on sleeping and rising they should protect themselves with the cross. Even a woman, like Umiltà of Faenza, might use the sign of the cross for imparting blessings.[84] Bonesvin provided short prayers to use with it. In the morning one could say, "I beg you, merciful Jesus, by the prayers and merits of Mary, to save me along the way and rule me each day." In the evening he suggested saying four times: "Jesus, living God, for the love of your holy Mother, be the guardian of my body and soul, and protect me from all snares of the Devil this night. I have sinned, I confess, have mercy on me."[85] Both Bonesvin and Filippo recommended using the sign of the cross as a blessing at table—where one made it with a knife over the bread before cutting it.[86] When Margherita of Cortona sat down to eat, after making the sign of the cross, she recited five Paters and five Aves over her food, recalling the five wounds of Jesus. She said the same five Paters when she was about to take Communion, so her prayer linked her material food with the spiritual food of Christ's true body and blood.[87] Most common at table was the recitation of an Ave Maria. In another version of the story of the miraculous tree whose leaves bore the word "ave," the man who died earned the marvel by always saying an Ave Maria over his food.[88]

Nonvocal forms of prayer were not unknown in communal Italy. Zucchero Bencivenni thought it fitting that priests, at least, set aside time to

83. Corrado of Cividale, *Vita Devotissimae·Benevenutae*, 12.94, p. 175.

84. Biagio of Faenza, *Vita [S. Humilitatis Abbatissae]*, 3.31, p. 213.

85. Bonvesin de la Riva, *Vita Scholastica*, 60, lines 291–302: "Sugens ac intrans lectum crucis exprime signum, ut stertas, vigiles tucius ipse tibi. Hec subscripta tuo Domini reverenter honore omni, cum surgis, carmina mane feras: 'Te rogo, Christe pie, precibus meritisque Marie, per loca salva vie me rege quaque die.' Ast omni sero, cum vis dare membra quieti, tucius ut stertas, quattuor ista canas: 'Christe, Deus vere, sancte Genitricis amore corporis ac anime sit tibi cura mee. Hostis ab insidiis cunctis hac nocte tuere. Peccavi, fateor, tu miserere mei.'"

86. Bologna, Biblioteca Universitaria, MS 1552, Filippo of Ferrara, *Liber de Introductione Loquendi*, 1.4, fol. 3ʳ; Bonvesin de la Riva, *Vita Scholastica*, 60, lines 303–4.

87. Giunta Bevegnati, *Legenda . . . Margaritae de Cortona*, 3.4, pp. 212–13; on her special devotion to the five wounds, see ibid., 4.19, p. 236.

88. Bologna, Biblioteca Universitaria, MS 1552, Filippo of Ferrara, *Liber de Introductione Loquendi*, 1.2, fol. 2ʳ; and see the version in Creytens, "Le manuel de conversation," 115–16, transcribing Vatican City, Biblioteca Vaticana, MS Pal. Lat 960, fol. 71ʳ.

meditate on the mysteries they were celebrating. He singled out the feasts of four general Communions—Christmas, Easter, Ascension, and Pentecost—as suitable occasions.[89] Zucchero Bencivenni had in mind what later ages would call "mental prayer"—a silent spiritual exercise rather than recitation of words. During the canonization process of Giovanni of Foligno, one witness reported that Giovanni "occupied himself in vocal prayer, saying the Lord's Prayer with the Ave Maria many times, and genuflecting so many times that his mother often found him with bloody knees, because he did not yet have the use of mental prayer."[90] Giovanni eventually did become a Franciscan and learned the spiritual discipline of mental prayer. One cannot rule out such practices by the laity, but hagiographic descriptions of mystical experience—usually those of female penitents or nuns—suggest a very verbal world. The visions of Oringa Cristiana, which her confessor kept secret until after her death, were not exalted experiences of the infinite. Rather, they were familiar chats with Jesus, Mary, apostles, martyrs, and founders of religious orders. For her confessor's benefit, she even listed the names of the saints she had met. Oringa's vocal prayer slipped easily into a conversation with heavenly personages.[91] There was a homeliness about the whole affair, recalling her affection for pet snakes. Oringa was not unique. Umiltà of Faenza, in a sermon to her nuns, recounted how she once had a chat with Saint John the Evangelist. He introduced her to her two guardian angels: one was an ordinary angel named Sapiel, the other a cherub named Emmanuel. Both angels were very beautiful, Umiltà remarked.[92] Mental prayer of this sort was very much like a chat with your neighbors of the contrada. When Jesus appeared, it was usually to have a little conversation. One day Margherita of Cortona was praying before the cross in a church, doubtless repeating her Paters and Aves. Suddenly the image of Christ addressed her. " 'What do you want, little lady?' Enlightened by the Holy Spirit, she immediately responded, 'My Jesus, I seek nothing, I want nothing, except you, my Lord.' "[93]

BOOKS OF DEVOTION

Peter the Chanter assumed that only the clergy could pray effectively, because only they could read the prayers of the liturgy and the sacred texts of the Bible. If prayer required reading a text with understanding, then only those who frequented the schools could pray.[94] That Peter's Italian contem-

89. Zucchero Bencivenni, *Sposizione*, 83–84.

90. *Acta [B. Joannis Firmani sive Alvernae]*, 1.4, p. 460: "Quia adhuc non habebat usum orationis mentalis, occupabat se ipsum in oratione vocali, dicendo toties orationem Dominicam cum Ave Maria, et toties in die flectendo genua, quod frequenter fuit inventus a matre cum genubus sanguine rubicatis."

91. *Legenda Beatae Christianae*, 69, pp. 248–50.

92. Umiltà of Faenza, "Sermo 4" (De Angelis Sanctis), 40–41.

93. Giunta Bevegnati, *Legenda . . . Margaritae de Cortona*, 1.1a, p. 181: " 'Quid vis paupercula?' Sancto illustrata Spiritu statim respondens ait: 'Non quaero nec volo aliud nisi vos, Domine mi, Iesu.' "

94. Trexler, *Christian at Prayer*, 25–27.

poraries had other ideas about prayer should be clear. But laypeople did feel the attraction of written prayers and devotions. The attraction grew stronger as literacy increased. As a young penitent, Oringa Cristiana recited a set number of Paters and Aves daily, since she was absolutely illiterate. After the founding of her convent, the Blessed Virgin appeared to her in the middle of the night. The Virgin was sitting in the "turn" where Oringa met with visitors. The Virgin held in her hands a beautiful book written in letters of gold. Oringa knelt beside the Virgin, who offered her the book and said, "Read this." Oringa responded, "Lady, I cannot read." This exchange happened three times, and the Virgin disappeared. Oringa took it as a sign that she should learn to read. She and six other lay sisters organized a study circle and eventually learned to read the first twelve psalms. Latin being spelled phonetically, it was not hard for the women to learn the entire Office. They probably never got the full sense of what they were reading—they consulted a priest to find out what the rubrics of the Office meant. Eventually, they sang the Office very well. On one occasion, a priest who had come to preside at the first Vespers of the feast of Saint John the Baptist failed to intone correctly the hymn "Ut Queant Laxis" in three attempts. The young sisters jumped in and intoned it so beautifully that the priest never forgot the sweetness.[95] Did they understand what they were singing by this time? Perhaps better than we might credit them.

Some people living in the world also supplemented their Paters and Aves with prayers from written, "learned," compilations. The first step to using these collections was to master proper pronunciation of the words. Learned prayer was just as "vocal" as unlearned prayer.[96] When still in her teens, Benvenuta Bojani had already learned to recite the little Office of the Blessed Virgin. She did so aloud—sometimes with help from Saints Catherine and Margaret, who appeared to make the responses. The noise woke up one of the servants, whom Benvenuta sent back to bed, saying, "Go to sleep and be still, there is nothing to worry about."[97] Margherita of Città di Castello learned to recite the little Offices of the Holy Cross and the Virgin. Eventually, she knew the entire Psalter.[98] These women were exceptional, not because they learned to read their prayers, but because of their choice in texts. In northern Europe, the classical thirteenth-century lay devotional book is the book of hours—the Little Office of the Virgin. Beyond Benvenuta and Margherita, one would be hard-pressed to find examples of its use in Italy. Among the confraternities, where one would most expect to find the Little Office, devotions took other forms, usually recitations of Paters and Aves.[99]

95. *Legenda Beatae Christianae,* 26–29, pp. 208–11.
96. Trexler, *Christian at Prayer,* 35.
97. Corrado of Cividale, *Vita Devotissimae Benevenutae,* 1.9, p. 153: "Dormi, quiesce et noli curare."
98. *Legenda B. Margaritae de Castello,* ed. Laurent, 21, p. 125.
99. Meersseman, *Ordo,* 2:948–49.

One scholar has suggested that the cost of books of hours restricted their use to the wealthy.[100] I doubt this was the only reason. Use of the Little Office in Italy seems restricted to those, like Oringa Cristiana and Margherita, who were in the process of becoming nuns or religious. The Office was clerical and monastic; its use suggested a departure from lay piety. During my searches of Italian manuscript collections, I only rarely found books of hours, and those were seldom local products.

While my sounding of manuscripts of devotion is admittedly provisional and hardly scientific, it is possible to inventory the contents of devotional collections likely to have been used by the laity. Bonvesin de la Riva gave examples of suitable prayers for lay use; they were mostly collects from the Church's liturgy, addressed to Christ, to the Virgin, to a martyr, to a virgin, to a confessor, or "to any saint."[101] After praising repetition of the Pater Noster and the Ave Maria, Peter the Chanter recommended for lay use the collects of the liturgical year and liturgical texts, like the Magnificat, the Gloria in Excelsis, and the Credo in Deum.[102] Both authors expected that these prayers would be read in Latin. Early-thirteenth-century Italian devotional collections follow this lead: most consist of Latin collects or collectlike prayers addressed to God, Christ, the Virgin, and the saints. Only later in the century do other forms appear, these often in the vernacular.

Paleographic and internal evidence can, with some certainty, identify devotional manuscripts as produced in communal Italy. I will restrict my discussion to manuscripts that can with some certainly be localized there. Only rarely does hard evidence indicate that a manuscript was intended for a lay audience. Language is not relevant. The habits of Oringa Cristiana and Benvenuta Bojani warn us that laypeople used Latin texts, even if they understood them only imperfectly. Some clerics probably preferred vernacular texts. Latin devotional manuscripts copied by monks or clerics might have passed into lay use. To some extent, the question of lay or clerical presents a false dilemma. The differences between the piety of the literate laity and that of the clergy can be exaggerated. Peter the Chanter and Bonvesin de la Riva suggested prayers for use by anyone who could read.

Two manuscripts, one preserved in Cesena, the other in Florence, suggest examples of clerical or monastic compilation. The Cesena manuscript is a small booklet $(5'' \times 7'')$ of fourteen leaves, probably copied in the early thirteenth century.[103] It once was property of the church of Sant'Andrea of Pergula, which pertained to the monastery of Avellena. The compiler excerpted sections from a work similar to the *De Sacramentis* of Hugh of Saint

100. Ibid., 2:942–43.
101. Bonvesin de la Riva, *Vita Scholastica*, 63–65.
102. Peter the Chanter, *De Oratione*, 226–27.
103. Ravenna, Biblioteca Comunale Classense, ms 95 (ca. 1200?), *Opusculum Liturgicum Anecdotum*.

Victor.[104] The text gives short allegorizations of clerical vestments, a summary of the seven gifts of the Holy Spirit, a brief commentary on the parts of the Mass (in particular the Sanctus and Gloria), and the text of Compline. The volume is well thumbed and dirty from use. A priest might have read this text to deepen his devotion to the liturgy he celebrated. On the other hand, the text would have been pretty much meaningless to a layperson. Its allegorism of priestly vestments and its commentary on the Hebrew and Greek words for offices like subdeacon would have been dry arcana. A second example of a text produced for clerics is a Camoldolese manuscript in Florence, which has two parts, a text of the monastic Office and a section entitled *Flos Omnium Orationum.*[105] This second part sounds like the kind of prayer recommended by Peter the Chanter, but it is not. These are nearly all "psalm prayers," intended for use after the psalms of the monastic Office. They use allegory to Christianize the Psalter. Such a devotional book made sense only for someone who regularly read or sang the Divine Office.

A search of clerical manuscripts might reveal occasional devotions suitable for nonclerics. A sumptuous Franciscan manuscript from the mid-1200s, for example, includes a drawing showing the measure of Christ's body size (fig. 57) and two poetic forms of the Ave Maria (fig. 53).[106] Is it possible that a devout layman might have enjoyed these items? Yes. Does the other content of the codex take us into the world of lay piety? No. Closer to the ideal of Peter the Chanter is a codex of "sacred prayers" (*preces sacre*) in Bologna.[107] This book is small, portable, a devotional pocket book. Its first part is twelfth-century and of monastic provenance, consisting of a commentary on Benedict's rule and prayers to monastic saints. On folio 28ʳ, however, the hand changes. From there on, the text is thirteenth-century, perhaps late, and includes a prayer honoring the Passion of Christ, with a rubric listing indulgences granted by "Pope Gregory" and confirmed by "Pope Nicholas." These would probably be the thirteenth-century popes Gregory IX and Nicholas III. But these later additions are monastic, too; they include a prayer for attention in singing the Office (fol. 34ʳ). The thirteenth century saw a rising lay desire to acquire indulgences, that is, Church grants of remission of punishment due for already confessed sins. The real proliferation of indulgences in prayer collections, however, is fourteenth-century. In any case, the feeling of this part of the manuscript is less clerical. The later

104. Hugh of St. Victor, *De Sacramentis,* 2.3–4, *PL* 173:421–38. But the parallel is not perfect; the text is also similar to the anonymous *Speculum Mysteriis Ecclesiae* (post-1180), *PL* 177, app., but the etymologies of the clerical Offices resemble those of Pseudo-Alcuin of York, *De Divinis Officiis,* 34–44, *PL* 101:1251–74.

105. Florence, Biblioteca Nazionale Centrale, MS Conv. Soppr. C.8.693 (XII cent.), fols. 1ʳ–52ᵛ: *Officium Monasticum;* fols. 52ᵛ–115ᵛ: *Flos Omnium Orationum.* For another example of a similar clerical prayer collection, see Florence, Biblioteca Nazionale Centrale, MS Magl. xxxvi.81ᵇⁱˢ. This codex includes four elevation prayers, which might have appealed to a lay audience.

106. Florence, Biblioteca Medicea Laurenziana, MS Pl. XXV 3, fol. 15ᵛ (Christ's body); fols. 210ᵛ–211ᵛ, 363ᵛ (versions of the Ave).

107. Bologna, Biblioteca Universitaria, MS 2858 (XII cent.).

prayers are often highly devotional, focusing on Christ's Passion and sometimes using litanic form, as in a prayer to the Blessed Trinity (fols. 26ᵛ–27ᵛ).
There is also a model confession (fols. 8ᵛ–10ʳ) of the sort examined in Chapter
7. Except when the prayers request monastic virtues or invoke monastic
saints, these might be the kind of devotions used by a literate layperson.

Another Bolognese miscellany has bound into it the *Elucidarium* ascribed
to Honorius Augustodunensis and some material for preparing for confession, both in a twelfth-century hand. But this insertion interrupts a later
florilegium of Latin prayers (fols. 16ᵛ–17ᵛ, 52ʳ–53ᵛ) in a distinct hand and on
different-size folios.[108] The selection of prayers is heavily Marian, and mostly
poetic, including the hymns "Gaude Virgo," "Ave Maris Stella," and "O
Sancta Virgo." There are also three hymns directed to the Trinity, and a
Eucharistic hymn, "O Vivens Hostium." The section closes with a prayer
against fever. This florilegium is heavily liturgical and hardly accessible to
those with weak Latin. Nonetheless, the prayers are poetic and pick up
themes popular in lay piety—the Virgin and the Eucharist. One could easily
imagine their use by nonclerics.

The clerical devotional collections considered so far contain, at best, sections that might have appealed to laypeople. The university library at Padua
has a Latin devotional volume from the mid–thirteenth century that is almost certainly lay in origin.[109] This small (4.5″ × 6″) collection of prayers is
filthy, literally worn out by use. The content may be taken as typical, except
for the little Office of the Virgin (fols. 65ʳ–95ᵛ). The focus of the book is on
penance and the Virgin. It includes the seven penitential psalms (fols. 3ʳ–11ᵛ)
and the gradual psalms (fols. 12ʳ–20ʳ), each set ending with a verse and collect. The penitential theme is picked up later in a section of prayers (fols.
104ᵛ–111ᵛ) that includes three prayers specifically focused on the crucified
Christ. Devotion to the Virgin is represented by eleven prayers (fols. 96ʳ–
104ᵛ), including a litanic invocation of her titles, each preceded by the greetings "Ave" or "Gaude." The collection ends with a prayer to the guardian
angel and a prayer honoring the cross. Perhaps the most interesting item in
this section is the litany of the saints (fols. 96ʳ–116ᵛ) (fig. 54). Although the
manuscript once passed through Franciscan hands, the litany contains no
Franciscans. It does include both Saint Omobono of Cremona and Saint
Raimondo Palmerio of Piacenza. The absence of mendicants and the inclusion of Lombard lay saints gives the book a very local feel. This is indeed the
world of communal piety: penitential, focused devotionally on the cross of
Christ and his Blessed Mother, the very world of Omobono and Raimondo.
This is a rare book. In spite of diligent searching in collections throughout
communal Italy, I found no other thirteenth-century Latin codex so unam-
biguously in accord with lay piety.

108. Bologna, Biblioteca Universitaria, MS 1563.
109. Padua, Biblioteca Universitaria, MS 469.

Vernacular texts are more promising. By the end of the thirteenth century, vernacular and partly vernacular manuscripts of prayers appear and can be compared with the Latin prayer collection at Padua. The Laurenziana in Florence has a remarkable early-fourteenth-century example.[110] This tiny prayer book is in a clear, readable hand, with virtually no abbreviations. It probably belonged to a woman, since a Latin prayer ascribed to Saint Augustine (fol. 17^v) uses *peccatrici* (feminine) instead of *peccatori* (masculine), and a prayer to the Virgin (fol. 18^v) similarly invokes her help for *tua famula*, not *tuo famulo*. The collection is heavily Marian in spirit. It opens with a long vernacular prayer, quasi-litanic in form, to the Virgin Mary (fols. 1^r–13^r). When said before her image for thirty days in succession, the user received an indulgence, supposedly by decree of Pope Gregory IX. Then comes a vernacular prayer, ascribed to Saint Jerome, directed to the guardian angel. Other Marian prayers follow. After these come the three Latin devotions of the book: a Marian prayer indulgenced by Pope Boniface VIII; a prayer for a good death (to be recited once a day), ascribed to Augustine; and another Marian prayer in litanic form. Regrettably, the manuscript is truncated at folio 19^v, in the midst of the litanic prayer. The litany first invokes the Virgin, using Gabriel's greeting, the "Ave." Then it invokes Gabriel and other angels according to the order of the heavenly choirs, and finally Jesus under his various titles. Overall, the Marian flavor of this book is pronounced, perhaps because of the owner's taste. But the concern for repentance at death and the invocation of the guardian angel link it to the earlier collection at Padua. The piety of this codex seems also typically lay in its use of litanic forms and repetitions and the inclusion of rubrics listing indulgences. All these qualities are absent from the clerical collections discussed earlier.

Two other vernacular booklets, one from Modena and the other from Siena, confirm the impression given us by the Paduan and the Laurenziana manuscripts. Both probably date near the end of the communal period. The Modena manuscript is a commonplace book, small (twelve folios), greasy and worn, copied by several untrained hands.[111] The texts are wholly in Italian, with the exception of the Apostles' Creed (fol. 4^r) (fig. 55), the opening words of John's Gospel (fols. 4^{r-v}), and the Magnificat (fol. 5^r). These were words of power that even those who preferred Italian devotions would want to recite in the liturgical language. The vernacular contents match the earlier examples. There are two short Marian prayers (fols. 0^v–1^v) and the opening psalm of the Office of the Virgin (fols. 9^{r-v}). The focus of the rest is Christological and penitential. The book includes Eucharistic prayers (e.g., "Anima

---

110. Florence, Biblioteca Medicea Laurenziana, MS Gaddi 231; this codex might be compared to Florence, Biblioteca Riccardiana, MS 1422, which, although later, also belonged to a woman, but in this case a nun.

111. Modena, Biblioteca Estense Universitaria, MS γ.W.2.40; on which, see Giuseppe Campori, *Catalogo dei codici e degli autografi* (Modena: Paolo Torchi, 1875), 11, no. 9.

de Christo," fols. 1ʳ⁻ᵛ) and a prayer to be recited before the cross (fol. 1ᵛ). The longest items (fols. 2ʳ–3ᵛ, 5ʳ–7ʳ, 9ᵛ–12ᵛ) in the collection are penitential. Two prayers recall Christ's sacrifice for sin and the need for repentance. The second of these is a truncated vernacularization of the "Miserere Mei" (Psalm 50 of the Vulgate). The rubric to the first penitential prayer promises that its use in times of sorrow will bring forgiveness and happiness (*alegreza*). The collection ends with litanic verses praising the Holy Name of Jesus, to which devotion was growing around 1300.

The second early-fourteenth-century collection is bound into the front of a codex in Siena.[112] Like those already examined, the format is small (4″ × 6″). It uses a mixture of Latin and vernacular. The collection opens with a series of Latin prayers under vernacular rubrics, including the ever popular "Anima Christi." All are Christological or Marian, except for a prayer to Saint Brendan, perhaps the owner's patron (fig. 56). The core of the collection (fols. 18ʳ–34ʳ) is a set of five long vernacular prayers to the Blessed Trinity, each to be recited with a Pater and a Credo. Then comes a miscellaneous collection of devotions (fols. 34ʳ–41ʳ): three Marian prayers (each again to be followed by a Pater and an Ave), the litany of the saints, a prayer against lightning, and a confessional formula (using the seven capital sins). On the last folio, the compiler has copied the Apostles' Creed in Latin.

While the evidence of these manuscripts is admittedly fragmentary and sometimes problematic, some tentative conclusions about the content of lay-people's prayer books at the end of the communal period are possible. First, in terms of content, the prayers and devotions chosen tend toward the penitential, focusing on the cross and repentance from sin. The Passion of Christ, his mercy, and his presence in the Blessed Sacrament figure prominently. As we will see, some of these prayers emphasize unexpected aspects of Christ's person, his nature as wisdom incarnate, for example. Second to the focus on the cross and repentance, and sometimes surpassing them in quantity, are added prayers and hymns to the Virgin Mary. Marian piety seems especially appealing to women, but it is present in all collections. Finally, other than the litany of the saints, these booklets of devotion do not give much space to the lesser saints. Only occasionally do they include prayers for special protection or against evils. While we do find rubrics stipulating repetitions and promising indulgences, these appear in the later manuscripts. The content is remarkably orthodox and "theologically correct."

As to the form of the prayers, compilers of Latin devotions show a predilection for litanic and simple prayers, suggesting that intelligibility was important to those using them. Vernacular manuscripts sometimes contain lengthy prayers. These are often especially penitential and resemble exami-

112. Siena, Biblioteca Comunale degli Intronati, MS I.VIII.21 (XIV cent.), fols. 1ʳ–42ᵛ. For another example of a macaronic prayer book of the fourteenth century, see Modena, Biblioteca Estense Universitaria, MS α.R.2.3.

nations of conscience. How common was the use of such booklets? The extant manuscripts are often heavily worn and cheaply produced. It is surprising that after such handling they survived at all. This suggests that there were many other little "pocket books" of devotion that have perished. By the early 1300s, such books had probably become quite common. But written prayers, themselves read aloud, never challenged the simple recitation of Paters and Aves before an image of Christ or the Virgin. Hagiographic sources suggest that this was the near-universal devotional practice of the laity. In contrast, the world of written prayer seems somewhat rarefied, even when focused on the cross.

Prayers to God, the Savior, and the Saints

To compose prayers is to theologize, to put into words the absolute dependence of the Christian on God. This is true even when the supplicant prays merely to obtain a temporal favor. One vernacular prayer from an early-fourteenth-century codex captures the majesty of the Deity addressed in stunning verses:

> No one can make any plan
>   without union to the First Creator.
> God has no dependence on anything,
>   for there was no creator before him.
> Rather, he always existed for himself;
>   he was first, with no predecessor.
> So also he has no ending,
>   no cause, nothing greater.
> The Creator could not be created,
>   for there was before him nothing prior;
>   To be created is to be unable to create.
> Filling all, above, below, and under the earth,
>   Formed by him, we ask you for life,
>   sense, power, benefit, love.[113]

This is an expression more elevated than the average, but it captures the dependence implicit in every act of prayer, no matter how simple or unsophisticated. Prayers before the cross powerfully combined the aspects of penance and Christocentricity so typical of thirteenth-century Italian piety with

---

113. Bologna, Biblioteca Universitaria, MS 1563, fol. 43ᵛ: "Non si formara alcuno ordinamento, senza lunati primo ordinatore. | Pero non abbe Deu conenzamento, la non fu nanzi a fie conditore. | Ma essu stessu ad essu sempre essento, fu prima senza primo antecessore. | Ande pero non a mai finimento, la non abbe conenzo ne maiore. | Non pottel creatore esser creato, per chel fu primo nanzi ad onne primo. | Abere creao sie non potte creare, sopra sotta infra teri pleno et dalato. | Essere forma da lui vitepemo vita; sentire, puovere, tenere, amare."

this sense of dependence on the Deity. One beautiful three-part Latin prayer may be taken as typical:

> O Lord Jesus Christ, I adore you hanging on the cross,
>> bearing the thorny crown on your head;
>> I ask you that your cross might free me from the avenging angel.
> O Lord Jesus Christ, I adore you wounded on the cross,
>> given gall and vinegar to drink;
>> I ask you that your wounds might be the healing of my soul.
> O Lord Jesus Christ, I adore you placed in the tomb,
>> and with the spices at rest;
>> I ask you that your death be the life of my soul.[114]

These verses not only focus on the redemptive sacrifice of the cross, but by their vivid imagery, they make it present to the imagination and affections. With their triple request for protection, healing, and life, they bespeak a deep personal dependence. The rubric that precedes the prayer promises that when the verses are recited, along with five Paters and five Aves, kneeling before an image of Christ Crucified, the supplicant will receive "fourteen thousand years of true indulgence by a grant of Pope Nicholas." The text is simultaneously a moving devotional exercise and an extraordinary promise of expiation.[115] The prayer's poetic and rhymed form commended it to the user's memory. Its formal simplicity is reminiscent of the litanic formulas so typical of lay participation in liturgical worship. This litanic form reappears in fifty-four epithets of Jesus, each incorporated into one line of a poem in a manuscript from the early 1300s. The poem's first four invocations focus again on the salvific power of the sacred cross:

> Fruitful cross with saving power,
> Watered from the living font,
> Whose is the aromatic flower,
> The fruit before all desired.[116]

Here the cross becomes a tree, which gives to humanity a saving fruit, Christ himself. Water from the font of Christ's body then nurtures the tree, which

114. Bologna, Biblioteca Universitaria, MS 2858, fol. 34ᵛ: "O Domine Iesu Christe adoro te in cruce pendentem, | coronam spineam in capite portantem; | deprecor te ut tua crux liberet me ab angelo percutienti. O Domine Iesu Christe adoro te in cruce vulneratum, | felle et aceto potatum; | deprecor te ut tua vulera sunt remedium anime mee. O Domine Iesu Christe adoro te in sepulcro positum, | aromatibusque conchietum; | deprecor te ut tua mors sit vita anime mee. Amen."

115. For similar indulgenced prayers before the image of Christ Crucified, see Modena, Biblioteca Estense Universitaria, MS γ.W.2.40, fol. 1ᵛ, and Bologna, Biblioteca Universitaria, MS 2530 (1308), fols. 32ʳ⁻ᵛ, the latter in the vernacular.

116. Milan, Biblioteca Ambrosiana, MS Y 5 Sup., fols. 44ʳ⁻45ʳ, here the opening: "Crux frutex salvificus, | Vivo fonte rigatus, | Cuius flos aromaticus, | Fructus desideratus."

gives as fruit the Eucharist, so central to the private and liturgical piety of communal Italy. The remaining fifty verses of this prayer pay further homage to the Eucharistic Christ offered on the altar daily and received by the faithful at general Communions. The trajectory of the entire prayer is summed up in its final acclamation: "Jesus, you are the end most hoped for" (*Ihesus finis optatus*). In the manuscript, these verses are appended to a text of Bonaventure's *Arbor Vitae*, his meditation on the cross and Passion.

These prayers are not monastic devotions, cloistered from everyday life. Their popularity lay in how their users could see their own trials, sorrows, and sufferings as crosses Christ could himself understand and remedy. The rubric before one long vernacular penitential prayer to the Trinity promised that if believers used it with a constant heart, their problems and sorrows would be turned into joys and consolations.[117] This was prayer for practical benefit more than an exercise in mystical union or pious contemplation. Although mostly lost, there must have been many other very practical formulas like one an Italian doctor copied onto the last folio of his medical codex, a prayer—better, a spell—against his enemies, including hostile lawyers: "In the name of Christ. Amen. I conjure you, O herb, that I conquer through the Lord, Father, [Son, and Holy Spirit,] and through the moon and stars; and that you conquer all my enemies, bishop and priests, all lay men and women, and all the lawyers opposing me."[118] The typical devotional collection, however, contains nothing quite so heterodox.

The evocative imagery of the most common prayers suggests a desire for direct contact with the physical person of Christ as a reality in this world. Similar longing lies behind one image in a collection of the late 1200s (fig. 57).[119] Here the standing Christ holds a cross-shaped staff and blesses the viewer. His feet stand on a carefully drawn "carpet line" some five inches in length. An inscription explains that if the line is extended "twice six times" (*bis sexties*), the result will be the exact measure of Christ's earthly body. The accuracy of the measure is certain, since it was copied from a golden cross in Constantinople made to Christ's exact size. The promise is fantastic, but the sentiment behind it is wholly orthodox. Christ had a real human body, with proportions like ours, and by its suffering he redeemed the world. Just as prayer needed to yield practical results, Christ's person needed to be experienced as present in this world.

Perhaps the most perfect, if also perhaps the most baroque, example of

---

117. Modena, Biblioteca Estense Universitaria, ms γ.W.2.40, fol. 3ᵛ.

118. Perugia, Biblioteca Comunale, ms 736 (I.130), fol. 267ʳ, text partly transcribed in *Inventari dei manoscritti delle biblioteche d'Italia*, ed. Giuseppi Mazzatinti et al. (Forlì: Bordandini, 1895), 5:190: "In nomine Christi. Amen. Coniuro te herbam vincham per dominum Patrem, etc., per lunam et stellas; et vinchas omnes inimichos, pontificem et sacerdotes et omnes laicos et omnes mulieres et omnes avocatos contra me." See also prayers against various afflictions in Florence, Biblioteca Nazionale Centrale, ms Conv. Soppr. F.4.776, fols. 76ʳ⁻ᵛ.

119. Florence, Biblioteca Medicea Laurenziana, ms Pl. xxv 3, fol. 15ᵛ.

this interpenetration of sacred power and worldly need is a vernacular Holy Week devotion from a fourteenth-century nun's prayer book.[120] Here, in a more cloistered environment, devotion skirts the edges of theological propriety. The devotion consists of a series of prayers, one for each day of Holy Week, not for meditation or reflection on the Passion, but to obtain "any benefit" (*per avere qualunche grazia*). For each day, the devotion prescribes a different posture: standing on Palm Sunday, and then, on the following days of Holy Week, kneeling, prostrate, standing, kneeling, standing, and standing. Numbers of Paters and Aves were to be recited each day: 12 on Palm Sunday, and 32, 48, 23, 22, 50, and 14 on the following days. There seems to be no special logic for the numbers and postures. After the Paters and Aves of each day, the supplicant recited a one-sentence invocation in the vernacular to request the desired *grazia*. These invocations focus on those present at the crucifixion: Mary Magdalene, the good thief, the Jews, John the Evangelist, and the Blessed Virgin, with each of whom the user associates or disassociates herself. The Triduum's verses recall Christ's last words, his cross, and his death. Only in those invocations did the rich affective piety seen in the prayers examined earlier make itself felt. The devotion closes, now wholly in Latin, on Easter Sunday with the psalm "Benedictus Deus" and a collect. This seemingly mechanical and somewhat self-interested exercise reflects the same union of the liturgical time and gesture, the centrality of the Pater and Ave, and the Christocentric piety that characterize communal devotional collections generally. It also joins that most central Christian mystery of the cross to concrete day-to-day needs.

More typical in manuscripts of devotion are prayers that associate the Incarnation and Christ's triumph over evil with the daily experience of the Eucharist. About 1300, one north Italian, perhaps a Franciscan, copied an extraordinary vernacular prayer of this type into his devotional miscellany:

> Divine Wisdom who concealed
> in human flesh the highest God,
> by this concealment you destroyed
> the one who teaches us sin by deceit.
> The pure humanity that you took on
> has put to death his wickedness.
> We ought to praise your great goodness,
> which for me put this evil so far off;
> we will see our flesh assumed to God.
> You made man in your own likeness;
> we adore it, that creation,
> in the Host made your own body.[121]

---

120. Florence, Biblioteca Nazionale Centrale, MS Palat. 150 (early XIV cent.), fol. 29ᵛ.

121. Bologna, Biblioteca Universitaria, MS 1563, fol. 17ᵛ: "Divina sapientia ke celasti, so carne humana lalta Deitate, | con quella celamentu debellasti kilui ke impari na offese a falzitate. | La pura humanitate

The charm of this prayer is somewhat lost in translation, which does not reproduce its rhymes, but the theological paradoxes remain. The Deity is hidden in Christ. Thus, the Devil, who tricked Adam, is himself deceived. God's great act of the Incarnation is possible only because he created human flesh in the first place. The creation of man in God's image receives honor through the miracle by which bread becomes Christ's human body on the altar at Mass. A Eucharistic doctrine so balanced in its theology and so expressive of the paradoxes of the Christian understanding of salvation would be hard to find in the schools of Paris or Bologna. The author wrote this prayer not in Latin, or even in formal Tuscanizing Italian, but in a regional dialect. Few Latin Eucharistic devotions rise to this level. One fourteenth-century owner copied a more conventional Eucharistic devotion on the verso of a blank folio at the beginning of his sumptuous thirteenth-century codex of works by the lay theologian Albertano of Brescia. The poem is one of many adaptions of the "Ave Corpus" model for Eucharistic prayers. The best known of these is the hymn "Ave Verum Corpus" itself, which is by far the most common Eucharistic devotion in the manuscripts examined. The short prayer is hardly more than a jingle, theologically unharmed by an attempt at verse translation:

> Hail, O Word, now incarnated,
>   on the altar consecrated.
> You, of angels, living bread,
>   Savior, hope for Christians fed.
> Praise, O body of Christ Jesus,
>   who descended and who frees us.
> Savior of the world and healing,
>   free us by your power annealing. Amen.[122]

Easy to memorize, the verses probably served as an elevation prayer. Rhymed Latin hymns in devotional collections sometimes rise to certain dignity and have considerable theological sophistication. Take, for example, the opening lines of a hymn from a miscellany of the early 1300s. In spite of the quadruple rhyme (not attempted in the translation), the verses are theologically suggestive:

> Hail living victim, truth, and life,
>   in whose sacrifice all others are ended.

---

ho pilglasti, deforusse a morte sua malignitate. | Laudare devemo tua gran boneneza, ke per mi fece si gran longinnitu; vedemo nostra carne assunta in Deu. | Fecestiti homo in vostra semelglanza; no ladoramo quellu operimentu, nel ostia mutata in corpu teu."

122. Florence, Biblioteca Nazionale Centrale, ms II.iv.iii (xiii cent.), fol. 1ᵛ: "Ave Verbum incarnatum, in altare consecratum. | Panis vivus angelorum, salus, spes Christianorum. | Salve Corpus Iesu Christi, qui pro nobis descendisti. | Salus mundi pro salute, libera nos cum virtute. Amen."

Through you infinite glory is given the Father,
   through you the Church stands united.[123]

Here the finality of the sacrifice of the cross becomes a springboard for
praising the work of Christ—who is truth and life—to the glory of the
Father. The stanza concludes with an ecclesiological association, in contrast
to the more privatized piety of the previous example. The stanza reflects the
ancient patristic vision of the Eucharist as the sacrament of Christian unity.
Elevated ideas, if not distinguished poetry.[124]

   The largest group of prayers in devotional collections is Christocentric
and Eucharistic. But close behind in popularity are compositions honoring
the Virgin Mary.[125] Marian miracles were beloved of preachers. They often
vindicate the honor the Virgin. One Paduan preacher of about 1300 recounted how a worldly cleric—clerics are often less devoted to Mary than
laypeople in these stories—dressed up in secular clothing and went dicing,
only to lose badly. On his way home, he jabbed his sword in the ground and
grumbled, "If only this were the Virgin Mary." The sword came out covered
with blood.[126] Italian devotional poetry of the period also focused on the
power of the Virgin. Bonvesin de la Riva dedicated one of his poems, "De
la dignitade de la Glorioxa Vergene," to this theme.[127] The work consists of
rhymed stanzas in praise of Mary and closes with an edifying example of
how she rewards those devoted to her.[128] A certain castellan had failed in his
duty to put down brigandage, but he did sing the Ave Maria many times a
day (*Spesse volte Ave Maria ognia dì cantava*). One day "Belzubù" came to take
him to hell, but Mary, remembering his devotion, protected him. So "Sa-
tanax" himself had to come to finish the job. Again the Queen of Heaven
intervened. The man was left safe but terrified and repented of his negligence:

Seeing that through the merits of the Virgin Mary
The man escaped body and soul, he returned to the good way,
And began to love the Virgin above all things that be,
And as much as he could render her honor and courtesy.[129]

123. Bologna, Biblioteca Universitaria, MS 1563, fol. 53ᵛ: "Ave vivens hostia, veritas, et, vita, | in qua
sacrificia cuncta sunt finita. | Per te Patris gloria datur infinita, | per te stat ecclesia igitur unita."
   124. For other Eucharistic devotions, consult Florence, Biblioteca Nazionale Centrale, MS Magl. xxx-
vi.81ᵇⁱˢ (XIII cent.), fols. 263ʳ⁻ᵛ, and Verona, Biblioteca Civica, MS 415 (early XIV cent.), fols. 1ᵛ–7ʳ, which
belonged to a woman.
   125. On the Christocentricity of communal piety, see Cinzio Violante, "Sistemi organizzativi della
cura d'anime in Italia tra Medioevo e Rinascimento: Discorso introduttivo," *Pievi e parrocchie*, ed. Erba et
al., 1:29.
   126. Padua, Biblioteca Universitaria, MS 717 (XIV cent.), fols. 1ʳ⁻ᵛ.
   127. Edited in *Poesie lombarde del secolo XIII*, 181–94. For another example, see the poem "Verzene
Gloriosa Anima Bella," in Bologna, Biblioteca Universitaria, MS 2727, fols. 39ᵛ–40ᵛ.
   128. *Poesie lombarde del secolo XIII*, 188–93.
   129. Ibid., 193: "Vezando ke per li meriti de la Vergine Maria | Scampato è om corpo e in anima, el
torna in bona via; | E prende ad amare la Vergene sopra tute le cosse che sia, | E quanto el pò ge rende
honore e cortexia."

So the poem ends, with the expectation that the reader will do likewise.

Extravagant claims for the Virgin's power did not cause Italians to separate Marian devotion from that to her son, Jesus. Their prayers and devotions did not make her a mother of mercy in contrast to a Christ of judgment, as happened in some late medieval piety.[130] There were moves in that direction, but focus on the crucified and Eucharistic Christ, himself the font of mercy, discouraged this division of roles. Rather, Marian prayers of the communal period are usually restrained, biblical, and Christologically sensitive. One "Gaude" prayer-poem from an early-fourteenth-century collection may be taken as typical:

> Rejoice, Virgin Mother of Christ,
>> who through your ear conceived,
>> hearing Gabriel's message.
> Rejoice, for filled with God,
>> you gave birth without pain,
>> the lily of modesty.
> Rejoice, for the one you bore,
>> whose death you grieved,
>> has a glorious resurrection.
> Rejoice, for, as you witnessed,
>> he to heaven ascended,
>> raised by his own power.
> Rejoice, for you ascended after him,
>> and great is your honor
>> in the heavenly palace.
> There the fruit of your womb,
>> is, through you, given us to enjoy
>> in happiness everlasting.[131]

In this lovely composition, Mary's joys are directly retraced to the works and triumph of her son. Her greatest glory was to be the first believer to be associated with him in his suffering, Resurrection, Ascension, and enthronement in heaven. The poem ends with an intimation of what is prepared for all good Christians in eternity. Marian prayers are typically of this sort.

130. For this division of roles in later piety, see Heiko Oberman, *The Harvest of Medieval Theology* (Durham, N.C.: Labyrinth, 1983), 313–17, on the sermons of Gabriel Biel.

131. Bologna, Biblioteca Universitaria, ms 1563, fol. 17ʳ: "Gaude, Virgo Mater Christi, que per aurem concepisti, Gabriele nunctio. | Gaude, quia Deo plena, perperisti sine pena, cum pudoris lilio. | Gaude, quia tui nati, quem dolebat mortem pati, fulget resurrectio. | Gaude, quia, te vidente, et in celum ascendente motu fertur proprio. | Gaude que post ipsum scandis, et est honor tibi grandis in celi palatio. | Ibi fructu ventris tui, quod te nobis datur frui, in perenni gaudio." For another example of this kind of Christocentric Mariology, see the thirteenth-century hymn "Ave Dei Genitrix et Immaculata," in Florence, Biblioteca Medicea Laurenziana, ms Pl. xxv 3, fols. 210ᵛ–211ᵛ. Note also the already mentioned biblical expansion of the Ave Maria in Florence, Biblioteca Medicea Laurenziana, ms Pl. xxv 3, fol. 363ᵛ.

Nevertheless, the Florentine woman's "Marian" devotional collection mentioned earlier reveals a more luxurious strain in popular Mariology. One rubric in it, which precedes a long devotional exercise, ascribed it to "Saint Gregory," who supposedly embellished it with an indulgence of 8,440 years "for mortal sins and the pain of purgatory." The rubric promised that those who said it, kneeling before an image of the Virgin, for thirty days, would receive "whatever just favor" (*ogni giusta gratia*) they might ask. Even more remarkably, should devotees perform the devotion every day until death, the Blessed Virgin would herself appear at that hour before their bodily eyes. But in contrast to its rubric, the prayer's piety is remarkably restrained and wholly conventional. The prayer focuses on Mary's experience at the foot of the cross; it gives equal attention to the suffering Christ and his work of redemption. Only near the end, when the user would ask the "just favor," does the Marian focus shoulder out the role of Christ and the prayer itself become a litany of the titles, biblical and popular, of the merciful Virgin.[132]

The collections also lack devotions focused on votive Masses—to celebrate a certain number of times with certain numbers of candles and prayers—like those that became so common in the late Middle Ages. But the scribe of the vernacular vita of Saint Petronio did include one such exercise, unique in the manuscripts examined, on the last pages of his manuscript. Its rubric promised that Christ would give strength in any adversity to all who recited a certain verse one hundred times and had three Masses celebrated in honor of the Blessed Trinity. The verse recited was itself a marvel of Trinitarian simplicity: "Ave Sancta Trinitas, equalis una Deitas, ut me facias constantem per tuam benignitatem" (Hail Holy Trinity, equally One Deity, make me constant through your kindness). During each Mass three candles were to burn on the altar, and three paupers were to receive alms. Each Mass was to have three collects, that of the Trinity, that of Our Lady, and that to God, "who does not fail to hear the cries of those afflicted." In spite of the rubric's mechanical implications and the devotion's repetitions, which for some moderns verge on superstition, the prayer was perfectly orthodox. The copyist assured the reader that if it did not bring benefit to the body, the devotion would aid the soul in the world to come. At the foot of the page he added his own simple prayer: "Mary, our advocate, pray for us. Amen."[133]

RELIGIOUS LITERATURE

To turn from collections of prayers to the other religious literature produced in the communes means taking a step away from lived piety. Reading devotional books must have been typical of only a very small fraction of the population; the circles that consumed ethical treatises and catechetical texts

132. Florence, Biblioteca Medicea Laurenziana, MS Gaddi 231, fols. 1ʳ–13ʳ.
133. "Ave Maria nostra advocata, ora pro nobis. Amen." Bologna, Biblioteca Universitaria, MS 2060 (XIV cent.), fols. 21ᵛ–23ᵛ.

were probably even smaller. Nonetheless, manuscripts containing such works are by no means rare in Italian libraries. In numbers they today far surpass collections of prayers, even if the latter were probably produced in greater number. There was more reason to preserve a fine codex of Albertano of Brescia than a cheap pamphlet of prayers. Since most prayer collections were short, codices that contain them, even when not created by modern binders, usually contain similar works. A manuscript from the early 1300s, in the Ambrosiana of Milan, may be taken as typical.[134] This collection assembles extracts from the *Arbor Vitae* of Bonaventure, a poetic prayer on the Passion, a sermon by Saint Bernard, the section on charity from a treatise on the virtues, an abstract from Augustine's *Soliloquies*, an anonymous treatise on hell, a treatise on the end of the world attributed to Saint Albert the Great, a versified guide to making a good confession, and a prayer to all the saints. This manuscript is in a single hand. A mostly vernacular collection of the late 1200s in the Biblioteca Nazionale at Florence provides another example.[135] It contains works of Albertano of Brescia, a moralizing collection on the virtues of the ancients called *De' filosafiadi e d'imperadori,* some Provençal poetry (entirely secular), and a couple of Latin prayers. Even ignoring their long selections in the vernacular, these manuscripts present a striking contrast to monastic or clerical compilations. Those usually consist of patristic sermons and theological treatises.[136] This contrast remains even when the content of the clerical manuscripts is more varied: such assemblages emphasize sermons, biblical commentaries, pastoral aids (particularly for hearing confessions), and an occasional theological treatise (e.g., Adso's *On the Antichrist*).[137]

The content of a manuscript like that of the Ambrosiana could be as idiosyncratic and unique as any collection of prayers. But certain generalizations are possible. Among the religious literature read in the communes, sermons did not enjoy the esteem typical of the later Middle Ages. Even collections of edifying stories remained, until well into the 1300s, a clerical preserve, used mostly to prepare homilies.[138] Codices with large vernacular content or Latin works intended for lay use include works from three general categories. The first and most common is "vices-and-virtues literature."[139] It ranges from versified catalogues of the cardinal and theological virtues to florilegia containing rules of life abstracted from pagan and classical sources. The most common subgroup in this category is confessional aids for lay-

---

134. Milan, Biblioteca Ambrosiana, ms Y 5 Sup.

135. Florence, Biblioteca Nazionale Centrale, ms Conv. Soppr. F.4.776.

136. E.g., Florence, Biblioteca Medicea Laurenziana, ms Conv. Soppr. 137, which is late-twelfth-century and clearly monastic.

137. This reflects the contents of the early-thirteenth-century Florence, Biblioteca Medicea Laurenziana, ms Aed. 37.

138. The vernacular collection of miracle stories in Bologna, Biblioteca Universitaria, ms 158, fols. 14^r–24^r, which dates to the 1300s, is among the earliest I know of.

139. This literature has been extensively catalogued in Bloomfield et al., *Incipits*.

people. The second group, still well represented but less so than the moralizing literature, consists of poems and treatises explaining the Creed or Catholic doctrines. Among these are short expositions of theological topics of popular interest, such as the end of the world or the causes of evil. I place in this category the fragmentary biblical translations occasionally encountered after 1300. I call this grouping "catechetical literature." Last in quantity come meditations and pious reflections. Among these, two compositions much outrank the rest in popularity. The first, and by far more common, is the meditation on the life of Christ falsely ascribed to Bonaventure. The second is a fascinating little work known as the *Piato di Gesu Christo*.[140] The Pseudo-Bonaventure is a clerical work that appealed to the piety of the communes; the *Piato* is probably a lay product and deserves special attention. I will not undertake here an exhaustive analysis of these three types of devotional literature. The small size of its audience counsels against that kind of emphasis. Instead I will present an overview, give some examples, and position these three categories within the piety that is the topic of this chapter.

For Zucchero Bencivenni, an understanding of the virtues and corresponding vices was essential for right living.[141] Treatises on the vices and virtues already existed in the Carolingian period, when Alcuin of York contributed an effort of his own.[142] In the wake of Lateran IV, clerical authors produced in great numbers updated versions, intended for use in sermons or when hearing confessions. The most widely distributed of these was the *Tractatus de Virtutibus* of the Dominican Guillaume Perault (Willielmus Peradus), which circulated in Latin. Other examples of the genre, including anonymous abridgments and reworkings, are common.[143] Only in the early 1300s did Francesco of Perugia, a Franciscan priest, produce a treatise of this type intended specifically for lay use, the *Tractatus de Septem Vitiis Capitalibus et Decem Preceptis*.[144] It dwelt on the vices, said little of the opposing virtues, and seemed mostly intended as an aid for going to confession. Like other clerical productions, it lacked concrete examples and smelled of the scholastic lecture room. As a popularizer, however, Fra Francesco was late off the mark. Vir-

140. I have completely omitted three items from consideration: vernacularized saints' lives, the hymns known as *laudi*, and the religious dramas known as *sacre rappresentazioni*. Nearly all examples are dated well into the 1300s, outside our period. In the case of *laudi*, of which thirteenth-century examples survive, there is no evidence these were ever used in private prayer or meditation.

141. Zucchero Bencivenni, *Trattato del ben vivere*, ed. Giuseppe Manuzzi (Florence: Passigli, 1848), 6.

142. His *De Octo Vitiis Principalibus*, which consisted of chapters 27–35 of his larger *Liber de Virtutibus et Vitiis* (*PL* 101:613–38), circulated in thirteenth-century Italy. E.g., Florence, Biblioteca Medicea Laurenziana, MS Mugellana 10, contains this treatise. See Bloomfield et al., *Incipits*, 304, no. 3593, on Alcuin's work.

143. Bloomfield's *Incipits* gives some idea of the extent of this literature. Merely for the sake of examples from our period, see Milan, Biblioteca Ambrosiana, MS H 168 Inf., fols. 54^r–116^v (Perault and other anonymous examples); Bologna, Biblioteca Universitaria, MS 2580 (XIV cent.), fols. 1^r–14^v (anonymous short treatment); Bologna, Biblioteca Universitaria, MS 1563, fol. 9^r (anonymous one-folio summary); Milan, Biblioteca Ambrosiana, MS Trotti 541 (XIV cent.), fols. 135^v–141^v (vernacular version similar to Alcuin's).

144. A copy is found in Florence, Biblioteca Nazionale Centrale, MS Magl. XXXV.

tues literature was the first religious literature written and consumed on a large scale by the Italian laity. Lay products differed from the clerical in that they elaborated the virtues and vices more by examples than analysis. These works gave pride of place to secular sources: tales of the Roman emperors and examples from pagan moralists like Seneca and Cicero were common. Christian and Old Testament figures complemented the pagan core, but the image was of a nonclerical world.[145]

This literature is virtually unedited, with the happy exception of the *Fior di virtù*, a mid-thirteenth-century vernacular treatment first printed in 1491 and now available in a modern translation.[146] In number of manuscripts, it overshadows all the rest.[147] What made it so popular? Certainly, its Italian dress and its focus on secular examples were critical. The organization by virtues and vices linked it to the growing desire for confessional preparation. There was also a distinctly "legal" feel to its piling up of "witnesses" and "authorities"—it is a massive text. This must have recommended it to readers touched by the revival of Roman law in communal Italy. Along with exempla, the *Fior* provided each vice and virtue with pithy proverbs and sayings that commended themselves to memorization. The exemplary stories are often entertaining, even amusing, and occasionally set in the cities of north Italy. The second most popular lay author of moralizing literature was Albertano of Brescia. He also wrote theological treatises that circulated among the laity, or at least among confraternity members.[148] Albertano wrote in Latin, but that did not hinder his popularity. He has recently been the subject of a fine study in English.[149] His works are all marked by a certain practicality and an engagement with the civic life. Both Albertanus and the *Fior di virtù* share a strikingly sympathetic attitude toward women.[150] The *Fior* author condemned writers who used only "bad women" in their examples. He declared: "In fact every day, we see examples of women strongly resisting and defending themselves against the violence of men, while the latter do not have to defend themselves against women. So that those who speak so badly of these poor and unfortunate women would do better to be silent since, naturally, they do not have a true and honorable foundation."[151] This attitude is a world away from the stereotyped misogyny sometimes showcased as typical of medieval moralists. Whether Albert's or the *Fior*'s enlightened views affected their readers is impossible to say. That two of the most

145. For examples, see the anonymous *Flores Moralium Auctoritatum* (XIV cent.) of Verona, Biblioteca Capitolare, MS CLXVIII (155), or the *Trattato delle quattro virtù cardinali*, found in Florence, Biblioteca Nazionale Centrale, MS II.IV.269 (XIV cent.).

146. Reprinted in *The Florentine Fior di Virtù of 1491*, trans. Nicholas Fersin (Philadelphia: Stern, 1953).

147. The Biblioteca Riccardiana of Florence, e.g., has no fewer than fifteen manuscripts of the work.

148. As evidenced, e.g., by their presence in Padua, Biblioteca Civica, C.M.215 (late XIII cent.), fols. 1ʳ–46ᵛ, a late-thirteenth-century codex. Here they share space with such "secular" texts as a *De Natura Animalium*, a *Notabilia Boetii* (recording remarkable dates and births), and a *Tractatus de Spera*.

149. See Powell, *Albertanus*.

150. Ibid., 116, compares the authors on women.

151. *Florentine Fior di Virtù*, 18; on this passage, see Powell, *Albertanus*, 116.

popular moralizing works have this "feminist" bent certainly suggests that they would also have appealed to women.

One thing is certain: the mere number of extant manuscripts indicates that communal readers liked religious literature treating the virtues and giving edifying exempla for them. Virtues literature collected exempla from classical authors, pagan philosophers, folklore and legend, the Bible, and saints' lives. In the special place it gave to "good pagans" (and their bad counterparts), virtues literature popularized the reappropriation of classical knowledge typical of the Aristotelian revival in scholastic theology. What Saint Thomas Aquinas did for the vices and virtues in the Secunda Secundae of his *Summa* for a clerical audience, the *Fior* and similar works did for the laity when they juggled contrasting pairs of vices and virtues.[152] This contrasting method appealed to readers. Umiltà of Faenza found it natural to oppose vices and virtues in sermons to her nuns, as did the otherwise unknown lay penitent Fra Cristiano, whose letter on the virtues of humility and fortitude to a *"fradelo"* appears in the codex of the vernacular life of Saint Petronio.[153]

One example, the treatment of friendship (*amicitia*) from the *Fior di virtù*, will suffice to give a sense of this literature's form and tone.[154] The treatment comes in the middle of the section listing the different kinds of love and their opposing vices. First, the author defines friendship: it is the kind of love that makes unrelated individuals want to be together (*stare insieme*). This is experiential and not very philosophical. But the author also knows that Aristotle divided the virtue of friendship three ways, so he gives three reasons for wanting to be together: mere utility, cooperation in some project, and desire for the other's good. This is an interesting reworking of Aristotle's division of friendship: a union in pursuit of the useful, the pleasurable, or the good. Pleasure has become business; the good pursued is no longer philosophical abstraction, but moral growth. In each section, after defining and dividing the virtue or vice, the author gives exemplary stories and aphorisms—the "authorities." For friendship, there are no stories, but there are some fine tags. These come from Solomon (friends help friends in adversity), Aristotle (people are social beings), Cicero (even heaven's glory would be sad without a friend there), Plato (test your friends), and finally the canon law in Gratian's *Decretum* (friendship with bad people is bad). Not only has the virtue been adapted to the way a person in the world (as opposed to a monk or philosopher) might experience it, but the reader has been equipped with pithy sayings to call to mind when trying to practice it. Is the *Fior di virtù* a "religious" work? Not if "religious" restricted its use to the cloister or the altar. If saintli-

152. See Casagrande, "Moltiplicazione," 267, on the pairing of vices and virtues.
153. E.g., Umiltà of Faenza, "Sermo 2," 18; Fra Cristiano's letter is in Corti, *Vita*, 53–58 (i.e., Bologna, Biblioteca Universitaria, ms 2060, fols. 21ᵛ–23ᵛ).
154. Bologna, Biblioteca Universitaria, ms 158, fols. 26ʳ⁻ᵛ; for a translation, see *Florentine Fior di Virtu*, 9–11.

ness can be found when carrying wine casks, selling combs, organizing hospitals, making shoes, and spending time with friends in the contado, then the practical moralism of the *Fior di virtù* is a road to saintliness. Citizens of the communes found in it the kind of moral wisdom suitable to their cities, thus its frequent recopying and imitation.

The communal period saw a multiplication of catechetical works second only to that of moralizing works on the virtues. The most celebrated was Zucchero Bencivenni's translation of the *Somme* of Laurent of Orleans, to which I have often referred. It commonly appears in manuscripts under the Latin title *Catechesimus Christianus Catholicus* or in the vernacular as *Queste rendite sono le virtudi*.[155] The work included hundreds of exempla. The section on the vices and virtues resembles Italian productions like the *Fior di virtù*. But this work was much broader than the typical virtues collection. It dealt with doctrine, prayer, the beatitudes, and other aspects of Christian teaching. It was patterned on sets of seven: seven sacraments, seven virtues, seven deadly sins, seven beatitudes, seven petitions of the Pater Noster, seven gifts of the Holy Spirit. Laurent drew heavily on exempla from sacred and profane history. The result was a practical guide that dealt, in simple fashion, even with technical theological issues such as unmerited and merited grace.[156] In the early 1300s, authors excerpted and adapted Zucchero Bencivenni's massive and unwieldy work.[157]

In contrast, the Apostles' Creed was brief, uncomplicated, and recommended by the Church as the doctrinal text for religious instruction.[158] Already by 1264, the north-Italian poet Pietro da Bescapé had produced the poem *No è cosa*, which followed the order of the Creed and elaborated each section with stories from Scripture.[159] In elaborating the material, Pietro added moral and biblical material. For example, after treating the unity of God and his act of creation, Pietro added a narrative of Adam's fall modeled on Genesis and an analysis of humanity's fallen state in terms of the seven capital sins.[160] When he turned to the birth of Christ, he merely mentioned the Creed. The poem's stanzas on this dogma report the birth narratives of Matthew and Luke.[161] The last things, which the Creed mentions briefly as

155. I have consulted the texts in Florence, Biblioteca Nazionale Centrale, MS II.vi.16, and Florence, Biblioteca Medicea Laurenziana, MS Conv. Redi 102. Small sections of the Italian have been edited in Zucchero Bencivenni, *Trattatello delle virtù*, ed. Luigi Barbieri (Bologna: Romagnoli, 1863); the Pater Noster section of this work is edited in id., *Volgarizzamento dell'esposizione del paternostro*, ed. Rigoli.

156. See, e.g., Zucchero Bencivenni, *Sposizione*, 6.

157. E.g., the anonymous thirteenth-century catechetical and moralizing material found in Florence, Biblioteca Nazionale Centrale, MS II.iv.111, fols. 74ʳ–103ʳ.

158. Yves M.-J. Congar, "Saint Thomas et les archidiacres," *Revue thomiste* 57 (1957): 660, traces the legal diffusion of the Lateran legislation. Thomas Aquinas commented on it in his opusculum on the Creed. It lies behind the profession of faith proposed in the decree *Firmiter* of the Gregorian Decretals (x 1.1.1).

159. Edited in *Poesie lombarde del secolo XIII*, 35–156, from Milan, Biblioteca Nazionale Braidense, MS AD.xiii.48.

160. *Poesie lombarde del secolo XIII*, 43–61.

161. Ibid., 62–68.

carnis resurrectionem, vitam aeternam, provided an opportunity to elaborate on the general judgment, the horrors of hell, and the joys of heaven.[162] Pietro's work had pretensions to literary grandeur and was long. Other anonymous poets, such as the one who recast the text into vernacular tercets, attempted less elaborate presentations of the Creed.[163] More common than poetic versions were short treatises explaining the Creed. The commentary on the Creed I discussed in Chapter 8, that prepared by a godfather for his godson, is a good example.[164] There were also small works on specific doctrinal topics. These often used numbers as a memory device. A tiny Latin treatise in a Bologna manuscript of the early 1300s gives the "five ways" in which God chastises people.[165] The author supplies biblical authorities for all except the last: when God decides to begin punishing people, while they are still alive, who are going to hell. God may also chastise people in order to prove their constancy to others, as in the case of Job or Tobit. He may afflict them so that Jesus or a saint can heal them in a display of power or mercy, as with the man born blind through no sin of his own or of his parents. Or, he may do it so that the person does not become proud, as with Saint Paul's thorn in the flesh. And so forth. Why bad things happen to good people is a perennial Christian problem.

Another theological summary is the tiny vernacular treatise on "fifteen signs to appear before the judgment," found in another Bologna codex.[166] This author claimed to draw on both the Bible and the sibyls, but all his signs were actually biblical. The list consisted of horrible cataclysms such as the sundering of oceans from their beds, starvation of all animals, and a rain of fire from heaven. The reader is left with a conviction that since none of this is happening yet, time remains for repentance before the dreadful day. Bridging the gap between doctrinal and moral treatises was a genre that rivaled both in popularity, confessional aids. These rank with the virtues literature in popularity and are often found in the same manuscripts. Since I have discussed the character of these works in Chapter 7, there is no reason to do so here.

PRAYING IN SILENCE

The devotional literature examined so far has a direct concrete quality, whether it concerns belief or morals. The prayers focused on Christ's redemptive death and the Virgin's loving intercession. They elaborated on the Pater Noster and the Ave Maria, the two mainstays of the lay office. Moralizing works focused on practical spiritual growth (virtues) and on the predica-

162. Ibid., 144–57.
163. Modena, Biblioteca Estense Universitaria, MS α.R.2.3, fols. 1ra–b.
164. Bologna, Biblioteca Universitaria, MS 158, fols. 47^v–50^v.
165. Bologna, Biblioteca Universitaria, MS 1563, fol. 9^v.
166. Bologna, Biblioteca Universitaria, MS 158, fol. 2^v. The "fifteen signs" would have a great vogue in the latter Middle Ages, as in England: Duffy, *Stripping of the Altars,* 70, 72, 82, 227.

ment of the penitent in confession (vices). Pietro da Bescapé's poetry served a catechetical purpose by elaborating on the Creed. But the people of the communes were not monks. Their prayer and reading had to fit into a day filled with work, community, and family responsibilities. Nonetheless, some people, a tiny spiritual "elite," probably spent time in meditation and mental prayer. What did they read? Versions of Gospel stories were probably the most important. The earliest life of Saint Francis, the first of the two by Tommaso of Celano, contains numerous allusions that reflect Francis's own taste in pious reading.[167] The allusions are almost exclusively from the synoptic Gospels, Matthew, Mark, and Luke. These are devoid of abstract doctrine and highlight Christ as an example of virtue or as the suffering Savior. When the life cites Paul or gives a doctrinal lesson, the voice is that of Celano, not Francis. Contemporary lay readers' taste in scripture was probably similar to that of Francis. Extant fragmentary translations of Scripture into the vernacular show a similar preference for the Gospels, especially those used at Mass.[168]

It is, then, no surprise that the text for contemplative reading most popular in communal Italy was the Pseudo-Bonaventurian *Meditationes Vitae Cristi*. These meditations appeared in Italian by the early 1300s, and manuscripts of them are found in nearly every major Italian library.[169] The meditations are affective, moving readers' attention from Christ's actions to the experiences of his disciples, in particular those of John the Evangelist, Mary Magdalene, and the Blessed Virgin. Women's encounters with Christ outnumber those of men by nearly two to one. The work, especially in its vernacular adaptation, pivoted on the Virgin Mother's sorrow that she would not be present for Jesus' celebration of the Passover. She asked that he hold a celebration of it for her and the other women, and Christ obliged.[170] As with Albertano of Brescia and the *Fior di virtù*, one might suspect a female readership. But, for all their adaption to lay and feminine sensibilities, the *Meditations* were a clerical product. They had more in common with the anchorhold than the palazzo.

One composition for devotional reading might conceivably be traced to a

167. See Étienne Delaruelle, "Saint François d'Assise et la piété populaire," *San Francesco nella ricerca storica degli ultimi ottanta anni, 13–16 ottobre 1968,* Convegni del Centro di studi sulla spiritualità medievale 9 (Todi: Accademia Tudertina, 1971), 128–30.

168. E.g., see the translation of the Gospels of Mass in Florence, Biblioteca Nazionale Centrale, MS Palat. 4, fols. 1ʳ–50ʳ (mid-1300s). Translations of other books, such as the Psalter, are even later. Florence, Biblioteca Nazionale Centrale, MS Palat. 2, contains a vernacular Psalter that might date to the late 1300s.

169. I counted four versions in the Riccardiana of Florence alone. The Latin *Meditations* are edited in Bonaventure, *Opera Omnia* (Paris: Vives, 1868), vol. 12. The vernacular version is edited in *Mistici del duecento e del trecento,* ed. Arrigo Levasti (Milan: Rizzoli, 1935). On this work's impact on Italian art, see Millard Meiss, *Painting in Florence and Siena After the Black Death: The Arts, Religion, and Society in the Mid–Fourteenth Century* (New York: Harper & Row, 1973), 125–30, esp. 128.

170. Meditazione 72, *Mistici del duecento,* ed. Levasti, 203; this motif of the women's Passover also appears in other meditations on the Passion, e.g., Florence, Biblioteca Medicea Laurenziana, MS Gaddi 187 (early XIV cent.), fols. 36ʳ–37ʳ.

lay author, the *Piato di Gesu Cristo*, the "Pleading of Jesus Christ." The idea of a court contest between Christ and the Devil over the salvation of humanity appeared first in French sermons of the early 1200s.[171] During the mid-1200s, an unknown Italian adopted the sermonic topos and turned it into an actual "court transcript." The pleading exists in a Pisan-Lucchese version, a Milanese version, and an abbreviated Latin adaption.[172] The trial begins with the Devil's opening argument. He claims his right over humanity by custom, because humanity has been in his power for a very long time; by imperial law, because they have overreached their rights; by natural law, because they ignored their Creator; by divine law, because Adam and Eve violated a revealed commandment; and by the law of Justinian, because they are his slaves, since he captured them in battle. Christ answers for humanity, arguing the defense *de dolo;* since the Devil deceived Adam and Eve, he got possession by fraud. The two lawyers trade a series of legal jabs. The Devil eventually claims the right to humanity by the Roman law of prescription, that is, the principle that even an unjust possessor gets title after long possession. Jesus counters that only uncontested possession grants title. The Devil replies that Eve sinned knowingly and willingly. Jesus counters that although Eve knowingly and willingly sinned, the Devil cannot advance his claim *in preiudizio del marito*—that is, by using a wife's error against her husband. The Devil counters that this would only hold if Eve had not been "emancipated," which she was by God's grant to her of free will. And so the contest goes.

Having exhausted his first round of arguments to no clear result, the Devil uses theology against Jesus: no human being can repent without grace, and Jesus has no right or legal entitlement to offer it. But Christ replies that he can use the legal title of the *buono amico*, the "good friend" of the accused. And we are back to another round of legal arguments. Again the debate reaches no clear conclusion, so, in the Pisan version, Christ invokes the logic of popular devotion. Just as one good coin is worth more than any number of bad ones, so one good work of the Blessed Virgin, who is a member of Adam's race, outweighs even six thousand years of sins. This was an argument than any pious Italian would have understood; Christ thinks like a pious layperson of the commune. This is a Savior who would have been perfectly at home in the law schools of Bologna, a Jesus that the men of the Italian republics could understand, just as the Jesus of the Pseudo-Bonaventure could speak to the needs and hopes of their wives.

171. Bloomfield, *Seven Deadly Sins*, 92–93, gives examples from Peter of Blois and Steven of Tournai.

172. The Pisan version, along with works by Albertano of Brescia, appears in Florence, Biblioteca Nazionale Centrale, MS II.VIII.49, fols. 209ʳ–212ᵛ, as "Piatto ch'ebbi Dio con l'inimicho"; the Milanese version (early 1300s), in Milan, Biblioteca Trivulziana, MS 768, fols. 48ʳ–53ʳ, as "Libro del piato che fece Cristo in su la croce col diavolo"; a Latin abbreviation (late 1300s), in Siena, Biblioteca Comunale degli Intronati, MS G.X.17. Barbi, "D'un antico codice," 277, suggests a late-thirteenth- or early-fourteenth-century date and a Pisan or Luccan origin for the *Piato*. Franz Roediger, ed., *Contrasti antichi: Cristo e Satana*, Collezione di operette edite ed inedite, 14 (Florence: Libreria Dante, 1887), edits the Florence manuscript. There are probably other versions.

Chapter Ten
World Without End. Amen.

In communal Italy there was a proper way to die; everyone knew it.[1] The chronicler Giovanni de' Mussi described the pious end of Umberto Palavicino in 1269. Umberto confessed, not just to one priest, but "many times to Dominicans, Franciscans, and prelates of the Church"; all absolved him of his sins. He received the last rites—confession, Communion, and anointing—while still conscious and clearheaded. His friends and relatives could certainly hope that his soul had ascended to heaven: "His was a good end."[2] In contrast, the Franciscan chronicler Salimbene described two "bad deaths." Giuliano de' Sessi of Reggio, a persecutor of the Church, in 1249 "passed from this world, wholly stinking, excommunicated, and cursed; without confession, without Communion, and without making satisfaction, on his way to the Devil."[3] Salimbene could imagine no greater horror than the death of a sinner like the worldly Bishop Obizzo of Parma. He supposedly refused deathbed Communion, saying he did not believe in it. But he also said he liked being bishop for the money. Fra Salimbene had no doubt he was rotting in hell.[4] The chroniclers observe good dying from a distance.

1. On death and dying, see Philippe Ariès's classic lectures, *Western Attitudes Toward Death: From the Middle Ages to the Present,* trans. Patricia M. Ranum (Baltimore: Johns Hopkins University Press, 1974). For a summary of other French studies, see Gabriella Severino Polica, "Morte e cultura ecclesiastica nel duecento," *Studi storici* 21 (1980), 909–14. On the anthropology of death, see Peter Metcalf and Richard Huntington, eds., *Celebrations of Death: The Anthropology of Mortuary Ritual,* 2d ed. (Cambridge: Cambridge University Press, 1991), esp. 24–37, and Maurice Block and Jonathan Parry, eds., *Death and the Regeneration of Life* (Cambridge: Cambridge University Press, 1982), 5–6. I thank Prof. Aletta Biersack of the University of Oregon for these references.

2. Giovanni de' Mussi, *Chronicon Placentinum* (1269), col. 476. See also Ariès, *Western Attitudes,* 5–6, on the survival of ideas on "proper ways to die."

3. Salimbene, *Cronica* (1249), 483, Baird trans., 332: "totus fetidus, excommunicatus et maledictus, sine confessione, sine communione, sine satisfactione de hoc mundo recessit, vadens ad diabolum." For the links between decay, damnation, and "bad death," see Block and Parry, *Death and the Regeneration of Life,* 16–17, and John Middleton, "Lugbara Death," ibid., 144–45.

4. Salimbene, *Cronica* (1233), 97–98, Baird trans., 46.

Sometimes we are privileged with a closer view. When Saint Pietro of Foligno received a revelation from God that he would soon die, he began his preparation. Each day until the Thursday before his death, he heard solemn Mass in the church of San Feliciano. When he could no longer assist at Mass, he called for a priest to make a general confession for the sins of his entire life. He received his last Communion, the viaticum. The next Sunday, lying ill in his little room in the church bell tower, he called for extreme unction, the anointing of the dying. He had himself laid down on the hard stones of the floor and took the sacred cross in his hands. Surrounded by his admirers and friends, he died. When his soul departed the earth, those in church for Sunday Mass saw the shrine candles he had so carefully tended miraculously come alight. The clergy buried him there in the church, near his beloved shrines, with great crowds assisting.[5]

Heretics and excommunicates forfeited the consolation of the last rites. A good death came in full union with the orthodox Church and the community of the faithful. As the thirteenth century wore on, authorities monitored the dying process ever more closely. In the late 1290s, Don Giacopo Benintendi of the church of San Tommaso in Bologna gave the last rites and a Christian burial to his parishioner Rosafiore, who years before had been penanced for involvement with heretics. The Bolognese inquisition punished him with a stiff fine and burned the woman's bones.[6] Earlier in the century a lifetime of devotion to God and service to neighbor rendered one worthy of the last rites. A good death was the promise of a good life. Zucchero Bencivenni opened his Italian adaption of Laurent of Orleans's treatise on the virtues with the assertion: "Who does not know how to live, does not know how to die; if you want to live authentically [*francamente*], learn to die happily."[7] A happy death followed a life in which the Christian chose the true goods (*veraci beni*) of divine grace over the inferior goods (*mezzani beni*) of earth: beauty, wealth, power, knowledge. Earthly goods were not bad, but only Christian love of God—charity—enabled the believer to master worldly allurements and not be mastered by them. Charity made the Christian a true lord (*signore*) of his life, with the prowess (*prodezza*) necessary to be a knight of God (*cavaliere di Dio*).[8] Authenticity of action (*franchezza*) was central to Zucchero Bencivenni's treatise. The one who possessed it—as sinners, children, and slaves could not—had true nobility (*vera nobilità*) and so true

5. Giovanni Gorini, *[Legenda de Vita et Obitu Beati Petri de Fulgineo]*, 11, *Analecta Bollandiana* 8 (1889): 367–68.

6. *ASOB*, no. 15 (April 1299) and no. 806 (20 April 1299), 1:37–39, 2:597–98; on this incident, see pages 444–46 below.

7. Zucchero Bencivenni, *Trattato del ben vivere*, 1: "che non sa vivere, e non sa morire. Se tu vuoli vivere francamente, appendi a morire lietamente."

8. Ibid., 8–20.

freedom.[9] That freedom gave the power to surrender one's soul to God without fear when death came.

To use Zucchero Bencivenni's chivalric language, the final battle with evil came on the deathbed. Here the enemy, the Devil, might visibly appear, even to good Christians, and tempt them to despair of heaven. Those assisting at the deathbed had to be ready with their prayers to help the dying fend off these manifestations of the Evil One.[10] No true Christian undertook the final battle alone; that would have been not the valor of a knight but the recklessness of a fool. It would have been pride, the sin that brought the fall of both Adam and the evil angels. Humility was to admit the need for mercy and accept the aid of God, one's neighbors, and the saints.[11]

Drama of the Deathbed

The vernacular vita of Saint Petronio, patron of Bologna, described his final days and showed readers how to prepare for a good death. Holy as he was, the bishop had to acknowledge his sins. He called his clergy and household to the bedside for his last words and prayers, and greeted them with an edifying discourse, charging them to love one another and, above all, to act always in ways pleasing to God. He received Communion and improvised a prayer of thanksgiving. He thanked God for his graces and gifts, both known and unknown. Next, in a prayer modeled on the articles of the Creed, he praised God for Christ's birth, death on the cross, and bodily resurrection. The prayer was proof of his Catholic orthodoxy. Then he turned to the Blessed Virgin, praying the Ave Maria in the Church's Latin. His Ave, as was then the form, lacked the verse requesting help "at the hour of our death." But Petronio's other prayers manifested his conviction that Mary was the surest help for sinners at that time. He praised the Blessed Mother for her role in the Incarnation and begged her intercession in his hour of need. He commended his city to her protection, asking that the crosses he had erected at its four corners drive off the powers of the Devil and any tyrant who might seek to destroy the city's liberties. Last of all, he placed himself under divine protection by making the sign of the cross and commending his spirit to God. Those about the deathbed heard a voice from heaven promising that God had heard his prayers. Saint Michael and the hosts of heaven, the author of his legend tells us, arrived rejoicing to take Petronio's soul to heaven.[12] "Last words" were no mere expression of piety.

9. Ibid., 20–24, esp. 22.

10. *Ordo Senensis*, 2.91, pp. 496–97. This author seems to have drawn his inspiration from Augustine, *Enchiridion ad Laurentium*, cc. 109–10, and from canon law, Gratian, *Decretum*, C. 13 q. 2 c. 23.

11. As explained in Bologna, Biblioteca Universitaria, ms 1767, fol. 98ʳ.

12. Corti, *Vita*, 46–48, from Bologna, Biblioteca Universitaria, ms 2060 (xiv cent.), fols. 19ʳ–20ᵛ. A deathbed scene, with a similarly edifying final discourse, is recorded at Bologna for Saint Dominic: see Jordan of Saxony, *Libellus de Principiis Ordinis*, pp. 92–94, and *Processus Canonizationis S. Dominici*, 128–30, as well as the introduction thereto, 69–70.

At the death of the righteous, they were pregnant with power. God himself directed them. The semiliterate Franciscan Giovanni of Alverna made many mistakes speaking Latin, but when he uttered words of consolation to the brethren from his deathbed, he spoke with flawless grammar.[13] At death, the believer could, like Saint Petronio, call down a blessing on the good or prophesy divine punishment on evil livers. Pietro Pettinaio, the combmaker of Siena, died surrounded by family and admirers, who sang "the holy offices instituted by the Church" for the dying. His vita, in rather formulaic words, reports that Pietro had properly confessed and received both viaticum and (unusually) extreme unction. He died with dire words on his lips: "Woe to you Pistoia; woe to you, Florence; and woe also to you, Siena!"[14] His biographer, Pietro of Monterone, explained that these utterances foretold the destruction of Pistoia, and Florence's defeats at Altopasso and Montecatini. He gave thanks that Siena was still safe, thanks to the patronage of the Virgin. Perhaps Siena's security was wishful thinking; Florence would soon be on the rebound.

Lives of holiness, like those of Petronio, Giovanni, and Pietro, might seem beyond the reach of most in communes, but the Church stood ready to aid the less perfect with her rites and sacraments. Excluding the excommunicated (and even their cause was not hopeless), anyone could convert, confess, and make a good end. But death might come at any time and place. Confession began the process of dying. Without it, all else was worthless. Preachers recommended practices to ensure that believers not face death without confession. A man fell mortally wounded in a battle between Bologna and Modena, we are told. Fortunately, he had fasted, eating only bread and water, on the vigils of all feasts of the Blessed Virgin Mary for seven years, trusting she would save him from unprepared death. The man died on the battlefield, but not before a priest had arrived to hear his sins.[15] Ordinary people imitated the patron of Bologna and availed themselves of the Virgin's help in their last hour. In a story dated about 1300, one dying woman sent for her priest to bring viaticum. He arrived to find that the Blessed Virgin was there and had just helped the woman make a peaceful death. The Virgin adored her son, Jesus, present in the Host brought by the priest. The priest, somewhat frightened, asked why the Queen of Heaven would assist at an ordinary laywoman's death. "The woman had said the Ave one hundred times a day and had done many other things in the Virgin's honor; thus it was fitting that she deserve it."[16] Preachers held up fasting in honor of Mary and ex-

13. *Acta [B. Joannis Firmani sive Alvernae]*, 5.49, p. 469. On the numinous quality of the deathbed, see Ariès, *Western Attitudes*, 7–8.

14. Pietro of Monterone, *Vita del beato Pietro Pettinajo*, 10, p. 115: "Guai a te Pistoia, guai a te Fiorenza; e guai ancora a te Siena!"

15. Pisa, Biblioteca Cateriniana del Seminario Arcivescovile, MS 139 (XIV cent.), fol. 139ᵛ.

16. Ibid., fol. 145ʳ. Other miracles in this collection focus on the power of recited Aves as a devotion; see, e.g., fol. 145ᵛ. But devotions claiming to protect the user from death in mortal sin, such as those

tolled her help at the time of death, but it was better to make more timely preparations.

Those visiting the sick, be they physicians or friends, were to urge those in even the slightest danger of death to confess quickly and be reconciled to God.[17] Priest, monk, nun, layperson, bishop, pope—all needed to confess. The first words addressed to a sick monk in one monastic sick-call ritual were an admonition that he call for the abbot and make a complete confession of sins.[18] Only after confessing was the monk ready for the other rites of the deathbed. But, as Zucchero Bencivenni reminded his readers, those who waited till they were dying risked forgetting to confess important sins and so failed to repent properly. This was a great sin.[19] Confession early in illness allowed the sinner time to reconsider his life and decide whether he needed to make a clean breast of forgotten crimes by confessing again. Good works were worthless without a complete and humble confession. One couple wanted children but failed to conceive. After trying other religious remedies, the husband went on pilgrimage to the Holy Land. His wife proved unfaithful and had two children by a "young man" during her husband's absence. When word came that her husband had died in the Holy Land, she repented and did many good works, but, out of shame, she failed to confess her sin. After she died, one of her sons longed to know her condition and asked a monk to say a "special Mass" for her. On the way to the altar, the monk had a vision of the woman in hell. Her good works had been worthless because of her failure to confess. The woman had told the monk: "There is no need to pray to God for me, because now I can never receive his mercy."[20] She had made a bad death.

The confession of those in danger of death, well prepared and prompt, involved a more elaborate rite than the routine confession of sins. For clergy and laity, the ritual was identical.[21] When, at the urging of his friends, family, and physician, a sick person "raised his mind to God" and called for a confessor, his priest put on the purple stole, took in hand his penitential manual, and went in procession to the sick bed. If the one dying were a monk, his abbot came, accompanied by the brothers; for a layperson, the parish priest came with his clerics. Those sitting (*sedentibus*) around the deathbed joined the ministers, who intoned the antiphon "Sana Eum Domine" (Heal him Lord) and chanted the seven penitential psalms and the litany of

---

found in the fourteenth-century Florence, Biblioteca Nazionale Centrale, MS Palat. 1, fols. 14ʳ⁻ᵛ, seem to be lacking in the communal period.

17. Lucca Synod (1300), 58, pp. 233–34; on the "ritualization" of dying, see Ariès, *Western Attitudes*, 11–13.

18. Florence, Biblioteca Nazionale Centrale, MS Conv. Soppr. D.8.2851 (XIV cent.), fol. 1ʳ.

19. Zucchero Bencivenni, *Sposizione*, 51.

20. Bologna, Biblioteca Universitaria, MS 158 (XIV cent.), fols. 20ᵛ–21ʳ: "Non é bisogno che tu preghi Idio per me, ch'io mai non posso avere misericordia da Dio."

21. *Ordo Senensis*, 2.87, pp. 487–90; the same chants and prayers are also prescribed in the *Rituale di Hugo [di Volterra]*, 283–85.

the saints. Generally, the faithful lacked this kind of musical skill. Those present simply joined in the easy response of the litany, "Ora pro eo," as Pietro Pettinaio did with his friends as he lay dying.[22] This part of the rite ended with several collects by the priest. The clerics and bystanders then departed, and the priest privately urged the one dying to draw up a will and determine his place of burial. Most important, those present were to urge satisfaction for past sins and offenses by almsgiving while the sick person still had control of his faculties.[23] Well over half of testators probably waited until their deathbed to make a will.[24] In such cases, the parish priest normally advised the penitent on what benefactions and bequests to include.[25] One cannot exclude the possibility of a bit of pious coercion by the priest, as in the case of one Perugian testator, Pascolo Rigoli, whose contribution to making his will in 1296 was the word *volo* ("I do") in response to the priest Don Angelo, who asked whether he wanted to leave half his money to the fraternity of the Misericordia—where he lay dying—and half to his nephew Mitole.[26] The testament produced would then be notarized and, after the death, proved by the city as a legal instrument.[27] Making a will was a personal religious act, part of the rites of dying. Only the will of an orthodox believer had legal effect. Should it be proved that the deceased had strayed from the Catholic faith, his will might be invalidated by law. The podesta of Bologna, Ranieri Zeno, did just that in 1250 with the will of Gerardo Palarini, when he was discovered to have died in heresy.[28] An assigned notary had responsibility to ensure that, after the testator's death, the will would be publicized and its provisions followed. The Church also acted to provide for prompt and careful execution of wills. In Lucca, the notary who failed to have a will executed within a month of the death was to be excommunicated.[29] The dying themselves seem to have taken the urging to make bequests ever more seriously. After 1300, the Italian cities saw a "boom" in the production of wills; even the relatively poor joined the well-to-do in drawing them up.[30]

What kind of bequests did they make? Examples from a group of published wills suggest that men and women approached death with rather dif-

---

22. Pietro of Monterone, *Vita del beato Pietro Pettinajo*, 10, p. 115.

23. *Ordo Senensis*, 2.87, pp. 490.

24. The proportion in Maria Immacolata Bossa, "I testamenti in tre registri notarili di Perugia (seconda metà del trecento)," *Nolens Intestatus Decedere*, 84, is about 63 percent, forty-two out of sixty-seven.

25. E.g., Novara Synod II (1298), 2.3.2, pp. 232–33, assumes that the parish priest helps the dying draw up their wills. On deathbed wills, see Samuel Cohn Jr., "Burial in the Early Renaissance: Six Cities in Central Italy," *Riti e rituali nelle società medievali*, ed. Chiffoleau, Martines, and Paravicini Bagliani, 39–57. Confraternity statutes reminded members to remember the group in their wills: e.g., Piacenza, Biblioteca Comunale, MS Pallestrelli 323 (1317), fols. 19ᵛ–20ʳ.

26. *Nolens Intestatus Decedere*, xiii–xiv.

27. Communal statutes include extensive sections regulating wills; for an early example, see Pisa Stat. II (1233), Leges 31–42, pp. 756–88.

28. Bologna Stat. I (1250), 7.101; repeated in ibid. (1259–60), 6.48.

29. Lucca Synod (1300), 52, p. 231.

30. See Gerardo Gatti, "Autonomia privata e volontà di testare nei secoli XIII e XIV," *Nolens Intestatus Decedere*, 17.

ferent concerns.[31] After 1260, at least, both men and women drew up wills, and they did so with almost the same frequency. This contrasts with practices before that date, when few, if any, women made wills.[32] Those represented in this sample were all lay penitents, but their wills are suggestive. The men thought first of making restitution for sin by generous gifts to the poor. Decco Caponsacchi of Florence, who drew up his will about 1296–97, left £500 flor. parv. for the ministers of the Brothers of Penance to buy clothing for the poor, after first deducting restitution for any usury he might have taken. He left the rest of his money, mostly in small £10–£25 donations, to religious houses, hermit groups, and hospitals. The largest sum went to the Franciscans.[33] Decco's focus on Christ's poor is mirrored in the 30 January 1275 will of Cittadino Bonasere of Passignano, a married Black Penitent who left everything to the penitent-fraternity leadership. They were to dispose of it "for the good of his soul and that of his family."[34] Lotteringo Orlandini, on 9 May 1258, left £400 to Christ's poor and to a long list of religious institutions in the city of Florence. His largest bequests went to the Dominicans at Santa Maria Novella and the Franciscans at Santa Croce (both £20). The next group of bequests (£10 each) went to three groups of sisters, a hospital, the Humiliati, and the abbey of Settimo, which was to purchase land to support the poor. Unique in this group of published wills, his also provided a £5 offering for a Requiem Mass.[35]

In contrast to these men, the *pinzochera* Donna Palmeria on 19 June 1281 left the bulk of her entire wealth, £325 flor. parv., to relatives; of it, £300 went to female relatives. Widows of her acquaintance received £50 and her household goods. The remaining £145 went for the Crusade, houses of nuns, local churches, and the Dominicans and Franciscans (£10 each).[36] Donna Lippa of Florence, a Gray Penitent, wrote a will resembling that of Palmeria. She favored individuals, all of them religious: Fra Taddeo Carini, O.F.M., got £50; Fra Giovanni Carini, O.P., £3; Fra Tommaso Carini, O.Hum.,

---

31. This sample is taken from "Cartulaire," 12–18, 22, 26–27, 28, Meersseman, *Dossier*, 193–202, 206–8, 212–16, 220. These are wills of penitents from Tuscany dating 1257 to 1300. A more comprehensive study could be done for Bolognese or Modenese wills, since these are well preserved. For Bologna, see Bertram, "Bologneser Testamente I" and "Bologneser Testamente II." On Modena wills, equally abundant, see ibid., pp. 237–40.

32. See the statistics in Bertram, "Bologneser Testamente I," 208–12, for the Dominican and Franciscan deposits. In the period 1260–1320, the Franciscan wills vary (by decades) from 35 percent to 55.3 percent women testators, the Dominican from 39.6 percent to 60.9 percent. In both cases, all but two decades have a female majority. Dominican preserved wills are always more heavily female than the Franciscan. The gender statistics for wills in notarial registers are similar: see id., "Bologneser Testamente II," 210–13; although in the years surveyed (1265–68 and 1348) the women represent a minority, in only one year are they under 40 percent, 1267 (30 percent). In the period before 1260, men always outnumbered women, by as much as 5 to 1: ibid., 205. There seems to have been a revolution in women's will-making in the 1260s. This deserves further study.

33. "Cartulaire," 26, Meersseman, *Dossier*, 212–13.

34. Ibid., 14, pp. 196–97.

35. Ibid., 12, pp. 193–95.

36. Ibid., 17, pp. 200–201.

£3; and Nuta, a *vestita*, £2. Perhaps strangely for a Gray Penitent, her one corporate donation (£50) went, not to the Franciscans, but to the Dominicans.[37] Only one male's will, that of Bello Ferrantini of Florence (27 May 1277), exhibits the concern for family and individuals seen in these women's wills. He left £800 flor. parv. to his daughters, and his horse to a friend. But his familial piety was overshadowed by a grant of £1000 flor. parv. to the poor and "pious places" (*piis locis*). This sum and some small grants to local churches were disbursed at the discretion of the ministers of the Black Penitents.[38] Perhaps he had neglected to make provision for his family earlier.

If this small sample reflects more general concerns, dying men thought first of the poor, perhaps because in life they had victimized them by taking usury. After that, they favored larger local religious communities. The women, perhaps unburdened by social sins, bestowed their charity on individuals, especially needy people they knew or simply on their friends. Mass bequests are rare. That duty normally devolved on the relatives, friends, and neighbors. The narrowly expiatory and personal focus of wills, even those of these professionally pious penitents, moved some communes to enact laws modifying testamentary provisions to provide for public charities. In 1250, Bologna ordered that one tenth of all testaments go to the reconstruction of the duomo, since "that church is the mother of all the churches of the clergy and laity of the city . . . and the Lord said to honor your father and mother."[39] A benefaction to the duomo would have worked to the glory of the city and pleased God, but it seems that the dying seldom made it. On the other hand, it does seem that the dying heard the call for more socially conscious benefactions generally. Over all, our period saw an increase in bequests to religious entities, especially hospitals.[40]

After the foreboding task of drafting a will, the ministering priest urged the one dying to make a full and humble confession, omitting nothing. Extant rituals give forms for this general confession.[41] These rites preserve the old dialogue format of the twelfth century. The priest began by examining the dying on the articles of the faith, using a question-and-answer format not unlike that used at baptism, although somewhat more extended. This examination not only excluded heretics from the consolations of the Church but reminded Catholics that confession was a "second baptism." If undertaken in faith, it left the one confessing in a state of innocence, ready to

---

37. Ibid., 30, pp. 219–20.

38. Ibid., 15, p. 198.

39. Bologna Stat. 1 (1250), 5.6, 1:443–44: "Quia ecclesia sancti petri episcopatus bon. mater est et capud omnium ecclesiarum clericorum et laicorum habitancium jn civitate predicta et eiusdem diocesis, et ab eis omnibus debeat exaltari et honorari dicente Domino honora patrem et matrem tuam ut sis longevus super terram, quod de matre spirituali que nos regenerat debeat intelligi."

40. A change that Antonio Rigon, "Orientamenti religiosi e pratica testamentaria a Padova nei secoli XII–XIV (prime ricerche)," *Nolens Intestatus Decedere*, 51, calls, using the words of Vauchez, a "révolution de la charité."

41. I follow here the forms found in the *Rituale di Hugo [di Volterra]*, 285–87 (ca. 1180).

meet the Lord. The priest reformulated the Latin questions of his ritual in a vernacular form. He inquired about the dying person's beliefs and spiritual disposition. A fourteenth-century model took the form of eight questions, and probably reflects as well as any the actual dialogue on the deathbed. Here the one dying was assumed to be a nun:

> *First Question:* Do you believe, my sister, those things which are of the Christian faith according to the teaching of the holy Church of God? *Answer:* I believe.
>
> *Second Question:* Are you happy to die in the Christian faith? *Answer:* I am very happy.
>
> *Third Question:* Do you acknowledge that you have not lived as well as you should have lived and have many times and gravely offended Christ? *Answer:* I acknowledge it and confess it.
>
> *Fourth Question:* Are you sorry for and do you repent of your offenses? *Answer:* For certain, I repent of them, and I am very sorry for them.
>
> *Fifth Question:* Do you have the will to amend your life, should you recover? *Answer:* I do.
>
> *Sixth Question:* Do you believe that Jesus Christ our Lord died for you? *Answer:* I firmly believe so.
>
> *Seventh Question:* Do you give him thanks? *Answer:* I give him all the thanks I can, and I would that I could and would do so even better.
>
> *Eighth Question:* Do you believe and hope that you cannot achieve the salvation of your soul except by the death of Christ and by his merits, and not by your own? *Answer:* I believe that and am certain of it.[42]

One could hardly find a more evangelical confession in the writings of the sixteenth-century reformers. The minister then reminded the penitent of God's mercy, and that salvation came from him alone, to which the penitent was to reply: "O my Lord, into your hands I commend my spirit; O Lord

---

42. Florence, Biblioteca Nazionale Centrale, ms Palat. 150 (early XIV cent.), "Ademande le quale sono da fare ad quello cristiano lo quale morira tosto," fols. 34ᵛ–35ʳ: "*Ademanda prima:* Creditu, sorella mia, quelle cose le quale sono della fede cristiana secundo la determinatione della sancta Ecclesia di Dio? *Responsione:* Credo. | *Ademanda secunda:* Sei lieta che muori in la fede cristiana? *Responsione:* Sono molto lieta. | *Ademanda tercia:* Recognoscite tu non avere cosi bene vixutu come debesti vivere et avere offeso Cristo spesse fiate et gravemente? *Responsione.* Recognoscolo et confessolo. | *Ademanda quarta:* Doliti et repentiscite delle tue offensioni? *Responsione:* Certamente me ne pento et molto me ne doglio. | *Ademanda quinta:* Ai voluntade de emendarte se scamperai? *Responsione:* Abio. | *Ademanda sexta:* Credi tu che per te sia morto Iesu Cristo nostro signore? *Responsione:* Credolo fermamente. | *Ademanda septima:* Rendili gratie? *Responsione:* Rendoli gratie quanto posso et vorreagli meglio potere et volere. | *Ademanda octava:* Creditu et speri non potere pervenire alla salute dell'anima tua, excepto che per la morte de Cristo et per li suoi meriti et non per li tuoi? *Responsione:* Credolo et sonne certa."

God of Truth, receive me."[43] The ritual then prescribed that the penitent make a general confession of all the principal sins of her life. This probably followed the forms found in the confessional manuals, since the priest had brought his "penitential" with him. The priest could thus help the dying one in her confession by again using a dialogue format. Sinners were to end their confession with some formula acknowledging the misuse of the senses: "I have sinned through my fault, Lord, before you and your saints, by my sight, hearing, taste, smell, and touch, and I beseech you, priest of God, that you pray for me to the Lord our God."[44] The priest then recited the absolution prayers, reconciling the sinner to God. To these prayers, he suitably added invocations asking the aid of the saints.

Confession and the preparation of a will allowed Christians to face declining health with a settled conscience. When they felt their strength declining, but while they still retained their faculties, they were to call for the most important rite of the deathbed, final Communion. In religious houses, this ceremony had long been embellished and elaborated. The canons of Siena made the rite even more impressive by holding their processions for viaticum immediately following the solemn Mass of the day.[45] When Communion was brought to a dying monk, a brother rang the bell of the chapter house. Monks gathered in the choir for a procession to the sickroom, with the celebrant vested in a chasuble and carrying the Host in a chalice. The priest would later cleanse his hands in that vessel after handling the Sacrament. Candle-bearers led the procession, during which the brothers sang the psalm "Miserere Mei." On arrival in the sickroom, the priest sprinkled it with holy water. The dying brother begged the community for prayers, and after recitation of the Confiteor and, in some places, the singing of the Agnus Dei, the dying monk (or nun) received the sacred Host.[46]

By the 1200s, viaticum also had become a solemn rite for the laity. Unlike the last confession, final Communion had a public nature and called on the dying person's neighbors to join the sacred drama. Taking viaticum to the dying, as an official rite of the Church, was the pastor's personal responsibility and could not be delegated to a layperson.[47] The parish priest donned the surplice, covered in winter by a closed cape, and took up before his

43. Florence, Biblioteca Nazionale Centrale, ms Palat. 150, fols. 35^(r-v): "O Signore mio, in le tue mane arecomando lo spirito mio; tu Signore, Dio della veritade, mi recomprasti." There follows in this manuscript a selection from the Latin commendation prayers for the dying from the Roman Ritual and the famous prayer "Anima Christi."

44. *Rituale di Hugo [di Volterra]*, 286–87: "Mea culpa peccavi Domine coram te et coram sanctis tuis in visu, in auditu, in gustu, in ordoratu et tactu preterea deprecor te sacerdos Dei ut ores pro me ad Dominum Deum nostrum."

45. On Sienese rites, see *Ordo Senensis*, 2.87–92, pp. 487–97, esp. 2.88, pp. 490–93.

46. Florence, Biblioteca Nazionale Centrale, ms Conv. Soppr. D.8.2851, fols. 1^(v)–3^(r), a Florentine example; Verona, Biblioteca Capitolare, ms DCCXXXVI (late XIII cent.), fols. 8^(r)–12^(r), an example from Pisa.

47. Novara Synod II (1298), 1.2.1.4, pp. 184–86. Nowhere is the observation of Ariès, *Western Attitudes*, 12–14, that premodern death was "public," more evident than in the rites of viaticum.

breast the Blessed Sacrament, concealed in a pyx covered with a clean white veil. He went in procession to the house of the dying, preceded by his clerics, who carried lighted candles—especially at night—and rang a small bell. On the way, he quietly recited the seven penitential psalms. The bell alerted neighbors of his mission.[48] That viaticum be always a public event, the church of Padua specifically forbade priests to bring Communion without bell and candles, or in such a way that they hid the sacred vessels under their cloak. The devout, hearing the bell or seeing the procession, not only venerated the sacrament, they also assisted the dying with their prayers. They knelt in the street as the Host passed, and bowed low, men uncovering their heads.[49] Sibyllina Biscossi never omitted these gestures and her prayer for the dying—except once, when by miraculous spiritual insight she realized that the priest mistakenly carried an unconsecrated Host. She immediately warned him of his oversight.[50]

Once viaticum reached the sickroom, the rite's audience shrank to the family and such close friends as had followed the procession to the house. Although a cleric and priest, Ambrogio Sansedoni took his final Communion in the same way as pious laypeople. He got out of bed to kneel before taking the Sacrament, first exchanging a kiss of peace with his brothers.[51] To the best of his ability, after Communion, he joined in saying the prayers for the dying. As these concluded, he quietly passed to his Maker.[52] Ambrogio also received extreme unction, the anointing of the dying, after his Communion. But there is little evidence that this sacrament played much part in the death-bed rituals of the laity.[53] Perhaps it was the complexity of the rite that discouraged it. Bishop Sicardo of Cremona explained that the anointing should properly be done by a group of seven priests, something possible only in a rather clerical environment.[54] The ritual books of Milan's Ambrosian Rite contained a ceremony that allowed for more frequent lay use of extreme unction. There, anointing preceded viaticum and, with the seven penitential psalms and the litany of the saints, was an integral part of the preparation for Communion.[55] The Milanese rite was also much simpler than the Roman usage, including only two anointings rather than the multiple anointings of

48. Piacenza Stat. Cler. (1297), pp. 531, 539; Padua Synod (1339), 11, p. 1137; Bologna Synod (1310), 491.

49. As Bonvesin de la Riva, *Vita Scholastica*, 68, lines 421–25, explains.

50. Tomasso of Bossolasco, *Vita [B. Sibyllinae]*, 3.15–16, p. 69.

51. On the universal desire to kneel when receiving viaticum, see Browne, "L'atteggiamento del corpo durante la Messa," 408.

52. Gisberto of Alessandria et al., *Vita [B. Ambrosii]*, 8.63, p. 193.

53. For the texts of this ritual, see Pont. Rom. (XII), 49A–B and 50, pp. 266–77; and, for local Italian usages, *Rituale di Hugo [di Volterra]*, 287–90, and *Ordo Senensis*, 89, p. 493, neither of which mentions the laity, implying that this is principally a clerical ceremony. But the goldsmith Saint Facio of Cremona received both viaticum and anointing: *Vita Beati Facii*, 42.

54. Sicardo, *Mitrale*, 6.12, col. 303. This is also reflected in Verona, Biblioteca Capitolare, MS MCIX (late XII cent.), fols. 28ᵛ–55ʳ.

55. Milan, Biblioteca Ambrosiana, MS A 189 Inf., fols. 73ᵛ–76ʳ.

the head, hands, feet, and five senses. Nor did it presuppose the presence of seven priests. Filippo of Ferrara wrote about visiting the sick a little after 1300. He included much medical advice and a little on prayer and Communion. But regarding extreme unction, he merely borrowed a description from the patristic author Cesarius of Arles and otherwise said it could be administered only once, during a terminal illness.[56] Although the saintly Dominican Reginald of Orleans was French, not Italian, he showed a similar lack of interest in extreme unction at the time of his death. On his deathbed, the possibility of anointing seems to have slipped his mind. When his prior suggested it, Reginald agreed, so that he "not seem to make little of the Church's anointing."[57] When diocesan statutes treated anointing, their concern was to prevent profanation of the blessed oil, not to ensure its delivery to the dying.[58] While anointing may well have had a vigorous life in some monastic communities, the central death ritual for lay men and women was Communion, the first taste of the banquet of heaven.[59]

FINAL HOURS

Reception of viaticum, which came as close to death as possible, began the final drama. Sicardo of Cremona described the ideal death:

> When the one dying reaches his last moment, let him be put down on ashes and straw, just like Saint Martin, who died lying on ashes, so showing that he was ashes and to ashes he would return. Before this, the Passion of Christ is read, or at least a part, so that he might be moved to greater sorrow for sin. A cross is also placed before his feet, so that looking down he might gaze upon it in fear. And he ought to lie with his face upward, so that he might look to heaven and, before he expires, commend his soul to the Lord.[60]

Dying was the final liturgy, celebrated equally by clerics and laypeople. The practice of lowering the dying onto sackcloth and ashes was known throughout Europe.[61] These signs of penance and Sicardo's formula of "ashes to ashes" recalled Ash Wednesday and the penance of Lent; meditation on the

---

56. Filippo of Ferrara, *Liber de Introductione Loquendi*, 4.34, in Bologna, Biblioteca Universitaria, MS 1552, fol. 21ᵛ. The Franciscan Jean of La Rochelle, [*Summa de Vitiis et Virtutibus*], in Florence, Biblioteca Medicea Laurenziana, MS Conv. Soppr. 145 (XIV cent.), fol. 147ʳ, shows the same limited focus.

57. *Vitae Fratrum Ordinis Praedicatorum*, 5.2, pp. 248–49, Conway trans., 229.

58. E.g., Novara Synod II (1298), 1.2.1.5, p. 187.

59. For a monastic rite of extreme unction, see Florence, Biblioteca Nazionale Centrale, MS Conv. Soppr. D.8.2851, fols. 4ʳ–7ᵛ.

60. Sicardo, *Mitrale*, 9.50, col. 427: "Moriturus itaque dum laborat in extremis, super cinere et palea deponatur, ad instar beati Martini, qui jacens in cinere vitam finivit, in quo innuitur quod cinis est et in cinerem revertetur. Antequam passio Christi, vel pars ejus, legatur, ut ad majorem compunctionem moveatur, crux etiam ante pedes ejus ponatur, ut mirens eam cernat, et magis conteratur, et debet recta facie jacere, ut coelum respiciat, et antequam expiret, ejus anima Domino commendetur."

61. *Vitae Fratrum Ordinis Praedicatorum*, 5.3, p. 250, Conway trans., 249.

cross and the commendation of one's soul, Christ's work on Good Friday; and the eyes' focus on heaven, Christ's Easter Resurrection and Ascension—a journey that dying Christians also hoped to make.[62] At Siena, after making the sign of the cross, those present knelt for the reading of the Passion.[63] The cross was the great shield of the dying, and ritual books urged the dying to look upon it.[64] Other weapons were at hand to fend off diabolical temptations. As Umiliana dei Cerchi lay dying, visions of demons afflicted her. Her companion Gisla ran (*cucurrit*) to get her image of the Blessed Virgin with Christ on the cross. She placed it directly on her writhing friend's body. Gisla then held up before Umiliana's face two lighted blessed candles so as to form a cross. She burned incense and sprinkled Umiliana's body with holy water. The demons fled in fear. Relieved, Umiliana looked up and saw the image of Christ. She asked that it be wrapped in a precious cloth and be "better positioned on her chest."[65] When the blessed Verdiana knew her death was near, she called for confession and Communion "in her usual way." She then knelt before the window of her cell, opened her Psalter to the "Miserere Mei," fixed her eyes on heaven, just as Bishop Sicardo recommended, and gave up her spirit. She died, as she wished, on Saturday, the day of Our Lady, and at the very hour she was accustomed to receive Communion. It was 1 February, the year 1242 by our reckoning.[66] Such was a good death—or, better, triumph over death's powers.

Umiliana and Verdiana were anchoresses; probably no more than a companion or confessor witnessed their passing. For most of the dying, lay or clerical, the sickroom was more crowded. Those crowds had a special, even liturgical, role to fulfill.[67] The priest Giacomo Salomone, although racked by cancer, joined those around him in chanting the litany as he lay on his deathbed.[68] When the founder of the Preaching Friars, Saint Dominic, lay dying at Bologna, he himself directed his brethren to chant the commendation of the dying, saying to them *incipe* ("start"). He then sang along with them, or at least moved his lips. He died as the cantor intoned the "Subvenite."[69] When bishop Lanfranco of Pavia died in 1194, he was staying with the monks of San Sepolcro. When he felt his strength departing, he called the monks to his side and joined them as best he could in the chanting of the

62. On this combination of death and rebirth in dying rituals, see Block and Parry, *Death and the Regeneration of Life*, 14–15.

63. *Ordo Senensis*, 90, p. 495, which mentions, like Sicardo, the model of Saint Martin.

64. *Ordo Officiorum della cattedrale [volterrana]*, 226 (Volterra, Biblioteca Comunale Guarnacci, MS 273, fol. 98ʳ).

65. Vito of Cortona, *Vita [B. Humilianae]*, 3.56–57, p. 399: "et aperiens oculos et videns ipsam tabulam supra pectus sibi positam, collocavit eam honorabilius in quodam panno serico mantelli sui, et supra petus suum melius collocavit."

66. *Vita Sancte Viridiane*, 10.

67. Contrary to Ariès, *Western Attitudes*, 4, I do not find any evidence that thirteenth-century Italian clergy discouraged "crowds" around the deathbed.

68. *Vita [Beati Jacobi Veneti Ordinis Praedicatorum]*, 3.42, p. 462.

69. *Processus Canonizationis S. Dominici*, Bologna Process 8 and 33, pp. 192–30, 152.

prayers for the dying. He asked to be dressed in full pontificals. At the end, he kissed the image of Christ Crucified and wept hot tears. He then recited the responsory "In Manus Tuas" from Compline, invoked the prayers of Saint Sirus, and gave up his spirit.[70] Not only bishops and priests met their Maker to the sound of chanted psalms. While Benvenuta Bonjani passed her last hours, her brother, the Dominican Fra Corrado of Verona, and his fellow friars circled her deathbed and chanted the commendation of the dying from the Roman Ritual.[71]

Adaptations allowed the illiterate and unmusical to participate. One four-teenth-century Augustinian friar from Florence reduced his well-used sick-call book to the sections that allowed participation by the unlettered: the penitential psalms, a short litany of the saints, and a series of collects requir-ing only the simple response "Amen."[72] The ex-minstrel Giovanni Buono may have had a good voice, but his Latin was shaky. During the commenda-tion of the dying, he sang along for the Credo in Unum Deum, which he knew from church each Sunday. He also joined in for the Pater Noster, the Ave Maria, and such as he knew of the psalms, in particular his beloved "Miserere Mei." Finally, he professed his faith *more laico*, that is, in his native Italian.[73] Everywhere people commended the dying to the Blessed Virgin by singing the Salve Regina, as they did at the death of Benvenuta Bojani.[74] A crowd of clergy and laity attended the death of the holy beggar Gualtiero of Lodi, singing chants, not those from the ritual of commendation, but those everyone would know: the Gloria in Excelsis from Mass and the great thanksgiving Te Deum Laudamus from Matins.[75] Judging from the music chosen, there was little lugubrious about that deathbed. The church of Milan was satisfied with a less musical send-off; the Ambrosian ritual prescribed only that the priest recite three collects over the one dying.[76] We can only guess at the emotional state of those present as they sang and prayed.

At the moment of death, or as soon as possible afterward, the cappella of the deceased sounded the "death bell" to invoke the prayers of the commu-nity. Those with means sent criers and family members through the city, asking for prayers.[77] The clergy of Ferrara and Reggio, at least until it was forbidden, dispatched *nuntii* to announce the deaths of clerics and beg pray-ers.[78] At Reggio, the great bell of the duomo responded to the cappella bell,

70. Bernardo Balbi, *Vita [S. Lanfranci]*, 2.31, p. 537.

71. Corrado of Cividale, *Vita Devotissimae Benevenutae*, 11.90, p. 174.

72. The friar's worn little book is Florence, Biblioteca Medicea Laurenziana, MS Gaddi 214 (early XIV cent.), fols. 1r–18r; see also Florence, Biblioteca Riccardiana, MS 1348, fols. 59v–60v.

73. *Processus . . . B. Joannis Boni*, 4.2.267–89, pp. 838–45.

74. Corrado of Cividale, *Vita Devotissimae Benevenutae*, 12.94, p. 175.

75. Bongiovanni of Lodi, *Vita Beati Gualterii Confessoris*, 8, pp. 22–24.

76. Milan, Biblioteca Ambrosiana, MS A 189 Inf., fols. 75v–76r.

77. See Reggio Stat. (1277), p. 45, which forbade sending criers.

78. Ferrara Clergy Const. (1278), cols. 434–35.

both sounding in unison the death knell.[79] All knew the meaning of the bells. For a layman, it tolled three times, symbolizing the Trinity whose image is found in every man. For a laywoman, the bell rang twice, since, in Eve, Adam found a second worthy of him. If the deceased was in holy orders, the bell rang once for each order he had received: doorkeeper, exorcist, lector, acolyte, subdeacon, and deacon—up to seven strokes for a priest.[80] And the people prayed. Something mysterious and potent attended the moment of death and the prayers around it. Folklore and pious story confirmed this. When Verdiana died, the bell of her parish church sounded the death call without a hand placed to the rope.[81] A sinful, scoffing woman failed to offer a prayer when she heard the death bell ring for Filippo Benizzi of Siena. She was struck mute. But she soon repented and received back her voice.[82] In Borgo San Giovanni at Parma during the late 1230s and early 1240s, a dog belonging to the de' Nauli could smell out deaths. The dog would become frantic to leave the house and go where someone had died. The dog stationed itself outside the house as long as the body remained there, in its own way begging prayers for the dead. Then it followed the corpse in the procession to the church and quietly took its place under the bier during the Requiem Mass. They called it the "dog of the dead." It was a dog that knew its pious duty.[83]

The liturgical books of Verona provided chants and prayers to be intoned over the body preceding its preparation for burial. They prescribed the responsory "In Paradiso," which also accompanied the funeral procession from the church to the cemetery. This beautiful chant was long and complex, and its use was probably restricted to monastic communities. For the laity, the preparation of the body was an intensely private task, the particular duty of the family, though lay custom probably differed little from that in religious houses, where members of the community, the deceased's spiritual family, had responsibility.[84] Bertramo del Foro, a canon of San Vincenzo at Bergamo, explained that when one of his community died, the canons themselves washed and prepared the body (and got to keep the deceased's clothing).[85] Washing the body had sacramental symbolism, recalling the deceased's first washing in baptism and the later washing of penance that pre-

79. Reggio Stat. (1277), p. 48.
80. Sicardo, *Mitrale*, 9.50, col. 427; *Ordo Senensis*, 2.93, pp. 498; Bologna Stat. II (1288), 4.91, 1:246; Pisa Stat. II (1313), 3.58, pp. 350.
81. *Vita Sancte Viridiane*, 10.
82. *Processus Miraculorum B. Philippi [Benitii]*, 2.6, fol. 54ʳ.
83. *Chronicon Parmense* (1246), 23.
84. As in Verona, Biblioteca Capitolare, MS MCIX, fols. 41ʳ–45ᵛ; the rituals of other cities provide no particular ceremony to precede the washing of the body: *Rituale di Hugo [di Volterra]*, 302; Florence, Biblioteca Nazionale Centrale, MS Conv. Soppr. D.8.2851, fol. 8ᵛ; Verona, Biblioteca Capitolare, MS DCCXXXVI, fol. 30ʳ (Pisa). The Milanese rite included prayers to be said while washing the body: Milan, Biblioteca Ambrosiana, MS A 189 Inf., 76ʳ⁻ᵛ.
85. "Instrumentum Litis" (September 1187), 1.2, p. 134; 2.12, p. 146. For a summary of the funeral material in these documents, see ibid., p. 73–82.

pared Christians to meet their Maker.[86] At Milan, the water used to wash the body was occasionally mixed with wine, to recall the Eucharist as well as baptism. It was perfectly proper to keep some of this mixture as a pious keepsake, as Don Mirano dei Garbagnati, priest of San Fermo, explained during the inquest into the cult of the pseudosaint Guglielma.[87] As preparation for burial, washing sufficed; embalming was rare or nonexistent. The only embalming I know of was for Saint Agnese of Montepulciano in 1317. Those preparing her body had to send all the way to Genoa to get the balsam. But their mail order proved unnecessary. Agnese's body proved miraculously incorrupt.[88] An incorrupt body testified to holiness; rapid decay suggested an evil life or a bad end. About the year 1322, the Augustinian preacher Filippo di Leonardo of Siena told of a beautiful woman whose husband indulged her whims for provocative and beautiful clothing. She became an occasion of sin for weak-willed men. When she died, in the middle of applying her makeup, we understand, her face immediately corrupted and presented a stinking (puzza) mess. Shamed by this revelation of her evil ways, her family buried her in a sealed coffin. Her serving maid let out the truth, however, and the family had to deny it in public.[89]

At least in the case of a cleric, the body was arrayed in the robe of his order. Clerics were not only washed; their beards were shaved and their tonsures renewed. Other members of religious orders, male or female, wore their order's habit. Occasionally laypeople received a religious habit on their deathbed and so associated themselves with the suffrages of the religious order.[90] Clerics wore the liturgical vestments proper to their rank: bishops full pontificals, priests their chasuble, deacons a dalmatic, subdeacons a tunical, and so forth. Sicardo of Cremona, however, conceded that, for those other than bishops and priests, a simple gown was enough in cases of poverty.[91] From his clerical point of view, ordinary men and women all belonged to a single order: the laity. So they should all go to the grave dressed alike: in sackcloth—a sign of the repentance suitable to their state. Sicardo admitted, a bit grudgingly, that the wealthy sometimes wrapped their dead in a shroud and shod them with hose and sandals. He gave this extravagance a religious gloss by suggesting that it was inspired by the burial shroud of Christ.[92]

86. As Sicardo, *Mitrale*, 9.50, col. 427, tells us.

87. *Atti inquisitoriali [contro i Guglielmiti]*, 2.27, p. 180.

88. Raimondo of Capua, *Legenda Beate Agnetis de Monte Policiano*, 3.2, pp. 70–71; see the anthropologists Metcalf and Huntington, *Celebrations of Death*, 193–97, on embalming practices.

89. Siena, Biblioteca Comunale degli Intronati, MS I.v.10 (early XIV cent.), fols. 1ʳ–2ᵛ.

90. See Louis Gougaud, *Devotional and Ascetic Practices in the Middle Ages* (London: Burns, Oates & Washbourne, 1927), 131–45; clothing with a monastic habit *ad succurrendum* is very old; the friars practiced it, too, at least by the 1300s.

91. Sicardo, *Mitrale*, 9.50, col. 427; councils repeated this legislation: e.g., Ravenna Council (1311), 2, p. 452.

92. Sicardo, *Mitrale*, 9.50, col. 427. See also *Ordo Senensis*, 2.93, pp. 498; Reggio Stat. (1277), p. 47; and Pisa Stat. II (1313), 3.58, p. 350, to the same effect.

The laity recognized, in fact, their own hierarchy and orders. Fra Salimbene recorded how Ser Lodovico of San Bonifacio, former podesta of Reggio, died on the feast of Saint Martin of Tours in 1283 in the presence of his Franciscan confessors, after "setting his soul in order in the finest manner." He left his horse and arms to the Franciscans of the city. All the townspeople came to view his body, which was dressed in scarlet, with a cape and cap of vair, girded with a sword, wearing golden spurs and fancy gloves.[93] Salimbene, cleric that he was, thought it a grand affair. At Bologna, home of the great law school, city fathers specifically stipulated that not only knights but also professors of civil and canon law go to the grave robed in scarlet silk.[94] Lay confraternities clothed their dead in the vesture of the society; flagellants held in their hands the discipline with which they had scourged themselves in life.[95] Lay penitents commonly held in their hands the Pater Noster cord.[96] In contrast to the clergy, who took their last vesture into the grave with them, the deceased laity surrendered their finery before burial, and it was given to the church as a burial offering. That was the rule in early-fourteenth-century Florence, unless the deceased had by will provided otherwise for dispersal of his clothing.[97]

Washed and properly dressed, the dead were ready for viewing by the mourners. In the case of clerics, lighted candles surrounded the bier, along with a processional cross at the head and a smoking censer at the feet.[98] Laypeople made do with just the candles. The "wake" took place at home and constituted the private, familial part of the obsequies. Liturgical books assumed that the funeral followed death immediately, on the morning after the preparation of the body. Some cities mandated rapid burials in the later communal period, but everywhere the body remained at home for at least a few days.[99] This allowed the gathering of family and neighbors, mutual condolences, and shared mourning. Close relatives sat by the catafalque and traditionally rose to give their seats to nearer relatives as they arrived.[100] Occasionally, a member of the family delivered a eulogy over the body.[101] When Francesco, the young son of Filippuzzo di Petronio Tudini, died, his family waked him for three days. To the surprise of all, on 21 September 1286, the day before the intended burial, Francesco came back to life, thanks,

93. Salimbene, *Cronica* (1283), 752–53, Baird trans., 524.
94. Bologna Stat. II (1288), 4.91, 1:247.
95. Lucca, Biblioteca Statale MS 1310 (1299), fol. 11ᵛ; Novara Battuti Stat. (XIV), 281.
96. As did Agnes of Montepulciano: Raimondo of Capua, *Legenda Beate Agnetis de Monte Policiano*, 3.1, pp. 68–69.
97. Florence Stat. II (1325), 5.10, p. 371.
98. *Ordo Senensis*, 2.93, pp. 499.
99. Ravenna Stat., 341, p. 159. Lett, *Enfant*, 204, notes that France synodalia in the 1200s also tried to end "superstitious" wakes and enforce rapid burials.
100. If I have correctly understood Ravenna Stat., 339, p. 158: "Et quod nullus sedens ad corroctum surgere debeat pro aliquo vel aliquibus, nisi surgerent occasione loci dandi."
101. Modena Stat. (1327), 2.46, p. 263, tried to forbid this practice.

this father said, to the intervention of the Servite saint Filippo Benizzi.[102] In an age when a coma might easily be mistaken for death, there were practical reasons to stretch out the wake, no matter what the liturgists and city fathers said.

The Community Mourns

Funeral rites in communal Italy taught lessons about community and social order; they were a catechism of the Catholic understanding of death.[103] Everywhere they took the same shape.[104] On the day after the wake, the death bell rang a second time, announcing the procession from the house to the church.[105] Mourners placed the body on a stretcher and covered it with the cappella's simple linen pall. Some families insisted on a more festive covering that would display their respect for the deceased and their wealth to their neighbors. Flowers and garlands decorated the body at little cost. The rich favored splendid silks, embroidered work, and sumptuous fabrics, much to the chagrin of city fathers, who restricted these honors to officials.[106] When the procession left the house, the funeral ceased to be a familial matter and involved the entire contrada. The mourners carried the body, not in a coffin, but on a bier, with the face uncovered so that all might have a last glimpse at their neighbor. The late-thirteenth-century communes tried to render the rite more anonymous, requiring that the face be covered—the reasons they gave were to protect women's modesty or to keep passing birds from defiling the corpse.[107] Families defied such laws. The dead remained individual members of their community until they vanished into the anonymity of the parish cemetery. Only monks and friars went to their funerals with their faces covered, a sign that in life they had already become dead to the world.[108] On arrival at the church, the clergy celebrated "Vigils of the

---

102. *Processus Miraculorum B. Philippi [Benitii]*, 1.34, fol. 53ʳ.

103. Giovanni Cherubini, "Parroco, parrocchie e popolo nelle campagne dell'Italia centro-settentrionale alla fine del Medioevo," *Pievi e parrocchie*, ed. Erba et al., 1:362, citing literary examples from the fifteenth-century *Motti e facezie del Piovano Arlotto*, nos. 15, 160 (available in an edition by Gianfranco Folena [Milan: Ricciardi, 1995], 30, 225). For liturgical forms of burial, see Pont. Rom. (xii), 51A–B, pp. 277–85. On the legal aspects of burial, see Elsa Marantonio Sguerzo, *Evoluzione storico-giuridica dell'istituto della sepoltura ecclesiastica* (Milan: Giuffrè, 1976).

104. The processions and rituals of the communal funeral liturgy parallel the three-stage death-ritual model (borrowed from van Gennep) in Metcalf and Huntington, *Celebrations of Death*, 29–30: those performed (1) while the dead person is treated as "present," (2) in transition to the other world, and (3) finally truly gone. These three steps were signaled in medieval Italy by the three principal chants of the rite: the "Subvenite" (from house to church), the "Libera" (at the church), and the "In Paradisum" (to the grave).

105. Sicardo, *Mitrale*, 9.50, col. 427.

106. E.g., San Gimignano Stat. (1255), 2.54, pp. 713; Florence Stat. I (1322), 5.7, pp. 223. For sumptuary legislation on funerals at Bologna, see Frati, *Vita privata*, 59–60, and, generally, Killerby, *Sumptuary Law in Italy*, 71–80.

107. Examples: Reggio Stat. (1277), p. 47; Bologna Stat. II (1288), 4.91, 1:246. See also Siena Stat. II (1310), 5.203, 2:318–19, and Florence Stat. I (1322), 5.7 and 5.11, pp. 225–26.

108. Florence, Biblioteca Nazionale Centrale, MS Conv. Soppr. D.8.2851, fol. 13ᵛ; see Metcalf and Huntington, *Celebrations of Death*, 6, on the social impact of such rites.

dead," Requiem Mass, and the blessing of the body. Then, for the last time, the chapel bell rang the death knell, and the procession went to the cemetery for deposition of the body, final prayers, and the closing of the grave.[109] Although it was not part of the Church's rites, a memorial meal for mourners hosted by the deceased's family always followed the deposition.

Funerals were an exercise in parish and neighborhood solidarity; a proper "send-off" was both a duty and an honor. Local priests took pride in a good clerical presence at parishioners' funerals; the family collected as many mourners as possible. Priestly confraternities required member priests to attend funerals at each other's chapels and to bring their laity with them. During the 1200s, funerals of ordinary people with more than ten priests in attendance were not at all unusual; in the next century cities sought to end such displays.[110] The chants of the Mass and burial were among the most evocative and well known of the entire liturgy. They were, however, complex, and only a good clerical presence ensured their proper execution. Family and neighbors expressed their solidarity and identity by a good turnout. Individual family members invited groups of *soci* (companions) to support them in their grief and swell the ranks of mourners.[111] Wealthier families competed to invite city officials, in particular council members and the captain of the people.[112] The podesta and his *familia* might attend funerals of prominent citizens. Brescia allowed its officials to attend the processions but made them wait outside the church during the funeral Mass.[113] Municipal societies, guilds, and confraternities required members, sometimes under pain of fine, to attend their wakes, processions, Masses, and depositions.[114] A poor turnout reflected badly on the bereaved and hindered the progress of the deceased's soul through purgatory.

Laypeople were no passive presence at funerals. They had their own "liturgy" to perform, the *pianto*, known in Latin sources as the *planctus*. There was nothing retiring about communal mourning: it was public, dramatic, obtrusive, and noisy. It was choreographed. Even in faraway Paris, Italian funerals were famous for their professional, paid mourners.[115] Wealthy Ital-

109. Sicardo, *Mitrale*, 9.50, cols. 427–30; *Ordo Senensis*, 2.93–100, pp. 498–506; for comparison, see Reggio Stat. (1277), pp. 45–48.

110. For priestly confraternity legislation on funerals, see Rigon, "Congregazioni," 16, citing Treviso, Archivio di Stato, Notarile, 1, 20, fol. 12ʳ; for city legislation limiting the number of priests at a funeral, see Bologna Stat. II (1288), 4.91, 1:247 (a limit of eight); Pisa Stat. II (1313), 3.58, pp. 350 (a limit of ten); Mantua Stat., 1.44, 2:94 (only two allowed).

111. Florence restricted such *soci* to three in town and two in the country: Florence Stat. 1 (1322), 5.7, pp. 222.

112. Pisa Stat. II (1313), Popolo 81 and 152, pp. 519, 627, forbade such appearances of officials "per coequalità dei nostri citadini."

113. Brescia Stat. (1313), 1.130, col. 40.

114. Bologna presents many examples: Bol. Pop. Stat., 2 (Callegari, 1254, c. 20), 253 (fines of 12d. bon.); 1 (Aquila, 1255, c. 10), 239 (3s. bon.); 1 (Vari, 1256, c. 27), 342; 1 (Matteo Griffoni, 1258, c. 10), 310 (10d.); 1 (Spade, 1262, c. 28), 332; 2 (Lana Bisella, 1288, c. 13), 364 (12d. bon.).

115. Trexler, *Christian at Prayer*, 42, citing Peter the Chanter, *Verbum Abbreviatum* (*PL* 205:97) on the "ploratores et ploratrices Longobardorum."

ians recruited peasants from the countryside and transported them to town. They filled up the empty space: in the house, during the processions, and at church.[116] Major responsibility for mourning still fell on family and neighbors. Mourners wailed, beat themselves with their hands, and poured out copious tears.[117] At the most extravagant, relatives rent their garments and threw off their mantles; women tore off their veils and let down their hair.[118] During the procession, mourners clung to the bier as it passed through the streets. In the church, lamentations continued during the vigil and the Requiem Mass; the overwrought threw themselves onto the body.[119] Although others participated in the pianto, the burden of mourning fell on close blood relatives: parents, siblings, children, grandchildren and, above all, widows. No commune dared forbid immediate kin from raising the pianto.[120] Some felt that wailing was contrary to the dignity of communal officials. Siena forbade its officials to *gridare i morti,* but only while they held office. Bereaved officeholders appointed substitutes to wail in their stead.[121] Tradition excluded the clergy from the pianto. Better that clerics shed tears *quietly* during the services and processions. Even the most staid of legislators did not forbid that. But some priests did forget themselves. After all, even Jesus wept for his friend Lazarus.[122] After the burial came another opportunity for demonstrations of grief, when the family returned home. The clerics, some perhaps with relief, went back to the church to celebrate the Office of the Dead.[123]

Women were the great mourners of the age. A devotional piece from the later communal period, *Il pianto della vergine Maria,* beautifully captures their special role in mobilizing sentiment at funerals.[124] This work presents the Blessed Virgin Mary's lament of her crucified son as a model for mourning. On receiving her son's body from the cross, Mary reversed the blessing of Gabriel, "Benedicta tu in mulieribus" (Blessed are you among women), crying out: "Anzi son la più maledetta di tutte l'altre femmine!" (Rather, I am the most cursed of all women!). She took Christ's body into her arms and addressed it directly, pouring out her desolation and abandonment. She called on Jesus to look down from heaven and see the pain his death had caused her. Mary choreographed the wailing of the other women, turning them into a choir of mourners. The two other Marys and Salome prostrated themselves on the ground, clung to the cross, and fell over Christ's body. The Virgin and Mary Magdalene (the theatrical mourner *par excellence*) lifted

116. As we known from Bologna Stat. II (1288), 4.91, 1:247, where the city forbids the practice.

117. Described in Parma Stat. I (before 1255), pp. 321–22.

118. Parma Stat. I (by 1255), p. 322; Bologna Stat. II (1288), 4.91, 1:245; Modena Stat. (1327), 4.172–74, pp. 475–77.

119. Modena Stat. (1327), 4.174, pp. 477.

120. E.g., Parma Stat. I (by 1255), p. 322; San Gimignano Stat. (1255), 2.54, p. 713.

121. Siena Stat. II (1296), 1.115–16, 1:113–14.

122. *Ordo Officiorum della cattedrale [volterrana],* 228 (Volterra MS 273, fol. 100ʳ).

123. Parma Stat. I (by 1255), p. 322.

124. Florence, Biblioteca Medicea Laurenziana, MS Gaddi 187 (early XIV cent.), fols. 76ʳ–84ʳ.

the body of Jesus into the tomb, refusing to allow the men to help.[125] They then "recommenced the pianto."[126] The apostles played a mere supporting role, assisting the women and sometimes offering consolation. The holy women took center stage; the men became an audience for the Virgin and her friends. Leaving the tomb, the holy women returned to the city, wailing in the streets, seeking out frightened disciples, and imploring—or better demanding—that these participate in a public outpouring of grief.

In Italy, although mourning the dead was not an exclusively female occupation, women led it, set the proper tone, and raised and lowered the intensity according to the time and place. Like Mary and her companions, the women of the communes practiced mourning as an art form, with its proper words and gestures. Although executed well after the communal period, the best snapshot of the pianto is Niccolò dell'Arca's famous sculpture, the *Compianto su Cristo morto* (1463), in the Church of the Vita at Bologna (fig. 58). The men hold back their emotions. Joseph of Arimathea stares at the viewer. John the Evangelist struggles to hold back sobs. In contrast, the women give full vent to their emotions: the Virgin collapses in tears; Mary of Cleopas shrieks in horror and recoils from the body; the Magdalene enters on the run, garments flying, her mouth frozen open in a scream.[127] "Has anyone seen a sorrow like my sorrow?"[128] Though wildly emotional, the pianto was a ritual. It began precisely at the tolling of the death bell, not before, and outside, not inside, the house of the deceased.[129] Women waiting in the street took up wailing only on the arrival of the catafalque. Once the body had arrived, they followed it to the church and then to the grave. At least, that was the preferred practice. Some women took advantage of the freedom given by mourning to wander the streets, raising the pianto in small unaccompanied groups, much to the horror of communal officials. The Virgin and Mary Magdalene would have understood.

Knowledge of the pianto comes mostly from sumptuary legislation to control it.[130] When legislators explained their intent, they singled out the indecorousness of crowds and the promiscuous mixing of men and women.[131] Already in the early 1200s, cities tried to prevent men from raising the pianto.[132] After the 1250s, they prohibited public wailing by women, but al-

125. On the Magdalene as model for grieving, see Katherine Ludwig Jansen, *The Making of the Magdalen: Preaching and Popular Devotion in the Later Middle Ages* (Princeton: Princeton University Press, 2000), 92–96.

126. Florence, Biblioteca Medicea Laurenziana, MS Gaddi 187 (early XIV cent.), fol. 80ᵛ: "Incomminciò a rinovellare il pianto."

127. Mario Fanti et al., *Le chiese di Bologna* (Bologna: L'inchiostroblu, 1992), 204–7.

128. Florence, Biblioteca Medicea Laurenziana, MS Gaddi 187, fols. 78ʳ⁻ᵛ.

129. Siena Stat. II (1310), 5.205–6, 2:319–20.

130. *Pace* Diane Owen Hughes, "Mourning Rites, Memory, and Civilization in Premodern Italy," *Riti e rituali nelle società medievali*, ed. Chiffoleau, Martines, and Paravicini Bagliani, 36. On regulation of the pianto, see Killerby, *Sumptuary Law in Italy*, 72–73, 106–7.

131. Siena Stat. II (1310), 5.211, 2:320–21.

132. See legislation from Como, Milan, Chieri, Novara, and Perugia, described in Hughes, "Mourning Rites," 26–27.

lowed it in the private space of the home.[133] In 1255, San Gimignano still permitted public wailing, but limited the number of women raising the pianto in the streets to twenty. Men might join the women's pianto only in the semiprivacy of the church at the Mass and vigil.[134] In the 1270s, communes attempted to forbid the pianto completely and even to reduce the numbers at funerals.[135] Some tried segregation. Early-fourteenth-century Lucca instructed men on how to conduct "their pianto." They should gather at a designated church, "make the pianto" for a suitable time, and then go straight home. Women were to wail on their own at some designated house. There was to be no more lamenting in the streets.[136] Siena tried to force the women to stay home during processions.[137] It seems that after 1300 the mixing of the sexes, the social competition, and the private occupation of public space was becoming intolerable. The late communes had become more oligarchical, religious expression ever more clericalized, and popular rites distasteful. Whatever the city fathers thought, the theatrical lamentation remained popular. Perhaps the clergy even joined in; at least in early-thirteenth-century Siena the liturgists had to remind them not to.[138]

Although men occasionally wailed, candle-carrying was their parallel to the women's pianto. Men carried candles before the bier, often in great numbers. Families vied to outdo each other by their candles, both in number and quality. Pious and civic societies kept a supply of mourning candles to enhance the ceremonies. Mourners from the neighborhood of Fraternità di Santa Lucia at Pisa carried their lighted candles into the church and held them throughout the service and the procession to the grave.[139] Families and confraternities did the same. When Saint Ranieri of Pisa died, people crowded the funeral procession as it went from the church of San Vito to the duomo of Santa Maria. They carried candles "as at Candlemas."[140] The lights presented an imposing spectacle at night.[141] The carpenters' society at Bologna only carried two candles in funeral processions (probably because of city regulation), but these were twelve-pounders, of the purest wax. They

133. Ibid., 31.
134. San Gimignano Stat. (1255), 2.54, pp. 713–14.
135. E.g., at Reggio; see Sagacino Levalossi and Pietro Della Grazata, *Chronicon Regiense, RIS* 18:8. On women's mourning, see Hughes, "Mourning Rites," 21–38.
136. Lucca Stat. (1308), 1.11, p. 15.
137. Siena Stat. II (1310), 5.218, 2:320; Lucca Stat. (1308), 1.11, pp. 14–16. The intent of some of this legislation was to keep women out of public view. Contemporary laws in Ravenna Stat., 160, pp. 89, forbade them to sit under porticoes or spin in public.
138. *Ordo Senensis*, 2.100, p. 506; this is the only regulation of clerical pianto that I have found.
139. E.g., Pisa Stat. I, pp. 705–6.
140. Benincasa of Pisa, *Vita [S. Raynerii Pisani]*, 12.125, p. 370.
141. A practice that San Gimignano Stat. (1255), 2.54, pp. 713, sought to curb. Even at the height of sumptuary regulations in the early 1300s, exceptions had to be made: e.g., Florence Stat. I (1322), 5.7, p. 225, allowed the "Sotietas Marie Virginis Orti Sancti Michaelis" to have many "cereos sive torchios ipsius sotietatis" carried at funerals. Florence tried to stop nocturnal funeral processions in 1322: Florence Stat. I (1322), 5.8–9, p. 225.

were stored in a protective case at the society chapel.[142] The carrying of such *doppieri* in procession eventually fell victim to sumptuary regulation. Cities tried to keep candle weight down to one or two pounds, and they often limited those carried them to fewer than a dozen.[143] Nevertheless, people defied the ban.

Solidarity in death dictated that pallbearers come from the same state as the deceased.[144] Priests were to carry a priest, deacons a deacon, confraternity members their brothers, and laypeople laypersons. Priests wore their stoles of office in the procession and recited prayers for the dead as they marched along. Organization of the funeral procession fell to the leaders of the deceased's state. At San Vincenzo at Bergamo, the canons' provost (*primicerio*) chose the pallbearers and assigned the other functions. He made sure that the cantors did not rush through the psalms of the Office.[145] The ministers of communal societies did the same at members' funerals.[146] Penitent societies took charge of members' funerals and those of their near relatives. The brethren first went to the cappella of the deceased. There the minister selected those to carry the body, and the rest formed up and marched before the parish cross to the house of the deceased.[147] Only at funerals of women did members of another state organize the procession. A deceased woman's near male relatives, not the females, carried her bier.[148] Bishop Sicardo of Cremona said this was because of the "risk of immodesty," but the rule effectively freed women to devote their undivided attention to raising the pianto—something the good bishop probably did not intend. In funeral processions men always went ahead of the body. Women marched behind the bier.[149] This made sense, since female mourners usually vastly outnumbered the men. Even nuns left their cloisters for funerals.[150] The widow in her robes of mourning, who followed immediately after the corpse, vied with it for attention. When the Sienese restricted funeral spectacle in the early 1300s, they limited the widow's escort to no more than twelve men and twelve women; only two candle-bearers were to carry wax torches (*doppieri*) at her side.[151] Even after sumptuary decrees, Sienese widows made a good showing.

142. Bol. Pop. Stat., 2 (Falegnami, 1264, c. 20), 203.
143. Treviso Stat. (1233), 745, 2:289 (limit of four candles); Reggio Stat. (1242), 62, p. 36 (limits candles to twelve); Brescia Stat. (1277), cols. (137)–(138) (two candles of ½ lb.); Bologna Stat. II (1288), 4.91, 1:246 (no *doppieri*); Lucca Stat. (1308), 1.11, p. 16 (limit of twelve candles or *doppieri*, total not weighing more than twelve lbs.); Siena Stat. II (1310), 5.210, 2:320 (eight candles of one lb.); Pisa Stat. II (1313), 3.58, p. 350 (nine lb. weight limit); Modena Stat. (1327), 4.173, p. 476 (two candles of one lb.). Brescia set up a "candle-control committee" to police their use at funerals: Brescia Stat. (before 1277), col. (203).
144. Sicardo, *Mitrale*, 9.50, cols. 427–28.
145. "Instrumentum Litis" (September 1187), 3.28, p. 173.
146. E.g., Bol. Pop. Stat., 2 (Ferratori, 1248, c. 31), 187; Lucca Stat. (1308), 1.11, pp. 14–16.
147. "Chapitre de Pénitents Lombards" (1280), 13–16, Meersseman, *Dossier*, 165–66.
148. A rule also found in Lucca Stat. (1308), 1.11, pp. 14–16.
149. San Gimignano Stat. (1255), 2.54, pp. 713.
150. See Milan Council (1287), 5, p. 874.
151. Siena Stat. II (1310), 5.211, 2:320–21. Other cities restricted female mourners in the same period: Reggio Stat. (1277), p. 46 (none more distantly related than three degrees); Florence Stat. I (1322), 5.7, pp.

Clergy from both the Mother Church and the chapel of the contrada had jealously guarded places in the funeral procession. In late-twelfth-century Bergamo, churches litigated over whose pall, processional candles, cross, holy-water vessel, aspergillum, and censer would be carried at funerals.[152] Don Alessandro of San Silo, the cross-bearer of Sant'Alessandro, who certainly knew the customs of his city, explained them in detail.[153] On the occasion of state funerals, the cross of San Vincenzo, the cathedral, went first, followed by the crosses of the various cappelle and their people. Then came the cross of the canons of Sant'Alessandro and the rest of the clergy. At the funeral of an ordinary citizen, the cross and candles of his own parish went before the bier.[154] The parish community dominated the funeral procession; the neighborhood had first place in committing its dead to God.[155] Clergy and commune legislated to protect the deceased's cappella cross from being overshadowed by those of other churches and corporations.[156] But citizens belonged to other corporations than the cappella. These brought their own paraphernalia and claimed their space, if not in the funeral itself, at least in a separate procession to the bereaved family's house to pay condolences.[157]

As the death bell of the cappella rang, the procession left the house. Led by the priest, acolytes and other clerics took up the cross and other items needed for the funeral. The men carrying candles followed, two by two. After them came the bier, the widow, and last of all the women. The procession might stop along the way to let the women raise the pianto; clerical liturgists preferred that the procession not stop until it reached the church.[158] Even if it did not stop, the procession passed through the major streets of the contrada, the deceased paying one last visit to his neighborhood.[159] Along the route, clergy and laity raised their voices in song. The laity had dirges in the vernacular to accompany the procession, but these are sadly lost.[160] The clergy usually intoned the chant "Subvenite" on approaching the church.[161] In this responsory, the community bade farewell to their deceased, com-

223–24 (no more than three mourning companions—*sotii*). Only Bologna Stat. II (1288), 4.91, 1:245–46, tried to exclude female mourners entirely.

152. "Instrumentum Litis" (September 1187), 6, p. 215; on which, see Valsecchi, *Interrogatus*, 77–78.

153. "Instrumentum Litis" (September 1187), 4, p. 192; repeated in ibid., 8, pp. 268–69.

154. *Rituale di Hugo [di Volterra]*, 304–5.

155. Vauchez, "Conclusion," *La parrocchia nel Medio Evo*, ed. Paravicini Bagliani and Pasche, 313.

156. E.g., Reggio Stat. (1277), p. 48; Bologna Stat. II (1288), 4.91, 1:246.

157. Milan, Biblioteca Nazionale Braidense, MS AC.VIII.2, fols. 32ᵛ–33ᵛ; Mantua Stat. (1303), 1.44, 2:94, allowed two crosses in ordinary funeral processions.

158. Reggio Stat. (1277), p. 46.

159. Pisa Stat. II (1313), 3.58, p. 350, provided for this, but forbade processions through the rest of the city.

160. Hyde, *Society and Politics*, 88.

161. Verona, Biblioteca Capitolare, MS DCCXXXVI, fol. 35ʳ; *Ordo Senensis*, 2.93, pp. 499 (where the "Credo Meus Redemptor" and the "Libera" might also be sung if the procession was long). Milan and Volterra rituals provided psalms during the procession: *Manuale Ambrosianum*, 1:101–2; Volterra, Biblioteca Comunale Guarnacci, MS 273, fol. 58ᵛ. At Bergamo, the usual chants were "De Terra Formasti Me" and then "In Regnum Dei" on entering the church: "Instrumentum Litis," 1.1, pp. 173–74.

mending them to the saints and angels who would lead them before the judge of all:

> R. Saints of God, come in aid; angels of the Lord, come in greeting, * receive his soul, * bring it into the presence of the Most High.
>
> V. May Christ, who has called you, receive you, and may his angels lead you into the bosom of Abraham, * bring your soul into the presence of the Most High. R.
>
> V. Eternal rest grant unto him, Lord, and let perpetual light shine upon him, * bring his soul into the presence of the Most High. R.[162]

At the church door, the deceased took leave of his family and friends. His face was covered. Mourners surrendered their candles and torches, sometimes offering them to the priest who would conduct the funeral.[163] Some mourners, however, held their candles throughout the Office and Mass and carried them to the grave, giving the rites the flavor of an Easter vigil. Bodies of laypeople entered the church feet first, facing the altar. The laity's bier stood in the nave, among the people, where the deceased had heard Office and Mass while alive. Clerics were laid in the choir, their proper place, with feet toward the congregation, as they would have faced them when giving a blessing or preaching. Wherever the location, mourners crowded around the body. At the funeral of the layman Ranieri of Pisa, who was laid out in the choir because of his holiness, the people invaded that clerical preserve to be near the body. They left so little room that the priests had to move his body up into the pulpit. Mourners refused to be put off. They climbed the stair in the choir screen to touch pieces of cloth to his body.[164]

Requiem Aeternam

The funeral Mass was conducted in the parish church.[165] When the mourners and body entered there, the focus of the funeral changed. The vigil and Mass of the dead were the most ecclesiastical of rites. The chants and prayers focused on Christ's dread judgment and the fearful consummation of the world. The church prayed, not only for the newly deceased, but for all who would one day die and stand before the divine tribunal. The rites at the church began with Vigils of the dead, an Office beginning with Vespers and

---

162. Text from the Roman Ritual: "R. Subvenite Sancti Dei; occurrite Angeli Domini. * Suscipientes animam eius. * Offerentes eam in conspectu Altissimi. V. Suscipiat te Christus, qui vocavit te, et in sinum Abrahae Angeli deducant te. * Suscipientes animam eius. Offerentes eam in conspectu Altissimi. V. Requiem aeternam dona eis Domine, et lux perpetua luceat ei. * Offerentes eam in conspectu altissimi."

163. Reggio Stat. (1277), p. 48; Treviso Stat. (1233), 745, 2:289; Modena Stat. (1327), 4.173, pp. 476 (which seeks to limit the offerings).

164. Benincasa of Pisa, *Vita [S. Raynerii Pisani]*, 12.125, p. 370.

165. Siena seems unique in having all funerals at the duomo: *Ordo Senensis*, 2.97, p. 503. On burial rights in canon law, see Marantonio Sguerzo, *Evoluzione*, 287–95.

completed by the morning hours of Matins and Lauds.[166] This Office was said in a simple and somber form beginning with the antiphon "Placebo Domino," by which it was often called. The vigil ended without a formal conclusion or dismissal, something that suggested the eternity of heaven to Bishop Sicardo.[167] Sienese commentators admitted that the chanting of this long Office produced some tedium, but one never knew if the deceased was dead or merely unconscious. The length provided a little more time for the "dead" to wake up.[168] A poor woman of Monte Pessulano once invoked the intercession of Saint Peter Martyr during the vigil for her son. To the surprise and shock of all, the boy woke up.[169] Clerics chanted the psalms; family and friends crowded around the body. In the church, the women resumed the cries of the pianto, competing with the clerical chants; some threw themselves on the corpse. If the person who had died possessed some reputation for sanctity, Vigils and Mass provided the last close contact with the remains. While Bishop Lanfranco of Pavia lay on his bier in the cathedral choir, a pious old woman hobbled in through the screen, took his hand, and blessed herself. His relics healed her of a two-year paralysis of her feet.[170] In 1240, Ranieri Rusticuzzi of Santo Stefano at Orvieto, who had hurt his arm throwing rocks, managed to get close to the catafalque of Fra Ambrogio of Massa. He rubbed the Franciscan's hand on his strained arm and promised to say twenty-five Pater Nosters yearly on the anniversary, if he got a cure. He did.[171] There was nothing restrained or reserved about funerals, even during the chanting of the solemn Offices.

Requiem Mass followed Vigils.[172] For the most part, the ceremonies of this Mass differed little from those of any other. As a sign of collective mourning, the priest wore black vestments, dropped most of the blessings, and omitted the circulation of the Pax.[173] People could make slight adaptions in the readings or chants to fit particular circumstances. At the funeral of Ser Guido of Bianello of Parma, they replaced the usual reading from 2 Macc. 12:43–46 (on praying for the dead) with Jer. 18:21–22, because it so beautifully evoked the tragedy of his murder.[174] The themes of judgment and the

166. *Rituale di Hugo [di Volterra]*, 305–12; "Instrumentum Litis," 3.28, p. 173.

167. Sicardo, *Mitrale*, 9.50, col. 246.

168. *Ordo Senensis*, 2.94–95, pp. 944–501.

169. *Vita S[ancti] Petri Martyris Ordinis Praedicatorum*, 10.75, p. 716.

170. Bernardo Balbi, *Vita [S. Lanfranci]*, 3.22, p. 537.

171. *Processus Canonizationis B. Ambrosii Massani*, 69, pp. 600–601. Bol. Pop. Stat., 2 (Fabbri, 1252, cc. 55–56), 238, required that the women following the corpse return home before the services in the church, which were for the men only.

172. The celebration of separate vigils for Benvenuta Bonjani (Corrado of Cividale, *Vita Devotissimae Benevenutae*, 12.94, p. 175) seems to have satisfied a desire to have one Office at the nun's convent and another at the church of the friars.

173. See, e.g., *Rituale di Hugo [di Volterra]*, 312–13. Eulogies seem to have been absent from most funerals; at least one city forbade them: Bologna Stat. II (1288), 4.91, 1:247. On the cross-cultural preference for black (along with white and red) as a mourning color, see Metcalf and Huntington, *Celebrations of Death*, 63.

174. Salimbene, *Cronica* (1286), 897, Baird trans., 622; the Milanese rites also included special forms of the service, e.g., for children: *Manuale Ambrosianum*, 1:102–4.

end of the world predominated. Nowhere was this better expressed than in the sequence before the Gospel, the "Dies Irae."[175] Written in the mid-1200s by Fra Giacopone of Todi, it was a meditation on Christ's judgment at the last day. By including it in the funeral Mass, the Church indicated that the judgment the deceased now faced would one day come to all.

At the end of Mass, the ministers left the choir for the blessing and commendation. The priest put off his chasuble and put on a black cope. The ministers brought the processional cross, holy water, and incense for the blessing of the body.[176] After the absolution prayer "Non Intres in Iudicium," the priest sprinkled the body with holy water and incensed it, walking around it counterclockwise, as he did when incensing the altar. The deacon assisted him, while the subdeacon stood at the head, holding the processional cross. At Siena, where all funerals took place at the cathedral, the deceased's pastor had a special role. At the blessing of the body, he came forward and took the aspergillum from the bishop or archpriest. After kissing the prelate's hand, he sprinkled his parishioner's body.[177] The cantor then intoned the "Libera," perhaps the perfect expression of the common fate of the living and the dead on the day of the judgment. Speaking for all Christians, the cantor alone sang the verses of the responsory:

> R. Deliver me, Lord, from eternal death on that dread day, * when the heavens and the earth shall be shaken, * when you come to judge the world by fire.
>
> V. That day is a day of wrath, a day of ruin and devastation, a great day and a very bitter one. * When the heavens and the earth will be shaken. R.
>
> V. I am seized with trembling and I fear, as the judgment and the wrath to come draw near. * When you come to judge the world by fire. R.
>
> V. I am most miserable, what shall I say, or what shall I do, when I have nothing good to say in front of such a judge? * When the heavens and the earth shall be shaken. R.
>
> V. Therefore, Christ, we ask you, we beg you, have mercy; you came to redeem the lost, do not condemn the redeemed. * When you come to judge the world by fire. R.
>
> V. O God, creator of all things, you formed me from the dust of the earth and wondrously redeemed me with your blood. Although my body may now decay, you will raise it up again from the tomb

---

175. On the association of the individual's death with the Second Coming of Christ in this hymn and in medieval death piety, see Ariès, *Western Attitudes*, 32–33.

176. "Instrumentum Litis," 1.1, p. 128; Florence, Biblioteca Nazionale Centrale, MS Conv. Soppr. D.8.2851, fols. 15r–16r; Verona, Biblioteca Capitolare, MS MCIX, fol. 48r.

177. *Ordo Senensis*, 2.97, pp. 504.

on the day of judgment. Hear me, hear me, and decree that my soul be gathered into the bosom of Abraham. R.[178]

The pallbearers then took up the body for the procession to the cemetery. When all had left the church for the procession, the women resumed the pianto, joined perhaps by the men and even some of the clergy.[179] When the procession approached the cemetery, the clergy intoned the last of the three great funeral chants of the medieval church, "In Paradiso."[180] Psalm 50, the penitential "Miserere Mei," provided the verses for this antiphon, if they were needed. Its words celebrated the deceased's entry into paradise, and so completed the soul's departure from the earthly city to the heavenly Jerusalem: "May the angels lead you into paradise; may the martyrs receive you at your coming, and take you into the holy city Jerusalem. May the choir of angels receive you, and may you find eternal rest with Lazarus, no longer poor."[181]

To enter a cemetery was to enter a sacred space.[182] The communes protected their burial grounds from both spiritual and physical pollution. They enacted laws to keep them free of trash and provided funds for their upkeep.[183] Religion absolutely excluded the unbaptized and criminals from burial in consecrated ground.[184] Churches set aside an unconsecrated plot next to the cemetery for unbaptized infants. Special rules governed women who died in childbirth and their unborn, unbaptized children. Their funeral rites were conducted outside the church building, as were those of people who died by violence—lest any blood desecrate the consecrated space. But no woman was ever to be denied burial in the cemetery because of the unbaptized fetus within her.[185] Those who unmistakably died in mortal sin— suicides, those dying in adultery or in a brothel, or in duels, tournaments, or as a soldier in an unjust war—these went to their grave not with Christians

178. As in Verona, Biblioteca Capitolare, MS DCCXXXVI, fol. 35ʳ. The "Libera" was used in a shortened form in the rites for the dying: e.g., Florence, Biblioteca Medicea Laurenziana, MS Gaddi 214, fols. 17ʳ–18ʳ.

179. For attempts to curtail wailing on the way to the grave, see *Ordo Senensis*, 2.100, p. 506; San Gimignano Stat. (1255), 2.54, pp. 713–14; Ravenna Stat., 341, p. 159.

180. Verona, Biblioteca Capitolare, MS MCIX, fol. 56ᵛ; Verona, Biblioteca Capitolare, MS DCCXXXVI, fol. 35ʳ; Florence, Biblioteca Nazionale Centrale, MS Conv. Soppr. D.8.2851, fols. 15ʳ–16ʳ; "Instrumentum Litis" (September 1187—Galdo, *primicerio* of San Vincenzo), 1.1, pp. 173–74 (but sometimes the "Dirige" was substituted: ibid., p. 215). *Manuale Ambrosianum*, 1:104–9, goes its own way, giving thirty psalms for use in the procession.

181. Text in the Roman Ritual: "In paradisum deducant te angeli: in tuo adventu suscipiant te martyres, et perducante in civitatem sanctam Jeruslem. Chorus angelorum te suscipiat, et cum Lazaro quondam paupere aeternam habeas requiem."

182. On cemeteries in medieval canon law, see Marantonio Sguerzo, *Evoluzione*, 84–86, 93–97.

183. E.g., Bergamo, *Antiquae Collationes Statuti Veteris Civitatis Pergami*, 9.62–63 (1236), col. 2035; Mantua Stat. (1303), 5.11, 3:96.

184. On medieval prohibition of Christian burial of public sinners, heretics, and those under ecclesiastical censure, see Marantonio Sguerzo, *Evoluzione*, 150–76. See also Bologna Synod (1310), 497–98.

185. Sicardo, *Mitrale*, 9.50, col. 430. For further comment, see Lett, *Enfant*, 211.

but in a place of dishonor, tossed on the trash heap like the carcasses of
animals. A hanged criminal was to be buried under his gallows. But in all
such cases, should the dying have sought confession and the ministry of a
priest, an exception might be made for a Christian burial.[186] The excommunicated could not rest in consecrated ground, at least until a judge relaxed
the ban or restitution was made, as the excommunicate's heirs could do for
withheld tithes.[187] The Lateran Council forbade, absolutely and irrevocably,
the burial of heretics in holy ground. The community of the sleeping dead,
like that of the living, should be an orthodox and pious commonwealth.[188]
Exhumation of heretics buried in holy ground reflected a desire for communal purity even in death more than an urge to inflict punishment on dead
dissenters.[189]

If a good Catholic Christian could not be buried in a cemetery, the
Church provided ceremonies to render an individual grave as holy as that of
the parish's consecrated ground. A priest blessed the isolated grave with holy
water and erected a cross, that all might know a Christian had been buried
there and that the demons might tremble. When a Catholic died at sea,
money for a proper funeral and burial was sewn into the shroud, in the hope
that a proper funeral would be conducted if the body should be found.[190]
Nearly all citizens of the communes went to rest in the chapel cemetery.
Christian cemeteries had been, from time immemorial, blessed with sacred
rites and marked out by sacred symbols.[191] Earth burial, after the model of
Jesus, was the universal norm. The medieval cemetery was free of private
monuments, its ground covered with symbolic plants. Vines and laurel, by
their green foliage, recalled the immortality of the soul. The favorite tree
was the cypress, whose sweet odor recalled holiness and hid any stench of
decay. It was an evergreen that recalled the resurrection to everlasting life as
it grew straight up. It symbolized, too, the finality of death in this age, since,
unlike other trees, it died completely when cut down, rather than sending up
new shoots.[192] The body was laid in the grave with the feet to the east,
toward the rising sun, the direction from which Christ would come at the
end of the world. The bodies of Christians would then rise from the grave to
greet him. Bishop Sicardo the liturgist discouraged separate burials of head

---

186. Sicardo, *Mitrale*, 9.50, cols. 429–30.

187. Aquileia, *Aquilejense Concilium a Raymundo Patriarca Aquilejensi Anno 1282 Habitum* (1282), Mansi 24: 437.

188. Michele Maccarrone, "'Cura animarum' e 'parochialis sacerdos' nelle costituzioni del IV Concilio Lateranense (1215): Applicazioni in Italia nel sec. XIII," *Pievi e parrocchie*, ed. Erba et al., 1:97, citing
Lateran IV, c. 66.

189. Gabriele Zanella, "L'eresia catara fra XIII e XIV secolo: In margine al disagio di una storiografia," *Bullettino dell'Istituto storico italiano per il Medio Evo e Archivio muratoriano* 88 (1979): 244.

190. See Sicardo, *Mitrale*, 9.50, col. 430, on these practices.

191. On the blessing of cemeteries in medieval canon law, see Marantonio Sguerzo, *Evoluzione*, 86–93.

192. So suggests Sicardo, *Mitrale*, 9.50, col. 428.

and body (something becoming ever more common in the late 1100s), since dismembering seemed also a countersign of the resurrection.[193]

Pisa was unusual in its great monumental *camposanto* at the cathedral complex. The city buried all its citizens there. The canons of the duomo, just as they strenuously defended their monopoly over baptisms throughout the 1200s, defended their rite to bury all their fellow citizens.[194] Pisa's single cemetery symbolized the unity of the larger city community, but it could not erase each Christian's link to the local chapel. Elsewhere, cemeteries were attached to each chapel (or occasionally groups of chapels). Parishioners needed special permission to be buried elsewhere.[195] In the tight urban environment, cemeteries were very small. Proximity to the church assured that those entering and leaving would remember their own mortality and their obligation to pray for the dead. The dead lay close to where they had received the spiritual food of the Eucharist, where they had assisted at Office and Mass. The union of cemetery and parish church showed the dead and the living's mutual sharing in the patrimony of Christ, salvation, and a future home in heaven.[196] Identity with the neighborhood chapel was deeply felt; it was one's community, both in life and in death. The dead lay with their relatives, ancestors, and neighbors, creating a community that transcended time.[197]

The small size of the cemeteries prevented permanent grave markers and memorial stones; the common burial site was anonymous. There were, however, exceptions. At Bologna, where an inventory has been made of marked tombs inside city churches, these unusual burials invariably have civic significance. In the postcommunal age, in-church burials with lustral plaques were mostly for priests or city officials.[198] The first authentic tomb slabs date to the late communal period and invariably mark the tombs of lawyers.[199] Bologna was the city of the law, and its professors and practitioners reflected honor on the entire commune. As ornaments of the city, these men deserved special commemoration in death and were also worthy of mention in the

193. Ibid. The prohibition entered canon law in Boniface VIII, *Detestandae Feritatis*, Extrav. Comm. 3.6 (Friedberg ed. 2:1271–73); on the practice, see Agostino Paravicini Bagliani, *The Pope's Body*, trans. David S. Peterson (Chicago: University of Chicago Press, 2000), 230 and 346 n. 39, with bibliography, and Elizabeth A. R. Brown, "Death and the Human Body in the Later Middle Ages: The Legislation of Boniface VIII on the Division of the Corpse," *Viator* 12 (1981): 221–70.

194. Ronzani, "Organizzazione," 61–62.

195. See, e.g., c. 31 from the Lucca Synod of 1302, in *Dei sinodi della diocesi di Lucca: Dissertazioni* (Lucca: Bertini, 1834), 59.

196. Sicardo, *Mitrale*, 1.4, col. 23.

197. Novara Synod II (1298), 1.2.4.1, p. 208.

198. E.g., that of Meo di Matteo di Madonna Chiara: *Iscrizioni medievali bolognesi*, 208, no. 1 (S. Giovanni in Monte, 1322); or those of Don Benvenuto di Santa Maria in Duno, Damiano di Don Giacomo, and Bonventura di Don Domenico: ibid., 307–8, no. 5 (San Giacomo Maggiore, 1294).

199. *Iscrizioni medievali bolognesi* includes only fourteen inscriptions from the period considered (1180–1340): four each from San Pietro and San Giacomo Maggiore, two from San Giovanni in Monte, and one each from San Vittore, Santi Naborre e Felice, Santo Stefano, and an unknown church. Nearly all commemorate lawyers.

Bolognese chronicles. Girolamo de' Borselli specifically mentioned the deaths of Guillelmus Durandus (the "Speculator"), Bassiano (the student of Bulgaro and teacher of Azzo), and Tancredo, all famous canonists or civilians.[200] For a handful of lawyers, early monumental inscriptions survive.[201] The most extraordinary funeral monuments at Bologna, however, are its great pyramid tombs. Again, all were for lawyers. Medieval observers commented on the splendor of the tombs for the glossator Accursio and the civilian Odofredo behind the apse of the Franciscan church.[202] They hailed the exquisite monuments of the notaries Egidio de' Foscherari and Rolandino de' Passaggeri before the church of San Domenico (fig. 59).[203] A citizen received special honor in death because he had brought special honor to the city during life. There was always a bit of distaste (perhaps envy?) when someone of lesser stature procured a marked tomb. The aristocrat Donna Mabilia, wife of the Ferrarese tyrant Azzo d'Este, got a special monument inside the Franciscan church there by making benefactions to the friars. Fra Salimbene, who recorded her burial, was a bit defensive about it.[204] Burial inside the church (without a monument) was for the chapel clergy; laypeople were buried there only by special dispensation. Others went to rest in the parish cemetery. There the pious dead lay in unmarked graves, undivided by rank, privilege, or wealth. Such a common end seemed natural and fitting.[205]

When the burial procession reached the cemetery, those accompanying the family were supposed to leave, so that only the immediate family, or at most a group of ten, would witness the deposition.[206] This counsel was probably honored only in the breach. The priest sprinkled the open grave with holy water to expel any demons that had stayed on after attempting to delude the deceased during life. Into the open grave, a cleric dumped the spent cinders from the thurible, since "nothing lasts longer than cinders underground." Thus, even after the body wholly decayed, the grave would be recognized should it ever be opened. At Siena, mourners placed aromatic herbs in the grave to recall their use at Christ's burial and, no doubt, to ward

200. Girolamo de' Borselli, *Cronica Gestorum* (1178), 16 (Durandus); (1197), 17 (Bassiano); (1197), 17 (Tancredo).

201. Tancredo: *Iscrizioni medievali bolognesi*, 77, no. 23 (San Pietro? XIII cent. original, now XVIII cent. copy); Bassiano: ibid., 61, no. 9 (San Pietro, 1197). Other lawyers with inscriptions are Bernardo Bottoni of Parma, the compiler of the Gloss on the Compilatio Prima, ibid., 64–65, no. 12 (XIII cent., of unknown origin, now at San Pietro), and Giacomo of Casalbuttano of Cremona, a doctor of both laws, ibid., 63–64, no. 11 (San Pietro? 1332). On the cult of lawyers at Bologna, see Hughes, "Mourning Rites," 35–36.

202. Francesco Pipino, *Chronicon*, 3.30, col. 703. Unfortunately, the tombs seen today are nineteenth-century reconstructions. On the tombs artistically considered, see Renzo Grandi, *I monumenti dei dottori e la scultura a Bologna (1267–1348)* (Bologna: Istituto per la Storia di Bologna, 1982).

203. Girolamo de' Borselli, *Cronica Gestorum* (1289), 33, 35.

204. Salimbene, *Cronica* (1250), 546, Baird trans., 378. On the canon law regulating burial inside the church, see Marantonio Sguerzo, *Evoluzione*, 61–70.

205. Bologna Synod (1310), 497; on the "anonymity" of medieval cemeteries, see Ariès, *Western Attitudes*, 47–49.

206. Bologna Stat. II (1288), 4.91, 1:247; Siena Stat. II (1310), 5.207, 2:320.

off odors. A cross was placed at the head, again to protect against demons.[207] The presiding priest then said a final prayer, and the clerics returned to the church, following the cross. In Siena, they assembled outside the choir and recited a commendation of the dead, at least if the deceased had been a priest.[208] The bereaved stayed on a while at the grave, saying their Paters and Aves and so commending the departed soul to God in lay fashion. Confraternities required such graveside suffrages; the common formula was ten repetitions each of the Pater and Ave.[209] In Verona, after deposition, the mourners accompanied the clerical procession to the church, where the clergy chanted seven psalms for them and the priest pronounced a final collect.[210] Elsewhere the family went straightaway to the house after the burial.[211] If the deceased was a married man, his widow traditionally led this procession, escorted by her mourning companions, numbering at Florence as many as ten men and six women. Before her, one companion carried a lighted candle of at least six pounds.[212]

After the deposition, the time of the main meal, midday, was nigh. Those who gathered at the house expected a funeral dinner with, at least, a generous supply of bread, wine, and "other side dishes."[213] Wine flowed freely. At Parma, wine merchants used to show up at the very graveside to peddle their wares—the city tried to stop that.[214] But no one stopped vendors from making deliveries to the house. Tradition dictated that the pallbearers and the criers who had announced the funeral receive a special meal with plenty to drink; societies provided for them in their statutes.[215] All who attended the funeral expected to take part in the banquet and festivities. A widow presided over her husband's funeral dinner, which provided a rare opportunity for gathering her female relatives and friends. By putting on a good meal, the family showed their appreciation to the neighbors and friends who had been with them in their time of grief. The wealthy, or would-be wealthy, had another chance to display their resources. So the later communes enacted sumptuary legislation, restricting funeral dinners to the immediate family. Siena excluded women beyond three degrees of relation to the deceased.[216]

207. On these practices, see Sicardo, *Mitrale*, 9.50, col. 428; *Ordo Senensis*, 2.98, p. 504; *Rituale di Hugo [di Volterra]*, 318 (which also provides for a Mass at the grave); Florence, Biblioteca Nazionale Centrale, MS Conv. Soppr. D.8.2851, fols. 26ᵛ–28ʳ.

208. *Ordo Senensis*, 2.100, p. 506.

209. E.g., "Statuto dei Disciplinati di Bologna" (1260), 19, Meersseman, *Ordo*, 1:486; "Statuto dei Disciplinati di Vicenza" (1263), 21, ibid., 1:487. Piacenza Battuti Stat. (1317), 65, prescribes twelve Paters and Aves.

210. Verona, Biblioteca Capitolare, MS MCIX, fol. 56ᵛ.

211. As we know from statutes, e.g.: Bol. Pop. Stat., I (Toschi, 1256, c. 38), 104.

212. Florence Stat. I (1322), 5.10, pp. 225–26.

213. Lucca Stat. (1308), 1.12, p. 17.

214. Parma Stat. III (1316), 269–70.

215. E.g., Bol. Pop. Stat., 2 (Formaggiari, 1242, cc. 3–4), 166–67.

216. Siena Stat. II (1310), 5.214, 2:322. For other attempts to limit funeral banquets, see Bologna Stat. II (1288), 4.91, 1:246; Lucca Stat. (1308), 1.11, p. 15; Siena Stat. II (1310), 5.207, 2:320; Modena Stat. (1327), 4.172, pp. 475.

Does the prohibition on distantly related and unrelated women mean that, with all the wine flowing, things occasionally got out of hand? In any case, the funeral banquet was a sign that, at least for the neighborhood, a society fractured by death was returning to normal.

For the immediate family, the funeral banquet began the period of public or solemn mourning. "When Baldovino di Giacomo Riccomanni, son and brother of the Calimala, died at Florence in 1272, his widow was supplied with only the traditional *benda,* waiting for three months before putting on what would become firmly fixed as the traditional black of widowhood. How the children were clothed we do not know, but his sole daughter-in-law immediately had her guarnacca [cloak] dyed *in sanguigno* and had made up a costume a few weeks later with the purchase of a bracio [a cloth measure of about two feet] of silk, which she also dyed *in sanguigno* to make a gonnella [gown]."[217] Brown and red were the mourning colors of communal Italy. Widows wore *panno bruno;* more distant female relatives wore red. The mark of deep mourning was the dark widow's *benda,* a headcovering that originally signified the loss of a spouse. In theory, only the widow herself could wear it, and she for only two weeks after the funeral.[218] She then put it aside for simple dark clothing, the attire used also to mourn the death of children under thirty.[219] But some widows, and even their friends, wore the *benda* for months or even years to express their sorrow.[220]

UNION WITH THE DEAD

Bishop Sicardo gave three possibilities for the soul after it left the body: "There are souls that, immediately after they leave the body, fly like a sparrow to the Lord. There are others that descend to hell. Others are in between, and they go to purgatory, to be helped by almsgiving, prayer, fasting, and the Mass. But because of the uncertainty, these things are done for all. For it is better that more be done for those whom it can neither help nor hurt, than that it be lacking to those whom it can help."[221] Death did not break the bonds of family, contrada, and city. Almsgiving, prayers, fasting, and the sacrifice of the Mass: by these, the living aided the needy dead, just as the saints helped the living by their prayers in heaven. No Christian was perfect, and even a saint might have to pass through some short purgation before entering God's presence. Saint Umiliana dei Cerchi appeared after

---

217. Hughes, "Mourning Rites," 33. The Calimala was a cloth guild.

218. Florence Stat. 1 (1322), 5.7, pp. 223.

219. At least in Siena, the two-week period was the norm: Siena Stat. II (1310), 5.204, 2:319.

220. Although cities tried to regulate its use: Lucca Stat. (1308), 1.11, p. 15; Pisa Stat. II (1313), 3.58, pp. 350–51.

221. Sicardo, *Mitrale,* 9.50, col. 430: "Sunt enim animae quae, statim ut exeunt a corporibus, ut passer volant ad Dominum; sunt aliae quae descendunt in infernum, sunt mediae, quae vadunt in purgatorium, quarum intuitu eleemosynae, oratione, jejunia et sacrificia, sed propter incertitudinem pro omnibus etiam fiunt; melius enim supererunt ista his, quibus nec prosunt, nec obsunt, quam derunt his, quibus prodesse possunt."

her death to her friend Gisla of Mucello in a dream. She told Gisla not to slacken in doing penance for her sins. Umiliana said, "Twelve days before my own death I foresaw it; and I passed through purgatory as innocent children do."[222] It was a mild purgatory because of Umiliana's penance on earth, but it was purgatory nevertheless. The Blessed Virgin's intercessory power for souls was celebrated, but it was safer to heed Umiliana's warning to do penance than merely to rely on the Virgin's help. A prior of San Salvatore at Pavia was lax in his life and talk, it is said, but he sang praises of the Virgin after every Office. One year after his death, the sacristan, Fra Uberto, heard someone calling his name in the night. It was the prior, who had gone to purgatory and suffered for a year before the Blessed Mother could rescue him.[223] The prior may have gotten out early, but even one year in what seemed like hell was a frightful prospect. It was good to pray for everyone—at least until they started working miracles. The most powerful aid to souls was the Mass, especially when said by a holy priest. God revealed to Saint Nicola of Tolentino that it had taken him only seven days of Masses to pray a soul out of purgatory.[224]

According to the Church calendar, the day to pray for the dead was 2 November, All Souls Day, following the solemnity of All Saints. This was a day of public fasting. The ritual books provided three Masses to be said for the dead by every priest.[225] At Siena, the last Mass ended with the chanting of the "Libera" and a procession to the cemetery to bless the graves with holy water.[226] At Verona, the clergy of the duomo had a similar procession every Friday. They chanted the "Libera" before the high altar and went to the cemetery to chant a short litany of the Blessed Virgin and an antiphon in honor of the cross before an image of the crucified Savior.[227] The people did come to these rites, but they had not achieved the popularity they would enjoy in later centuries. People preferred particular Masses for their own relatives and neighbors. The traditional days for such Masses were the burial day, the third day after, and the seventh day after. Bishop Sicardo suggested that the Masses on these three days purged the three parts of the soul, the concupiscible, irascible, and rational faculties. More likely, the Mass on the third day symbolized Christ's Resurrection, that on the seventh the Sabbath rest of the just. Bishop Sicardo also knew of Requiems on the fortieth day— supposedly a symbol of the Ten Commandments and the four Gospels—and on the fiftieth day—the Ten Commandments and the five senses. These memorial Masses were not so common, and Sicardo did not like them.

222. Vito of Cortona, *Vita [B. Humilianae]*, 6.1, p. 400: "Duodecim diebus prius mortem meam praescivi, et per purgatorium transivi sicut pueri faciunt innocentes."

223. Pisa, Biblioteca Cateriniana del Seminario Arcivescovile, MS 139, fol. 144ʳ.

224. Pietro of Monte Rubiano. *Vita [S. Nicolai Tolentinatis]*, 2.12, p. 647.

225. Sicardo, *Mitrale*, 9.50, cols. 424–30.

226. *Ordo Senensis*, 1.421, p. 379–80.

227. Verona, Biblioteca Capitolare, MS DCCXXXVI, fols. 55ᵛ–57ᵛ.

The most popular of all Masses for the dead was that on the anniversary of death.[228] The widow of Count Lodovico of San Bonifacio remembered his first anniversary by sending a samite and purple pallium for the altar of the Franciscan house where his Requiem was celebrated.[229] Second in popularity was the one-month anniversary Mass. Legend had it that Saint Gregory the Great had prayed the emperor Trajan out of hell after thirty days of Masses, and this founded the practice of a "trentine" of Masses leading up to the thirty-day anniversary. That devotion would have a great vogue in the later Middle Ages, but it had only just started its long career in the communal period.[230] The one-week and one-month anniversaries were especially popular with families of the deceased. They provided an opportunity to reaffirm family and neighborhood solidarity in the face of loss. Pious women gathered on those days for a pianto in the local church.[231] The wealthy endowed Masses for themselves and their relatives. Rolando Taverna, bishop of Spoleto, beautified buildings, including the church of the Holy Sepulcher in his hometown of Parma. There he installed a chapel with marble columns and endowed Requiem Masses for his relatives buried there.[232] He combined familial piety with home-city patriotism. Account books of the Franciscan church in Bologna track the popularity of suffrages for the dead, since nearly all the *entrate* are Requiem Mass alms—in a typical recording period, 19 April to 17 July 1299, the take was £196 10s., a princely sum for the poor brothers of Saint Francis.[233]

Each Sunday, the parish remembered its dead during the bidding prayers before the Canon.[234] At Ferrara, when the priest had finished the biddings, he announced the names of the recently deceased. The congregation knelt and prayed a Pater and an Ave for each. On the first Sunday of the month, they said seven Paters and seven Aves for all the faithful departed; whenever a priest died, they said twelve.[235] In proper proportion, lay Paters could be just as helpful to the dead as clerical Masses. Among the Dominicans, a cleric might replace the suffrage of a Requiem Mass with the recitation of the penitential psalms and the litany. A lay brother's version of the suffrage

---

228. Sicardo, *Mitrale*, 9.50, cols. 244–45; *Rituale di Hugo [di Volterra]*, 301–20; *Ordo Senensis*, 2.103, pp. 509–10; Florence, Biblioteca Nazionale Centrale, MS Conv. Soppr. D.8.2851, fols. 23ʳ–24ᵛ (a monastic example).

229. Salimbene, *Cronica* (1283), 752–53, Baird trans., 524–25.

230. *Ordo Senensis*, 2.102, p. 509; see Gregory the Great, *Dialogi*, 4.5, *Dialogues*, ed. and trans. Adalbert de Vogüé (Paris: Cerf, 1978), 3:33–39.

231. See Ravenna Stat., 341, p. 159; Modena Stat. (1327), 2.46, p. 263; Lucca Stat. (1308), 1.14, p. 17.

232. Salimbene, *Cronica* (1285), 865–66, Baird trans., 600–601. For another example of a chantry, see *Iscrizioni medievali bolognesi*, 334, no. 38 (San Giacomo Maggiore, 1310).

233. See Bologna, Biblioteca dell'Archiginnasio, MS B.490 (1769, from XIV cent. original), pp. 10–11.

234. Nicole Lemaître and Jean-Loup Lemaître, "Un test des solidarités paroissiales: Le prière pour les morts dans les obituaires," *La parrocchia nel Medio Evo*, ed. Paravicini Bagliani and Pasche, 260; for other examples of such prayers for the dead, see Jean-Loup Lemaître, *Répertoire des documents nécrologiques français* (Paris: Imprimerie Nationale, 1980), nos. 1459, 1752, 2182.

235. Ferrara Clergy Const. (1278), col. 437.

was one hundred Paters and Aves.[236] Who could tell whether God might not be more pleased with the Paters of a pious lay brother than with the elaborate prayers of clerics? Prayers for the dead had their greatest power during the Communion at Mass, just as the sacrifice was complete. One thirteenth-century Florentine priest collected Communion devotions, including prayers for the dead. His collection recommended that, on entering a cemetery, one say a Pater for the dead, remembering that what they were now all would one day be. For the literate he excerpted two Latin prayers from the Mass of the dead, which could be added to this Pater to make it more specific. One was for all the dead in the cemetery, the other for one's parents. Death did not cancel the Fourth Commandment. But for those with no Latin, the Pater was wholly sufficient; it was the Lord's own prayer.[237]

Whether a family, a pious association, or the commune itself, every corporation was especially responsible for its dead. In 1278, the clergy confraternity of Ferrara got bishop Guglielmo to promise that on the first of each month he would chant Mass and the Office of the dead for his deceased priests. The cathedral clergy, for their part, bound themselves to attend under a penalty of £6 ven. parv., to be dispensed as alms for the poor by the archdeacon.[238] When a priest died, four priests of his contrada read the Psalter over his body, and the bishop or archpriest of the duomo said the funeral Mass. All priests chanted seven Requiem Masses for him within a month of his death. The laity were not forgotten by these clerics; they too could enroll in the confraternity for prayers and temporal benefits. A deceased priest's clothing and goods went to the poorer lay members from his neighborhood.[239] Bishops also stipulated that the clergy recite Masses and prayers for them after their death. In the province of Ravenna, the bishops, cathedral canons, and collegiate-church clergy all chanted a Mass and fed three paupers each day for an entire month when their archbishop died.[240]

Lay confraternities and communal societies recited their own Paters and Aves for the dead after Mass, usually on the first Sunday of the month.[241] Innocent III's 1201 provisions for Humiliati lay tertiaries required them to attend each other's funerals and recite there twelve Paters and the psalm "Miserere."[242] The most ancient parts of the Bolognese Popolo's statutes are probably their suffrage provisions.[243] At Pisa, the society of Santa Lucia kept a necrology listing dead members and recited three Paters and three Aves

236. *ACGOP*, 267.
237. Florence, Biblioteca Nazionale Centrale, MS Magl. XXXVI.81bis, fols. 37ʳ⁻ᵛ.
238. Ferrara Clergy Const. (1278), cols. 433–34.
239. Ibid., cols. 434–35.
240. Ravenna Council (1311), 2, p. 452, and Ravenna Council (1317), 21, p. 620.
241. E.g., Lucca, Biblioteca Statale, MS 1310, fol. 9ʳ; Piacenza, Biblioteca Comunale, MS Pallestrelli 323, fols. 17ʳ–19ᵛ; Meersseman, "Statuto dei Disciplinati di Bologna" (1260), 10, Meersseman, *Ordo*, 1:480; id., "Statuto dei Disciplinati di Vicenza" (1263), 29, Meersseman, *Ordo*, 1:497.
242. On the Humiliati rites for the dead, see Andrews, *Early Humiliati*, 225–29.
243. Epstein, *Wage Labor*, 84–85.

daily for them.[244] Associations updated their necrologies regularly, and some of these continued in use for over a hundred years. The necrology of the Ospedale of Reno near Bologna includes names of lay penitents and clerics in equal number. The hospital continued to add names throughout the communal period—in over a hundred different hands.[245] Some of the most elaborate suffrages come from flagellant statutes in the later communal period, but these are probably no different from earlier, lost legislation. The Pavia *battuti* had two annual suffrages for the dead, on the feast of their patron Saint Agatha and on the feast of the Assumption of Mary. They gathered on each for a Requiem and recited together twenty-five Paters and Aves. They had a weekly Mass of the dead, too; members who could not attend it said fifty Paters and Aves instead.[246]

Suffrages always included almsgiving, that most powerful of good works for souls in purgatory. Even the priests did not rely on Mass alone. Feeding the poor made the banquet of heaven visible here on earth. At Ravenna, annually on 4 June, the clergy fed twelve paupers in memory of the deceased benefactors and patrons of their churches.[247] The annual meal for the dead was especially a family event. People ate and prayed for their dead parents and relatives, and most also provided something for the poor. Donna Giacobba di Don Bonadio of Careno considered it perfectly orthodox that the friends of the dubious Guglielma of Milan meet at her tomb for *convivia* in her memory on the date of her death.[248] Hints in sumptuary legislation at Siena suggest that memorial banquets on the anniversary of death were a vital part of lay commemoration of the dead.[249] As the community prayed and remembered the dead, it reaffirmed the link between the *Citade Sancta* here on earth and its fulfillment in the celestial Jerusalem to come.

244. Pisa Stat. I, pp. 705–6.
245. The necrology is edited in Bocchi, "Necrologio," 121–32; on this book, see ibid., 65–86.
246. Milan, Biblioteca Nazionale Braidense, MS AC.VIII.2, fols. 10ᵛ, 36ʳ; cf. also Piacenza, Biblioteca Comunale, MS Pallestrelli 323, fols. 17ʳ–20ʳ; Novara Battuti Stat. (XIV), 280.
247. Ravenna Council (1311), 4, p. 453.
248. The inquisitors of her cult found nothing odd in this: *Atti inquisitoriali [contro i Guglielmiti]*, esp. 2.33, 3.8, pp. 190, 218.
249. Siena Stat. II (1310), 5.212–14, 2:321–22.

Epilogue
Communal Piety and the Mendicants

So far this book has said little about the mendicant orders or heretics, the two topics that, along with the papacy, especially fascinate students of religious life in high medieval Italy. Communal piety, especially its penance culture, inspired Saint Francis and his followers.[1] The Minorites and other orders that adopted aspects of their piety, especially the Dominicans, came to dominate the religious life of the cities. Their presence affected city space, communal charity, political practice, and spirituality. It also brought remarkable changes in the religious life of women, at least among a spiritual elite. The friars cooperated in the policing of doctrinal orthodoxy, a pressing concern for the thirteenth-century Roman Church. There truly were dissenters, Cathars and others, about in the Italian cities. And inquisitions and less dramatic forms of persuasion, such as revived preaching and new confraternities supervised by both Dominicans and Franciscans, also monitored the traditional piety of the laity. By the later 1200s, long-venerated lay saints might become posthumous heretics, and seemingly devout members of the local cappella might end up at the stake. These changes are the subject of this epilogue.

MAKING SPACE FOR THE FRIARS

The arrival of the mendicants at Bologna was unusual for northern Italy only in its precocity. When Saint Francis preached there in the Piazza Maggiore during 1222, his followers had already arrived three years earlier. They had located near Porta Stiera, where the first Mass was chanted at their

---

1. On the impact of the mendicants, see first the essays edited by André Vauchez, *Ordres mendiants et la ville en Italie centrale (v. 1220–v. 1350)* (*Mélanges de l'École française de Rome: Moyen Âge–temps modernes* 89 [1977]): 557–773, in particular, Luigi Pellegrini, "Gli insediamenti degli ordini mendicanti e la loro tipologia: Considerazioni metodologiche e piste di ricerca," 563–73.

convent in 1221.[2] Dominicans arrived at about the same time. Jacques of Vitry penned his famous description of the new "canons of Bologna" after his visit in 1222.[3] The Dominicans preached, practiced poverty, and attracted vocations from the university. Other mendicants, Augustinians and Carmelites, followed soon after. Bologna chronicles noted the arrival of even minor offshoots of the begging tradition, like the Brothers of the Sack, who settled outside Porta San Mamolo in 1256.[4] Individual communes gave birth to mendicant groups peculiarly their own. Some, like Florentine Servites, flourished; others, like the Apostolici at Parma, descended into heresy and incurred the wrath of inquisitors. The communes themselves were less discriminating than the Church. In 1250, Parma recognized the Apostolici and, by 1262, enrolled them on the city alms list, along with more respectable orders—much to the disgust of Fra Salimbene, who called them a fraudulent imitation of his own Franciscans.[5] The mendicant vogue touched smaller cities, which lured foundations by promises of alms and real estate. In 1230, Treviso appropriated £50 for constructing a convent to attract the Dominicans. But Franciscans always seemed the better catch. In 1231, Treviso ordered its new podesta, Don Caccianimici of Bologna, to expend £1,000 to build a house for the poor brothers of Saint Francis.[6] In 1233, the people of Reggio Emilia, perhaps inspired by the Alleluia devotion of that year, gathered and carried stones for the Dominican's new church. At Reggio, both young and old carried bricks; the weaker escorted them with lighted candles and banners. Bishop Nicola and his archpriest, Giacomo, came to bless the work and lay the friary cornerstone.[7]

The mendicants quickly placed their mark on the cities. At Bologna, the Dominicans took over the church of San Nicolò delle Vigne in 1221. Almost immediately, they began new construction and expansion that would last into the 1300s.[8] Franciscan building at Bologna began in Porta Stiera during 1236, and their great Gothic church was finished in 1263.[9] Pope Innocent IV recognized the prestige of both foundations by visits during his journey back from the Council of Lyons. On 14 and 15 October 1250 respectively, he

2. Matteo Griffoni, 7–8; on Mass: *CCB*: Vill. (1221), 83. For mendicant impact on the contado, see Charles M. De La Roncière, "L'influence des Franciscains dans la campagne de Florence au XIVᵉ siècle (1280–1360)," *Mélanges de l'École française de Rome: Moyen Âge–temps modernes* 87 (1975): 27–103.

3. Jacques of Vitry, *Historia Occidentalis*, 27, p. 143; on this passage, see Hinnebusch's remarks, in ibid., pp. 6, 19–20.

4. *CCB*: B (1256), 139.

5. Parma Stat. 1, 115–16; Salimbene, *Cronica*, 580, Baird trans., 404; see Orioli, *Venit Perfidus Heresiarcha*, 65–67.

6. Treviso Stat. (1230), 686, 2:268; (1231), 690, 2:269–70.

7. Alberto Milioli, *Liber*, 509.

8. See I. B. Supino, *L'architettura sacra in Bologna nei secoli XIII e XIV* (Bologna: Zanichelli, 1909), 3–41, esp. the plan on 25; for the implantation of the Dominicans in Bologna, see Tommaso Alfonsi, "Le chiesa di s. Nicolò delle Vigne in Bologna dal 1221 al 1251," *Il rosario: Memorie domenicane*, 3d ser., 2 (1915): 317–320, 372–84. For French comparisons, see Jacques Le Goff, "Ordres mendiants e urbanisation dans la France médiévale: État de l'enquête," *Annales: Économies—sociétés—civilisations* 25 (1970): 924–46.

9. Supino, *Architettura*, 43–48.

consecrated the new high altars of the Franciscan and Dominican churches in two grandiose ceremonies. He gave the Franciscans a sumptuous set of paraments in commemoration of the occasion.[10] The Augustinians at Bologna began the construction of their large church of San Giacomo in 1267 and completed it in 1290, just as the Carmelites began their San Martino dell'Aposa, a project that would last into the 1300s.[11] Setbacks in these projects concerned the entire city. When two vaults under construction at San Francesco collapsed in 1254, causing many injuries and breaking the legs of the director of construction, Fra Andrea, the podesta, Ubertino of Udine, came with his council to console the friars. The city took over the construction costs.[12]

Monumental mendicant churches affected the spaces around them. Cities rerouted streams and canals to provide the new communities with water.[13] The friars acquired land around their convents for expansion and for gardens and vineyards. The acquisition process often spanned many decades. Dominican land purchases at Bologna left a paper trail extending more than thirty years.[14] Siena undertook some of the earliest urban planning, helping the friars acquire and clear areas in front of their churches so as to create monumental squares and wider access streets.[15] Cities evicted unseemly neighbors, such as brothels and taverns, from the new mendicant preserves.[16] The friars could be quite aggressive. At Reggio, the sons of Saint Francis expended large sums of money evicting their neighbors and pulling down houses to expand the streets and piazza fronting on their church of San Giacomo.[17] Such construction generated resistance. At Bologna, the city forbade the Dominicans' neighbors from throwing trash and dead animals onto convent property. The commune also reined in rock throwers around the Franciscan convent, who were disturbing the Mass and Office.[18]

This construction added an overlay of major churches that redefined the city's religious space. These new squares and churches created cultic centers that competed with that of the duomo. The sacred space of the city was "decentered." Mendicant buildings usually formed a ring outside the early

10. Matteo Griffoni, 112; *CCB:* Vill., 130.

11. Supino, *Architettura*, 55–75. These projects competed for support with those at San Michele in Bosco and San Giovanni in Monte: ibid., 85–91.

12. *CCB:* Bol., 136–37.

13. E.g., at Bologna and Parma: Bologna Stat. 1 (1250), 7.144, 2:147 (for the Dominicans), and (1252), 9.351, 2:520 (for the Franciscans); Parma Stat. 1 (before 1255), pp. 379 (for the Franciscans) and 381 (for the Dominicans).

14. See Mario Fanti, "Il ritrovato originale del contratto fra s. Domenico e Pietro di Lovello del 7 giugno 1221," *AFP* 36 (1966): 389–94, and V. Alce, "Documenti sul convento di s. Domenico in Bologna dal 1221 al 1251," *AFP* 42 (1972): 5–45.

15. Siena Stat. 1 (1262), 1.276, pp. 109–8; Bologna Stat. 1 (1250–67), 2:373.

16. E.g., at Reggio: Reggio Stat. (1265, 1270), 4.5, pp. 238–39, for the Dominicans and Franciscans.

17. *Mem. Pot. Reg.* (1272), col. 1134; Sagacino Levalossi and Pietro Della Grazata, *Chronicon Regiense* (1272), col. 5.

18. Bologna Stat. 1 (1250), 8.66–70 and 82, 2:257 and 268–69 (Dominicans); (1250, 1252, 1259, 1260–67), 8.31, 2:226–27 (Franciscans).

communal walls. They were located in the *borghi,* which would be enclosed with the last ring of walls, constructed just before the population drop after the Black Death.[19] Mendicant convents dominated these new neighborhoods. Their location put mendicant churches in areas of mercantile and population growth and linked them geographically to the class that dominated the later communes. The friars sponsored confraternities and established "chapters" of their third orders, which drew people away from their neighborhood cappelle and the earlier religious associations of the commune.[20] In small cities, mendicant foundations literally overshadowed the older cultic center. A triangle of sanctuaries—Dominican, Franciscan, and Augustinian—typically reordered the geography of the communes. Late communal Bologna, Florence, Padua, Vicenza, and other smaller cities were defined by their mendicant triangles.[21]

City statutes suggest the monetary impact of the mendicants' arrival and its transformation of communal almsgiving. The 1228 statutes of Verona, among the earliest extant, reveal the premendicant pattern of municipal charity. Verona exempted six churches from taxes and provided special legal protection to the monastery of San Zeno.[22] The city allotted new tax exemptions, on a small scale, into the 1270s.[23] The largest share of public funding in the early 1200s probably went to the duomo, although financial records are lacking. The pattern changes radically after 1250. Almsgiving to the mendicants began with ad hoc grants for limited periods, usually to meet some particular need. In 1250, the Bologna city council voted an annual £500 (£300 from Altedo and £200 from the city) to the Minorites for a five-year period, after which the sum was lowered to £200 a year.[24] This funding alone dwarfed any earlier support for the duomo. Little communes followed the lead of the larger. In 1255 San Gimignano voted its Franciscans £20 pis. a year to repair their habits.[25] Siena followed the older practice of individual grants for specific purposes into the 1260s. But these came to resemble annual doles, as the city underwrote construction costs for the Dominicans, Franciscans, Crutched Friars, Humiliati, Carmelites, Augustinian Hermits, Servites, and six new houses of nuns. Such construction added up to a sizable

19. Anna Benvenuti Papi, "Mendicanti a Firenze," *In Castro Poenitentiae,* 4–6.
20. Ibid., 11–13.
21. On this new geography, see *Storia della città* 9 (1978), in particular: Angiola Maria Romanini, "L'architettura degli ordini mendicanti: Nuove prospettive di interpretazione," 5–15; Giuseppina Inga, "Gli insediamenti mendicanti a Cortona," 44–55; and Sandra Farina, "I conventi mendicanti nel tessuto urbanistico di Bologna," 56–61. More generally on Bologna, see Massimo Giansante, "Insediamenti religiosi e società urbana a Bologna dal x ad xviii secolo," *L'Archiginnasio* 89 (1994): 217–22; and on Italian cities generally, see Enrico Guidoni, *La città dal Medioevo al Rinascimento,* 2d ed. (Bari: Laterza, 1985).
22. Verona Stat. i (1228), 139, p. 103; 234, pp. 177–78. In this early period there were provisions for older Benedictine houses: e.g., Padua Stat. (1230), pp. 424–25, no. 1365 (for Santa Giustina); p. 264, no. 1366 (Santa Maria di Procilla).
23. Verona Stat. ii (1276), 1.229, p. 187.
24. Bologna Stat. i (1250), 5.13, 1:450.
25. San Gimignano Stat. (1255), 4.48, p. 729.

sum, although actual figures are lacking.[26] With money came city involvement. At Pisa in 1286, the city appointed its own overseer for city-financed construction at the Franciscan convent, supposedly at the friars' request.[27]

Ad hoc grants and exemptions never disappeared, but after the 1260s, cities regularized their almsgiving.[28] Only Padua seems to have resisted making support for the mendicants a recurring budget item, but ad hoc construction subsidies to the friars proliferate in city statutes from 1265 to 1277.[29] Elsewhere, cities established rosters of subsidized entities, each of which received yearly or twice-yearly donations. To itemize these alms lists would be tedious, but overall patterns emerge clearly. Alms grants were generally smaller than outlays for construction. Alms usually ran between £20 and £50 a year and sometimes included provision of food.[30] Recipients multiplied, and the burden increased over time. The provisions created a customary and perpetual burden. Such grants eclipsed or put pressure on municipal support for the duomo and the cathedral complex. Only at Siena, where the late 1200s saw a major new cathedral-building project, did expenditure on the old cultic center outclass grants to new orders and foundations. But even there the three major orders each received a recurring £100 a year.[31]

In the early 1200s, the lay Brothers of Penance provided their cities with needed public servants. They served in sensitive positions, overseeing charity, finances, elections, and other tasks demanding nonpartisanship and integrity. After the friars arrived, this changed. During 1240, in an early example of government involvement by friars, Cremona decided that henceforth mendicants would select the notary who assisted the city financial officer (*massarius*).[32] Reggio in 1260 determined that the *massarius* would himself be a friar.[33] Within twenty years, the friars would come to predominate. Bologna's statutes reveal the creeping mendicant takeover. By the end of the 1250s, those advising the podesta on selection of his successor had to be Dominican, Franciscan, or Augustinian friars. They sat "on the bench" with the podesta during the election. By the 1260s, the Augustinians of San Giacomo Maggiore had become responsible for keeping Bologna's books of condemnations and lists of those under the city ban.[34] The Lombardi made the Dominicans custodians of their statute book in 1291.[35] By the end of the

26. Siena Stat. I (1262), 1.40–91, pp. 36–47.
27. Pisa Stat. I, 1.180, p. 337.
28. For examples of later ad hoc charity, see Girolamo de' Borselli, *Cronica Gestorum* (Bologna, 1313), 37; Cremona Stat. (1313), 105; Florence Stat. II (1325), 4.62, p. 351; Modena Stat. (1327), 1.61, pp. 52–53; Mantua Stat., 5.4–9, 3:94–99.
29. Padua Stat., 4.12, pp. 351–52, no. 1151–55; 4.13, p. 355, no. 1163.
30. See examples of such alms lists in Parma Stat. II (1266), 100–101; Pisa Stat. I (1286), 1.57, pp. 133–43; Bologna Stat. II (1288), 11.5, 2:191–92; Ravenna Stat., 355, pp. 169–70.
31. Siena Stat. II (1310), 1.54, 1:77–83.
32. Cremona Stat., 99.
33. Reggio Stat., 2.3, pp. 150–51.
34. Bologna Stat. I (1262), 11.125, 3:386–87.
35. Bol. Pop. Stat., I (Lombardi, 1291, c. 23), 70–71.

century, municipal elections at Bologna were wholly in the control of the Dominican prior and the Franciscan guardian. They selected the sixteen men from each quarter who chose the consuls and "ancients" of the Popolo. They supervised elections.[36] Other cities show similar patterns.[37] As friars took over sensitive posts, lay penitents disappeared. By the end of the century, the Brothers of Penance had completely lost their role in city administration. Friars accumulated other political duties besides administration. In 1299, the Bolognese named the Dominican prior of Faenza as agent in their negotiations with the Romagnol communes harboring the exiled Lambertazzi faction. He met with representatives of these communes in the Franciscan house near Monte del Re, a dependency of Dozza (Imola).[38] Exemptions followed on duties. In 1252, the Bolognese allowed friars to hold office simultaneously as syndics of the university and their own religious corporations, a kind of pluralism forbidden to secular corporations. At Pisa, the Humiliati were exempted from regulation by the wool guild. The Bolognese granted exemption from the calumny oath, once a unique privilege of the bishop and lay penitents, to friars of all orders in 1288.[39]

Conversely, the mendicants drew the cities into religious activities that earlier had been alien to them. The communes had always sought to preserve the appearance and reality of Catholic orthodoxy. But after the 1230s, mendicant inquisitors demanded city muscle in policing heretics. In letters of 11 and 12 May 1252, Pope Innocent IV ordered the northern cities to impose the "imperial penalty," that is, death by fire, for heresy. He instructed the region's Dominican priors to report on city compliance.[40] After the murder of the inquisitor Peter of Verona in 1253, papal letters first rewarded municipal repression with indulgences and finally commanded it on pain of excommunication.[41] The cities were slow to comply, and some even claimed to have privileges exempting them from doing the ecclesiastical tribunals' dirty work. Pope Innocent was complaining to the friars about passive resistance within a year.[42]

Friars impinged on the traditional role of the parochial clergy, first by hearing confessions and attracting people to their Masses and Offices, and later by doing sick calls and burials. Although the originally clerical Domini-

36. Bologna Stat. II (1293, but enacted originally in 1288), 5.153, 1:565.
37. Bologna Stat. I (1259–60), 11.101, 3:353; Pisa Stat. I (1286), 1.177, p. 335; Brescia Stat. (1313), 1.160, col. 48. But Brescia excluded religious from city office: Brescia Stat. (before 1277), col. (161); (1313), 1.170, col. 51–52.
38. Pietro Cantinelli, *Chronicon* (1299), 91.
39. Bologna Stat. I (1250), 4.21, 1:403; Pisa Stat. I (1286), 1.162, p. 294; Bologna Stat. II (1288), 6.42, 2:34.
40. Bologna, Biblioteca dell'Archiginnasio, MS B.3695, doc. 5 (*BOP* 1:205) and doc. 6 (originals both dated 1252).
41. Innocent IV (31 May 1254), in ibid., doc. 19 (*BOP* 1:248), granted forty days to those attending Dominican sermons against heresy.
42. Ibid., doc. 15 (*BOP* 1:231).

cans were probably the first to compete with the seculars, the Franciscans had become so thoroughly clericalized that by 1227 the pope had already recognized and protected their exercise of parochial functions such as confessions and funerals. With sick calls and funerals came bequests, which previously would have gone to the cappelle. Above all, the encroachment on burial rights, with its influence over bequests, rankled and provoked lawsuits.[43] From the secular clergy's point of view, the friars' encroachment was not merely financial, it also disrupted pastoral care and weakened parish unity and identity.[44] This synopsis may exaggerate mendicant-secular friction—lawsuits leave paper trails, friendly relations do not—but the Franciscan Salimbene reported, with distaste, the accusations made by the secular clerics. The mendicants failed to encourage people to pay tithes, buried the dead in their own cemeteries and took the burial fees, heard parishioners' confessions and solicited alms, and even usurped the parish priest's office of preaching.[45]

The cities admittedly loved the friars, but there were always misgivings about their growing domination of communal religious life. Some friars lacked integrity. In 1308, Lucca enacted draconian sanctions against Fra Francesco, an Augustinian who had betrayed the commune. His death sentence was not repealed until a year later, and then only at the demand of the papal legate.[46] Mendicant churches provided sanctuary for malefactors. In 1277, much to one Bolognese chronicler's disgust, the Franciscans helped the youthful Bastardino de' Griffoni escape communal justice by hiding him and smuggling him out of the city dressed as a friar. He had murdered a knight of the podesta in the Piazza San Salvatore.[47] By the 1300s, Florence and Siena started barring friars from holding communal office.[48] The Pisans lynched several Dominicans in 1313, after hearing a rumor that a friar had poisoned the emperor Henry VII.[49] The friars were no longer petted darlings.

NEW INSIDERS, NEW OUTSIDERS

Spiritually, the mendicant arrival brought winners and losers. The lay penitents had always counted women in their number, but the movement was predominantly male. The public life of the commune was a man's preserve; the neighborhood societies were military and so excluded women. A look at

43. For litigation between friars and parish clergy over burial rights, see Florence, Biblioteca Medicea Laurenziana, MS Acq. e Doni 263.

44. See Meersseman, *Ordo*, 1:157–58.

45. Salimbene, *Cronica* (1250), 584, Baird trans., 407. See also Luigi Pellegrini, "Mendicanti e parroci: Coesistenze e conflitti di due strutture organizzative della Cura Animarum," *Francescanesimo e vita religiosa dei laici nel '200*, 133–34.

46. Lucca Stat. (1308), 3.62–74, pp. 180–83; pp. 340–41.

47. Matteo Griffoni, 22, 27.

48. Siena Stat. II (1310), 1.379, 1:267; Florence Stat. II (1325), 3.108, p. 262.

49. *CCB*: A (1313), 290.

the gender ratio of the lay saints reinforces the masculine image of communal religiosity. The popular communal saints were men like Pietro Pettinaio,
Omobono of Cremona, and Ranieri of Pisa. The later thirteenth century
saw a slow but real gender shift in the spiritual life. The mendicants played
a central, if not always willing, role in this change. Admittedly, the female
saints who proliferated in the later 1200s were not all mendicant protégées.
Saint Margherita of Cortona, who was initially drawn to the Franciscans,
spent her later years distancing herself from them. The reasons for this
change are unclear; perhaps she felt they were limiting her independence.
But on the whole, women found in the friars a support lacking in the secular
clergy and the city cappelle. Saint Oringa Cristiana got help from the Franciscans when she started her hermitage, and many of her miracles aided
Franciscans and Dominicans.[50]

In the later 1200s, the focus of women's religious life moved from the
country to the city. The period saw the first large-scale urban competition
to the rural life of the Benedictine nuns. Mendicant patronage facilitated
this.[51] Female religious foundations during the communal period were nearly
all under mendicant patronage or affiliated with some mendicant-inspired
reform movement in the monastic orders.[52] Older houses of women had
links to aristocratic patrons and always remained outside communal piety.[53]
The mid-1200s saw a boom in women's foundations within the city walls. Of
the thirty-six known convents of women at Bologna in 1250, only seven predated 1200; nineteen were mid-thirteenth-century creations. Never again
was Bologna to know such a large female religious establishment. From the
high of thirty-six houses in the 1200s, women's convents began a slow decline
until the 1500s, when there were only twenty houses.[54] New foundations took
the Augustinian rather than Benedictine rule and huddled around the houses
of their mendicant patrons.[55] Most invisible to us are the countless new "mi-
croconvents" of *pinzochere*, which proliferated in the last decades of the 1200s.
As with the mendicants themselves, communal almsgiving underwrote this
explosion of women's houses. At Bologna, the larger houses of Dominican
and Franciscan nuns received annual grants comparable to those of the friars.[56] Even when grants going to women's houses were not as large as those

---

50. *Legenda Beatae Christianae*, 16, pp. 200–201; miracles: ibid., 45–47, pp. 223–26.

51. Gabriella Zarri, "I monasteri femminili a Bologna tra il xiii e il xvi secolo," *AMDSPPR*, n.s., 24
(1973): 133.

52. Ibid., 157.

53. Significantly, perhaps, when Ezzelino III da Romano cast off his wives, they took refuge in older
Benedictine foundations, Gisla di Sambonifacio at Sant'Agnese and Selvaggia at Santi Narborre e Felice.
See Luigi Simeoni, "Due mogli di Ezzelino rifugiate nei monasteri bolognesi," *L'Archiginnasio* 38 (1943):
87–92.

54. Zarri, "Monasteri," 135–36. Extinctions began after 1310: ibid., 139–40.

55. E.g., the cluster of Dominican nuns' houses around San Domenico in Bologna: ibid., 151–58.

56. Bologna Stat. 1 (1252), 5.19, 1:454 (£50 to the Dominicans at Ronzano); (1253), 5.20, 1:454 (£50 a
year to the Franciscan nuns).

to the men, they outstripped them in sheer numbers.[57] Female foundations rode the coattails of the friars' popularity. Women drifted into the mendicant orbit in part because of the secular clergy's lack of appreciation for their freelance spirituality and independence.[58] Where confraternity matricula exist, as at Bergamo, these record the growing, even dominant female presence in mendicant-sponsored confraternities in the late 1200s.[59] It was hard to be a "Sister of Penance" in 1200, but these early pious women, like their male counterparts, enjoyed a great degree of autonomy and independence. The mendicants, on the other hand, though they made a place for women, also exerted control over them. In the later 1200s, confraternities of female penitents under mendicant supervision were turned into regular monasteries; the *pinzochere* became nuns.[60]

The mendicants sought to evangelize the whole population. As they kindled a more vibrant piety, they also created a lay clientele. The churches of the mendicants may have been stark and austere—the Dominicans, like the Franciscans, originally forbade sculpture and made do with painted decoration[61]—but they developed crowd-pleasing devotions. After 1224, the Dominicans ended Compline with a procession to the people's part of the church for the singing of the Salve Regina to the Blessed Virgin. "Crowds of people came running to see this out of devotion."[62] The Preachers had to forbid friars from remaining in the people's church to socialize after the procession.[63] After attracting the devout, the friars reorganized them. The mendicant takeover of the penitents dates to 1282, when an attempt was made to impose a Franciscan form of their rule on all Italian lay penitents.[64] Local groups of penitents had already come under Franciscan influence, but this move caused resistance. Some Black Penitents sought protection from the Dominicans and negotiated new statutes to govern their lives[65] Eventually the lay penitents evolved into "third orders" subordinate to the mendicants. They lost their old prerogative of selecting spiritual directors from any order or even from the secular clergy. Mendicant direction meant that the penitents would be infused with the spirituality of their clerical guides. In the

57. See examples of such alms lists in Parma Stat. I (1261), p. 435; Siena Stat. I (1262), I.40–91, pp. 36–47; Brescia Stat. (1252), col. (105); Parma Stat. II (1266), 100–101; Pisa Stat. I (1286), I.57, pp. 133–43; Bologna Stat. II (1288), 11.5, 2:191–92; and Ravenna Stat., 355, pp. 169–70.

58. So Benvenuti Papi, "Donne religiose nella Firenze del due-trecento," *In Castro*, 631.

59. See Brolis, "A Thousand and More Women," 231–46.

60. On this phenomenon, see De Sandre Gasparini, "Laici devoti," 225, and Antonio Rigon, "Penitenti e laici devoti fra mondo monastico-canonicale e ordini mendicanti: Qualche esempio in area veneta e mantovana," *Ricerche di storia sociale e religiosa*, n.s., 17/18 (1980): 71–72.

61. *ACGOP* (1239), 11; (1240), 13.

62. Girolamo de' Borselli, *Cronica Gestorum*, 21: "Multi currebant de populo ex devotione ad videndum."

63. *ACGOP* (1245), 32.

64. "Regula di fra Caro" (1284), Meersseman, *Ordo*, 1:394–400.

65. Such as the *Ordinations* given by Munio of Zamora to the *vestitae* at Orvieto in 1286: ed. Maiju Lehmijoki-Gardner, "Writing Religious Rules as an Interactive Process: Dominican Penitent Women and the Making of Their *Regula*," *Speculum* 79 (2004): 683–87.

late 1200s, penitents under Franciscan direction emphasized penance; those under Dominican control, doctrinal orthodoxy or Marian devotions.[66] Only the flagellants preserved their freedom to select spiritual directors and conduct their own affairs.[67] They were the last refuge of the freelance lay piety of the republics, although even among them the Franciscans made inroads.[68] As cities lost their republican institutions, the new princes often suppressed flagellant groups. The princes and the mendicants were allies, perhaps unwittingly, in the decline of the old style of communal piety.[69]

Nowhere was the mendicant impact on religiosity more dramatic than in attitudes toward heresy.[70] The cities had always been "orthodox"; heretics were "sectarians," intentional outsiders to communal religion.[71] The cities always legislated against heresy, especially if it had a public face. Modern studies have concluded that actual heresy, formal dissent from approved Catholic doctrine, was not common in the cities, contrary to older generalizations. Catharism, the preeminent heresy of the communal period, was a phenomenon of the hill country, not the great cities. Thirteenth-century Italians recognized this. When Archbishop Federico Visconti preached on the feast of Saint Dominic at the church of Santa Catarina in Pisa around 1277, he suggested that the Cathar heresy had been cooked up in the hills of Languedoc by men preaching against the violence of the rural nobility.[72] Even in the hills, heretics tended to pass through, rather than become part of, the settled population.[73] This tendency was even more consistent in the cities. Nor were heretics very numerous. For the period 1260 to 1308, one expert puts the total number of heretics active in northern Italy between 700 and 750. Perhaps a quarter to a third were women. Bologna counted about 100 heretics out of a population approaching 40,000. Verona and its contado

66. Giuseppina De Sandre Gasparini, "Movimento dei disciplinati, confraternite e ordini mendicanti," *I frati minori e il terzo ordine*, 110–11. And on the clerical control of the penitents in the late 1200s generally, see Casagrande, *Religiosità*, 127–38.

67. As observed by Meersseman, *Ordo*, 1:512.

68. On the flagellants, see *Il movimento dei disciplinati nel settimo centenario dal suo inizio (Perugia, 1260)* (Perugia: Deputazione di Storia Patria per l'Umbria, 1962); and for Bologna particularly, see Fanti, "Gli inizi del movimento dei disciplinati a Bologna e la confraternita di Santa Maria della Vita." See De Sandre Gasparini, "Movimento," on the growing Franciscan influence over these groups; and on these groups' independence from clerical models, see Casagrande, "I veri laici: I disciplinati," *Religiosità*, 438–41.

69. De Sandre Gasparini, "Movimento," 86–87, notes that the Devotion of 1260 did not occur in cities controlled by the Pallavicino or the da Romano. For Este laws forbidding *battuti* in Ferrara, see *AIMA* 6:471–74. It appears that the signoria of Mastino della Scala precluded the devotion in Verona: Parisio of Cerea, *Annales* (1260), 16.

70. For a brief overview of the extensive literature on heresy in communal Italy, see Gabriele Zanella, "Malessere ereticale in valle padana (1260–1308)," *Hereticalia*, 18–21.

71. So Eugène Dupré Theseider, "Gli eretici nel mondo comunale italiano," rpt. in *Mondo cittadino e movimenti ereticali nel Medio Evo (saggi)* (Bologna: Pàtron, 1978), 233–59, esp. 258, who agrees with Manselli and Volpe.

72. André Vauchez, "Les origines de l'hérésie cathare en Languedoc d'après un sermon de l'archevêque de Pise Federico Visconti (+ 1277)," *Società, istituzioni, spiritualità: Studi in onore di Cinzio Violante* (Spoleto: Centro Italiano di Studi sull'Alto Medioevo, 1994), 2:1022–36

73. Powell, *Albertanus*, 25; Zanella, "Malessere ereticale," 49.

were a virtual hotbed of dissent; the local heretics numbered 250. Inquisition records reveal that the most common heresies detected were rationalist doubts about God and the sacraments, not developed Cathar dualism.[74] Dissent there was, but it had neither the numbers, concentrations, nor coherence to produce a true alternative religious culture.[75] Heretical sympathies expressed, rather, a generalized discontent with the religious and spiritual establishment, not preference for some doctrinal alternative.[76] I have emphasized the *relative* insignificance of dissent in communal religion because it throws into stark relief the mendicants' skepticism about the orthodox lay religiosity of the age. Ordinary people wondered why inquisitors came after their seemingly harmless neighbors. One did not need to be a heretic to object to aggressive policing of orthodoxy. In a celebrated incident at Parma in 1279, the inquisitor Fra Florio sent to the stake a certain Todesca, wife of Ubertino Blancardo, from the contrada of San Giacopo. She had been a servant of an authentic heretic, the well-to-do Donna Oliva de' Fredolfi. Todesca's neighbors objected to this imputation of guilt by association. They stormed the Dominican convent, looted and burned it, and killed one of the friars, Fra Giacomo de' Ferrari. The friars left the city in procession and complained to the papal legate at Florence, Cardinal Latino. He excommunicated the commune and put the city under interdict. Parmese opinion was outraged: the city itself had no guilt in the matter. Negotiations to remove the censures lasted until 1282, when the commune paid large fines and imposed draconian punishments on the looters. The incident became, in popular lore, a classical example of clerical overreaching.[77] Executions of people like Todesca provoked bad feeling against *questi frati,* "these friars." To the friars themselves, their detractors were suspect of heresy.[78] A man at Gubbio, on seeing a new image of Saint Peter Martyr in the Dominican church there, blasphemed the saint, saying: "Those friars have painted a picture of that Peter showing him dying for the Christian faith, but I have it for certain that he was killed, not for the faith, but on account of a certain bad woman."[79]

74. Zanella, "Malessere ereticale," 41–47. For Bologna in the 1270s and 1280s, Zanella (ibid., 45) estimates forty heretics total: twenty-three known by name, thirty referred to in inquisition processes.

75. So ibid., 62–63; conclusions repeated in id., *Itinerari ereticali,* 5–45, esp. 44–45.

76. Id., "L'eresia catara fra XIII e XIV secolo: In margine al disagio di una storiografia," *Bullettino dell'Istituto storico italiano per il Medio Evo e Archivio muratoriano* 88 (1979): 246, esp. n. 15, echoing Raffaello Morghen, "Problèmes sur l'origine de l'hérésie au Moyen Âge," *Hérésies et sociétés dans l'Europe pré-industrielle, 11ᵉ–18ᵉ siècles,* ed. Jacques Le Goff (Paris: Mouton, 1968), 130–31.

77. The most complete version of the incident is in *Chronicon Parmense,* 36, 41, 43; other versions may be found in Salimbene, *Cronica,* 732, 736–37, 744, Baird trans., 511, 514, 518; *Mem. Pot. Reg.,* col. 1146; Sagacino Levalossi and Pietro Della Grazata, *Chronicon,* col. 9. See also the papal letter treating the matter in Bologna, Biblioteca dell'Archiginnasio, MS B.3695, doc. 37 (*BOP* 2:129–30; MS original of 1282).

78. So Zanella, "Malessere ereticale," 62–64.

79. *Vita S[ancti] Petri Martyris Ordinis Praedicatorum,* 8.61, p. 713 (text from Miracles of Berenguer, 1310s): "Fratres isti pingere faciunt figuram istius Fr. Petri, quomodo mortuus fuerit, quasi subierit pro fide Christiana martyrium: sed ego pro certo habeo, quod ipse non pro fide, sed propter mulierem quamdam malam occisus fuit."

There is no reason to assume the man was himself a heretic, or even a sympathizer.

By the 1290s heresy hunting was on a collision course with lay piety. Saint Pietro of Foligno got dragged before the Franciscan inquisitor of Assisi, who grilled him on the Incarnation, Passion, Resurrection, and Ascension of Christ, and then sent him off under detention to Spoleto. It was a sorry affair in the eyes of Pietro's biographer.[80] Already in the 1260s, an inquisitor's suspicions about the orthodoxy of Giovanni Buono of Mantua brought his canonization process to a halt and then ended it permanently.[81] Inquisitors scrutinized the cults of long-dead communal saints. Perhaps they undertook a systematic review of all such devotions.[82] Guido Da Loca of Brescia, a lay penitent who had imitated the penances of John the Baptist, had long enjoyed a popular cult, a tomb in the Brescia duomo, and a reputation for miraculous healings. A posthumous inquest under the Dominican bishop of Brescia, Bartolomeo of Braganze, condemned him of heresy. Familiars of the inquisition broke open his tomb and burned his bones in the presence of "nearly forty thousand people." When they were thrown into the fire, his bones miraculously floated above the flames and remained unharmed. The crowd began to cry, "Death to the bishop and the friars!" But the clerics escaped harm, supposedly by producing the Blessed Sacrament and chasing off the demons protecting the false saint's relics. Such is the story told by Filippo of Ferrara.[83] In any case, Saint Guido's cult was suppressed. More notorious still was the case of Saint Alberto of Villa d'Ogna, the wine porter of Cremona. Saint Alberto worked miracles in Cremona at his tomb, at Parma in San Pietro near Piazza Nuova, and at Reggio in the churches of San Giorgio and San Giovanni Battista. At Parma, his devotees processed through town with his relics, carrying crosses and banners and singing. The offerings at his shrine amounted to £300 imp., sufficient to buy a house in the contrada of Santo Stefano and open a hospital named in his honor. Parish priests erected images of him in their churches, and people had his image painted on porticoes and city walls. But Alberto was a drunkard, said Fra Salimbene, and his devotees were a pack of wine guzzlers and silly women.[84] Thank goodness a Franciscan inquisitor finally got around to suppressing his cult.

No suppression of a cult equaled in notoriety that of Saint Armanno Pun-

---

80. Giovanni Gorini, *[Legenda de Vita et Obitu Beati Petri de Fulgineo]*, 2.14, *AS* 31 (Jul. IV), 668, and ibid., 9b, *Analecta Bollandiana* 8 (1889): 365.

81. Golinelli, "Dal santo," 33–34.

82. So suggests Wessley, "Thirteenth-Century Guglielmites," 302 n. 68, and Orioli, *Venit Perfidus Heresiarcha*, 80–81.

83. Filippo of Ferrara, *Liber de Introductione Loquendi*, 2.25, in Bologna, Biblioteca Universitaria, MS 1552 (XV cent., original ca. 1330), fols. 8ᵣ⁻ᵛ, and the version edited by Creytens in "Le manuel de conversation," 120–21, from Vatican City, Biblioteca Vaticana, MS Pal. Lat. 960, fol. 94ᵛ.

84. Does he by these terms simply mean laypeople? Salimbene, *Cronica* (1279), 733–36, Baird trans., 512–13. Alberto's cult is also described in *Chronicon Parmense* (1279), 34–35.

gilupo of Ferrara.[85] Although a son and relative of Cathars, his neighbors were sure that Armanno had rejected the false faith from childhood. He confessed regularly and fervently took Communion until his death in 1269, said his usual confessor, Don Rainaldo of San Nicolò.[86] At the posthumous inquest, another priest, Don Alberto, testified to Armanno's holiness, describing how he piously confessed to him when sick and during Lent. If Armanno's wife was sick, he always sent for a priest.[87] Given his family background, he had trouble avoiding contact with Cathars. The local inquisitor, Fra Aldobrandino of Ferrara, had him arrested and interrogated. Perhaps he was tortured. Armanno admitted the heretical associations, abjured all heresy, and paid a fine of £100 fer.[88] Inevitably, he had new encounters with heretics in the 1250s and 1260s. But his Catholic devotion seemed impeccable. He went to confession regularly at San Nicolò and, after 1266, took the precaution of confessing to Don Zambono, the bishop of Ferrara's own chaplain. Three days before his death he confessed for the last time, to Don Alberto, another chaplain of the bishop. In some Cathar circles they called him an apostate and "worse than a beast."[89] To his neighbors, he was a devout Catholic, loved for his generosity and good works.

After his death on 15 December 1269, a popular cult sprang up immediately. The clergy of the duomo and the Augustinians (who were also devotees of Saint Giovanni Buono) promoted it.[90] The cult spread, only to encounter resistance. A merchant arrived at Bergamo from Venice, having passed through Ferrara. Speaking to Fra Arasino of Bergamo in the Franciscan convent, he reported all the good things happening around Armanno's tomb in Ferrara. It seemed that there was a new saint. But Dominicans and Franciscans, he said, were out to kill the cult—claiming the saint was a heretic.[91] Fra Salimbene, no lover of the Armanno cult, opined that the Ferrara clergy and laity had cooked up the new saint because they were jealous of how many saints the Franciscans had produced. Or was Saint Armanno drawing off donations from Minorite shrines? When a relic of Saint Armanno (the little toe of his right foot) arrived at Parma, the people formed a procession to carry the toe to the cathedral and place it on the high altar. There, Don Anselmo of San Vitale, the episcopal vicar, exposed it for veneration—only

---

85. On Armanno, see Amedeo Benati, "Armanno Pungilupo nella storia religiosa ferrarese del 1200," *Atti e memorie della Deputazione della provincia ferrarese di storia patria*, 3d ser., 4/1 (1966): 85–123, and now Zanella, "Armanno Pungilupo, eretico quotidiano," *Hereticalia*, 3–14. Zanella, *Itinerari*, 48–102, edits the extant materials on Armanno Pungilupo as they appear in Modena, Archivio di Stato, Biblioteca MS 132, fols. 11ʳ–33ᵛ. I have silently corrected quoted texts from the errata list published in Zanella, *Hereticalia*, 225–29.

86. Zanella, "Armanno Pungilupo," 7–8.

87. "Acta contra Armanum [Punzilupum]," 87.

88. Ibid., p. 67.

89. Ibid., pp. 50–51, 57, 59, 87; on these texts, see Zanella, *Itinerari*, 16–19, 20–21, 22.

90. "Acta contra Armanum [Punzilupum]," 79–80.

91. Zanella, "Armanno Pungilupo," p. 9; "Acta contra Armanum [Punzilupum]," 66.

to find that it was a clove of garlic, Salimbene jeered.[92] Fra Aldebrandino opened an inquest, lasting from the spring of 1270 to the summer of 1274. He took depositions on Armanno's belief and behavior but then dropped the case. The next inquisitor, Fra Florio of Vicenza, reopened it in 1284. The canons of the Ferrara cathedral checked him by sending an inventory of Armanno's miracles to the pope in 1286. Fra Florio sent his own report to Rome in 1288. Nothing happened. Meanwhile, at Ferrara, the cult grew. Saint Armanno enjoyed a traditional stone arca raised on pillars, an altar in the duomo, and statues and paintings in local churches. The arca had been constructed from a Paleo-Christian sarcophagus dating to the reign of the emperor Honorius, a precious vessel indeed. Everywhere his images and reliquaries were decorated with ex-votos honoring his cures.[93] In spite of mendicant grumbling, the cult continued for some thirty years.[94] Then, in 1299, a new inquisitor, Fra Guido of Vicenza, reopened the investigation. He collected his predecessors' work and took new depositions.[95]

The accusations against Pungilupo were an odd lot. Donna Duragia said that Pungilupo once prepared a large loaf of bread and a carafe of wine to celebrate with his friends on Easter. After the meal, he supposedly joked that the priests were wrong in thinking that the Corpus Domini could never be consumed, "because they had just eaten a big one."[96] On another occasion he told a joke about a priest's getting drunk on sacramental wine. Armanno had criticized the inquisition and the friars for burning "good men."[97] Armanno did dislike the friars and the inquisitor who had fined him, but was that heresy? More disturbing was that some Cathars said that Armanno was "one of us." But others cursed him as a Catholic.[98] The accusations were all hearsay. The shoemaker Castellano admitted that at Armanno's burial he had condemned the saint as a Catholic and a traitor to Catharism. But in damning testimony, Castellano admitted that his friend Odoberto, another Cathar, had rebuked him for the curse, stating that Armanno had received Cathar "baptism" (the *consolamentum*) in the same ceremony as his own wife.[99]

The case against Armanno was founded on circumstantial and secondhand evidence. I do not find it convincing.[100] Armanno was an independent-thinking layman, he indulged in anticlerical humor, his charity included her-

---

92. Salimbene, *Cronica* (1279), 735–36, Baird trans., 513–14.

93. As we know from Pope Boniface VIII's order that these be destroyed: "Acta contra Armanum [Punzilupum]," 90–93, 95.

94. On this long delay in the investigation, see Zanella, *Itinerari*, 32.

95. "Acta contra Armanum [Punzilupum]," 48–72, contains Guido's work. On the steps in the long process against Armanno, see Zanella, *Itinerari*, 25–28.

96. "Acta contra Armanum [Punzilupum]," 56.

97. Ibid., 54–55 (on the friars), 59 (on the drunk priest).

98. Ibid., 60–61, 63–63.

99. The testimony appears twice: ibid., 51, 59. Others repeated the same story: ibid., 56–59.

100. *Pace* Malcolm D. Lambert, *The Cathars* (Oxford: Blackwell, 1998), 281–82, who believes that Pungilupo was a convinced Cathar dissimulating as a Catholic.

etics, and he harbored intense dislike for the friars. Whatever Armanno's true beliefs, Guido's investigation resulted in a summons of the Ferrara cathedral clergy to Rome. There on 13 January 1301, in a process presided over by Fra Guido, the local saint was declared a heretic and his family's property forfeit.[101] Fra Guido returned to Ferrara and entered the duomo in the middle of the night. He and inquisition familiars then took sledgehammers to Armanno's shrine and burned his bones. What did the canons think about these events? What would they think three years later, when the new pope, Benedict XI, rewarded Fra Guido's industry by making him the new bishop of Ferrara?[102] We know what the laity thought. Finding the shrine in pieces on the morning after the raid, a mob attacked the Dominican monastery of San Domenico and tried to lynch the inquisitor. He was saved by a detachment of soldiers dispatched from Azzo d'Este, the lord of Ferrara.[103] In the struggle over the cult of Saint Armanno Pungilupo the views and attitudes of the inquisitor Guido and the clergy of Ferrara are much more visible than those of the laity. In a later clash between Fra Guido and the people of Bologna we can begin to hear echos of the voices of these laypeople themselves.[104]

The Death of a Pursemaker

The medieval "man in the street" almost never speaks in medieval documents. In the spring of 1299, thanks to an inquisition inquest, we come very close to hearing ordinary people giving their opinions on orthodoxy, heresy, and the mendicants.[105] The incident that triggered the inquest may not be unique, but its extensive documentation is.[106] The affair began on the morning of 12 May 1299, when Fra Guido ordered his messenger to bring two prisoners from their cells to hear his sentence. On their appearance in the office of the inquisition at the church of San Domenico in Bologna, the

101. Zanella, *Itinerari*, 27–28.

102. Francesco Pipino, *Chronicon*, 3.48, col. 712.

103. Benati, "Armanno Pungilupo," 114.

104. What made one a heretic? See Zanella, "Eresia catara," 239–58; Mariano D'Alatri, "'Eresie' perseguite dall'inquisizione in Italia nel corso del duecento," *The Concept of Heresy in the Middle Ages (11th–13th C.)*, Mediaevalia Lovaniensia, ser. 1, stud. 4 (Louvain: Louvain University Press, 1976), 211–16 and 240 n. 3.

105. I thank Fr. Arturo Bernal, O.P., of the Dominican Historical Institute, Rome, for permission to reproduce here in a slightly different format my "Lay Versus Clerical Perceptions of Heresy: Protests Against the Inquisition in Bologna, 1299," from *Praedicatores Inquisitores 1: The Dominicans and the Mediaeval Inquisition: Acts of the First International Seminar on the Dominicans and the Inquisition, Rome 23–25 February 2002*, Dissertationes Historicae 30 (Rome: Istituto Storico Domenicano, 2004), 701–30.

106. See Eugène Dupré Theseider, "L'eresia a Bologna nei tempi di Dante," rpt. in *Mondo cittadino e movimenti ereticali nel Medio Evo (saggi)* (Bologna: Pàtron, 1978), 261–315; and Lorenzo Paolini, *L'eresia catara alla fine del duecento*, L'eresia a Bologna fra XIII e XIV secolo 1 (Rome: Istituto Storico Italiano per il Medio Evo, 1975), 63–79; and Lansing, *Power and Purity*, 151–58, on these events. Guido's register is edited by Lorenzo Paolini and Raniero Orioli, *Acta S. Officii Bononie ab Anno 1291 usque ad Annum 1310*, 2 (continuously paged) vols. (Rome: Istituto Storico Italiano per il Medio Evo, 1982), with index vol. (1984). Fra Guido was also a poet; his unedited poems are preserved in Vicenza, Biblioteca Civica Bertoliana, MS 526 (early XIV cent.).

inquisitor formally condemned Bompietro di Giovanni, a pursemaker from the parish of San Martino dell'Aposa, and Giuliano di Salimbene, another pursemaker from the same parish, as relapsed heretics.[107] In the presence of his vicar, Fra Omobono of Bologna, his assistants, the prior of the Carmelite friars Fra Pietro de' Ricolfi, and the archpriest of the cathedral Don Arpinello, he excommunicated the two prisoners and released them to the secular authorities. Among the "many others" witnessing this act were a judge, a notary, a jurist, and four knights, representatives from the secular government of the commune of Bologna. The knights included members of the powerful Caccianemici and Ramponi clans. The notary of the tribunal, Alberto de' Carboni, was instructed to publicize this judgment by announcing it in the church of San Martino dell'Aposa after the reading of the Gospel at the solemn Mass on the following Sunday, 17 May.

Since the rest of the day would be taken up by the prisoners' condemnation before the podesta of Bologna at the Palazzo Comunale, Fra Guido's only other formal act that morning was to remove the excommunication that Giuliano's proctor, the archdeacon of Pievenda, Don Manfredo Maschara, had incurred when he suggested that his client flee the city if he were indeed guilty of the Cathar heresy.[108] While Don Manfredo was free to give Giuliano legal advice, in this suggestion he had overstepped the bounds of his office. If a suspect's counsel learned that he was guilty, the counsel was expected to urge him to confess his guilt and beg for mercy. To do otherwise would amount to concealing the crime and becoming a *fautor*, that is, an abetter of heresy. Because Manfredo had merely given advice imprudently and had confessed his error to Fra Omobono, he was let out on £100 bon. bail, which could be returned at the inquisitor's discretion.[109] We know of no other business conducted at the tribunal that day.

The releasing of a relapsed heretic, much less of two, to the secular authorities was not an everyday event in late-thirteenth-century Bologna. Between 1297 and 1310 at least ten executions of heretics were considered by the court. Of these, six are known to have been carried out, three for Catharism, three for association in the heresy of Fra Dolcino.[110] If we assume that

107. *ASOB*, no. 125, 1:151–52. See sentences of Giuliano, ibid., no. 566, 1:302–6, and Bompietro, ibid., no. 567, 1:306–9. On Giuliano, see Paolini, *Eresia*, 126–35; on Bompietro, see ibid., 110–26.

108. *ASOB*, no. 124, 1:151. See also Paolini, *Eresia*, 44–45. On this heresy, see Malcolm D. Lambert, *Medieval Heresy: Popular Movements from Bogomil to Hus* (London: Arnold, 1977), 108–50. On inquisition procedure and witnesses, see A. Shannon, "The Secrecy of Witnesses in Inquisitorial Tribunals and in Contemporary Secular Criminal Trials," *Essays in Medieval Life and Thought in Honor of A. P. Evans* (New York: Columbia University Press, 1955), and, more broadly, T. Buehler-Reimann, "Enquête-Inquesta-Inquisitio," *Zeitschrift der Savigny-Stiftung für Rechtsgeschichte: Kanonistische Abteilung* 91 (1975): 53–62.

109. Innocent III provided for fining fautors; see Bologna, Biblioteca dell'Archiginnasio, MS B.3695, doc. 13 (*BOP* 1:223).

110. Extant condemnations for Catharism name Bonigrino (*ASOB*, no. 10, 1:20–25) and the previously mentioned Giuliano and Bompietro; for Dolcinism, Rolandino (no. 585, 2:347), Pietro Dal Pra (no. 586, 2:350), and Giovanni (no. 917, 2:704). Legal advisors recommended release to the secular authorities of four others (see ibid., no. 809, 2:599–600; no. 868, 2:624–25; no. 819, 2:606; no. 865, 2:623–24). Since

every other execution the legal experts recommended took place, the rate of execution was less than one heretic a year in more than thirteen years for the area of jurisdiction, Lombardy—that is, most of northern Italy. Medieval inquisitors believed in deterrence as an important aspect of capital punishment, and this rate was high enough for the procedure to seem routine, while keeping the burnings rare enough to attract attention.[111] The condemnation of two heretics at once was unusual, but Fra Guido probably had no expectation that the death of one of them would trigger an extraordinary outburst of popular anger against his tribunal and its procedures.

Bompietro di Giovanni was about thirty-eight years old in 1299. Giuliano, with whom he would be executed, had years earlier been a friend of Bompietro's father, Giovanni, who had entertained Cathars while Bompietro was still young and then had received the *consolamentum* in Ferrara before his death. Bompietro's was a Cathar family, but perhaps not so inveterately heretical as Giuliano's, whose father, Salimbene, may be identical to the Salimbene whose consolation is recorded, like a baptism in the family Bible but hidden in code, at the end of the manuscript containing the famous Cathar treatise, the *Liber de Duobus Principiis*.[112] Bompietro's mother, Dolcebona, had gone to the stake years before, condemned by Fra Guido himself.[113] Indeed, Bompietro's neighborhood, the cappella of San Martino dell'Aposa and that of San Tomasso del Mercato, seems to have had a number of heretical families (*domus*), enough to be called a "heretical zone." This area was centered on the Aposa itself, an urban stream that attracted leather-working establishments.[114]

The young Bompietro had been well acquainted with heretics and inquisitors. Bompietro told Fra Guido how, when he was about twelve years old, his family gave hospitality to the notorious Cathar preacher Pietro of Rimini and the one-eyed *perfecta* Maria of Vicenza.[115] Such granting of hospitality for transient heretics seems pretty much typical of "unorthodox" behavior of late-thirteenth-century Bologna, which lacked a large resident heretical

the records for 1291–97 may not be complete, these numbers represent a low estimate for the whole twenty years.

111. On such statistics and medieval inquisition generally, see Bernard Hamilton, *The Medieval Inquisition* (New York: Holmes & Meier, 1981), 56–57.

112. Edited by C. Thouzellier as *Liber de Duobus Principiis: Livre des deux principes* (Paris: Sources Chrétiennes, 1973); Eng. trans. in *Heresies of the High Middle Ages*, ed. W. Wakefield and A. Evans, Records of Western Civilization 81 (New York: Columbia University Press, 1969), 511–91.

113. As would appear from the testimony of Giovanna di Bartolomeo, who suggested that Fra Guido had burned her because she would not give him her daughter, *ASOB*, no. 349, 1:228.

114. Lorenzo Paolini, "Domus e zona degli eretici: L'esempio di Bologna nel XIII secolo," *Rivista di storia della chiesa in Italia* 35 (1981): 371–87. Dupré Theseider, "Eresia a Bologna," 277–81, reaches similar conclusions about the trade connections of Bolognese heretics, but his tabulation shows that the heretics of the Bologna Register are nearly all non-Bolognese.

115. On Bompietro's experiences at Ferrara, see his first two interrogations by Fra Guido, *ASOB*, no. 11–12, 1:25–33.

population.[116] Sometime between 1272 and 1273, Giovanni rented a house at Ferrara in the contrada of San Romano from another Cathar, Menaboi Pizoli. Their home became a virtual hospice for heresy.[117] They harbored Cathar believers, worshiped the perfects as the presence of the Good God, and provided them with fish, the one flesh food they could eat. To Bompietro the perfects seemed "the best men in the world"; it was their piety, not, as we will see, their doctrine, that attracted him.

In 1276, at the age of fifteen, Bompietro had his first brush with an inquisition. Cited on 10 November before the inquisitor Fra Guglielmo of Cremona, the youthful suspect perjured himself, denying any knowledge of heresy. Convicted on 7 December, he was sentenced to wear yellow crosses and make a pilgrimage to Rome.[118] Instead of complying, he followed his family to Bologna, where they settled in the house that his parents had constructed in the cathedral parish of San Pietro, near the center of the city. There his parents continued to patronize heretics, including Giuliano, Pietro, and Maria—all of whom they worshiped in the Cathar fashion.[119] During this period, Bompietro also acquired a wife, a Bolognese woman named Contessa di Constantino from San Martino dell'Aposa, the parish in which he would eventually settle.

In 1283, after a short return with his family to Ferrara, Bompietro and his wife settled permanently in Bologna. His father and mother stayed behind in Ferrara. Bompietro was about twenty-one years of age. Throughout this period, he continued to consort with heretics. Contrary to the terms of Fra Guglielmo's sentence, he listened to them, fed them, and even worshiped them. Before the inquisitor Fra Guido, he later named thirty-three of them, some from influential circles in Bologna. These accusations led to only two new trials that are recorded in the inquisition register, that of Bompietro's wife and that of the aristocratic Donna Rengarda degli Aldigeri.[120] The latter was the widow of the noble Erriguccio de' Galluzzi and the wife of the famous jurist Francesco, son of the glossator Accursio. Whether because of his wife's heresy or more likely because of Francesco's own habits (Dante placed him in hell with the Sodomites), the couple separated at Rengarda's request in 1288.[121] Neither process brought a conviction. Bompietro's household seems to have taken on the character of a "conventicle," like that of his parents in Ferrara.

Nevertheless, Bompietro insisted that he had abandoned his childhood

---

116. Paolini, *Eresia*, 174. See also Zanella, "Armanno Pungilupo," 6. Orthodox clerics—e.g., Salimbene, *Cronica* (1248), 395–96, Baird trans., 269, speaking of the Apostolici—saw vagrancy as one of the marks of a heretic.

117. *ASOB*, no. 11, 1:26–27.

118. Ibid., no. 567, 1:307.

119. Ibid., no. 11, 1:29.

120. For a catalog of these accusations, see Paolini, *Eresia*, 114–21.

121. Dante, *Inferno*, 15.110. On this separation, see Paolini, *Eresia*, 117 n. 117. On the Aldigeri family, see ibid., 116 n. 113.

belief in Catharism, which had never amounted to anything more theologically sophisticated than condemning marriage, denying the Eucharist, and
worshiping the perfects. His claim has the ring of truth, since, as Fra Guido
discovered, Bompietro was incapable of distinguishing one Cathar sect from
another. The pursemaker confessed that he could not bring himself to turn
in Giuliano, knowing that his father's old Cathar friend might end up at the
stake. He ascribed his contact with the other Cathars to his own foolishness
(*ex simplicitate*). Knowing that his actions were risky, and that he had thereby
incurred excommunication, he had confessed his lapses (probably spontaneously) to Fra Guido's predecessor, the inquisitor Fra Florio of Vicenza. Faced
with such a case, Florio scourged him "a bit" (*aliquantulum*) on the shoulders
with a rod and gave him absolution, with a warning to watch himself. The
easygoing Florio did not even bother giving him a written copy of the absolution.[122] One senses that the sterner Guido was not pleased.

Unlike the elderly Cathar Giuliano, Bompietro was well known to his
fellow residents in San Martino dell'Aposa and the surrounding neighborhood. His parish was located off the Market (the Piazza del Mercato, or
Campus Fori) on the north side of Bologna, between the old and new city
walls. San Martino was a center for leatherworking and for Bompietro's
trade, pursemaking. As well as a pursemaker, Bompietro was a respected
small-scale businessman, a member of the merchants' society, dealing in
wine. From his own stocks, Bompietro supplied Mass wine to the Carmelite
friars who had established themselves in his parish. He attended the Office,[123] which the friars sang, along with his friend, the tailor Zambonino di
Bongiovanni from San Bendetto in Galliera.[124] This parish was opposite San
Martino on the northwest corner of the Market. He was established, well
respected, generous, to all appearances a good Catholic—but a Catholic
who gave alms indiscriminately to Catholic and Cathar alike, even after his
second warning by Fra Florio.

After Bompietro's arrest and two appearances before Fra Guido on 23
and 25 March 1299, the inquisitor referred Bompietro's case to a panel of
four experts in canon law. They submitted their opinion on 4 April. The
panel included famous names: Guido of Baiso (known to canon-law history
as "the Archdeacon"), Giovanni of Monte Merlo, and Marsilio Manteghelli.

122. *ASOB*, no. 12, 1:33. Fra Florio was charged with peculation in 1307: Zanella, "Malessere ereticale," 34.

123. Lansing, *Power and Purity*, 92–93, is willing to consider Bompietro a Cathar "believer" in spite of
his Catholic conformity. I see no particular reason to doubt his good faith; as she admits, ibid., 95–96,
most Cathars and Catholics had only vague views on abstruse theological constructs and dogma.

124. As we know from a denunciation by Giovanni Bonmercati, a heresy hunter from the Societas
Crucis, *ASOB*, no. 180, 1:175. He had overheard Zambonino say this in his lamentation over Bompietro's
death while sitting on a bench outside the church of San Michele del Mercato di Mezzo, just around the
corner from the Palazzo Comunale. On his business connections, see ibid., 1:48 n. 1. It appears that Fra
Guido did not have Zambonino summoned. On the Societas Crucis, see Lorenzo Paolini, "Le origini
della 'Societas Crucis,'" *Rivista di storia e letteratura religiosa* 15 (1979): 173–229.

These, along with Aimerico, the lector of San Domenico, considered Bompietro relapsed. The canonist Bonincontro, the Dominican Fra Giovanni of Faenza, and two Franciscans were less certain. Another interrogation before Fra Guido followed on 7 April.[125] While Bompietro's status as a *relapsus* doomed to the stake may have seemed obvious to the learned canonists, it was not so evident to those who knew him. At least in his parish, skepticism about his arrest surfaced almost immediately. Some parishioners, such as the two sisters Maria and Bitina di Zacarello of Saliceto and Francesca di Bulgaro de' Gattaresi, could not believe he was a heretic. "If he was a heretic, the friars could make anyone a heretic," Donna Maria later declared.[126] This initial incredulity would continue to harden, even if some skeptics, like Donna Tommasina di Pietro degli Orsi from the parish of San Donato, decided after his condemnation that he must, in fact, have been guilty.[127]

Not all were polite in voicing their disapproval. Francesco di Giacomo Ramisini from San Benedetto in Galliera had said after the arrest that Bompietro seemed to be a "good Catholic," and that if he were in Bompietro's position, he would take a knife and stab the inquisitor—intemperate words for which he would later be fined £50 bon.[128] Some were even more imprudent in expressing their outrage. The merchant Giacomo di Arardo de' Musoni went to see Bishop Giovanni Savelli at his office in the episcopal palace. When he heard that the bishop was still in conference with the inquisitor and his advisors, he let out a stream of oaths. Outside the bishop's chapel, in the presence of three messengers of the inquisition, he raged: "Is that inquisitor here? I would happily stab him with a knife; I would rather do that than eat. If I didn't fear the commune more than God, I'd happily stab him." When one of the messengers, Milanino of Milan, reprimanded him, saying such talk was a sin against God, Giacomo said he cared little for God. He then revealed the reason for his outburst: the newly arrested Bompietro was a good man. There was no reason to detain him; the inquisition had done it merely to get his money.[129] Although later (the inquisition only caught up with Giacomo on 1 June) he claimed to have changed his mind about Bompietro's guilt after the sentence, and he insisted that he had only spoken out of love for the man,[130] Giacomo's anger was shared by many more people than the inquisitor probably suspected.

But whatever the talk and threats, Fra Guido soon lost interest in Bompietro. After Bompietro identified Giuliano in March, the inquisition's attention

---

125. See their "consilium," in *ASOB*, 2:804, 596. On inquisition experts, see C. Douais, "La formule 'communicato bonorum virorum consilio' des sentences inquisitoriales," *Compte rendu du quatrième Congrès scientifique international des catholiques* (Fribourg: Oeuvre de Saint-Paul, 1898), 316–67.

126. See *ASOB*, nos. 347–48, 1:227–28.

127. Ibid., no. 546, 1:290.

128. Ibid., no. 503, 1:280.

129. Ibid., nos. 328–29, 1:219–20.

130. Ibid., no. 333, 1:223–24. He was let go after posting the enormous bond of £100 imp. on 2 June, ibid., no. 345, 1:226–27.

was taken up with the arrest and interrogation of this more dangerous deviant. Giuliano's questioning before Guido and Omobono took place on the same day that the experts gave their opinion on Bompietro. Fra Guido gave Bompietro three days to prepare a defense.[131] The three days stretched to a month while Giuliano testified, admitting that he had perjured himself before the inquisitor Florio and that he had failed to wear his penitential crosses. But he denied that he was still consorting with heretics.[132] In light of Bompietro's testimony to the contrary, Giuliano was at first given three days to reconsider. Then eight more days were added so that the inquisition's messenger Benincasa di Martino could announce the charges and solicit defense witnesses in the Piazza Maggiore (the Platea Communis in front of the government buildings) and in the streets around Giuliano's house.[133] No new witnesses were found, and Giuliano seems to have gone into hiding.

On 29 April, a panel of legal experts determined, in the light of Bompietro's testimony and Giuliano's own admissions, that it would be legal to try him in absentia as a relapsed heretic; the following day, the archdeacon of Piedvenda, near Padua, Don Manfredo Maschara, presented an instrument from Giuliano, giving him the power to represent him in court. By presenting the "power of attorney," Manfredo prevented the tribunal from trying his client Giuliano in absentia. So, on 1 May, a messenger went to summon Giuliano to appear in court and order Manfredo to appear with his client by the following Friday. Don Manfredo came and admitted that neither he nor Giuliano had paid the fine of £10 bon. incurred for failing to respond to a lost earlier summons.[134] Both appeared before the court on the following Monday, 11 May.

That morning, a panel of experts under the master of theology Fra Ramberto advised Guido that the evidence collected and the suspects' confessions had more than fulfilled the requirement of at least one trustworthy witness, which was needed to permit judicial torture. The request for this advice is a sign of Fra Guido's ruthlessness in pursuing Giuliano; the register indicates the use of torture on only one other occasion.[135] Since they already had the testimony of the two witnesses required for a condemnation, the experts' consent was probably solicited for the sake of eliciting new accusations. No mention of torture appears in the depositions of either suspect on 11 May, and perhaps it was not used, at least in the case of Bompietro. His deposition repeats his previous testimony, admitting in addition that his wife had associ-

---

131. Ibid., no. 90, 1:129. On inquisition suspects' right to a defense, see Walter Ullmann, "The Defense of the Accused in the Medieval Inquisition," *Irish Ecclesiastical Record* 73 (1950): 481–89. A defense proctor, such as Manfredo Maschara, might be appointed by the judge if the defendant could not afford one: ibid., 483.

132. *ASOB*, no. 14, 1:35–36.

133. Ibid., no. 91, 1:129–30; no. 99, 1:134.

134. These matters are contained in ibid., no. 807, 2:598, and nos. 113–15, 1:144–45.

135. Ibid., no. 810, 2:600–601. The other use of torture is recorded in ibid., no. 691 (2 August 1304), p. 473.

ated with heretics and given them fish.[136] Giuliano's deposition may well reflect fear or pain—he confessed to Bompietro's accusations that he had spread Catharism at Padua, even after his sentencing to crosses by the inquisition, and to more: that he had been spreading heresy for the last five years in Florence, that he had come north at Bompietro's bidding, and that he had spread heresy there in Bologna. Even if elicited under fear or pain, the old Cathar preacher's confession was probably essentially true. We have no reason to believe he had any remorse for his missionary work. The stage was now set for the two men's sentencing and the events that would follow. No other business was to be conducted at the tribunal that day, or on the following day, the date of the execution.

By his sentences on the morning of 12 May (which were witnessed by, among others, Giuliano's hapless proctor Don Manfredo), Fra Guido declared the two *relapsi* excommunicated and released to the secular authorities. On hand to receive them in the name of Don Ottolino of Mandello del Lario, podesta of Bologna, were his judge and assessor Giacomo of Baradello and his knight Andriotto. Guido placed at their disposal the notary Alberto to draw up the document of condemnation.[137] Although the executions would take place under the auspices of the communal government in accord with the statutes of Bologna, which made heresy a capital offense, the process before Fra Guido would be the only trial. It was the podesta's duty to condemn and execute those identified as relapsed by the inquisition.[138] Accompanied by the inquisitor and the friars, the agents of the commune conveyed Bompietro and Giuliano to the Palazzo Nuovo, the seat of the podesta.

The procession of friars and officials probably attracted some attention as it crossed the Piazza Maggiore (fig. 60). This square, which already had its spacious modern size, would have been filled with people, since Tuesday, 12 May, was a business day.[139] Benches for trade were set up in the square, some even at the foot of the tower of the Arenga in the center of the palazzo complex (fig. 61), and under the arcade of the Palazzo Vecchio, which faced the square. An official of the podesta rang the bell of the commune, announcing that an official act was about to be performed. Attention would

136. Contessa would later be cited herself, ibid., nos. 46, 47, 68, 1:78–80, 102–3.

137. Ibid., pp. 304–5, 1:308–9.

138. See the podesta's oath in Bologna Stat. 1, 1:67.

139. Of those who made depositions, twenty-two identified themselves as present in the Platea Communis or at the Arenga. These must be understood as the core group of the protest on 12 May, the *die condempnationis*. Paolini, *Eresia*, 66–67, identifies 355 participants in the *tumulto* (which he places on 13 May, at the execution), by counting the depositions related to the protests. This number is lower than that of Dupré Theseider, "Eresia a Bologna," 414, whose calculation is 362 (larger because he includes individuals who protested but were identified by Paolini as *fuori tumulto*). My computerized tally is as follows: All individuals (some represented by more than one deposition) involved in protests: 345. Those protesting in the Piazza Comunale: 22. Total of those acting *any place* on the day of the condemnation: 46. Those at the execution: 12. Those acting *any place* on the day of the execution: 19. How many actually shouted protest at the Arenga is impossible to say, but a number much over fifty, let alone over one hundred, seems very unlikely.

have been focused on the loggia of the Arenga, from which the podesta would pronounce his sentence. A number of those waiting in the square were from Bompietro's parish and that of Santa Maria della Mascarella, the parish next to it on the northeast corner of the Market. He had been under investigation for over a month, and the expectation of his sentence had attracted attention.

Don Ottolino of Mandello then appeared with the friars. Guards brought Bompietro and Giuliano onto the loggia. Fra Guido formally handed the prisoners over to the podesta, who judged them as relapsed into heresy and condemned them to burn at the stake. But Bompietro suddenly cried out in a loud voice, asking to make his confession as a Catholic and receive Communion. He insisted that although he had been reared in Catharism by his family, he had abandoned the heresy twenty years earlier.[140] It was an unforeseen and startling development. Fra Guido refused the request. Not everyone in the large piazza could hear Bompietro or the inquisitor's response. But word quickly passed through the crowd that Bompietro wanted to die in the Church and was asking for the body of Christ. Someone in the crowd began to shout, "Take Bompietro to the fire!" but Ugolino di Martino, an acquaintance of Bompietro's from San Martino dell'Aposa, shouted him down.[141] At least eight men, mostly from Bompietro's neighborhood, then began shouting to release Bompietro and let him live because he had asked for the body of Christ. One cried out, demanding to know why he had been arrested by the inquisition at all.[142]

Fra Guido's spies or informants would later identify one of these protesters as of particular importance in inciting the crowd. The butcher Gonto di Taviano was yelling that since Bompietro wanted Communion, it should be given to him immediately; otherwise the friars would be committing a great sin.[143] Witnesses, including a canon lawyer, reported seeing Gonto standing below the Arenga, shouting at the top of his lungs, "The inquisitor is doing this because Bompietro refused to give him his sister, and she would not consent to the inquisitor either," and then yelling that Bompietro could have saved himself if he had paid off the inquisition.[144] Gonto's scurrilous shouts later earned him a fine of £100 and a warning.[145] Perhaps they went unheard beyond the area around the Arenga and were less significant than his accuser thought.

---

140. See the testimony on this of Pace of Salicetto, *ASOB*, no. 23, 1:50.

141. See his confession of 12 July, ibid., no. 559, 1:293, "'Ducatur Bompetrus ad ignem': 'Noli clamare ista.'"

142. See *ASOB* deposition numbers 260 (1:199), 267 (1:201—which specifically mentions the podesta's judgment), 307 (1:213—a deposition by two men), 368 (1:237—from S. Biagio), 526 (1:285—from S. Tecla in Curia), 558 (1:293—an objection to detaining Bompietro in prison).

143. *ASOB*, no. 132, 1:155–56; no. 328, 1:219.

144. Ibid., no. 139, 1:158, "Inquisitor facit hoc quia dictus Bompetrus noluit ei dare sororem suam, nec consentire eam ipsi inquisitori." And ibid., no. 140, 1:158–59.

145. See his sentence of 22 May, ibid., nos. 246, 328, 1:196, 204–5.

But others in the piazza were becoming hysterical as the mood turned ugly. Valeriano di Guido from the parish of Santa Maria Maddalena began to thrash about (*volvando se*), crying in tears to those around him that the condemnation was a great sin because Bompietro was asking for the sacrament of the Lord's body. Although later, on 16 May, he would deny those words, Fra Guido exacted from him a security of £100 bon., one of the highest required of a protester, and threatened him with jail should he dare to speak against the judgment again.[146] One of the women present, Dotta di Giovanino, from San Tommaso del Mercato, added her cries to the men's protest against the denial of Communion, shouting and repeating what Valeriano had said. Their cries may well have turned the crowds against the friars and the judgment, since they were the only protesters in the square whom Fra Guido would later threaten with imprisonment.[147] The onlookers' logic was summed up beautifully by the wholly respectable Don Giovanni of Vernazza, who was standing just under the Arenga.[148] He turned to the crowd and shouted, "How can this be? This man seems to be a good Christian. I have seen that heretics despise the body of Christ, and this one is asking for it. How is it possible to be a heretic when one is asking for the body of Christ? This is not possible." To the simple faithful and, no doubt, to many of the clergy, his logic seemed impeccable. Pope Alexander IV had specifically commanded that under no circumstances (*nequaquam*) was a heretic, even if relapsed, to be denied confession and Communion if he asked for it, a decree repeated by Pope Boniface VIII in 1298 as part of his *Liber Sextus*.[149] Execution of a relapsed heretic who had repented, although theoretically possible, was also virtually unknown.[150] How could the friars turn away one who showed signs of repentance? It could only be the work of the Devil.

The shouts to free Bompietro were joined by other voices calling for the death of the inquisitor and the friars.[151] Saviabona di Gerardo of Venice, a vendor of bands and belts, whose bench stood at the foot of the Arenga, under the arcade next to that of the meat vendor Giacomo di Rolanduccio,[152] took up the cry of "death to the friars." She turned toward the crowd and shouted that the friars should be burned instead of Bompietro and that, were it not for the pictures of the saints there, their church of San Domenico should also be put to the torch. She was heard by all those under the portico,

---

146. Ibid., no. 147, 1:162–63.

147. He released her on £25 bon. bail. See her testimony, ibid., no. 131, 1:155, and sentence, no. 143, 1:160.

148. He was an official of his Società delle Armi, the Lombardi; see Bologna Stat. II, 2:377.

149. *Liber Sextus*, 5.2.4, in vol. 2 of *Corpus Iuris Canonici*, 2d ed., ed. E. Friedberg (Leipzig: Tauchnitz, 1881).

150. Hamilton, *Medieval Inquisition*, 56.

151. *ASOB*, nos. 264–65, 1:200–201.

152. Saviabona's whole process is preserved in ibid. (see, in order, nos. 26, 37, 247, 278, 330, 42, 379, 385, 568, 575). See also Paolini, *Eresia*, 69–72.

including a lay sister from San Domenico, Sor Migliore di Giuliano, who objected. Saviabona flew at her, shouting that the Dominicans were sons of the Devil and that they had turned her into a pauper through a fraudulent will, perhaps that of her parents.[153] The confrontation between the two women was noticed by others further back in the crowd, like Angeleria di Simone Guidolini from San Martino dell'Aposa, who asked someone in front what the ruckus was about. "Saviabona is attacking the friars," she was told.[154] On 9 June, Fra Guido fined Saviabona £30 bon., required her to wear crosses, attend sermons on all Sundays and feast days, fast every Friday, and say twenty-five Aves and Paters each day. But five days later, in consideration of her age and poverty, he relented, reducing her punishment to hearing sermons on feast days. He canceled the fine.[155]

Among those leaving the piazza after the podesta's sentence, some simply grumbled against the injustice of Bompietro's condemnation, cursing the inquisitor and the friars under their breath.[156] But some, such as Tommaso di Porcondino and Giovanni di Caldario, agreed with Saviabona that people should go burn San Domenico, just as they had burned the house of the inquisition in Parma.[157] It was dangerous talk. Word spread that Bompietro would spend the night in the prison of the commune at the foot of the Arenga and then go to the stake unshriven and without Communion.[158] Donna Contessa di Ugolino from Santa Maria della Mascarella, who did not know Bompietro well enough to know which one of the communal societies he belonged to, demanded among her friends, "What are the members of the Società dei Vari doing that they don't go to the Palazzo Comunale and free Bompietro?"[159] Others also suggested that the militia take up their arms and storm the friars' convent at San Domenico.[160] Meanwhile, some women prayed that Christ would come to the good Bompietro's aid and miraculously free him.[161] At least one matron urged her servants to destroy

---

153. See *ASOB*, nos. 26, 37, 379, 1:54, 66, 240: "Isti fratres predicatores vellent comburri cum Sancto Dominico, nisi essent picture, que sunt in ecclesia." "Fratres conduxerunt me ad paupertatem, propter malum testimentum quod fecerunt fieri."

154. Ibid., no. 42, 1:71.

155. Sentence: ibid., no. 568, 1:310–12; reduction: 2:329–31.

156. E.g., ibid., nos. 167, 199, 270.

157. Ibid., no. 150, 1:164. Others mistakenly thought this had occurred at Padua or "in alia civitate," ibid., nos. 284, 349, 1:207–8, 228.

158. Twenty-four of those interrogated identify themselves as speaking on the day of the condemnation, but give no place or a place other than the Piazza Maggiore. In contrast to those present in the piazza, most of these are women, who would logically have heard about the events from returning male relatives. Those who are represented by a single entry in the register follow. From S. Martino dell'Aposa: ibid., nos. 155, 202, 203, 206, 207, 211, 235, 212, 277; from S. Maria de Mascarella: nos. 193, 236, 237, 261, 280; from other parishes: nos. 200, 201, 208, 239, 242, 248, 313, 420.

159. Ibid., no. 380, 1:241, "Quid faciunt illi, qui sunt de societate varorum, quare on vadunt ad pallatium communis et non liberant ipsum Bompetrum?" It was a natural error; the Vari met in the church of S. Martino dell'Aposa. See Bol. Pop. Stat., 2:347–61.

160. E.g., *ASOB*, no. 241, 1:194; no. 300, 1:212.

161. See ibid., nos. 238, 277, 351, 1:193, 206, 229.

the scaffold being prepared for the execution.[162] At San Martino, Donna Tommasina di Bonaiolo suggested that the inquisitor was himself a heretic and that those who gave alms to the friars would have a year of bad luck.[163] Bologna being a male-dominated society, this probably amounted to little more than wishful thinking in the kitchen or at the water fountain, but such feelings seem to have been prevalent throughout the city.

The mood of many in the city became obvious to the friars as they returned home. Don Nicola di Guido de' Borromei was sitting under the portico of his house, a couple of blocks from the Palazzo Comunale, near San Bartolo di Porta Ravennate, when a throng including three of his friends arrived with news of the events in the piazza. A heated discussion ensued, during which two Dominicans, Fra Giacomo Casotti and Fra Albergitto of Bologna, passed by and overheard Nicola ranting against the inquisition and in favor of the condemned. Someone said that if Bompietro had given the friars £40 bon. as a payoff, they would not have condemned him, and that it would be better if the friars were burned in his stead. The friars turned Nicola in. He appeared before the tribunal on 14 May, and Fra Guido gave him three days to prepare his defense.[164] Although Nicola then disappears from our records, similar incidents multiplied as word spread. On the very day of the sentence, one woman was overheard praising Bompietro and damning the inquisitor and the friars to hell in the very church of San Domenico.[165]

In the twenty-four hours that separated the condemnation from the execution, older grievances merged with the anger against the treatment of Bompietro. Although it was forgotten during the clamor in the piazza, Fra Guido had earlier that year begun the posthumous investigation of a woman from the parish of San Tommaso del Mercato. Rosafiore di Nicola of Verona was the widow of the well-known Cathar Bonigrino Delay, who had been sent to the stake as relapsed on 12 September 1297, the first execution recorded in the register.[166] She and her husband had been investigated in 1287 for receiving heretics and sentenced to wear crosses. Although her husband relapsed into his old ways, Rosafiore watched herself. She seems to have become close to her parish priest, Don Giacomo Benintendi, who visited her when sick, heard her confession, and gave her Communion.[167] On 3 April

162. Ibid., no. 438, 1:260.
163. Ibid., no. 155, 1:166–67.
164. On Nicola, see ibid., nos. 127–30, 1:152–54.
165. Ibid., no. 420, 1:255–56.
166. Ibid., no. 10, 1:20–25; on Bonigrino and Rosafiore, see Paolini, *Eresia,* 96–110, and id., "Bonigrino da Verona e sua moglie Rosafiore," *Medioevo ereticale,* ed. Ovidio Capitani (Bologna: Il Mulino, 1977), 213–44. Bonigrino's process and condemnation are continued in *ASOB,* nos. 3–10, 1:11–25. On the significance of Rosafiore's legal condition as a "convicted" heretic, see O. Ruffino, "Ricerche sulla condizione giuridica degli eretici nel pensiero dei glossatori," *Rivista di storia del diritto italiano* 46 (1973): 30–190.
167. Giacomo appears in the 1300 tithe list for Bologna as rector of San Tomasso; see Sella, "Diocesi di Bologna," 107. He paid 30s. bon., which suggests his parish was one of the larger in the city, although not among the largest.

1297, she made her will, giving as her largest monetary bequest £200 bon. for distribution to Christ's poor. In addition she provided 100s. for Masses and prayers for her soul. All her property in Verona she left to her niece, Bonafiglia.[168] When the end came, Don Giacomo gave her the last rites and buried her in the cemetery of San Tommaso del Mercato.[169] One would have thought it an edifying story of a genuine return to orthodoxy and a pious death.

The inquisitor did not think so. The priest of San Tommaso had buried a penanced heretic without permission of the Holy Office; never mind that she was his parishioner. We have no record of her posthumous condemnation for relapse, but it had occurred before Giacomo's arrest. At his interrogation, Fra Guido grilled Giacomo on his behavior. Yes, Don Giacomo admitted that some people had said she was a heretic; yes, he knew that Guido had interrogated her and her niece Bonafiglia at home concerning possible relapse into heresy. Why did he give her the last rites and burial without permission of the inquisition or the bishop? As far as he knew, Rosafiore had lived a blameless life after being penanced. Indeed, Rosafiore's good name was known throughout her parish. On Easter Sunday, 19 April, in the church of San Domenico, when her posthumous condemnation had been read by the inquisitor, a Sister of Penance from San Tommaso del Mercato, Sor Agnese, was heard to mutter in disbelief that Rosafiore was "a good woman, among the best in that contrada."[170] The inquisitor was impressed neither by pubic opinion nor by the parish priest's excuses. Don Giacomo was excommunicated, suspended from office, required to post bail of £200 bon., and given ten days to prepare a defense. Guido would eventually fine him £25 imp. for his act of compassion.[171]

More humiliating for the rector was the order that he personally exhume the body of his parishioner and turn her bones over to the inquisition.[172] On Sunday, 3 May, in the presence of Fra Guido and the agents of Ottolino of Mandello, after the Gospel at the principal Mass in San Tommaso del Mercato, the order was read to exhume Rosafiore's bones on the following Saturday, 9 May, for burning. They would go into the fire along with Giuliano and Bompietro on 13 May. Although present, the parish's pastor could not even sing the Mass—his excommunication would not be removed until he showed proper contrition four days later. Fra Guido's order included a judgment against Rosafiore's niece Bonafiglia.[173] We have no documents from

168. Her testament, found in Bologna, Archivio di Stato, MS *Memoriali* 92 (1297): fol. 535ᵛ, is transcribed in Paolini, *Eresia*, 109–10 n. 86.

169. Don Giacomo described his ministries to Rosafiore in *ASOB*, no. 15, 1:37–39.

170. Ibid., no. 122, 1:149, "Dicta Roxaflore fuerat bona mulier et de melioribus, que essent in contrata illa."

171. Giacomo's process is found in ibid., nos. 15, 103, 806, 564, 565. On his case, see Paolini, *Eresia*, 40–45.

172. Part of the penalty provided by canon law for burying heretics: *Liber Sextus* 5.2.2.

173. *ASOB*, no. 117, 1:145–46.

the process against her. Since she was Rosafiore's heir, the suspicion that this entire affair was engineered to seize the family's property soon began to circulate.[174]

On the morning of 13 May, the attitude in the city was sullen. Police of the inquisition and commune were in evidence, and most people guarded their lips more carefully than on the day before. Only half as many people would later admit to protesting on the day of the executions as confessed to protesting on the day of the condemnations. Nevertheless, the bitter and threatening talk of the night before had brought out a couple of hotheads. When a communal jailer, Francesco di Marco, arrived in the Piazza del Mercato for the completion of the scaffolding, he found Giacobino di Riccio de' Colombi and Pietro Madiane throwing rocks at the scaffold, cursing at the jailers, and shouting against the inquisition and in favor of Bompietro.[175] When Francesco tried to stop them, Giacobino pulled out his sword. Francesco drew his knife, and Giacobino backed off and fled.[176] Considering popular feelings, it is surprising that this was the only recorded attempt to stop the execution.

On the morning of the execution, the inquisitor would have delivered a sermon in the piazza. He was no doubt well guarded after that morning's incident. Fra Guido would have imposed any other lesser penances and again announced the execution of the two *relapsi* and the burning of Rosafiore's bones. Then he would have departed. The execution of the condemned was a secular matter. We have no description of the execution. Giuliano certainly died defiant. No one speaks of any repentance, and no deposition indicates the least sympathy for him. But the unshriven Bompietro, perhaps invoking Christ and the saints, went to the stake calling forth the murmured sympathy of most of those present. As much as Bompietro, Rosafiore's bones generated bitter comment. Two women spoke aloud. Mina, a butcher's wife from San Giuseppe, cried out, "O Donna Rosafiore, none of this can hurt you!"[177] Bompietro's neighbor Donna Bitina cursed the inquisitor more colloquially, "O gli nascha'l vermo cane!"[178] The words would cost her £10 bon.[179] The crowd at the execution seems to have been a more feminine one than at the condemnation, perhaps more pitiful and less defiant as well.[180]

174. Indeed, it was against canon law to seize a wife's property merely because of her husband's heresy: *Liber Sextus* 5.2.14.

175. *ASOB*, no. 220, 1:185–86.

176. Ibid., no. 271, 1:203–4; Giacobino was later cited, ibid., no. 330, 1:221, but nothing else remains from his process, if there was one.

177. Ibid., no. 444, 1:262, "O domina Rosaflore, nichil nocet vobis."

178. Which might be translated, "May he give birth to a worm dog!" Or perhaps, "May a dog-worm grow in him!" It does lose something in translation.

179. *ASOB*, no. 163, 1:169.

180. Of those at the 12 May condemnations, seventeen out of twenty-one were men. Of the thirteen (or eleven, if we omit the two morning rock throwers) at the site of the execution on 13 May, ten were women. See Dupré-Theseider, "Eresia a Bologna," 278–79, and Paolini, *Eresia*, 57, for an attempt at a socioeconomic analysis of the crowd.

Others present seem to have looked on in silence. At least some probably blessed Bompietro in their hearts and cursed the injustice of the proceeding against him. The burning of the old widow's bones stirred a revulsion seemingly equal to that of the execution.[181] To the onlookers it seemed not just wrong to desecrate the remains of someone who had died in communion with the Church, but also foolish and stupid, a *truffa*.[182] Some were curious how they could be sure Don Giacomo had found the right bones in the unmarked graves of the cemetery.[183] Others even smelled something heretical in the idea that burning the bones of the dead would hurt them. One parishioner of San Tommaso, Donna Diana di Alberto degli Scalami, who may well have known Rosafiore, would later wryly remark that it is better to burn heretics while they are still alive.[184]

That evening, under cover of darkness, Brandano, the son of one of the most distinguished members of Bompietro's parish, the notary Don Pace di Giovanni of Salicetto, organized (with the help of Salvitto di Salvitto of the same place) the gathering of the ashes and their decent burial in the marketplace. Brandano savored this quiet act of defiance against an inquisition that had not only killed Bompietro but was also harassing (for reasons unknown to us) his friend Benvenuto, a watchman on the city walls. A shoemaker from Santa Maria della Mascarella, Bernardino di Biagio, led the large group of men who dug the grave. When finally summoned before the inquisition, on 26 June, Brandano and Salvitto were each fined £25 bon. for their act of mercy.[185] The shoemaker, who on 19 May was the first member of the burial party to be identified, paid only £10 bon., being a man of humbler rank.[186]

LAYPEOPLE SPEAK

When the Holy Office reopened on Thursday, 14 May, Fra Guido and his associates began their initial investigation into the disturbances of the preceding two days. That day they examined two protesters against whom accusations had been filed. Dotta di Giovanino, who had shouted support of Bompietro in the Piazza Maggiore, gave no new leads. Nicola di Guido de' Borromei, the malcontent whom passing friars had overheard attacking the inquisition, must have seemed the tip of an iceberg of discontent in the parish of San Bartolo di Porta Ravennate. Summonses were sent out. Fra Guido spent a good part of the next day interrogating five other parishioners—perhaps Nicola's friends and acquaintances.[187] Everything turned up dry.

181. Of the eleven people identifiable as present at the execution, six confessed objections to the burning of the bones, and of these, three confessed to nothing else.

182. Of the eighty-four who confessed to objecting to burning the bones, thirty-six described it as a *truffa*, or words to that effect.

183. E.g., *ASOB*, no. 183, 1:176, "Quomodo scire, que sint sue?"

184. Ibid., no. 239, 1:193, "et melius fuisset comburere vivos quam mortuos."

185. Ibid., nos. 475–76, 1:274.

186. Ibid., no. 225, 1:187–88. Paolini, *Eresia*, 126, suggests he was a friend of Bompietro.

187. *ASOB*, nos. 134–38, 1:157–58.

Asked whether they had been making noise (*faciendo rumorem*) or shouting (*clamando*), or had heard anyone voicing support for Bompietro or Giuliano, each one denied it. They knew nothing.

As these fruitless interrogations were going on, the Dominican Fra Bonifacio di Leonardo of Bologna arrived at the tribunal and made a deposition accusing a barber from San Vitale, just outside the old walls beyond San Bartolo, of praising Bompietro. He had threatened the friar and his companion, Fra Giovanni Gosberti, saying, "You clergy are going to have your turn too."[188] Fra Bonifacio did not know the man's name. By the next morning, the barber had been identified as Bartolomeo di Gianni. Summoned in midmorning, he scornfully refused to come. Unidentified measures were taken, and within hours the suspect appeared before Fra Guido. He denied making any threats but reported that a certain Francesco di Gerardello of Budrio had yelled that the friars ought to be flogged.[189] Depositions were received against two other suspects. Valeriano di Guido, the man who had been seen sobbing at the sentencing, was summoned and denied having said anything in favor of the heretics, as did Alberto di Lorenzo from San Damiano parish.[190] The inquisitor's patience was now wearing thin. He threatened both men with prison and demanded £100 bon. security from each.

Two other accusations were the only other business that day. A man reported that the notary Francesco di Pasquale of Gubbio had been in the piazza, shouting in favor of the heretics and urging that San Domenico be burned. This may have seemed a more promising lead, but no charges were filed. Finally Fra Giovanni, who appears to have been roaming the city looking for clues and waiting to be insulted, returned to report that Donna Contessa Ravagnani had yelled at him, "Believe you me, whatever contrada you friars go to, you will be butchered."[191] When she later appeared before the tribunal, she also admitted mocking friars passing through her neighborhood, yelling, "Don't bother looking in this house; it may be large, but there is not much in it, and if I were a man . . ."[192] Guido was not amused; he fined her £100 bon., thereby certainly confirming her in the suspicion that the friars were after people's property. Three days' work had borne no fruits other than the punishment of random insults, the collection of worthless tips, and the identification of one hysteric. The inquisitor would certainly not have suspected that the next day would bring a startling new development.

On Sunday, 17 May 1299, the notary Alberto arrived for the principal Mass at the church of San Martino dell'Aposa to read, after the Gospel, the condemnation of Bompietro and Giuliano and to declare the seizure of their

188. Ibid., nos. 144–45, 1:161–62, "Vos habebitis una vice super clerichatas."
189. Ibid., no. 146, 1:162.
190. Ibid., nos. 147–48, 1:162–63.
191. Ibid., no. 149, 1:163.
192. Ibid., no. 154, 1:166, "Dixit, 'Nolite respicere in domum, quia domus magna est, tamen parum est in ea et si essem homo,' et ulterius non processit in verbis."

property. Summoned to come and witness this act were the vicar general Fra Benvenuto, three Carmelite friars with their subprior Fra Guglielmo Angelico, and two eminent laymen, the notary Don Pace of Salicetto (who probably did not know that his son had organized Bompietro's burial) and Ser Paolo Trintinelli.[193] But as Alberto began to announce the sentences, Trintinelli exploded with rage.[194] Paolo was a man to be reckoned with; he was a past consul of the Società dei Linari and a director of the Società dei Linaiuoli.[195] In front of the entire congregation, he denounced the inquisitor in a loud voice. He did not give a bean (*fabam*) for the judgments. The inquisitor could write whatever he wanted; Bompietro was a good man. The one who tried to calm him, Pace the notary, was, if anything, an even more distinguished citizen. Pace had served on a committee that revised the city statutes in 1286–87; he was a official (*anzianus*) of the linenworkers' society, a member of the leatherworkers' society, an official for criminal justice (*officialis ad officium bannitorum*), a councilor (*sapiens*) of the quarter of San Pietro, and a councilor of the Società dei Vari, and thus very visibly involved in city government.[196] "Ser Paolo," he said, "you are speaking badly; you could be excommunicated for such talk." "I don't care about such excommunications," Ser Paolo retorted. "Watch yourself, if the inquisitor summons and condemns you, you will have to pay," replied Pace, now appealing to Trintinelli's more earthly sensibilities. "I do not care and I am not afraid," came the answer. Others, including the parish notary and the friars, tried to reason with him.

Trintinelli turned from them in disgust and denounced the impending ruin of Bompietro's family. It would be better to rob the altar of the cathedral of San Pietro than to rob Bompietro's widow and children. Turning on the Carmelite friars, he berated them as "vile wretches" for not having defended their old benefactor. Again Don Pace tried to reason with Trintinelli, reminding him that Bompietro, when he was condemned on the Arenga, had himself admitted being reared in heresy. This piece of irrelevant information appears to have worked some effect on Ser Paolo, who replied sullenly, "What happened to Bompietro was unfortunate, but I'll be quiet." But now it was the turn of one of the burial party to attack the judgments. Salvitto di Salvitto of Salicetto denounced the court at length and praised Bompietro, saying that he was a good man and that the friars were the real heretics. "You're excommunicated!" yelled Pace. "I don't care about this excommunication, and I'll never go before that inquisitor to do penance," Salvitto retorted.

193. As seen on the witness codicil of Bompietro's condemnation, ibid., no. 567, 1:309. On Trintinelli, see Paolini, *Eresia*, 56–61.
194. For the events that followed, see the testimony against Trintinelli, in *ASOB*, nos. 22–23, 27–32, 1:47–51, 55–60, especially that of Pace, no. 23, 1:50–51.
195. Bologna Stat. II (1288), 1:406 and 1:408; he continued to hold the latter office in 1293, ibid. 1:593.
196. Bologna Stat. II, 1:150, 372, 396, 419, 471, 530.

By this time, other leading men from the parish and from Santa Maria della Mascarella had joined in denouncing the condemnation. They said that they had already supported Bompietro while he was in jail awaiting trial, and that the prosecution had been nothing but a ruse to steal his money. Not everyone in the church could hear what the shouting was about, but when it became clear that some of their leaders were disputing the sentence, ordinary people in the congregation added their voices in support of Bompietro. Finally, in the name of the inquisitor, the Carmelite Fra Giacomo of Tuscany, who was singing the Mass, declared the excommunication of everyone present who had objected to the judgments. Still defiant, Ser Paolo called the excommunication worthless, adding that the friars were more excommunicate than Bompietro. The two messengers of the inquisition, Benincasa di Martino and Nascimbene di Adelardo, sped back to the office of the inquisition and reported the incident to Fra Guido. The interrogation of suspects would begin on Monday.

The outburst of Paolo Trintinelli was in the eyes of the authorities profoundly disturbing. Here was a powerful civic leader, a banker with vast property (valued at £8,261 in 1297), and he had publicly denounced the Holy Office.[197] Furthermore, this had incited protests by other leaders and common people. The inquisitor and his associates spent Sunday afternoon and evening planning their strategy. On Monday, Ser Paolo was dragged before the tribunal. When presented with the charges, he denied them with an oath (*Domine quod non!*). Guido released him into the hands of the two men who would stand surety for him on a bond of £2,000, and gave him three days to reconsider his testimony.[198] Guido then collected depositions from those involved in the incident.

Three days later, Trintinelli relented, retracted everything he had said in favor of Bompietro, and asked for pardon.[199] On 10 June, his bail was reduced to £200 imp., and he was sentenced.[200] In issuing his sentence, Fra Guido took the unusual step of consulting the bishop, his fellow Dominican, Giovanni Savelli. Ser Paolo was ordered, for one year, to attend a sermon every Sunday and feast day, if not at the public preaching sponsored by the commune in the Piazza Maggiore,[201] then at the Franciscan or Dominican church. He was also ordered to make a "deposit" of £200 imp. with the inquisition, which was to be expended at Fra Guido's discretion. Considering the gravity of his offense and his wealth and public stature, it seems a light sentence. Three days later, Trintinelli made his deposit with the inquisition banker Don Brunino di Bianco Cose, counting out two hundred Vene-

---

197. On Trintinelli's wealth and positions, see Paolini, *Eresia*, 56 n. 211, and *ASOB*, 1:47–48 n. 1.
198. *ASOB*, no. 179, 1:174–75.
199. Ibid., no. 28, 1:56.
200. Ibid., no. 389, 1:254; sentence: no. 569, 1:312–14.
201. Bologna Stat. 1, 1:443.

tian *grossi*. Fra Guido was *contentus*.[202] The next day, with his head bare and a rope around his neck, Ser Paolo knelt in the bishop's palace, confessed that he had lied at his first interrogation, and begged for mercy. He was then silent out of shame and respect. At the request of the bishop, the podesta, the guild directors, the city councilors, and other officials of the commune, Fra Guido refunded the money deposited and reduced the sentence out of consideration for Trintinelli's age and health. Ser Paolo would only have to attend sermons for the remaining two weeks of June.[203] The most prominent critic of the condemnation had been humiliated and could be reintegrated into the life of the city. Or had the communal government and bishop tired of Fra Guido's high-handed procedures and the witch hunt for protesters, which had now touched even the ruling class?

In the wake of the excommunication in San Martino, a flood of self-denunciations had begun to pour into the Holy Office on the same Monday Ser Paolo made his first appearance.[204] A procession of twenty-five women and two men, eighteen from the parishes of San Martino dell'Aposa and Santa Maria della Mascarella, and five from parishes next to them, came to confess their transgressions and asked to be absolved from excommunication. Their confessions were virtually identical; they had criticized the inquisitor, the friars, and the condemnation of Bompietro. They often made reference to the denial of Communion. Four women, only one of whom was from Bompietro's parish, admitted to having been at the execution and having spoken against the burning of Rosafiore's bones. Fra Giacomo's dragnet excommunication at Mass had produced its first haul. Most who confessed on Monday were probably present when Ser Paolo exploded, and had incurred the ban by voicing support. The inquisitor may have been surprised to hear objections to the bone-burning. Fra Guido took £10 bon. bail from fifteen and let the rest go with a warning.[205]

The following day, 19 May, saw the largest number of self-denunciations of the entire period of the investigation; forty-six confessed. They included Bompietro's son Giacomo, who was let go with a warning after admitting he thought the inquisition had treated his father badly.[206] Santa Maria della Mascarella was more heavily represented (thirteen depositions) that day, so the excommunications may have been announced there after the haul of penitents from San Martino on Monday. From the total of 320 self-denunciations, 144 would be made by 26 May. All the rest, except for two, would be

202. *ASOB*, no. 397, 1:247.

203. Ibid., nos 45, 574, 1:75–76, 2:326–29.

204. The depositions from this inquest form a collection in their own right in Bologna, Biblioteca dell'Archiginnasio, MS B.1856 (ca. 1300). Fol. 36r is the title page of the inquest. Fol. 35v is blank. The depositions begin on fol. 36v.

205. Cf. Paolini, *Eresia*, 69 (who thinks the *cautiones* were imposed only four times); the imposition of *cautiones* was common, especially in the early days of the inquest.

206. *ASOB*, no. 214, 1:184.

received by 12 July. After 24 June, all but twelve of the self-denunciations would cluster in groups, on every fourth or fifth day: 26 June (thirteen), 29 June (eleven), 3 July (twelve), 8 July (seventeen), 12 July (twelve). Mondays and Fridays often saw heavy traffic. None would come on Thursdays, although the tribunal was open. It seems likely that Fra Guido concentrated on the parishes around the Market where Bompietro was well known, announcing days on which those denouncing themselves should appear. Announcements were probably made at Mass on Sundays and then again (by heralds?) on Thursdays. Those who had uttered rash statements knew they could be turned in, and after the first week of depositions, Fra Guido only imposed the token £10 bail sporadically. It is not surprising that so many came and confessed.

The parishes with over ten self-denunciations each—San Martino dell'Aposa (sixty-four), Santa Maria della Mascarella (fifty-seven), San Tommaso del Mercato (eighteen), Santa Maria Maggiore (sixteen), San Benedetto in Galliera (thirteen), and San Sinesio (twelve)—were all located on the sides of the Market. Except in the case of San Tommaso, the depositions are concentrated on particular dates, with about half from each coming together: San Martino (18–19 May), Santa Maria della Mascarella (19–21 May), Santa Maria Maggiore (19 May), San Benedetto (25 May), and San Sinesio (15–17 June). Even the depositions from less well represented parishes appear together chronologically.[207] We may assume that each parish was summoned for a particular day or time. If one could not come to the inquisition to turn oneself in, Fra Guido was happy to send a messenger over to take down the confessions—as he did for the family of Pietro Pizzoli of Argelato on 19 June, when Fra Tommaso della Cena and Benincasa di Martini took down his confession and those of the five women of his house.[208]

The publication of excommunications in the parishes and the occasional long lines of offenders at the tribunal would have been a regular reminder of the presence of the inquisition. As the investigation proceeded, the object of new protests shifted to the Dominicans themselves, away from the injustice done to Bompietro. Oddo di Albertino Lasagnoli, a master carpenter from Santa Tecla di Porta Nova, which was directly on the Piazza Maggiore, wandered about his neighborhood bad-mouthing the friars and longing for a popular uprising to exterminate them. He also cursed the pope and the clergy. On 2 June, Bondiolo, a tavern keeper from the contrada, denounced him for defending Bompietro.[209] Another resident, Don Vacondio Amati, probably worried that Lasagnoli's behavior would draw suspicion to the par-

207. E.g.: S. Nicola degli Albari, six of eight on 20–21 June; S. Agata, all six on 3 July; S. Cristina della Fondezza, all four on 12 July.

208. *ASOB*, nos. 429–34, 1:258–59; on 26 June, another family of four confessed at home, ibid., no. 477–80, 1:275–76.

209. Ibid., no. 354, 1:230.

ish, slipped a *cedula*, which Alberto di Bartolomeo de' Lancei helped him write, into the hands of Fra Simone di Bertolo Belondini. The two men added that Oddo was known to blaspheme Christ and the Virgin Mary.[210] The inquest was on; seven other residents of the neighborhood were called in to testify about Oddo.[211] He was known to hate both usurers and friars, claiming that the friars were glad to bury usurers in consecrated ground, provided they shared the ill-gotten gains in the moneylenders' wills. The friars had used their money for bribes to get Saint Peter of Verona made a saint—an accusation that, if made on the inquisitor saint's feast day of 29 April, suggests Oddo had been bad-mouthing the friars throughout the period of the two Cathars' trials.

Oddo's hate for the friars was focused on their rapacity and lust. Seeing friars pass through the city, he said, "Those there are lurking robbers; they keep concubines and lovers, and there are few who don't. They wander about the city after women and fool them by saying, 'If you have any money, give it to us for your salvation,' and the women are stupid and give it to them."[212] Challenged for such talk by the wholesale merchant Giacomo Mercadelli, Oddo insulted him: "Eatis vos, quod vobis naschatur vermus canis."[213] When Oddo finally appeared before Fra Guido, on 19 June, he candidly admitted everything except having defended Bompietro—that accusation was both false and unjust. Asked whether he was willing to name any heretics, he said yes, one—Alberto di Bartolomeo de' Lancei. Fra Guido fined him £100 bon.

Such outspokenness toward the friars seems to have been the exception. Rather, as Fra Guido's agents (more and more, it was Fra Omobono or some other subordinate, rather than the inquisitor, who did the processing) took down the depositions, the expressions of quiet anger fell into set patterns. Even discounting for the formulaic structure taken by the depositions within days of Trintinelli's citation, the overall pattern of complaint seems clear and believable. Nearly all confessed to mere spoken remarks, not actions or even shouting. The remarks seem to have often been made in private or at home. Grumbling focused on the injustice of Bompietro's death. Of the total 320 self-denunciations, 270 specifically condemned Bompietro's sentence or the inquisition or inquisitor for making it. Ten merely praised Bompietro without attacking his persecutors, but that amounted to the same thing. Some eighty-one explicitly mentioned his desire for repentance and the denial of Communion. Biagia, the daughter of Don Bernardo from Santa Maria della Mascarella, probably summed up the opinion of many about

---

210. Ibid., no. 356, 1:231.

211. Ibid., nos. 354–62, 364, 1:231–34.

212. Ibid., no. 359 (testimony of Bartolomeo de' Lancei), 1:232: "Iste sunt latrones cavati, et tenent concubinas et amaxias et pauci sunt qui non teneant, et vadant per civitatem ad mulieres et decipiunt eas et dicunt eis: 'Si habetis pecuniam, date nobis in salvamento,' et mulieres sunt symplices et dant sibi."

213. Ibid., no. 361, 1:233. This seems to have been a popular Bolognese curse; see page 446 above.

Bompietro when she said, "Those cursed friars should have received him, because Christ accepts everybody."[214] It was the refusal of confession and Communion that elicited the most violent reactions. Many labeled Fra Guido's actions a cause of heresy.[215] Yes, the inquisitor was a devil, the Antichrist.[216] The aristocratic Donna Lucia, wife of the jurist Pace de' Paci, repeated the prophesy that Bompietro's condemnation would cause such heresy to flood the world that priests would hide their clerical state, "just as Fra Giovanni said."[217] The repetition of this prophesy cost her £25 bon.

Although twenty-nine mentioned Giuliano in conjunction with Bompietro, only two mentioned the old Cathar in his own right.[218] Many who showed pity for Giuliano seem only to have done so because they thought that he too had repented.[219] To burn a convinced Cathar did not trigger protest. But the burning of Rosafiore's bones was widely decried (eighty-one depositions mention it). It seemed pointless, stupid, and, in the popular mind, perhaps even heretical. Protest against the bone-burning was not localized in any part of the city—in Rosafiore's own parish, only four out of the eighteen self-denunciations mentioned it. But the two women who admitted criticizing the fining of her priest, Don Giacomo, for burying her were both from the parish.[220]

The miscarriages of justice not only brought down popular curses on the heads of the friars, they also brought speculation about why Bompietro had died. One self-denouncer out of five confessed having voiced the opinion that the prosecutions were made to seize money or property. One had even heard that Fra Guido tried to shake Bompietro down for 200 gold florins in return for acquitting him.[221] Although the "take" of the entire affair, including the fining of protesters, would hardly have enriched Fra Guido and his assistants, the posthumous condemnation of Rosafiore does seem suspicious. The register contains no accusations or evidence to substantiate her "relapse." But the property listed in her will was worth less than the bond Guido exacted from the priest who buried her.[222] The Bolognese inquisition, like all medieval courts, depended on the fines it levied to pay expenses. To that extent, the accusation of venality may have a certain basis in truth. Five women smelled other forms of corruption behind the injustice: the inquisitor

214. Ibid., no. 197, 1:180, "Illi fratres maledicti debebant recipere eum, quia Christus recipit omnes."
215. E.g., ibid., nos. 257, 311.
216. Ibid., nos. 158, 159, 351.
217. Ibid., no. 524, 1:285, "Dixit quod venerat id quod dixerat frater Iohamnes, quod mundus veniret in tanta heresi quod presbiteri cooperirent sibi clericas." Could this "Fra Giovanni" be the Franciscan apocalypticist Pietro di Giovanni Olivi? Donna Lucia's husband, Pace, became podesta of Padua in 1305; see *Liber Regiminum Padue*, 347; *CCB*: Vill., 268.
218. *ASOB*, nos. 398, 399.
219. E.g., ibid., no. 341, 1:225–26.
220. Ibid., nos. 297, 298.
221. Ibid., no. 165, 1:169–70.
222. See Paolini, *Eresia*, 108–10.

was taking revenge on Bompietro and Rosafiore because they had thwarted his sexual advances on a sister, daughter, or niece.[223] It was not only Oddo Lasagnoli who harbored suspicions about the friars' morals.

What may well have attracted Fra Guido's attention most were the forty-one who said that they had hoped for vengeance or some calamity to be visited on the inquisition and the friars. Perhaps there was an incendiary among the five men in twenty-four who said it was better to burn the inquisitor or San Domenico than Bompietro, but this seems little more than idle talk. One might expect that some of the five women who wanted to end almsgiving to the Dominicans would put their words into action. But hopes for a boycott did not materialize. Although bequests to San Domenico were off slightly in 1298 (51) and 1299 (48) from the high in 1297 (66), they rebounded to an all-time high of 174 during the Holy Year of 1300 and remained at around 50 to 60 a year until the mid-1320s.[224] The years 1295 to 1323 were the Bolognese Dominicans' peak period of popularity in wills. In the end, the Dominicans and mendicants generally were too much in tune with the piety of the age to be rejected in themselves. In spite of popular condemnation of inquisition abuses and other kinds of friction, the mendicants never lost their popularity. Nor would those people who turned themselves in to the Holy Office (243 of whom were women) have caused Fra Guido much lost sleep. His personal attentions were directed exclusively toward the notable, the violent, and those who might have more information.

In the end, popular outrage was not directed at the repression of heresy or even against the inquisition as such.[225] Rather, the Bolognese railed against the treatment of Bompietro because he was a respected friend and neighbor, a good and generous man, one who insisted that he was a Catholic and venerated the Blessed Sacrament. Known Cathars could go to the stake, and the inquisition would be merely feared; when it attacked people like Bompietro or Rosafiore or took their children's money, popular sensibilities were outraged. Already by early June, however, public expression of dissent seems to have all but disappeared. The last man apprehended by the inquisition in the affair was interrogated on 19 June. On 16 and 19 June, the porters of San Domenico reported that about a week earlier they had heard Filisino di Ardizzone de' Libri defending Bompietro's orthodoxy and attacking the inquisition. He did so in the courtyard outside the very door of the Dominican monastery and in the presence of the wardens of the contrada and a

223. *ASOB*, nos. 196, 250, 305, 349, 404.

224. See Bertram, "Bologneser Testamente I," 211–15.

225. *Pace* Lorenzo Paolini, "Gli ordini mendicanti e l'inquisizione: Il comportamento degli eretici e il giudizio sui frati," *Mélanges de l'École française de Rome: Moyen Âge–temps modernes* 89 (1977): 695–709, esp. 706–8, who thinks the protests of these ordinary Catholics represented a dissent from enforcing orthodoxy. This is too sweeping; they rejected prosecution of those who met lay standards of practical orthodoxy.

large group of laypeople. When one porter challenged him, Filisino announced that he had no fear of the inquisition and that the condemnation of Bompietro had been an offense to God. He also jeered that the inquisitor had bought his job at the Roman Curia for 2,000 gold florins.[226] Hauled before Fra Guido, the bold Filisino showed less valor; he admitted his guilt and begged for mercy.[227] Guido fined him £100 bon. and paternally warned him to stay out of taverns and give up dicing and bad company. The protests that had begun with righteous indignation ended with the ranting of a tavern haunter.

226. *ASOB*, nos. 412, 424, 1:252, 256.
227. Ibid., nos. 422, 425, 1:255–56.

Bibliography

MANUSCRIPTS

Bologna, Archivio di Stato. MS Comune Governo. Vol. 4. *Statuti del comune dell'anno 1259*.

Bologna, Biblioteca dell'Archiginnasio. MS B.490. *Entrata e spesa di S. Francesco dall'anno 1292 al 1352*.

————. MS B.1856. *Liber Confessionum et Citationum Haereticorum*.

————. MS B.3695. *Bolle e brevi riflettenti gli eretici*.

————. MS Gozz. 158. *Parrocchie di Bologna*. Incl. "Parrocchie di Bologna da una pergamena dell'Archivio della Vita," fol. 1ᵛ.

————. MS Gozz. 210, vol. 8. [*Miscellanea*.] Incl. *Statuta Anni 1258 et matricula [Annorum 1258–1310] Societatis S. Eustachii*, fols. 123ʳ–152ᵛ.

Bologna, Biblioteca Universitaria. MS 89.VI.5. *Constitutiones Ecclesiae S. Mariae Majoris Anno 1310*, fols. 1ʳ–18ʳ.

————. MS 89.XI.I.

————. MS 158. [*Miscellanea*.] Incl. [Miracoli], fols. 14ʳ–24ʳ; *Fiore di Virtù*, fols. 24ᵛ–45ᵛ; [Moralia], fols. 45ᵛ–47ʳ; "Confexione," fols. 52ʳ–56ᵛ; [Sonetti sui peccati capitali], fols. 70ʳ⁻ᵛ.

————. MS 1473. *Vitae Sanctorum et Vita S. Petronii*.

————. MS 1515. [*De Officio Inquisitionis*.]

————. MS 1552. Filippo of Ferrara. *Liber de Introductione Loquendi*.

————. MS 1563. [*Miscellanea*.] Incl. [Monitio Quaedam Vitam Spiritalem Adiuvans], fol. 8ᵛ; [Definitio Vitiorum Capitalium], [Rithmici Perfectionem Religiosae Vitae Completentes], [De Flagello Dei], [Rithmici de Vanitate Mundi], "Dies Irae," fol. 9ʳ; [Praeces et Orationes], fols. 16ᵛ–17ʳ; [De Vitiis et Virtutibus], fols. 37ʳ–41ᵛ; [Oratio ante Confessionem], fols. 42ʳ–43ʳ; [Praeces et Orationes], fols. 52ʳ–53ᵛ.

————. MS 1767. Giovanni Italo. *Liber de Miraculis*. Incl. [Missa pro Sponsis], fols. 114ʳ–115ᵛ.

————. MS 1785. Rolando the Deacon of Pisa. *Liber de Ordine Officiorum [Ecclesie Pisane.]*

————. MS 2060. *Vita e li meriti del glorioso messer s. Petronio*.

————. MS 2530. [*Miscellanea*.] Incl. [La pistola di S. Gironimo a Eustachio], fols. 1ʳ–24ᵛ; "Di molti virtudi e di molte altre cose," fols. 25ʳ–29ᵛ; "Sermone il quale fece sancto Bernardo," fols. 29ᵛ–31ʳ; "Confessione di cinque sensi corporali," fols. 31ʳ–32ʳ; "Oratione che fece Sancto Tomaso d'Aquino," fol. 32ʳ; "Orationi quando si vede il corpo di Cristo," fols. 32ʳ⁻ᵛ.

————. MS 2580. *Vitutues Principales Sunt Septem*.

————. MS 2727. Jean Rigaud. *Formula Confessionum*. Incl. "Verzene gloriosa anima bella," fols. 39ᵛ–40ᵛ.

————. MS 2858. *Praeces Sacrae*. Incl. "Confessio Sancti Gregorii et Alie Confessiones," fols. 8ᵛ–18ʳ.

Cesena, Biblioteca Comunale Malatestiana. MS D.XVI.3. Augustine of Hippo. *De Veritate Catholice Fidei*. Incl. [Confiteor], fol. 342ᵛ.

Florence, Biblioteca Medicea Laurenziana. MS Acq. e Doni 263. *Acti facti contro al clero fiorentino*.

————. MS Acq. e Doni 336. *Statuti e ordinatione de la Compagnia over Fraternitade de la Purificatione de la Virgine Maria*.

————. MS Aed. 37. [*Miscellanea*.] Incl. [Haltigarus Cameracensis], "De Septem Criminalibus Vitiis," fols. 1ᵛ–2ʳ; "De Interrogationibus et Admonitionibus Penitentie a Sacerdotibus Faciendis," fols. 107ʳ–109ᵛ.

————. MS Aed. 214. [*Miscellanea*.] Incl. "Quomodo Infantes Catechumeni Efficiantur," fols. 42ʳ–59ʳ.

————. MS Conv. Redi 102. Zucchero Bencivenni. *Catechesimus Christianus Catholicus*.

————. MS Conv. Soppr. 137. [*Sermonarium*.]

————. MS Conv. Soppr. 145. [*Miscellanea*.] Incl. [Jean of La Rochelle (Iohannes de Rupella), *Summa de Vitiis et Virtutibus*], fols. 145ᵛ–153ᵛ.

————. MS Gaddi 187. *Le meditationi de la vita di Cristo*, fols. 1ʳ–75ʳ; *Il pianto della vergine Maria*, fols. 76ʳ–84ʳ.

————. MS Gaddi 214. [*Rituale ad Visitandum Moribundum*.]

————. MS Gaddi 231. [*Preci vari*.]

————. MS Pl. XIX 29. [*Miscellanea*.] Incl. "Interrogationes Fatiende per Confessorem in Confessione," fols. 132ʳ–133ᵛ; "Missae Gratiarum," fol. 236ᵛ; "Quam Bonum Sit Audire Missam," fol. 257ᵛ.

————. MS Pl. XXV 3. [*Supplicationes Variae*]. Incl. [Mensura Dominici Corporis], fol. 15ᵛ; "Ave Dei Genitrix," fols. 210ᵛ–211ᵛ; "Ave Maria," fol. 363ᵛ.

Florence, Biblioteca Nazionale Centrale. MS II.IV.111. [*Miscellanea*.] Incl. "Ave Verbum Incarnatum," fol. 1ᵛ; [Kalendarium], fols. 2ʳ–7ᵛ; "Sopra li diece comandamenti dati da Dio," fols. 74ʳ–75ʳ; [Poesia di argomento religioso], fols. 104ᵛ–105ʳ.

————. MS II.IV.269. *Delle quattro virtù cardinali*.

————. MS II.IV.686. *Laude*. Incl. "Offitio a disciplina," fols. 3ʳ–9ʳ; "Officio per li morte," fols. 9ᵛ–20ᵛ.

————. MS II.VI.16. Zucchero Bencivenni. *Queste rendite sono le vitudi che'l Sancto Spirito arrosa di gratia*.

————. MS II.VIII.49. [*Miscellanea*.] Incl. "Liber de xv signi," fols. 192ᵛ–208ʳ; "Piatto ch'ebbi Dio con l'inimicho," fols. 209ʳ–212ᵛ.

————. MS II.IX.49. *I capitoli e hordinamenti della Compagnia della Santa Croce*.

————. MS Conv. Soppr. C.8.693. *Officium Monasticum; Flos Omnium Orationum*.

————. MS Conv. Soppr. D.8.2851. *Ordo Infirmorum Fratrum Secundum Consuetudinem Monasticam Abbatie Sancte Marie Florentine*.

————. MS Conv. Soppr. F.4.776. *Miscellanea*. Incl. [Orationes], fols. 76ʳ⁻ᵛ.

————. MS Magl. XXXVI.81ᵇⁱˢ. [*Miscellanea*]. Incl. "Quod Intente in Ecclesia Verbum Dei Est Audiendum," fols. 35ʳ–37ʳ.

————. MS Palat. 1. *Miscellanea*. Incl. "Versus Tante Eficacie ad Salutem quod qui eos Dixerit illa Die sine Penitentia Mori non Potest," fol. 14ᵛ.

————. MS Palat. 2. *Saltero di David*.

————. MS Palat. 4. [*Miscellanea*.] Incl. "Tanti vangeli disposti di latino in volgare," fols. 1ʳ–50ʳ; "Dodici articoli della fede," fol. 76ᵛ.

————. MS Palat. 150. [*Miscellanea*.] Incl. "Questi sono gli paternostri li quagli si vuolgliono dire la domenica dulivo," fol. 29ᵛ; "Ademande le quale sono da fare ad quello cristiano lo quale morira tosto," fols. 34ʳ–35ʳ.

Florence, Biblioteca Riccardiana. MS 256. [*Miscellanea*]. Incl. [Traditio Orationis Dominicae], fols. 137ᵛ–139ʳ.

———. MS 1316. [*Miscellanea.*] Incl. "Formula di confessione," fols. 22ʳ–24ᵛ.

———. MS 1419. *Meditazioni sulla vita di Gesù Cristo.* Incl. "Ordine della comunione," fols. 70ᵛ–71ʳ.

———. MS 1422. [*Miscellanea.*] Incl. [Chonfesione], fols. 143ᵛ–144ᵛ.

Lucca, Biblioteca Statale. MS 333. *Constitutum Domus Filiorum Corbelani Consortium, 1288.*

———. MS 1310. *Li capitoli e ordinamenti della Compangnia nova della passione di Gesu Christo 1299.*

Mantua, Archivio di Stato. Fondo Gonzaga, Busta 3305. *Processus et Alie Scripture Pertinentes ad Canonizationem Sancti Iohannis Boni.*

Mantua, Biblioteca Comunale Centrale Teresiana. MS 331. [*Miscellanea.*] Incl. "Rationale de Baptismo," fols. 31ʳ–38ᵛ.

———. MS 399. Iohannes Teutonicus. *Confessionale.*

———. MS 954. *Statuti et ordinatione instituiti per el reverendo episcopo fra Iacobo di Benfacti per la Compagnia de fratelli disciplinanti in del loco de Sancta Maria de la Misericordia posto dal pozzo de Salveto in Mantua.*

Milan, Biblioteca Ambrosiana. MS A 98 Sup. Giacomo of Varazze. *Legenda Aurea.* Incl. "Hymnus de Sacramento Eucharistiae," fol. 297ᵛ.

———. MS A 189 Inf. *Manuale Ambrosianum cum Calendario.*

———. MS E 15 Sup. Incl. "Schema Fragmentum Virtutis et Vitiis," fol. 84ᵛ.

———. MS H 168 Inf. *Miscellanea.* Incl. *Tractatus de Virtutibus Theologicis et Cardinalibus et de Septem Donis,* fols. 1ʳ–51ᵛ; [Fragmenta Moralis Doctrinae], fols. 52ʳ–53ᵛ; [Guillaume Perault], *Summa de Viciis et Virtutibus,* fols. 54ʳ–116ᵛ.

———. MS N 43 Sup. *Tractatus de Poenitentia; sive, Plurium Miraculorum Enarratio.*

———. MS Q 38 Sup. *Miscellanea.* Incl. [Materia Confessialis]: "De Quatuor Virtutibus Principalibus," fols. 52ʳ–53ᵛ; "De Septem Petitionibus et Septem Donis Spiritus Sancti," fols. 61ᵛ–62ᵛ; "De Sex Legibus et Earum Praeceptis et de Octo Mandatorum Generibus," fols. 62ᵛ–66ʳ; "De Articulis Fidei et de Septem Virtutibus," fols. 66ʳ–67ʳ; "De Septem Sacramentis," fols. 67ʳ–70ʳ; "Quomodo se Debet Habere Confessor erga Penitentem," fols. 70ʳ–75ᵛ.

———. MS Y 5 Sup. *Miscellanea.* Incl. [Rithmus de Iesu Christo], fols. 44ʳ–45ᵛ; [Tractatus Brevis de Virtutibus], fol. 64ʳ; "Tractatus de Inferno," fols. 68ᵛ–92ᵛ; "De Confessione," fol. 107ʳ.

———. MS Z 256 Sup. *Rotulus Letaniarum in Letaniis Minoribus Ambrosianis.*

———. MS Trotti 541. *Miscellanea.* Incl. "Informatorium," fols. 12ᵛ–28ᵛ; "De Confessione Peccati," fols. 124ʳ–159ᵛ.

Milan, Biblioteca Nazionale Braidense. MS AC.VIII.2. "Li statuti e ordinamenti de la Confraternitade di Recomendati a Madona Sancta Maria."

———. MS AD.xiii.48. *Esposizione rimata di storia sacra del Vecchio e Nuovo Testamento in dialetto milanese.*

Milan, Biblioteca Trivulziana. MS 768. *Miscellanea.* Incl. "Libro di santo Paulo appostolo," fols. 42ᵛ–48ʳ; "Libro del piato che fece Cristo in su la croce col diavolo," fols. 48ʳ–53ʳ; "Le cinque chiavi de la sapientia," fols. 53ᵛ–69ᵛ.

———. MS 1335. Guglielmo della Torre. *Costituzioni date ai canonici di S. Maria di Torello.*

Modena, Archivio di Stato. Biblioteca MS 132. [*Acta Contra Armannum Punzilupum.*]

Modena, Biblioteca Estense Universitaria. MS α.R.2.3. *Poesia antica volgare.*

———. MS γ.W.2.40. *Miscellanea.*

Padua, Biblioteca Antoniana. MS 109. Gregory the Great, *Regula Pastoralis.* Incl. "Reconciliatio Paenitentium in Caena Domini," fols. 148ᵛ–154ᵛ.

———. MS 217. *Miscellanea.* Incl. Berengario Fredelli, *Summa Confessionis,* fols. 91ʳ–98ʳ.

————. MS 532. Peter the Chanter, *De Oratione et Speciebus Illius.*

Padua, Biblioteca Civica. MS C.M.215. [*Miscellanea.*] Incl. Albertano da Brescia, *De Doctrina Dicendi*, fols. 1ʳ–18ᵛ; id., *De Amore et Dilectione Dei*, fols. 18ᵛ–46ᵛ; *De Natura Animalium*, fols. 46ᵛ–53ʳ.

Padua, Biblioteca Universitaria. MS 469. [*Psalmi et Orationes.*] Incl. "Psalmi Penitentiales," fols. 3ʳ–11ᵛ; [Psalmi Graduales], fols. 12ʳ–20ʳ; "Officium Sancte Marie," fols. 65ʳ–95ᵛ; "Litanie et Orationes," fols. 96ʳ–116ᵛ.

————. MS 717. [*Speculum Exemplorum.*]

————. MS 1359. *Ordinamenta [Fratalie Notariorum Vicentinorum, 1272–1304].*

Parma, Biblioteca Palatina. MS Par. 44. *Rituale delle monache benedettine di Sant'Alessandro in Parma.* Incl. "Missa pro Pugnatoribus."

————. MS Par. 996. [*Missale ad Usum Ecclesiae Mutinensis.*]

Piacenza, Biblioteca Comunale. MS Pallestrelli 323. *Libellus Verberatorum Sancte Marie de Placentia, 1317.*

Pisa, Biblioteca Cateriniana del Seminario Arcivescovile. MS 139. [*Miscellanea.*] Incl. "Miracula de Beata Virgine," fols. 136ᵛ–150ᵛ.

————. MS 177. *Biblia.* Incl. [Expositio Symboli], fols. 3ʳ–4ʳ; [Themata in Articulis Fidei], fols. 4ʳ–6ʳ; "Themata in Festivitatibus Sanctorum," fols. 6ʳ–10ʳ.

Ravenna, Biblioteca Comunale Classense. MS 95. *Opusculum Liturgicum Anecdotum.*

San Gimignano, Biblioteca Comunale. MS 3. *Ordo Officiorum Vulterranae Ecclesiae Plebis Sancti Geminiani.*

Siena, Biblioteca Comunale degli Intronati. MS F.VIII.12. *Breviarium Fratrum Minorum.* Incl. "In Festo et Translatione Beatissimi Ansani Martiris," fols. 573ʳ–81ᵛ.

————. MS G.I.2. Incl. [*Vita Sancti Galgani*], fols. 195ʳ–96ᵛ.

————. MS G.V.8. *Ordo Officiorum Ecclesiae Senensis.*

————. MS G.X.17. *Essempla Sanctorum et Philosophorum.* Incl. "Disputatio inter Christum et Diabolum de Liberatione Hominis," fols. 201ʳ–202ᵛ.

————. MS I.V.10. Simone di Cascia, OSA. *Spositione sopra de' vangelii e' quali frate Giovanni da Salerno de' frati romitani di santo Agostino extrasse e reduxe in volgare.* Incl. Filippo di Leonardo of Siena, OSA, "Esempio d'una donna della citta di Siena che fu lisciata dal diavolo," fols. 1ʳ–2ᵛ.

————. MS I.VIII.21. [*Orationi.*]

Verona, Biblioteca Capitolare. MS LXXXIV. *De Divinis Officiis et Missis per Annum.*

————. MS XCIV. *Carpsum sive Ordo Veronensis Ecclesie.* Incl. "Ordo Reconciliationis Penitenitum," fols. 88ʳ–94ᵛ.

————. MS CLXVIII. *Flores Moralium Auctoritatum.*

————. MS CXCIX. *Liber Iuris Civilis Civitatis Verone.*

————. MS DCCXXXVI. *Ordo Benedicendi seu Rituale ad Usum Ecclesie Pisane.* Incl. "Benedictiones," fols. 2ʳ–8ᵛ; "Ordo ad Commundicandum Infirmum," fols. 8ʳ–12ʳ; "Ordo ad Ungendum Infirmum," fols. 12ʳ–19ᵛ; "Ordo Commendationis Anime," fols. 19ᵛ–30ʳ; "Orationes pro Defunctis," fols. 30ʳ–54ᵛ; "Ordo Processionis," fols. 55ᵛ–57ᵛ.

————. MS MCIX. *Manuale sive Rituale Antiquum Veronensis Ecclesiae.* Incl. "Litanie, fols. 1ʳ–4ʳ; "Ordo ad Catecuminum Faciendum," fols. 4ᵛ–15ʳ; "Ordo ad Penitenitam Dandam," fols. 15ʳ–20ᵛ; "Canones de Homicidiis et de Ieiuniis," fols. 20ᵛ–28ᵛ; "Ordo ad Visitandum Infirmum," fols. 28ᵛ–41ʳ; "Commendatio Anime," fols. 41ʳ–55ʳ; "Benedictiones," fols. 55ʳ–71ᵛ.

Verona, Biblioteca Civica. MS 415. *Orationi inanti e dopo la comunione.*

Vicenza, Biblioteca Civica Bertoliana. MS 526. Guido of Vicenza. *Versus de Dominicis et de Alio Tempore Totius Anni.*

————. MSS 533–34. *Statuta et Ordinamenta Fratalee Notariorum Vincentie; Reformationes Fratalee Notariorum Vincentie [1273–1332].*

————. MS 564. *Statuta et Ordinamenta Communis Vincentiae, 1264.*

Volterra, Biblioteca Comunale Guarnacci. MS 222. *Libellus de Ordine Officiorum Vulterrane Ecclesie.*

————. MS 273. [*Rituale Ecclesie Volterrane.*]

LEGAL AND STATUTORY SOURCES

Acta Capitulorum Generalium Ordinis Praedicatorum 1: Ab Anno 1220 usque ad Annum 1303. [ACGOP] Edited by Benedictus Maria Reichert. MOPH, 3. Rome: Polyglotta, 1898.

"Acta contra Armanum [Punzilupum]." Edited by Gabriele Zanella. *Itinerari ereticali: Patari e catari tra Rimini e Verona,* Studi storici, 153. Rome: Istituto Storico Italiano per il Medio Evo, 1986. 48–102.

Acta S. Officii Bononie ab Anno 1291 usque ad Annum 1310. [*ASOB*] Edited by Lorenzo Paolini and Raniero Orioli. 2 vols. Rome: Istituto Storico Italiano per il Medio Evo, 1982.

Alberto of Castellario. "Inquisicio que Fit et Fieri Intenditur per Fratrem Albertum de Castelario de Cuneo Inquisitorem (1335)." Edited by Grado G. Merlo. *Eretici e inquisitori nella società piemontese del trecento.* Turin: Claudiana, 1977. 163–255.

Aquileia (ecclesiastical province). *Aquilejense Concilium a Raymundo Patriarca Aquilejensi Anno 1282 Habitum.* Mansi 24:427–38.

————. *Constitutiones Provinciales Aquilejenses Bertrandi Patriarchae Anno 1339.* [Aquileia Constitutiones] Mansi 25:1109–32.

Atti inquisitoriali [contro i Guglielmiti]. Milano 1300: I processi inquisitoriali contro le devote e i devoti di santa Guglielma, edited by Marina Benedetti. Milan: Scheiwiller, 1999. 51–305.

Bergamo. *Antiquae Collationes Statuti Veteris Civitatis Pergami.* Edited by Giovanni Finarzi. Historiae Patriae Monumenta 16: Leges Municipales 2:2. Turin: Regius, 1876. Cols. 1921–2086.

Biella. *Statuta Comunis Bugelle et Documenta Adiecta.* [Biella Stat.] Edited by Pietro Sella. Biella: Testa, 1904.

Bologna. "La Compagnia di s. Maria delle Laudi e di San Francesco di Bologna." Edited by Candido Mesini. *AFH* 52 (1959): 361–89.

————. "Costituzioni della chiesa bolognese emanate nel sinodo diocesano del 1310 al tempo del vescovo Umberto." [Bologna Synod] Edited by Leandro Novelli. *Studia Gratiana* 8 (1962): 448–552.

————. *Statuti delle società del popolo di Bologna.* [Bol. Pop. Stat.] Edited by Augusto Gaudenzi. Fonti per la storia d'Italia: Statuti secolo XIII, 4–5. Vol. 1: Società delle armi. Vol. 2: Società delle arti. Rome: Istituto Storico Italiano, 1889/96.

————. *Statuti di Bologna dell'anno 1245 all'anno 1267.* [Bologna Stat. I] Edited by Lodovico Frati. 3 vols. Bologna: n.p., 1869–77.

————. *Statuti di Bologna dell'anno 1288.* [Bologna Stat. II] Edited by Gina Fasoli and Pietro Sella. Studi e testi, 73 and 85. 2 vols. Vatican City: Biblioteca Apostolica Vaticana, 1937–39.

Brescia. *Statuti di Brescia.* [Brescia Stat.] Edited by Federico Odorici. Turin: Paravia, 1877.

Corpus Iuris Canonici. 2d ed. Edited by E. Friedberg. 2 vols. Leipzig: Tauchnitz, 1879–81.

Cortona (bishop). "Visite pastorali a Cortona nel trecento." Edited by Noemi Meoni. *Archivio storico italiano* 129 (1971): 232–56.

Cremona. *Dei documenti storici e letterari di Cremona.* Edited by Francesco Robolotti. Cremona: Feraboli, 1857.

Cremona (cathedral chapter). "Gli statuti dei canonici della cattedrale di Cremona del 1247." [Cremona Cath. Stat.] Edited by Francesco Novati. *Archivio storico lombardo* 30 (1903): 451–60.

Ferrara. *Statuta Ferrariae Anno* MCCLXXXVII. [Ferrara Stat.] Deputazione provinciale ferrarese di storia patria: Monumenti 3. Modena: Casa di Risparmio di Ferrara, 1955.

Ferrara (clergy). *Constitutiones Factae a Parochis Civitatis Ferrariensis pro Suae Congregationis Regimine, Anno 1278.* [Ferrara Clergy Const.] *AIMA* 6:433–40.

Florence. *Statuti della Repubblica fiorentina.* [Florence Stat.] Edited by Romolo Caggese. Vol. 1: Capitano del popolo (1322–25). Vol. 11: Podestà (1325). Florence: Galileiana, 1910–20.

Franceschini, Adriano. *I frammenti epigrafici degli statuti di Ferrara del 1173 venuti in luce nella cattedrale.* Ferrara: Deputazione Provinciale Ferrarese di Storia Patria, 1969.

Giacomo Benfatti. *Li statuti et ordinatione per la compagnia de' fratelli disciplinanti in del loco de Sancta Maria de la Misericordia.* Edited by Augustine Thompson. In "New Light on Bl. Giacomo Benfatti, Bishop of Mantua, and the Mantua Disciplinati," *AFP* 69 (1999): 161–79.

Grado (ecclesiastical province). *Concilium Gradense in quo Plura tum ad Disiciplinam Ecclesiasticam cum ad Divinorum Officiorum Ritus Clerive Mores Pertinentia Sancita Sunt et Synodus Torcellana in qua Praedicti Gradensis Concilii Constitutiones Promulgatae Sunt.* [Grado Council] Mansi 24:1163–72.

Hostiensis (Enrico of Susa). *Summa Aurea.* Venice: Sessa, 1570.

Imola. *Statuti di Imola del secolo* XIV 1: Statuti della città (1334). Edited by Serafino Gaddoni. Corpus Statutorum Italicorum, 13. Milan: Hoepli, 1931.

"Inquisitio quam fecit Albertus de Baxiano (1332)." In Arnaldo Segarizzi, "Contributo alla storia di Fra Dolcino e degli eretici trentini," *Tridentum* 3 (1900): 292–97.

"Instrumentum Litis de Matricitate." Edited by Giangiuseppina Valsecchi. *"Interrogatus . . . Respondit": Storia di un processo del xii secolo.* Bergamo: Biblioteca Civica, 1989. 127–271.

Liber Vite. [Piacenza Battuti Stat. (1317)] Edited by C. Mesini. In "Statuti piacentini-parmensi dei disciplinati," *Archivio storico per le province parmensi* 12 (1960): 55–70.

Lombardy (ecclesiastical province). *Constitutiones Domini Coelestini Legati in Lombardia.* Mansi 24:881–86.

Lottieri della Tosa. *Il codice di Lottieri della Tosa.* Edited by Giovanni Lucchesi. Faenza: Banca Popolare di Faenza, 1979.

Lucca. *Statuto del commune di Lucca dell'anno* MCCCVIII. [Lucca Stat.] Edited by Salvatore Bongi and Leone Del Prete. Memorie e documenti per servire alla storia di Lucca, 3:3. Lucca: Giusti, 1867.

Lucca (diocese). *Constitutiones Domini Lucani Episcopi.* [Lucca Synod (1300)] In "La sinodo lucchese di Enrico del Carretto," edited by Raoul Manselli. *Miscellanea Gilles Gérard Meersseman.* Edited by Michele Maccarrone et al. Italia Sacra, 15. Padua: Antenore, 1970. 1:210–46.

———. *Dei sinodi della diocesi di Lucca: Dissertazioni.* Edited by Paolino Dinelli. Memorie e documenti per servire all'istoria del ducato di Lucca, 7. Lucca: Bertini, 1834.

———. *Lucana Synodus sub Henrico Lucensi Episcopo circa Annum 1308 Habita.* [Lucca Synod (1308)] Mansi 25:173–98.

Mansi, Giovanni Domenico, ed. *Sacrorum Conciliorum Nova et Amplissima Collectio.* [Mansi] 54 vols. 1901. Reprint, Graz: Academische Druck, 1960.

Mantua. *Statuta Dominorum Raynaldi Botironi Fratrum de Bonacolsis, Anno 1303.* [Mantua Stat.] Edited by Carlo d'Arco. *Studi intorno al municipio di Mantova dall'origine di questa fino all'anno 1863; Ai quali fanno seguito documenti inediti o rari.* Mantua: Gaustalla, 1871–74. 2:45–309; 3:5–299.

Mantua (cathedral chapter). "Constitutiones Antiquae Aecclesiae Mantuanae." Edited by Petro Torelli. *L'archivio capitolare della cattedrale di Mantova fino alla caduta dei Bonacolsi.* Pubblicazioni della R. Accademia virgiliana di Mantova, serie 1: Monumenti 3. Verona: Mondadori, 1924. 230–34.

Milan. *Gli atti del comune di Milano fino all'anno* MCCXVI. Edited by Cesare Mamaresi. Monumenta Historiae Patriae 16: Leges Municipales 2. Milan: Capriolo, 1919.

————. *Liber Consuetudinum Mediolani Anni MCCXVI.* Edited by Giulio Porro Labertenghi. Historiae Patriae Monumenta 16: Leges Municipales 2:1. Turin: Regius, 1876. Cols. 859–960.

Milan (ecclesiastical province). *Concilium Mediolanense in Causa Disciplinae Ecclesiasticae Habitum Anno Domini 1287.* [Milan Council (1287)] Mansi 24:867–82.

————. *Synodus Provincialis Pergami habita in Castono sive Cassono Mediolani Archiepiscopo anno MCCCXI.* Edited by Carlo Castiglioni. *RIS²* 9:3.

Modena. *Respublica Mutinensis (1306–1307).* [Modena Stat. (1306/7)] Edited by Emilio Paolo Vicini. 2 vols. Milan: Hoepli, 1932.

————. *Statuta Civitatis Mutine Anno 1327: Testo.* [Modena Stat. (1327)] Edited by Cesare Campori. Monumenta di storia patria delle province modenesi: Serie degli statuti, 1. Parma: Fiaccadori, 1864.

Novara (diocese). *Canones Episcopales Ecclesie Novariensis.* [Novara Synod II] Edited by Giuseppe Briacca. *Gli statuti sinodali novaresi di Papiniano della Rovere (a. 1298).* Milan: Vita e Pensiero, 1971. 168–279.

————. "Per la storia della chiesa novese: Gli statuti del vescovo Gerardo (1209–1211) con le aggiunte del vescovo Sigebaldo (1249–1268)." [Novara Synod I] Edited by Carlo Salsotto. *Bollettino storico per la provincia di Novara* 44 (1953): 28–35.

Padua. *Statuti del comune di Padova dal secolo XII all'anno 1285.* [Padua Stat.] Edited by Andrea Gloria. Padua: Sacchetto, 1873.

————. "Statuti extravaganti [padovani]." Edited by Maria Antonietta Zorzi. *L'ordinamento comunale padovano nella seconda metà del secolo XIII: Studio storico con documenti inediti.* Miscellanea di storia veneta 5:3. Venice: Deputazione di Storia Patria per le Venezie, 1931. 199–223.

Padua (diocese). *Constitutiones Paduanae ab Ildebrandino Paduano Episcopo in Synodo Anni 1339 Conditae.* [Padua Synod] Mansi 25:1131–44.

Parma. *Statuta Communis Parmae ab Anno 1266 ad Annum circiter 1304.* [Parma Stat. II] Monumenta Historica ad Provincias Parmensem et Placentinam Pertinentia, 1. Parma: Fiaccadori, 1857.

————. *Statuta Communis Parmæ ab Anno 1316 ad 1325.* [Parma Stat. III] Monumenta Historica ad Provincias Parmensem et Placentinam Pertinentia, 1. Parma: Fiaccadori, 1859.

————. *Statuta Communis Parmae Digesta Anno 1255.* [Parma Stat. I] Monumenta Historica ad Provincias Parmensem et Placentinam Pertinentia, 1. Parma: Fiaccadori, 1856.

Perugia (diocese). *Synodus Perusina sub Episcopo Fr. Francisco circa Annum 1320 Habita.* Mansi 25:639–48.

Piacenza. *Statuta Antiqua Mercatorum Placentiae. Statuta Varia Civitatis Placentiae,* Monumenta Historica ad Provincias Parmensem et Placentinam Pertinentia, 1. Parma: Fiaccadori, 1855. 3–184.

Piacenza (clergy). *Statuta Clericorum Placentiae.* [Piacenza Stat. Cler.] *Statuta Varia Civitatis Placentiae.* Monumenta Historica ad Provincias Parmensem et Placentinam Pertinentia, 1. Parma: Fiaccadori, 1855. 529–55.

Pisa. *Statuti inediti della città di Pisa dal XII al XIV secolo.* [Pisa Stat.] Edited by Francesco Bonaini. Vol. I: Statutes of 1275 and 1286. Vol. II: Statutes of 1233–81 and 1313–23. Florence: Vieusseux, 1854–70.

Pistoia (diocese). *Constitutiones Synodi Dioecesanae Pistoriensis sub Episcopo Ermanno Editae Anno 1308.* Mansi 25:169–74.

Ravenna. *Statuto del secolo XIII del comune di Ravenna.* [Ravenna Stat.] Edited by Andrea Zoli and Silvio Bernicoli. Ravenna: Ravegnana, 1904.

Ravenna (ecclesiastical province). *Concilium Ravennate I Causa Reformandae Disciplinae Celebratum Anno Domini 1286.* [Ravenna Council (1286)] Mansi 24:615–26.

————. *Concilium Ravennate II pro Disciplina et Moribus Ecclesiae Reformandis Celebratum Anno 1311.* [Ravenna Council (1311)] Mansi 25:449–76.

————. *Concilium Ravennate III de Disciplina Ecclesiastica Celebratum Anno 1314.* [Ravenna Council (1314)] Mansi 25:535–50.

————. *Concilium Ravennate IV Celebratum Bononiae Anno 1317.* [Ravenna Council (1317)] Mansi 25:599–628.

Reggio. *Consuetudini e statuti reggiani del secolo XIII.* [Reggio Stat.] Edited by Aldo Cerlini. Milan: Hoepli, 1933.

Regula et Constituciones Regule Congregationis et Elemosine Fratrum Sancte Marie Nove cum Indulgentie eidem Regule Concesse in Novara. [Novara Battuti Stat. (XIV)] Edited by Pier Giorgio Longo. In "Penitenti, battuti, devoti in Novara tra XIII e XVI secolo (Documenti e appunti per uno studio)," *Bollettino storico per la provincia di Novara* 72 (1981): 278–85.

Robolini, Giuseppe. *Notizie appartenenti alla storia della sua patria.* Pavia: Fusi, 1832.

San Gimignano. "Statuti del comune di San Gimignano compilati nel 1255." [San Gimignano Stat.] Edited by Luigi Pecori. *Storia della terra di San Gimignano.* Florence: Galileiana, 1853. 662–741.

Siena. *Il constituto del comune di Siena dell'anno 1262.* [Siena Stat. 1] Edited by Lodovico Zdekauer. Milan: Hoepli, 1897.

————. *Costituto del comune di Siena volgarizzato nel MCCCIX–MCCCX.* [Siena Stat. II] Edited by Alessandro Lisini. 2 vols. Siena: Lazzari, 1903.

Statuti di confraternite religiose di Padova nel Medioevo: Testi, studio introduttivo e cenni storici. Edited by Giuseppina De Sandre Gasparini. Padua: Istituto per la Storia Ecclesiastica, 1974. Incl. "Statuti della Confraternita dei Servi di Dio e della s. Madre del Duomo," 1298 (Statuti D), 10–23; "Statuti della Confraternita di s. Lucia," 1334 (Statuti L), 67–77.

"Gli statuti di un'antica congregazione francescana di Brescia." Edited by P. Guerrini. *AFH* 1 (1908): 544–68.

"Statutum Obizonis Marchionis Estensis et Populi Ferrariensis contra Flagellantes Anno 1269." *AIMA* 6:471–74.

Treviso. *Gli statuti del comune di Treviso.* [Treviso Stat.] Edited by Giuseppe Liberali. Monumenti storici pubblicati dalla Deputazione di storia patria per le Venezie, n.s., 4. 2 vols. Venice: Deputazione di Storia Patria, 1951.

Vercelli. *Statuta Communis Vercellarum ab Anno MCCLXI.* [Vercelli Stat.] Edited by Giovambatista Adriani. Historiae Patriae Monumenta 16: Leges Municipales 2:2, cols. 1089–389. Turin: Regius, 1876.

Verona. *Liber Juris Civilis Urbis Veronae.* [Verona Stat. 1] Edited by Bartolomeo Campagnola. Verona: Bernum, 1728.

————. *Gli statuti veronesi del 1276 colle correzioni e le aggiunte fino al 1323 (Cod. Campostrini, Bibl. Civica di Verona).* [Verona Stat. II] Edited by Gino Sandri. Monumenti storici pubblicati dalla Deputazione di storia patria per le Venezie, n.s., 3. Venice: Deputazione di Storia Patria, 1940.

Vicenza. *Statuti del comune di Vicenza MCCLXIV.* [Vicenza Stat.] Edited by Fedele Lampertico. Monumenti storici pub. dalla Deputazione veneta di storia patria, ser. 2: Statuti 1. Venice: Deputazione Veneta, 1886.

Volterra. *Statuti di Volterra (1210–1224).* [Volterra Stat.] Edited by Enrico Fiumi. Florence: Casa di Risparmio, 1951.

LITURGICAL SOURCES

Carpsum. L'orazionale dell'archidiacono Pacifico e il Carpsum del cantore Stefano: Studi e testi sulla liturgia del duomo di Verona. Edited, with an introductory study, by G. G. Meersseman, E. Adda, and J. Deshusses. Spicilegium Friburgense, 21. Fribourg: Edizioni Universitarie, 1974. 203–312.

Guillelmus Durandus. *Rationale Divinorum Officiorum.* Edited by A. Davril and T. M. Thibodeau. Corpus Christianorum Continuatio Mediaevalis, 140–140a. 2 vols. Turnout: Brepols, 1995–98.

Manuale Ambrosianum ex Codice Saec. xi olim in Usum Canonicae Vallis Travalliae. Edited by Marco Magistretti. Monumenta Veteris Liturgiae Ambrosianae, 2–3. 2 vols. Milan: Hoepli, 1904–5.

Martène, Edmund. *De Antiquis Ecclesiae Ritibus.* 2d ed. 4 vols. Antwerp, 1736. Reprint, Hildesheim: Olms, 1967.

Ordo Officiorum della cattedrale [volterrana] (anno 1161). De Sancti Hugonis Actis Liturgicis. Edited by Mario Bocci. Documenti della Chiesa volterrana, 1. Florence: Olschki, 1984. 29–229.

Ordo Officiorum Ecclesiae Senensis ab Oderico eiusdem Ecclesiae Canonico Anno mccxiii Compositus. [Ordo Senensis.] Edited by Giovanni Crisostomo Tombelli. Bologna: Longi, 1766.

Peter the Chanter. *De Oratione et Speciebus Illius. The Christian at Prayer: An Illustrated Prayer Manual Attributed to Peter the Chanter (d. 1197).* Edited by Richard C. Trexler. Binghamton, N.Y.: Medieval and Renaissance Texts and Studies, 1987. 178–234.

Le pontifical romain au Moyen Âge. Edited by Michel Andrieu. Studi e testi, 86–88. 3 vols. Vatican City: Biblioteca Apostolica Vaticana, 1938–40.

Pontificale Guillielmi Durandi. [Pont. Rom. (Durandus)] *Le pontifical romain au Moyen Âge,* 3:327–662.

Pontificale Romanum Saeculi xii. [Pont. Rom. (xii)] *Le pontifical romain au Moyen Âge,* 1:123–302.

Pontificale secundum Consuetudinem et Usum Romanae Curiae. [Pont. Rom. (xiii)] *Le pontifical romain au Moyen Âge,* 2:327–522.

Rituale di Hugo [di Volterra], secolo xii con aggiunte. De Sancti Hugonis Actis Liturgicis. Edited by Mario Bocci. Documenti della Chiesa volterrana, 1. Florence: Olschki, 1984. 275–327.

Sicardo of Cremona. *Mitrale; seu, De Officiis Ecclesiasticis Summa.* PL 213:13–432.

HAGIOGRAPHIC SOURCES

Acta Alia [B. Joannis Firmani]. AS 36 (Aug. ii), 470–74.

Acta [B. Joannis Firmani sive Alvernae]. AS 36 (Aug. ii), 459–69.

Acta [B. Torelli Puppiensis]. AS 8 (Mar. ii), 495–99.

Acta [S. Contardi Peregrini]. AS 11 (Apr. ii), 444–48.

Acta Sanctorum quotquot Toto Orbe Coluntur vel a Catholicis Scriptoribus Celebrantur ex Latinis et Graecis Aliarumque Gentium Antiquis Monumentis Collecta, Digesta, Illustrata. [AS] 2d ed. Edited by Godefridus Henschenius et al. 60 vols. in 70. Paris: Palme, etc., 1867–1940.

Antonino of Florence. "De Joanne Bono Cive Mantuano." (*Chronicae,* 24.13.) *AS* 57 (Oct. ix), 746–47.

Apographum Processus Informationis circa Vitam, Mortem, Translationem et Miracula B. Odonis. In "Documenta de B. Odone Novariensi Ordinis Carthusiani," *Analecta Bollandiana* 1 (1882): 324–54.

Bartolomeo Albizzi. *Legenda Sancti Gerardi Ordinis Fratrum Minorum.* Edited by Filippo Rotolo. In "La leggenda del b. Gerardo Cagnoli, O. Min. (1267–1342) di Fra' Bartolomeo Albizzi, O. Min. (+1351)," *Miscellanea Francescana* 57 (1957): 397–46.

Benincasa of Pisa. *Vita [S. Raynerii Pisani].* AS 24 (Jun. iv), 345–81.

Bernardo Balbi. *Vita [S. Lanfranci Episcopi Papiensis].* AS 25 (Jun. v), 533–42.

Biagio of Faenza. *Vita [S. Humilitatis Abbatissae].* AS 18 (May v), 207–23.

Bongiovanni of Lodi. *Vita Beati Gualterii Confessoris.* Edited and translated by Alessandro Caretta. In "La vita di s. Gualtiero di Lodi," *Archivio storico lodigiano* 88 (1968): 14–27.

Corrado of Cividale. *Vita Devotissimae Benevenutae de Foro-Julii. AS* 61 (Oct. XIII), 152–85.

Cristoforo of Parma. *Legenda Beati Francisci de Senis Ordinis Servorum B. M. V.* Edited by Peregrine Soulier. *Analecta Bollandiana* 14 (1895): 174–97.

De Vita et Actibus Galgani. Edited by Fedor Schneider. In "Der Einsiedler Galgan von Chiusdino und die Anfänge von S. Galgano," *Quellen und Forschungen aus italienischen Archiven und Bibliotheken* 17 (1914–24): 71–77.

Giordano of Città di Castello. *Vita Beati Ubaldi Eugubini Episcopi.* Edited by François Bolbeau. In "La vita di sant'Ubaldo, vescovo di Gubbio, attribuita a Giordano di Città di Castello," *Bollettino della Deputazione di storia patria per l'Umbria* 74 (1977): 95–112.

Giovanni of Orvieto. *Vita [S. Petri Parentii]. AS* 18 (May v), 86–99.

Giovanni Gorini. *[Legenda de Vita et Obitu Beati Petri de Fulgineo.]* Chaps. 1–2 (i.e., 1–9a): *AS* 31 (Jul. IV), 665–68. Chaps. 9b–11: *Analecta Bollandiana* 8 (1889): 365–69.

Gisberto of Alessandria et al. *Vita [B. Ambrosii Senensis]. AS* 9 (Mar. III), 181–200.

Giunta Bevegnati. *Legenda de Vita et Miraculis Beatae Margaritae de Cortona.* Edited by Fortunato Iozzelli. Grottaferrata: Collegium Bonaventurae ad Claras Aquas, 1997.

Hippolito of Florence. *Miracula intra Triennium ab Obitu Patrata [B. Humilianae de Cerchis]. AS* 17 (May IV), 402–7.

Inquisitio Facta Cremonae per d. Homobonum Episcopum Cremonensem de Vita et Moribus b. Joannis Cazefronte Abbatis Sancti Laurentii de Cremona postea Episcopi Vicentini. Edited by Alessandro Schiavo. *Della vita e dei tempi del b. Giovanni Cacciafronte cremonese, vescovo di Mantova poi di Vicenza.* Vicenza: Paroni, 1866. 235–60.

Jordan of Saxony. *Libellus de Principiis Ordinis.* Edited by M.-H. Laurent. MOPH, 16: Monumenta Historica Sancti Patris Nostri Dominici, 2. Rome: Institutum Historicum Fratrum Praedicatorum, 1935. 25–98.

Legenda Beatae Christianae Virginis de Castro S. Crucis Vallis Arni Lucanae Dioecesis. Edited by Giovanni Lami. *Vita della b. Oringa Cristiana fondatrice del venerabile convento di S. Maria Novello e di S. Michele Arcangelo dell'Ordine Agostiniano nella terra di Santa Croce in Toscana.* Florence: Albiziniani, 1769. 189–258.

Legenda Beati Fratris Venturini Ordinis Praedicatorum. Edited by A. Grion. *Bergomum* 30 (1956): 38–110.

Legenda B. Margaritae de Castello. Edited by M.-H. Laurent. In "La plus ancienne légende de la b. Marguerite di Città di Castello," *AFP* 10 (1940): 115–28.

Miracula [B. Ambrosii Senensis]. AS 9 (Mar. III), 200–209.

Pierdomenico of Baone. *Vita B. Henrici Baucenensis. AS* 22 (Jun. II), 365–69.

Pietro of Monterone. *Vita del beato Pietro Pettinajo da Siena.* Translated by Serafino Ferri. Edited by Maestro de Angelis. Siena: Rossi, 1802.

Pietro of Monte Rubiano. *Vita [S. Nicolai Tolentinatis]. AS* 43 (Sept. III), 644–64.

El processo della canoniçatione de sancta Chiara. Edited by Zeffirino Lazzeri. In "Il processo di canonizzazione di S. Chiara d'Assisi," *AFH* 13 (1920): 439–93.

Processus Apostolici Auctoritate Innocentii Papae IV Annis 1251, 1253, et 1254 Constructi de Vita, Virtutibus et Miraculis B. Joannis Boni Mantuani. AS 57 (Oct. IX), 778–885.

Processus Canonizationis B. Ambrosii Massani. AS 68 (Nov. IV), 571–608.

Processus Canonizationis S. Dominici [Bononiae]. Edited by M.-H. Laurent. MOPH, 16: Monumenta Historica Sancti Patris Nostri Dominici, 2. Rome: Institutum Historicum Fratrum Praedicatorum, 1935. 123–67.

Processus Miraculorum B. Philippi [Benitii]. Edited by Arcangelo Giani. *Annales Sacri Ordinis Fratrum Servorum Beatae Mariae Virginis.* Florence: Giunta, 1618. Vol. 1, fols. 51^r–55^r.

Raimondo of Capua. *Legenda Beate Agnetis de Monte Policiano.* Edited by Silvia Nocentini. Florence: Galluzzo, 2001.

Recupero of Arezzo. *Summarium Virtutum et Miracula [B. Ambrosii Senensis]*. *AS* 9 (Mar. III), 209–39.

Rufino of Piacenza. *Vita et Miracula B. Raymundi Palmarii*. *AS* 33 (Jul. VI), 644–57.

Sermone de Inventione Reliquiarum [S. Petronii]. Edited by Francisco Lanzoni. *San Petronio vescovo di Bologna nella storia e nella legenda*. Rome: Pustet, 1907. 240–50.

Summarium Processus Vitae et Miraculorum B. Simonis a Collazzone Discipuli S. Francesci Fabricatum A. 1252 et 1253. Edited by D. M. Faloci Pulignani. In "Il b. Simone da Collazzone e il suo processo nel 1254," *Miscellanea Francescana* 12 (1910): 117–32.

Tomasso of Bossolasco. *Vita [B. Sibyllinae Papaiensis]*. *AS* 9 (Mar. III), 68–71.

Umiltà of Faenza. "Sermones." Edited and translated by Adele Simonetii. *I sermoni di Umiltà da Faenza: Studio e edizione*. Spoleto: Centro Italiano di Studi sull'Alto Medioevo, 1995.

Vita B[eatae] Iohannae de Signa. *AS* 68 (Nov. IV), 283–88.

Vita Beatae Margaritae Virginis de Civitate Castelli. Edited by A. Poncelet. *Analecta Bollandiana* 19 (1900): 23–36.

Vita [Beati Andreae de Galleranis]. *AS* 9 (Mar. III), 53–57.

Vita Beati Facii. Edited by André Vauchez. In "Sainteté laïque au XIIIᵉ siècle: La vie du bien-heureux Facio de Crémone (v. 1196–1272)," *Mélanges de l'École française de Rome: Moyen Âge–temps modernes* 84 (1972): 36–49.

Vita [Beati Jacobi Veneti Ordinis Praedicatorum]. *AS* 20 (May VII), 452–66.

Vita Beati Nevoloni. Edited by Francesco Lanzoni. In "Una vita del beato Nevolone faentino, terziario francescano," *AFH* 6 (1913): 645–53.

Vita di s. Omobono. Edited by Giuseppe Bertoni. In "Di una vita di s. Omobono del secolo XIV," *Bollettino storico cremonese* 3 (1938): 163–75.

Vita di san Petronio con un'appendice di testi inediti del secoli XIII e XIV. Edited by Maria Corti. Scelta di curiosità letterarie inedite o rare del secolo XIII al XIX, 260. Bologna: Commissione per i Testi di Lingua, 1962.

Vita di s. Petronio vescovo di Bologna. Edited by Giuseppe Guidicini. *Notizie relative ai vescovi di Bologna da san Zama ad Oppizzoni*. Bologna: Compositori, 1883. 75–96.

Vita [Sanctae Bonae Virginis Pisanae]. *AS* 20 (May VII), 142–61.

Vita [Sanctae Zitae Virginis Lucencis]. *AS* 12 (Apr. III), 504–15.

Vita Sancte Viridiane. Edited by Olinto Pogni. *Vita di S. Verdian d'incognito autore estratta dal codice latino trecentesco esistente nella Biblioteca Medicea Laurenziana di Firenze dal fiorentino monaco Biagio*. Empoli: Lambruschini, 1936. 7–13.

Vita Sancti Galgani. Edited by Eugenio Susi. *L'eremita cortese: San Galgano fra mito e storia nell'agiografia toscana del XII secolo*. Spoleto: Centro Italiano di Studi sull'Alto Medioevo, 1993. 185–213.

Vita Sancti Homoboni. Edited by Francesco Saverio Gatta. In "Un antico codice reggiano su Omobono il 'santo populare' di Cremona," *Bollettino storico cremonese* 7 (1942): 111–15.

Vita Sancti Lucensis Confessoris. Edited by Martino Bertagna. In "Note e documenti intorno a s. Lucchese," *AFH* 62 (1969): 452–57.

Vita S[ancti] Petri Martyris Ordinis Praedicatorum. Edited by Ambrogio Taegio. *AS* 12 (Apr. III), 694–727.

Vita [Sancti Pilingotti Urbinatis]. *AS* 21 (Jun. I), 145–51.

Vita vel Acta Sancti Petronii Episcopi et Confessoris. Edited by Francisco Lanzoni. *San Petronio vescovo di Bologna nella storia e nella legenda*. Rome: Pustet, 1907. 219–40.

Vitae Fratrum Ordinis Praedicatorum. Edited by Benedict Maria Reichart. MOPH, 1. Louvain: Charpentier & Schoonjans, 1896. (Translated by Placid Conway as *Lives of the Brethren of the Order of Preachers, 1206–1259*. New York: Benziger, 1924.)

Vitale de' Avanzi. *Leggenda del beato Pellegrino*. Edited by Benedetto Angelo Maria Canali. *Vita del beato Pellegrino Laziosi da Forlì*. Lucca: Marescandoli, 1725. 165–67.

Vito of Cortona. *Vita [B. Humilianae de Cerchis]*. *AS* 17 (May IV), 385–402.

OTHER MEDIEVAL SOURCES

Alberto Milioli. *Liber de Temporibus et Aetatibus.* Edited by Oswald Holder-Egger. *MGH.SS* 31:353–580.
Annales Foroiuliensis. Edited by Wilhelm Arndt. *MGH.SS* 19:196–222.
Annales Sanctae Iustinae Patavini. Edited by Philip Jaffé. *MGH.SS* 19:148–93.
Annales Veteres Mutinenses ab Anno 1131 usque ad 1336. Edited by Lodovico Antonio Muratori. *RIS* 11:53–86.
Annales Veteres Veronenses. Edited by Carlo Cipolla. *Archivio Veneto* 9 (1875): 89–98.
Antiquitates Italicae Medii Aevi. [*AIMA*] Edited by Lodovico Antonio Muratori. 6 vols. 1738–42. Reprint, Bologna: Forni, 1965.
Auvray, Lucien. *Les registres de Grégoire IX.* 3 vols. Paris: Thorin, 1896–1955.
Bartolomeo of Vicenza. *Sermones de Beata Virgine (1266).* Edited by Laura Gaffuri. Padua: Antenore, 1993.
Bocchi, Francesco. "Il necrologio della canonica di Santa Maria di Reno e di San Salvatore di Bologna: Note su un testo quasi dimenticato." *AMDSPPR*, n.s., 24 (1973): 53–132.
Bonvesin de la Riva. *Vita Scholastica.* Edited by Anežka Vidmanová-Schmidtová. *Liber Quinque Clavium Sapientiae.* Leipzig: Teubner, 1969. 41–102.
Breve Chronicon Mantuanum. Edited by Carlo d'Arco. In "Cronichette di Mantova di autore anonimo dal 1095 al 1299," *Archivio storico italiano,* n.s., 1:2 (1855): 25–58.
Bullarium Franciscanum Romanorum Pontificum. [*BF*] Edited by Giovanni Giacinto Sbaraglia. 7 vols. Rome: Propaganda Fidei, 1758–68.
Bullarium Ordinis Fratrum Praedicatorm. [*BOP*] Edited by Thomas Ripoll and A. Brémond. 8 vols. Rome: Mainardi, 1729–40.
Chronica XXIV Generalium Ordinis Fratrum Minorum. Analecta Franciscana, 3. Quaracchi: Collegium S. Bonaventurae, 1897.
Chronicon Faventinum. See Maestro Tolosano.
Chronicon Marchiae Trevisinae et Lombardiae. Edited by L. A. Botteghi. *RIS²* 8:3.
Chronicon Parmense ab Anno 1038 usque ad Annum 1338. Edited by Giuliano Bonazzi. *RIS²* 9:9.
Corpus Chronicorum Bononiensium. [*CCB*] Edited by Albano Sorbelli. *RIS²* 18:1. Incl. *Cronaca A* detta volgarmente *Rampona* [A]; *Cronaca B* detta volgarmente *Varignana* [B]; *Cronaca* detta dei *Bolognetti* [Bol.]; Pietro and Floriano da Villola, *Cronaca* [Vill.].
Dante Alighieri. *La Commedia secondo l'antica vulgata.* Edited by Giorgio Petrocchi. 2d ed. Florence: Le Lettere, 1994.
Dossier de l'ordre de la pénitence au XIII⁴ siècle. [Meersseman, *Dossier*] Edited by Gilles Gérard Meersseman. Spicilegium Friburgense, 7. Fribourg: Editions Universitaires, 1961.
Francesco Pipino. *Chronicon ab Anno MCLXXVI usque ad Annum circiter MCCCXIV. RIS* 9:587–752.
Galvano Fiamma. *Cronica Maior Ordinis Praedicatorum.* Edited by Gundisalvo Odetto. In "La Cronaca maggiore dell'Ordine Domenicano di Galvano Fiamma: Frammenti inediti," *AFP* 10 (1940): 319–73.
———. *Manipulus Florum. RIS* 11:537–739.
Giordano of Pisa. *Quaresimale fiorentino 1305–1306.* Edited by Carlo Delcorno. Florence: Sansoni, 1974.
Giovanni de' Mussi. *Chronicon Placentinum. RIS* 16:447–634.
Giovanni Villani. *Cronica.* 8 vols. Rome: Multigrafica, 1980.
Girolamo de' Borselli. *Cronica Gestorum ac Factorum Memorabilium Civitatis Bononie.* Edited by Albano Sorbelli. *RIS²* 23:2.
Iscrizioni medievali bolognesi. Edited by Giancarlo Roversi. Bologna: Istituto Storico di Bologna, 1982.
Jacques of Vitry. *The "Historia Occidentalis" of Jacques de Vitry: A Critical Edition.* Edited by John Frederick Hinnebusch. Spicilegium Friburgense, 17. Fribourg: University Press, 1972.

Kantorowicz, Hermann. "Una festa studentesca bolognese per l'Epifania del 1289." *AMDSPPR*, 3d ser., 24 (1905/6): 321–22. "Documenti," 323–26.

Laurent of Orleans. *Somme du roi*. See Zucchero Bencivenni.

Liber de XV signi. Edited by Michele Barbi. In "D'un antico codice pisano lucchese di trattati morali." *Raccolta di studii critici dedicata ad Alessandro d'Ancona*. Florence: Barbèra, 1901. 253–59.

Liber del piato ch'ebbi Dio con l'inimico. Contrasti antichi: Cristo e Satana. Edited by Franz Roediger. Collezione di operette edite ed inedite, 14. Florence: Libreria Dante, 1887. 31–48.

Liber Regiminum Padue. Edited by Antonio Bonardi. *RIS²* 8:1:291–376.

Maestro Tolosano. *Chronicon Faventinum*. Edited by Giuseppe Rossini. *RIS²* 28:1.

Matteo Griffoni. *Memoriale Historicum de Rebus Bononiensium*. Edited by Lodovico Frati and Albano Sorbelli. *RIS²* 18:2.

Memoriale Potestatum Regiensium. [*Mem. Pot. Reg.*] Edited by Lodovico Antonio Muratori. *RIS* 8:1071–180.

Monumenta Germaniae Historica inde ab Anno Christi Quingentesimo usque ad Annum Millesimum et Quingentesimum: Scriptores. [*MGH.SS*] Edited by Georg Heinrich Pertz et al. 33 vols. in 36. 1826–1913. Reprint, Stuttgart: Hiersemann, 1976.

Muzio of Modena. *Annales Placentini Gibellini*. Edited by Georg Heinrich Pertz. *MGH.SS* 18:457–581.

Novellino. Edited by Cesare Segre. *La prosa del duecento*. La letteratura italiana: Storia e testi, 3. Milan: Ricciardi, 1959. 793–882.

Ordo Fraternitatis: Confraternite e pietà dei laici nel Medioevo. [Meersseman, *Ordo*] Edited by Gilles Gérard Meersseman, with the collaboration of Gian Piero Pacini. Italia Sacra, 24–26. 3 vols. Rome: Herder, 1977.

Parisio of Cerea. *Annales*. Edited by Philippus Jaffé. *MGH.SS* 19:2–18.

Patrologiae Latinae Cursus Completus. [*PL*] Edited by Jean-Paul Migne. 221 vols. Paris: Garnier, 1878–90.

Pietro Cantinelli. *Chronicon*. Edited by Francesco Torraca. *RIS²* 28:2.

Poesie lombarde del secolo XIII. Edited by Bernardino Biondelli. Milan: Bernardoni, 1856.

Rationes Decimarum Italiae nei secoli XIII–XIV: Aemilia, le decime dei secoli XIII e XIV. [Rat. Dec. Aem.] Edited by Angelo Merati et al. Studi e testi, 60. Vatican City: Biblioteca Apostolica Vaticana, 1933.

Rationes Decimarum Italiae nei secoli XIII–XIV: Lombardia et Pedemontium. Edited by Maurizio Rosada. Studi e testi, 324. Vatican City: Biblioteca Apostolica Vaticana, 1990.

Rationes Decimarum Italiae nei secoli XIII–XIV: Venetiae-Histria, Dalmatia. [Rat. Dec. Ven.] Edited by Pietro Sella and Giuseppe Vale. Studi e testi, 96. Vatican City: Biblioteca Apostolica Vaticana, 1941.

Regesta Honorii Papae III. Edited by Pietro Pressutti. Rome: Vaticana, 1895.

Rerum Italicarum Scriptores. [*RIS*] Edited by Lodovico Antonio Muratori. 25 vols. in 28. 1723–51. Reprint, Bologna: Forni, 1965.

Rerum Italicarum Scriptores: Raccolta degli storici italiani dal cinquecento al millecinquecento. [*RIS²*] Edited by Giosue Carducci et al. 103 vols. in 142. Città di Castello: Lapi, 1908–16.

Rolandino of Padua. *Cronica in Factis et circa Facta Marchie Trivixiane*. Edited by Antonio Bonardi. *RIS²* 8:1:3–175.

Sagacino Levalossi and Pietro Della Grazata. *Chronicon Regiense*. *RIS* 18:5–98.

Salimbene of Parma. *Cronica*. Edited by Giuseppe Scalia. 2 vols. Scrittori d'Italia, 232–33. Bari: Laterza, 1966. (Translated by Joseph L. Baird et al. as *The Chronicle of Salimbene de Adam*. Medieval and Renaissance Texts and Studies, 40. Binghamton, N.Y.: Center for Medieval and Early Renaissance Studies, 1986.)

Zucchero Bencivenni. *La sposizione di questa santa orazione del paternostro*. [From Laurent of Orleans, *Somme du roi.*] Edited by Luigi Rigoli. In *Volgarizzamento dell'esposizione del paternostro.* Florence: Piazzini, 1828.

———. *Trattatello delle virtù.* [From Laurent of Orleans, *Somme du roi.*] Edited by Luigi Barbieri. Bologna: Romagnoli, 1863.

———. *Trattato del ben vivere.* [From Laurent of Orleans, *Somme du roi.*] Edited by Giuseppe Manuzzi. Florence: Passigli, 1848.

SELECTED MODERN SCHOLARSHIP

Airaldi, Gabriella. "Il matrimonio nell'Italia medievale." *Atti dell'Accademia ligure di scienze e lettere* 34 (1977): 220–36.

Alexandre-Bidon, Danièle. "Des femmes de bonne foi: La religion des mères au Moyen Âge." *La religion de ma mère: Les femmes et la transmission de la foi.* Edited by Jean Delumeau. Paris: Cerf, 1992. 91–122.

Andrews, Frances. *The Early Humiliati.* Cambridge: Cambridge University Press, 1999.

Ariès, Philippe. *Western Attitudes Toward Death: From the Middle Ages to the Present.* Translated by Patricia M. Ranum. Baltimore: Johns Hopkins University Press, 1974.

Arnaldi, Girolamo. *Studi sui cronisti della Marca Trevigiana nell'età di Ezzelino da Romano.* Studi storici, 48–50. Rome: Istituto Storico Italiano per il Medio Evo, 1963.

Atti dell'11° Congresso internazionale di studi sull'alto Medioevo, Milano, 26–30 ottobre 1987. Spoleto: Centro Italiano di Studi sull'Alto Medioevo, 1989.

Audisio, Gabriel. *The Waldensian Dissent: Persecution and Survival, c. 1170–c. 1570.* Translated by Claire Davison. Cambridge: Cambridge University Press, 1999.

Baldelli, Ignazio. "La lauda e i disciplinati." *Rassegna della letteratura italiana* 64 (1960): 396–418.

Barbi, Michele. "D'un antico codice pisano lucchese di trattati morali." *Raccolta di studii critici dedicata ad Alessandro d'Ancona.* Florence: Barbèra, 1901. 241–59.

Barsocchini, Domenico. *Dissertazioni sopra la storia ecclesiastica lucchese.* 2 vols. Memorie e documenti per servire all'istoria del ducato di Lucca, 4–5. Lucca: Bertini, 1818–44.

Benati, Amedeo. "Armanno Pungilupo nella storia religiosa ferrarese del 1200." *Atti e memorie della Deputazione della provincia ferrarese di storia patria,* 3d ser., 4/1 (1966): 85–123.

Benvenuti Papi, Anna. *In Castro Poenitentiae: Santità e società femminile nell'Italia medievale.* Italia Sacra, 45. Rome: Herder, 1991.

———. "Santità femminile nel territorio fiorentino e lucchese: Considerazioni intorno al caso di Verdiana da Castelfiorentino." *Religiosità e società in Valdelsa nel basso Medioevo.* Florence: Società Storica della Valdelsa, 1980. 113–44.

Bertram, Martin. "Bologneser Testamente I: Die urkundliche Überlieferung." *Quellen und Forschungen aus italienischen Archiven und Bibliotheken* 70 (1990): 151–233.

———. "Bologneser Testamente II: Sondierungen in den *Libri Memoriali.*" *Quellen und Forschungen aus italienischen Archiven und Bibliotheken* 71 (1991): 193–240.

Bloch, Maurice, and Jonathan Parry, eds. *Death and the Regeneration of Life.* New York: Cambridge University Press, 1982.

Bloomfield, Morton W. *The Seven Deadly Sins: An Introduction to the History of a Religious Concept, with Special Reference to Medieval English Literature.* East Lansing: Michigan State College Press, 1952.

Bloomfield, Morton W., et al. *Incipits of Works on the Virtues and Vices.* Cambridge: Medieval Academy of America, 1979.

Blumenfeld-Kosinski, Renate, and Timea Szell, eds. *Images of Sainthood in Medieval Europe.* Ithaca: Cornell University Press, 1991.

Boesch Gajano, Sofia. *Agiografia altomedievale.* Bologna: Il Mulino, 1976.

———. "Il culto dei santi: Filologia, antropologia e storia." *Studi storici* 23 (1982): 119–36.

Boesch Gajano, Sofia, and Lucia Sebastiani, eds. *Culto dei santi, istituzioni e classi sociali in età preindustriale.* L'Aquila: Japadre, 1984.

Boldorini, A. "Aspetti e momenti della *Cura Animarum* nel basso Medioevo ligure (secc. XIII– XV) con appendice documentaria." *Archivum Ecclesiae Ianuensis* 1 (1981): 1–50.

Bornstein, Daniel. "The Uses of the Body: The Church and the Cult of Santa Margherita da Cortona." *Church History* 62 (1993): 163–77.

Boyle, Leonard. *Pastoral Care, Clerical Education, and Canon Law.* London: Variorum, 1981.

Brentano, Robert. *Two Churches: England and Italy in the Thirteenth Century.* 2d ed. Berkeley and Los Angeles: University of California Press, 1988.

Briacca, Giuseppe. *Gli statuti sinodali novaresi di Papiniano della Rovere (a. 1298).* Milan: Vita e Pensiero, 1971.

Brolis, Maria Teresa. "A Thousand and More Women: The Register of Women for the Confraternity of Misericordia Maggiore in Bergamo, 1265–1339." *Catholic Historical Review* 88 (2002): 231–46.

Brooke, Christopher. *The Medieval Idea of Marriage.* Oxford: Oxford University Press, 1991.

Browne, Pietro. "L'atteggiamento del corpo durante la Messa." *Ephemerides Liturgicae* 50 (1936): 402–14.

Butler, Alban. *Lives of the Saints.* Complete ed. Edited by Herbert Thurston and Donald Attwater. 4 vols. Westminister, Md.: Christian Classics, 1991.

Canetti, Luigi. *Gloriosa Civitas: Culto dei santi e società cittadina a Piacenza nel Medioevo.* Cristianesimo antico e medievale, 4. Bologna: Pàtron, 1993.

Cannon, Joanna, and André Vauchez. *Margherita of Cortona and the Lorenzetti: Sienese Art and the Cult of a Holy Woman in Medieval Tuscany.* University Park: Pennsylvania State University Press, 1997.

Casagrande, Carla. "La moltiplicazione dei peccati: I cataloghi dei peccati nella letteratura pastorale dei secc. XIII–XV." *La peste nera: Dati di una realtà ed elementi di una interpretazione: Atti del XXX Convegno storico internazionale dell'Accademia tudertina.* Spoleto: Centro Italiano di Studi sul Basso Medioevo, 1994. 253–84.

Casagrande, Giovanna. *Religiosità penitenziale e città al tempo dei comuni.* Rome: Istituto Storico dei Cappuccini, 1995.

———. "Un ordine per i laici: Penitenza e penitenti nel duecento." *Francesco d'Assisi e il primo secolo di storia francescana.* Turin: Einaudi, 1997. 237–52.

Centro studi e ricerche sulla antica provincia ecclesiastica ravennate. *Atti del convegno di Parma (1976).* Ravennatensia, 7. Cesena: Santa Maria del Monte, 1979.

Chiffoleau, Jacques, Lauro Martines, and Agostino Paravicini Bagliani, eds. *Riti e rituali nelle società medievali.* Spoleto: Centro Italiano di Studi sull'Alto Medioevo, 1994.

Chiovaro, Francesco. "Le mariage chrétien en occident." *Histoire vécue du peuple chrétien.* Toulouse: Pivat, 1979. 1:225–55.

Christian, William A., Jr. *Local Religion in Sixteenth-Century Spain.* Princeton: Princeton University Press, 1981.

Congar, Yves M.-J. "Saint Thomas et les archidiacres." *Revue thomiste* 57 (1957): 657–71.

La conversione alla povertà nell'Italia dei secoli XII–XIV: Atti del XXVII Convegno storico internazionale, Todi, 14–17 ottobre 1990. Spoleto: Centro Italiano di Studi sull'Alto Medioevo, 1991.

La coscienza cittadina nei comuni italiani nel duecento, 11–14 ottobre 1970. Convegni del Centro di studi sulla spiritualità medievale, 11. Todi: Accademia Tudertina, 1972.

Creytens, Raymond. "Le manuel de conversation de Philippe de Ferrare, O.P. (+ 1350?)." *AFP* 16 (1946): 105–35.

Dalla penitenza all'ascolto delle confessioni: Il ruolo dei frati mendicanti: Atti del XXIII Convegno internazionale, Assisi, 12–14 ottobre 1995. Spoleto: Centro Italiano di Studi sull'Alto Medioevo, 1996.

d'Avray, David. "Marriage Ceremonies and the Church in Italy After 1215." *Marriage in Italy, 1300–1650*. Edited by Trevor Dean and K. J. P. Lowe. Cambridge: Cambridge University Press, 1998. 107–15.

De La Roncière, Charles M. "Dans la champagne florentine au xɪv^e siècle: Les communautés chrétiennes et leurs curés." *Histoire vécue du peuple chrétien*. Toulouse: Pivat, 1979. 1:281–314.

Delumeau, Jean, ed. *La religion de ma mère: Les femmes et la transmission de la foi*. Paris: Cerf, 1992.

De Sandre Gasparini, Giuseppina. "Laici devoti fra confessione e penitenze." *Dalla penitenza all'ascolto delle confessioni: Il ruolo dei frati mendicanti: Atti del xxɪɪɪ Convegno internazionale, Assisi, 12–14 ottobre 1995*. Spoleto: Centro Italiano di Studi sull'Alto Medioevo, 1996. 211–61.

———. "Movimento dei disciplinati, confraternite e ordini mendicanti." *I frati minori e il terzo ordine: Problemi e discussione storiografiche, 17–20 ottobre 1982*. Convegni del Centro di studi sulla spiritualità medievali, 23. Todi: Accademia Tudertina, 1985. 79–114.

———. *Statuti di confraternite religiose di Padova nel Medioevo: Testi, studio introduttivo e cenni storici*. Padua: Istituto per la Storia Ecclesiastica, 1974.

Diehl, Peter D. "Overcoming Reluctance to Prosecute Heresy in Thirteenth-Century Italy." *Christendom and Its Discontents: Exclusion, Persecution, and Rebellion, 1000–1500*. Edited by Scott L. Waught and Peter D. Diehl. Cambridge: Cambridge University Press, 1996. 47–66.

Dinelli, Paolino. *Dei sinodi della diocesi di Lucca: Dissertazioni*. Memorie e documenti per servire all'istoria del ducato di Lucca 7. Lucca: Bertini, 1834.

Dondaine, Antoine. "Saint-Pierre-Martyr: Études." *AFP* 23 (1953): 67–73.

Duffy, Eamon. *The Stripping of the Altars: Traditional Religion in England, 1400–1580*. New Haven: Yale University Press, 1992.

Dupré Theseider, Eugène. "L'eresia a Bologna nei tempi di Dante." Reprinted in *Mondo cittadino e movimenti ereticali nel Medio Evo (saggi)*. Bologna: Pàtron, 1978. 261–315.

———. "Gli eretici nel mondo comunale italiano." Reprinted in *Mondo cittadino e movimenti ereticali nel Medio Evo (saggi)*. Bologna: Pàtron, 1978. 233–59.

Elliott, Dyan. *Spiritual Marriage: Sexual Abstinence in Medieval Wedlock*. Princeton: Princeton University Press, 1993.

Epstein, Steven A. *Wage Labor and Guilds in Medieval Europe*. Chapel Hill: University of North Carolina Press, 1991.

Erba, A., et al., eds. *Pievi e parrocchie in Italia nel basso Medioevo (sec. xɪɪɪ–xv)*. Italia Sacra, 35–36. 2 vols. Rome: Herder, 1984.

Fanti, Mario. "Gli inizi del movimento dei disciplinati a Bologna e la confraternita di Santa Maria della Vita." *Bollettino della Deputazione di storia patria per l'Umbria* 66 (1969): 181–232.

———. "Sulla costituzione ecclesiastica del bolognese ɪv: La decima del 1315." *AMDSPPR*, n.s., 17–19 (1965–68): 107–45.

Farina, Sandra. "I conventi mendicanti nel tessuto urbanistico di Bologna." *Storia della città* 9 (1978): 56–61.

Ferrali, Sabatino. "Pievi e clero plebano in diocesi di Pistoia." *Bullettino storico pistoiese*, 3d ser., 8 (1973): 39–62.

Fisher, J. D. C. *Christian Initiation: Baptism in the Medieval West: A Study in the Disintegration of the Primitive Rite of Initiation*. London: SPCK, 1965.

Francescanesimo e vita religiosa dei laici nel '200: Atti dell'vɪɪɪ Convegno internazionale, Assisi, 16–18 ottobre 1980. Assisi: Università di Perugia, 1981.

Frati, Lodovico. *La vita privata di Bologna nel sec. xɪɪɪ al xvɪɪɪ con appendice di documenti inediti*. Bologna: Zanichelli, 1900.

I frati minori e il terzo ordine: Problemi e discussione storiografiche, 17–20 ottobre 1982. Convegni del Centro di studi sulla spiritualità medievali, 23. Todi: Accademia Tudertina, 1985.

Gatta, Francesco Saverio. "Un antico codice reggiano su Omobono il 'santo populare' di Cremona." *Bollettino storico cremonese* 7 (1942): 107–15.

Giansante, Massimo. "Insediamenti religiosi e società urbana a Bologna dal x ad xviii secolo." *L'Archiginnasio* 89 (1994): 205–28.

Golinelli, Paolo. *Città e culto dei santi nel Medioevo italiano.* 2d ed. Bologna: CLUEB, 1996.

———. "Dal santo del potere al santo del popolo: Culti mantovani dall'alto al basso Medioevo." *Quaderni medievali* 19 (June 1985): 12–34.

———. *Indiscreta Sanctitas: Studi sui rapporti tra culti, poteri e società nel pieno Medioevo.* Studi storici, 197–98. Rome: Istituto Storico Italiano per il Medio Evo, 1988.

Grundmann, Herbert. *Religious Movements in the Middle Ages: The Historical Links Between Heresy, the Mendicant Orders, and the Women's Religious Movement in the Twelfth and Thirteenth Century, with the Historical Foundations of German Mysticism.* Translated by Steven Rowan from the 2d German ed., of 1961. Notre Dame: University of Notre Dame Press, 1995.

Guidicini, Giuseppe. *Notizie relative ai vescovi di Bologna da san Zama ad Oppizzoni.* Bologna: Compositori, 1883.

Gy, Pierre-Marie. "Du baptême pascal des petits enfants au baptême *quamprimum.*" *Culture, éducation et société: Études offertes à Pierre Riché.* Edited by Michel Sot et al. Paris: Erasme, 1990. 353–65.

———. "Le précepte de la confession annuelle et la nécessité de la confession." *Revue des sciences philosophiques et théologiques* 63 (1979): 531–47.

———. "Le précepte de la confession annuelle (Latran iv, c. 21) et la détection des hérétiques: S. Bonaventure et S. Thomas contre S. Raymond de Peñafort." *Revue des sciences philosophique et théologiques* 58 (1974): 444–50.

Hamilton, Bernard. *The Medieval Inquisition.* New York: Holmes & Meier, 1981.

Hay, Denys. *The Church in Italy in the Fifteenth Century: The Birkbeck Lectures, 1971.* Cambridge: Cambridge University Press, 1977.

Herrmann-Mascard, Nicole. *Les reliques des saints: Formation coutumière d'un droit.* Paris: Klincksieck, 1975.

Hessel, Alfred. *Storia della città di Bologna, 1116–1280.* Translated by Gina Fasoli. Bologna: ALFA, 1975.

Hyde, J. K. *Society and Politics in Medieval Italy: The Evolution of the Civic Life, 1000–1350.* New Studies in Medieval History. London: Macmillan, 1973.

Jones, Philip. *The Italian City-State: From Commune to Signoria.* Oxford: Clarendon Press, 1997.

Kantorowicz, Hermann. "Una festa studentesca bolognese per l'Epifania del 1289." *AMDSPPR,* 3d ser., 24 (1905/6): 321–22.

Kempers, Brian. "Icons, Altarpieces, and Civic Ritual in Siena Cathedral, 1100–1530." *City and Spectacle in Medieval Europe.* Edited by Barbara A. Hanawalt and Kathryn L. Reyerson. Medieval Studies at Minnesota, 6. Minneapolis: University of Minnesota Press, 1994. 89–136.

Kennedy, V. L. "The Moment of Consecration and the Elevation of the Host." *Medieval Studies* 6 (1944): 121–50.

Kieckhefer, Richard. "Holiness and the Culture of Devotion: Remarks on Some Late Medieval Male Saints." *Images of Sainthood in Medieval Europe.* Edited by Renate Blumenfeld-Kosinski and Timea Szell. Ithaca: Cornell University Press, 1991. 288–305.

Killerby, Catherine Kovesi. *Sumptuary Law in Italy, 1200–1500.* Oxford: Clarendon Press, 2002.

Kirshner, Julius, ed. *The Origins of the State in Italy, 1300–1600.* Chicago: University of Chicago Press, 1995.

Klauck, Hans-Joseph. *The Religious Context of Early Christianity: A Guide to Graeco-Roman Religions.* Translated by Brian McNeil. Studies of the New Testament and Its World. Edinburgh: Clark, 2000.

Ladner, Gerhart B. "The Gestures of Prayer in Papal Iconography of the Thirteenth and Early Fourteenth Centuries." *Didascaliae: Studies in Honor of Anselm M. Albareda, Prefect of the Vatican Library*. Edited by Sesto Prete. New York: Rosenthal, 1961. 245–75.

I laici nella Societas Christiana dei secoli XI e XII: Atti della terza Settimana internazionale di studio, Mendola, 21–27 agosto 1965. Milan: Vita e Pensiero, 1968.

Landotti, Giuseppe. "La 'Preghiera dei fedeli' in lingua italiana da secolo XIII al secolo XX." *Ephemerides Liturgicae* 91 (1977): 97–131.

Lansing, Carol. *Power and Purity: Cathar Heresy in Medieval Italy*. New York: Oxford University Press, 1998.

Lanzoni, Francisco. *San Petronio vescovo di Bologna nella storia e nella legenda*. Rome: Pustet, 1907.

Lett, Didier. *L'enfant des miracles: Enfance et société au Moyen Âge (XII*ᵉ*–XIII*ᵉ *siècle)*. Paris: Aubier, 1997.

Little, Lester K. *Liberty, Charity, Fraternity: Lay Religious Confraternities at Bergamo in the Age of the Communes*. Bergamo: Lubrina, 1988.

———. "Pride Goes Before Avarice: Social Change and the Vices in Latin Christendom." *American Historical Review* 76 (1971): 16–49.

Lobrichon, Guy. *La religion des laïcs en Occident, XI*ᵉ*–XV*ᵉ *siècles*. Paris: Hachette, 1994.

Lomastro, Francesca. *Spazio urbano e potere politico a Vicenza nel XIII secolo dal "Regestrum Possessionis Comunis" del 1262*. Vicenza: Accademia Olimpica, 1981.

Lugano, Placido. "Delle chiese della città e diocesi di Foligno nel secolo XIII." *Bollettino della R. Deputazione di storia patria per l'Umbria* 10 (1906): 435–78.

Maccarrone, Michele, et al., eds. *Miscellanea Gilles Gérard Meersseman*. Italia Sacra, 15–16. 2 vols. Padua: Antenore, 1970.

Magli, Ida. *Gli uomini della penitenza: Lineamenti antropologici del Medioevo italiano*. Bologna: Cappelli, 1967.

Manselli, Raoul. *La religion populaire au Moyen Âge: Problèmes de méthode et d'histoire*. Quebec: Institut d'Études Médiévales Albert-le-Grand, 1975.

Manzini, Enrico Bottrigari. *Cenni storici sopra le antiche e sulla odierna cattedrale di Bologna*. Modena: Vincenzi, 1877.

Marantonio Sguerzo, Elsa. *Evoluzione storico-giuridica della sepoltura ecclesiastica*. Milan: Giuffrè, 1976.

Marchetti, Mino. *Liturgia e storia della chiesa di Siena nel XII secolo: I calendari medioevali della chiesa senese*. Roccastrada: Istituto Storico Diocesano di Siena, 1991.

Meersseman, Gilles Gérard. *Dossier de l'ordre de la pénitence au XIII*ᵉ *siècle*. Spicilegium Friburgense, 7. Fribourg: Editions Universitaires, 1961.

———. *Ordo Fraternitatis: Confraternite e pietà dei laici nel Medioevo*. Italia Sacra, 24–26. 3 vols. Rome: Herder, 1977.

Meersseman, Gilles Gérard, E. Adda, and J. Deshusses. *L'orazionale dell'archidiacono Pacifico e il Carpsum del cantore Stefano: Studi e testi sulla liturgia del duomo di Verona*. Spicilegium Friburgense, 21. Fribourg: Edizioni Universitarie, 1974.

Meluzzi, Luciano. "Le soppresse chiese parrocchiali di Bologna." *Strenna storica bolognese* 12 (1962): 113–40; 13 (1963): 167–97; 14 (1964): 165–88; 17 (1967): 291–317; 18 (1968): 227–39; 19 (1969): 141–72; 21 (1971): 141–74.

Menant, François. "La transformation des institutions et de la vie politique milanaises au dernier âge consulaire (1186–1216)." *Atti dell'11° Congresso internazionale di studi sull'alto Medioevo, Milano, 26–30 ottobre 1987*. Spoleto: Centro Italiano di Studi sull'Alto Medioevo, 1989. 113–44.

Menestò, Enrico, and Roberto Rusconi. *Umbria: Una strada delle sante medievali*. Rome: Rai, 1991.

Merlo, Grado G. *Eretici e inquisitori nella società piemontese del trecento*. Turin: Claudiana, 1977.

———. "Militia Christi come impegno antiereticale (1179–1233)." *Militia Christi e crociata nei secoli XI–XIII: Atti della undecima Settimana internazionale di studio, Mendola, 28 agosto–1 settembre 1989.* Milan: Vita e Pensiero, 1992. 355 86.

Metcalf, Peter, and Richard Huntington, eds. *Celebrations of Death: The Anthropology of Mortuary Ritual.* 2d ed. Cambridge: Cambridge University Press, 1991.

Miccoli, Giovanni. "La storia religiosa IV: Limiti e contraddizioni della restaurazione postgregoriana." *Storia d'Italia* 2:1. Turin: Einaudi, 1974. 431–1079.

Miller, Maureen C. *The Bishop's Palace: Architecture and Authority in Medieval Italy.* Ithaca: Cornell University Press, 2000.

Molin, Jean-Baptiste. "L'"Oratio Communis Fidelium' au Moyen-Âge en Occident du Xe au XVe siècle." *Miscellanea liturgica in onore di sua eminenza il Cardinale Giacomo Lercaro,* 2. Rome: Desclée, 1967. 313–467.

———. "Le prières du prône en Italie." *Ephemerides Liturgicae* 76 (1962): 39–42.

Morris, Colin. "San Ranieri of Pisa: The Power and Limitations of Sanctity in Twelfth-Century Italy." *Journal of Ecclesiastical History* 45 (1994): 588–99.

Mundy, John Hine. "In Praise of Italy: The Italian Republics." *Speculum* 64 (1989): 815–35.

Murray, Alexander. "Piety and Impiety in Thirteenth-Century Italy." *Popular Belief and Practice: Papers Read at the Ninth Summer Meeting and the Tenth Winter Meeting of the Ecclesiastical History Society.* Edited by G. J. Cuming and Derek Baker. Studies in Church History, 8. Cambridge: Cambridge University Press, 1972. 83–106.

Muzzarelli, Maria Giuseppina. *Penitenze nel Medioevo: Uomini e modelli a confronto.* Il mondo medievale, 22. Bologna: Pàtron, 1994.

Nolens Intestatus Decedere: Il testamento come fonte della storia religiosa e sociale: Atti dell'incontro di studio (Perugia, 3 maggio 1983). Perugia: Editrice Umbra Cooperativa, 1985.

Norman, Diana. *Siena and the Virgin: Art and Politics in a Late Medieval City State.* New Haven: Yale University Press, 1999.

Orioli, Raniero. *Venit Perfidus Heresiarcha: Il movimento apostolico-dolciniano dal 1260 al 1307.* Studi storici, 193–96. Rome: Istituto Storico Italiano per il Medio Evo, 1988.

Orselli, Alba Maria. *L'idea e il culto del santo patrono cittadino nella letteratura latina medievale.* Bologna: Zanichelli, 1965.

———. "Vita religiosa nella città medievale italiana tra dimensione ecclesiastica e 'cristianesimo civico': Una esemplificazione." *Annali del'Istituto storico italo-germanico in Trento* 7 (1981): 361–98.

Osheim, Duane. "Conversion, *Conversi,* and the Christian Life in Late Medieval Tuscany." *Speculum* 58 (1983): 368–90.

Ousterhout, Robert G. "The Church of Santo Stefano: A 'Jerusalem' in Bologna." *Gesta* 20 (1981): 311–22.

Paravicini Bagliani, Agostino, and Véronique Pache, eds. *La parrocchia nel Medio Evo, economia, scambi, solidarietà.* Italia Sacra, 53. Rome: Herder, 1995.

Pasquini, Emilio, and Antonio Enzo Quaglio. *Lo stilnovo e la poesia religiosa.* Letteratura italiana Laterza, 2. Bari: Laterza, 1980.

Peyer, Hans Conrad. *Stadt und Stadtpatron im mittelalterlichen Italien.* Zurich: Europa, 1955.

Pini, Antonio Ivan. "Le arti in processione: Professioni, prestigio e potere nelle città-stato dell'Italia padana medievale." *Lavorare nel Medio Evo: Rappresentazioni ed esempi dall'Italia dei sec. X–XVI, 12–15 ottobre 1980.* Convegni del Centro di studi sulla spiritualità medievale, 21. Todi: Accademia Tudertina, 1983. 67–107.

———. *Città, comuni e corporazioni nel Medioevo italiano.* Bologna: CLUEB, 1989.

———. "Problemi di demografia bolognese del duecento." *AMDSPPR,* n.s., 17–19 (1965–68): 147–222.

Powell, James M. *Albertanus of Brescia: The Pursuit of Happiness in the Early Thirteenth Century.* Philadelphia: University of Pennsylvania Press, 1992.

Religion and the People, 800–1700. Edited by James Obelkevich. Chapel Hill: University of North Carolina Press, 1979.

Rigon, Antonio. "Congregazioni del clero cittadino e storia della parrocchia nell'Italia setten-trionale: Il problema delle fonti." *La parrocchia nel Medio Evo, economia, scambi, solidarietà.* Edited by Agostino Paravicini Bagliani and Véronique Pache. Italia Sacra, 53. Rome: Herder, 1995. 2–25.

———. "Dévotion et patriotisme communal dan la genèse et la diffusion d'un culte: Le bienheureux Antoine de Padoue surnommé le 'Pellegrino' (+ 1267)." *Faire croire: Modalités de la diffusion et de la réception des messages religieux du XIIᵉ au XVᵉ siècle.* Collection de l'École française de Rome, 51. Rome: L'École Française, 1981. 259–78.

Ronzani, Mauro. "L'organizzazione della cura d'anime nella città di Pisa (secoli XII–XIII)." *Istituzioni ecclesiastiche della Toscana medioevale.* Edited by C. Fonseca and C. Violante. Galatina: Commissione Italiana per la Storia delle Pievi, 1980. 35–85.

Rusconi, Roberto. "Immagine della confessione sacramentale (secoli XII–XVI)." *Dalla penitenza all'ascolto delle confessioni: Il ruolo dei frati mendicanti: Atti del XXIII Convegno internazionale, Assisi, 12–14 ottobre 1995.* Spoleto: Centro Italiano di Studi sull'Alto Medioevo, 1996. 272–74.

———. "Ordinate Confiteri: La confessione dei peccati nelle 'Summae de Casibus.'" *L'aveu: Antiquité et Moyen Âge.* Rome: EFR, 1986. 297–313.

Samaritani, Antonio. "Circoscrizioni battesimali, distrettuazioni pastorali, congregazioni chiericali nel medioevo ferrarese." *Analecta pomposiana* 4 (1978): 69–176.

Segarizzi, Arnaldo. "Contributo alla storia di Fra Dolcino e degli eretici trentini." *Tridentum* 3 (1900): 273–97.

Sella, Pietro. "La diocesi di Bologna nel 1300." *AMDSPPR,* 4th ser., 18 (1927/28): 105–55.

Sensi, Mario. *Storie di bizzoche: Tra Umbria e Marche.* Rome: Edizioni di Storia e Letteratura, 1995.

Severino Polica, Gabriella. "Morte e cultura ecclesiastica nel duecento." *Studi storici* 21 (1980): 909–14.

Sorbelli, Albano. "La 'Sancta Jerusalem' stefaniana." *L'Archiginnasio* 35 (1940): 14–28.

Spufford, Peter. *Handbook of Medieval Exchange.* London: Boydell & Brewer, 1986.

Supino, I. B. *L'architettura sacra in Bologna nei secoli XIII e XIV.* Bologna: Zanichelli, 1909.

Thompson, Augustine. "Lay Versus Clerical Perceptions of Heresy: Protests Against the Inquisition in Bologna, 1299." *Praedicatores Inquisitores 1: The Domincans and the Mediaeval Inquisition: Acts of the First International Seminar on the Dominicans and the Inquisition, Rome 23–25 February 2002.* Dissertationes Historicae 30. Rome: Istituto Storico Domenicano, 2004. 701–30.

———. "New Light on Bl. Giacomo Benfatti, Bishop of Mantua, and the Mantua Disciplinati." *AFP* 69 (1999): 147–79.

———. *Revival Preachers and Politics in Thirteenth-Century Italy: The Great Devotion of 1233.* Oxford: Clarendon Press, 1992.

Tocco, F. "Guglielma Boema e i Guglielmiti." *Atti della R. Accademia dei Lincei: Classe di scienze morali, storiche et filologiche rendiconti,* 5th ser., 8 (1900): 3–32.

Trexler, Richard C. *The Christian at Prayer: An Illustrated Prayer Manual Attributed to Peter the Chanter (d. 1197).* Binghamton, N.Y.: Medieval and Renaissance Texts and Studies, 1987.

———. "Diocesan Synods in Late Medieval Italy." *Vescovi e diocesi in Italia dal XIV alla metà del XVI secolo: Atti del VII Convegno di storia della chiesa in Italia (Brescia, 21–25 settembre 1987).* Edited by Giuseppina De Sandre Gasparini et al. Rome: Herder, 1990. 295–335.

———. *Public Life in Renaissance Florence.* New York: Academic Press, 1980. Reprint, Ithaca: Cornell University Press, 1991.

Tucci, Hannelore Zug. "Il carroccio nella vita comunale." *Quellen und Forschungen aus italienischen Archiven und Bibliotheken* 65 (1985): 1–104.

Valsecchi, Giangiuseppina. *"Interrogatus . . . Respondit": Storia di un processo del xii secolo.* Bergamo: Biblioteca Civica, 1989.

Van Os, Henk W. *Sienese Altarpieces, 1215–1460: Form, Content, Function.* Groningen: Bouma, 1984.

Vauchez, André. *The Laity in the Middle Ages: Religious Beliefs and Devotional Practices.* Edited by Daniel E. Bornstein. Translated by Margery J. Schneider. Notre Dame: University of Notre Dame Press, 1993.

———. "Lay People's Sanctity in Western Europe: Evolution of a Pattern (Twelfth and Thirteenth Centuries)." *Images of Sainthood in Medieval Europe.* Edited by Renate Blumenfeld-Kosinski and Timea Szell. Ithaca: Cornell University Press, 1991. 21–32.

———. "Une nouveauté du xiie siècle: Les saints laïcs de l'Italie communale." *L'Europa dei secoli xi e xii fra novità e tradizione: Sviluppi di una cultura: Atti della decima Settimana internazionale di studio, Mendola, 25–29 agosto 1986.* Milan: Vita e Pensiero, 1989. 57–80. (Translated as "A Twelfth-Century Novelty: Lay Saints of Urban Italy." *The Laity in the Middle Ages: Religious Beliefs and Devotional Practices.* Edited by Daniel Bornstein. Notre Dame: University of Notre Dame Press, 1993. 51–72.)

———. "Reliquie, santi e santuari, spazi sacri e vagabondaggio religioso nel Medioevo." *Storia dell'Italia religiosa 1: L'antichità e il Medioevo.* Edited by André Vauchez. Rome: Laterza, 1993. 455–83.

———. *La sainteté en Occident aux derniers siècles du Moyen Âge d'après les procès de canonisation et les documents hagiographiques.* Bibliothèque des Écoles françaises d'Athènes et de Rome, 241. Rome: École Française de Rome, 1981.

———. "Sainteté laïque au xiiie siècle: La vie du bienheureux Facio de Crémone (v. 1196–1272)." *Mélanges de l'École française de Rome: Moyen Âge–temps modernes* 84 (1972): 13–53.

———. "Le 'trafiquant céleste': Saint Homebon de Crémone (+ 1197), marchand et 'père des pauvres.'" *Mentalités et sociétés.* Vol. 1 of *Horizons marins, itinéraires spirituels (v^e–xviiie).* Edited by Henri Dudois, Jean-Claude Hocquet, and André Vauchez. Paris: Sorbonne, 1987. 115–22.

———. "La valorisation de la pratique sacramentelle." *Histoire du christianisme des origines à nos jours.* Edited by Jean-Marie Mayeur et al. Paris: Desclée-Fayard, 1990. 5:745–48.

———, ed. *Ordres mendiants et la ville en Italie centrale (v. 1220–v. 1350) (Mélanges de l'École française de Rome: Moyen Âge–temps modernes* 89 [1977]).

Vodola, Elisabeth. *Excommunication in the Middle Ages.* Berkeley and Los Angeles: University of California Press, 1986.

Vogel, Cyrille. *Introduction aux sources de l'histoire du culte chrétien au Moyen Âge.* Spoleto: Centro Italiano di Studi sull'Alto Medioevo, n.d.

———. "Les rites de la pénitence publique au xe et xie siècles." *Mélanges offerts à René Crozet à l'occasionne de son soixante-dixième anniversaire.* Edited by Pierre Gallais and Yves-Jean Riou. Poitiers: Société d'Études Médiévales, 1966. 1:137–44.

Waley, Daniel Philip. *The Italian City Republics.* 3d ed. New York: Longman, 1989.

Webb, Diana. "Cities of God: The Italian Communes at War." *The Church and War.* Edited by W. J. Sheils. Studies in Church History, 20. Oxford: Ecclesiastical History Society, 1983. 111–27.

———. *Patrons and Defenders: Saints in the Italian City-States.* London: Tauris Academic Studies, 1996.

Weissman, Ronald. "From Brotherhood to Congregation: Confraternal Ritual Between Renaissance and Catholic Reformation." *Riti e rituali nelle società medievali.* Edited by Jacques Chiffoleau, Lauro Martines, and Agostino Paravicini Bagliani. Spoleto: Centro Italiano di Studi sull'Alto Medioevo, 1994. 77–94.

Wenzel, Sigfried. "The Seven Deadly Sins: Some Problems of Research." *Speculum* 43 (1968): 1–22.

Wessley, Stephen E. "The Thirteenth-Century Guglielmites: Salvation Through Women." *Medieval Women*. Edited by Derek Baker. Oxford: Blackwell, 1987. 289–303.

Wickstrom, John. "The Humiliati: Liturgy and Identity." *AFP* 62 (1992): 195–225.

Zanella, Gabriele. *Hereticalia: Temi e discussioni*. Spoleto: Centro Italiano di Studi sull'Alto Medioevo, 1995.

———. *Itinerari ereticali: Patari e catari tra Rimini e Verona*. Studi storici, 153. Rome: Istituto Storico Italiano per il Medio Evo, 1986.

Zarri, Gabriella. "I monasteri femminili a Bologna tra il XIII e il XVI secolo." *AMDSPPR*, n.s., 24 (1973): 133–224.

Index

Medieval people are alphabetized under their given names, modern people under their surnames.